THE ENCYCLOPEDIA OF 20TH CENTURY CONFLICT

AIR
WARFARE

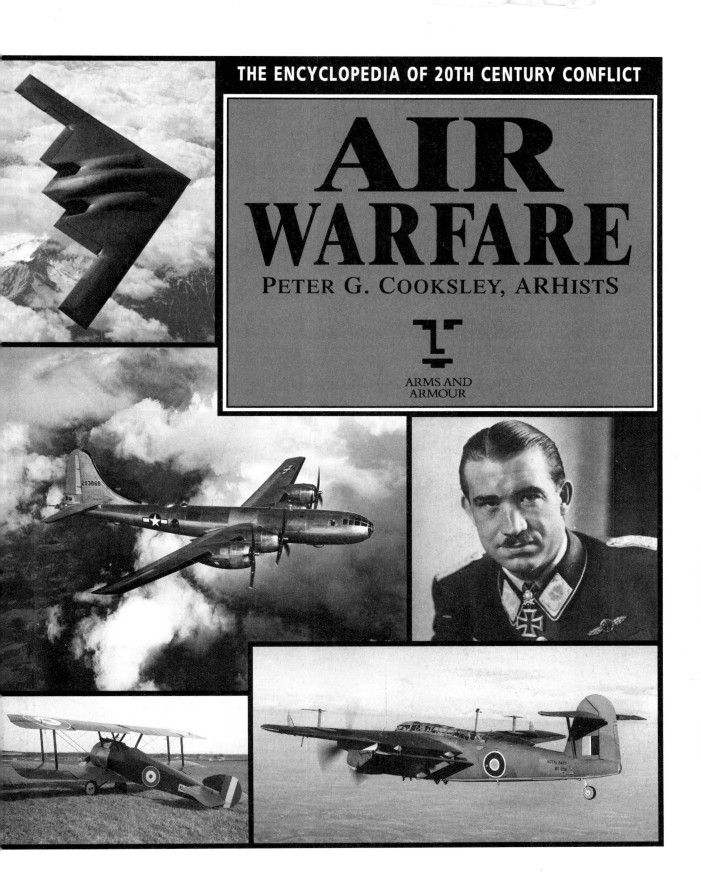

THE ENCYCLOPEDIA OF 20TH CENTURY CONFLICT

AIR WARFARE

PETER G. COOKSLEY, ARHistS

ARMS AND
ARMOUR

Arms and Armour Press
An Imprint of the Cassell Group
Wellington House, 125 Strand, London
WC2R 0BB

Distributed in the USA by Sterling
Publishing Co. Inc., 387 Park Avenue South,
New York, NY 10016-8810.

British Library Cataloguing-in-Publication
Data:
a catalogue record for this book is available
from the British Library

ISBN 1-85409-223-5

Printed and bound in Great Britain.

BY THE SAME AUTHOR
FLYING BOMB
SKYSTRIKE
OPERATION THUNDERBOLT
1940. THE STORY OF No. 11 GROUP, FIGHTER
COMMAND
FOCKE-WULF 190A
MESSERSCHMITT 109E
ADVANCED JETLINERS
FLIGHT ROYAL
AVIATION ENTHUSIASTS' GUIDE TO
LONDON AND THE SOUTH EAST

AVIATION ANNIVERSARIES 1979
CROYDON AIRPORT FLYPAST
WELLINGTON, MAINSTAY OF BOMBER COMMAND
THE SKYBIRD STORY
SOPWITH FIGHTERS IN ACTION
THE BATTLE OF BRITAIN
THE BE2 IN ACTION
BRISTOL FIGHTERS IN ACTION
THE DH9 IN ACTION
VCs OF THE FIRST WORLD WAR: AIR VCs
SKILL AND DEVOTION (Editor)

ACKNOWLEDGEMENTS

In compiling and writing this work I have
been most grateful for the enthusiastic
assistance and the guidance of Arms and
Armour Press, and in addition for access to
the published researches of the Cross &
Cockade Society (International) and the
Croydon Airport Society. Acknowledgements and thanks for other assistance are
due to Messrs G. Constantine, N. W.
Cruwys, E. R. Hooton, Bruce Robertson
(who also contributed the biographical section) and H. N. R. Wylie, and, of course, the
staffs of the Royal Air Force and Imperial
War Museums.
Peter G. Cooksley
London, 1997

JACKET ILLUSTRATIONS:
Back, top left: Ilyushin Il-2; see page 145.
(Bruce Robertson collection).
Back centre, upper left: Hawker Typhoon;
see page 135. (BAe via Bruce Robertson)
Back centre, lower left: Albatros D.Va; see
page 64. (Author's collection)
Back, bottom left: Grumman Avenger; see
page 127. (Bruce Robertson collection)
Back, top right: Short Sunderland; see
page 228. (RNZAF)
Back, bottom right: Panavia Tornado; see
page 231. (BAe)
Front, top left: Air Chief Marshal Sir Hugh
Dowding; see page 258. (Bruce Robertson
collection)
Front centre, upper left: B-24 Liberator;
see page 69. (J. W. A. Bowden)
Front centre, lower left: Mitsubishi A6M5a
Zero (Zeke); see pages 158, 248. (Bruce
Robertson collection)
Front, bottom: Tupolev Tu-20 Bear; see
page 76.
Front, top right: Anthony Fokker; see page
262. (Bruce Robertson collection)
Front centre, upper right: de Havilland
Mosquito; see pages 46, 95. (de Havilland)
Front centre, lower right: Sopwith Camel;
see pages 31, 86. (RAF Museum)

TITLE SPREAD ILLUSTRATIONS:
Top, left to right: Bristol Bloodhound; see
page 80. (Author's collection) Lt-Gen James
Doolittle (left); see page 256. (Bruce
Robertson collection) B-2 bomber; see page
225. (Northrop)
Centre, left to right: Sea King. (Author)
SEPECAT Jaguar; see page 217. (Author's
collection) B-29 Superfortress; see page 71.
(Bruce Robertson collection) General Adolf
Galland; see page 264. (Bruce Robertson
collection)
Bottom, left to right: Manfred von
Richthofen (centre); see page 274. (IWM
Q42262) F-9F fighter; see page 217.
(Author's collection) Sopwith Camel; see
page 220. (E. T. Maloney) Fairey Barracuda;
see page 111. (Bruce Robertson collection)

CONTENTS

INTRODUCTION

In the history of warfare, that waged in the air is alone confined to the twentieth century since powered flight only became possible one December day at Kill Devil Hill, Kitty Hawk, three years after the century had begun. However, the majority of military uses to which man's ability to make controlled flight was subsequently put had been anticipated for hundreds of years, so that, having designed an ingenious 'flying boat' in 1670, the Jesuit priest Francesco de Lana-Terzi had cautioned that such vessels might be able to cause 'a ship to capsize by flinging down pieces of iron, kill the crew and set the ship ablaze with artificial fire, with bullets and with bombs. Not only ships but also houses, castles and towns might be served in this way, without risk to those who cast down such objects from immeasurable heights.' In the following century these fears were being echoed by Dr Samuel Johnson in his Rasselas, writing that the good would be gravely endangered if the wicked were able to attack them at will from the air, and just ten years after Johnson's death there occurred almost such an action, by balloons and probably the first, taking the form of a reconnaissance of Fleurus in Belgium on 26 June 1794 when Capitaine Coutelle signalled such information to General Jourdan that it materially contributed to the French victory. The consequence was the formation of a 'Company of Aerostiers' equipped with new cylindrical balloons, but when these proved of limited use the Company was disbanded six years later.

Certainly the first bombing attack in history was that made in 1849 when the Austrians sent over Venice specially equipped hot-air balloons, thus heralding the Japanese 'Fu-Go' weapons of the Second World War

Above: A Belgian military balloon of the Compagnie des Ouvriers et Aerostatiers A second occupant is perched in the leading lines below the crow's feet. (Author's collection)

which, apart from being gas-filled, were similarly unmanned. This year also was that in which Henry Coxwell was commissioned to look into the question of evolving gas balloons of 50,000 cubic feet capacity for British Army reconnaissance, signals and dropping high explosive, interest in these operations having probably been stimulated by the success of McClellan's captive balloons in 1861 during the American Civil War, though Coxwell was to see his efforts gain little attention and he was soon to move to Germany. There in 1870 he became an instructor to a pair of Cologne balloon detachments and thus saw the beginning of the Franco-Prussian War that was to witness the use of sixty-six gas balloons to evacuate from besieged Paris more than one hundred VIPs and nine tons of mail and distribute the occasional propaganda leaflets to the Prussians en route.

By now the British Army authorities had at last realized the military possibilities of balloons and were to fly them for observation above the battlefields of Bechuanaland in 1884 and again the following year in the Sudan. Five years later a Balloon Section was officially created as part of the Royal Engineers.

Fourteen years were to pass before any real acceptance of heavier-than-air craft for military purposes was gained, this finally coming from the United States, where the Government made available the sum of $50,000 for aviation trials by Samuel P. Langley, who was successfully to fly a half-scale model of his proposed machine in 1901. However, the tests carried out from the Potomac River with a full-size craft termed the *Aerodrome* in 1903 failed at both the October and December attempts.

It was at about this period, too, that experiments were begun in the use of man-lifting kites for observation, since the preparation of these seemed to offer relief from the three hours needed to fill a gas balloon as well as other problems associated with their operation in hot climates. But despite advantages offered by such types as the Baden-Powell and Cody kites, both bearing the names of their inventors, it was the gas balloon that seemed to present the greater threat to ground forces, so that it was not long before

Above: The *Ville de Paris*, a French Clement-Bayard/Astra dirigible with a 17,657 cu ft gas capacity, flown during 1907—08. It made a noteworthy 148-mile triangular journey from Verdun to Sartrouville-Valmy and back to base on 15 January 1908. (Author's collection)

investigations into possible countermeasures evolved such weapons as the German Erhardt and Krupp-Daimler balloon destroyers and the similar Cadillac gun in the USA. All were mounted on motorized chassis and were introduced before 1910, their official titles accurately signifying just how little the military potential of powered flight was realized in some quarters. However, following Blériot's successful cross-Channel attempt France formed a useful aeroplane force for deep reconnaissance ahead, and in cooperation with, the cavalry, despite which General Foch was to remark that 'Aviation is good sport, but for the Army it is useless.' This was a surprising observation from an officer who had previously shown

shrewd perception, and one with which Colonel Capper, Officer Commanding the British Army Balloon Section, disagreed, as shown in the conclusion of an address he delivered in 1906 to the Royal United Services Institution which ran: 'In a few years we may expect to see men moving swiftly through the air on simple surfaces just as a gliding bird moves. Such machines will move very rapidly, probably never less than twenty, and up to a hundred miles an hour. Nothing but the heaviest storms will stop them. They will be small and difficult to hit, and very difficult to damage, and their range of operations will be very large.' Four years later the British & Colonial Aeroplane Company of Bristol was to sign a contract in

Above: The restricted view and cramped pilot's position of a Blériot XI monoplane. The bright hemispherical object beyond the rudimentary instrumentation is the end of the cylindrical brass fuel tank. (Author)

November agreeing to supply eight Boxkite aircraft to Czarist Russia. In 1910 also Japan sent two Army officers to Europe to be trained as her first military pilots.

Abroad, the next year saw Italian Sottotenete Giulio Gavotti drop the first bombs on an enemy from a powered aircraft, a German Etrich Taube monoplane; Turkish troops at Taguira Oasis in the Libyan desert being the target for the picric acid (lyddite) Cipelli bombs that were used on 1 November; the exhibition of a gun-carrying Voisin at the Paris Aero Show, thus anticipating the Lewis machine gun fitted to a Wright biplane of the United States Army in June 1912; and, in England, a Bristol Prier monoplane being used for wireless trials. In German military aviation experiments seemed to be taking a different route by concentrating on development of the Zeppelin, the warlike potential of which was regarded at the time as representing the ultimate weapon against which no defence was possible. However, at the outbreak of war in August 1914 it became clear that this concentration had not been at the expense of heavier-than-air craft, since the total force of the latter numbered 260 (about half of the 500 estimated in some quarters), while France could find 156 warplanes and the Royal Flying Corps 53.

The opening of hostilities saw the aeroplane still envisaged in a reconnaissance role, but it naturally followed that opposing forces performing such identical duties soon created demands that their opponents be eliminated if only to free ground troops from the threat of having their movements reported. Therefore crude methods were at first resorted to, for example taking aloft missiles such as bottles and bricks with the intention of flinging these into an enemy's propeller arc. More orthodox methods found flyers taking into the air various firearms, and it was only a little later that the idea of substituting machine guns was put into practice, although there remained the problem of firing these through the disc swept by the propeller. Thus the first fighter air-

Above: Unarmed Sopwith Tabloid 326 was delivered to the Royal Flying Corps in mid-May 1914 and associated with Nos I and 5 Squadrons before going to the Central Flying School at the end of the year. (Author's collection)

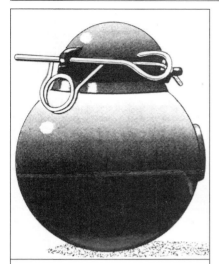

Above: A 4lb Cipelli lyddite bomb of 1911. (Author's collection)

craft, still known as 'scouts' from their immediate ancestry, either had such weapons fitted at an angle to fire outside the swept area, or were 'pushers' with the airscrew at the back. Early solutions to the problem took the form of interrupter gears, used by the British, which prevented a round being fired while a propeller blade was passing; fitting propellers with deflectors, favoured by the French; and synchronization, a method by which the pro-

peller in effect fired the gun, favoured by the Germans. As a result, flexible weapons became confined to those for defence, with fixed guns for offence, the early single firearms being doubled in number before the end of the war. Thus were evolved the first fighter aircraft, later to be developed in specialist directions such as the armoured ground attack type and the interceptor. Individual tactics soon followed.

Bombing had an earlier lineage but was equally crude since the first such missiles were simply dropped by hand, the only aiming being performed by the human eye. Racks (one of them rotary) evolved before 1914 were soon forgotten, the only containers being for the contemporary flechettes, sharpened steel darts about 15cm in length which could be dropped on to troops lacking head cover. Flechettes were particularly effective against such targets, although otherwise they were incapable of inflicting much harm, although they earned the gruesome reputation of having the ability to pass right through a horse if dropped from a sufficiently high altitude. These, together with the rope-bound incendiary bombs which preceded the development of the sophisticated thermite type were all missiles that were collec-

tively little more than the primitive ancestors of an armoury which within a span of four years was to include high-explosive bombs weighing 3,300lb. The latter were not used operationally, but those of 1,650lb were, along with incendiary bombs. Meanwhile torpedo planes had sunk ships, airborne cameras had changed the concept of reconnaissance and aircraft were able to operate from first seaplane and later aircraft carriers at sea, along with which flying boats had been developed, able to enforce the first checks on the menace of the U-boat. In parallel with these developments were such specialist aircraft as those intended for new long-range work, the delivery of poison gas and dive bombing, as well as improvements in engine design (the evolution of the rotary motor, for example, reached its zenith during this period).

The once-feared Zeppelins had proved vulnerable, with the result that larger strategic bombers had replaced them, not only in Germany but also in Britain, establishing a policy that was soon to be followed in France and later the United States, and together with these developments had gone advances in interception techniques, by night as well as by day. By 1918, too, the world's smaller countries had begun to show an interest in military

Above: A Bristol Boxkite. The slightly later variant, marketed as the 'military' version, was distinguished by its extended upper wing tips. The British War Office ordered four of these on 14 March 1911, and models went to Russia and Spain. (Author's collection)

Above: The wreck of L33, shot down at Little Wigborough on 23 October 1916, shows the distinctive structure of Zeppelin airships. (Author's collection)

Above: A British Cody man-lifting carrier kite. Above this, a linked team of three provided the lift, with a pilot kite at the top. Here the observer is about to ascend in a wicker chair, which has replaced the standard basket. The simpler Baden-Powell system designed by the brother of the Boy Scouts' founder saw operational service in South Africa. (Author's collection)

aviation and had acquired machines, while among the larger nations even in the East, China had gained experience in aerial warfare four years earlier, successfully using four Caudrons as part of its 'White Wolf' operation, and Japan had formed a single air force with Naval and Military Wings as a result of the government having voted ¥100,000 for the establishment of such an arm in 1912.

But naturally, as a result of the war, Europe could boast the widest experience and largest air forces. That of France was one of the most powerful, with a total of 127,630 officers and men, of whom over 12,000 were aircrew, and second only to Great Britain's total of 293,532, and both countries had vast industries to draw upon. Only Russia and the United States lacked these, the former being rent by revolution while still attempting to operate the motley collection of chiefly French machines used by its air force, while surprisingly the latter had entered the war with such suddenness that France's industry had been looked to for aircraft and plans were afoot to produce British designs under licence. Only in the field of engine development was the United States' industry in a better position, such motors as the Liberty and Curtiss powerplants eventually proving their value for military purposes

The years following the European cataclysm were to witness a reduction in the pace of developing aerial warfare, and although those years immediately following the cessation of the 'war to end wars' were to see continued operations in Russia (where such novel spectacles were to be witnessed as Sopwith Camel dive-bombers) as well as the Chanak crisis of 1922, war continued to be waged from the air very much in the style and manner that had evolved between 1914 and 1918, this even being true of the 'police' operations carried out by the Royal Air Force over the North-West Frontier and in Iraq. The potential for troop movements by means of aircraft was to be shown for the first time in the civilian evacuation from Kabul at the beginning of 1929.

This period between the two world wars was one during which naval aviation made immense strides, however, with the evolution of the aircraft carrier as it was to be later understood and such innovations as the exchange of converging longitudinal arrester wires for those rigged laterally and the first use of catapults for launching aircraft, although the original experiments had been conducted before the war. On land, long-range flights were very much the order of the day, endurance tests that were to assist both engine and airframe development as well as aerial medicine – all occurrences that were exploited for their propaganda value, at the same time giving no hint of the parallel development in weapons that was being conducted. Poison gas warfare, it is true, occupied the attention of civilians and politicians alike, with the result that an attempt to outlaw it was made in the Washington Treaty of 1922, the Articles of which were closely followed three years later by the Geneva Gas Protocol, a declaration that also embraced bacteriological warfare. Nevertheless, horrific reports were forthcoming of the effects of mustard gas used by Mussolini's Regia Aeronautica during Italy's annexation of Abyssinia in 1935–36.

Italy had attempted a similar conquest in 1896 but this had resulted in a humiliating defeat at the Battle of Adowa. The new assault had the advantage of the use of air power, against which the poorly armed tribesmen that made up the Ethiopian Army stood little chance of success. The only hope of stopping the conflict lay in the imposition of oil sanctions, but the largely ineffectual League of Nations was reluctant to impose such measures, although they were discussed, .and in the meantime Italy's conquest was successfully completed in 1936.

The following year saw the eruption of war between Japan and China with an all-out attack by the former that largely continued the assault on Manchuria of six years before. This, too, the League of Nations had proved incapable of halting, and the fresh conquest surprised the Western world because of the modernity of the Japanese Air Force's equipment, previously believed to be made up of poor copies of European designs. This struggle was to drag on until absorbed by the greater one in the Second World War and provided an obvious pointer

to the inevitability of a fresh world holocaust, with air power playing a major part. European developments also indicated this trend, with the National Socialists firmly in power in Germany by 1933, the clandestine Luftwaffe now publicly acknowledged and a series of Expansion Schemes being effected for Britain's Royal Air Force.

Alone among those of the major European countries, France's air arm was suffering from the political changes which had been initiated in mid-1936 when the left-wing Popular Front government had instituted the nationalization of the aircraft industry, which had already slipped into decay. However, although 200 airframes a month were being produced in an attempt to make good the earlier production deficits (no more than forty airframes over the same period of time), the erratic delivery of armament, engines and equipment was further hampered by administrative bottlenecks so that complete aircraft were received only irregularly by the Armée de l'Air. Thus it slowly became clear, as the European political situation became increasingly threatening, that no measures taken at home could correct matters, and France began to look abroad for military aircraft, placing orders with the United States.

Full-scale war was being waged between Japan and China by 1937, and in the previous year civil war had erupted in Spain, providing a proving ground for the weapons and air crews of Nazi Germany (which supported General Franco) and Soviet Russia (which assisted the Republican forces). The Russians withdrew before long, but the Condor Legion remained until just before the Fascist victory in March 1939. One contribution to this victory was a pointer towards future trends: the air lift of Moorish troops across the Straits of Gibraltar in a fleet of Junkers Ju 52/3ms, establishing Franco's grandiosely titled 'Army of Africa'.

The Munich Crisis of September 1938 was solved from the viewpoint of Western Europe by the appeasement of Nazi demands, but the fact that only a short period of grace had been achieved became clear by March the following year when Hitler's troops occupied Bohemia, Moravia and the

Lithuanian city of Memel. Six months later the attempt to annex Poland triggered the Second World War. Elsewhere, eight weeks later, another conflict broke out, this time between the Soviet Union and Finland, and although this contributed nothing to the development of air warfare it did show the comparative inadequacy by European standards of the aircraft of US design, some of which were flown by the Finns. This was particularly the case with regard to armament and performance, and these shortcomings were again demonstrated by the types originally ordered by France when these were taken over by Great Britain after the collapse of the former country in 1940.

Meanwhile in Europe both sides new embarked on a period since known as the 'Phoney War' from its near-complete inactivity, although there was sufficient to indicate that there was little to choose between the training and equipment of the RAF and the Luftwaffe. France, meanwhile, soon suffered collapse, leaving Britain to fight alone for her survival in the Battle of Britain – the only time in history when the existence of a nation has depended almost solely on air activity. It is well known that the victory of 1940 was in no small measure aided by the existence of 'radio location', later known as radar.

The widening conflict over the following years saw many other developments in the waging of aerial warfare, including the use of paratroops, gliders, helicopters, suicide aircraft and flying bombs, but of greater significance was the advent of jet propulsion, transforming the whole concept of war in the air and even spreading to the field of naval aviation which had enjoyed change only slowly during 1939–45.

The preconception widely held in some quarters that all aircraft operating from carriers had to carry a two-man crew had been abandoned, as was the concept that biplanes were the only suitable designs, a realization that increased the speeds of naval aircraft and endorsed the importance of the carrier which had existed in little more than pioneer form in the 1914–18 conflict some twenty years previously. This was to be proved by naval aviation turning the tide of the

Pacific War at the Battle of Midway. That this was greater than anything conceived earlier was indicated by the Japanese loss of 280 machines compared to 179 by the Americans, many of these latter machines being obsolescent Douglas Devastator and Vindicator torpedo aircraft. Indeed, it had been carrier-borne aircraft that had precipitated America's entry into the European war when, on 7 December 1941, afterwards to be called 'a day of infamy' by President Roosevelt, 350 bomber and torpedo aircraft, operating in two waves from six of Japan's eleven carriers, had attacked, without warning, the US naval base at Pearl Harbor.

In other directions, the years of the Second World War had seen huge changes, one of the most significant being that affecting aircraft armament. Rifle-calibre machine guns and those of 0.5in calibre favoured by America, formerly used for both defensive and offensive purposes, were now being augmented by all nations with cannon, experimentally in 1915/16 and again as early as 1927 in Great Britain by the 37mm Coventry Ordnance Works guns. Except in rare instances, single flexibly mounted defensive gun positions had been replaced by power-operated turrets (another innovation conceived during the 1930s), some of which had their guns radar-controlled, for example the British Boulton Paul 'D' turret with its external scanner. The Second World War had also seen the large-scale introduction of offensive aerial rockets, an idea which had tentatively been employed during the war of twenty-five years before.

However, the greatest innovation of the Second World War was without question the use of atomic weapons, allied in the West to the possession by the United States of the mightiest strategic bombing force in history, so that the end of the conflict in 1945 placed America in the historically unique position of having complete military ascendancy over the remainder of the globe. With its very limited strategic bomber force, manned by inexperienced crews, and lack of nuclear know-how and production facilities on a mass basis, Soviet Russia saw the situation as a threat and thus was set in motion the 27-year arms race which was not to be slowed until

agreement was reached between the superpowers at the conclusion of the Strategic Arms Limitation Talks (SALT) of 1972.

The Berlin Air Lift of 1948 had added a fresh dimension to aerial warfare by the dissemination of succour rather than death for a period of fifteen months when an entire population were supplied by air with the means of survival. Elsewhere a fresh outbreak of fighting followed from the suggestion that Palestine be divided between Jews and Arabs. This eventually resulted in the proclamation of the State of Israel on 14 May 1948. The new nation, naturally, took immediate steps to establish an air force, this being initially equipped with such aircraft as ex-Czech Messerschmitt Bf 109G-14s – now redesignated Avia C-210 Mezecs (Mules), which had been procured by an underground purchasing commission and dismantled in order to be delivered secretly in C-54 Skymasters and C-46 Commandos – three B-17s and some A-20s from surplus dumps in Oklahoma and Florida. All were flown by volunteer air crews.

Two years later a new flashpoint erupted in Korea, brought about by the invasion of the South by the North, which was ordered to withdraw by the United Nations. The directive being ignored, sixteen nations were soon involved in an attempt to push the Communist forces that were already threatening Pusan in the south back beyond the 38th parallel. At first there was little opposition to Allied air power, some of the United States' strike missions being flown from Japan, but when the North Korean forces were joined by the Chinese, aerial combat took on a more serious aspect and mass flights of F-84G Thunderjets were sent across the Pacific with the aid of flight refuelling. MiG-15 jets, allegedly powered by Soviet copies of the British Rolls-Royce Nene, were soon encountered in numbers, and these were met by such aircraft as F-86 Sabre jets and Sea Furies of the Royal Navy. This conflict was to see the first large-scale use of napalm attacks since 1944, with air supply and paratroop drops on a greater scale than any carried out at any time during the Second World War. Towards the middle of the three-year campaign, Boeing B-29 Superfortress bombers

were used to pound the North, although many of the Chinese bases were safely located beyond the Yalu River in Manchuria.

Aside from this conflict, the period was one which was to see the evolution of a form of air warfare that was to continue to the end of the century with the introduction of semi-automatic interception. A pilot was guided to the vicinity of an enemy by ground control, his aircraft then flew to within range by means of the automatic pilot and the rocket armament fired automatically, previously 'locking on' to, for example, an enemy's heat emissions. In the strategic field the array of nuclear weapons saw hydrogen bombs supplant the atomic weapons that had destroyed Hiroshima and Nagasaki in 1945, and these could be delivered over perhaps a 6,000-mile range by such aircraft as the 200-ton Boeing B-52 Stratofortress powered by eight turbojets. Elsewhere, a year before the conclusion of the Korean conflict the RAF was engaged in a very different type of war, making rocket attacks against the jungle hideouts of Mau Mau terrorists in Kenya after having flown in a large ground force at the beginning of the campaign; and, four years later, a limited war called for Britain's and France's involvement in the actions against Egyptian installations during the Suez conflict.

The 1960s opened with the destruction of a US U-2 spyplane by an anti-aircraft missile while on a sortie over Soviet Russia, an indication of the advances that had been made in the field of military aerial reconnaissance, while April of 1961 was marked by the little-remembered wholesale destruction of the Second World War-vintage Martin Marauder bombers sent to support the abortive American attempt to topple Fidel Castro's regime at the Bay of Pigs landings. However, graver events for the United States were to begin to unfold three years later in the form of warfare in Vietnam.

The beginning was deceptive, involving no more than guerrilla risings throughout 1955-56, but these suddenly escalated in August 1964 with mythical Communist torpedo boats attacking US warships in the Gulf of Tonkin, Aircraft from US carriers immediately made reprisal attacks on North Vietnamese naval bases.

Soon ground troops from the North were swarming down from Hanoi, and these were quickly locked in combat with those of the United States in battalion strength. In an effort to cut off the flow of enemy troops, bombing attacks were directed against targets north of the 17th Parallel, only to face losses from both anti-aircraft missiles and also the new MiG-21 interceptors with which the NVAAF were now equipped. It was only when the pace of the war had begun to slow that the number of B-52 missions was reduced, operating from bases in Thailand and Guam, although attacks were also now being made on Cambodia. While these events were unfolding, other wars calling for air support had broken out between India and Pakistan, first in 1965 and then in 1971, the air force of the former being in part equipped from Soviet sources while the latter – which operated with relative success in the first encounter – was soon to turn to China, adopting Shenyang F-6s (Chinese-built MiG-19s) to augment its new French Mirage IIIs and Canadian Sabre 6s with Cessna Bird Dogs for liaison and training etc. Elsewhere another of the world's trouble spots had seen, at 0845hrs on 5 June 1967, a pre-emptive attack by Israeli aircraft on targets and installations in Egypt. This accounted for 79 of the total of 452 United Arab Republic aircraft destroyed in the Six Days' War at a cost of 46 Israeli jets.

The war against the Vietnamese Communists dragged on, spawning such additions to the armoury of air warfare as defoliation, to deny the enemy the cover provided by dense jungle and gunships, both fixed-wing and helicopters, and also seeing the re-emergence of retrieving gliders by means of the 'snatch' procedure by low-flying tug machines such as had been perfected in the closing days of the Second World War. However, the opening of 1975 brought with it the fall of Phuoc Binh, the capital of the main southern province, and the tempo of US involvement began to slow, in part bowing to opposition to the war from home. This in turn brought about the largest fixed-wing air evacuation in history. It was well under way eight weeks later, ferrying out civilians and later, in an orderly withdrawal, troops, before the Viet

Cong seized Saigon on 30 April, thus effectively bringing the conquest to an end. The official onset of peace, however, would be years in coming.

Two years before this, the antagonism between Israel and Egypt had flared once more in the form of the October or Yom Kippur War. The reason for this outbreak is said to have been the agreement of the American-sponsored ceasefire of 7 August 1970 which ended the inconclusive three years of fighting that had preceded it, but now, when the Israelis attempted to counter the UAR attack, their pilots found themselves flying into a seeming wall of carefully laid radar-controlled anti-aircraft fire from guns and missiles alike which inflicted grave losses in the first few days of action. The front was stabilized, however, allowing the Israeli Air Force to shift to the offensive, systematically destroying oil installations, power stations and military concentrations. Perhaps the single most outstanding feat of this conflict was the destruction by two IAF Mirage pilots of a 'Kelt' missile fired at Tel Aviv from an Egyptian Tu-16 medium bomber, and it was said to be due to this force gaining air supremacy that the war was finally ended at a total cost to the Arab forces of 334 aircraft shot down and many destroyed on the ground.

Unfortunately a skirmish was to take place once more between aircraft of Syria and Egypt on 27 June 1979, but the next aerial conflict was that which was part of the war between Iraq and Iran that erupted in 1980 and was to last for the next eight years. Iraq was accused in the closing twelve months of the conflict of using mustard gas bombs, the first known employment of this type of warfare since Italy's war against Ethiopia in 1935. Meanwhile, 1982 witnessed the outbreak of war between Great Britain and Argentina, triggered by the latter's attempt to annex the Falkland Islands on 2 April 1982.

The resultant 'Operation Corporate' was largely a naval and army campaign, but the contribution made by the aircraft of the Royal Navy and Royal Air Force was nevertheless significant. The RAF opened the air operation with the first of four attacks on Port Stanley airfield by Vulcans carrying 1,000lb high-explosive bombs on a

8,000-mile round trip from the Ascension Is with the aid of flight-refuelling, which caused the enemy to re-deploy part of his fighter force to safeguard Buenos Aires in case this city should be attacked.

The Falklands war also saw much use of the Harrier, the revolutionary British 'jump-jet' that had begun to take over the role of close air support in July 1969 and had been ordered for the Royal Navy six years later. At first during mid-May some had operated from HMS *Hermes*, later transferring to a landing strip at San Carlos, the type as a whole performing over 1,500 sorties, during which none was lost in air-to-air combat. Also significant were the Hercules transports fitted for in-flight refuelling, supplying ships at sea and flying in stores and fuel; the Victor tankers which were also involved; and the Nimrods for maritime reconnaissance, some armed with Harpoon anti-ship missiles augmented by Sidewinders for self-defence. In addition such helicopters as the Sea Kings lifted hundreds of troops, prisoners and cargo.

The following year the world received a jolt when it was announced on 6 September that Soviet MiGs had brought down Flight 007 of Korean Air Lines over Sakhalin Island off Siberia. The victim was a Boeing 747, in which all 269 lives were lost. The danger point passed without further incident, only to be replaced by another in 1986 in which air power was exclusively used to strike against a country in retaliation for alleged crimes against the injured party's citizens abroad. On 15 April aircraft of the United States Sixth Fleet were joined by those of the US Air Force to attack targets in Libya, and although the raids conducted by the US Navy were part of a series of encounters between Colonel Qadhafi's aircraft and those of the USS *Coral Sea* (CV-43), the participation of the USAF raised a political storm when it became clear that the attackers had taken off from the British bases at Upper Heyford and Lakenheath, being refuelled by tankers from Mildenhall.

However, air warfare of a different kind was to be waged during Operation 'Just Cause' in support of the United States' invasion of Panama in 1989 with the declared intention of

Above: A contrast representing the progress of air war in the twentieth century –
the nose of a Fairchild A-10. (Author)

capturing the Panamanian leader, General Noriega, to face indictment for drug offences. He had 'declared war' on the US five days before the operation was mounted on 20 December with the ferrying in of a large number of troops, some to make air drops, by a force of seventy-seven StarLifters, Hercules and Galaxies. Although the subsequent troop movements were supported by such fixed-wing aircraft as Vought A-7Ds and AH-64A Apache helicopters (in use for the first time), the event is of historical significance in being that in which 'stealth' aircraft were used in quantity for the first time. These were Lockheed F-117 'Wobblin' Goblins', later known as Nighthawks, reportedly flying non-stop to Panama from the Tonopah Test Range, Nevada, with the aid of in-flight refuelling, and at night, also on 20 December, bombing the barracks at Panama City.

But the world had to wait until January 1991 for the first large-scale demonstration of the capabilities of modern aircraft, when the invasion of Kuwait by the forces of Iraq triggered

Operation 'Desert Storm', the action by Coalition forces to throw back the invader. That, from an air warfare viewpoint, Kuwait was incapable of such an action is demonstrated by the fact that this country could at the time only find fifteen serviceable military aircraft. The numbers found by the other participants cast an interesting light on the potential of the weapons used at the end of the century: the United States employed 48 bombers, the balance being made up of 236 aircraft from three other nations.

These figures clearly show that there would never again be anything like the thousand-bomber attacks against a single target such as were mounted during the Second World War. The potential for destruction had increased beyond recognition, even using non-nuclear weapons, and although 'toss-bombing' of the type developed and practised during World War II by RAF Mosquito squadrons was still used, employing 1,000-pounders, the most severe of the Iraqi defences were now being avoided by a stand-off manoeuvre using deadly

'smart' bombs such as the GBU-15 released perhaps ten miles from the target and flown the remainder of its journey with the aid of a television picture.

Also banished by modern technology was the concept of destruction by the sheer weight of an attack, and although defence systems were now universally taken to include hardened aircraft shelters, yielding only to a direct hit by a powerful weapon, airfields could be and were made useless by such specialist bombs as the JP.233 anti-airfield device, each containing 30 runway-cratering submunitions with 215 intended for area-denial to make repairs hazardous, and all usually delivered after the attention of attacking electronic countermeasures aircraft such as F-4G Wild Weasels and EF-111A Ravens, plus the use of HARM and ALARM anti-radiation missiles to incapacitate weapon-laying radar, the whole generally monitored and controlled by AWACS machines.

A few weeks after the commencement of operations against Iraqi invading forces, a new device was to be employed for the first time – the Thermal Imaging Airborne Laser Designation (TIALD) pod. This was an aid to making bombing effective by night as well as during daylight and made possible a degree of precision undreamed of some eight decades before when the embryo days of air warfare had seen small spherical bombs weighing four pounds and filled with lyddite manually tossed from the cockpit of an unstable aircraft which had continually to be flown 'hands-on'!

'Desert Storm' was a long way from the days when the forgotten Carinthian border war* provided a postscript to the First World War with Austria's early air arm locked in combat with the machines of the National Council of Serbs, Croats and Slovenes in 1918–19, and an even greater distance in both time and technology from 1912 which found the Blériot monoplanes and Henry and Maurice Farmans of Serbia committed to the Balkan wars.

*South Austrian Alpine province bordering Italy and the then new Yugoslavia, by which country it was occupied after the First World War.

Vought F4U-1 Corsair.
(Bruce Robertson collection)

CHRONOLOGY

1900

7 March *The Bristol*, an 11,500 cu ft balloon of the 1st Balloon Section of the Royal Engineers, is attached to the Cavalry Division in South Africa and takes part in the advance on Bloemfontein and later the engagements at the Vet and Zand Rivers. It is not finally emptied until three weeks after inflation – a record for the time.

2 July Zeppelin's first airship, *Luftschiff Zeppelin 1* or *LZ1*, makes its maiden flight at 2000 hrs over Lake Constance, where it had been housed in a large, floating hangar. Problems are caused by the method of trimming, which consists of a movable lead weight sliding along a 85.3ft rail between the gondolas; this becomes jammed and an emergency landing has to be made on the lake. LZ1 is the world's first rigid dirigible airship, from which will be developed others having military potential.

19 July The British Royal Engineers' No 1 Balloon Section, having marched from Pretoria, joins General Pole Carew's force for operations in the Eastern Transvaal, but a fortnight later, on reaching Brugspruit, its oxen are taken to replace animals lost by the heavy artillery and Naval Brigade so the immobilised Section is forced to return to Pretoria by train and balloon operations cease. During the summer of this year also, the two sons of Milton Wright, Wilbur (33) and Orville (29), build their first glider to prove their theories on wing warping for lateral control. Their new craft, which has a wing area of 165 sq ft, is taken to remote Kitty Hawk to be flown as a kite after the first flight indicates that it has insufficient lift. The spot for these trials has been chosen for its prevailing winds, which average a speed of 21mph.

1901

13 October A balloon flight across the Mediterranean is made by de la Vailx from Toulon to Algeria. It has no military overtones but is viewed with disquiet by the few who know of the attempt to bomb Venice just over half a century before. The Wrights now build a second glider, a biplane with a wing area of 305 sq ft. Thoroughly tested during October and November, it is joined by a third. A total of almost one thousand flights are carried out.

1902

Now, towards the end of the year, the Wrights settle down to serious work on a powered aircraft based on experience from their gliders. Failing to find a car manufacturer to supply a suitable motor, they decide to produce a four-cylinder horizontal water-cooled engine themselves.

1903

17 December From Kitty Hawk, North Carolina, the Wright brothers achieve the first, sustained man-carrying flight in history using a controllable powered aircraft. This lasts twelve seconds with Orville at the controls, and covers a distance of 112ft at a maximum altitude of 14ft. It is followed by other flights the same day, the fourth with Wilbur aboard covering 852ft and lasting 59 seconds. The *Flyer*, as the machine becomes known, had been assembled and was ready for testing on 12 December but it was damaged by the wind during a launching attempt two days later. Construction had begun the previous June.

1904

9 November Wilbur Wright, flying an improved version of the original machine, completes nearly four circuits of an 80-acre field in a time of 5min 4sec. During the winter of the same year, detachments of the 1st and 2nd Balloons of the Royal Engineers under Lts T. H. L. Speight and P. W. L. Brooke-Smith conduct ballooning experiments in Malta and Gibraltar, and Cody man-lifting kites are about to replace those designed in 1894 by Major B. F. S. Baden-Powell of the Scots Guards for the British Army. The year has also seen the first use of the heterodyne principle for transmitting and receiving wireless signals, the first investigation of the possibilities for radio direction-finding, and also the first use of a vacuum diode valve in a receiver — all advances that are profoundly to affect the use of radio in air warfare.

1905

6 October A new, enlarged Wright biplane flies a distance of a little over 24 miles in 38min 3sec and the brothers immediately realise the enormous military potential of their machine for reconnaissance. They therefore offer one to the United States Army.

24 October A reply to the Wrights' offer states that the Board of Ordnance and Fortification 'does not care to formulate any requirements for the performance of a flying machine or take any action on the subject until a machine is produced which by actual operation is shown to be able to produce horizontal flight and carry an operator'. Meanwhile S. F. Cody is engaged in England as Chief Kiting Instructor by the Balloon Factory at Farnborough, and during this year he first flies his new glider design. Elsewhere, the German-designed kite-balloon, with its elongated envelope equipped with three fins so that it resembles the barrage balloons of the two world wars, is being evaluated for observation purposes by several countries although in the Russo–Japanese war of 1904-05 they are recorded as being singularly unsuccessful.

1906

May Colonel (later Major-General Sir John) Capper, CB, RE, Commandant of the British Army's Balloon School, is appointed Superintendent of the Balloon Factory. The former had been constituted in April, absorbing the earlier miniature balloon companies and, in addition to conducting experiments in handling balloons for manoeuvres and war, is also to look into the military potential of powered aircraft.

The year also sees the adoption by the British Army of Cody Kites, capable of lifting an observer to an altitude of some 1,500ft. The record, achieved in the previous year, is more than double that figure, and drill ensures that a kite can be set up, flown, hauled down and repacked in the twenty minutes usually taken to fill and fly a balloon. Kites have the added advantage of being easier to handle in high winds. The year sees the French Minister for War send a mission to the United States to begin negotiations with the Wrights for a manufacturing licence for their aeroplane.

1907

1 August An Aeronautical Division is created in the United States Army Signal Corps, responsible for 'balloons, air machines, and kindred subjects'. Thus is established the world's first heavier than air military aviation organization.

10 September On this date the maiden flight of the British Army airship, Dirigible No 1, better-known as the *Nulli Secundus*, takes place, piloted by Col Capper and crewed by Captain King and S. F. Cody, the latter in charge of the 50hp Antoinette engine which only he is strong enough to start. It had been bought in Paris by Capper since no suitable motor of British design was obtainable. The airship has a gas capacity of 55,000 cu ft, is 26ft in diameter and, measuring 122ft long, has an envelope of gold-beater's skin, and although of the non-rigid type has a stiffening framework suspended below with a car for the motor and crew. The suspension is by cord netting attached to fabric bands round the envelope owing to the difficulty of attaching lines to the gas-proof material. A speed of 16mph is achieved.

5 October Another flight by this vessel is made, this time over London, where both St Paul's Cathedral and Buckingham Palace are circled as part of a 3½ hour flight. During attempts to set course for home, it proves impossible to make any progress against the prevailing headwind and a forced landing is made near Crystal Palace.

This is the year during which the US Army's Brigadier-General James Allen officially issues the world's first specification for a military aeroplane. It calls for an armed machine, carrying a crew of two and capable of being used for reconnaissance. The speed demanded is 40mph and the duration one hour.

1908

2 February The US Army accepts a tender from the Wrights to build a military aircraft for two occupants and able to fly at 40mph. The cost is $25,000.

24 July The first flight takes place of the improved and remodelled *Nulli Secundus II*. Reconstructed as a semi-rigid airship, she has her gas capacity increased to 85,000 cu ft, but the maiden voyage lasts only eighteen minutes. After two further flights she is broken up. The year also sees the successful transmission of wireless messages by Army operators on the ground to the balloon *Pegasus*, 20 miles distant.

1909

25 July Louis Blériot makes the first successful aeroplane crossing of the English Channel using a monoplane of his own design. The military indications are summed up by a British newspaper the following day which announces 'England is an island no more', and Major Herbert Musgrave, a British witness to the event, is sufficiently impressed to go to the War Office and draw attention to the threat which aviation poses. On the Continent the success gives a tremendous fillip to French aviation. This is demonstrated at the Bethany aviation meeting the following month, at which Général Roques, newly appointed commander of the aviation section of the Sapper Corps (also responsible for the Army's balloon section), details a mission to select an aircraft suitable for military use. The following month orders are placed for one Blériot monoplane, two Farman biplanes and a pair of Wrights after approval from Général Brun, Minister of War. Finance is officially voted for further purchases, this time for use by the Etablissement d'Aviation at Vincennes, the commander of which, Commandant Estienne, orders a pair of Antoinette monoplanes powered by 40hp motors, three Farman biplanes with 50hp Gnome rotary engines and two more Wrights with 30hp Wright-Bériquands. Fitting these to the Wrights had been decided on a year before when it was realized that the standard engine, capable of giving only 11hp, was insufficient so that Ets Mariquand et Marre was ordered to increase the rating of the motors it was to produce under licence.

25 July The first officially recognized flight of a heavier-than-air powered aircraft takes place in Russia, made by van den Schkrouff from Odessa, flying a Voisin biplane.

2 August In the United States a Wright Model 'B' is accepted by the Army at Fort Worth to act as a test vehicle to determine the suitability of heavier-than-air craft for war and becomes the first warplane in the world. In England Captain H. P. T. Lefroy RE takes charge of Army wireless experiments.

1910

19 February Sir George White founds four companies that are to have a profound effect on the international availability of military aircraft and also undertake the very first production orders for such types in the world. The four companies are The Bristol Aeroplane Company Limited, The Bristol Aviation Company Limited, The British and Colonial Aeroplane Company Limited and The British and Colonial Aviation Company Limited.

9 June The first successful reconnaissance by a powered aircraft takes place in France, using a Henry Farman

Above: The British Army Airship *Nulli Secundus* (Second to None), which, after a 3½hr flight from Aldershot to London on 5 October 1907, was forced to land near Crystal Palace on account of deteriorating weather. The subsequent storm wrecked it.
(Author's collection)

biplane flown by Lieutenant Féquant, with Capitaine Marcormet as observer. Having taken off from Camp de Châlons, the pair take several photographs of Vincennes, some 90 miles distant, after 2½ hours' flying time.

10 June The licence-built Wright biplane ordered during 1909 is finally delivered to the French Army to be test-flown by Capitaine Etève of the Sapper-balloonists. Although this machine retains the skid undercarriage of the original, it will be replaced by wheels on subsequent machines, which will also have a different stabilizer.

30 July At Larkhill, Hampshire, the first flight of the Bristol Boxkite prototype takes place with M. Edmond, the French test-pilot at the controls. This machine has the well-known appearance with upper and lower wings of equal span, although it is not long before a new model is announced as a 'military version' with the upper planes of greater span.

10 August In France, Lieutenant Féquant successfully spots for, and directs, guns in the Nancy region – the first recorded occasion that this has been done.

27 August In the United States the first transmission of radio messages between an aircraft and a ground transmitter takes place, conducted by James McCurdy flying a Curtiss biplane. The messages are sent and received via an H. M. Horton wireless set at Sheepshead Bay, New York State.

September Large-scale French Army manoeuvres are held in the Picardy region with two Henry Farmans supporting the 9th Army Corps, a Sommer and a Blériot the 2nd, and two further Farmans, another Blériot and a Wright for other Corps. British Army manoeuvres held during the same month are supported by two Bristol Boxkites, No 8, flown by Lieutenant Loraine being fitted with a Throne-Baker wireless transmitter, accompanied by Captain Dickson in No 9. Dickson is later to predict the coming of fighter aircraft with these words: 'Both sides would be equipped with large corps of aeroplanes, each trying to obtain information of the other. The efforts which each would exert in order to hinder or prevent the enemy from obtaining information' would lead to a battle for air supremacy 'by armed aeroplanes

Above: British Naval Airship No I (R.1), unofficially known as the *Mayfly*, never took to the air as its back was broken when being manoeuvred from its floating hangar at Barrow on 22 September 1911. Its gas capacity was 663,000 cu ft, its length 512ft and the diameter 48ft. (Author's collection)

against each other.' June of this year has already seen the first missile dropped from an aircraft when Glenn Curtiss aimed dummy bombs at the outlines of a warship marked by buoys, while, also in the United States, Jacob Fickel has experimentally fired a rifle from an aircraft in flight during August.

26 September The US Navy Department designates Captain W. I. Chambers to handle all matters concerning aviation, including the establishment of a framework on which a maritime flying service might be based.

1 October The new airfield at Colindale, north of London, is opened, taking its name from nearby Hendon.

22 October In France, following a request from the Senate, an Order in Council is made granting a certain degree if independence to the Aéronautique Militaire. Général Roques is thereupon appointed Inspector of the force, relinquishing his command of the Sapper Corps.

14 November The world's first take-off from a ship is made in the United States by Eugene Ely flying a Curtiss Biplane from the deck of the US cruiser *Birmingham* at Hampton Roads, Virginia.

15 November The British and Colonial Aeroplane Company secures the first military aircraft contract in the world following negotiations via William

Rebitkoff, the Russian Attaché in Paris. This is to supply eight Bristol Boxkites fitted with enlarged fuel tanks and triple rudders. These aircraft, numbered 18 to 25, will be delivered to St Petersburg in the following April, plus No 32, the 50hp Gnome motor of which had been replaced by one of 70hp to bring it up to the standard of the others (it also has an enclosed nacelle). In July of the following year the two oldest of the eight Boxkites will be exchanged for Nos. 26 and 30.

19 December Two European-trained officers of the Japanese Army demonstrate two imported aircraft in their homeland, a Henry Farman and a Grade.

1911

18 January Curtiss demonstration pilot Eugene Ely again distinguishes himself in the United States, this time by landing on a specially constructed deck on USS *Pennsylvania* moored in San Francisco Bay, using a Curtiss biplane. The undercarriage of his aircraft is fitted with hooks which engage ropes stretched across the flight deck and attached to sandbags, serving to halt the aircraft.

28 February In England an Army order is issued creating, with effect from 1 April, an Air Battalion of the Royal Engineers consisting of two Companies, No 1 operating airships and No 2 five aeroplanes, a Wright biplane, a Farman, a Blériot, a Paulan biplane and a de Havilland. Later the total is increased to 17, with 11 different types. The Air Estimates the following month provide £85,000 for the purchase of new aircraft.

1 July The initial flight takes place of the United States Navy's first aircraft, a Curtiss A-1 hydro-aeroplane.

24 September The Royal Navy's rigid airship, popularly known as the *Mayfly* but officially as HMA No 1, ordered in 1908, breaks its back during a squall while being manoeuvred from its floating hangar. The damage means that no flight can ever be made and the 512ft monster, with a gas capacity of 663,000 cu ft is abandoned to deteriorate in its shed at Barrow.

11 October During a war in Tripolitania against the Turks, Capitano Piazza reconnoitres enemy lines flying a Blériot monoplane, one-ninth of the entire strength of the Italian air arm, which consists of two Blériots imported from France, together with three Nieuports and two Farmans, plus a pair of Etrich Taubes supplied by Austria. Two non-rigid airships are also maintained for bombing.

1 November Sottotenente Giulio Gavotti, flying an Etrich Taube, drops a bomb on Ain Zara and three over the Taguira oasis.

1 December Lt A. M. Longmore successfully lands his Short S.38 No 2 on the River Medway.

4 December In Britain, the first flight of the B.E.1 takes place. The pilot is Geoffrey de Havilland and the machine the first of a dynasty of warplanes, the chief being the B.E.2 that will, in derivative form, be used extensively during the coming European war. During this year also, Germany purchases its first eight monoplanes for military use, a pair of Grades, five Rumplers and a Schultze as well as 25 biplanes, 22 of them being of the Farman type, plus three Albatroses. Meanwhile, in America, one Lt Riley Scott has invented a primitive bomb sight. January has seen both the first landing on the deck of a warship, successfully carried out by Eugene Ely, and Glen Curtiss making a landing and take-off from water for the first time, while in Italy Capitano Guidoni has launched the first marine torpedo from an aircraft. Sweden has taken her first steps in military aviation with the purchase by the Navy of a Blériot monoplane.

1912

10 January Lt C. R. Samson makes the first flight of an aircraft from a warship in Great Britain using a 50hp Gnome-powered Short S.38 from improvised staging on the forecastle of HMS *Africa*, a *King Edward VII* class predreadnought, while at anchor off Sheerness.

1 February In England the maiden flight of the B.E.2 takes place during the morning with Geoffrey de Havilland at the controls, followed by three other flights that day. Although the aircraft will be one of the chief types in the Royal Flying Corps (yet to be formed), no armament is carried.

17 February As a result of a request made by the Governor-General of French West Africa for aircraft to support the 19th Army Corps, 400,000 francs are voted for the purchase of six aircraft to form a desert air corps. These are stationed in Algiers for operations in Afrique Occidentale Française.

29 February A law passed in France, effective from August, organizes the Aéronautique Militaire into three Groups with headquarters at Versailles, Reims and Lyon. These are to be completely independent, commanded either by a Colonel or Lieutenant-Colonel and composed of 'centres aéronautiques' (aircraft stations), as well as companies of non-flying personnel at aerodromes and special centres, among the latter being the military aviation research centre at Chalais-Meudon.

22 March In North Africa Lts de Lafargue and Reimbert, in a two-seat aircraft, begin the region's first reconnaissance flight, flying from Biskra to Touggourt.

26 March The first recorded flight of the new B.E.2 aircraft takes place in Great Britain after the aircraft has been fitted with a wireless transmitter.

13 April The Royal Flying Corps is formally constituted by Royal Warrant. The new service is to consist of a Naval Wing, a Military Wing and a Central Flying School to train pilots for both. No 2 (Aeroplane) Company of the earlier Air Battalion is to become No 3 Squadron RFC; Farnborough's pilots are formed into No 2 Squadron; and the former No 1 (Airship) Company now becomes No 1 Squadron.

9 May Eastchurch-trained Lt C. R. Samson RN flies a Short S.38 biplane from a runway erected on the fore deck of HMS *Hibernia* while the vessel is steaming at 15kt during a Review of the Fleet by HM King George V. The aircraft is fitted with air bags in case it should be necessary to alight on the water, but in fact Samson lands safely at Lodmore. The aircraft is No 2 once more, the same machine that was successfully used for the trials in January.

13 May The Air Battalion of the Royal Engineers, with its reserves, is officially absorbed into the Military Wing of the new Flying Corps.

2 June A Lewis gun mounted on a Wright Model 'B' of the US Army is fired at a cheesecloth ground target measuring 6ft by 7ft over College Park, Maryland. The gunner is Capt Charles de Forest Chandler and the pilot Lt T. de Witt Milling.

12 June The new Central Flying School, situated at Upavon, Salisbury Plain, is officially opened. It has an initial establishment of 180 men of all ranks, including a commandant, Captain G. M. Paine; a secretary, Assistant Paymaster J. N. Lidderdale; two chief instructors, Lt H. R. Cook specializing in Theory and Construction and civilian Mr G. Dobson in charge of meteorology; five officers to instruct in flying, Capt J. D. Fulton, Capt E. L. Gerrard, Lt P. A. Shepherd, Maj H. M. Trenchard and Capt J. M. Salmond; and an Inspector of Engines, Eng-Lt C. R. J. Randall, a medical officer, Capt E. G. R. Lithgow, and, as Quartermaster, The Hon Lt Kirby. To these are added 63 NCOs to assist in training the 68 pupils. Buildings, fourteen in all, including those for transport, workshops and hangarage, are erected not far from the Netheravon Cavalry School.

2 July The total of aeroplanes listed to participate in the Military trials (more correctly called the Military Aeroplane Competition) scheduled to take place at Larkhill on August is 32 from 21 entrants, and although the majority are of British design, some are of overseas origin. The winner is a Cody biplane, the judges seemingly being over-influenced by the view afforded to the pilot: the type is totally unsuited to waging war.

27 August When the trials end on this date, wisely only two Cody machines are ordered. The actual competition machine, entry No 31, described as a Cody V, is one that is officially taken on charge on 27 November to become the RFC's No 301, and another is specially constructed and delivered on 20 February the following year. This is No 304, which will be presented to the Science Museum, South Kensington, with a total flying time of under three hours. Both Cody biplanes are powered by 120hp Austro-Daimler motors.

6 September The British Army's Deperdussin monoplane No 258 suddenly breaks up in flight while over Graveley, near Hitchen, flown by Capt Patrick Hamilton with Lt Wyness-Stuart as passenger. Both men are killed.

10 September A fatal crash of Bristol-Coanda monoplane No 263 occurs due to accidental operation of the quick-release of the flying wires. The machine falls near Port Meadow, Oxford, killing Lts E. Hotchkiss and C. A. Bettington.

13 September Coupled with the fact that two fatal civilian aeroplane crashes have taken place not long before, the Secretary of State places a ban on the future use of monoplanes by the military in Great Britain as a precaution against that type of configuration being inherently dangerous.

16 September At the British Army's autumn manoeuvres two squadrons of eight aircraft participate with promising results.

28 September A Military and Naval Aircraft Review is held at Hendon. Here monoplanes are still to be seen, but all are operated by the Royal Flying Corps' Naval Wing since Winston Churchill, First Lord of the Admiralty, has not followed the Army example and imposed a similar ban.

1 October While a fund-raising campaign encourages civilian contributions, the German Air Arm is inaugurated. Eighty million marks - equivalent to £400,000 - is provided for Army aviation, including dirigibles, plus a substantial share of the 800 million marks reserved for work over the next five years. The new air force is to be commanded by two Inspector-Generals and divided into four battalions with stations at Aachen, Allenstein, Cologne, Darmstadt, Doeb-

ritz, Freiburg, Grandenz, Hannover, Insterburg, Juterborg, Königsberg, Metz, Posen, Strassburg and Zeithain. Diedenhofen, Döberitz, Metz, Oberwiesenfeld bei München, Saarburg and Sperenberg bei Juterborg are the planned locations for Army flying schools. In addition to the aircraft purchased in 1911, the following are taken on charge during this year: 20 Bristols, one Dornier, two Etrich Taubes, two Grades, six Harlans, 20 Mars and 40 Rumpler Taubes. All these are monoplanes, to which must be added biplanes comprising 50 Albatroses, twelve Aviatiks, 30 Eulers, ten Ottos, a pair of LVGs, ten Mars and six Wrights, making a grand total, with those bought in the previous year, of 244, about 200 of which, according to contemporary comment are 'war effective'. Meanwhile the German Navy is currently adding to its Curtiss floatplane bought during 1911 two more of these, four Eulers and four 'Albatros hydros' (floatplanes), and to these biplanes are added four Rumpler monoplane 'hydros'.

12 November During a series of experiments in the United States to determine the possibilities of catapult-assisted aircraft take-offs, Lt Theodore G. Ellyson, the US Navy's first qualified pilot (soon joined by Lt John Rodgers), makes the first successful launch of this type using a Curtiss A-1 flown from a compressed-air catapult.

Other significant events in aviation this year include steps by Turkey to obtain aircraft and pilots from Germany for her use in the war being waged in the Balkans; the placing of an order by Britain with the German Parseval company for the non-rigid 330,000 cu ft airship PL-18 (to become Naval Airship No 4); and the Argentine authorities' laying of the foundations of the Fuerza Aérea Argentina by establishing in September a Military Aviation School at El Palomar, equipping it with machines of French design.

1913

26 February The French military air arm embarks on a long-distance flight linking Biskra with Tunis via Tozeur, Gabès, Sfax and Sousse using four Henry Farmans, the pilots being Lts Reimbert, Cheutin and Jolain, plus Sgt-Maj Hurars.

3 March The eight French flyers (mechanics were carried in the second seats) arrive safely despite violent thunderstorms at what was later to be known as El-Aouina.

30 March It is announced that the total number of aircraft expected on the strength of the Naval Wing of the Royal Flying Corps within the year is 'about 32', including those on order and trainers. This number includes seven monoplanes made up of one Blériot, two Deperdussins and two Shorts, one Etrich and one Nieuport. Fifteen biplanes are made up of single examples of an Avro, Breguet, Caudron and Maurice Farman, with pairs of Bristols, Henry Farmans and Sopwiths together with five of Short design. Ten floatplanes completed the total, from which 16 are said to be available at short notice for war purposes, including an Astra, an Avro, a Donnet-Leveque, a Henry and a Maurice Farman, plus a pair of Borels and three Shorts.

2 May A new British altitude record of 8,400ft is established by Maj E. L. Gerrard, who also takes a passenger on the attempt. Although this is made purely for aeronautical achievement, its significance is not lost on military planners.

9 May A Royal Review by King George V, accompanied by the Queen and the Princesses Mary and Victoria, takes place at Farnborough to inspect 'all the aircraft of the British Army available for immediate service, namely, 17 aeroplanes and two airships'. On the same day, at Buc, France, King Alfonso of Spain reviews 'four squadrons of the French flying corps'.

13 May In Russia, the first flight is made from St Petersburg (later Leningrad) of Igor Sikorsky's four-motor Bolshoi biplane. A derivative, Le Grand, will fly at that summer's Army manoeuvres, and another, the Ilya Mourometz type, is to be developed into a bomber eventually capable of taking a 920lb bomb and setting new military standards.

3 June The Royal Flying Corps is reviewed on Laffan's Plain, near Salisbury, Wiltshire.

12 June The French-built non-rigid dirigible later to become Naval Airship No 3, begins her trials at Farnborough and is accepted the following month after slight modifications. It is described as 'the fastest airship in the world'. The only British airship of its time to be armed, it carries a single Hotchkiss machine gun.

30 June The Parseval airship ordered from Germany is officially accepted at the end of her trials in England to became Naval Airship No 4, 'so that,' comments *The Aeroplane*, 'we come into the possession of two really practical airships'.

1 September Capt Becke, of No 2 Squadron RFC, flies the 375 miles from Montrose to Limerick, including the crossing from Stranraer to Limerick, in a single day.

25 September The Royal Flying Corps succeeds in contributing two airships and 45 aeroplanes to an autumn Army exercise, flying a total, it is claimed, of some 10,000 miles in the process.

22 November A British record is set up by Capt Longcroft flying from Montrose to Portsmouth and then back to Farnborough non-stop using 'a Bristol-built B.E. with a 70hp Renault engine'.

29 November A new British type, the Sopwith Tabloid, is assessed at Farnborough and proves to have an astonishing maximum speed of 92mph and an initial rate of climb of 1,200ft/min. The immediate official reaction is an order for nine, costing £1,075 each, with the idea of using them for fast communication and scouting, the latter indicating that aeroplanes are still looked on as successors to the balloons of the previous century and originating the type name by which fighter aircraft are to be known for many years to come.

22 December During acceptance tests for the French Army, a Voisin powered by an 80hp Gnome climbs to an altitude of 3,300ft in 13min 45sec with M. Rugere at the controls. This is claimed to be the first time that a military biplane with an engine of 80hp has risen to that height in less than 15min. Genuine naval air operations still lie in the future, although the opening eight weeks of this year find the United States' embryonic naval air arm participating in exercises with the Fleet. In Europe, the Royal Navy employs aeroplanes in its July manoeuvres for the first time and HMS *Hermes*, a 5,600-ton *Highflyer* class protected cruiser, has been fitted with an aeroplane launching platform (which, however, is little used as most of the aircraft participation is from shore stations). In March the sum of £321,000 is set aside in the Naval Estimates for aviation, providing an interesting comparison with the 50 million marks (equivalent to £250,000 at the time), plus a generous proportion of a 'special fund', voted for naval air expenditure in Germany. Six German naval air stations have been set up by this year, at Cuxhaven, Emden and Hombourg on the North Sea and at Kiel, Putzig and Königsberg on the Baltic coast, while there now exist flying schools at Holminsal and Putzig for the instruction of German naval aviators. Towards the close of the year a Grahame-White with a machine gunner seated below the pilot is demonstrated at Bisley, and at the Olympia Air Show in London, France has exhibited an armoured biplane. Meanwhile new regulations have been issued for future warplanes of the German Army. These machines must (a) 'henceforth be entirely of national manufacture'; (b) 'be capable of being fitted with bomb racks and reconnaissance cameras'; (c) 'have a minimum speed of 56mph'; (d) 'measure no more than 49 feet in wing span, have a length no greater than 32 feet and not exceed 13 feet in height, and have engines of no more than 100hp'; and (e) have a minimum endurance of four hours.

Elsewhere Brazil has formed a naval seaplane school with a single Italian Bossi seaplane, Holland established the Lucht Vaart Afdeling as part of the Army in July, and Norway has undertaken her first army and naval air operations. This year has also seen the establishment of a new naval air station on Calshot Spit under the command of Lt Spencer D. A. Grey RN during March, the same month as the 1st Aero Squadron was established at Texas City with Curtiss R-3 biplanes. However, disgusted with the official lack of interest in his having fitted a machine gun to a Wright biplane, Col Isaac N. Lewis leaves the United States and sets up a factory to produce machine guns at Liége, Belgium.

1914

25 April US naval aircraft are called upon during the crisis in Mexico, their purpose being – with the aid of five aircraft and seven pilots sent as detachments aboard the USS *Birmingham* and USS *Mississippi* – to support the Atlantic Fleet.

28 June In Sarajevo, the capital of Bosnia, a political fanatic named Gavrilo Princip murders the only man who could have held together the turbulent factions of the Austro-Hungarian Empire, the Archduke Francis Ferdinand of Austria. This was the catalyst that inflamed the underground power struggles taking place in Europe. One commentator foresees events, remarking that 'The sky is about to become a battleground.'

30 June The first Sopwith SS.1 Tabloid aircraft, No 381, is issued to No 5 Squadron RFC at Netheravon, having been flown from Farnborough by Maj Higgins.

1 July The Naval Wing of the RFC becomes the Royal Naval Air Service under the command of the pioneer Cdr C. R. Samson. All military airships are transferred to this service at the same time.

2 July The 'Camp of Concentration' for the RFC is held at Netheravon, from where all the Corps' squadrons, Nos 1 from Farnborough, 2 from Montrose, 3 and 4 already at Netheravon, and the nucleus of a fifth, disperse after a month. The idea of such a mock mobilization has seemingly come from the commander of the Military Wing, Lt-Col F. H. Sykes and the set programme follows a daily pattern of devoting the mornings to practical trials and experiments and the afternoons to lectures and discussions.

18 July The United States' Aeronautical Division of the Army's Signal Corps is redesignated the Aviation Division with 60 officers and 260 men. In Great Britain between this date and 22 July a Royal Review of the Fleet and manoeuvres take place at Spithead, most of the aircraft being concentrated at Calshot, Portsmouth and Weymouth.

20 July A formation flight of seventeen aircraft, plus two airships, takes place over the assembled vessels.

28 July A successful experiment is carried out in which an 810lb, 14in torpedo is dropped from a Short seaplane powered by a 160hp Gnome motor.

26 July It is decided that the Fleet should not disperse as previously ordered on this date owing to the deteriorating international situation, the aeroplanes being instead kept ready for action at Grain, Felixstowe and Yarmouth.

30 July Czar Nicholas II of Russia finally orders general mobilization at 1800 hrs.

1 August Germany orders general mobilization at 1700 hrs and declares war on Russia. France orders general mobilization at 1705 hrs.

3 August Germany declares war on France.

4 August Germany invades Belgium and receives a British ultimatum to withdraw. No reply is received, so Great Britain automatically enters the war at 2300 hrs. The outbreak of the First World War finds Britain with 110 military aircraft and seven airships; France has 160 warplanes and about 15 airships, although most were of doubtful military value. The RFC and RNAS have 197 officers and 1,647 men. Belgium has no lighter-than-air craft and only 25 aeroplanes. Russia at the same time allegedly has 300 military aircraft and eleven dirigibles, although how many of the former are suitable for operational use or are airworthy is in doubt; certainly the total is fewer than the 500 unofficially announced at the time. The outbreak of war also finds Austria-Hungary with one airship and 35 aeroplanes. The German total is 246 machines organized in 41 flight sections, plus eleven airships, many of Zeppelin design. About half of the former consist of 'Taubes' (a title describing the appearance, not the manufacturer, and covering both single- and two-seaters), plus Albatros and Aviatik two-seat biplanes, although all are in fact unsuited to real military tasks.

5 August Naval Airship No 4 (NA.4, the Parseval) carries out the first air action of the war, escorting troop ferries between Dover and Calais.

6 August German airship Z.VI bombs Liége, its fortress lying in the path of Moltke's push across Belgium. The airship lacks proper bombs, so eight heavy artillery shells are carried fitted with pieces of horse blanket to act as fins, but on descending through cloud to find its target the airship is so severely shot up by ground fire that a return towards friendly territory has to be made, which ends in a crash-landing in the forest outside Bonn.

Above: The plaque on the Royal Flying Corps memorial at Swingate Downs, Dover, marking the spot from which Nos 2, 3, 4 and 5 Squadrons departed for war between 13 and 15 August 1914. (Author)

13 August. The RFC begins to ferry by air the machines of Nos 2, 3, 4 and 5 Squadrons from Swingate Downs, Dover, to Amiens. They carry no armament, so the pilots, wearing the inner tubes of motor tyres in case they have to land in the English Channel, are ordered to ram any enemy which might be encountered. Squadron distribution by November sees Headquarters retain control over No 4, the Wireless Unit and Aircraft Park at St Omer, while the allocation to formations is as follows: No 2 to IV Corps, No 3 (later) to the Indian Corps, No 5 to III Corps and No 6 to II Corps.

21 August Germany loses two of her surviving front-line dirigibles, one to French ground fire and the other to fire from friendly troops who mistake its identification flares.

25 August At a little after 1100 hrs Lts Harvey-Kelly and Mansfield, in a B.E. two-seater accompanied by two others, succeed in driving down a photographic Taube, which nevertheless lands safely in a field near Merville, the crew, a sergeant and observer officer, escaping into a wood. Hopes of exam-

ining the aircraft are prevented when it is set alight by British troops.

26 August On the Eastern Front, Russian Staff Captain Nesterov dies as a result of deliberately ramming an aircraft of the Austrian Air Corps. The Austrian pilot, Lt Baron von Rosenthal, also dies.

30 August Four light bombs are dropped from a German Taube flown by Lt von Hiddessen on the outskirts of Paris

22 September The first use of wireless from aeroplanes to artillery is made as a result of the attachment of Lt Swain Lewis and Baron Trevenen James to No 4 Squadron to experiment in this field, although the crew are hampered by bulky equipment weighing some 75lb which takes up the whole of the observer's cockpit and part of the pilot's. In June these officers had made a flight from Netheravon to Bournemouth in a pair of suitably equipped B.E.s, and, although flying ten miles apart, they had experienced no difficulty in keeping in touch with each other by wireless telegraphy throughout the journey. On this date also the RNAS sends four aircraft from Antwerp to bomb the airship sheds at Düsseldorf and Cologne. Only Flt Lt C. H. Collet manages to find the first, but his bombs miss their target.

5 October Cpl Quenault (observer) and Sgt Joseph Frantz (pilot) in a Voisin of the Aéronautique Militaire bring down an Aviatik in flames near Rheims.

6 October No 6 Squadron RFC finally leaves Farnborough for Bruges, its departure delayed as a result of its numbers having been reduced in order to bring the other squadrons up to strength for their earlier departure. The flight is formed by Maj J. H. W. Becke, the commanding officer, in B.E.2a 667; Capt F. J. L. Cogan in B.E.2b 646, Capt A. C. E. Marsh in B.E.2a 492 and Capt C. L. N. Newall in B.E.2a 488, these being the flight commanders. The remaining personnel consist of Capt G. H. Cox in B.E.8 636, Capt A. Ross-Hume in Henry Farman 440, Capt W. Lawrence in an similar type numbered 680 and Lt P. Rawson-Shaw in an

unidentified B.E., with Lt J. B. J. Leighton in B.E.8 632, Lt L. G. Hawker in Henry Farman 653 (he was to take over 'B' Flight's B.E.2c 1780 at Bailleul on 1 January 1915), Lt C. Y. McDonald in another Henry Farman, number 669, and Sgt C. Gallie with B.E.2a 470.

8 October An attack is mounted by the RNAS against airship sheds at Cologne which had escaped during the earlier operation. The pilots are Sqn Cdr Spencer D. Grey in Sopwith Tabloid 167, which takes off at 1320 hrs, and Flt Lt Reginald L. G. Marix in 168, which takes off ten minutes later. Mist obscures the ground so that bombs dropped from 600ft cause a massive explosion from the hangar, destroying the Army Airship LIX inside; the vessel had made its first flight only on 29 July.

21 November Another attack is made on airship sheds, this time at Friedrichshafen on Lake Constance by four RNAS Avro 504s. The force consists of pilots Sqn Cdr E. Featherstone

Briggs, Flt Cdr J. T. Babington, Flt Lt Sidney Vincent Sippe and Flt Sub-Lt R. P. Cannon flying Nos 873, 875, 874 and 179 respectively.

27 November Japanese naval seaplanes make the first air attack in history against maritime installations when two Maurice Farman Longhorn floatplanes, operating from the seaplane tender *Wakamiya Maru*, bomb the fortress at Tsingtao as well as German and Austro-Hungarian warships in nearby Kiaochow Bay.

29 November The RFC in France is organized into Wings, Nos 2 and 4 Squadrons forming the 1st Wing while Nos 5 and 6 constitute the 2nd.

8 December The Wireless Flight attached to No 4 Squadron RFC now becomes No 9 Squadron and is to take charge of all the developmental wireless work in France.

25 December The RNAS attempts to attack the airship base at Cuxhaven using seaplanes — the first offensive strike by this type of aircraft in the

Above: An example of a reconnaissance photograph, of which thousands were taken between 1914 and 1918. This shows the Yser Canal cutting through devastated country. It was taken by Lt Wilson of No 7 Squadron from an R.E.8. (Dr A. G. Wilson)

history of air warfare. The aircraft and seaplane carriers involved were:

Type/number	Vessel	Crew
Short Folder/119	*Engadine*	Flt Cdr Ross
Short Folder/120	*Engadine*	Flt Lt Miley Short
Folder/122	*Engadine*	Flt Cdr Gaskell
Short 135/135	*Riviera*	Flt Cdr Hewlett
Short 135/136	*Riviera*	Flt Cdr Kilner, Lt Childers*
Short 74/811	*Riviera*	Flt Lt Edmonds
Short 74/812	*Empress*	Flt Lt Bone, AM Waters
Short 74/814	*Empress*	Flt Sub-Lt Blackburn, CPO Bell
Short 74/815	*Empress*	Flt Cdr Oliver, CPO Budds

*Author of *The Riddle of the Sands* (1903)

Also this year, during an action in Mexico, an operation in direct support of a naval sweep is carried out by a Curtiss AB flying boat while searching for mines in Vera Cruz harbour.

1915
7 January The German High Command decides to attack British military installations with rigid airships. This decision is soon changed to include London, though avoiding royal residences.

19 January The first enemy Zeppelin raid on Britain is made by L3, L4 and L6 carrying both 110lb high-explosive bombs and incendiaries. Despite fog patches and freezing rain bombs are dropped on Sheringham and Snettisham in Norfolk.

19 February RNAS aircraft assist in the bombardment of fortresses in the Dardanelles.

21 February The first night attack on a target in the British Isles is carried out by a single Friedrichshafen FF29, No 203, crewed by pilot Stephan Prondzynski and observer Fähnrich zur See Heym, two incendiary bombs being dropped on Braintree and one high-explosive bomb each near Coggeshall and on Colchester between 1945 and 2045 hrs.

10 March British troops on the Western Front open what is to become the Battle of Neuve Chapelle, the first ground operation in which an air arm plays an integrated part, directing artillery fire by means of the 'Clock System', systematic patrols of the battlefield, air attacks synchronized with the battle plan and on railway junctions and headquarters, and photographic reconnaissance, from an experimental branch directed by Lt J. T. C. Moore-Brabazon (later Lord Brabazon of Tara), who is assisted by Lt C. D. M. Campbell, Flt Sgt Laws and 2/AM W. D. Corse, all experts in photography and the use of the Type 'A' cameras that are employed. Battery ranging from the air by wireless is also carried out.

21 March The first attack by an airship on Paris results in one person being killed and eight wounded.

24 March Five British naval aircraft mount an attack on the German submarine base at Antwerp, where intelligence sources indicate a small type of U-boat (UB class) is being prepared. The attack is led by Sqn Cdr A. M. Longmore, but only two machines penetrate the defences, those flown by Sqn Cdr Ivor T. Courtney, who drops 20lb bombs on the Hoboken workshops, and by Flt Lt Harold Rosher, who attacks from only 1,000ft. It is decided to restrict future attacks to Zeebrugge and Ostend.

1 April French pilot Roland Garros achieves his first victory using a gun firing through the airscrew arc by means of deflectors fitted to the blades, a device perfected by Raymond Saulnier.

7 April Begun in February, experiments in England are now deemed to show that naval gunfire can be directed from aircraft, although several indications of this have already taken place on a local level in various theatres.

26 April A violent assault using poison gas is made on Allied positions in the Ypres sector. This is to trigger an air reprisal exactly a month later. German casualties are reported to be 800,000 by this time.

8 May The first Kite Balloon Section of the RNAS reaches France.

26 May An attack directed against the chemical factory at Ludwigshafen by a formation of Voisins is led by Cdt de Goys, using modified 90mm and 115mm artillery shells as bombs. They left their home base shortly before dawn and claim to have damaged the target.

31 May The first night attack on London is made by Army Zeppelins LZ38 (Hpt Linnarz) and LZ37.

7 June Airship LZ37 is brought down from 11,000ft over Ghent at about 0215 hrs as a result of having been bombed from above by Flt Lt R. Warneford RNAS flying Morane Type 'L' 3253 using six 20lb bombs.

4 July Oswald Boelcke wins his first victory in the air while flying a two-seater when his observer is successful in bringing down a Morane after twenty minutes stalking their quarry. The victims are pilot Tétu and observer Comte de la Rofoucauld.

1 August The first victory with a forward gun firing through the airscrew disc of a Fokker E.1 is claimed over the Western Front by Immelmann.

10 August Airship L12 (Peterson) is brought down by ground fire from the 3in naval guns at Dover into the English Channel at 0240 hrs. Unsuccessful attempts to destroy it with 20lb bombs are made as it lies beside the quay at Ostend whence it had been towed by a German torpedo boat at first light.

12 August The first successful attack against a ship by means of a torpedo dropped from an aircraft is made by Short Type 184 seaplane No 185 flying from the Gulf of Xeros against a Turkish vessel in the Straits. The British pilot, Flt Cdr Edmonds from the carrier *Ben-My-Chree*, descends to 15ft above the water to make sure of his aim.

In the year that the London Aerodrome, later to be generally known merely as Hendon, becomes a military station for the use of the RNAS, German Fokker E.IIIs are beginning to make things uncomfortable for the Allies on the Western Front, a state of affairs that is later to be known as the 'Fokker Scourge' but which begins with the introduction of these monoplanes fitted with synchronized guns in July. One of the attempts to counter this is the tactic of flying in close formation, introduced in August by French Capitaine Felix Happe. New types of aeroplane are also being introduced by the

Above: A German rope-bound incendiary bomb dropped in the yard of Charlton Road Fire Station, London, during September 1915. (Via P Lamb)

Allies, such as the British F.E.2b and de Havilland D.H.2 (both aircraft appearing in February and retaining the pusher configuration) and the French Nieuport 11, a tractor machine appearing in July which overcame the problem of the forward-firing gun by having it mounted above the upper wing to fire outside the arc of the airscrew. Earlier in the year an LVG E.VI fitted with a gun firing through the airscrew disc with the aid of a Schneider interrupter gear, based on trials that took place before 1914, had been dispatched to the Front but was

destroyed before being used operationally.

1916

31 January Nine German naval airships, L11 (Kptlt von Buttlar), L13 (Kptlt Mathy), L14 (Kptlt Bocker), L15 (Kptlt Breithaupt), L16 (Oblt z S Peterson), L17 (Kptlt Ehrich), L19 (Kptlt Loewe), L20 (Kptlt Stabbert) and L21 (Kptlt Dietrich) set out to attack Liverpool in the evening, causing the deaths of 70 persons and injuring 113.

16 February The British War Office reassumes responsibility for the aerial

defence of the country from the Admiralty.

21 February The Battle of Verdun opens in France. During this, the enemy uses aircraft for Contact Patrols on a large scale for the first time, employing 145 machines. The patrols are at first regarded as a failure but later prove of extreme value to corps commanders in the field who have lost contact with forward troops. In addition to harassing Allied forces, the enemy maintains communication with isolated battalions and companies by means of message drops and coloured streamers or pennants, receiving replies in the form of strips of cloth laid out on the ground. To oppose the German assault, France alone flies a total of 1,149 sorties.

15 March Punitive action under the command of US Gen Pershing begins on the Mexican border against the forces of Pancho Villa, with air support by the 1st Aero Squadron's Curtiss JN-4s marked with the original US national marking of a small red, five-pointed star on the rudder and under the lower wing tips. The machines are entirely clear-doped and are identified by large black numbers on the fuselage sides just aft of the rear cockpit and at the mid-point of the semi-span. Examples are '42', '43' (Lt Dargue) and '44' (Capt Dodd). Capt Foulois is the squadron commander. This is the first ever military operation to be carried out by US Army aircraft. Ten pilots and 85 men with eight machines had originally been sent out, but such are the climatic conditions that by April only two JN-4s remain airworthy.

19 March German seaplanes carry out daylight attacks on targets in Dover, Deal and Ramsgate just before midday. This is regarded as the most ambitious raid on the Kent coast to date.

1 April London is attacked by airships of the German Navy, while those of the Army set out for targets in East Anglia but return because of bad weather. Of the Navy vessels, L13 (Kptlt Mathy), L14 (Kptlt Bocker), L15 (Kptlt Breithaupt), L16 (Oblt z S Peterson) and L22 (Kptlt Deitrich), the third is brought down in the Thames Estuary by anti-aircraft fire. L9 and L11 had also been included in the force, but suffered engine trouble.

12 April Work is completed on fitting the seaplane carrier *Campania* with a flying-off deck. The ship is also to be used for experiments with kite balloons.

14 April British naval aircraft carry out an attack on Constantinople (later renamed Istanbul) and Adrianople.

15 April Between this date and the 29th, 16,800lb of food supplies are air-dropped to the British 6th Division in Kut-el-Amara, besieged since 7 December 1915, 5,000lb of flour, sugar, salt etc being required daily. The threat of interception and the difficulties of reaching an operational ceiling in the heat and of aiming sacks without the aid of parachutes, so that many fall into the hands of enemy Turks, all add to the problems of the operation. The only means of protecting the supplies is by using double hessian sacks. In command of the garrison is Maj-Gen Townshend, who had sent a radio message appealing for assistance at the end of March emphasizing the grave position in which the 13,840 troops and 3,700 town Arabs found themselves. With no alternative source of supplies, his requirements are based on an estimate of a 6oz ration per man per day, and to meet this demand pilots take a 50lb bag of flour lashed above each lower wing and dropped by simply cutting the rope. Under the fuselage of each aircraft a hastily designed beam fitted with a crude release gear takes a pair of 25lb bags, all adding to the load, which is such that no observers can be carried by the Army aircraft (chiefly B.E.2s of No 30 Squadron) and Navy aircraft involved. Some pilots make as many as four trips a day.

20 April The 'American Squadron' in France, later to become N124, commanded by French officer Lt de Meux, is created with seven US pilots, Thaw, Prince, Cowdin, Rockwell, Hall, McConnell and Chapman (see 18 May).

23 April New measures are taken to protect bombers operating by daylight, and on this date nine Sopwith 1½ Strutters carry out a photographic sortie on enemy targets, in company with a similar number of bombers, the whole formation escorted by twelve Sopwith Pups and three Spads.

29 April By this date 140 individual flights to supply Kut have been made (see 15 April) and surrender negotiations have begun with the Turks three days before, since the end of the operation finds only one pilot passed fit to fly. One-third of the 12,000 troops taken prisoner will die in captivity.

18 May American Kiffin Rockwell, flying a Nieuport Bébé, gains N124's first victory near Mulhouse, France (see 20 April).

31 May On this date and on June 1 the Battle of Jutland takes place in the North Sea, the Germans employing five airships for reconnaissance, while the British seaplane carrier HMS *Engadine* launches Short 184 floatplane, No 8395 shortly after 1500 hrs, crewed by Flt Cdr Rutland and Assistant Paymaster Trewin to make a reconnaissance. (The fuselage of this aircraft is still preserved.)

10 June Belgian Lts Behaeghe (pilot) and observer Colignan fly one of four seaplanes specially obtained from the RNAS at Zanzibar to bomb the German warship *Graf von Goetzan* at Kigoma, 145 miles from their base at M'toa on Lake Tanganyika. A sortie by three floatplanes two days later is aborted due to mist. Aircraft used are 150hp

Above: A composite SS-type airship envelope and a B.E.2c were tried out by Cdr Usborne and Lt-Cdr Hicks in an attempt to gain early altitude before separating for airship interception, but it unfortunately crashed into the goods yard of Strood railway station on 21 February 1916 and both men were killed. (JMB/GSL collection)

Sunbeam Crusader-powered Short 827s 3093, 3094, 3095 (all built by Short Bros) and 8219 (built by Parnall & Son)

25 June Four balloons are destroyed by British aeroplanes armed with Le Prieur rockets.

1 July At 0730 hrs the Battle of the Somme opens, an Anglo-French offensive which finds the RFC in France with 386 aircraft on charge equipping 27 squadrons so that the first British contact patrols are carried out. On the ground, 30,000 men are lost in the first hour, and double that number by the end of the day. This engagement will last for twenty weeks, France alone losing 200,000 men on the ground during that time.

16 July The second prototype of the new R.E.8 is sent to France for evaluation but the heaviness of the controls and the aircraft's sluggish turn characteristics come in for unfavourable comment.

31 July London and counties in the south-east of England are raided by eight enemy naval airships after dark, but the force is scattered by high winds and bombs have to be dropped from above the cloud.

24 August Eight die when airships raid London's outskirts.

28 August Italy enters the European conflict with a declaration of war on Germany.

30 August Oswald Boelcke's Jagdstaffel 2 is formed and member Manfred von Richthofen claims his first victory over a British aircraft eighteen days later above Cambrai while flying an Albatros D.II during the new unit's first patrol.

3 September During a night patrol Lt W. L. Robinson of No 39 (HD) Squadron RFC brings down enemy Schütte-Lanz Army airship SL11 (Hpt Schramm) over Cuffley, Hertfordshire, while flying B.E.2c 2693.

6 September Trials are conducted investigating the possibility of refuelling non-rigid airship C.1 from the light cruiser HMS *Canterbury*.

12 September On Long Island in the United States, the first tests begin of Dr Elmer Sperry's Hewlett-Sperry aerial torpedo, a 600lb radio-controlled biplane flying bomb with a 40hp Ford engine.

15 September The Battle of Fleurs-Coucelette opens on the Western Front

and sees the first use of tanks. These are manned by the newly formed Heavy Section of the Machine Gun Corps. Forty-nine such vehicles take part and aircraft are ordered to cooperate, this being the first combination of the two new forms of warfare.

23 September Two naval Zeppelins are destroyed, L32 (Oblt zur See Peterson) near Billericay by Lt Sowrey flying B.E.2c 4112 and L33 (Kptlt Bocker) over Little Wigborough as the result of ground fire and engagement with Lt L. de B. Brandon in B.E.2c 4544. The intended targets for the twelve airships sent were London and the Midlands.

1 October Enemy Zeppelin L31, commanded by Kptlt Mathy, is brought down over Potters Bar by 2/Lt Tempest flying B.E.2c 4577 of No 39 Squadron. The loss of the experienced Mathy is a severe blow to the Kaiser's Navy. Eleven airships were dispatched for targets in London and the Midlands, but one, L30 (Kptlt von Buttlar), was forced to return to base.

9 October On the Western Front initial deliveries of the new French Spad VII scouts begin to No 19 Squadron, RFC. The type made its first flights in April, but subsequent deliveries have been slow. The first deliveries to French units began on September 2.

22 October The first delivery of the new Sopwith Pup scout (A627, constructed by the Standard Motor Co) is made to No 54 Squadron RFC. By the end of the year a total of 20 will have brought the unit to operational strength.

9 November The first HE bomb weighing 500lb is dropped on Ostend during a night attack by a Short 184 seaplane. An air fight takes place north-east of Bapaume involving an estimated total of 56 machines, 30 German and 26 British a very considerable number for the time.

22 November The first flight takes place of the first of the three prototype S.E.5s, piloted by Frank Gooden. On the next day the aircraft is test-flown by Albert Ball who, although later to change his opinion, is known to have remarked of the S.E. 'It's a bloody awful aeroplane' (see 7 May 1917).

28 November An audacious daylight raid on London is made by an LVG C.IV, No 272/16. Six 22lb bombs are

dropped between Brompton Road and Victoria Station.

2 December France's Ministère de la Guerre advises the Commander of the French Army, Général Joffre, that the former 'American Squadron' will henceforth be known as the *Escadrille Lafayette*. Part of the French forces, it will be termed SPA124 after receiving Spads as replacements for its Nieuports and will finally be absorbed by the United States Army in France on 19 February 1918.

4 December An official return mentions a proposed adaptation of a Sopwith Pup to be powered with a 110hp Clerget, replacing the standard 80hp engine and enabling work to begin on what will become the Sopwith Camel. By the end of 1916 the RFC's cumbersome wireless sets are being replaced by a lighter apparatus produced by the Stirling Telephone Co. H. P. Holland has collaborated with Prof A. M. Low to produce a radio-controlled, monoplane guided missile that has been built by the Royal Aircraft Factory and termed the 'Aerial Target' to conceal its real purpose.

In Germany, Hans Burkhardt has evolved the two-motor Gotha G.II which first flew in March and will later see active service on the Western Front with such units as Bogohl III at Ghent. Other new aircraft appearing in the year have been France's Caudron R.IV and Britain's D.H.2 in February, Sopwith Pup in September and Sopwith Triplane three months later. In November a force of RFC B.E.2cs is formed to assist the troops of the Sheriff of Arabia, who was about to revolt against the Turks. In the United States, August has seen the foundation of a Naval Flying Corps with 150 officers and 350 men, while provision has also been made for a Naval Reserve Flying Corps. With a few Castaibert two-seat monoplanes, Uruguay has established an air service, the Escuela Militar de Aeronautica. In Japan designers Lts Nakajima and Magoshi have seen the construction of the first indigenous floatplane, the Type Yokosho, while the Yokosuka Naval Air Corps was activated (the first of two) in April.

1917

3 January The first meeting of the reconstituted British Air Board takes place under the presidency of Lord Cowdray.

13 January Reported as missing over the Western Front on this date are Lts Bentley and Hinckley of No 5 Squadron's B.E.2d 5755 in which they took off at 1430 hrs for 'liaison practice with a klaxon horn', this being a semi-experimental method of air-to-ground communication in use at the time. Poor weather over the Front, which will show no signs of lifting until the week beginning the 21st, causes the abandonment of all but a few operations on both side of the lines.

1 February This date sees the commencement of unrestricted submarine warfare by the enemy, a change in naval policy which is to have a widening effect on the tasks carried out by aircraft, including those in the lighter-than-air category. Although used for convoy escort from the first days of the war, these craft were modified and introduced for eight-hour duration patrols after hasty improvisation over a period of three weeks by the British.

11 February The first air attack on the submarine assembly yards at Antwerp, using 25lb high explosive bombs.

12 March The first events in Russia take place which will become the revolution that overthrows the power of Czar Nicholas II and the Romanovs as well as concluding all organized warfare against the Kaiser's Germany.

17 March Royal Flying Corps Communiqué No 79 is the first not to include a list of casualties suffered on the Western Front during the previous week, a security measure that reflects mounting losses which will, in association with the planned offensive, culminate in 'Bloody April'.

23 March British reports continue to describe reconnaissances of the Hindenburg Line in preparation for a new offensive. Photographic sorties of this part of the line have been carried out since the preceding October. Among the squadrons carrying out this work is No 70, flying Sopwith 1½ Strutters, its Commanding Officer being Maj (later Air Chief Marshal) A. W. Tedder.

6 April The United States of America joins the Allies in the war against Germany.

7 April No 56 Squadron RFC takes its new S.E.5s to France, only to be ordered home again in June to augment Home Defence. On the return of the Squadron to France, it re-equips with S.E.5as.

13 April The 'Spider Web' Anti-Submarine Patrols begin from the sea-plane station at Felixstowe, Suffolk, the first sortie being made by Curtiss H.12 flying boat 8661.

19 April Six German floatplanes, three of them carrying torpedoes, fly from bases in Belgium to carry out attacks on British shipping off Ramsgate, Kent. This is the first torpedo sortie made by aircraft in Western Europe.

25 April Royal Naval Air Service floatplanes succeed in sinking a German destroyer off Ostend.

1 May Air-dropped torpedoes from two German seaplanes sink the first vessel to be accounted for during the war in British waters, this being the SS *Gena*, which went down off Lowestoft. On this day, too, the floatplane station at Great Yarmouth initiates its flying boat patrols with that made by Curtiss H.12 8660.

7 May British pilot Capt Albert Ball, who has claimed 44 victories in the air, is killed in action while flying S.E.5a 4850.

12 May In an attempt to prevent attacks by Marinefeldjasta aircraft such as that which had been responsible for the attack of 19 April, British Sopwith Pups from Dunkirk intercept a formation of Albatros scouts and claim five shot down into the sea. The exact variant is not reported, although pilots at this time describe meeting 'a new type' only six days before. This would have been the Albatros D.V, which entered service with Jagdstaffeln earlier in the month.

14 May During the afternoon enemy airship L22 (Kptlt Lehmann) is intercepted about eighteen miles NNE of Texel by Curtiss H.12 flying boat 8666 from Great Yarmouth, crewed by Flt Sub-Lt Leckie, Flt Lt Galpin, CPO Whatling and AM Laycock, and the British gunner, using a mixture of Brock, Pomeroy and Buckingham ammunition, destroys the dirigible, which bursts into flames and falls into the water.

17 May The first Sopwith F1 Camels intended for the RNAS have arrived in France by this date.

20 May The first German submarine to be destroyed by an aircraft, *UC36*, is sunk by Flt Sub-Lts Morrish and Boswell flying a Curtiss H.12 flying boat. This is the first submarine to be destroyed by an aircraft.

25 May The first concentrated attack on Britain during daylight is delivered at about 1400 hrs by a formation of 22 Gotha bombers against targets in Folkestone and Shorncliffe. One of the raiders is destroyed and another crashes, possibly damaged, before reaching base after being fired on by interceptors from Dunkirk. German sources claim that three British aircraft from the very large number of interceptors sent up have been destroyed.

7 June At 0310 hrs, on the Western Front, the Battle of Messines begins with the simultaneous detonation of nineteen deep mines driven under the German fortifications during many months of work, 1,000,000 lbs of high explosive having been laid in the excavations. Immediately a massive artillery barrage begins and Allied infantry move forward under an umbrella of low-flying support — the first time air cover has been used in this manner for a major attack.

13 June In a daylight raid on London, fourteen of the twenty unescorted Gotha G.IVs which have taken off reach their target on a fine but hazy morning in loose formation and drop 72 high-explosive bombs within the square mile of the City limits. The attack, in which 162 persons are killed and 432 wounded, causes a public outcry.

17 June The first Sopwith F1 Camel for the RFC in France is allocated, although the machine originally intended is accidentally damaged and has to be replaced.

26 June Germany orders the permanent grouping of her Jagdstaffeln on the Western Front, a decision taken after the success of the experience gained in April; hence, for example, Jastas 4, 6, 10 and 11 combine to form Jagdgeschwader I.

4 July Five Sopwith Camels successfully intercept a formation of sixteen Gotha bombers south-west of Ostend. The bombers are returning from a raid on Harwich and Felixstowe. Flt Lt Shook succeeds in bringing down one of the enemy in flames, while another is claimed as having been sent down out of control.

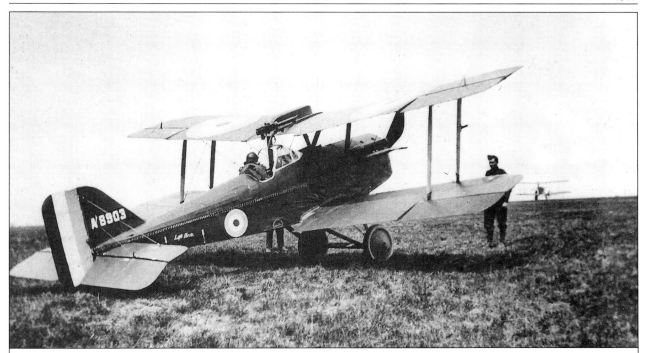

Above: An S.E.5, with the early semi-glazed cockpit, from No 56 Squadron RFC, photographed on 17 August 1917. (JMB/GSL collection)

7 July An air raid on London is carried out in daylight by 22 Gothas, from a total of 24 setting out. A number of intercepting aircraft are sent up to defend the capital, but with little success other than breaking up the already loose formation. The first bombs are dropped in the Tower Hill and Hackney areas at about 1025 hrs.

9 July RNAS Handley Page O/100 3124, specially flown the 2,000 miles from England, bombs the German battlecruiser *Goeben* in Stenia Bay on the Black Sea.

10 July In Flanders, Germany launches the first attack by a complete Staffel in support of a ground offensive, and the experience gained immediately gives birth to a number of specialist ground attack units.

2 August The first landing by an aircraft on a ship under way is made by Sqn Cdr Dunning RN in a Sopwith Pup aboard HMS *Furious*. Arrester wires, which at first ran fore and aft, and later laterally, have yet to be introduced, and no sandbags and ropes such as were employed on USS *Pennsylvania* seven years previously are used, the machine being prevented from running off the flight platform only by a deck party. In June the same

officer had taken off in a Pup from the same vessel.

18 August The German submarine *UB32* is claimed to have been sunk by an RNAS Wright floatplane.

21 August The temporary 20ft forward flying deck of HMS *Yarmouth* is used to launch a Sopwith Pup flown by Flt Sub-Lt B. Smart in an attempt to intercept a Zeppelin which has been shadowing the vessel and the accompanying 1st Light Cruiser Squadron off the Danish coast. Zeppelin L23 is destroyed, and orders have already been issued (on August 17) that one vessel in each light cruiser squadron is to have a flying-off platform fitted over its forward turret.

22 August There is an attack on targets in Great Britain when a force of ten enemy bombers is sent against Margate, Ramsgate and Dover. Originally fifteen Gotha G.IVs were dispatched (a considerably greater force was intended, but losses are now becoming felt), but five have been forced to turn back before the lead aircraft appears over the Kent coast at 1006 hrs. The barrage of ground fire from the North Foreland accounts for two almost immediately, one going into the sea and the other crashing in

flames on Margate's Hengrove golf course, killing the crew and losing an engine as it falls. Twelve persons are killed and 27 injured in the attack, which costs the enemy a total of three Gothas, one being brought down by a defending aircraft and two by gunfire. In the light of this attack, and in view of those which are imminent, it is timely that in the previous month the London Defence Area was formed under General Ashmore.

2 September Although modest in scope, the attack delivered on this date must be regarded as the opening of the enemy night bombing offensive using aeroplanes, two of which drop bombs on Dover at about 2300 hrs. The type of bombers used will never be established, but it is believed in some quarters that AEGs are employed.

3 September In contrast with the single victim of the previous night's raid, 132 people are killed by the bombs dropped by the four (of five) Gothas which deliver a much more ambitious assault on Chatham approaching midnight. Only defending RFC aircraft are sent up to try to thwart the raid, as it is not Admiralty policy to attempt night interceptions. On this date also the United States' 1st Aero Squadron reaches Europe.

4 September Following a decision probably taken in order to take advantage of good weather which is not expected to last, nine out of a total of eleven bombers dispatched set course for London. However, only five are to carry out the attack on the capital. Difficulties are encountered intercepting the raiders, since they have been dispatched at five-minute intervals rather than in a single formation. Nineteen civilians die on the ground, and an aeroplane, presumed to be one of the raiders, is reported crashing into the sea off Eastchurch after appearing to have suffered engine damage.

8 September A monitor is reported to have bombarded Middlekerke with the aid of a spotting aeroplane.

11 September At 0825 hrs, Capitaine Guynemer and Sous-Lieutenant Bazon-Verduraz of SPA 3 take off on a routine patrol over their sector of the Front in France, the former being the acclaimed victor in fifty-three combats. What happens thereafter will never be satisfactorily established: all that will be known will be contained in a report that both men have vanished while in combat with an enemy aeroplane above Poelcapelle. On this day, too, one of the pre-production Fokker Triplanes, piloted by Lt Kurt Wolff, victor in thirty-three combats, is shot down by a Sopwith Camel.

22 September Curtiss H.12 flying boat 8695 takes part in the sinking of enemy submarine *UC72*, reflecting both the foreshadowed activities of this branch of naval warfare and the increasing efficiency of measures against submarines.

23 September An epic dog-fight takes place. In it Lt Werner Voss, leader of Jasta 10, flying a Fokker Triplane, is finally shot down by Lt Rhys-Davies of No 56 Squadron.

25 September During a night attack by fourteen Gotha bombers on London, the first example of the type to be brought down by night over England falls into the sea off the Essex coast.

28 September The sinking of another submarine, *UC6*, by a Curtiss H.12 flying boat is claimed by Flt Sub-Lts Hobbs and Dickey.

30 September The defensive 'Balloon Apron' is installed around London.

1 October A Sopwith Pup is successfully flown by Flt Cdr Rutland RN from a platform built on the 15in gun turret of HMS *Repulse* with the structure turned at 45 degrees to the bow. This introduces the facility for aircraft to be turned into the wind without the vessel having to alter course.

11 October The 41st Wing of the Royal Flying Corps is formed in France to operate from Nancy against objectives in Germany. In command is Lt-Col C. L. N. Newall.

19 October A determined attack by airships takes place on targets in England by Navy Zeppelins, these being L41 (Hpt Manger), L44 (Kptlt Stabbert), L45 (Kptlt Kolle), L46 (Kptlt Hollender), L47 (Kptlt von Freudenreich), L49 (Kptlt Gayer), L50 (Kptlt Schwonder), L52 Oblt z S Kriemel), L53 (Kptlt Prolss), L54 (Kptlt von Buttlar) and L55 (Kptlt Flemming). The weather encountered during this intended mighty attack (preventing two further airships from leaving their sheds) brings about the loss of five of the raiders, but it also gives the name by which the sortie will be known for many years — the 'Silent Raid' (due to the climatic conditions dispersing the sound of the high-flying airships' motors).

10 November VII Brigade is dispatched to the Italian Front and the Third Battle of Ypres (Passchendaele) effectively closes. During this, aircraft have proved effective in protecting troops on the ground in II Brigade's area, no losses of Corps aircraft being reported on the opening day of the offensive which had been hampered throughout by poor visibility and heavy rain.

20 November An Allied experiment is carried out in the area of Cambrai whereby an attack, spearheaded by a heavy concentration of tanks and supported by D.H.5s and Sopwith Camels in a ground attack role, is not preceded by an artillery bombardment. Complete surprise is achieved and a deep penetration made (see 15 September 1916).

21 November Zeppelin L59 (Kptlt Bockholt) leaves Jamboli (Bulgaria) en route for East Africa with some fifteen tons of supplies for German guerrilla detachments, but while nearing Khartoum orders are received to return as the German forces have been defeated. Despite the difficulties

involved, the vessel completes a 4,200-mile journey in 95 hours.

29 November The Air Force (Constitution) Act 1917 receives Royal Assent, effectively creating the Royal Air Force.

30 November During a counter-attack in the Cambrai area German aircraft are used as ground attackers for the first time. Every available Schlacht-staffel, previously used singly, is now pressed into use, supporting JG I (see 7 December).

7 December Harried from the air, British troops are forced to withdraw to the line of the Flesquières Ridge, but despite the success of the German counter-attack the air operations will continue during the periods when the weather permits. The year has seen several developments in air warfare, among them being the virtual defeat of the airship as a weapon, once regarded as the ultimate in bombers. In its place, the heavier-than-air machine is fast developing into a strategic weapon for both day and night use, in its turn hastening the evolution of the techniques and weapons of night interception and specialist fighters. Indeed, Maj Murlis Green, in England, has even gone so far as to envisage the advent of twin-engine fighters for this purpose, foreshadowing developments that will not take place until the Second World War when, as a Group Captain he will specialize in solving the problems of early night interception.

Both sides during 1917 introduce new types of aircraft, Germany sending the new Albatros D.IIIs to the front in January, followed by the Fokker Dr.I Triplane in August and, in November, the Rumpler C.IV for two-seat reconnaissance and photographic work which takes the aircraft deep behind Allied lines, relying on its high-altitude performance to escape detection. Meanwhile France introduces the Breguet XIV in June. Of metal construction and employed for day bombing and reconnaissance, this aircraft will remain in service until 1930, and will also be employed by the United States in France. Spad units begin to adopt the S.XIII in September, and three months later the first D.H.9s enter service despite opposition at certain levels because of the known unreliability of its Puma engine. Outside the European theatre, the foundations of the Cuban Aviation Corps are laid in 1917 with the acquisition of six Curtiss machines to be used as trainers. These will last until they are destroyed in a hurricane in 1926, a fresh start being made with a small number of D.H.4s and some Vought reconnaissance aircraft in 1931 when separate Army and Naval Aviations will be established.

In other theatres of war, June sees the formation of the first RFC fighter unit in the Middle East, using in part Bristol M.1C monoplane scouts. Four months later Austria-Hungary, whose air arm was then at its zenith, launches with the aid of German reinforcements the Battle of Caporetto, in which the opposing Italian pilots distinguish themselves, although five British and three French air units are rushed to help stem the Italian retreat. In Japan the Yokosuka Naval Arsenal constructs its first native-designed operational naval aircraft.

1918

1 January RFC bombers operating from Italian bases carry out an attack on targets at Vittorio.

3 January In Britain the foundation an Air Council to regulate affairs anticipates the new Air Force. Lord Rothermere, Secretary of State, is the Council's first President.

18 January In France, Major-General Salmond assumes command of the Royal Flying Corps.

28 January An enemy force of seven Gotha G.Vs (out of thirteen dispatched) and one Staaken R.IV Giant (of two) is sent against targets in London in a night attack which stimulates the largest operation by interceptors to date, one bringing down in flames their first Gotha.

1 February The 41st Wing, commanded by Lt-Col Newall (see 11 October 1917) and formed from Nos 55 (D.H.4), 100 (F.E.2b) and 16, formerly Naval 'A'; (Handley Page O/100) Squadrons to bomb Germany, is now redesignated No VIII Brigade.

21 February British troops under General Allenby capture Jericho after severe fighting with the aid of air support.

7 March Night attacks against British targets have hitherto been confined to moonlit nights (hence 'bomber's moon'), but a raid on London by five Staaken Giants is the first on a moonless night.

21 March On the Western Front, at dawn, Ludendorff's army launches a last offensive between Scarpe and Oise in a bid to break the Allied line before US troops can be effectively deployed. The brunt of the attack is suffered by the Fifth Army in the St Quentin sector, and for a time the whole British line, where the casualties will total over 300,000, is in peril. The struggle, freely using tanks and aircraft, will continue for several months, and German heavy bombers will be committed to targets behind Allied lines.

1 April A new British service, the Royal Air Force, officially comes into existence, created by an amalgamation of the former Royal Flying Corps and the Royal Naval Air Service, the personnel of the first being absorbed and retaining their former Army numbers in the new service. No 1 in the RFC had been a Pte H. Edwards, who joined the Army in 1895, but he left the service on 16 October 1913, and although he is nominally also No l in the RAF he will never serve in it. The muster role of serving

Above: A Sopwith F.1 Camel marked 'Lucifer', believed to be numbered B3871. (RAF Museum)

Above: A late-production Fokker D.VII constructed by the parent factory shows its four-colour lozenge-printed fabric. (Author's collection)

RAF men begins with No 5, one W. E. Moore, who enlisted in the Army on 9 December 1889 and by the time of the amalgamation held the rank of Warrant Officer. Army ranks will persist for the first eighteen months of the RAF's existence, until 1 October 1919. Members of the RNAS were temperoraly given army type status, effective to 1 October.

4 April The US 94th Pursuit ('Hat in the Ring') Squadron becomes the first US-trained pursuit unit to see action on the Western Front.

12 April Navy Zeppelins L60 (Kptlt Flemming). L61 (Kptlt Ehrlich). L62 (Hpt Manger), L63 (Kptlt von Freudenreich) and L64 (Kvtkpt Schütze) make the final attack by night on British targets in the Midlands, killing seven and injuring 20.

14 April The US 94th Pursuit Squadron becomes the first unit to see combat when Lts Campbell and Winslow shoot down a pair of enemy aircraft. The 94th and 95th (which arrived in France in March) will later form the nucleus of the 1st Pursuit Group. Groups will be enlarged to form Wings as more squadrons became available.

15 April The US 1st Aero Squadron makes its first mission over the lines.

18 April France forms the Division Aérienne, a force made up of almost 600 aircraft consisting of two Groupements, one with twelve units of Spads and nine Breguet XIV bombers, the other with nine units of Spads and six Breguet bombers. The intention is that this Division be moved from front to front as the situation demands (see 18 July).

27 April The first flight takes place of the Sopwith TF.2 Salamander, a single-seater specifically designed for 'trench fighting' in place of adapted Sopwith F.1 Camels, variants which never entered production. Late in the month the first Fokker D.VIIs appear over the Front, operated by Jagdgeschwader I comprising Jastas 4, 6, 10 and 11.

14 May French Breguet XIV bombers raid an ammunition dump at Bois de Champion sufficiently heavily for the Dutch Meteorological Institute erroneously to record a minor earthquake! This type of operation attracts heavy casualties, exemplified by those of Escadrille 117, which in thirteen weeks loses forty-five machines and 116 aircrew.

18 May To appease British public opinion, inflamed by attacks at home, an increased number of raids are begun by RAF bombers on German cities. Cologne receives a daylight attack.

19 May German attacks on British targets nevertheless continue, London being raided at around midnight by 28 Gotha G.Vs and three Staaken R.IVs of Bogohl 3, at least one of which is carrying a 2,200lb bomb. Six of the raiders are brought down, two certainly falling to anti-aircraft fire. Forty-nine civilians die and 177 are injured.

24 May In the United States the Division of Aeronautics is created, the operational arm of which is to be known as the Army Air Service.

31 May In France the first enemy machine to be successfully intercepted during the hours of darkness is shot down, and the first submarine definitely accounted for by land-based aircraft - *UC49* - is sunk.

6 June The RAF's Independent Force is formed from the earlier VIII Brigade, which had been created from 41 Wing in February. The Brigade made a total of 142 attacks on enemy targets, including 57 in Germany. The com-

Above: A Spad in French service, the star marking being a personal insignia and not denoting Soviet use. (Bernd Totschinger)

mander of the new IF is Maj-Gen Sir Hugh Trenchard. The specialized force is established to permit coordinated bombing attacks without diverting air effort from the Western Front (see 11 October 1917 and 1 February 1918).

7 June RAF bombers of the 9th and 51st Wings of IX Brigade assist in stemming an enemy attack on the Noyon Montdidier Front, part of an offensive against the French VI Army on a 35-mile front on the Aisne, north-west of Reims, which is supported by a considerable part of Germany's fighter and Schlacht force. The push was not halted until the previous day, when the enemy reached the Marne. Opposing the offensive, the modernized French air arm is supported by the newly arrived USAS, and on the ground by the British IX Corps.

16 June No 151 Squadron RAF, formed four days earlier and equipped with night-flying Sopwith F.1 Camels, arrives in France to become the leading night interception and intruder force. It will make its operational debut on 20 June.

18 June Sopwith 2.F1 Camels from HMS *Furious*, while on anti-Zeppelin patrol over the North Sea, engage four enemy floatplanes at 21,000ft over the Skagerrak. In the resulting fight, the first in air warfare involving carrier aircraft, one of the enemy is shot down and the remainder are claimed to have been driven off.

18 July A counter-offensive involving British, French and United States troops, with strong support from France's Division Aérienne and aircraft from IX Corps, is launched between Château-Thierry and Soissons, but the price in the air is to exceed 500 machines a month for the Allies (see 18 April).

19 July Four Sopwith 2.F1 Camels from HMS *Furious* successfully drop 50lb bombs on the enemy airship sheds at Tondern, destroying both L54 and L60 which are inside.

23 July No 151 Squadron RAF scores its first victory when an enemy bomber is shot down over Etaples by Captain Yuille (see 16 June).

31 July Nine D.H.9 aircraft of the RAF bomb railways and blast furnaces at Mainz. They are intercepted by fighters of the newly formed Kampfeinsitzerstaffeln, or Kestas, manned by second-line pilots, and only two of

the British aircraft escape. Also on this date the first successful take-off by a Sopwith 2.F1 Camel is accomplished from the 30ft long platform of a 58ft by 16ft towed lighter. The original purpose of these vessels was the transport of large flying boats across the North Sea, thereby increasing their operational radius over the area of the Heligoland Bight. The pilot is Lt S. D. Culley (see 11 August).

2 August RAF units, flying a variety of aircraft including Sopwith F1 Camels, 7.F1 Snipes, R.E.8s and D.H.9As which had been deployed to Archangel in support of White Russian forces in May, begin operations against the Bolsheviks.

5 August The flagship of the Zeppelins, L70 (Kptlt von Lossnitzer), commissioned on 8 July and part of a force made up of it and L53 (Kptlt Prolss), L56 (Kptlt Zaeschmar), L63 (Kptlt von Freudenreich) and L65 (Kptlt Dose), is brought down by Capt Leckie and Maj Cadbury (pilot) flying D.H.4 A8032 at Wells-next-the-Sea, Norfolk.

8 August In France the first contact patrols are made in cooperation with cavalry. This day also sees the greatest

Above: LFG Roland D.VIa 1219/18, a German scout, showing the wooden 'clinker' construction of its fuselage. (Author's collection)

number of air casualties, 83 machines being lost, compared to 49 by the enemy. In Germany, however, the date will be regarded as the 'Black Day', since it is the one when a combined French and British offensive commences, supported along the entire front by concentrated ground attack and bombing sorties, many of these directed against enemy airfields in order to keep aircraft grounded (see 16 August).

9 August No 97 Squadron RAF, flying Handley Page O/400s, is sent to augment the Independent Force.

11 August The last enemy airship to be destroyed during the war is brought down by Lt S. D. Culley flying Sopwith 2.F1 Camel N6812 from lighter No H5 towed by the destroyer HMS *Redoubt*, three other lighters having carried flying boats to the vicinity of the Heligoland Bight the previous day. At 0830 hrs L53 (Kptlt Prolss) is sighted and Culley takes off. Almost an hour later he reaches 300ft above the airship's altitude and is within range of it. Two minutes before the hour he opens fire but No 1 gun jams after five rounds. However, a double burst from No 2 sets the Zeppelin alight. The aircraft, armed with twin Lewis guns above the upper centre-section, is later preserved and placed on exhibition in the Imperial War Museum, London, and Culley, recommended for the

Victoria Cross, is in fact awarded the DSO (see 31 July).

12 August As part of the policy of attacking German towns and cities from the air, a force of RAF bombers raids Frankfurt.

15 August Advancing British troops are reported to have crossed the River Ancre, a tributary of the River Somme.

16 August A typical attack connected with the Allied offensive is carried out when a force of 65 ground-attack aircraft bomb and machine gun the enemy base at La Bassée (see 8 August).

25 August An attack similar to that made against Frankfurt is directed against targets in Mannheim.

31 August No 115 Squadron is added to Independent Force (other sqns were being added to RAF) (see 9 August).

16 September In company with HM Drifter *Young Crow*, a Sea Scout Zero (SS.Z) non-rigid airship depth-charges and sinks enemy submarine *UB103*.

19 September In Palestine the retreating Turkish Seventh and Eighth Armies massed on the Tulkeram—Nablus road are harried for three days and finally destroyed by air attack, a pair of aircraft appearing every two minutes where the Turks are trapped in a ravine; at half-hourly intervals an additional six bombers attack. These assaults on Wadi el Far'a are spearheaded by No 1 Australian Squadron.

22 September On the Salonika Front, similar operations are conducted against retreating Bulgars.

26 September American ground and air forces, having moved into the Meuse—Argonne area of France, are thrown into an assault on enemy positions, General Mitchell relying on massive blows against the Germans for success. About three-quarters of the aircraft available are employed.

2 October The problem of supplying the rapidly advancing Belgian Army is met by an air-drop of rations by a force of some 80 British and Belgian aircraft, the latter drawn from an air arm that was modernized and expanded during the spring. Its three fighter escadrilles, equipped with Spad XIIIs, Hanriot HD.ls and Sopwith Camels, complement a bombing and reconnaissance force of Breguet XIVs, Royal Aircraft Factory R.E.8s and Caudron G.IIIs and G.IVs, plus a small number of surviving Sopwith 1½ Strutters.

13 October In France, German troops are reported to be in retreat along a 100-mile front, harried by air attacks where possible.

14 October This day sees the first recorded use by the RAF of the largest type of British bomb, weighing 1,600lb and carried by a Handley Page O/400.

24 October A series of attacks with bombs and gunfire is made by aircraft against Turkish troops retreating at Monsul on this date and over the following four days.

31 October Only 37 examples of the new Sopwith TF.2 Salamander Trench Fighter are reported to be on charge with the RAF at this date, two being in France. Said to be the British answer to the German specialist AEG and Junkers machines used for trench-strafing, it appears too late for service in numbers over the Front.

4 November The battle of Vittorio Veneto opens. Ammunition is air-dropped to advanced troops while a series of offensive sorties quickly demoralizes retreating Austrian forces.

9 November German troops are reported to be in general retreat, and most of the Central Powers forming Germany's allies have either given up or are near to collapse, although the enemy still has an air service with 2,390 first-line aircraft on charge either at the Front or employed on

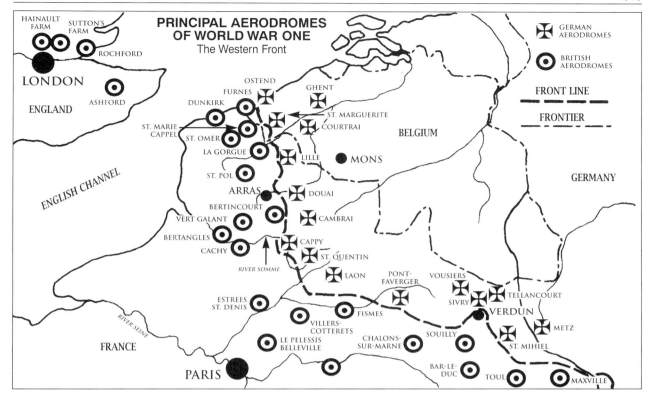

PRINCIPAL AERODROMES
OF WORLD WAR ONE
The Western Front

Home Defence. France has at this time 4,511 aircraft making up twelve independent escadrilles, ten bombing groups, 124 reconnaissance escadrilles and a number of observation units collaborating with the artillery, while the United States can find a total of 1,481 machines making up 45 squadrons. Great Britain possesses 22,647 aeroplanes, including seaplanes and trainers, plus 103 airships.

10 November Revolution is reported from Berlin.

11 November At 1100 hrs fighting ceases as a result of an Armistice signed by the Allies and Germany. During the four years of fighting Germany and Austria-Hungary have produced 67,982 aircraft, a high percentage in the final year, Great Britain 55,093, France 67,982, Italy 12,021 and the United States 11,227.

8 December The first RAF squadrons are ordered to Bickendorf in Germany as part of the Army of Occupation, Nos 4(AFC), 29, 43, 48, 70, 79, 149 and 206 arriving before the end of the year.

Thus ends the final year of the first large-scale war since the invention of heavier-than-air craft, and a period of twelve months which has seen the advent of such pointers to the future as the first flight in May of the Handley Page V/1500, conceived to take the war far into enemy territory. In the same month the RAF had sent a token establishment to Russia, although the original intention was less to intervene in the conflict between Red and White forces than to forestall any possibility of the Germans establishing a U-boat base at Murmansk on the Arctic coast. Nevertheless, three months later a flight of D.H.4s is operating in support of troops in the fighting that is to result in the taking of Archangel. Meanwhile Poland, having regained her national identity in October, believes herself threatened, so that she is soon to make use of an army in exile that has already been trained and equipped in France, complete with its own air section. Among the little-recorded events of the year have been the steps taken to combat the submarine threat to British shipping routes, one of these being the establishment of 'Scarecrow' patrols over inshore waters, so named because they were frequently carried out by inadequately armed and unsuit-

able machines, the presence rather than the attacking ability of which, it was hoped, would deter U-boat commanders. In Japan the year 1918 sees the activation of the Sasebo Kokutais of the Naval Air Corps in March (see 1916), while in another part of the world the establishment of the Finnish Ilmailuvoimat, or Aviation Force, takes place: for the next quarter of a century, latterly under the revised name Suomen Ilmavoimat, it will be involved in fighting with the Soviet Union.

Had the war continued, the promising Franco-American Le Père Lusac two-seat fighter of 1918 would have almost certainly ushered in a new era of air combat, as also the Fokker D.VIII monoplane, popularly known as the 'flying razor' from its clean design, might have done, but two British machines of the period which have rolled back the frontiers of air warfare are the Sopwith Cuckoo, a torpedo carrier without the handicap of floats and thus capable of operation from either shore bases or carriers, and the Sopwith 7.F1 Snipe, powered by the ultimate development of the rotary engine, the 250hp Bentley BR2. A number of Snipes became operational with

No 43 Squadron RAF in September, while a pair of long-range Mk Ias were allocated to No 45 Squadron as escorts for the bombers of the Independent Force.

1919

20 February In Afghanistan Habibollah Khan is assassinated, and the succession of Ambullah to the throne triggers the Third Afghan War involving RAF units on the North-West Frontier of India (see 24 May).

19 April The 80 aircraft which make up the air force of the re-emergent Poland are now constantly in action. Its first encounter takes place on this date when a Fokker D.VII, flown by Lt Stee, shoots down a Nieuport escorting a Brandenburg two-seater.

16 May Many of the post-First World War long-distance flights have military overtones, designed to test new engines and equipment. That made by the US Navy NC flying boats across the Atlantic via the Azores between this date and 31 May is in part intended to test the utility of airborne wireless telegraphy.

24 May Drawn into the war in Afghanistan which was to last until August, the RAF uses a Handley Page V/1500 bomber to attack the capital at Kabul. Two RAF squadrons already there are now augmented by a further four flying Bristol F.2Bs, D.H.9As and D.H.10s.

8 June A formation of Fairey IIIC floatplanes from the North Russian Expeditionary Force carry out a bombing attack on four Bolshevik naval vessels, having been taken to the vicinity aboard HMS *Pegasus*.

11 December In Britain, an official publication presented by Winston Churchill, the Secretary of State, and written by Maj-Gen Sir Hugh Trenchard (later Marshal of the Royal Air Force Viscount Trenchard) under the title 'The Permanent Organisation of the RAF' is to have a strong effect on the Government's decision to permit the RAF to remain an independent service.

Also during this year US Brig-Gen Mitchell, called to assist operations on the Mexican border, has introduced twice-daily air patrols between Brownsville, Texas, and San Diego, California, to spot illegal border crossings and discourage marauding bandits. The period has seen attempts made to smuggle examples of Fokker D.VII warplanes to places of safety with an eye to selling them to several of the world's emergent air forces, while the former wartime Allies have been doing their best to enforce the provision of Article IV of the Armistice Agreement which called for the handing over of German warplanes, *'In erster Linie alle Apparate D.VII'* ('especially all machines of the D.VII type'). Elsewhere Peru has founded a military air corps with French assistance and twelve aircraft, British and French, while Argentina has built on the foundations of an air arm laid in September 1912 by receiving an Italian aviation mission bringing with it six Ansaldo fighters, four Caproni bombers and some support types. The growing realization of the value of air power is illustrated by the fact that this year Chile, which had only established an air arm six years before, can now boast the foundation of a Naval Aviation Service flying a small number of seaplanes.

1920

April No 25 Squadron RAF becomes, until September 1922, alone responsible for the defence of the United Kingdom. In Venezuela a Presidential decree establishes a military air service based at Maracay, while Mexico can boast fifty available aircraft, although these will not officially constitute an air force until 1924. Ecuador, with Italian assistance, founds her Cuerpo de Aviadores Militares, also using some German machines.

16 August Throughout this day and the next, about fourteen surviving Polish aircraft fly 190 sorties against the Bolshevik ground forces and contribute to the withdrawal of the Bodenny Cossacks who have been threatening Lvov – a significant testimony to the value of air power since only some three weeks earlier the thirty aircraft available had been thrown into an attempt to halt Russian forces approaching Warsaw. In 35 air battles waged between the spring and October 1920, the Poles will claim eleven enemies destroyed for a cost of three to themselves, although 43 will have been lost on the ground.

The early part of the year also sees a dozen D.H.9s sent aboard the carrier *Ark Royal* for the RAF 'Z Force' in Somaliland, supporting a small part of the Camel Corps and successfully putting down the insurrection led by Mohammed bin Abdullah in three weeks. Similar British operations are carried out against Garjak Nuers in the Sudan. Perhaps the largest operations of this nature, however, have been those created by the League of Nations mandate to supervise the orderly development of Iraq and Palestine before independence. These overtures are not recognized by Turkey or by the Arabs, so that clashes, often calling for air support, are inevitable.

1921

10 March 'Flew to Aberdeen [USA] to witness dropping of bombs,' writes Brig-Gen 'Billy' Mitchell, the American disciple of all-out air power when describing an early part of his demonstration during which redundant US and captured German warships are sunk. In the main, MB-2s are used to bomb such vessels as the 'unsinkable' *Ostfriesland* in Chesapeake Bay, although critics point out that it is simple to attack unmanned ships from low altitude (see 1923).

In Italy this year, General Giulio Douhet, the international exponent of independent air power, publishes his book *Command of the Air*, advocating the bombing of cities and destroying an enemy's will by terrorizing civilians, with the result that armies and navies can be reduced and finally unified. Meanwhile calls are being made by the American Chief of the Air Service, Maj-Gen Mason M. Patrick, for a 'properly balanced air service' with 80 per cent of its strength made up of combat machines and only 20 per cent comprising observation machines. The Irish Air Corps is founded as part of the Army. In Venezuela the first elements of a flying school are set up, equipped with a small number of Caudron and Farman aircraft by a French aviation mission, but little official interest is displayed and the school is disbanded (see 1920). However, Chile can now boast a small bomber force made up of ex-British D.H.4s.

1922

April The beginnings of the Fuerza Aérea Colombiana are laid with the establishment at Flandes of a Caudron G.III trainer-equipped army air arm. Nicaragua forms its Air National Guard to make protective patrols over the Panama Canal Zone with US-supplied D.H.4s and Curtiss JN-4s.

7 June Capts Sacadura Cabral and Gago Coutinho of Portugal complete their attempt to fly the South Atlantic from Lisbon to Rio de Janeiro in Fairey IIID floatplane No 17 *Santa Cruz*. The planned route is via the Cape Verde Islands and St Paul's Rocks, which are so small that a ship is sent in advance to aid identification! The departure was on 30 March, and Las Palmas was reached after 8½ hours in a special long-span Fairey IIID, *Lusitania*, but bad weather delayed a resumption of the journey to Cape Verde. Superb navigation found the tiny island, but landing on the rough sea broke up the seaplane's floats so that another aircraft was requested. This took the crew to Fernando de Noronha, but the machine was wrecked and the trip was completed in No 17 (which is currently preserved).

The flashpoint of the year is when the armies of Mustafa Kemel defeat the Greeks at Sakarya River and seem likely to advance into Europe, only to find the way blocked at Chanak by 1,200 British soldiers supported by No 1 Squadron RAF. However, although newspapers bear such headlines as 'Chanak Crisis — War Almost Inevitable', Kemel backs down. He will later overthrow the Sultan and become the first President of a modern Turkey.

This year also finds the RAF dealing with a revolt in Transjordan and cooperating with the 120,000 British troops in Iraq. Japan's first torpedo-bomber, the Mitsubishi BLM, is designed, first flying in the following January. The fleet carrier HMS *Eagle*, the first vessel of the type to have an offset 'island' superstructure, is commissioned.

1923

February The governor of Southern Kurdistan, Sheikh Mahmud, descends with a large army reinforced by hill Arabs on the British garrison at Kirkuk, the invaders believing that no support can be sent to the outnumbered defenders since the roads are impassable because of heavy rains. The garrison is so greatly outnumbered that the assistance of the RAF is

sought. Drawing on the experience gained supplying Kut, the response comes in the form of airlifting, with Vickers Vernons, some 480 officers and men of the 14th Sikhs into the town – so promptly that the invaders withdraw.

22 August This is the date on which the first flight takes place of the United States' 'super-bomber' deterrent, the Barling XNBL-l, a four-motor biplane with a span of 120ft. It is, however, underpowered and has a range of only 170 miles.

27 August On this and the following day a US Army D.H.4B makes a 37-hour endurance flight with the aid of in-flight refuelling over a 31-mile course at San Diego, California. The record-making aircraft is crewed by Lts Lowell Smith and John Richter, and the 'tanker', which passes fuel to the other aircraft on fifteen occasions, is a second US-built D.H.4 flown by Lts Virgil Hines and Frank Seifert.

Elsewhere recognition of the value of air power is taking different forms, and in the Soviet Union the first society of 'Friends of the Workers' and Peasants' Red Air Forces' is set up for engineering and glider-pilot training, a similar organization to the German 'Sports Flying Association' which gives training for air warfare while avoiding any infringement of the victors' ban on the country's possessing an air force. Brig-Gen Mitchell's demonstration bombing of old warships continues, and in September the obsolete US warships *Virginia* and *New Jersey* are sunk off Cape Hatteras. In El Salvador, a Military Aviation Service is established with five German Aviatik trainers.

1924

6 April Route-finding is still being carried out by a number of air forces, and on this date four US Douglas World Cruiser aircraft, powered by single 400hp Liberty engines, developed from the Douglas DT-2 torpedo bomber depart from Lake Washington for Tokyo on a flight round the world via Canada, Alaska and the Aleutians. No 1, *Seattle* (Maj Martin and Sgt Harvey), is lost when it flies into a mountain early on, but the survivors reach Japan by 24 May and Croydon, England, on 16 July. After leaving Britain, engine trouble accounts for No 3, *Boston* (Lts Wade and Ogden), at sea,

leaving No 2, *Chicago*, and No 4, *New Orleans* (Lts Nelson and Harding), to have new motors fitted at Greenland. At Nova Scotia the pair are joined by the prototype, which, being a replacement for the lost *Boston*, is now named *Boston II* and is crewed by the original airmen, and the three machines complete the course. Nos 1 and 4 will be preserved.

This year too, a secret Soviet-German agreement is signed, creating a flying school at Lipetsk in exchange for which Soviet officers are allowed to study administration and command at the German General Staff School in Berlin. In Britain the first four squadrons of the (later Royal) Auxiliary Air Force are formed.

1925

1 May Japan's Army Air Corps attains status with infantry, artilery etc with 3,700 officers and men and about 500 aircraft.

3 September The US Navy airship ZR-1 *Shenandoah*, based on the Zeppelin pattern, is lost in a storm. Type trials which have shown the craft to be difficult to handle in bad weather are discontinued.

5 September The RAF uses 29 assorted aircraft to begin the evacuation of British subjects from Kirkuk before starting to bring in troop reinforcements and drop supplies.

Minor wars elsewhere find France opposing Beni-Zerouel's forces in Morocco as well as Abd el Krim's Riffs, escadrilles in Syria supplying the besieged citadel of Soueida for 61 days as well as flying over 6,000 combat missions. British wartime experiments with aeroplanes carried by airships are resumed with R33 and Gloster Grebe fighters and the D.H.53 Humming Bird. No 25 Squadron RAF demonstrates ground-to-air radio.

1926

1 March The RAF start a long-distance formation flight from Cairo to the Cape and back using four Fairey IIIDs, covering 10,600 miles in 140 hrs over seventeen days.

16 March The launch of the world's first liquid-fuelled rocket is made in the United States by R. H. Goddard.

1 July Swedish naval and army air components combine to form the Kungl. Svenska Flygvapnet (see 1911).

Above: The original Fairey Long-Range Monoplane. This is J9479 (c/n F.1131) of 1929. The subsequent K1991 (c/n F.1671) of two years later differed in such external features as streamlined wheel covers. (Fairey)

22 October The United States demonstrates the potential of dive-bombing over the Pacific Fleet, introducing a new anti-ship tactic that is not lost on Germany or Japan.

Also this year the US Congress grants the Navy permission to build two rigid airships, ZRS-4 *Akron* and ZRS-5 *Macon*, and in Britain trials with fighters launched from R33 are continued (see 1925).

1927

8 May At 0517 hrs Nungesser and Coli, flying a Lavasseur PL8 named *Oiseau Blanc* (which has been developed from a carrier-borne three-seater), take off to fly the Atlantic from east to west and are never seen again.

14 October Four Supermarine Southampton flying boats of the RAF's Far East Flight depart from Felixstowe on a 27,000-mile round trip of the East. The year also sees the Soviet Tupolev TB-1, claimed to be the first twin-motor monoplane bomber, make its first flight, while in Japan the Kawasaki Army Type 88 bomber is officially accepted in August and the Mitsubishi BLM Type 87 torpedo bomber is adopted by the Army (see 1922).

1928

15 September In France, the Ministère de l'Air is created, paving the way for an independent air force.

1929

26 March In Britain the first flight takes place of the Handley Page Hinaidi. Of metal construction, it signals the discarding of wooden construction for military aircraft in Europe until the appearance of the Mosquito.

17 September An 8hp motor driving a pusher propeller is experimentally fitted to Dr Lippisch's tailless Storch V glider The basic concept of this layout will lay the foundations for the Messerschmitt 163 Komet fighter of the Second World War.

30 September The first flight takes place in Germany of the world's first rocket-propelled aircraft, a sailplane designed by car manufacturer Fritz von Opel.

In this year Germany announces that her Deutscher Luftsportverband (DLV), formed to give glider instruction to potential pilots, now has 50,000 members. Meanwhile Guatemala founds its Cuerpo de Aeronáutica Militar.

1930

1 September Costes and Bellonte leave Paris to fly successfully non-stop to New York in a Breguet XIX, a modified bomber named *Point d'Interrogation*.

12 December The first flight takes place of the massive Soviet Tupolev TB-3 (Ant-6). Powered by four motors, it has a span of 129ft 7in, a range of 839 miles and a 4,850-lb bomb load.

During the year the British Air Ministry issues Specification F.7/30, resulting in the first Supermarine design to be named 'Spitfire'. However, the aircraft does not go into production.

1931

18 September A bomb beneath a train of the South Manchurian railway signals an invasion of that country by the Japanese Army. The latter is supported by Nieuport 29s and Salmson A2s, flying against Chinese Potez 25s.

27 October A Curtiss F9C

Sparrowhawk makes a successful hook-up on to the airship USS *Los Angeles* over Lakehurst, New Jersey (see 1925 and 1932).

3 December The first Soviet trials launching a pair of I-4 fighters from a TB-1 parent machine take place over Monino (see 1934).

In Britain the Westland COW (Coventry Ordnance Works) Gun Fighter flies for the first time, armed with a 37mm cannon. Japan's first completely indigenous fighter, the Navy A2N, enters service, while the Type 88 joins the Army in October.

1932

26 January HM submarine *M2*, equipped to carry a Parnall Peto float-plane, is lost with 52 crew aboard in West Bay, three miles off Portland Bill. Divers find the hangar doors open.

5 February Japanese and Chinese aircraft engage during the Shanghai Incident. The Japanese are supported by the carriers *Notoro*, *Kaga* and *Hosho* with a total of 75 machines.

29 June The first successful hook-up to the airship USS *Akron* by a Curtiss F9C is made (see 1931).

1933

8 February The RAF gains the world long-distance record with a non-stop flight of 5,309 miles from Cranwell to Walvis Bay, South West Africa, by Fairey Long Range Monoplane K1991.

Meanwhile France declares her aim of fielding 1,544 first-line aircraft, with 1,297 reserves.

1934

March In Britain the decision is taken to concentrate on the new Rolls-Royce P.V.12 aero-engine. This will later become the Merlin.

April A Russian TB-3 (see 1930) successfully flies carrying two I-5s, two I-16s and an I-2. All the aircraft are released without problems (see 1931).

1 December The Hawker Hurricane prototype is ordered in Britain.

1935

24 February The first flight takes place of the Heinkel He 111, described as a high-speed transport since the existence of the secret Luftwaffe is not revealed until March, about the time that the prototype Junkers Ju 87 first flies.

9 July Bristol's proposals for converting the Type 142 to the Blenheim bomber are tabled.

28 July The first flight of the US Boeing B-17 takes place. It is to be quickly dubbed 'Flying Fortress' by the Press.

3 October Italy invades Ethiopia with land forces supported by some 320 aircraft. A little later mustard gas as well as high-explosive bombs are dropped.

6 November The Hawker Hurricane prototype makes its initial flight. At the beginning of the year an Air Ministry committee looks into the potential of aircraft detection by radio (radar) and in the late spring the first experimental system is set up off the East Coast.

1936

29 February The United States demands the 'highest priority' for the development of anti-aircraft radar.

5 March The first flight of the Spitfire prototype takes place from Eastleigh, Southampton.

20 July First air actions of the Spanish Civil War.

Above: Model 299, the Boeing B-17 prototype, which made its first flight on 28 July 1935. It had been designed to Army Air Corps Requirement 5/34 calling for 'a bomber to be used against fleets of vessels'. It had five defensive positions and a bomb load of 4,800lb. The location of the wing insignia is interesting. (Author's collection)

Above: The prototype Supermarine Spitfire, K5054, is seen here during mid-June 1936, showing the modified rudder balance and a finish of Cellon Seaplane Grey (a light blue-grey shade). (Author's collection)

28 July Twenty Kondor Legion Junkers Ju 52/3m transports airlift the first of 13,520 troops from Morocco, plus supplies, to support Gen. Franco's Nationalist forces in Spain.

14 August A Ju 52 bomber scores two direct hits on the Republican battleship *Jaime I*, and the first Italian air support for the Nationalists (the Aviacione Legionari) arrives in Spain.

Soviet aid for Spanish government forces begins in September, and the Nazi Condor Legion develops new tactics, including the replacement of stiff 'vic' formations by the fighter Schwarm. In America $100,000 is allocated to radar development, but work had already begun setting up five such stations 25 miles apart to protect England's Thames valley. Development work on Sqn Ldr Whittle's jet engine begins, similar work having taken place in Germany by Dr von Ohain in March. Also in 1936 the Nazi experimental station at Peenemünde opens and the USAAC accepts its first two B-17s.

1937
14 August Undeclared war breaks out between Japan and China. The former has almost 900 aircraft, the latter rather fewer but with American-trained personnel.

18 September In the first major air engagement, Japan claims all but five from an enemy formation of sixteen aircraft destroyed.

12 October In Britain, the initial flight of the first production Hawker Hurricane takes place.

December The first RAF squadron (No 111) to be equipped with Hurricane fighters.

A Handley Page Heyford bomber is the first aircraft 'seen' by trial radar during this year. An He 112 experimental fighter, powered by a liquid-fuel rocket motor, flies in Nazi Germany (see 1938).

1938
17 May A contract is secretly signed with the United States for the supply of 100 Curtiss Hawk 75A-ls and 173 Pratt and Whitney Twin Wasp engines to France.

July The Air Defence Cadet Corps (later ATC) is formed, anticipated in 1927 by the Young Airmen's League. The 22,000-ton fleet carrier HMS *Ark*

Royal, capable of accommodating 70 aircraft, is commissioned.

31 August The Armée de l'Air announces that 161 Bloch 200 bombers are in service, although the design dates from 1932.

11 October The same service commences a mass flight to North Africa using Amiot 143 bombers designed to a 1928 specification. These are to be the backbone of France's bombing force in the coming war. Meanwhile a Purchasing Commission is examining US military aircraft for possible RAF purchase. In Germany, an He 176 rocket fighter makes its first flight (see 1937).

1939
March The Spanish Civil War ends and the Ejercito del Aire becomes an independent service.

1 April The prototype Mitsubishi A6M (Zero) makes first flight from Kagamigahara.

27 August The world's first jet aircraft, the He 178, flies successfully in Germany.

1 September The Nazis' invasion of Poland is supported by 1,581 warplanes of various types and the unopposed use of dive bombers adds to the legend of their invincibility.

3 September Britain and France declare war on Nazi Germany.

4 September The RAF uses Blenheim and Wellington bombers to strike shipping near Wilhelmshaven by day.

16 September A peace formula is agreed between Japan and the Soviet Union, ending a minor war that had begun on 24 August. The Soviets had committed 400 aircraft to the struggle.

30 November War breaks out between the Soviet Union and Finland, in which the former use largely obsolescent aircraft.

1940

4 January The first flight takes place of a Wellington bomber fitted with a 49ft 9in degaussing ring to sweep magnetic mines. Twelve similar aircraft are secretly modified in 'D' hangar at Croydon Airport.

6 January Seven Soviet Ilyushin bombers are destroyed by two Finnish Fokkers over Utti.

31 January Britain attempts to buy 300 Re 2000 fighters from Italy but the deal is vetoed by Germany.

14 February Finland complains that the Soviet bombing of towns and railways is 'illegal'.

23 February Very severe weather throughout Europe restricts flying but the RAF makes one of many leaflet raids over German and occupied territory. The first had been made on 12/13 January.

2 March An RAF reconnaissance Spitfire photographs the entire Ruhr industrial area in a single sortie.

8 March France diverts 175 aircraft to aid the Finns.

11 March The RAF sinks its first U-boat (*U31*), with a Blenheim IV (P4852) of No 82 Squadron.

13 March There is a cease-fire in Finland. The air losses of the Finns are said to be 61 aircraft, those of the Soviets '750 to 900'.

6 April RAF leaflet ('Nickel') raids cease, although they are continued by France.

9 April The Nazis invade Norway with the assistance of paratroops, supported by reportedly 1,000 aircraft, and Denmark with 60 aeroplanes. These countries are reported to have 80 and 100 warplanes respectively.

10 April The first Battle of Narvik takes place. The German cruiser *Königsberg* is sunk at Bergen by fifteen FAA Skua dive bombers, the first major warship sunk by air action alone.

11 April The first RAF raid on a continental target (Stavanger-Sola airfield) takes place.

13 April The Second Battle of Narvik takes place. HMS *Warspite*'s Swordfish aircraft bombs *U64*.

10 May The Nazis invade Holland (126 aircraft) and Belgium (179) and paratroops attempt to abduct the former country's Queen Wilhelmina.

11 May French Leo 451 bombers attempt to stem the Nazi advance and later destroy strategic bridges. The first RAF attack on the German mainland takes place.

13 May In their first action, French Dewoitine D.520 fighters destroy four enemy aircraft over the Meuse.

14 May Rotterdam is destroyed by 60 Heinkel 111 bombers. The Germans break through on the Sedan front.

24 May The first British civilian casualties of the war are suffered in a raid on Middlesbrough.

26 May The Dunkirk evacuation begins.

3 June Operation 'Dynamo' ends, 338,226 servicemen having been rescued. The Luftwaffe has lost over 103 aircraft in the period, the RAF 106. 'Haddock' Force is created, to prepare for the RAF bombing of Italy.

5 June Operation 'Rot' (Red) begins the Battle of France.

7 June The former mailplane F-ARIN *Jules Verne* bombs Berlin by night.

10 June Italy declares war on the Allies and raids Malta the next day.

13 June Japanese bombers deliver a fire raid on Chungking and Italy raids the French naval base at Toulon.

14 June Nazi forces enter Paris.

21 June Guided by the new Knickebein, 50 bombers make first use of the device to attack targets in Britain.

25 June Hostilities end in France. It is reported that l'Armée de l'Air has lost 892 aircraft.

1 July Guy Gibson drops a 2,000lb bomb near the German battlecruiser *Scharnhorst* at Kiel.

10 July Widespread attacks on Channel shipping opens the Battle of Britain.

18 July Nazi Stukas are intercepted in a disciplined manner, disproving the legend of the aircraft's invincibility although they continue in use. The RAF bombs invasion barges.

20 July A German night fighter wing (Nachtjagdgeschwader 1) is created.

22 July The first night success by the RAF with the aid of AI (Airborne Interception) radar is recorded near Brighton.

1 August Luftwaffe propaganda leaflets are dropped over southern England.

20 August A heavy attack is made on Chungking by Japanese bombers.

25 August The RAF raids Berlin for the first time, with 81 aircraft.

27 August Anti-U-boat patrols are mounted from Iceland using Fairey Battles.

31 August The Luftwaffe continues attacks on British fighter bases and industrial areas in daylight. Berlin is raided for a fourth time.

7 September A massive incendiary raid on London, using reportedly 350 bombers.

15 September The RAF, erroneously, claims 185 victories in air fighting during 'The Greatest Day'.

18 October Targets in Italy are raided by the RAF. The Japanese bomb the Burma road.

25 October Bf 109 fighter-bombers make a further attempt to reach London and Fiat bombers of the Corpo Aereo Italiano attack Harwich, both by day.

31 October This is the date officially regarded as marking the end of the Battle of Britain.

3 November Poor weather temporarily halts the Luftwaffe 'Blitz'.

11 November Twenty-one Swordfish aircraft from HMS *Illustrious* attack Italian warships at Taranto.

14 November A heavy night attack is mounted by the Luftwaffe on Coventry.

15 November 350 German bombers attack London.

19 November Three raids are made on Birmingham. Press reports tell of 350, 116 and 200 bombers. Others raids will follow on 22/23 November.

8 December A second fire raid carried out on London, with 413 bombers, lasts for fourteen hours.

16 December The first area bombing, by 134 RAF aircraft on Mannheim, takes place.

21 December First major intruder sortie is mounted, by six Blenheim IFs from No 23 Squadron over Normandy/Artois.
29 December 136 bombers drop 30,000 incendiary bombs on the City of London in the first of 57 consecutive night attacks.

1941

2 January Cardiff is bombed by 100 aircraft at night.
3 January Bristol is bombed by 170 aircraft at night.
9 January In Britain, the Air Training Corps is formed from the nucleus of the ADCC (see 1938).
16 January Ju 87s raid Malta, which is later subjected to almost continuous attacks.
10 February British paratroops flying from Malta begin Operation 'Colossus'.
24 February RAF Manchester bombers are used for the first time, raiding Brest.
March The only action using the Soviet parasite aircraft, or *zvyeno* system (see 1934), takes place when a TB-3-AM-34 launches two SPB dive bombers (converted I-16s) to attack a bridge.

10 March Halifax bombers are employed for the first time, attacking Le Havre.
12 March The first sorties by Halifax bombers over Germany are flown when RAF aircraft raid Hamburg.
13 March The Luftwaffe attacks Glasgow and Clydeside, killing 460.
2 April The first flight takes place of the He 280 experimental jet aircraft at Rostock (see August 1939).
13 April Between this date and July German and Italian bombers make 437 attacks associated with the siege of Tobruk, dropping 350 tons of bombs.
18 April The first flight of the Messerschmitt Me 262 takes place in Germany, but the aircraft is powered by piston engines as jets are not available (see November).
1 May The prototype North American Mustang flies in the United States.
3 May Radio equipment from three Heinkel 111s downed over Liverpool provide information enabling the Y-Gerät blind-bombing system to be jammed.
10 May The climax of 'Blitz' starts 2,200 serious fires in London.

15 May The first test flight of the British Gloster E.28/39 jet takes place at Cranwell.
16 May 111 aircraft bomb Birmingham and the West Midlands.
20 May The Germans invade Crete (Operation 'Merkur'), using paratroops, airborne infantry and DFS gliders in conjunction with bombers.
26 May RN Swordfish aircraft disable *Bismarck*, enabling British heavy units to sink the German battleship the next day.
1 June Manchester is attacked by 110 aircraft, adding to the 39,678 killed and 46,119 injured since September 1940.
14 June The first of RAF's fighter sweeps over France is conducted.
18 June The existence of British 'radio location' (radar) is announced.
22 June The Germans invade the Soviet Union (Operation 'Barbarossa'). 1,800 aircraft are destroyed, mostly on the ground.
25 June Despite the official end of the Russo-Finnish war, Soviet aircraft bomb Helsinki.
28 June The Germans drop 3,870 'block-busters' on Brest-Litovsk.

Above: A Pe-2 of the Soviet Red Air Fleet. This reconnaissance bomber was in full production during 1941–45. (Author's collection)

July US Gen Arnold is given details of the Whittle turbojet.

6 July Peruvian aircraft and paratroops are in action against Ecuador (see 1919 and 1920).

8 July The first operation (daylight) by RAF Fortress Is takes place (see July 1935).

21 July German He 111s, led by pathfinders, attack Moscow by night.

3 August The first success by a CAM-ship Sea Hurricane is achieved.

7 August Soviet 4-motor Petlyakov Pe-8s bomb Berlin.

8 August The first of 40 consecutive raids on Chungking is carried out by Japan.

25 September German paratroops are dropped over the Crimea.

2 October The initial flight of the prototype Me 163 rocket fighter takes place.

22 October The first patrol by a No 1453 Flight Turbinlite (Helmore) Havoc takes place.

November The first Fw190A-1s are delivered to JG26. The first of the new Mustang fighters are also delivered to the RAF.

25 November First Me 262 flight with jet engines takes place (see April).

7 December 350 Japanese Navy aircraft from six carriers attack Pearl Harbor; 35 raiders are brought down.

28 December The Japanese bomb Manila. This is the year in which the RN made its first use of RATOG (Rocket Assisted Take-Off Gear) and that in which the Sea Hurricane is introduced.

1942

2 January The first of eleven RAF night raids on German warships at Brest takes place.

10 January The first of six RAF raids on Emden takes place.

11 January Japanese paratroops land at Menado in the Celebes.

1 February The Japanese raid Rangoon by day and night, and Port Moresby two days later.

11 February Operation 'Cerberus', in the English Channel, sees German warships, including *Scharnhorst*, *Gneisenau* and *Prinz Eugen*, succeed in breaking through to German territorial waters. British air attacks are unsuccessful.

17 February The Japanese submarine *I-25* launches an E14Y1 seaplane to reconnoitre Sydney.

20 February The Germans organize an air lift, using 300 aircraft by May, to supply the 16th Army trapped north of Smolensk.

27 February The Japanese launch a fire raid on Toungoo (Burma Road).

4 March Malta receives its 394th air attack in 60 days.

April The new Messerschmitt 323 is tested in Germany.

1 April The new Ju 87D makes its debut over Malta.

4 April Operation 'Eisstoss' is launched against Leningrad.

5 April Japanese carrier aircraft strike against Colombo.

10 April Bomber Command aircraft set off to attack Essen with its new 8,000 lb bomb for the first time.

13 April The 'Royce Raid' of three B-17s and ten B-25s flies from Australia to Philippines to bomb Japanese targets and returns to base three days later.

17 April The RAF uses Lancasters in a daylight raid on Augsburg.

18 April US B-25s, led by Lt-Col Doolittle, fly from the carrier *Hornet* to attack Tokyo.

Above: An Allison-powered North American Mustang I (AM148) of No 26 (AC) Squadron RAF in 1942. (Author's collection)

23 April The Germans begin the 'Baedeker Raids', attacking historic British cities.

15 May The first tests take place of the Soviet BI-1 (Berezniak Isnaev) rocket-powered fighter.

30 May The first RAF 'Thousand Bomber' raid (Operation 'Millennium') is launched against Cologne, although some operational training aircraft have to be used to make up the number.

1 June There is an RAF 'Thousand Bomber' (actually 956) raid on the Ruhr.

3 June Wellington GR.VIIIs are now flying with twin torpedoes, and the first fitted with a Leigh Light attacks a U-boat.

4 June The Battle of Midway opens. The Japanese carriers *Akagi*, *Kaga*, *Soryu* and *Hiryu* are sunk, but the USS *Yorktown* is also lost with its aircraft.

6 June The RAF's Hawker Hurricane IID makes its début in Libya and a Leigh Light Wellington sinks a U-boat.

25 June There is an RAF 'Thousand Bomber' raid on Bremen. 'Gee' blind-bombing equipment is successfully tested against a major target.

1 July The First Battle of El Alamein opens.

5 July Luftwaffe torpedo-equipped He 111s of I/KG26, newly introduced in June, score a signal success in attacking convoy PQ17.

15 July 200 RAF Spitfires carry out a massive sweep over France.

26 July Soviet Pe-8s of ADD (Long-Range Bombing Force) begin round-the-clock attacks in support of the 62nd Army south-west of Stalingrad.

30 July Explosive incendiary bombs are used by the Germans during raids on Britain.

17 August The first American attack on a European target takes place when twelve B-17s, escorted by RAF Spitfires, bomb the rail centre at Rouen.

19 August Commandos with air support attack Dieppe after photographic reconnaissance by North American Mustangs (Operation 'Jubilee').

25 August 600 Luftwaffe aircraft raid Stalingrad. 40,000 are killed.

24 August A special Spitfire V destroys a Ju 86P at an altitude of 42,000ft.

26 September The RAF abandons high-altitude sweeps over France.

October RAF Mustangs first fly over Germany.

2 October The first flight takes place of the Bell XP-59 Airacomet fighter, powered by two General Electric gas turbines based on British Whittle-type jet motors.

November The new Hawker Typhoon is taken into operational service by the RAF.

25 November An attempt is made to keep the German 6th Army at Stalingrad supplied by air. The total number of aircraft used rises to 850 by December, with 489 lost.

18 December Panzers at Stalingrad are attacked by 74 Pe-2s, ten Il-2ms and 28 Yaks.

27 December Supplies are parachuted to starving Japanese forces on Guadalcanal.

Early in the year, Focke Achgelis had been asked to design the Fa 330 powered kite for submarines and the first Seafires had joined the RN.

1943

6 January Round-the-clock air attacks are made on a Japanese convoy heading for Lae in New Guinea, heralding the Battle of Huon Gulf.

11 January US bombers attack Naples.

13 January The RAF opens a new series of attacks on the Ruhr. Eight are to be made in the month.

16 January RAF resumes raids on Berlin and uses new marker bombs to indicate targets.

30 January The Australians airlift 800 men to Wau, where the garrison faces a huge Japanese force.

February The Mosquito VI fighter flies for the first time.

5 February Airfields on Rabaul are subjected to a fire raid by US bombers.

13 February The U-boat base at Lorient receives 1,000 tons of bombs from the RAF.

17 Feb RAF Mediterranean Air Command is created, to include Middle East Command, NW Africa Air Forces, RAF Malta and Strategic, Coastal and Tactical Air Forces, as well as the Western Desert Air Force and US Air Support Command.

15 March Pontoon bridges over the River Don are bombed by Soviet aircraft.

18 March U-boat building yards at Vegesack near Bremen are attacked by US B-17s and B-24s in daylight.

22 March Hawker Hurricane IIDs deci-

mate a Panzer column with 40mm cannon.

4 April Fourteen Ju 52 transports fall to P-38 Lightnings off the coast of Tunisia.

7 April A massive Japanese attack on shipping off Guadalcanal costs the Allies US destroyer *Aaron Ward* and HMNZS *Moa* among other vessels.

16 April The first night attack by Luftwaffe fighter-bombers, with 30 FW 190s, is sent against London.

20 April The first 'nuisance' raid on Berlin is made by eleven RAF Mosquitos. In fact a diversional tactic.

30 April The RAF attacks Essen for the fifty-fifth time.

6 May Fierce air battles result from Soviet raids on the Bryansk-Orel, Novgorod and Ukraine areas.

7 May Further German day and night attacks using fighter-bombers are made on targets in Britain (Great Yarmouth and Lowestoft).

16 May Operation 'Chastise', the 'Dambusters' raid on the Ruhr, takes place.

20 May In Sardinia, seven Messerschmitt 323 Gigant transports are encountered and shot down by P-40 Warhawks.

28 May The oil refinery at Leghorn is raided by 100 B-17s.

8 June Pamphlets are dropped by the Allies demanding the surrender of the Italian garrison at Pantellaria.

10 June Airfields in the area of Kursk are raided by 700 night bombers.

13 June This day sees the first large-scale use of 'butterfly' anti-personnel bombs over Great Britain during an attack on Grimsby.

20 June The first Allied shuttle raid takes place when 60 RAF Lancasters fly to Algiers, bombing Friedrichshafen on the way, then return to base, attacking Spezia en route.

30 June 'Serrate' operations (fighter interception by homing on to enemy transmissions) begin against German AI-equipped night fighters.

2 July The Germans attempt the air-to-air bombing of B-24s attacking airfields in southern Italy.

10 July The Allied invasion of Sicily (Operation 'Husky') takes place using 3,680 aircraft.

17 July The British FIDO (Fog Investigation Dispersal Operation) system is used for the first time.

24 July 700 RAF bombers attack Hamburg using 'Window' strips to deceive enemy radar. The first tests of the Gloster Meteor jet take place.

27 July An RAF raid on Hamburg maintains the fires started on 24 July.

1 August 164 B-24s raid the Ploesti oil fields (Operation 'Tidal Wave')

13 August B-24s from North Africa attack the Messerschmitt works.

17 August 597 RAF bombers attack Peenemünde (Operation 'Hydra') and the US Eighth Air Force raids the Schweinfurt ball-bearing works with 230 aircraft (see 14 October).

23 August For the first time since 1941 the Japanese raid Chungking.

6 September Airfields near Naples are bombed round-the-clock.

11 September Do 217s use Fritz X and Hs 293 radio-controlled missiles against shipping off Salerno.

11 October The Japanese bomb Madras.

14 October 'Black Thursday': 228 B-17s bomb Schweinfurt (see 17 August)

3 November 500 B-17s and 100 B-24s use 'Mickey Mouse' H2X radar to bomb Wilhelmshaven through dense cloud.

16 November Molybdenum mines at Knaben are bombed by B-17s and B-24s, as is the Norsk hydroelectric power station.

18 November The RAF begins a series of raids on Berlin with 50 diversionary attacks.

5 December Japanese aircraft bomb Calcutta.

11 December The US Eighth Air Force claims 138 interceptors shot down during a daylight attack on U-boat yards at Emden. A total weight of 25,000 tons of bombs has been dropped on Berlin in 32 raids for the loss of 1,047 RAF aircraft this year. The Germans have begun training pilots for the new Me 163 Komet rocket-propelled fighter.

1944

5 January The RAF drops 1,100 tons of high explosive on Stettin.

8 January The Lockheed XP-80 Shooting Star flies for the first time, from Muroc Dry Lake.

21 January The first raid associated with Operation 'Steinbock' includes Heinkel He 177s.

27 January The most concentrated of all raids on Berlin by the RAF takes place: 1,500 tons of HE are dropped at the rate of 75 tons a minute.

6 February 200 Soviet bombers attack Helsinki.

11 February A night attack on the German battleship *Tirpitz* in Alta Fjord is made by a Soviet heavy bomber squadron.

15 February The monastery at Monte Cassino is hit by 493 tons of HE from 135 B-17s.

18 February Operation 'Jericho': nineteen RAF Mosquitos from Nos 464 and 487 Squadrons pin-point Amiens jail and breach the walls to allow the escape of 250 French Resistance prisoners. No 21 Squadron is held in reserve and does not attack. Gp Capt 'Pick' Pickard, who has led the entire operation, is lost (he had become known to the general public following his appearance in the film *Target for Tonight*).

20 February The US Eighth and Fifteenth Air Forces, with escort, bomb fighter assembly plants in Operation 'Big Week'.

24 February The ninth London raid in Operation 'Steinbock' takes place.

26 February 600 Soviet bombers attack Helsinki.

4 March The first raid on Berlin by US aircraft takes place using 30 B-17s.

5 March Allied aircraft support the second Chindit operation inside Japanese-occupied Burma.

6 March There is a very heavy attack on Berlin by 730 B-17s and B-24s.

15 March Allied bombers obliterate Cassino, also attacking Stuttgart and making a diversionary raid on Munich.

18 March In the heaviest raid of the war to date, 3,000 tons of bombs are dropped by the RAF on Frankfurt.

19 March Operation 'Strangle', a three-week air attack against Italian communications, begins.

24 March Berlin is attacked, with a diversionary raid on Kiel.

April The Tempest V enters service with the RAF.

11 April Six low-flying RAF Mosquitos destroy Gestapo records at The Hague.

18 April The final raid on London (see 21 January) takes place. The total number of civilians killed is 1,493, with 2,841 injured.

25 April The first of series raids on Portsmouth, Plymouth and Devonport take place.

5 May Torre Dam in Italy is dive-bombed by RAF Mustangs.

6 May This day sees the first flight of the Mitsubishi A7M, intended to replace the A6M Zero.

16 May Soviet bombers raid Minsk railway junction.

20 May Allied bombers are sent against twelve rail and nine airfield targets on the continent. 5,000 sorties are flown.

1 June The RAF's strength is stated to total 8,339, aircraft against the Luftwaffe's 6,967.

2 June The first shuttle raid by B-17s of the Fifteenth Air Force (Operation 'Frantic') takes place.

5 June RAF diversionary attacks are made (Operation 'Taxable').

6 June The Allied D-Day landings take place in France (Operation 'Overlord') and preliminary smoke screens are laid by white-nosed RAF Douglas Bostons.

Allied Strengths involved in Operation 'Overlord'

Heavy bombers	3,467
Medium bombers	1,645
Fighters	5,409
Transports	2,355
Gliders	867
Airborne troops landed (British)	7,900
Airborne troops landed (US)	15,500

13 June The first ten V-1 flying bombs are launched against London.

14 June The first attack by the new B-29 Superfortress bombers is made on Japan.

15 June There is a concentrated attack on London and the south-east of England by 244 V-1s.

19 June In the Battle of the Philippine Sea, 372 Japanese carrier aircraft are launched against US carrier forces.

22 June The Luftwaffe raids the Eighth Air Force's shuttle base in the Ukraine by night.

23 June A Soviet offensive in Byelorussia involves 6,000 aircraft against 1,300 German.

4 July The RAF drops 12,000lb bombs on V-1 stores outside Paris.

8 July 1,700 barrage balloons are redeployed in south-east England to meet the threat from V-1 flying bombs.

12 July Gloster Meteor jet fighters join the RAF.

17 July 1,596 anti-aircraft guns are redeployed in south-east England to meet the V-1 threat.

11 August The Germans test the Ruhrstahl-Kramer X-4 wire-guided, rocket-propelled missile intended for use with the Messerschmitt Me 262 jet being delivered.

15 August Airborne forces, supported by 1,300 aircraft, land behind the beachhead established in southern France. (Operation 'Dragoon')

16 August Messerschmitt 163 rocket-propelled fighters make their first interception of Allied bombers (see 2 October 1941).

17 September The Battle of Arnhem (Operation 'Market Garden') sees Allied troops transported in 3,500 aircraft and 500 gliders.

October The first tests take place of Japan's Yokosuka MXY 7 manned flying bomb (Baka or Okha)

12 October The Japanese use new Ki-67 torpedo aircraft in the Battle of Formosa.

25 October Kamikaze aircraft from the Shikishima Unit of Japan's Special Air Corps are used for the first time, sinking the escort carrier *St Lo* (CVE-63) during the Battle of Leyte Gulf (see 1977).

31 October Nos 21, 464 and 487 Squadrons carry out a low-level attack on the Gestapo headquarters at Aarhus, Denmark. (see 21 March 1945)

12 November The German battleship *Tirpitz* is sunk in Tromsø Fjord by Lancasters of Nos 9 and 617 Squadrons using 12,000lb bombs.

24 November The first raid by B-29s is made on Tokyo. Flying from India, 111 aircraft take part.

6 December The first flight of the Heinkel He 162 jet fighter takes place in Germany.

This year Norway's army and navy air arms have merged to become the RNorAF (Kongelige Norske Luftforsvaret). Between June and the following January, the US Eighth Air Force uses old B-17Es and Fs as radio-controlled flying bombs, each filled with ten tons of Torpex (Projects 'Aphrodite' and 'Castor').

1945

1 January 800 German fighters make low-level raids on Allied airfields in Holland and Belgium.

6 January Kamikaze attacks damage the battleship USS *California* in the Pacific.

26 January Operation 'Thunderclap' (new attacks on Berlin, and on Dresden) is proposed.

February The first manned flight of the Bachem Ba 349 Natter (Viper) rocket-propelled interceptor takes place.

3 February 1,000 B-17s, escorted by 900 fighters, raid Berlin.

13 February Dresden is heavily raided by 773 Lancasters and 311 B-17s and burns for seven days (see 26 January).

16 February US paratroops take Corregidor.

20 February 900 B-17s escorted by 700 fighters raid station and marshalling yards at Nuremberg.

22 February 900 bombers attack a huge range of continental targets (Operation 'Clarion').

Above: A de Havilland Mosquito with a bulged bomb bay capable of accommodating a 4,000-lb bomb. (de Havilland)

Above: An Avro Lancaster I bomber, the prototype of which (a converted Avro Manchester) first flew on 9 January 1941. A total of 745 were committed to operations in March 1945. (Author)

3 March 100 Luftwaffe night intruders attack twenty British airfields.

9 March An incendiary raid by 900 B-29s is made on Tokyo using napalm and oil.

18 March 1,300 bombers over Berlin are intercepted by jet fighters.

21 March RAF Mosquitos from Nos 21 Sqdn, RAF, 464 Sqdn, RAAF and 487 Sqdn, RNZAF, destroy the Gestapo HQ in Copenhagen in a low-level attack.

23 March The British Army crosses the Rhine, supported by 8,000 aircraft and 1,300 glider sorties on connected sorties (Operation 'Varsity'). Artillery fire practically obliterates Wesel.

29 March The last of 2,419 V-1s (air-launched from He 111s since about August 1944) crosses the British coast. 6,184 people have been killed in these attacks, and 17,918 have been injured.

6 April Kamikaze raids are made on the US invasion fleet (Operation 'Kikusui').

9 April The RAF raids Kiel by night. The 'pocket battleship' *Admiral Scheer* capsizes.

10 April The last enemy sortie is flown over Britain, by an Arado Ar 234 jet of KG76.

15 April Ki-84s strafe US bases on Okinawa and B-29s bomb Tokyo.

17 April B-29s begin a series of raids on kamikaze bases.

7 May Germany surrenders unconditionally to the Western Allies and USSR.

14 May A daylight fire raid on Nagola takes place using napalm and oil bombs.

23 May 1,000 B-29s raid Tokyo on this and following night.

2 June US attacks on kamikaze bases in the south of Japan force a redeployment north.

9 July Operation 'Eclipse' – to photograph from the air the total eclipse of the sun – is mounted using PRU Spitfire X4492/'F' (Flt Lt T. Percival) and a North American B-25 Mitchell, both operating from Rivers, Manitoba.

17 June B-29s carry out attacks on Japanese industrial targets.

16 July This day sees the first successful explosion of an atomic bomb, at 0529 hrs at Alamogordo, New Mexico, as part of the 'Trinity' trials. Anglo-American production of the first atomic bombs is coded the 'Manhattan Project'.

27 July 660,000 leaflets are dropped by B-29s on eleven Japanese cities.

6 August Hiroshima is hit by a 20kT atomic bomb ('Little Boy') dropped by B-29 *Enola Gay* of the 509th Composite Group, Twentieth Air Force. The order to make such an attack had been given by US President Truman in an attempt to force Japan to surrender as it has been calculated that an invasion would result in tremendous US casualties. The speed of the Allied advance in Europe removed the need to use such a weapon against Nazi Germany.

7 August The first flight takes place of a Japanese jet based on the Me 262, the Nakajima Kikka (Orange Blossom).

9 August A second atomic bomb is detonated over Nagasaki (the 20kT 'Fat Man'), dropped by the B-29 *Bock's Car*.

An estimated 106,000 people are killed in this blast and that of 6 August.

15 August Japan surrenders. Vice-Admiral Ugaki, commander of kamikaze operations, leads a final mission against Okinawa, but all seven piloted bombs are shot down short of the target.

18 August A pair of B-24s converted for reconnaissance to F-7s are damaged by fighters and AA fire over Tokyo despite the surrender.

22 August Soviet airborne forces land at Port Arthur.

November The Bristol Centaurus V-powered Hawker Tempest II joins the RAF (with No 54 Squadron).

7 November A Gloster Meteor IV breaks the world's absolute air speed record at Herne Bay. The aircraft used are EE454 (Gp Capt Wilson) which achieves 606mph and EE455 (Eric Greenwood) at 603mph.

December The Angkatan Udara Republik Indonesia is formed.

4 December De Havilland Vampire LZ581 (Lt Cdr Brown RNVR) becomes the first jet aircraft to land on an aircraft carrier (HMS *Ocean*).

1946

1 January A US experimental detonation of an atomic bomb at Bikini Atoll sinks three ships and damages 31 out of 73.

25 January A submarine atomic bomb test takes place.

24 April The first flight takes place of the Soviet Union's Yak-17 jet, a hasty improvisation based on the Yak-3.

May This month sees the beginning of the 180-day Project 'Ruby', using Lancasters and modified B-29s experimentally to bomb the nearly completed U-boat pens at Farne near Bremen with 12,000lb 'Tallboys'. The B-29s also carry two 4,500lb rocket-assisted armour-piercing bombs each.

21 July An FH-1 Phantom jet operates from the carrier USS *Franklin D Roosevelt*.

15 November The first public exhibition takes place (at Cleveland, USA) of the German X-4 air-to-air rocket, the US Navy's KDN-1 and KAN-2 'Little Joe' and the US Air Force's annular wing ROC missiles.

1947

24 July The first flight takes place of the Soviet Union's pioneer jet bomber the Il-22, although development is later abandoned.

1 October Tests begin of the US Air Force's first swept-wing fighter, the North American XP-86.

1948

26 June The first flights of the Berlin Air Lift (Operation 'Plainfare' formerly 'Carter Paterson') are made by US aircraft. (Operation known as 'Vittles' in the US)

28 June RAF aircraft join 'Plainfare'.

19 August The first offensive actions of Operation 'Firedog' (against Communist terrorists in Malaya) take place. The anti-guerrilla campaign will last until 31 July 1960.

1949

11 May The blockade of Berlin is officially lifted at 0000 hrs, but the air lift continues until October in order to build up stocks.

23 October A successful test explosion of a Soviet atomic bomb takes place.

This year Chinese Nationalist forces are defeated on the mainland and a new air force is constituted under Soviet supervision.

1950

31 January Plans are announced for the United States to develop a hydrogen bomb.

22 March The first Boeing B-29 is supplied to the RAF as the Washington.

25 June North Koreans cross the 38th

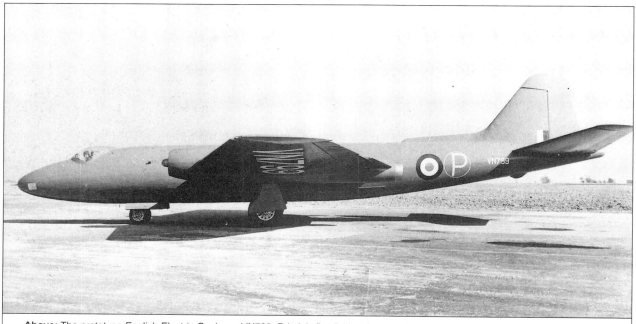

Above: The prototype English Electric Canberra VN799, Britain's first jet bomber, made its maiden flight at Warton on 13 May 1949. The aircraft was intended for radar bombing with a crew of two. (Author's collection)

Parallel and trigger the Korean War with the air support of 132 Il-10s, Yak-3s, -7s and -9s. F-82 Twin Mustangs shoot down three of the last on the same day. Soviet equipment, supplied via China, which has been delivered to the North allows it to be tested 'by proxy'.

1951
24 May The first Canberra jets enter service with the RAF.
22 August The RN's first jets enter service with 800 NAS at Ford.
October Over Korea, the obsolescent B-29s are relegated to night attacks.

1952
3 October The trial explosion of a British atomic weapon takes place over the Monte Bello Islands off the north-western coast of Western Australia.

1953
20 November 13,000 French para-troops land in the valley of Dien Bien Phu to block the route to Laos in Indo-China.

During the summer of this year certain sections of the RAF are placed on a temporary war footing during the Coronation of HM Queen Elizabeth II.

1954
RAF Venoms replace Vampire fighters in the Middle East.

1955
8 February The first of the V-bombers, the Valiant, joins the RAF.
23 February The first action involving the Canberra takes place during 'Firedog' when China Rock, Malaya is bombed (see 1948).

During this year also l'Armée de l'Air reinstates its F-47s in preference to jets for use in Algeria against the Fedaheen and the Soviet Tu-20 bomber makes its first public appearance over Moscow on a national Aviation Day.

1956
26 July Egypt nationalizes the Anglo-French Suez Canal and armed conflict results.
24 September The first official flight of an aircraft belonging to the new German Luftwaffe takes place.
11 October The first live drop of a British atomic bomb takes place over Maralinga, South Australia, from Valiant WZ366 of No 49 Squadron.

29 October Sixteen C-47s of the Israeli Air Force drop 395 paratroopers over the Mitla Pass with Meteor and Mystère support to open the Sinai campaign (Operation 'Kadesh')
31 October The first bombs in the Suez conflict are dropped by Canberra WH853 of No 10 Squadron RAF and hit Almaza airfield.

This year is also that in which the MiG-21 makes its debut.

1957
4 April A British Defence White Paper envisages that missile development is likely to be more useful than that of bombers.
15 May The first British H-bomb is test-dropped over Christmas Island by a No 49 Squadron Valiant (XD818) in Operation 'Grapple' (see 11 October 1956).
21 May The first Vulcans enter RAF service with No 83 Squadron.

1958
21 February It is announced that British Canberras are to have a nuclear capability and that in-flight refuelling trials are to be speeded up.
9 April The first Victor bombers join No 10 Squadron RAF.
24 September Nationalist F-86F Sabres armed with heat-seeking Sidewinder missiles engage Communist MiG-15s over Formosa.
17 December The first public announcement of the TSR-2 project is made in Britain.

1959
20 February Details of the proposed TSR-2 are announced.

This year too, sees the formation of the SOAF (Sultan of Oman's Air Force) and that of the Royal Libyan Air Force using machines donated by the RAF (see 1969).

1960
2 March A long-distance, 8,500-mile flight by a Valiant bomber takes 18hr 5min and twice calls for air refuelling.
1 May A US U-2B spy plane flown by CIA pilot Gary Powers from Peshawar, Pakistan, is shot down by a series of SA-2 missiles over Sverdlovsk in the USSR and provokes an international incident.
19 November Britain's P.1127 VTOL aircraft, from which the Harrier 'jump-

jet' will to be developed, makes its first free flight.

1961
26 May A Convair B-58 bomber completes a flight from New York to Paris in 3hr 19min.
1 July Hunter fighters, and transport aircraft, answer an appeal from Kuwait. Canberras stand by in the Persian Gulf, as do V-bombers in Malta.

1962
23 February It is announced that the RAF will be issued with Blue Steel stand-off missiles during the year, and that Canberras will have AS.30s.
November The cancellation of Skybolt is announced.

The Indo–Pakistan conflict of this year sees the pilots of the latter nation make successful use of a Sidewinder/gun combination.

1963
February Two RAF squadrons prepare for Blue Steel capability; one (No 617) is already fully equipped (see 23 February 1962).

1964
5 August 65 Aircraft from two US carriers launch raids on North Vietnam.

This year an announcement is made regarding the unification of services planned to form the Canadian Armed Forces.

1965
18 March A strategic air offensive is begun to force the North Vietnamese to negotiate (Operation 'Rolling Thunder').
4 April Four North Vietnam MiG-17s destroy two US F-105Ds.
24 July A USAF F-4C is shot down south of Hanoi by a North Vietnamese missile.

1966
25 March A low-level 'penetration flight' of 1,045 miles made by a US F-111A from Edwards AFB, California, to Fort Worth, Texas.
27 May The first flight takes place of a McDonnell F-4J Phantom which is equipped with AWG-10 Westinghouse radar and the AJB-7 Sieger bombing system.
24 November Sweden's Saab 37 Viggen STOL combat aircraft is rolled out at Linköping.

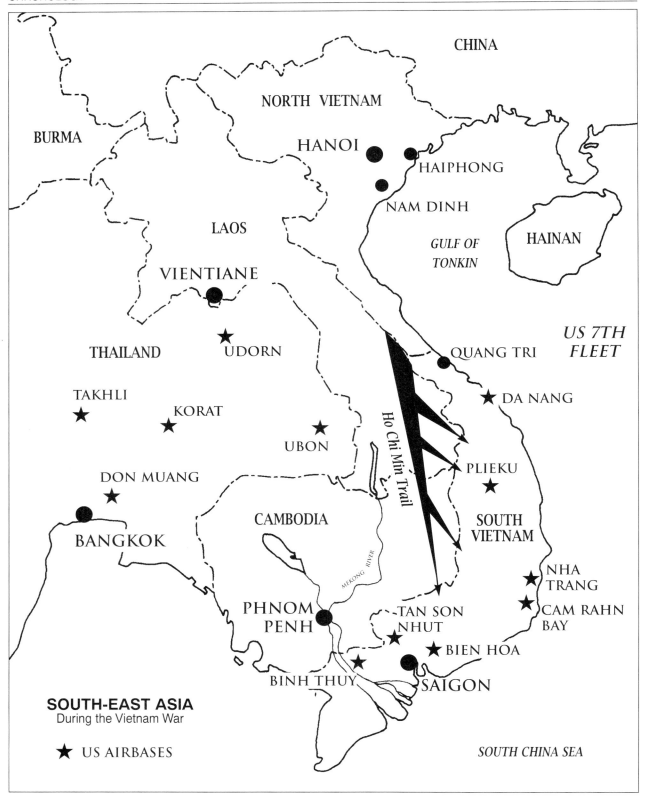

SOUTH-EAST ASIA
During the Vietnam War

★ US AIRBASES

Above: Beginning its existence under the designation A2F-1, the Grumman A-6 Intruder was to play a significant part in the Vietnam War, replacing the elderly piston-engined machines with which the US Navy and Marines were attempting to answer demands for an increasing number of attack missions. Equipment included multi-mode navigation/attack radar, sophisticated armament control and the ability to video strikes and thus assess the damage inflicted. (Bruce Robertson collection)

30 November The strength of the Japanese Air Self-Defence Force (JASDF) announced as being 1,625 aircraft.

This year also Morocco adopts the Northrop F-5 and Spain acquires her first aircraft carrier, the former US light carrier *Cabot*, on loan for five years.

1967
22 February US infantry make the first airborne assault in the Vietnam War on Tay Ninh City (Operation 'Junction City Alternate').
5 June The Arab—Israeli Six-Day War opens with a series of pre-emptive air strikes by the Israelis on airfields in Egypt.
2 October The announcement is made that Polaris-armed submarines will take over as Britain's nuclear deterrent.

The beginning of the year is marked by the announcement that US tactical air power consists of 4,800 combat aircraft, while the closing months see RAF Vulcans of Nos 12

and 101 Squadrons test-drop 1,000lb bombs, those dropped from low level being of the new retarded type. Hunter FGA.9s conduct trials with armour-piercing rockets (SNEB rocket pods). Meanwhile Israeli–Arab hostility continues with the War of Attrition.

1968
21 January US B-52s fly the first of 2,700 missions in defence of the heavily attacked Marine base at Khe Sanh (Operation 'Niagara')
30 April The RAF's Bomber and Fighter Commands merge and form RAF Strike Command.
July The first Soviet Sukhoi Su-15 all-weather fighters enter operational service.
31 October President Nixon halts the bombing of North Vietnam (Operation 'Rolling Thunder').

1969
14 April North Korean fighters shoot down a US Navy EC-121 electronic sur-

veillance aircraft over the Sea of Japan.
30 June The RAF's V-bomber force ceases to act as Britain's nuclear deterrent (see 2 October 1967).
8 October The first General Dynamics FB-111A (strategic bomber version of the F-111) is delivered to the US Air Force.

Following a military coup, Libya is declared a republic this year and the equipment of its new air arm becomes largely French (see 1959),

1970
7 January A deep-penetration attack is made by Israeli Phantoms on an Egyptian Air Force supply depot near Cairo.
18 March US B-52 bombers begin a series of attacks on Cambodian targets at night.
May Sukhoi Su-17 variable-geometry aircraft enter service with the Soviet Air Force. During the latter part of the month Egyptian Su-7s attacked Israeli sites in the Suez area.
21 November US HH-53 helicopters,

escorted by Skyraiders, fly from bases in Thailand, 400 miles distant, hoping to rescue US prisoners-of-war believed to be held captive near Hanoi. No prisoners are found.

1971

February Heavy sorties are flown by US aircraft against North Vietnam (Operation 'Slugger')

21 September A tactical strike is made by 196 US aircraft against three storage depots at Dong Hoi, firing some 350,000 gallons of fuel.

7 November US Air Force and US Navy aircraft open heavy attacks on North Vietnamese airfields.

3 December War breaks out between India and Pakistan and lasts until the 15th of the month. Indian attacks on Pakistani troop concentrations are later switched to armour and rolling stock using rocket-armed Hunters, plus Sea Hawks from the carrier *Vikrant*. The first use of Soviet-built AWACS is also made, to direct Indian night raids on targets 230 miles distant.

This year Mirage 5s enter service in Belgium and Viggens in Sweden (see 24 November 1966).

1972

30 March Every available US and South Vietnamese aircraft, plus B-52s from home bases, is pressed into use to stem a massive triple offensive launched by North Vietnam.

2 April Huge enemy forces press forward in what has evolved into a full-scale invasion of South Vietnam, although they begin to be hampered by the limited air support available.

8 May President Nixon authorizes full-scale air attacks on North Vietnam again (Operation 'Linebacker').

9 May US A-6 Intruders lay thousands of magnetic, acoustic and pressure mines to seal off North Vietnamese ports.

June MiG-23s and MiG-27s enter service in the Soviet Union.

18 December Bombing attacks on North Vietnamese targets north of the 20th Parallel are resumed (Operation 'Linebacker II').

1973

15 January All offensive operations by the United States against North Vietnam are to be suspended during resumed peace talks in Paris, with effect from the 18th.

15 August The final air strike by US aircraft (A-7s) is flown against Khmer Rouge targets in Cambodia.

6 October Egypt launches an attack on Israel supported by various MiGs and Su-7s, triggering the Yom Kippur War (see 19 August 1981).

24 October A cease-fire is arranged after Egypt's 10th Army is encircled. The Israelis have lost 118 aircraft, Egypt 113 and Syria 149.

1974

20 January The General Dynamics F-16 air superiority fighter flies for the first time. The aircraft is described as 'the most important combat aircraft for the rest of the century' (see 7 June 1980).

14 August The first flight of the Panavia MRCA Tornado multi-role variable-geometry aircraft takes place. The aircraft has been manufactured by a British/German/Italian consortium (see November 1982).

23 December The first flight takes place of the variable-geometry Rockwell B-1 four-seat strategic bomber. Production versions will have internal provision for 24 SRAM thermonuclear missiles, with eight carried externally. This year also sees the Sukhoi Su-24 strike aircraft entering service in the Soviet Union.

1975

May Israel's Kfir multi-role combat aircraft becomes operational.

September The Soviet Union's Tu-22M variable-geometry anti-shipping strike aircraft enters service.

1 November Developed from the Boeing 747 airliner, the Boeing E-4A airborne command post enters service in the United States (see 3 December 1971).

1976

July The Soviet Union's first V/STOL aircraft, the Yak-38, is reported in use from the carrier *Kiev* in the Mediterranean.

1977

March The US Air Force's first Boeing E-3A Sentry AWACS joins Tactical Air Command, the idea for such types having been evolved by the US Navy in 1944–45 to deal with kamikaze aircraft attacking via the gap under conventional radar (see 25 October 1944).

5 August The first 'ski-jump' launch of a single-seat Harrier aircraft (XV281) takes place (see 1978).

1978

June The new IAe 58 Pucará strike aircraft enters service in Argentina (see 3 April 1982) and the first post-war all-Japanese fighter, the Mitsubishi F-1, is delivered to the JASDF.

September The British SBAC display publicly demonstrates the 'ski-ramp' launching technique for carrier-borne aircraft, claimed to have been devised by Lt Cdr Taylor RN. The penultimate angle of the platform is 17½ degrees and the optimum 20, thus giving the lift formerly associated with a vessel steaming into a Force 7 wind (see 5 August 1977).

1979

18 June The first Sea Harrier, an FRS.1, for Britain's Royal Navy is delivered for tests with the Intensive Flying Trials Unit.

1980

7 June A precision bombing attack against a nuclear reactor near Baghdad, carried out at low level by a force of eight Israeli F-16s with an escort of F-15s, strikes a crushing blow at atomic development in Iraq (see 16 January 1991).

23 September War breaks out between Iran and Iraq with a large land offensive by the latter along Iran's southern border supported by air strikes against airfields and oil refineries.

1981

June The F-117A 'stealth' fighter makes its maiden flight in the United States.

19 August A pair of armed Sukhoi Su-22 fighter-bombers of the Libyan Air Force are destroyed by two F-14 Tomcats over the Gulf of Sirte when they are detected approaching US naval forces.

The Soviet Air Force adds the Sukhoi Su-25 tactical support aircraft to its inventory this year.

1982

3 April Argentine forces invade the Falkland Islands and war with Great Britain results.

Above: Panavia Tornado prototype XX946, which first flew on 30 October 1974. The aircraft was originally known as the MRCA (which legend it carries on the port air-intake). (BAe)

5 April A British Task Force is dispatched to the South Atlantic (Operation 'Corporate'), headed by the aircraft carriers *Invincible* and *Hermes*.
25 April Two RN helicopters successfully attack the Argentine submarine *Santa Fe* with rockets.
1 May An RAF Vulcan makes a 7,000-mile round trip with the aid of flight refuelling to bomb the airfield at Port Stanley. It is the longest-range air strike in the history of warfare.
9 May Two RN Sea Harriers intercept the intelligence-gathering fishing vessel *Narwal*.
12 May Two Argentine Skyhawk fighter-bombers are destroyed by Seawolf missiles
21 May An Argentine reconnaissance Pucará reconnaissance aircraft is shot down by a Stinger SAM and a Macchi MB.339 hits HMS *Argonaut* with cannon fire and 5in rockets; late in day the ship is hit by two 1,000lb bombs from a Skyhawk. During the night HMS *Ardent* is sunk by seven bomb hits; she had been hit by

Snakeye retard bombs earlier in the day.
22 May Two Sea Harriers of 800 NAS disable the Argentine supply ship *Rio Iguazu*, while four RAF Harriers attack Goose Green.
28 May British paratroops advancing on Goose Green are attacked by Argentine Pucarás, one of which is shot down by a Blowpipe SAM. Enemy positions at Goose Green are attacked by Harriers of No l Squadron with cluster bombs and rockets.
1 June An Argentine radar reconnaissance C-130 is destroyed by a Sea Harrier with cannon fire and an AIM-9L missile. One of these 801 NAS Sea Harriers is shot down in the afternoon by a Roland missile and four enemy Canberras make a high-altitude attack on San Carlos.
3 June Leaflets calling for an Argentine surrender are dropped on Port Stanley and an RAF Vulcan lands at a Brazilian airport after flying from Ascension.
9 June The Israelis launch the first of

a series of attacks intended to destroy Syrian SAM systems in the Lebanon.
14 June Argentine resistance in the Falkland Islands ends with 102 aircraft reported lost for Britain's 36.

Principal Missiles Used in the Falklands Campaign

Name	Used by	Details
Exocet	Britain/ Argentina	Anti-ship missile, 20-mile range.
Seacat	Britain/ Argentina	AA missile, 3-mile range.
Sea Dart	Britain/ Argentina	AA missile, 24-mile range.
Seaslug	Britain	A/A and anti-ship missile, 24-mile range
Seawolf	Britain	Close-range SAM
Side-winder	Britain/ Argentina	Air-to-air missile, 24-mile range

November The Panavia Tornado becomes fully operational with the

Above: A Tornado IDS (Interdictor/Strike) aircraft of the Royal Saudi Air Force surrounded by a selection of offensive stores. The machine is finished in a stone and dark earth disruptive camouflage scheme with small patches of dark green. In the foreground is a Sea Eagle anti-ship missile. (Author's collection)

RAF's No 9 Squadron (see 14 August 1974).

1983
25 October The United States invades Grenada, using troops of the Airborne Division with support from aircraft flown from the carrier USS *Independence* and AC-130 Spectre gunships (Operation 'Urgent Fury').

During the year Soviet MiG-31s enter service and Lockheed F-117A 'stealth' fighter-bombers are sent for operational evaluation with the US TAC.

1984
16 January Developed from British Harrier, the first McDonnell Douglas AV-8Bs are issued to the Marine Training Squadron in the United States
26 March Two-week Soviet exercises in collaboration with the Fleet find Tupolev Tu-22M bombers simulating attacks on warships.

Later in the year Mirage 2000 fighters are issued to French operational units, and in September Soviet TAF accepts its first Su-27s.

1985
7 July The first operational Rockwell B-1B bombers are delivered to the 96th Bomb Wing in the United States (see 23 December 1974)
1 October Israeli F-15s, with the aid of flight refuelling, destroy the headquarters of the Palestine Liberation Organisation at Tunis.

The opening months of 1985 have seen MiG-29s enter service with the Soviet Air Force.

1986
14 April Fifteen US F-111s supported by three EF-111s for electronic countermeasures leave from RAF bases at Lakenheath and Upper Heyford to make the 2,800-mile journey, with the aid of flight refuelling, to attack targets in Libya. Tripoli Airport and the port at Sidi Bial are hit by Mk 20 Rockeye 500lb laser-homing bombs, and the command centre with Mk 82 2,000lb laser-guided missiles. Meanwhile Grumman A-6 Intruders and Vought A-7 Corsairs drop 500lb and 2,000lb 'iron' bombs on a military barracks near Benghazi and on Benina airfield. Cover is provided throughout by F-14 Tomcats and F-18 Hornets of the US Sixth Fleet under the direction of a Grumman E-2C Hawkeye command aircraft. Additional countermeasures are provided by EA-6 Prowlers and subsequent reconnaissance is made by a Lockheed SR-71A. One F-111 is lost.

1987
1 July The Harrier GR.5 STOVL aircraft enters service with No 233 OCU at RAF Wittering.

1988
18 April US A-6E Intruders from the

Above: External offensive stores under the wing of a Harrier 'jump-jet'. The two containers in the foreground are for cluster bombs. (Author's collection)

USS *Enterprise* sink the Iranian frigate *Sahand* and damage the *Sablan* in the Persian Gulf.

12 September ZA195, the new Sea Harrier FRS.2, makes its first flight.

December The first production AGM-65G air-to-surface missile is delivered to the USAF.

1989

4 January A pair of Grumman F-14 Tomcats from the carrier USS *John F. Kennedy* shoot down two Libyan MiG-23s over the Mediterranean.

9 February The first Tornado F2 ADV, armed with four Sky Flash missiles, is issued to the Royal Saudi Air Force.

13 February The one hundredth Mirage 2000 is added to the strength of the French Air Force.

July The Tupolev Tu-160 variable-geometry strategic bomber becomes operational in the Soviet Union and the Lockheed F-117A makes its operational début, using 2,000lb laser-guid-ed bombs to attack a military barracks in Panama (see 1983).

17 July The first flight of the B-2 'stealth' bomber is made from Palmdale, California.

1990

30 January The Royal Navy makes its first deployment of a Sea King helicopter on a frigate, an HAS.5 embarking on HMS *Brave*.

2 August Iraqi forces invade Kuwait, initially attacking air bases at Ali al Salin and Ahmad al Jabir so that Kuwaiti Skyhawk aircraft have to be flown from road sites. Following this event, Great Britain, France and the United States deploy military aircraft to the Middle East (Operation 'Desert Shield'). The US Navy provides the carriers *Independence*, *Dwight D. Eisenhower*, *Midway*, *Ranger*, and *Theodore Roosevelt*, while Strategic Air Command deploys two B-52G Wings, at first to Diego Garcia in the Indian Ocean.

November A limited number of RAF Tornado crews are deployed to the Gulf to gain experience with and devise tactics for ALARM (Air-Launched Anti-Radar Missiles).

1991

16 January The opening assault of Operation 'Desert Storm' takes place with an attack on two Baghdad radar stations.

17 January The first MiGs are claimed destroyed by F-15Cs.

18 January One RAF and one Italian Tornado are shot down. The French attack a munitions dump using AS.30 laser-guided bombs.

19 January RAF Tornados and USAF F-15Es use thermal imaging to hunt mobile 'Scud' missiles.

23 January The RAF drops 1,000lb 'iron' bombs on Iraqi airfields.

24 January Lynx helicopters from HMS *Cardiff* call up A-6Es to destroy various small enemy craft.

28 January F-111s use GBU-15 infrared-guided bombs on pumping stations pouring crude oil into Gulf.

30 January A Lynx helicopter from HMS *Gloucester* using Sea Skuas disables an enemy vessel armed with Exocet missiles.

31 January An AC-130H gunship is destroyed.

2 February Pave Spike laser designator pods are used for the first time to illuminate targets for Tornado attacks with Mk 84 laser-guided bombs.

5 February US B-52s are redeployed to RAF Fairford.

6 February F-111s use GBU-12 laser-guided bombs against Iraqi Army units.

7 February Fuel-air bombs are used for three days to clear minefields.

10 February Pave Spike laser designator pods and Mk 84 laser-guided bombs are used by Tornados against hardened shelters.

24 February Over 2,000 troops are airlifted in position, to open the ground invasion of occupied Kuwait the next day.

27 February F-111s use GBU-28 laser-guided bombs on an enemy underground command post near Baghdad.

28 February The offensive against Iraq is ordered to cease. Coalition air losses are stated to be 68, against an estimated Iraqi total of 141.

10 May In France the first flight takes place of the Dassault Rafale C.

1992

13 January Over 100 British, French and US aircraft carry out strikes on Iraqi SAM bases and their control centres in the Air Exclusion Zones imposed by the UN after the end of the Gulf War. The strikes are joined by aircraft from the USS *Kitty Hawk*.

29 February The first flight takes place of the new British Hawk Mk 102D (ZJ100), the production prototype for the '100' series.

27 March Trials begin of the Westland Super Lynx Mk 95 (ZH580/1001) ordered for Portuguese military service.

14 April Another helicopter makes its début in the United States — the McDonnell Douglas AH-64D Longbow Apache (89-0192).

3 July NATO begins an airlift of supplies and medical equipment into Sarajevo.

This year also sees Russia announce the export of Sukhoi Su-27s, one of the world's most advanced fighters, to China. The Russian Su-30 appears, as does the MiG-33 shipboard aircraft, in addition to a pair described as 'stealth' designs.

1993

4 March The first flight takes place of the Saab JAS 39A Gripen, 39102, the second production machine and the first for the Swedish Air Force. It has a high performance and is capable of delivering a variety of missiles.

1 April RAF Tornados are ordered to stand by to enforce a No-Fly Zone over Bosnia. They are supported by Jaguars from the Iraqi No-Fly Zone, French fighters from Egypt and US machines operating from carriers. All come under AWACS control.

12 April The first sortie takes place in Operation 'Deny Flight', patrols to enforce NATO's No-Fly Zone over Bosnia-Herzegovina

This year the Rockwell Industries/Deutsche Aerospace X-31A ETM enhanced manoeuvrability research aircraft completes its flight trials, and construction begins of the first Mitsubishi FS-X single seat fighter (a heavily redesigned F-16C) intended to replace the Mitsubishi F-1.

1994

31 January The United States agrees to sell 36 McDonnell Douglas A-4 Skyhawk bombers to Argentina.

10 February NATO sends an ultimatum to the Bosnian Serbs demanding the withdrawal of their heavy artillery from the outskirts of Sarajevo within ten days; otherwise they risk air strikes against the positions. To enable these to be carried out the key stations at Gioia del Colle, near Bari, acts as the base for eight RAF Jaguars and Rivolto that for eight of the same type under French command, and there are six Dutch F-16s at Villatranca and twelve US A-10s at Aviano. In addition the carriers *Saratoga* (US), *Clémenceau* (French) and *Ark Royal* (British) are based in the Adriatic.

14 February RN Sea Harriers from *Ark Royal*, carrying free-fall bombs, are reported to be making round-the-clock patrols over Sarajevo.

20 February Gen Sir Michael Rose, commander of the UN Forces in Bosnia, states that the threatened air strikes are not necessary as all heavy guns have been removed from the perimeter of Sarajevo, are under UN control or have been disabled.

21 February Reconnaissance flights, some armed, confirm the general's statement on this, the day the UN ultimatum runs out.

28 February Four Serbian Super Galebs (Seagulls) from a formation of six are shot down by four US fighters over Bosnia in the NATO No-Fly Zone. Sidewinder and other missiles are reported to have been used including the first use of AMRAAM.

27 March In the afternoon, Peter Wegel makes the first flight of the Eurofighter 2000 at Manching, Germany. It lasts for 45 minutes. A DASA X-31 digital control system from Rockwell had been suggested originally for this aircraft.

7 April The first flight of ZH653, the first of thirteen British Aerospace/McDonnell Douglas Harrier T.10 night-attack aircraft, takes place at Warton. Acting as a trainer for the GR.7, the type is scheduled to enter service in 1995.

9 April Using five Lockheed C-130 transports, Belgium flies into Kigali Airport, Rwanda, a force of 1,600 paratroops to meet the threat to foreign nationals after the outbreak of serious unrest in the African state.

10 April A pair of US F-16s, flying under UN command from a base in Italy, drop two bombs on Bosnian Serb artillery shelling the town of Gorazde.

11 April A single F-18 drops three bombs in a similar 20-minute attack.

16 April A-10s under NATO command are reported attacking Serbian tanks on the heights above Gorazde, and a Royal Navy Sea Harrier is shot down.

7 May The public début takes place of ZH588, the second prototype EF2000 single-seat Eurofighter, piloted by Chris Yeo at Warton.

9 May Attack aircraft having made many strikes against ground targets in the renewed war between North and South Yemen, 225 refugees (180 of them British) are evacuated in a civilian DC-10 flying from San'a Airport direct to Gatwick, England.

1 June Israeli jets attack a target, alleged to be a training base for the Palestinian Hizbollah group, near the city of Baalbek in the Syrian-controlled

Bekaa Valley. Twenty Muslim casualties are reported.

8 July As a result of the war in Rwanda, Operation 'Turquoise' begins a daily airlift of food into the French-controlled 'safe area'.

15 July An upgrading programme for the RAF's 142 Tornado strike aircraft to extend the type's long-range capability is announced and an order is placed for new Paveway III 'smart' bombs plus TIALD pods, thus doubling Britain's precision-bombing capability. CASOM long-range air-to-ground missiles are examined.

3 August Gen Sir Michael Rose warns that he will use air strikes if threats to regain Bosnian Serb heavy artillery taken into UN safekeeping are carried out (see February).

5 August After Bosnian Serbs seize a quantity of impounded equipment, including a T-55 tank, from an arms dump at Ilidza, a suburb of Sarajevo, two US A-10s and two RAF Jaguars, with Dutch and French jets, make a punitive attack on a Serb position six miles to the south. The equipment is returned the next day.

18 September Sixty-one Lockheed Hercules transports carrying troops of the US 82nd Airborne Division to invade Haiti are recalled when it appears that the allegedly oppressive ruling junta had been overcome by peaceful means.

19 September US troops of the 10th Mountain Division, the first of 15,000 men, are flown in to Haiti's Port au Prince airport in helicopters from the carrier *Eisenhower* to support the reinstatement of President Aristide.

8 October 82,000 Iraqi troops forming two mechanized and one armoured division are reported to be heading south and within twenty (and later eight) miles of the Kuwait border. US, British and French aircraft capable of making a response from Turkey are reported to total some 60, while in Saudi Arabia there are 36 US F-15 and F-16 fighters with AWACS guidance types as well as six RAF Tornados. The carrier *George Washington*, with 50 aircraft, is simultaneously ordered to the Red Sea.

10 October The United States announces a proposed rapid build-up of 'at least 200' combat aircraft in the Gulf region. The total Iraqi air strength is estimated as 300 combat machines,

comprising Mirage fighters, MiG-23s and MiG-29s.

11 October Despite Iraqi assurances, the US arms build-up in the Gulf is to continue and the dispatch of 350 aircraft, including B-52 bombers, A-10 strike aircraft and F-117A 'stealth' types, is announced.

12 October War having been averted by the United States' acceptance of Iraq's withdrawal from the frontier, it is announced that Allied forces in the area will be engaged in an extensive exercise before leaving.

18 November Two Serbian Yugoslav-made Orao fighter-bombers bomb north-west Bihac at 1100hrs having flown from their base about 30 miles distant at Udbina. Cluster and two PLAB M17 napalm bombs are dropped from 200ft.

19 November During an assault on the centre of Cazin, south of Bihac, the target is strafed and a pair of bombs dropped. One of the two attacking aircraft is shot down and the pilot killed.

21 November In Operation 'Deny Flight', NATO jets from the United States, France, Holland and Britain, flying from Aviano, Giola del Colle, Istrana and Villafranca in Italy, raid a target in Serbian-held Croatia at 12 noon. Four of the 39 attackers are RAF Jaguars, two armed with 1,000lb HE bombs, while Sea Harriers from HMS *Invincible* provide top cover.

23 November Two strikes by warplanes from the same countries are made against the Serbian missile site at Otokar near Bihac in western Bosnia. Although tracking radar is destroyed in the first, which involved 24 aircraft, the missiles escaped damage, calling for a second attack by 'about 30' machines which is reported to be successful. HARM missiles are used.

1 December Following Chechnya's unilateral declaration of independence, Russian bombers target the airport, a housing estate and the home of the separatist leader Gen Dudayev in three attacks on the capital, Grozny, while troops and armoured vehicles are flown in to the surrounding areas.

17/18 December Russian fighter-bombers attack the village of Petropavlovskaya, north-east of Grozny, overnight.

18 December Jets bomb strategic targets on the outskirts of Grozny at

0700 hrs GMT. The following day the targets are stated as having been a gas refinery and the capital's television tower.

22 December In support of tanks, Grozny is attacked from the air for the first time in daylight.

29 December It is announced that henceforth only laser-guided bombs will be used against targets in Chechnya.

The first half of this year has seen the successful trials in the United States of the Sea Harrier FRS.2 with the AMRAAM (Advanced Medium-Range Air-to-Air Missile) using GEC-Marconi Blue Vixen look down/shoot down Doppler radar, thus permitting the engagement of targets beyond visual range.

1995

5 January The death occurs at 69 years of age after a long illness of Ben Rich, who led Lockheed's F-117 'stealth' aircraft (q.v.) development team.

16 January Russian aircraft operating against Chechnya use cluster bombs for the first time.

17 January It is announced that twelve Sukhoi Su-34s (first designated Su-27 IBs) are to be produced at Novosibirsk by 1998. The aircraft is a two-man side-by-side tactical bomber with an unrefuelled range of 2,000 miles, equipped with multi-function radar and inertial satellite-linked navigation and armed with air-to-ground missiles or bombs.

4 February The first Russian jet fighter to be destroyed over Chechnya (an Su-24) is brought down by ground fire.

10 February Peruvian and Ecuadorian aircraft attack each other's positions during a border dispute. Two of sixteen Peruvian machines bombing Tiwinza are lost and one is damaged by AA fire, while Ecuador attacks positions north of Cueva de los Tayos.

11 February Unmanned US drones operating from the Croatian island of Brac are reported to be reconnoitring Bosnian communication lines from an altitude of 25,000ft.

30 March The RAF disbands its Balloon Operations Squadron. Balloon Command had been created under the auspices of Fighter Command in November 1938.

28 April Velupillai Prabhakran's Tamil

Tigers shoot down a military aircraft over the Jaffna peninsula.

29 April Tamil Tiger guerrillas bring down a second military aircraft near Palaly, killing all 51 on board. Two Serb aircraft attack the Muslim enclave of Bihac in northern Bosnia before heading for Croatia.

25 May At 1600 hrs local time six UN aircraft from Italy make a 20-minute attack on an ammunition depot at Pale, nine miles south-east of Sarajevo.

26 May Another strike is made at the same target, while two aircraft carriers are ordered to the area, one French and one US.

28 May Russian aircraft carry out two attacks on the Chechnyan guerrilla headquarters at Vedeno.

2 June An F-16C of the US 555th Squadron based at Aviano, Italy, is brought down while flying a UN mission near Mrkonjic Grad, 25 miles south of Banja Luka by a Serbian SAM-6 missile. Pilot Scott O'Grady ejects.

8 June At 0644 hrs Capt O'Grady, located twenty miles south-east of Bihac, is rescued by a 40-man Marine helicopter force from USS *Kearsarge*. The two CH-53 Super Stallions are fired at from a portable SAM-7 launcher.

11 July Two UN F-16s attack Bosnian Serb forces threatening the safe haven of Srebrenica.

23 July A French Mirage flying from Mont-de-Marsan is reported to have attacked Pale, the home of Bosnian Serb leader Radovan Karadzic's aide, releasing a 'one-ton' laser-guided bomb from 10,000ft at 1300 hrs.

26 July Germany agrees to augment NATO air strength over Bosnia with a force of Tornado and transport aircraft.

1 August Three Serbian jets attack Croat positions with rockets.

4 August Two USA EA-6Bs on patrol from the USS *Theodore Roosevelt* fire missiles at Serbian positions in the Kniri area of Krujina when discovering that they are about to come under attack. Croat Galebs and Super Galebs attack the Serb communications centre at Gracac, while Udbina and Bihac are also bombed.

7 August Serb jets from Banja Luka attack Croat targets, while two of five are lost while making strikes at Mackovac and Savski.

10 August Israeli helicopters fire rockets at Hizbollah guerrilla targets in Louwaizeh and the Mitla hills.

30 August Carrier-borne F-14s open four massive NATO attacks by over 60 aircraft on Serb missile, radar and communications sites at Sarajevo, Gorazde, Tuzla and Pale, using rockets and laser-guided bombs. One French Mirage is lost. This day is the first of Operation 'Deliberate Force', 300 sorties being mounted against twenty targets.

31 August Further afternoon attacks are followed by night operations by RAF Harriers flying from Bari in southern Italy.

1 September Following early morning sorties, NATO attacks over Bosnia are suspended for twenty-four hours to allow negotiations to proceed.

5 September NATO attacks are resumed with RAF Harriers flying from Gioia del Colle in southern Italy.

The year has also seen exploratory talks between Britain and Spain with a view to the joint development of a new class of aircraft carrier intended to replace HMS *Invincible* by the year 2015. Russian air defences are reported to be in 'deep crisis' owing to deteriorating equipment and disintegrating organizational policies.

1996

1 January The 1,915th supply sortie into Sarajevo, made by an RAF Lockheed Hercules on Flight No IFN94, closes the longest airlift in history. United States and French sorties are similarly terminated.

18 January Russian helicopter gunships are used to flush out Chechen rebels said to be holding between 70 and 120 persons hostage

15 February The death is reported of Adolf Galland.

24 February Two Cuban MiGs shoot down two light aircraft at a spot variously described as being 'in Cuban air space' and 'over international waters between Havana and Florida'.

6 March Russian helicopter gunships make their first attempt to drive out rebels loyal to Dzhokhar Dudayev during renewed fighting in the Chechen capital of Grozny.

This year the RAF closes its historic station at Scampton, Lincolnshire, the former base of No 617 Squadron.

Royal Navy Westland Sea King helicopters.
(Author)

A — Z

A- (1) The United States Navy designation for attack aircraft introduced in 1946, examples being the Douglas A-4 Skyhawk and Vought A-7 Corsair II. Originally used by the United States Army Air Corps and Army Air Force but also included dive and light bombers such as the Martin A-30 Baltimore during the years of WWII. (2) A-type airship (see DN-1).

A-Stoff Liquid oxygen.

AAM Air-to-air missile, fired from one aircraft against another. Towards the close of the century often the principal armament carried by interceptors. AAMs are now essentially weapons guided by radar, infra-red-seeking sensors or a combination of these but at first could only be fired on a more or less straight course during clear weather and were unreliable above sources of heat and in conditions of high humidity, although proving superior to conventional guns due to the increased speed of aircraft. The beginnings of like weapons were made during the First World War when such aircraft as Nieuport 17s and B.E.2cs were equipped with Le Prieur rockets chiefly intended for use against balloons with their potentially explosive gas content. The idea was reintroduced by the Soviet AF in 1938 and later still by the Luftwaffe when Messerschmitt 262 fighters were thus equipped to counter high-flying US daylight raiders although the missiles were still unguided.

Aasen bombs Converted Italian grenades in use before WWI.

Abstellknopf The red button on the Zahlwerk control unit fitted to Heinkel 111 bombers adapted to air-launch V-1 flying bombs during WWII. This button stopped the motor of the missile in an emergency.

ACE Allied Command, Europe. NATO designation for one of the two subordinate Commands falling under SHAPE, Supreme Headquarters, Allied Powers in Europe. About 3,000 combat aircraft came under the former during the 1970s.

Ace A term first applied in France during WWI to a pilot who had shot down five enemy aircraft and as a consequence was mentioned in official communiqués. The United States later adopted the same qualifying figure entering the field later, although Germany and Austria required ten as the qualifying number. Only Great Britain officially shunned the system after Field Marshal Sir Douglas Haig pointed out the injustice of giving to one Corps of the Army greater publicity than any other, the British air arm having no separate existence at the time. Be that as it may, although the ace system enjoyed no military importance, its psychological significance was immense, for both raising and maintaining morale, including that of civilians, and, although by no means accurately, giving an impression of military success applicable to the war as a whole. The major recorded aces and their victories (indicated here by an asterisk if including unconfirmed) are:

Above: Georges Guynemer, the French ace of WWI. On the wall of the Parthenon crypt, Paris, is a marble plaque reading: 'Fallen on the field of honour on September 11th, 1917 – a legendary hero, fallen in glory from the sky after three years of fierce struggle. He will remain the purest symbol of the qualities of his race, indomitable tenacity, ferocious energy, sublime courage; animated by the most resolute faith in victory, he bequeaths to the French soldier an imperishable memory which will exalt the spirit of sacrifice.' This dedication exemplifies the attitude adopted by all nations, in every age, towards their ace fliers. (Author's collection)

FIRST WORLD WAR

Australia
Captain R. A. Little	47
Maj R. S. Dundass	39

Belgium
2/Lt W. Coppens	37
Adj A. de Meulemeester	11
2/Lt E. Thieffrey	10

Canada
Maj W. A. Bishop	72
Maj R. Collishaw	60
Capt D. P. MacLaren	54
Maj W. G. Barker	52
Capt F. R. McCall	37
Capt W. G. Claxton	36
Capt J. S. T. Fall	36

France
Capitaine R. P. Fonck	75
Capitaine G. M. L. Guynemer	54
Lt C. E. J. M. Nungesser	45
Capitaine G. F. Madon	41
Lt M. Boyau	35

Germany and Austro-Hungary
Rittmeister M. von Richthofen	80
Oblt E. Udet	62
Oblt E. Loewenhardt	53
Lt W. Voss	48
Hpt B. Loerzer	45
Lt F. Rumey	45
Hpt R. Berthold	44
Lt P. Baumer	43
Lt J. Jacobs	41
Hpt O. Boelcke	40
Hpt G. Brumowski	40
Lt F. Buchner	40
Oblt L. von Richthofen	40
Lt K. Menckhoff	39
Lt H. Gontermann	39
Lt M. Müller	36
Lt J. Bucker	35
Lt G. Dorr	35
Hpt R. R. von Schleich	35

Great Britain and Ireland
Maj E. C. Mannock	73*
Maj J. T. B. McCudden	57
Capt P. F. Fullard	52
Capt G. E. H. McElroy	49
Capt A. Ball	47
Maj T. F. Hazell	43
Maj J. Gilmour	40
Capt J. I. T. Jones	40
Capt H. W. Woollett	36

Italy
Mag F. Baracca	34
Ten S. Scarsoni	26
Ten-Col P. R. Piccio	24
Ten F. T. Baracchini	21
Cap F. R. di Calabria	20
Sgt M. Cerutti	17
Ten F. Ranza	17
Ten L. Olivari	12
Ten G. Ancillotto	11
Sgt A. Reali	11

Russia
Staff-Capt A. A. Kazakov	17*
Capt P. V. d'Argueeff	15
Lt-Cdr A. Seversky	13
Lt I. W. Smirnoff	12
Lt M. Safonov	11
Capt B. Sergievsky	11
Ens E. M. Tomson	11

South Africa
Capt A. W. Beauchamp-Proctor	54
Capt S. M. Kinkead	35*

USA
Capt E. V. Rickenbacker	26
Capt S. C. Rosevear (RFC)	23
Capt W. C. Lambert (RFC)	22
Capt F. W. Gillette (RFC)	20
Capt J. J. Malone (RN)	20
Maj A. M. Wilkinson (RFC)	19
Capt F. Hale (RFC)	18
Capt P. T. Iaccaci (RFC)	18
2/Lt F. Luke Jr	18
Maj R. G. Lufbery (AM)†	17
Lt H. A. Kullberg (RFC)	16
Capt O. J. Rose (RFC)	16
Lt C. T. Warman (RFC)	15
Capt F. Libby (RFC)	14
Lt G. A. Vaughn	13
Lt F. L. Baylies	12
Lt L. B. Bennett (RFC)	12
Capt F. E. Kindley	12
Lt D. E. Putnam	12
Capt E. W. Springs	12
Lt T. A. Iaccaci (RFC)	11
Capt R. G. Landis	10
Capt J. M. Swaab	10

Unless otherwise stated, all the above served with either the American Expeditionary Force or with the Lafayette Escadrille. †Aéronautique Militaire.

SINO–JAPANESE, SPANISH CIVIL, RUSSO–FINNISH WINTER WARS AND SECOND WORLD WAR

Australia
Wg Cdr C. R. Caldwell	28

Canada
Flt Lt G. Beurling	31

Czech
Capt J. Franntisek	28
Lt K. M. Kuttelwascher	18

Finland
Lentomestari E. I. Juutilainen	94
Kapteeni H. Wind	78
Majuri E. Luukkanen	54
Lentomestari U. Lehtovaara	44
Kapteeni R. O. Puhakka	43
Lentomestari O. Tuominen	43
Lentomestari N. Katajainen	36
Luutnantti K. Puro	35
Luutnantti L. Nissinen	32
Majuri J. Karhunen	31

France
Capitaine M Albert	23

Germany (day)
Maj E. Hartmann	352
Maj G. Barkhorn	301
Maj G. Rall	275
Oblt O. Kittel	267
Maj W. Nowotny	258
Maj W. Batz	237
Maj E. Rudorffer	222
Obst H. Bär	220
Obst H. Graf	212
Maj H. Ehrler	209
Maj W. Herget (see below)	14

Germany (night)
Maj H. W. Schnaufer	121
Obst H. Lent	102
Maj H. Sayn-Wittgenstein	84
Obst W. Streib	65
Hpt M. Meurer	65
Obst G. Radusch	64
Hpt H. Rökker	64
Maj R. Schönert	64
Maj P. Zorner	59
Maj W. Herget	57

Great Britain and Ireland
Gp Capt J. E. Johnson	34
Wg Cdr B. Finucane	32
Wg Cdr J. R. D. Braham	29
Wg Cdr R. R. S. Tuck	29
Gp Capt F. R. Carey	28*
Sqn Ldr N. F. Duke	28

Italy
Cap F, Lucchini	26

Japan
WO H. Nishizawa	87
Lt T. Iwamoto	80*

PO S. Sugita	70*
Lt S. Sakai	64
WO H. Shinohara	58
PO T. Okumura	54
M/Sgt S. Anabuki	51
Lt M. Tarui	38
WO I. Saski	38
PO T. Ohta	34

South Africa

Sqn Ldr M. T. St J. Pattle	51*
Gp Capt A. G. Malan	32*

Soviet Union

I. N. Kozhedub	62
A. I. Pokryshkin	59
G. A. Rechkalov	58
N. D. Gulayev	57
A. V. Vorozheikin	52
K. A. Yevstigneyev	52
D. B. Glinka	50
A. F. Klubov	50
I. M. Pilipenko	48
V. N. Kubarev	46
(Ranks not available.)	

Spain

Cdte Castano (National)	40

USA

Maj R. I. Bong	40
Maj T. B. McGuire	38
Cdr D. S. McCampbell USN	34
Lt-Col G. Boyington USMC	28
Col F. S. Gabreski	28
Maj R. S Johnson	28
Col C. H. MacDonald	27
Maj J Foss USMC	26
Lt R. M. Hanson USMC	25
Maj G. E. Preddy	25

KOREAN WAR

USA

Capt J. McConnell USAF	16
Maj J. Jabara USAF	15
Capt M. J. Fernandez USAF	14
Maj G A. Davis USAF	14
Col R. N. Baker USAF	13

VIETNAM WAR

Vietnam People's Air Force

Col Tomb	13
Capt N. V. Bay	7*

USA

Capt C. D. Bellevue USAF	6
(Radar operator)	

It seems likely that, in future wars, the victory scores of flyers such as these will be considerably smaller due to the reduced number of aircraft flown on any single operation compared with earlier conflicts, although the destructive powers of these, massive by all earlier standards, will be further increased. But whatever future conflicts will indicate, the 'ace' situation and its propaganda overtones was summed up long ago by one who was just such a pilot himself, the British Maj James Byford McCudden VC, DSO, MC, MM, Croix de Guerre, who observed that 'we're just hired assassins'.

ACLANT One of two major NATO commands, Allied Command Atlantic had its headquarters at Norfolk, Virginia, and was responsible for security from the North Pole and southwards to cover the northern tropics, concentrating on anti-submarine work with the aid of land-based aircraft in company with a smaller proportion of US Navy carrier-borne machines and surface vessels from a variety of member nations.

AEG Allgemeine Elektrizitaats Gesellschaft. A German aircraft manufacturer of the First World War of which probably the best-known product was the AEG C.IV, a two-seat reconnaissance or artillery observation machine introduced in 1916 of a type in which the firm tended to specialize from the earliest years of the conflict. The C.IV was followed by a night bomber and a triplane single-seat fighter during the following year. All these were designed by the AEG organization, but in addition it also produced Rumpler Taube military monoplanes.

Aerfer-Aermacchi A manufacturer formed of two Italian organizations to produce the AM.3 light army liaison and AOP machine, a short take-off three-seater with a range of 500 miles which was in Italian service during the 1970s.

Aerial mines See Mines.

Aeritalia An Italian airframe manufacturer which commenced work shortly before the end of WWI, based on the Fiat concern. The first product of the new company was the R-2, a reconnaissance bomber which marked the beginning of a long series of military aircraft for the Regia Aeronautica. The new title was adopted in 1972.

Aermacchi An Italian aircraft manufacturer which first entered the field during the period of WWI with the Macchi M.14 scout and Macchi-Nieuport designs. These were followed by a long succession of types throughout the 1930s. During the post-WWII period de Havilland Vampires were constructed under licence as well as Lockheed F-104 Starfighters. In 1960 a resumption of its own designs included the successful MB.326 jet trainer.

Aero A Czechoslovakian aircraft manufacturer dating from the establishment of that country's independence after the end of WWI which was responsible for a number of military designs, the first being the Aero A-18, a fighter, followed by the A-24 bomber and a succession of further types for the Czech Army Air Force throughout the 1930s. Immediately before the outbreak of WWII manufacture of the Aero B-17, a licence-built version of the Soviet Tupolev SB-2 bomber, was begun.

Aerobatics A contraction of 'aerial acrobatics', the term was first used to describe what were essentially display manoeuvres during the earliest days of aviation. These were soon being used for recoveries from certain flight conditions such as stalling and involuntary spinning, and a widening repertoire was adopted by military pilots of WWI for purposes of escape or to gain advantage over an adversary. Lt Nesterov of the Imperial Russian air arm is credited with performing the first loop on 27 August 1913 while flying a Dux-built Nieuport Type 4 monoplane – a feat marked by the naming of the town of Sholkiv after him in December 1951.

Aéronautique Militaire The title for the air arm of the French Army throughout the period of WWI and lasting until 2 July 1934 when it was changed to l'Armée de l'Air', an alteration which now signified complete independence from the army.

AEW Airborne early warning. A system whereby electronic surveillance equipment is fitted to an aircraft, the advantages being that attackers are detected attempting to intrude into a country's air space below the level of surface-based radar coverage.

AFCENT A subordinate command within the SHAPE organization, being one of the two NATO commands. The headquarters of this one, Allied Forces Central Europe, was at Brussum in Holland and was itself divided into a pair of sub-sections, NORTHAG, the Northern Army Group, and CENTAG, the Central Army Group, these being supported by the Second Allied Tactical Air Force and the Fourth Allied Tactical Air Force respectively.

AFNORTH A subordinate command within SHAPE covering Norway (where its headquarters was situated at Kolsaas), Denmark, the Baltic and Germany. Two Luftwaffe wings and the air forces of Norway and Denmark provided support for this, the Allied Forces Northern Europe.

AFSOUTH Allied Forces Southern Europe, a SHAPE subordinate command responsible for the defence of Italy, Greece, Turkey, the Mediterranean and the Black Sea, the air forces of these countries in addition to that of the United States Sixth Fleet supplying support together with the Royal Air Force based on Malta and Cyprus.

AGM An alternative, and widely used, abbreviation for a stand-off bomb, meaning air-to-ground missile (air-to-surface missile is a more accurate term). However, the concept of such a missile is that it allows a manned aircraft to hit a target and fly free from the explosion zone, which is also likely to be heavily defended. Early attempts to introduce such missiles were made with some success during the closing period of WWII by the United States; the weapon was known as BAT and was employed against Japanese warships. Post-war years saw a succession of further devices, the Rascal for the United States, the British Blue Steel and the Anglo-French Martel to name only a few.

Air Arm A term usually regarded now as referring to an arm of an army, navy or marine corps, but in a wider sense it may be taken as indicative of the military air service of a nation.

Air corps The air arm of an army or marine corps.

Aircraft carrier See Seaborne Aircraft.

Aircraft recognition The craft of visually recognizing an aircraft type, and therefore whether it is 'friendly' or an enemy. Practised at first by airmen of all nations during WWI, it was later adopted by civilians at home, partly as a hobby, the first official recognition experts in Great Britain being probably the Police, who were expected to telephone to the authorities sightings of enemy aircraft. During the period between the world wars the art lapsed except among a small number of chiefly civilian enthusiasts, but immediately upon the outbreak of WWII it began to be taught to the armed forces of participating nations and encouraged among civilians. In Great Britain there were the Harkers' Clubs, whose members were mainly the 'spotters' responsible for keeping watch for enemy aircraft approaching essential factories, and the Observer Corps Clubs, after members of that Corps began to identify aircraft types (which they were not expected to do in the early months, sightings being merely reported as 'a plane'). Instruction saw the use of silhouettes, augmented by films and models.

Air launching The launching of one aeroplane from another while airborne. Various methods of doing this have been attempted, among the first probably being that which took Bristol 'C' Scout 3028 on the upper wing of a Porte Baby flying boat in May 1916 to form an anti-Zeppelin weapon, the launching of single-seaters from airships was employed during the same period by the RAF and continued afterwards by Great Britain, the United States and Soviet Russia. The Mistel (q.v.) composite used by the Germans in WWII mounted manned, single-motor fighters above unmanned twin-engine aircraft acting as self-propelled bombs. Air launching FZG 76 (or V-1) flying bombs under Heinkel He 111H-22s towards the end of WWII was another example of the same idea. Only Germany adopted air launching operationally, although most of the tri-als showed promise. See also Parasite Aircraft, Samolyot.

Air observation posts Light aircraft which had their beginnings established during the First World War as artillery observation ('Art Ob') machines to spot for the guns in much the same way as the military use of balloons was first conceived, as well as carrying out tactical reconnaissance. The envisaged role changed little until after 1945 when, with the increasing vulnerability of such aircraft to ground fire, its importance tended to decline, so that the role tended to be delegated to helicopters. Although the work was included among the duties expected from army cooperation machines, the tasks of these were in fact wider. During 1939–45 AOP squadrons were regarded as RAF units under army control, each commanded by a major of the Royal Artillery. The air crews were captains from the same regiment, although an adjutant and equipment officer came from the RAF. The first British AOP squadron of the sixteen formed was No 651, established on 1 August 1941. All had been disbanded or redesignated by the summer of 1947 and the work became the responsibility of the Army Air Corps, a true corps having the same status as the Royal Artillery or Royal Engineers.

Air Raid Precautions Measures to meet anticipated air attack, introduced in Great Britain as ARP and in Germany as Luftschutz in 1938 with a free issue of gas masks to civilians, the formation of an Auxiliary Fire Service, the recruitment of street wardens, rescue workers etc, the provision of public and private air raid shelters and the laying in of stocks of food, first aid equipment, cardboard coffins and the like. France and Japan took similar steps.

Air–Sea Rescue A wartime facility to save the lives of aircrews having to abandon their aircraft over the sea. Both Great Britain and Germany organized similar services, those of the latter being the better in the earlier years of WWII. The RAF based its service on high-speed rescue launches of which several types were in use (these being armed and of British Power Boat, Thornycroft, Vosper and Walton

Above: Royal Naval type SS airship No 3 returning from a patrol to Mudros in 1916. (Author's collection)

Thames design), augmented by flying boats and land-based aircraft, some of these latterly being equipped with a dinghy that could be dropped with the aid of parachutes. During 1939–45 both sides also provided moored rescue vessels for airmen. These were equipped with first aid facilities, blankets and food. Anchored perhaps 25 miles out in the North Sea as well as in the English Channel, they were visited regularly by patrolling launches. After 1945 air–sea rescue was reorganized using helicopters in collaboration with long-range fixed-wing aircraft and the RNLI.

Airship A lighter-than-air craft used for bombing by Germany in WWI and for sea patrol by the RNAS at the same time. The latter were small, non-rigid vessels which ceased to be used after the end of hostilities, although similar dirigibles continued to be used at home by the US Navy into World War II.

Air superiority fighter A fighter designed for the express purpose of giving a user control of the air, this on the assumption that the opposing side has available aircraft of equal potential. The description is used as much for commercial and propaganda purposes but from a military viewpoint it is meaningless: intelligence, training, organization and leadership all play parts that are collectively more important than the design of a single piece of manned military hardware.

Air support Generally a description of the use of aircraft against enemy artillery or armour opposing friendly ground forces, but also used to describe the provision of food, ammunition and medical supplies where these cannot be supplied by any other method, such as over difficult terrain or because of enemy action. Alternatively the rapid redeployment of infantry etc by ordinary air transport or by helicopters may be described in this way.

Above: The Albatros D.Va was introduced to supersede the D.V in the autumn of 1917, manufacture being discontinued in favour of the Fokker D.VIIs in 1918. Nevertheless, the Albatros continued in service until the end of WWI. This example was captured by the French. (Author's collection).

Air-to-air bombing Bombing one aircraft from another, a technique used against US bomber formations by both Japanese and German Air Forces in WWII.

ALARM The British radar-seeking Air-Launched Anti-Radiation Missile, the most advanced weapon of its kind in the world.

Albatros A manufacturer of military aircraft during WWI, at first specializing in reconnaissance two-seaters of the 'B' class but later designing the Albatros D.I to D.Va scouts, one or other of which types was to see service in numbers with all the Jagdstaffeln created in readiness for the German spring offensive of 1918.

Albino Free balloon barrage (previously 'Pegasus').

'Alkali' The code name for an air-to-air guided missile which equipped all air forces of the Soviet bloc during the early 1970s. Capable of being launched from all types of fighter, it relied on radar to find its target.

All-weather fighter An aircraft designed to have a high performance and long endurance and the ability to intercept enemy bombers flying at great altitude and high supersonic speeds, equipped with electronic and radar devices enabling it to fulfil these demands under all weather conditions, by day or by night. The first type for this role in the RAF was the Gloster Javelin, the FAW.1 entering service with No 46 Squadron at Odiham in February 1956.

Aluminium Drive An appeal launched by the British Minister of Aircraft Production on 10 July 1940 for aluminium articles to be donated from civilian sources and subsequently be converted for aircraft production. Organized at much the same time as the Allied withdrawal from Dunkirk and with the potential invasion of England a probability in the immediate future, it generated an enormous response although it probably contributed nothing to the production of aircraft in time for the daylight air fighting which came. Subsequent 'historians' have made much of this fact to denigrate the cam-paign, not realizing that the metal gained in this way was indeed subsequently utilized and ignoring the massive psychological fillip the nation received as a result of participating.

So great was the response, aluminium items flooding into Women's Voluntary Service collecting centres, that a fortnight later it became necessary to call a halt, Lord Beaverbrook conveying his thanks to the nation via special notices in newspapers thus: 'To the fine-spirited, the kind-hearted, the patriotic members of the public, who gave us their pots and pans. The collection of aluminium for aircraft closes on Saturday next, July 27. If any of you still have gifts of aluminium to send us, will you please take them to the collecting stations of the WVS before that date. The contributions have been immense. The generosity shown us, the consideration shown us has been heartening to a degree. The response has been a real encouragement to us. But our needs are growing all the time. We will return again, therefore, asking on another occasion for the aluminium which is still available in the country.' In fact no further campaigns of this type were organized.

American Volunteer Group The Group, known as the AVG, was formed by Major Claire Lee Chennault (brigadier-general in the Chinese Army) after a tour of the United States in November 1940 to recruit 100 pilots for a fighting force to assist China's war with the Japanese. It was officially formed in August 1941 when 100 Curtiss P-40Bs were diverted from British contracts for use by this Group, which was regarded as part of the Chinese Air Force, although the final number of pilots had fallen short of the figure required, 80 having been selected. Ninety of the P-40Bs, now painted with shark's teeth nose markings in emulation of those of No 112 Squadron of the RAF's Desert Air Force, reached Burma and began operations from two bases, Kunming and Mingaladon, in December, the first action taking place on the 20th when the P-40s from Kunming shot down six from a force of ten Japanese bombers attacking the area. Three days later the Mingaladon squadron was in action, being unfortunate in losing two of its pilots at once. The final credit of vic-tories gained by the AVG was 286, scored over South China and Burma, before it became the USAAF's 23rd Pursuit Group, most machines of the three squadrons having been identified by a narrow band round the rear fuselage, white identifying the 1st and blue and red indicated the 2nd and 3rd respectively. As a component of the Chinese Air Force, the 'Flying Tigers' had developed tactics enabling the superior speed and sturdy construction of the P-40s to balance the Japanese' superior manoeuvrability, but in doing so the aircraft were slowly to be lost by enemy ground strafing and the increasing cannibalization called for by a lack of spares, so that when only twenty P-40s were left, the US Government granted an augmentation of the force by 30 P-40Es in March 1942. The P-40 aircraft used were finished in a green and brown disruptive upper camouflage paint scheme and carried the Chinese white and blue twelve-pointed star national insignia above and below the wings only, while the AVG insignia carried by some consisted of a cartoon, leaping, winged tiger; also winged were the nude girls which, in various poses. constituted the machines' individual markings.

Amphibian An aircraft constructed for use from either land or water, the best-known military example probably being the PBY-5A version of the Consolidated Catalina of WWII, although there were others. The Grumman G-44 Widgeon, for example, was used by the US Coast Guard in about 1941 after several years' employment of the Grumman G-21A Goose amphibian, both US designs that were anticipated by the US Army Air Corps' use of Douglas Dolphins a decade previously. Britain's Supermarine Walrus (Seagull in Australia) and Sea Otter were also amphibious warplanes.

'Anab' A guided missile of the heat-seeking variety also relying on this guidance system alternating with radar homing devices. This air-to-air guided missile was used by many of the Warsaw Pact countries during the 1970s and is known to have formed the armament of such Soviet machines as the MiG-21 and Yak-28 all-weather fighter and tactical strike aircraft.

Angled deck A type of construction for aircraft carriers introduced after WWII for the Royal Navy by Capt D. R. F. Campbell DSC RN, and since widely copied, that replaces the axial layout first by splitting a flight deck diagonally. The angle by which the deck is offset varies from vessel to vessel, but all eliminate the need for a safety net to protect parked machines from overshooting aircraft. Aircraft carriers fitted with these decks can be equipped with waist as well as forward catapults if space permits. The first British carrier fitted with an angled deck was HMS *Centaur*, commissioned in September 1953. This immediately proved the ease with which landing machines that missed the arrester wires could make a second attempt.

Anstellknopf The black button in the Zahlwerk of a Heinkel bomber adapted to carry a V-1 flying bomb by means of which the motor of the missile was started prior to launching. See Abstellknopf.

Anti-aircraft guns Weapons which were developed for the destruction of aerial craft, beginning with balloons in the latter part of the nineteenth century (hence their original name of 'balloon guns'.) The first of these mounted on a vehicle was the Erhardt car produced on a chassis modified by Rheinmetall of Düsseldorf in 1906 and incorporating a 5cm 30-calibre gun which had just been developed by the same company. It was hand-elevated and traversed on a pedestal in the rear of the car so that it had an all-round traverse, coupled to which was a depression angle of 5 degrees and an elevation of 70 degrees. Three years later a 7.5cm Krupp-Daimler mobile gun was developed, based on the field gun of similar calibre, and with an elevation of 75 degrees was capable of sending a 14lb shell one and a half miles. A version of 6.5cm calibre was also tried out. Both were fitted with 'differential' recoil systems and telescopic sights. Krupp developed a shell for these guns which also left a smoke trail in flight, thus assisting gunlaying. Improved models of this and the later 8.8cm version were used operationally by the German Army in WWI. A contemporary of the 7.5cm Krupp was the 5.7cm Flak auf Daimler Panzerkraftwagen, another mobile anti-aircraft gun developed by the same firm and known as the L/30. It was mounted on a turntable, with the crew enclosed in a cramped but protective cylinder of 3.5mm armour, although in 1910 a version was introduced in which this was discarded (a worker would later describe it as 'completely useless').

Meanwhile a Cadillac with twin Colt machine guns was being tried in America, the idea being that, with it, balloons could be chased across country and destroyed. In Britain anti-aircraft measures were seen at first as being the responsibility of the Royal Navy as the nation's traditional defender, although the Army was later to take over. The chief weapon was one version or another of the French 75mm field gun, described as quick-

Above: A British 3.7in quick-firing anti-aircraft gun. The earlier Mk III model, in use circa 1940, fired a 28lb shell to an engagement ceiling of 25,000ft, the practical rate of fire being 10rds/min. (Author)

Above: A 40mm Bofors anti-aircraft gun fitted for automatic loading. The earlier version, hand-loaded with clips of four 2lb shells, was adopted by Britain in 1938. (Author)

firing auto-cannon and either fixed or fitted to mobile chassis for use; others consisted of 3in, 20cwt, high-velocity, quick-firing, high-angle guns on either trailers or Daimler lorries and 3pdr high-angle Vickers guns on Lancia lorries, as well as 3pdr Vickers QFs, also on Lancias. Adapted 13pdr field guns were also used, and the emphasis on high angles was important since the 13pdrs, for example, pressed into use and re-mounted after service with the RHA, could not be fired at an elevation greater than 60 degrees without a danger of the recoil knocking out the bottom boards of the lorry. In addition a Royal Navy Anti-Aircraft Mobile Brigade existed. Based at Kenwood House, North London, its purpose was to turn out after the manner of the Fire Brigade and drive at high speed with sirens blaring, to put up a curtain of fire in the reported path of raiding airships. The first gun to fire in the defence of London was a 1lb pompom.

By the end of WWI anti-aircraft guns had become so large that a tendency developed to mount mobile versions on trailers, this being the case with the British 3in, 20-cwt QFs which were to remain in service until 1941. First mounted on a Peerless truck in the second European conflict, they were augmented by 40mm Bofors guns in 1938. In Italy an attempt was made towards the end of the 1920s to evolve a 75mm 'Auto-Cannone' mounted on a Ceirano (Fiat) self-propelled chassis, and these were produced in numbers for the Italian Army so that they were still in service in WWII. German AA guns in a surprisingly large number of cases were augmented by captured weapons, including 10.5cm and very heavy 12.8cm Flak 40 guns introduced during 1943 and towards the end of the war sometimes used in pairs with common elevating and traversing, plus Oerlikons and multiple pom-poms such as had been used throughout. However, the backbone of German AA artillery was formed by the 88mm series, of which the Flak 18, first introduced in 1933, was used in the Spanish Civil War, firing a 19.8lb shell. This was followed by the similar Flak 36, which differed chiefly in having an improved mounting, from which was evolved the Flak 37 with better instrumentation.

Complete re-design of the Flak 18 resulted in the Flak 41 with its power rammer introduced in 1943. British 3.7s outranged them, however, by some 5,000ft.

Adopted before WWII, the German 10.5cm Flak 38 could fire a 32.2lb shell, had electric ramming and power-assisted laying and was still in service as the war drew towards its close, when Great Britain was to introduce the 'Z' gun (q.v.) which fired 3in rocket-propelled projectiles. As such it was the precursor of modern anti-aircraft weapons, guided missiles. Conventional anti-aircraft guns of other warring nations during 1939–45 included France's 7.5cm type, the Russian 7.62cm and 8.5cm weapons, the 9cm Ansaldo and the 10.2s of Italy plus the little-known Czechoslovakian 7.65cm type. As the century draws towards its close, missile systems such as the Rapier 2000 reign almost supreme, but that there was still a use for 'light flak' was proved by captured 36mm Oerlikon-Buhrle twin-type GDF guns being refurbished along with their Skyguard radar systems after the Falklands War. See Flakhelfers.

Anti-personnel bombs Bombs scattered by aircraft, either in free batches or by means of containers, intended to kill or maim individuals discovering or attempting to handle them. One used by Germany during WWII was known, from its appearance, as the 'Butterfly bomb' (officially an SD-2 fragmentation bomb) and consisted of a small cylinder about 7cm in diameter attached to which, by means of a short length of stout wire, were a pair of curved 'wings' which opened while descending and thus armed the weapon. A bomber could carry well over 300 of these, fighters or smaller machines 96, and, fused to detonate on impact, after a delay or when disturbed, they were effective against not only troops but also parked aircraft and vehicles. See Daisycutter.

Anti-submarine warfare The use of, among other measures, aircraft to track, hunt and destroy submarines. During 1914–18 the RNAS used various types of non-rigid airships to do this, while heavier-than-air craft included such types as the D.H.6. During the years between the wars, such measures fell to both landplanes and flying boats armed with bombs or depth charges, and these methods were continued into the conflict of 1939–45, to be translated into such electronic-aided systems post-war as, for example, the dropping of sonar buoys into the sea to transmit their findings to aircraft, while magnetic anomaly detectors via MAD tail 'stingers' can also detect the presence of submarines from the small changes in the earth's magnetic field that they create. Any attack which follows can be delivered by means of depth charge, missile or torpedo from either specially equipped conventional aircraft or helicopters.

Apache The Hughes AH-64 Apache helicopter was designed for ground attack work where large heavy enemy

Above: The Hughes AH-64 Apache helicopter. (Bruce Robertson collection)

Above: Armstrong Whitworth Whitley bombers – this is a Mk V – were introduced into service in March 1937, and Whitley IIIs, powered by Tiger VI radial motors, made the RAF's first war sortie on the night of 3–4 September 1939, ten aircraft of Nos 51 and 58 Squadrons dropping leaflets over enemy territory. (Author's collection)

troop concentrations were encountered. It is armed with sixteen Hellfire missiles or 76 FFAR rockets and a 30mm Chain Gun having a rate of fire of 800rds/min. Its maximum speed is 220mph. (See overleaf)

Armstrong Whitworth Whitley A twin-engined British bomber which was already in RAF service at the outbreak of WWII together with the Handley Page Hampden and Vickers Wellington. At first operated in daylight attacks, it was better known for its use in leaflet-dropping sorties and a little later in mine-dropping. The first of the type had entered service as a heavy bomber, powered by Armstrong Siddeley Tiger motors, in 1937, the initial examples being identified by wings without dihedral.

The Whitley II, the first RAF aircraft fitted with superchargers, soon followed, and this was succeeded by the Mk III powered by 920hp Tiger motors instead of those of 795hp fitted earlier. Next came the Mk III in August 1938, unusual in having a 'dustbin' ventral defensive position. The Mk IV followed, having 1,030hp Rolls-Royce Merlin engines and a Nash & Thompson power-operated rear turret replacing the original manual type. The Mk V was the major production model, with a 15in increase in fuselage length and 1,145hp Merlin X engines first introduced on the Mk IVA. The curved fins were also replaced by fins with straight leading edges. The bomb load, carried in a fuselage rack and centre-section cells, was 7,000lb. The Whitley was the first type to drop bombs on German territory (on 19 March 1940) since 1918.

In addition to its use as a bomber, the aircraft also saw service in coastal patrol, in which capacity 146 GR.VIIs with extended range were employed. They carried ASV radar, and Coastal Command claimed its first U-boat 'kill' (*U206*) with the type on 30 November 1941, the Whitley involved being Z9190 of No 502 Squadron.

The arrival of more advanced bombers meant that the Whitley was replaced in the spring of 1942, the type's final operation as a bomber being an attack on Ostend during the night of 29—30 April. The aircraft was subsequently used as a glider tug and for early paratroop trials and training flights, relegated Mk IIs having been used for this work at Ringway (Manchester), the base of No 1 Parachute Training School, since the summer of 1940.

'Archie' WWI slang for anti-aircraft fire.

Armour Protective plating to shield either the crew or vital parts of an aircraft against gunfire. The beginnings were laid during WWI when pilots strapped a steel helmet under their seats. By the end of the war the armoured aeroplane intended for ground attack work had been evolved, the British Sopwith Salamander being an example of this. During WWII most military aircraft offered the occupants some degree of armour plating protection, the most obvious example being the place behind the head of a pilot, sometimes marked with a large yellow disc to indicate its type. The near-ultimate in protection would seem to be that fitted to the US Fairchild A-10, with the pilot virtually enclosed in an armour 'bath'.

Army Air Corps In Britain, the corps for which the War Office took financial responsibility with effect from 1 September 1957 within the Army, although a corps of the same name had been officially constituted to include the Glider Pilot Regiment on 24 February 1942. In the United States, this was the official term for the American air arm from 2 July 1926, abolishing the former title of Army Air Service adopted on 24 May 1918. The new title was itself replaced by that of Army Air Force on 20 June 1941 by Regulation 95-5.

Army Air Force See Army Air Corps.

Army Air Service See Army Air Corps.

'Aspirin' British radio jammer of WWII.

Astra Torres British Naval Airship No 3, used for Channel patrols from 10 August 1914. A non-rigid airship, it was the only one of its period to be armed.

AS11 An anti-tank/assault missile with a range in excess of 3,000 yards and a high degree of penetration. Carried by a variety of helicopters including Royal Marine Wessex and Wasps. It is an air launched derivative of the surface-to-surface SS11 missile.

AS12 Air-to-surface wire guided, spin stabilized missile developed from the SS11. With a range of almost 20,000 yards it equipped RN Wasp and Wessex helicopters among a variety of other helicopters. It is an air launched derivative of the surface-to-surface SS12 missile.

Asymmetric aircraft The sole example of an asymmetric military aircraft known to have seen operational service is the WWII German Blohm und Voss Bv 141 three-seat tactical reconnaissance machine which, introduced to the Luftwaffe in 1943, consisted of a single motor extended to a boom supporting the offset tail unit. The crew were accommodated to starboard of this motor in a nacelle, giving an excellent view through 180 degrees in azimuth which could be widened to port by merely rolling the machine.

Atomic bomb A bomb dependent for its explosive power on splitting very heavy atoms and also known as a nuclear fission bomb, the material used being uranium-235 or plutonium-239. The first such bomb to be used in war was dropped by the USAAF on Hiroshima at 0816 hrs on 6 August 1945. This was 'Little Boy', a 10ft 6in by 2ft 5in, 9,700lb device detonated at 1,890ft to destroy the city of Hiroshima. The second was the 10ft 8in by 5ft, 5-ton 'Fat Man' dropped at 1102 hrs and detonated at 1,650ft over Nagasaki (Kokura had originally been the intended target) on 9 August. The United States had exploded her first trial bomb on 17 July 1945. Britain exploded her first atomic bomb in Australia during 1956. See Hydrogen Bomb, Neutron Bomb.

Autogyro An aeroplane deriving its lift from a rotor which, unlike that of a helicopter, is unpowered. Ten Cierva

C-30A autogyros built under licence by Avro of Manchester were supplied to the RAF from August 1934 mainly for the School of Army Cooperation, Old Sarum, being named Avro Rotas Mks I and II. They later served with No 1448 Squadron. One Sea Rota was supplied in January 1935. The US Army used Kellet YG-1s from 1935 under various designations until 1945.

Autolycus A short-range instrument for the detection of diesel fumes from submarines either on the surface or recently submerged, or while using its snorkel. The device is not capable of detecting nuclear-powered submarines.

Auxiliary Air Force A term describing a reserve air force, and in Great Britain, the AAF, which was created by the Air Force Reserve Act of 1924, the first four squadrons being formed within a year and the number having risen to twenty flying squadrons and 44 of barrage balloons by September 1939. The AAF was granted the prefix 'Royal' after WWII but was disbanded in 1957. Members were distinguished by a small letter 'A' worn as a collar flash by officers and beneath the eagle shoulder badge by others.

Avro 504 A British WWI two-seat aircraft which was originally conceived as a trainer but was eventually used for reconnaissance, bombing and single-seat Home Defence night fighting, finally existing chiefly in 'J', 'K' and 'N' versions. Produced in very large numbers, it lasted well into the period between the two world wars in many of the world's air forces.

AWACS Airborne Warning and Control System. An aircraft maintaining lengthy patrols, fitted with electronic equipment enabling its crews to perform similar tasks to those defined under AEW but in addition maintain a controlling facility. These aircraft are usually identified by the large, flat, rotating scanner disc above the fuselage, but other systems exist which dispense with this.

Azon bombs Guiding tails for standard bombs first used by the USAAF on 17 December 1944 over Burma. They were capable of course correc-

tion in azimuth only, and chiefly used for attacks on bridges, ships etc.

B- (1) The designation for bombers used by the United States services. During the Second World War, this was in part anticipated by the 'A' (Attack) designation. (2) (B-Series) The designation for the US Navy's first production non-rigid airship, ordered in March 1917.

B-1 The designation for the North American Rockwell bomber, a variable-geometry design capable of speeds in excess of Mach 1.0 which was in service from the mid-1980s.

B-17 The designation for the Boeing bomber popularly known as the Flying Fortress and used by the United States and in small numbers as the 'Fortress' by the RAF in WWII. The first flight of the type was made on 28 July 1935 and several variants were quickly developed, twenty B-17Cs going to the RAF in the spring of 1941 to be used as bombers by No 90 Squadron alone and the B-17D seeing action in the opening stages of the war in the Pacific. The B-17E underwent modifications which included the introduction of an extended fin strake, and the B-17H versions were B-17Gs converted to carry an airborne lifeboat for air–sea rescue missions. The main versions used were the B-17F and B-17G. In March 1944 the peak of 4,574 B-17s in service with US forces was reached.

B-24 The designation for the Consolidated Liberator, the most widely employed US bomber of WWII. A total of 18,188 were built, of which the first was delivered in June 1941. Changes of armament and equipment resulted in a dozen versions, including the initial XB-24, but it was not until the introduction of the XB-24K that a marked change to the external appearance resulted, from the introduction of a single fin and rudder. Both Bomber and Coastal Commands of the RAF operated the type, the B-24B model being known as the Liberator I, the B-24C as the Liberator II and the B-24D as the Liberator III. In addition, the B-24H and J were both supplied under Lease-Lend, becoming RAF Coastal Command's GR.VI, to join the

Above: Boeing B-17s were dubbed 'Flying Fortresses' by the popular press on account of their heavy defensive fire power, but under daylight battle conditions they proved vulnerable until such variants as this B-17F were evolved. They formed the backbone of the US Eighth Air Force operating from Britain in WWII. (Author's collection)

Above: An RAF B-24 Liberator with its port inner motor ablaze over a target in northern Italy, March 1945. (J. W. A. Bowden)

GR.V (B-24G) already in service. Some RAF Liberators were fitted with Leigh Lights (q.v.) – airborne searchlights for anti-submarine work – while Liberator bombers saw extensive RAF service in the Middle East.

B-25 Designation for the North American Mitchell bomber, named after the unjustly disgraced William Mitchell. Claimed by some to be the best all-round medium bomber of WWII, its first flight was made on 19 August 1940, the NA-40-2 which immediately preceded it having a more bulbous appearance but otherwise resembling the later silhouette. Ten variants were to follow, including that armed with a 75mm cannon in the nose and a ground attack version with a formidable array of 0.5in Colt-Browning guns. Those operated by the RAF were employed chiefly as light day bombers from October 1942 and continued in service until superseded by Mosquito XVIs. United States versions are best remembered for the attack on Tokyo and other targets in Japan on 18 April 1942, operating from the USS *Hornet*.

B-26 The designation for the US Martin Marauder bomber of WWII. At first unofficially known as the 'Flying Torpedo', the prototype made its maiden flight in November 1940 and production versions were to earn a reputation for being difficult to land. Some six variants were developed and a total of 5,157 were constructed, the early examples having wings spanning 5ft less than the later standard of 71ft. B-26As served with the RAF as Marauder Is, followed by B-26Cs and B-26F/Gs as Marauder IIs and IIIs respectively, and were used in the Middle East. A small number were operated by the South African Air Force.

B-29 The designation for the Boeing Superfortress. Entering service in 1943, the type was not used in Europe, but in the East it was used by the US to bomb Japanese industrial targets, which attacks commenced in June 1944. The type, which had first flown on 21 September 1942, is of historic interest in that it was used for the first delivery of atomic bombs on 6 and 9 August 1945 and was significant in having pressurized cabins and a remote-control fire system for its armament of gun turrets which lay outside this area. It was the largest bomber of any type operated during WWII, and sixty-one B-29 squadrons were flying when hostilities ended in August 1945; a total of 4,221 had been delivered when production ceased in May 1946. A development was the B-

50. From March 1950 a number of RAF Squadrons operated these bombers under the name 'Washington' but by December 1954 all had been withdrawn. The aircraft used to deliver the atomic bomb on Hiroshima was *Enola Gay*, a B-29-45 flown by Col Paul Tibbets from the 393rd Bomb Squadron, 315th Bomber Group. The Soviet Tu-4 bomber (and the Tu-70 transport) were copies of the B-29, three examples of which had been forced to make emergency landings in the Soviet Union.

B-47 The designation for the Boeing Stratojet, the first swept-wing jet bomber, which first flew in the closing months of 1947. It could carry 20,000lb of bombs at a maximum speed of 600mph over a range of 4,000 miles. It was fitted with a 20mm cannon in a remotely controlled tail turret. Photographic, electronic, and weather reconnaissance versions were respectively, the RB-47B, ERB-47H and WB-47E.

B-52 Designation for the Boeing Stratofortress, which first flew in 1952 and was the world's largest bomber. Three examples from the 93rd Bomb Wing were sent round the world from their base in California on a 24,325-mile non-stop trip of 45 hours in

Above: The Boeing B-29A Superfortress was being evolved as early as March 1938 and eventually set entirely new technical standards for bomber design. With a bomb load of 20,000lb and a range with half that load of 3,250 miles, it is chiefly remembered for its ability to deliver the first atomic bombs. (Bruce Robertson collection)

Above: In the foreground, the B-52B Stratofortress represents the first production version of this mighty Boeing bomber. It had an endurance of some ten hours. Later models were expected to remain in service until the year 2000, despite the prototype having first flown in 1952. (Bruce Robertson collection)

January 1957, the average speed being 530mph. As an alternative to conventional and nuclear bombs, Hound Dog missiles could be carried. Construction ceased in June 1962 with 744 built. It is still in service and capable of operating cruise missiles.

B-57 The designation for the US version of the English Electric Canberra jet bomber built under licence by Martin and General Dynamics. Seven variants were produced, one of which, the RB-57F, had an extended wingspan.

B-Stoff Aviation fuel for reciprocating engines.

B/A The abbreviation for bomb aimer, sometimes described as 'air bomber' (particularly in the United States).

Bachem Ba 349A See Natter.

Baedeker Raids A series of attacks on targets in Great Britain during the spring and early summer of 1942 in which towns and cities of particular historical or cultural interest were bombed. The name was based on that of the author of a German guide for visitors to England in 1842, Karl Baedeker. Civilians killed in these attacks totalled 1,600, with 1,760 injured. Damage was caused in such cities as Bath, Exeter, Canterbury and York.

Baika See Kawanishi.

Baka See Kamikaze.

Balbo, General (later Marshal) Italo Balbo was responsible for the two-year preparatory work which preceded a mass return flight from Rome to Chicago initially of twenty-four Savoia-Marchetti S55X twin-hulled flying boats in the summer of 1933 to mark the tenth anniversary of the 'Fascist Revolution'. For some time afterwards large formations were known as 'Balbos'. A brilliant pilot and organizer whose attention to detail extended to the testing of eighty-eight types of airscrew until a suitable design was found for the 11,800 mile journey, he was appointed Governor of Libya in November when Mussolini felt himself threatened by Balbo's popularity.

Balkenkreuz See Crosses.

Balloons, Apron Captive Caquot-type balloons were used for the defence of London during World War I, flown in groups of three linked together with a single cable from which nine others, 1,000ft long, were freely suspended to act as a defensive 'apron' in the path of enemy aircraft. Flown at between 8,000ft and 10,000ft, they suffered from the tendency of the weight between each balloon to draw them together. The idea was borrowed from Italy, where a similar method was used to protect Venice from Austrian bombers. British airship pioneer E. T. Willows experimentally added spherical balloons.

Balloons, Barrage Tethered unlinked balloons frequently flown from mobile winches to protect target areas during World War II, those in Great Britain being manned by male and female personnel. They were introduced in Britain in the late 1930s on land, and later for shipping, these latter being smaller and having more sharply triangular fins than those of their 20,000 cu ft land-based counterparts which only became inflated with air, not gas, as height was increased. With an approximate flying altitude of 4,000ft, these 'L2s' measured 62ft in length and had a diameter of 25ft. Most of the warring nations used similar devices, the US Marine Corps, for example, having 'ZK' balloons, six squadrons of which protected Navy bases and depots.

BATTLE OF BRITAIN

The daylight air fighting in defence of the British Isles in the summer of 1940 was unique in that never before had the survival of a nation depended solely on the outcome of air combat.

Some ten months beforehand Britain had gone to war in support of promises made to Poland, which country had, nevertheless, succumbed to the Germans, as had Norway, Denmark, Belgium and France, from which last the British Army had been driven, only saved by its last-minute evacuation from the Dunkirk beaches in May and June (Operation 'Dynamo'). The RAF meanwhile had lost some 450 fighters and 430 pilots, so that Fighter Command's strength had been cut by 50 per cent in six weeks, although it could still boast the best-organized defence system in the world, built up over many years, and pilots who included a hard core of vocational flyers augmented by Auxiliaries and Volunteer Reservists who were, it is now agreed, the products of the finest training system in Europe and probably the world. Set against these, however, the Luftwaffe could find aircrews who were battle-hardened from experience and aircraft that had been tried and perfected in conflict.

At a higher level, the RAF's Fighter Command operated a reporting and control system that was second to none, dominated by Headquarters at Bentley Priory and administered in the various Groups via the individual headquarters of each, that of No 11 Group having the defence of south-east England, with London at its heart, as its responsibility. Each of these Groups, of which only three existed initially, was divided into Sectors with responsibility for the squadrons operating from it. But by-passing these and enjoying direct communication with both Command and Group Headquarters was the world's first radar chain, the 'sightings' of which could be passed back to fighter leaders via a linkage which was superior to anything available to the Luftwaffe.

The actual day on which the Battle of Britain opened is quite impossible to establish, although at one time this was regarded in England as 8 August. Yet by the end of the first week in July attacks were being mounted against convoys off the south and east coasts, although the numbers of aircraft were small by comparison with the vast armadas of aircraft the enemy was later to find. The Germans finally launched Adlerangriff (Attack of Eagles) on 13 August after several postponements, and the later part of this period, when attacks were concentrated against airfields, was long regarded as Stage Two, but the whole question of dividing the air fighting in British skies into neat periods of time is very much one of personal viewpoint. However, despite the several advantages which the RAF enjoyed, there is no doubt that the Battle of Britain was, as the Duke of Wellington had described Waterloo, 'a close-run thing', due chiefly to the shortage of pilots which the RAF suffered, a famine of manpower which indicates why the list of Allied pilots included over 50 from the Fleet Air Arm, plus those drafted from other Commands. The gravity of the situation is indicated by the tales, widespread in the service at the time, of fighters being taxied in after sorties by pilots who, a few moments later, were found still in their cockpits, fallen into a coma-like sleep from exhaustion.

It was not until the afternoon of 13 August that the German air arm got properly into its stride, using the three Luftflotten (Air Fleets) based on the Continent and in Scandinavia, but, when it did, attacks were made on Southampton, the decoy target near Portland and Middle Wallop airfield, and in the evening raids were made on the Spitfire factory at Castle Bromwich and the Stirling bomber production line at Sheppey, targets that had to be made without the aid of fighter escort, since the latter's range was insufficient. Two days later Luftflotte 5's big assault took place, mounted from Norway against the north-east of England. It was believed that the attacks on the south had already drained Britain of all fighter opposition, although, in point of fact, in this respect the enemy was wrong and the assaults were broken up and more than a dozen of the raiders brought down.

Meanwhile the fine, warm weather that covered most of the country was permitting considerable activity in the south, this being in the main the interception of attacks on Fighter Command's airfields using fighters and both conventional and dive bombers in such numbers that it was clear that an attempt was being made to swamp the defences and the radio location system (radar). By 1100 hrs Lympne and Hawkinge were being dive-bombed by escorted Stukas, despite the mauling that these aircraft had received a little earlier when used against convoys in the English Channel – a trouncing that proved that the much-vaunted Junkers 87 was not the invincible weapon made out by propaganda. Meanwhile other attacks aimed at the Rye and Dover radar stations had succeeded in putting both off the air for a few hours by destroying the electricity mains.

Such actions typified the battle, which was in the last analysis the attempt by Göring's Luftwaffe to achieve the three objectives necessary to a successful seaborne invasion of the British Isles – the destruction of the RAF's fighter force, including its all-important radar facility; to make unusable its airfields; and so to damage the British aircraft industry that it became incapable of replacing lost aircraft in sufficient numbers to enable Fighter Command's strength to be restored before the summer faded into autumn. ▶

Balloons, Bombing Japanese 'Fu-Go' (q.v.) unmanned bombing devices used at the end of WWII to drift across the Pacific and indiscriminately drop high-explosive and incendiary bombs which were automatically released. Envelopes were of paper and later silk and were often assembled by children. More than 9,000 such weapons were dispatched. British leaflet or incendiary-carrying free balloons were launched over occupied France from Kent in 1940.

Balloons, Observation Tethered kite balloons with an observer in a suspended basket were used by both sides along the Western Front during WWI. Strongly defended, they were flown by the Allies after midday and by the enemy in the morning due to the direction of the light and therefore the way in which the sun lit the terrain. See Caquot.

Barbette A remotely controlled housing for an aircraft's defensive gun(s). A WWII example is the pair, each carrying a single 13mm MG 131 gun, fitted to German Messerschmitt 210 and 410 Hornisse designs, although the idea is no different from that of controlled defensive turrets, devices which were investigated for the Avro Lincoln and carried by both the Boeing B-29 and B-50 designs, each of which were defended by four such. The B-47 and the US Navy A-3 Skywarrior boasted a single remotely controlled barbette in the tail armed with twin 20mm cannon, this being similar in concept to the weapon envisaged for the tail

BATTLE OF BRITAIN

▶ By the end of August it seemed that these might be achieved, for, although new fighters were being delivered at a growing rate, it appeared that the shortage of pilots to fly them (526 had been killed in action by now) would not be overcome. August 16 saw Winston Churchill at No 11 Group's Operations Room for the greater part of the day, and it was from this experience that he pronounced the historic comment, four days later repeated in the House of Commons, 'Never in the field of human conflict was so much owed by so many to so few', at the same time bestowing the sobriquet ('The Few') by which RAF Fighter Command's pilots of 1940 have been known ever since.

It was not until October that the unexpectedly severe losses inflicted on the enemy forced him to shift the thrust of the main attacks to the larger cities, thus reducing the chances of a continued mauling of a similar intensity to that which had been endured up to now, and also to strike at civilians who might, just conceivably, suffer so hideously that the direction of government policy could be altered. However, when this too was met with stubborn resistance, allied with the onset of autumn, plans to conquer England with the aid of an invading army were set aside.

However, before these plans were finalized a switch of daylight targets away from the long-punished fighter fields to London itself took place on 7 September, and twenty-four hours later night attacks were added to the capital's suffering. Increased effort seemed to mark the 15th, when moderate attacks by both day and night did moderate damage but during which also the enemy losses were the highest suffered since 13 August, it being believed when the September day closed that 185 of the enemy had been accounted for. Time has proved this

wrong, but historical niceties are given scant regard when the enemy is 'at the gates'. Since the claim was made in good faith, the date is still kept as Battle of Britain Day.

There was no neat and tidy conclusion to the greatest air battle of all time: it simply faded away as the enemy changed the

emphasis of his assaults to less costly targets, as the weather deteriorated and as concentration was increasingly made on the night attacks which would pass into the English language as an anglicized abbreviation of the German term 'Blitzkrieg'. ▪

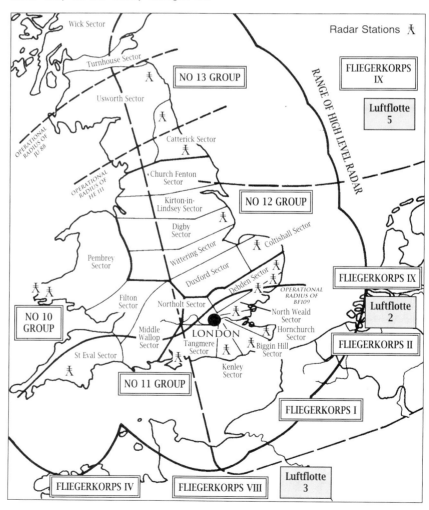

defence of the Heinkel He 177 housing two 20mm MG 151/20 cannon.

Barracuda A Fairey design for a Royal Navy, monoplane, carrier-borne, torpedo aircraft to replace Fairey Albacore biplanes used in 1943. It was unusual in having a retractable undercarriage folding into shoulder-mounted wings. It was used at the Salerno landings in September 1943 and many subsequent actions, including the attack on the German battleship *Tirpitz* in 1944, and was not finally replaced until super-seded by Grumman Avengers in 1954. Three main versions were produced.

Baynes Bat A British carrier wing intended to convert army tanks to tailless gliders. Successfully tested as a one-third scale model in July 1943 at Boscombe Down, Farnborough and Beaulieu, RA809 was not proceeded with.

B.E.2 A British two-seat biplane designed by the Royal Aircraft Factory in 1912 and used in several versions (of which the B.E.2c is the best known) by the RFC for reconnaissance, artillery observation, bombing, Home Defence and training. Produced in large numbers which incurred proportionate losses, it caused the declaration in the House of Commons by Noel Pemberton-Billing that the crews had been 'murdered, rather than killed'. The designation 'B.E.' had indicated 'Blériot Experimental', a term no longer appropriate, and as a military aircraft it suffered from 'inherent stability', impairing its manoeuvrability.

PRINCIPAL AIRCRAFT OF THE BATTLE OF BRITAIN

British

Vickers-Supermarine Spitfire Mk I Armed with eight 0.303in Browning machine guns.
Vickers-Supermarine Spitfire Mk IIA Armed as above.
Some cannon armed Spitfires were used and these were specially modified Mk Is.
Hawker Hurricane Mk I Armed with eight 0.303in Browning machine guns. A single Hurricane with twin 20mm cannon was flown during the Battle of Britain. See Oerlikon.
Boulton Paul Defiant Mk I Armed with four 0.303in machine guns in a power-operated turret. Relegated to night interception after both squadrons cut to pieces in daylight.
Bristol Blenheim Mks IF and IVF Armed with six 0.303in machine guns in a pack under the fuselage, one in the port wing and one, hand-operated, in a dorsal turret.

German

Messerschmitt Bf 109E Armed with two 20mm cannon and two 7.9mm machine guns. Fighter-bomber versions capable of delivering either four 110lb or a single 551lb bomb were introduced during September.
Dornier Do 17Z Bomb load 2,200lb. Photographic reconnaissance versions of this were also used.
Heinkel He 111H-3 Bomb load 4,400lb.
Junkers Ju 87B Bomb load 1,100lb.
Junkers Ju 88A-1 Bomb load 3,968lb.
Messerschmitt Bf 110C-4 Bomb load 1,102lb. Fighter-bomber and fighter-reconnaissance versions also used.

Italian*

Fiat CR.42 Falco Armed with two 12.7mm machine guns.
Fiat G.50bis Freccia Armed with twin 12.7mm machine guns.
Fiat BR.20 Cicogna Bomb load 2,550lb.

*The main Italian participation did not take place until after the recognized dates for the Battle of Britain, although assistance for Luftflotte 2 had been offered by the Duce as early as July but was then rejected. The offer was later renewed, with the result that the Gruppo Aereo Italiano, consisting of 80 BR.20 bombers from 13 and 43 Stormi, were based at Melsbroek and Chièvres, Belgium, respectively, in September, the fighter arm, made up of 50 CR.42s of 18 Gruppo and 48 G.50s of 20 Gruppo, being simultaneously deployed at Malden and Ursel. The first sortie of the Gruppo was an attack by sixteen ▶

Above: Lt Peter Krug, the wounded pilot of a 6/KG 3 Dornier 17Z, is taken into custody at 1245 hrs on Wednesday 28 August 1940, having been shot down into Walpole Bay off Forness Point near Margate, Kent. His captors are a British private and lance-corporal, while a civilian policeman brings up the rear. (Bruce Robertson)

Above: The Bear, the only Soviet Turbo-prop bomber to enter service.

BATTLE OF BRITAIN

▶ escorted BR.20s on Harwich on 26 October which was intercepted over Ramsgate without loss to either side, although one Italian had crashed on take-off and two were forced down into the sea en route having run out of fuel. The main attack followed on 11 November, directed again against Harwich and carried out by twelve BR.20s and an equal number of CR.42s, and this was intercepted over Ramsgate at 1330 hrs by Hurricanes of Nos 17, 46 and 257 Squadrons. Without loss to themselves these British fighters accounted for a number of raiders, including the Fiat CR.42 still preserved by the RAF Museum, which was brought down virtually intact at Orfordness.

British Fighter Production, 1940

	Planned	Produced
February	171	141
March	203	177
April	231	256
May	261	325
June	292	406
July	329	496
August	282	476

Battle of Britain Personnel Strengths and Casualties

Allied pilots	Killed in action	
1,822	RAF and Commonwealth	339
56	Fleet Air Arm	9
21	Australian	14
73	New Zealand	11
88	Canadian	20
21	South African	9
2	Southern Rhodesian	0
8	Irish	0
7	US	1
141	Polish	29
86	Czechoslovak	8
26	Belgian	6
13	Free French	0
1	Israeli	0

Luftwaffe	
Bomber crews	1,176
Ju87 crews	85
Fighter-bomber crews	212
Fighters	171
Others (missing believed killed)	1,445

RAF Casualties, August 1940 (Month of Maximum Losses)

Date	Losses	Date	Losses	Date	Losses
1	5	12	11	24	10
2	1	13	14	25	13
3	-	14	4	26	7
4	1	15	11	27	4
5	1	16	11	28	10
6	1	17	-	29	1
7	-	19	4	30	9
8	20	20	1	31	9
9	1	21	-		
10	-	22	2		
11	22	23	-		

As an emergency measure during 1940, Miles Master trainers N7780–7782 and N7801–7822, with N7412 as the prototype, were adapted as six-gun single-seat fighters, but they were not used.

Beams Electronic aids to navigation and target identification introduced during WWII by both the RAF and the Luftwaffe. The former's included 'Gee' and 'Oboe', which depended on ground transmitters.

'Bear' The NATO code-name for the Soviet Tupolev Tu-20/95/142, the only turboprop heavy bombers ever to enter service (in 1955). Nine versions were identified, the 'Bear-F' running to three sub-variants. The maximum speed was 570mph and the range 9,200 miles carrying a 25,000lb bomb load or alternatively 'Kangaroo', 'Kelt' or 'Kitchen' missiles. Latterly the 'Bear' was employed on reconnaissance and electronic countermeasures duties.

Beddington Aerodrome The original, western, part of Croydon Aerodrome, Surrey. See Croydon, National Aircraft Factory.

Beethoven See Mistel.

'Benito' The RAF code-name for the Y-Verfahren radio navigation system (q.v.).

Berlin Air Lift Operation 'Plainfare/ Vittles' was conducted by the Western Allies to transport food and fuel to the former German capital between 29 June 1948 and 19 May 1949, during which it was calculated that 2,000 tons of essential supplies would be required per day to maintain the 2.5 million inhabitants who were suddenly denied all surface communication by the Soviets on 31 March. Berlin reception points for land-based aircraft were Gatow, Tegel and Tempelhof, while flying boats put down on Lake Havel. At the peak of the operation twenty aircraft an hour were landing at any one airfield in good weather by day and night.

'Bersatu Padu' The name of an exercise conducted during April and May 1970 in which 2,265 passengers, more than 750 tons of cargo, 350 road vehicles and twenty helicopters were deployed from the United Kingdom to Malaysia. Lifts such as this were necessitated from 1967 by the political decision to withdraw the RAF from 'East of Suez' but still retain a rapid reinforcement capability.

Bessoneaux A type of hangar officially termed Type 'H' Canvas Hangar, used by the Royal Flying Corps, Royal Air Force and others during and after WWI at home and in France, Canada, Russia and the Middle East. The type measured 65ft 6in by 78ft 9in in ground area and consisted of a lightweight timber frame covered in heavy canvas with opaque panels to admit light to the interior. Its name was taken from that of its designer (Etablissements Bessoneaux, 10 Rue d'Uzes, Paris) and it could be rigged in two ways with the sides either vertical, leaving the diagonal buttresses exposed, or covered, resulting in sloping sidewalls.

Biggin Hill An RAF fighter station in Kent 1916–57.

Bird Dog In a competition for light aircraft in 1950, the design submitted by Cessna was selected by the US Army, Navy and Marine Corps. The three-seat Bird Dog was also built under licence in Japan by Fuji and saw service with several air arms in Latin America.

'Bison' The NATO code-name for Soviet Myasischev Mya-4 long-range, heavy bomber which entered service in 1955–56. Its estimated speed was 560mph and it had a bomb load of over 20,000lb. Less than 200 examples are believed to have been delivered, the later ones lacked the nose glazing of the first but were fitted with a flight refuelling probe. The defensive armament consisted of paired 20mm cannon.

'Biting' The code-name for the airborne combined operation against enemy radar installations at Bruneval on night of 27 February 1942.

Blimp The popular generic term for non-rigid airships, particularly those used operationally during WWI. It is said to be onomatopoeic, imitative of the sound produced by lightly drumming on tight fabric with the fingernails.

Blind Boys Sightless male adolescents said to have begun employment with Fascist Italy's anti-aircraft defences during WWII, making use of their more highly developed hearing to identify aircraft by sound alone. A similar experiment was tried on a small scale using adults in Great Britain during WWI.

Blitz The popular British contraction of the German term 'Blitzkrieg' during WWII, generally taken to refer to the protracted period of bombing by the enemy between 7 September 1940 and 11 May 1941, the longest sustained period being that carried on for 57 consecutive nights when a total of 18,000 tons of bombs were dropped on London. The peak is regarded to be the attack delivered on Sunday 29 December, which began at 1815 hrs and took the form of an attempt to destroy the City with incendiaries, 1,500 individual fires at one time burning simultaneously, six of them graded conflagrations and sixteen others classified as 'major fires'.

Bloch MB.131 A French military aircraft designed to meet a 1933 specification calling for a machine capable of carrying out bomber, fighter and reconnaissance missions. The initial order was very quickly changed, and 155 machines were delivered as medium bombers, although they were finally used mostly for reconnaissance in 1940 to replace the MB.210 (q.v.).

Bloch MB.210 A French low-wing, twin-motor bomber with a retractable undercarriage which made its first flight in June 1934, the first examples of the 224 ordered subsequently being delivered at the end of the same year. Those of the 11th Bombardment Group were used operationally in the summer of 1940, despite being officially scheduled for retirement, and 37 were taken over by the Germans after the French collapse, some being used on the Bulgarian Front.

Blohm und Voss Financial incentives offered during the formative years of the Nazi Party in Germany resulted in several firms accepting and entering the aviation industry Among them was this heavy engineering firm which specialized in large flying boats, which included the Bv-138 twin-boom, three-motor anti-shipping boat used extensively over the Baltic from 1940 but designed two years before and the six-engine Bv 222, the largest flying boat to attain operational status in WWII with a span of just under 151ft. In other fields designs included the asymmetric Bv 141 and the Bv 40, a fighter-glider which would be towed into combat by a conventional interceptor before being cast off to give battle with its twin 30mm cannon. The Bv 40 was eventually abandoned in favour of the Messerschmitt 163 (q.v.) rocket fighter.

Above: There were several ways in which a Bessonneau canvas hangar could be erected and rigged. This one is set up to cover an area 76ft by 104ft. (Author)

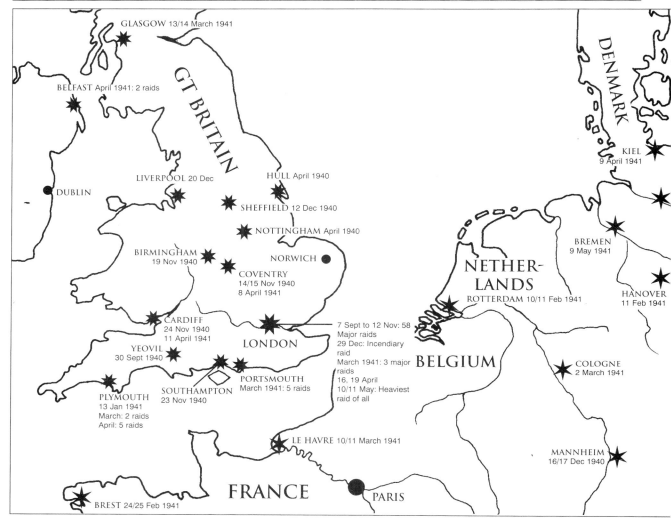

GLASGOW 13/14 March 1941

GT BRITAIN

DENMARK

BELFAST April 1941: 2 raids

KIEL
9 April 1941

LIVERPOOL 20 Dec

HULL April 1940

DUBLIN

SHEFFIELD 12 Dec 1940

NOTTINGHAM April 1940

BREMEN
9 May 1941

BIRMINGHAM
19 Nov 1940

NORWICH

NETHER-
LANDS

HANOVER
11 Feb 1941

COVENTRY
14/15 Nov 1940
8 April 1941

ROTTERDAM 10/11 Feb 1941

CARDIFF
24 Nov 1940
11 April 1941

LONDON

BELGIUM

COLOGNE
2 March 1941

7 Sept to 12 Nov: 58
Major raids
29 Dec: Incendiary
raid
March 1941: 3 major
raids
16, 19 April
10/11 May: Heaviest
raid of all

YEOVIL
30 Sept 1940

PORTSMOUTH
March 1941: 5 raids

PLYMOUTH
13 Jan 1941
March: 2 raids
April: 5 raids

SOUTHAMPTON
23 Nov 1940

MANNHEIM
16/17 Dec 1940

LE HAVRE 10/11 March 1941

FRANCE

PARIS

BREST 24/25 Feb 1941

Blohm und Voss Bv 246 See
Hailstone.

Blue lamps Experimental formation-
keeping lamps carried by RAF
bombers during the spring of 1940 but
later abandoned. They are known to
have been tried out on Vickers
Wellington bombers of No 149
Squadron flying from RAF Mildenhall
on the night of Tuesday 25 April and
also, it is said, by some FAA Swordfish.
Blue Steel An air-to-surface guided
missile, or stand-off bomb, produced
by Hawker Siddeley and intended for
use from Vulcan and Victor bombers.
Capable of being fitted with a conventional or nuclear warhead, it was powered by a liquid fueled rocket which
gave a range of some 200 miles if
released from sufficient altitude,

although this was reduced for those
weapons which were converted for
low-level operations after a change of
tactics took place. The body measured
35ft in length and the speed is reported to have been in the region of Mach
2. Guidance was entirely by means of
an automatic navigational system, and
target information could be updated
by the crew of the 'mother' aircraft
before release.

Blue Streak An inter-continental ballistic missile of British origin, the
launching sites for which were deemed
too vulnerable to an enemy attack,
resulting in the cancellation of the project at the end of the 1950s.

Body Armour Magnesium steel and
canvas protection first worn by US air-

crew in December 1942. Each 'flak
vest' weighed 20lb, and 20g (approximately 1mm) metal was employed.

Bolo House A slang term for the
Headquarters of the RNAS for three
years during WWI. It was situated in
the former Hotel Cecil, which was not
derequisitioned until 1920, being
eventually demolished to make way
for Shell-Mex House on London's
Victoria Embankment in August–
October 1930.

Bomber Command During WWII RAF
Bomber Command was responsible for
389,809 sorties, losing 10,882 aircraft
in the process and having 5,572 damaged. In addition to bombing attacks
against enemy targets, aircraft of the
Command carried out the laying of

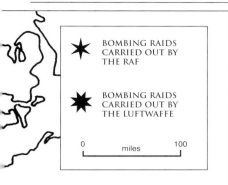

HAMBURG 16 Nov 1940,
May 1941, 11 May 1941

BERLIN
26 August 1940
23/24 Sept 1940
8 Oct 1940
16 Dec 1940
21 Dec 1940
24 March 1941

GERMANY

'THE BLITZ' AND BRITISH RETALIATORY BOMBING
Autumn 1940 to Spring 1941

mines, dropped leaflets ('bomphlets' in the RAF slang of the time), made decoy attacks and carried out electronic counter-measures flights. Just before the end of WWII the strength of the Command consisted of 3,691 aircraft. Its most publicized raid was probably the first of the 'Thousand Bomber' attacks, carried out on the night of 30/31 May 1942, although aircraft from Operational Training Units had been used to make up the number.

Bomb sniffers Groups operating ahead of bomb disposal units to determine the validity of reported UXBs during WWII.

Boulton and Paul Sidestrand A twin-motor biplane bomber used by the RAF from 1928, when it was issued only to No 101 Squadron, to December 1934. The design was remarkable for its ability to be flown on a single engine and the ease with which it could be spun and rolled. It was officially described as a medium bomber, the first time that the designation was used in Britain. Four variants were produced, the engines of the last having Townend rings.

Boulton Paul Overstrand A replacement bomber produced by the same manufacturer (renamed) and operated alone by the same squadron as the foregoing. It was more powerful, carried a greater load and had a power-operated gun turret in the nose, the first RAF machine thus equipped. The prototype first flew in 1933 under the designation Sidestrand V, but this was changed in March 1934. The last was delivered at the end of 1936 so that, although superseded by the outbreak of WWII, some were still flying as gunnery trainers.

Boulton Paul Defiant A two-seat RAF fighter armed only with four machine guns in a power-operated turret which first joined No 264 Squadron in December 1939. These aircraft saw service on 12 May 1940 during the withdrawal of troops from Dunkirk and were mistaken for single-seaters and so scored a number of victories, but the success was short-lived and the type was converted for night-fighting. Target-tug and EW versions also existed.

Boy Scouts Mounted on bicycles in WWI, these sounded the Morse 'G-C' on bugles as the civilian 'All Clear' in Britain.

Brandenburg A German manufacturer of a large number of designs, chiefly biplanes, although the term generally refers to the monoplane W.29s operated from North Sea air stations with 26 of the larger but similar W.33s during WWI.

Breguet 19 A French biplane bomber of the 1920s constructed of duralumin. The most significant was the civilian long-range *Point d'Interrogation*.

Brewster Buffalo The name adopted for the RAF version of the US Navy's Brewster Model F2A-2, examples of which had originally been ordered by the Belgian government but were taken over by Great Britain when the former country was overrun in 1940. The type proved unsatisfactory in service and so the 0.50in guns were exchanged for lighter 0.303in calibre and the type was diverted to the Far East, where it participated in the defence of Singapore, after the fall of which the sixteen survivors were added to the American Volunteer Group defending Burma.

Bristol Beaufighter A two-seat, twin-motor derivative of the Bristol Beaufort, which first entered RAF service as a night fighter in December 1940. Its introduction was surrounded by great secrecy so that silhouettes, when eventually permitted, were forbidden to show the rear of the fuselage. It was the second fighter to be fitted with AI (airborne interception) radar during the German air attacks of the 'Blitz' (q.v.) period in 1940–41 (the first British aircraft to be thus fitted was the earlier Bristol Blenheim fighter, the standard armament of which was augmented by a tray of four fixed machine guns under the fuselage centre-section, a modification produced by the workshops of the Southern Railway). The Beaufighter Mk I was powered by Bristol Hercules radials and the Mk II by Rolls-Royce Merlins. Originally the tailplane was level, but to improve lateral stability in flight dihedral was added on the production line and retrospectively to examples in service. Other variants, including the torpedo-bomber, acquired a dorsal strake and were fitted with a glazed defensive position above the fuselage replacing the original streamlined cupola.

Bristol Beaufort A twin-motor torpedo-bomber operated by the RAF from December 1939 and later by South Africa, Canada, Turkey and Australia, in which last country they were also produced from 1941.

Bristol Blenheim A British-designed medium bomber (sometimes erroneously described as a light bomber) which, derived from the Bristol *Britain First*, owned and later presented to the nation by Lord Rothermere, caused something of a stir in November 1936 when the first example left the factory: capable of a maximum speed of 260mph and of delivering a bomb load of 1,000lb, the aircraft could outpace contemporary fighters.

The first variant was distinguished by an ultra-short nose and was allocated to 30 RAF squadrons at home and abroad, while export models went to Finland and Yugoslavia (both of which later built some under licence) and to Turkey. A British night fighter version appeared in 1938 armed with four 0.303in machine guns under the belly, firing forward from bolt-on trays produced by Southern Railway workshops, and it was these aircraft which pioneered airborne radar during 1940—41.

The Mk IV with an extended nose appeared in 1939, having increased tankage, armour and provision for an extra 320lb of bombs externally, while the single gun in the dorsal cupola was now increased to a pair. One of these Blenheims, N6215 of No 139 Squadron, flown from Wyton by Fg Off A. Macpherson, was the first RAF aircraft to cross the German frontier on 3 September 1939, taking photographs which were used the next day to direct a raid by ten of the type from Nos 107 and 110 Squadrons on shipping in Schillig Roads. This was the first of a series of daylight raids that were to continue until late in 1941, the final sortie by Blenheim IV bombers being made on 18 August the following year. Fighter versions similarly armed to the earlier type also existed.

A lesser known version was the Mk V, which had a disappointing performance despite different Mercury engines. It offered no increase in range, speed or bomb load when it appeared in November 1942, and, although retaining a similar dorsal armament, now in a high-speed traversing turret, and an improved version of the Mk IV's rearward-firing armament under the nose (now increased to a pair of 0.303s), it was never popular. The Mk V flew with ten squadrons in the Middle and Far East until 1943 and was identified by its semi-transparent, extended nose.

Bristol Bloodhound A surface-to-air anti-aircraft missile used for defence by the RAF from the second half of the 1950s, propelled by Thor-type ramjets.

Above: A Bristol Bloodhound surface-to-air missile. These supersonic weapons, powered by Thor-type ramjets, were adopted by the RAF and a number of overseas countries in the 1950s and were based on the results of tests both at home and in Australia. (Author's collection)

Above: The Bristol Blenheim I prototype K7033 which made its first flight in 1936. (Author's collection)

BOMBING

Although the first bombs were of the 4lb picric acid type used by Italy in 1911, these were little more than modified hand grenades, and it was Germany which produced the first true bomb, the APK of 1912, its two types consisting of either 11lb or 22lb of explosive contained in a cast iron sphere. However, these were of too simple a nature to be of any significant value, and they had been discarded by the time war broke out two years later. Meanwhile a whole dynasty of bombs was being quietly evolved in Italy which gave birth to the series that was to be used throughout the four years of the conflict. This was the Carbonit range, the largest weighing 110lb, which was to introduce something resembling the later accepted shape with a nose fashioned to assist penetration and a stabilizing tail.

As is so often the case, parallel development was being carried out in several countries, so that in Britain the 20lb Hales bomb was being evolved specially for the Royal Naval Air Service, which used them for all its early sorties despite the fact that its designation (in fact it only weighed 18½lb) was something of a misnomer as the actual explosive weight was a mere 4½lb of Amatol. The use of this explosive marked a change in British policy since the filling was still TNT (trinitrotoluene) with the addition of 25 per cent by weight of ammonium nitrate, a substitution as great as the earlier replacement of picric acid. The Hales bomb was an anachronism, too, in having a loop-handle aft of its fins (between which the fuse was carried), an indication that the earliest bombs were dropped over the side of an aircraft by hand,

a simple method of delivery, since these measured only 23¼in long and 5in at their greatest diameter.

That bomb racks were still to become the norm is surprising since at least one form had been publicized since mid-August 1914 as having been in use on the Bristol-Coanda T.B.8 biplane at the end of the previous year. It consisted of a circular frame supporting a horizontal drum about the circumference of which twelve bombs were arranged in the manner of revolver chambers. A button in the base of the cockpit could be pressed to release all the bombs in the space of 21sec, it was claimed, while if it was desired to drop the load individually the rack could be mechanically programmed to do this. The total weight of each bomb was 10lb, only 2lb of which consisted of TNT. When these were scattered independently the whole device revolved to bring the following missile to the bottom ready for dropping.

In order to allow the pilot of the T.B.8 to make a crash landing if necessary with the bombs still aboard, they were not fused until having fallen some 100ft, a windmill arming device for this being among the first of a whole range which was still being used over three decades later. This was not all, for in order to ensure that no bombs remained caught up in the mechanism a strong spring flung each clear in the direction of flight. This type of aircraft was also equipped with a prismatic sight that was superior to the rough-and-ready measures that marked the early war years, which were soon to see the RFC and the RNAS using bombs weighing 100lb.

Meanwhile France was modifying 75mm artillery shells as bombs by fitting them with stabilizing tail fins and special fuses developed by Canton-Unné, these being quickly followed by others based on 90mm and

Above: A 20lb Hales bomb. The wire handle above the fins illustrates the early method of dropping these by hand. The more aerodynamically shaped Cooper bomb, also designated a 20pdr, was introduced later. (Author)

155mm calibre shells, and although France later developed proper bombs the 75mm adaptation was the most widely used bomb throughout 1914–18.

As the war progressed, larger bombers capable of taking increased loads were evolved, although the 20lb Cooper bomb containing either Trotyl or Mamotal 80/20 was replacing the Hales of similar weight and 50lb and 112lb bombs were developed by the Woolwich Royal Laboratory (q.v.), but it was not until the introduction of such Handley Page aircraft as the 0/100 and 0/400 that even heavier bombs became commonplace. These culminated in the 3,300lb bomb for the HP V/1500. Although the weapon was never used operationally, now that an aircraft with sufficient range was available it had been intended to use the bombs against targets in Berlin.

Germany, however, was progressing along a different route, which ultimately resulted in the 660lb PuW bomb, very sophisticated for 1915, with a steel rather than ▶

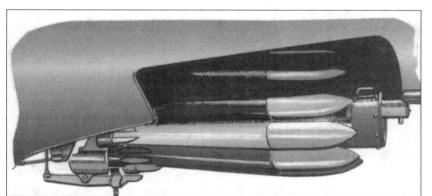

Above: First publicized in mid-1914, although introduced for the Bristol-Coanda T.B.8 biplane at the end of the previous year. (Author's collection)

BOMBING

a cast iron casing and offset fins that not only imparted rotation to the bomb as it fell but also allowed a system of centrifugal arming in the manner of an artillery shell. In addition, an attempt had been made to evolve an aerodynamic shape for the PuW, so that it remained but a short step to the development of the war's heaviest operational bombs, the 2,200pdrs which giant Zeppelin-Staaken biplane bombers associated with the late attacks on London could carry. The period also saw the evolution of rope-wound incendiaries, themselves based on the first crude, petrol-filled canisters. Flieger-Leutnant Caspar dropped the first HE bombs over England at Dover.

By 1918 development had reached an advanced stage with 100lb and 250lb general-purpose RAF bombs augmented by those intended for such specialized purposes as armour-piercing (for use against capital ships), but this and allied types came in for greater attention with the outbreak of WWII. 1941 saw the British 4,000lb 'Cookie' first used operationally by a Wellington bomber over Emden on 1 April. After one of the new 8,000lb high-explosive bombs had been dropped on Essen on the night of 10/11 April two years later by a Handley Page Halifax, a 12,000lb bomb was dropped by a Lancaster of No 617 Squadron RAF during 15/16 September 1943 on the Dortmund–Ems Canal.

However, the introduction of the first of Dr Barnes Wallis's 12,000lb deep-penetration 'Tallboys' saw it used by Lancasters on the Saumur Tunnel on 8/9 June 1944, to be joined by the 22,000lb 'Grand Slam', first delivered to destroy two spans of the Bielefeld Viaduct by No 617 Squadron and

followed by a further forty on other targets. The year 1944 was to see the introduction of a new device, the napalm bomb, its jellied mixture of naptha and palm oil not only giving it a name but being also designed to adhere and burn.

It is generally agreed that the most spectacular of bombs were those used against the Möhne and Eder dams in Germany which were cylinders, Again the brainchild of Dr Barnes Wallis, these weapons were designed to bounce across the surface of the water and then sink against the dam, and explode there, causing shockwaves to burst the wall. It is a matter of history that the attack was made at night on 16 May 1943 by nineteen Lancasters, once more from No 617 Squadron RAF, preliminary tests having been made at Reculver Bay near Margate and over The Fleet, the inland waterway behind the Chesil Beach, Dorset. Hardly less dramatic were the 4,000lb spherical 'Highball' bombs designed to be dropped by de Havilland Mosquitos to sink the battleship *Tirpitz*. However, all these were eclipsed by the atomic bombs dropped on Japan to end WWII and the hydrogen bombs that followed.

Modern weapons include bombs with parachutes and flip-out air brakes to allow aircraft dropping them to escape from the delivery zone. Old methods of delivery have been rendered redundant in the closing years of the century by the introduction of 'smart' and laser-guided bombs (q.v.), the remarkable accuracy of which was demonstrated over Iraq during the Gulf War of 1991, The same conflict was able to confirm the operational efficiency of a fresh avenue in bomb development, the use of anti-airfield weapons, variants of which were first used operationally by the Israelis in 1967.

See 'Chastise', Retard bombs, Royal Laboratory, Slick bombs, 'Smart' bombs.

Above: The British 22,000lb 'Grand Slam' bomb reverted to a more traditional aerodynamic shape after the blunt-nosed cylindrical contours of the preceding 12,000lb blast bomb. (L. Sorrell)

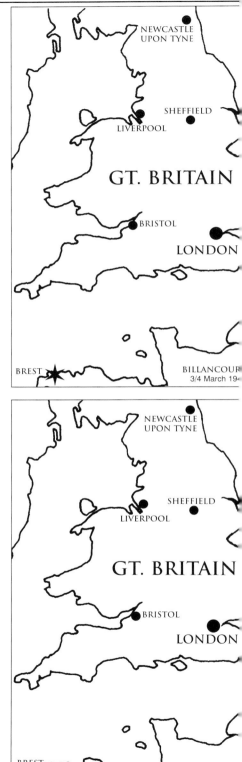

NEWCASTLE UPON TYNE

SHEFFIELD

LIVERPOOL

GT. BRITAIN

BRISTOL

LONDON

BREST

BILLANCOUR
3/4 March 19

NEWCASTLE UPON TYNE

SHEFFIELD

LIVERPOOL

GT. BRITAIN

BRISTOL

LONDON

BREST

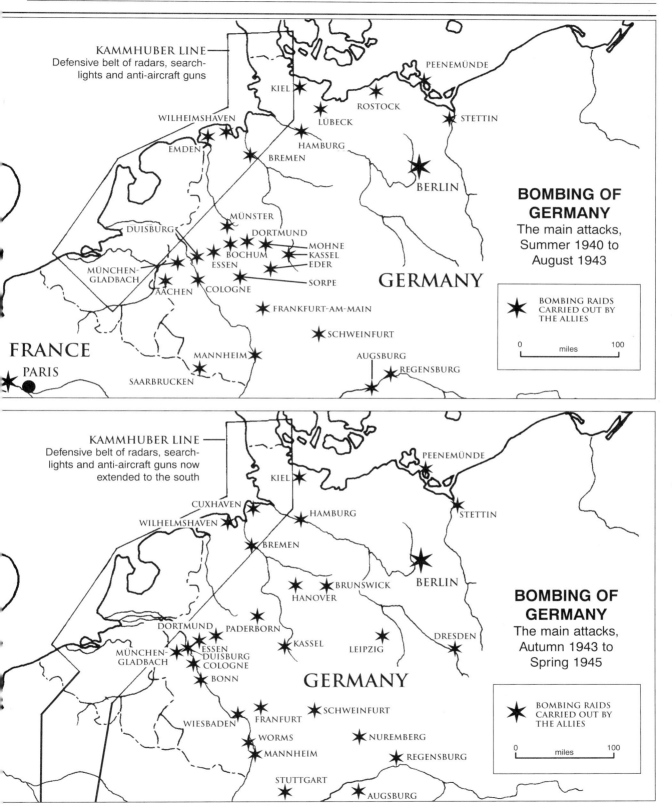

BOMBING OF GERMANY
The main attacks, Summer 1940 to August 1943

KAMMHUBER LINE
Defensive belt of radars, search-lights and anti-aircraft guns

BOMBING RAIDS CARRIED OUT BY THE ALLIES

0 — miles — 100

GERMANY

FRANCE
PARIS

PEENEMÜNDE
KIEL
ROSTOCK
LÜBECK
STETTIN
WILHEIMSHAVEN
HAMBURG
EMDEN
BREMEN
BERLIN
MÜNSTER
DUISBURG
DORTMUND
MOHNE
BOCHUM
KASSEL
ESSEN
EDER
MÜNCHEN-GLADBACH
SORPE
AACHEN
COLOGNE
FRANKFURT-AM-MAIN
SCHWEINFURT
MANNHEIM
AUGSBURG
SAARBRUCKEN
REGENSBURG

BOMBING OF GERMANY
The main attacks, Autumn 1943 to Spring 1945

KAMMHUBER LINE
Defensive belt of radars, search-lights and anti-aircraft guns now extended to the south

BOMBING RAIDS CARRIED OUT BY THE ALLIES

0 — miles — 100

GERMANY

PEENEMÜNDE
KIEL
CUXHAVEN
HAMBURG
STETTIN
WILHELMSHAVEN
BREMEN
BERLIN
BRUNSWICK
HANOVER
DRESDEN
DORTMUND
PADERBORN
KASSEL
LEIPZIG
MÜNCHEN-GLADBACH
ESSEN
DUISBURG
COLOGNE
BONN
SCHWEINFURT
WIESBADEN
FRANFURT
WORMS
NUREMBERG
MANNHEIM
REGENSBURG
STUTTGART
AUGSBURG

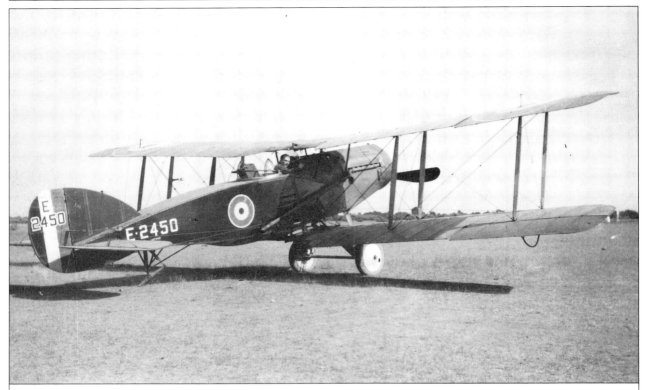

Above: The Bristol F.2b Fighter was at first deemed a failure because pilots were mistakenly expected to adopt established two-seater tactics. Later the policy of flying it in combat in the manner of a single-seater proved it an enormous success, and the type remained in use at home and overseas long after the end of WWI. (Author's collection)

Bristol Bulldog A biplane fighter adopted by the RAF, finally serving with nine squadrons until 1936, the first going to No 3 in May of 1929. During the Abyssinian Crisis, created by Fascist Italy's imperial ambitions in 1936, the Bulldogs of No 3 Squadron were redeployed to the Sudan. The type was widely exported to serve with a number of foreign air arms, and those Mk IIs originally supplied to Latvia saw active service in the Spanish Civil War, when a number, manned by volunteer pilots, were operated from Lamiaco during 1936–37.

Bristol Fighter The Bristol F.2b, officially classified as a two-seat army cooperation type, was one of the mainstays of the RAF both during and after WWI, at the end of which 3,100 had been delivered. During the years that followed, versions were introduced with improvements, including oleo undercarriages and Handley Page slots, and a trainer model was produced. The first sortie

of the newly formed RAF was flown by one of the type from No 22 Squadron at dawn on 1 April 1918. A vast number saw service with foreign air forces.

Bristol-Prieur See Prieur.

Brock A machine-gun bullet developed by Cdr Frederick Arthur Brock RN which was successfully demonstrated in October 1915 and adopted the following July. Designed to explode between the outer covering and gas cells of an airship, it was used by the RFC only until early 1917 when it was superseded, but it was retained by the RNAS throughout the war.

'Bromide' RAF code-name for jamming X-system navigation signals.

Brushfire War The term for local engagements which have to be met and dealt with quickly to prevent their spread. A number of aircraft types were developed for this work, particu-

larly during the early 1950s, one being the US Fletcher Defender. The aircraft are also known as 'co-in' or counter-insurgency types.

Buckingham An incendiary, phosphor-based bullet developed by James Francis Buckingham, patented in January 1915 and, as the Mk VII bullet, adopted by the RFC for use against airships. An incendiary filling percolated through an annular hole, the seal of which melted on firing, and took fire on contact with the outside air. It was also used by the United States and France.

Buddy See In-flight refuelling.

'Buffalo' The code-name for trials of the British atomic bomb carried out in September–October 1956 at Maralinga, Australia. Two Vickers Valiant bombers of 'C' Flight, No 49 Squadron, were involved, a 'Blue Danube' atomic weapon being successfully dropped on 11 October.

'Bulldog' The code-name for an important air-defence exercise carried out over England on Sunday 23 September 1949 involving the Belgian and United States Air Forces as well as the Royal Air Force, Royal Auxiliary Air Force, Royal Observer Corps (q.v.) and the Territorial Army.

Bullets See Brock, Buckingham, Pomeroy.

Bullpup The term for the Maxson Electronic AGM-12 air-to-surface guided missile issued to most NATO air forces. It existed in a number of versions, including the AGM-12B with a liquid-propellant rocket and HE warhead, the AGM-12D with a nuclear warhead, and the AGM-12E with a high-fragmentation head.

Burma See India and Burma.

Byakko The fighter version of the Nakajima P1Y1. It was among the best Japanese aircraft of WWII, being comparable with the Junkers 88. It had been designed by the Yokosuka Naval Arsenal to cope with the prevailing twin shortages of labour and material, but a reliable aircraft nevertheless resulted which was also immensely strong, being able to cope with 60-degree bombing dives with the assistance of dive brakes, conventional flat trajectory bombing, torpedo attacks and reconnaissance missions, but the heavy fighter model produced in 1944 was significant in having an armament of four 20mm cannon as well as a 13mm machine gun. A night fighter version was designated P1Y-2, and all aircraft of the type were code-named 'Frances' by the Allies, irrespective of their role.

C- (1) The designation used both by the US Navy and Air Force for transport or cargo aircraft. (2) The designation for British 'Coastal' type non-rigid airships of WWI. An improved model was the 'Coastal Star' (C*) type. (3) (C-Series) The US Navy's non-rigid airship designation, introduced in 1918.

C-9A The designation for the McDonnell Nightingale used by the US Air Force alone, being a 'medevac' or aero-medical version of the DC-9 short-range jet equipped for forty stretcher cases. Deliveries were first made in November 1965.

C-46 Otherwise the Curtiss Commando, this type was originally conceived as an airliner and first flew on 26 March 1940, the prototype, after the adoption of a single fin and rudder, being evaluated by the USAAF as the C-55-CS before being sold in 1941, becoming G-AGDI St Louis. The entry of the United States into WWII prevented the manufacture of civilian versions, but the aircraft was adopted for military use, 3,340 being delivered to the US Army Air Force and Marine Corps. Unlike the original design provision, the 'double bubble' fuselages of these aircraft were unpressurized.

C-47 Better-known as the Douglas Dakota, this was probably the most famous transport aircraft of all time, being originally conceived as the DC-3, an improved successor to the DC-2. It first flew in 1936 in civil form, and the bulk of the 13,000 produced were manufactured during WWII and used by just about every air force in the world, including that of the Soviet Union, which knew it as the Lisunov Li-2 (NATO code-name 'Cab'). It long outlasted the war years, when it was used as a normal transport and freight-carrier and for glider-towing and the dropping of parachute troops, to see service in the Vietnam campaign as the AC-47 gunship ('Puff the Magic Dragon') and final upgrade as the US Navy and USAAF C-117 Skytrain.

C-54 The Douglas Skymaster, a four-motor airliner design, pressed into service chiefly as a troop-carrier during WWII and capable of taking 50 fully armed men or 22,000lb of freight. A total of 1,084 had been produced by August 1947, both as C-54s and as R5Ds for the US Navy. It is interesting to note, in view of its useful military career, that the C-54 was at first rejected for civilian use in the belief that a smaller aircraft would be more commercially viable. The prototype and first production models were distinguished by triple fins. 23 were delivered to the RAF.

C-87 The designation for transport versions of the Consolidated Liberator.

The RAF's twenty-four Liberator VIIs were known as the C-87 Liberator Express in the US, or RY-1 by the US Navy. The Liberator IX, with its single fin and rudder, was termed the C-87C in the United States (RY-3 in the US Navy); twenty-seven were scheduled for service with the British, but not all were delivered.

C-130 Known more widely as the Lockheed Hercules, this aircraft is one of the most successful transports of all time. It first flew in August 1954 and a large number of variants have appeared since including a gunship, designated the AC-130, used in Vietnam and a transport adopted by the RAF which affectionately terms it 'Fat Albert'. Fighting in the former Yugoslavia saw the type used for evacuation and a large number of mercy missions.

C.200 A Macchi-designed fighter, also known as the Saetta (Arrow), designed by Mario Castoldi and which first flew in 1937. It was powered by a Fiat A-74 RC.38 radial motor which not only gave great manoeuvrability but also a low thrust-line, allowing the pilot an excellent forward view characterized by a nose-down attitude. Although used by Italy during WWII, its armament of two fuselage-mounted 12.7-mm machine guns was poor for the period.

C.202 From a pilot's viewpoint, this, the Macchi Folgore (Lightning), was an excellent aircraft, but it suffered from its light armament and a licence-built, liquid-cooled Daimler-Benz 601A1 engine, manufactured by Alfa Romeo, capable of delivering only 1,150hp at take-off. The armament consisted of twin 12.7-mm fuselage guns and provision for two of 7.7-mm calibre in the wings, plus two 220lb bombs. The first of the type reached Libya on 25 November 1941 and were operated by 1° Stormo Caccia Terrestre. Other units equipped with the C.202 included the 21° Gruppo, fighting over the Russian Front until May 1943.

C.205 A development of the foregoing, the Macchi Veltro (Greyhound) was intended to give a better performance and was thus powered by a more powerful Daimler-Benz engine, the DB

605A-1, and was armed with two 12.7-mm fuselage guns, plus two 20-mm Mauser 151 cannon. Issued to operational units at the same time as Italy's surrender on 8 September 1943, the Veltro saw service and was known to have flown escort to Spitfire fighter-bombers.

Cable-cutter A device fitted to the leading edges of the wings of hardly any bombers during WWII. It was situated towards the tips, and a balloon barrage cable meeting a wing would slide along the taper until striking the spring-loaded cutter, which would then automatically sever the cable.

Camel The unofficial name for a British single-seat scout designed by the Sopwith (q.v.) company and used during WWI mainly by Great Britain but also by Australia, Belgium, Greece and the United States. The majority were powered by Clerget rotary motors, although Le Rhône and Bentley Camels existed, but, whatever the motor, the aircraft was tricky to fly, although those who mastered it found it to be a potent fighting machine. In addition to the standard F.1 Camel, a 2F.1 version existed for the Navy, being constructed with a dismountable rear fuselage for ship stowage; these aircraft were Bentley-powered. 'TF' (Trench Fighting), two-seat training and night-fighting models were available, the last with a relocated cockpit and revised armament. The first F.1s entered service with No 70 Squadron RFC in July 1917. Some 2.F1s could be found in Estonia and Canada in 1919, the last giving long service.

Camouflage Usually dope schemes to make an aircraft inconspicuous, the general practice being to colour the upper parts to blend with the local terrain or disrupt the outline of the machine and the lower surfaces with the sky (hence some form of blue is almost universal here).

Campania A Fairey two-seat floatplane design of 1916, the first British naval aircraft specifically intended for operating from a carrier vessel, taking its title from the fact that the first such ship was the converted Cunard liner thus named. Take-off was with the aid

Above: A British Caquot-type observation balloon at 'Suicide Corner', Kemmel, Belgium, in November 1917. The fins, filled with air, not gas, would automatically self-inflate at altitude. (Cross & Cockade, Hastings)

of a wheeled trolley, and a maximum of ten Campanias could be handled.

CAM-ships Catapult Armed Merchant ships, the term referring to those vessels equipped with a Sea Hurricane for the interception of aircraft attacking convoys. The first were available in January 1941 and regarded as expendable, the pilot being expected to land on the sea if landfall was too far distant. This method of interception was temporarily suspended in the winter of 1941–42 owing to the weather. See Shipborne Aircraft.

Canberra See English Electric Canberra.

Cannon Shell-firing guns of heavier calibre than machine guns, with a slower rate of fire but increased destructive power. An early demonstration was that of 1913 when a COW (Coventry Ordnance Works) gun was fired from an F.E.3 at Farnborough, and towards the end of WWI the Swiss Oerlikon company perfected a gun of 13mm calibre. In WWII, cannon were

used essentially for offensive armament, but subsequently such guns were carried by bombers for defence.

Caproni An important WWI Italian aircraft manufacturer responsible chiefly for a series of heavy bombers until 1918 and transport aircraft thereafter until reverting to the first with such types as the Ca.73. The Ca.46 bomber was significant for being produced by some seven factories in Italy and two in France simultaneously, and in 1917 it was chosen by the United States to be licence-built, although, of the thousand produced, only five were delivered for military use.

Caquot balloon A type of tethered balloon named after its inventor, a French captain. With its three fins, it soon became the archetype 'L' and 'M' observation and barrage balloon. It proved more stable than the German Drachen kite balloon which it later replaced, and it was produced with four gas capacities, the 'P' of 26,486 cu ft, the 'P2' of 28,958 cu ft, the 32,843-cu ft 'M2' and the Navy's 35,315 cu ft 'R'.

'Carpet' The code-name for an airborne radio jamming device intended to interfere with enemy ground radar installations operating on the 300-600Mc band used by the RAF during WWII.

CASA A Spanish aircraft manufacturer, established in 1923, at first responsible for light aircraft but later building military designs under licence. After a period after WWII constructing Heinkel He 111s with Rolls-Royce Merlin motors, among the aircraft it undertook the manufacture post-war was the Northrop Freedom Fighters designated SF-5A and 5B.

Catalina The name for the Consolidated PBY flying boats and amphibians ordered in the United States to take advantage of new design techniques in 1933. The design was destined to become one of the most widely produced flying boats of WWII. Four main variants saw service with the US Navy, some of them continuing in use after 1945 chiefly for air-sea rescue, frequently with a lifeboat under one wing. The RAF operated seven variants for general reconnaissance.

Catapult Devices used to assist aircraft with heavy wing-loadings to take off from a restricted space, generally a naval vessel.

Caudron A French aircraft manufacturer eventually absorbed by SNCAN. Its early designs all owed something to the G.II of 1913 in having a nacelle for the occupants and/or motors, with the tail unit supported on slim booms. The single-engine G.III was used for reconnaissance and training in WWI by both Great Britain and France, while the G.IV, used mainly by France, performed both reconnaissance and bombing duties. On 19 January 1919 Jules Vedrines achieved the first landing on the roof of a building (the Galeries Lafayette in Paris) using one of the former.

CCIP Continuously Computed Impact Point. Spot on the sight which tells constantly where ordnance will hit.

CCRP Continuously Computed Release Point. Similar to the foregoing but with auto weapon release.

CENTO Central Treaty Organization of 1955 with the UK, US, Iran, Iraq, Pakistan and Turkey as members with the aim of meeting a Communist attack on one of the member states. Iraq withdrew in 1958 and Pakistan in 1972. No longer exists

CF-100 The Avro Canada CF-100, sometimes called the Canuck, made its first flight on 19 January 1950 and production versions of this long-range, all-weather fighter proved excellent, five versions, with a number of sub-types, being produced before manufacture terminated in 1957. In addition to those used by the Canadian Armed Forces, fifty-three examples went to Belgium. A Mk 6, envisaged as having afterburners and being armed with Canadian Sparrow 2 missiles, was not proceeded with.

Chaff Strips of metal foil used to confuse enemy radar systems. See Window.

Chance Vought A US aircraft manufacturer specializing in designs for the Navy. Probably its best-known product was the F4U Corsair of WWII, some of which were even involved in the Vietnam campaign. Its first jet, the F7U-3 Cutlass, appeared in 1951. The company was absorbed into Ling-Temco Electronics in 1961. Subsequent types included the A-7 Corsair II, based on the earlier Crusader design.

'Channel Stop' The code-name for the operation mounted as a preliminary to the D-day landings by the Allies in WWII to prevent the passage of enemy shipping through the Straits of Dover during the hours of daylight.

'Chastise' The code-name for the operation carried out by nineteen Lancasters of No 617 Squadron RAF on the night of 16/17 May 1943 against the Möhne, Eder and Sorpe dams in the Ruhr valley using the new 'bouncing bombs' designed by Dr Barnes Wallis. The raid was led by Wg Cdr Guy Gibson, who was later awarded the Victoria Cross; 32 other members of the Squadron were decorated. The aircraft, in numerical order, and the captains involved were: ED864/'B' (Bill Astell); ED865/'S' (Lewis Burpee); ED886/'O' (Bill Townsend); ED887/'A'

('Dinghy' Young); ED906/'J' (David Maltby); ED909/'P' (Micky Martin); ED910/'C' (Warner Otley); ED912/'N' (Les Knight); ED918/'F' (Ken Brown); ED921/'W' (Les Munroe); ED923/'T' (Joe McCarthy); ED924/'Y' (Cyril Anderson); ED925/'M' ('Hoppy' Hopgood); ED927/'E' (Robert Barlow); ED929/'L' (Dave Shannon); ED932/'G' (Guy Gibson); ED934/'K' (Vernon Byers); ED936/'H' (Geoff Rice) and ED937/'Z' (Henry Maudsley). At least 36 practice attacks had previously been made with concrete-filled bombs on the Ashley Walk Range, under the supervision of the ROC. See Bombing.

Chel Ha'Avir The Israeli (q.v.) Defence Force/Air Force (Hebrew), established on 27 May 1948 on the basis of the former Sherut Avir (q.v.).

Chengdu F-7 Chinese version of the Soviet MiG-21 fighter.

'Cherry' Allied term for the Japanese Yokosuka H5Y, the Navy Type 99 flying boat of WWII. A medium-size, twin-engine patrol craft, its production was suspended after some twenty examples had been delivered between 1936 and 1941 as it proved to be underpowered.

CHH Chain Home High. British radar stations identified by twin masts some 250ft in height, one being used for transmitting and the other for receiving. One such station, situated on Hengistbury Head, Dorset, was able to 'see' aircraft over Paris.

Chinook The Boeing-Vertol 114 medium cargo helicopter begun in 1956 when the US Army demanded a turbine-powered, all-weather machine capable of operating under a wide variety of conditions. Over 500 examples served in Vietnam, airlifting troops and weapons on the battlefield as well as salvaging abandoned aircraft. From this was developed the heavy-lift Model 179, which differed in having a single lifting rotor.

CHL Chain Home Low. 'CH' was the earliest type of British ground-based defence radar, the first RDF stations for which were set up in 1937. Nineteen had been constructed by September 1939. The system was able to detect aircraft up to an altitude of 30,000ft and at distances up to 100 miles plus under favourable conditions; the size of a formation could also be estimated, but aircraft flying at low altitude could not be detected. To remedy this, twenty-seven CHL stations were in use by the summer of 1940. They operated on a wavelength of 1.5m, had rotating antennae at the top of 20ft and 185ft towers and were thus able to 'see' low-flying intruders 30 miles away. Receiving towers for the CH system were wooden and 350ft tall; those for transmitters were of steel, operation being on a wavelength of 10m.

Church bells During WWII the ringing of church bells was forbidden in Britain, except to give warning of enemy parachute troops (q.v.) landing.

'Cigar' The code-name for the WWII British jamming of enemy VHF radio communications to airborne fighters.

'Circus' An RAF daylight fighter-bomber escort operation against short-range targets, mounted with a view to drawing German fighters to interception, thereby preventing their redeployment to the Eastern Front.

'Claude' The Allied code-name for the Japanese Mitsubishi A5M naval fighter. First flown on 4 February 1935, it was first delivered during 1937 so that it was in time to see action against the Chinese before WWII It was phased out of first-line use in 1942, by which time an Army version, the A5M4 had been produced and had entered service. It was fitted with a fixed undercarriage and, initially, a cockpit hood, though the latter proved unpopular and was discarded.

Climbing attack A WWII Luftwaffe tactic using SG 500 Jagdfaust (Fighter Fist) rockets to shoot upwards when triggered by the shadow of a bomber above a photo-electric cell. Five such tubes in each wing root fired 50mm shells, while an equivalent weight shot downwards cancelled the recoil. An FW 190 thus fitted claimed a B-17G, but the twelve Me 163B-1s equipped in this way were not used operationally.

Cluster Bomb Unit (CBU) A free-fall device capable of scattering a number of submunitions over a target area which varies according to the altitude at which the unit is set to open. Includes Beluga or BL-91, 92 or 755 according to content, such a weapon was anticipated during WWII by the Luftwaffe's AB 1000, AB 500 and AB 36 anti-personnel and incendiary bomb containers. An example of their use as the century drew towards its close was that during the Russian actions over Chechnya during 1994–95, when pictures showed the submunitions to contain metallic balls about 8mm in diameter.

Coanda A Romanian-born aircraft designer employed by the British and Colonial Aircraft Company (Bristol) in 1912, producing a two-seat monoplane the same year. On this was based the Bristol-Coanda T.B.8 biplane, a small number of which saw service with the RNAS. At least one of these had a two-wheel undercarriage which replaced the four-wheel type inherited from the monoplane, and aileron-control

CHINA

The Air Force of the People's Liberation Army of China is said to be the third largest in the world, with an estimated strength approaching 5,000 aircraft, and organised along Soviet lines. Four squadrons, made up of some fifteen aircraft each, constitute an air regiment, four of which form an air division. However, China's technical poverty, in part due to the emphasis placed by Mao Tse-tung on alternative technology in its formative years, and an increasing isolation from the Communist Bloc later on, means that it is one of the world's least modern major air arms. Thus increased efforts were made to purchase military aircraft and associated equipment from the West, and when these were only partially successful China's new regime attempted to push forward with the necessary advances without this aid.

After the 1949 defeat of the Nationalist forces on the mainland, the Communists received large numbers of modern aircraft, particularly from the Soviet Union, and these rose to a peak during the Korean War, thus setting the pattern which was to follow into the next decade. Soviet types such as the Tu-4 were made available for tactical operations, but mostly the support took the form of such types as the Tu-16 and some 300 Il-28s for light bombing, coupled with Beriev Be-6s for maritime reconnaissance. In so vast a country transport aircraft assume an importance almost unequalled elsewhere, so that, backed up by the availability in an emergency of a fleet of civil airliners, An-2s, Li-2s, Il-14s and Il-18s were made available to a total of some 400 machines, while training was taken care of by the supply of Yak-11s, Yak-18s and MiG-15UTIs trainers.

The naval air arm was less well supplied, but a comprehensive force was assembled nevertheless, some 100 Il-28s for torpedo-bombing being supported by about four times as many MiG-15s (Jian-4s), -17s (Jian-5s) and -19s (Jian-6s), a total number of about forty regiments flying the last type. The naval fighters were not confined to maritime support duties but constituted an integral part of the defence system which was organized across the country as a whole, divided into protected geographical districts and administered from the headquarters in Peking.

Nearer the end of the twentieth century a few Chengdu Jian-7s (otherwise MiG-21s) were adopted to augment the ageing fighters of the Army, but meanwhile Chinese engineers had not been idle, developing from the Jian-6 a new attack aircraft, the Qiang-5, which presented a similar silhouette to its parent design but was distinguished by a new radar nose and eight attachment points for external stores.

That measures of this nature were necessary indicates the crisis that was developing in the supply of Chinese military aircraft, since, in the normal course of events, the obsolete fighters, for example, would have been replaced by large numbers of MiG-21s, followed no doubt by Sukhoi Su-7s and MiG-23s: that these were not forthcoming is an illustration of the slowly developing ideological dispute between Moscow and Peking which can be traced back to the 1960s. It was not long before 1,400 Soviet advisers to China were withdrawn – at a time when the still-embryonic aircraft industry was in no position to meet the demands that almost immediately would be placed on it.

Clearly, the situation called for desperate measures if the Army and Navy were not to suffer a famine of reasonably modern types. One such was the ordered dismantling of some MiG-21s so that drawings could be pre-

replaced the wing-warping of the earlier versions. From a military viewpoint their rotating bomb rack was remarkable (see Bombing), and one of the type attacked enemy batteries at Middelkerke as early as 25 November 1914. The maximum speed of the aircraft was up to 75mph, according to the engine fitted.

Cockpit The control position for an aircraft, a term borrowed from naval parlance where it indicated a similar position on sailing vessels.

COD The abbreviation for Carrier Onboard Delivery, the use of transport aircraft, usually converted from other roles, for the delivery of personnel and supplies direct to an aircraft carrier at sea.

Code, manufacturers' See Prototype Codes.

Code markings (aircraft) These evolved from the single letter or numeral used as individual aircraft identification marks carried by the belligerents during WWI. Many European countries were using extended letter or letter/number systems by the outbreak of WWII. In Britain two-letter combinations denoted the unit and the single character the individual aircraft identification with the pre-war introduction of camouflage schemes, and although these were mostly altered after 1939 the same system was followed, the darker grey first used being replaced by a lighter shade during the Battle of France. Dark red letters were later adopted for night bombers and a few aircraft had 'squared' (e.g. M2) individual letters when these duplicated single letters already in existence. Modern codes consist of either single letters or letter/number combinations. The pre-1939 Luftwaffe scheme of in some cases five characters was replaced by four black letter/number combinations during WWII, although in both schemes colour was used to a predetermined system to denote the Staffel, and the Gruppe within which it operated. The French system in use at the end of the century was not dissimilar, although this consisted of a number and a two-letter combination separated by a hyphen. The codes 'G-X' and 'G-K' were allocated to captured Allied aircraft flight testing.

Coin The abbreviation of 'counter-insurgency', a military aircraft duty not very different from the 'police' actions carried out by certain imperial nations between the world wars. Fixed-wing aircraft have tended to be specially designed or adapted for this work since the late 1950s, although helicopters have also been increasingly used.

'Colossus' The airborne combined operation against an aqueduct at Tragino in southern Italy carried out on the night of 10/11 May, 1941. See Parachute Forces.

Specialists, Officers and men Participating in 'Colossus'
'X' Troop commander:
Maj T. A. G. Pritchard (Royal Welsh Fusiliers)
Location planning:
Lt A. J. Deane-Drummond (Royal Signals)

---

pared with a view to home production, for although plans were in hand to manufacture the new J-8 'Finbacks', these were of a long-term nature. However, there still existed the manufacturing licence secured in 1958 to manufacture the J-6 (Jianjiji, or Fighter Aircraft), otherwise the MiG-19, and to this end the Shenyang National Aircraft Factory rapidly tooled up and had produced its first aircraft of the type by the end of 1961. The aircraft were eventually delivered at a rate of sixty per month, including such variants as an all-weather version and a trainer, some fifteen years later. In addition a 'stretched' variant, with repositioned intakes and cockpit, was not long in procuring orders from such customers as North Korea and Pakistan, so that, today, the Nanchang Q-5 III 'Fantan', using French and Italian avionics, ensures that the air arm of Communist China, with the red star and bar national insignia on which the characters 8 over 1 are superimposed, is likely to maintain for the present a strength of numbers which is still not complemented by its modernity.

Some might argue that the lineal descendant of the Kuomintang or Government Air Force which was established in 1914 is the pair of Taiwanese air arms. The force evolved from a flying school at Nan Yuan which enjoyed US instruction. The main operational foundations, however, were laid soon after the end of WWI by an Italian mission, and although British influence resulted in the establishment of a large school at Chengdu, equipment and procedure remained primarily Italian. The Central Government Air Force that emerged in 1934 was augmented by those of several independent provinces, that of Kwangsi being among the most active. These were later absorbed by the government, but the fighter arm of the main force was virtually annihilated by the Japanese in August 1937, at a time when its US and Italian equipment was being added to from Soviet stocks following the signing of a non-aggression pact between the two countries.

During the war years the Chinese air arm was organized on the basis of five air forces designated after the routes they protected: the First Route Air Force, with its HQ at Chungking; the Second, with its HQ at Kweilin; the Third, based on Chengtu; the Fourth, based on Lanchow; and the Fifth Route Air Force, with its headquarters at Kungming. Of these, the Third and Fifth were largely training organizations and the Fourth was orientated towards Mongolia and Tibet. The Second was disbanded with the fall of Kweilin, leaving the surviving Route Forces to carry out operations which were in the main fighter sweeps, with occasional missions by medium bombers made by the Second Bomb Group based at Chinkiang. Later in WWII US influence once more dominated with the formation of the AVG (American Volunteer Group), and this continued when the Taiwan Air Force and Army Air Arm were put on a war footing during the Communist take-over of the mainland. F-84 Thunderjets, including FS-920, 961 and 996 were presented during 1953 to replace the ageing aircraft then in use, and the CNAF continued to be kept up to date with the passage of time, receiving such types as the Lockheed U-2 to augment the output of the Taiwanese factories.

The end of the century found the Communist PLAAF (People's Liberation Army Air Force) with relatively archaic, mostly ex-Soviet technology without AEW capability. Some 4,500 aircraft were distributed through 45 air divisions, with 700 fighters and strike aircraft serving with the Navy. Reports of F-104s of the 5th Fighter Wing from Ching Chuan Kang engaging mainland MiGs in combat have remained unconfirmed.

Interpreters:
Sqn Ldr Lucky MC (RAF)
Pte Nastri (Rifle Brigade)
Pte Fortinato Picchi*
Sapper commander:
Capt G. F. K. Daly (Royal Engineers)
Air preparations:
Wg Cdr J. B. Tate DFC (RAF)
Photo reconnaissance:
Fg Off A. Warburton DSO, DFC (RAF)

Charge covering party:
Capt C. G. Lea (Lancashire Fusiliers)†
Sgt Clements†
Sgt Lawlay†
Charge-laying:
Sgt Drury (Royal Engineers)
Pte Pritchard
For the withdrawal, the Troop was formed into three groups command-ed by Maj Pritchard, Capt Lea and

2/Lt G. Jowett (Highland Light Infantry). *Strictly, this man was a civilian recruited from the staff of the Savoy Hotel, London, for his regional linguis-tic knowledge.
†These three were responsible for the party covering those laying the charges to destroy the aqueduct which was the target.
The operation had, in practical terms,

CODE-NAMES
Military operations

The following is a select listing of code-names applied to air war and associated operations:

'Abigail' RAF attack on Mannheim of 16/17 December 1940 in retaliation for raids on Coventry and Southampton.

'Anvil'/'Dragoon' Landing of Allied 7th Army in Southern France on 15 August 1944.

'Avalanche' Allied landings on Salerno beach-es with air support on 9 September 1943.

'Balak' Czechoslovak–Israeli ferry operation to introduce Avia S.199s into use between May and August 12 1948, flown between Zatec, Dov and Ekron AFBs.

'Barbarossa' German attack on the Soviet Union on 22 June 1941.

'Bellicose' RAF shuttle-bombing raid on Friedrichshafen, 20 June 1943.

'Bell Tone II' USAF operation in Vietnam in 1962.

'Biting' Combined operation near Bruneval to capture Würzburg radar parts, 27/28 February 1942.

'Black Buck' RAF series of bombing missions during Falklands campaign in 1982.

'Bodenplatte' German offensive operation against Allied airfields on 1 January 1945.

'Bolo' US counter-air operation Vietnam War, 2 February 1967.

'Bone Deep' US F-102A deployment, 1960.

'Carter Paterson' Original name for Berlin Air Lift, later changed to Operation 'Plainfare/Vittles'.

'Cerberus' German code-name for the 'Channel dash' of warships *Scharnhorst*, *Gneisenau* and *Prinz Eugen* on 12 February 1942. See 'Thunderbolt'.

'Chariot' British Commando landing at St Nazaire on 27 March 1942. 'Chastise' RAF attack to breach the Möhne, Eder and Sorpe dams on 16/17 May 1943.

'Cold Water' RAF attempt to pre-empt attacks on Britain by bombing enemy bases.

'Colossus' (q.v.) Airborne operation to destroy aqueduct at Tragino, southern Italy, 10/11 February 1941.

'Corkscrew' Air bombardment of Pantellaria, opened on 23 May 1943, gaining surrender after twenty days.

'Corporate' British operations in the Falkland Islands, 1982.

'Cottage' Allied invasion of Japanese-occu-pied island of Kiska, 15 August 1943.

'Creek Claxon' Standby of US Air National Guard at Ramstein AFB, Germany, while regular units converted.

'Crossbow' Allied defence measures against flying bomb attacks on the British Isles, 1944.

'Crusader' British offensive in Western Desert to relieve pressure on Tobruk, 18 November 1941.

'Deliberate Force' NATO attacks on Serbian targets, August/September 1995.

'Deny Flight' NATO attack on Udbina, 13 November 1994.

'Desert Shield' Build-up of Coalition forces opposing the Iraqi occupation of Kuwait, 1990–91.

'Desert Storm' Operation to liberate Kuwait, 1991

'Detachment' US landing on Iwo Jima, 19 February 1944.

'Dragoon' See 'Anvil'.

'Dynamo' Evacuation of the British Expeditionary Force from Dunkirk, May/June 1940.

'Eagle Claw' US attempt to rescue hostages in Teheran, 1981.

'Eclipse' Attempt to photograph, from the air, a total eclipse of the sun on 9 July 1945. Also name for operation by the Allied Air Disarmament Wings to destroy stocks of 1,368 flying bombs and 3,002 V-2 rockets after end of WW2.

'Eisenhammer' Proposed use of Luftwaffe *Mistel* pick-a-back aircraft against Soviet power stations planned for 1 February 1945.

'Eisstoss' Ice Strike. German attack against Soviet Baltic Fleet, 4 April 1942.

'Eldorado Canyon' US air attack against selected targets in Libya, April 1986.

'Eruption' Attacks on Japanese airfields, 3/4 November 1944.

'Exodus' Air repatriation of ex-POWs, April 1945.

'Fall Gelb' Yellow Plan. German plan for limit-ed offensive in West, drastically revised by Manstein Plan of February 1940.

'Firedog' RAF operations against Communist-inspired terrorist forces in Malaya, 1949–60.

'Flashlamp' Preparatory operations for D-day landings against targets in Northern France, 5 June 1944.

'Flax' Allied air operation to intercept Axis transport supplying troops in Tunisia. The first victories were achieved on 5 April 1943.

'Frantic' First US shuttle raid with B-17s, 2 June 1944.

'Fuller' Operation against German warships in the Channel, 12 February 1942. See 'Cerberus'.

'Gaff' Parachute drop by Belgian and SAS force to destroy petrol dumps in the Rouen area, 25 July 1944.

'Glimmer' Diversionary pre-'Overlord' RAF attack of 5/6 June 1944.

'Global Shield' Annual US SAC exercise to scramble B-52 bombers in minimum time.

'Grandero I' US action in Honduras, 1984.

'Gunboat' June 1986 programme for heavy-calibre cannon on a special C-130A gun-ship.

'Ha-Go' Japanese offensive in Arakan, begun 4 February 1945.

'Herkules' Planned German airborne invasion of Malta, 1942.

'Husky' Allied air and seaborne landings in Sicily, 9/10 July 1943.

'Hydra' RAF attack on Peenemünde, 17 August 1943.

'Ichigo' Major Japanese offensive against US air bases, begun 25 May 1944.

'Intruder' Begun on 21 December 1940. Name used for offensive night patrols over enemy territory to destroy aircraft and dislo-cate enemy night organisation.

'Jericho' RAF low-level raid on Amiens jail, 18 February 1944.

'Jubilee' Allied raid on Dieppe, 19 August 1942.

'Judgement' RN air attack on Italian warships in Taranto harbour, 11 November 1940.

little effect on the war effort in either Albania or North Africa, since the aqueduct was promptly restored, but it was of importance in the history of air warfare in that, as an experiment in the use of a new instrument, it pointed the way to the immediate future.

Commonwealth Air Forces The establishment of the chief Commonwealth,

ex-Empire and former Dominion air forces were all initiated as a result of WWI, that of Australia, for example, originating from an air unit established at Point Cook in 1912 which later became the Australian Flying Corps. This gave invaluable service during the following conflict, notably in Mesopotamia and Palestine. It was disbanded after 1918, only to reappear

as the Royal Australian Air Force (RAAF) in September 1923. On the outbreak of WWII the Australians provided the first overseas force to operate in Europe, with a Sunderland squadron of Coastal Command in January 1940. Four years later the RAAF in Europe was to fly a total of 34,000 sorties taking up 161,000hrs, its bombers dropping 57,000 tons and its fighter-

'Junction City' First US airborne assault of Vietnam War, 22 February 1967.

'Kadesh' Israeli operation at beginning of Sinai campaign, 29 October 1956.

'Kikusui' Floating Chrysanthemum. The first of ten kamikaze attacks on US invasion vessels off Okinawa, 6 April 1945.

'Linebacker' Resumption of US bombing of North Vietnam from 8 May 1972.

'Manna' Supply drop by RAF bombers over Holland, 29 April–8 May 1945.

'Market Garden' Airborne landings at Arnhem, 17 September 1944.

'Merkur' Mercury. German airborne invasion of Crete, 20 May 1941.

'Millennium' First RAF 1,000-bomber attack on Cologne, 30/31 May 1942.

'Mondlicht Sonate' Moonlight Sonata. Luftwaffe raid on Coventry, 14 November 1940.

'Musketeer' RAF bombing attack on Egyptian airfields in Suez War, October/November 1956.

'Mutton' Laying of aerial mines by HP Harrows of No 93 Squadron RAF in 1940.

'Niagara' US operation in defence of marine base at Khe Sanh, begun 21 January 1968.

'Olympic Coronet' Planned Allied invasion of Japan, 1945.

'Overlord' Allied invasion of Europe, 6 June 1944.

'Peace Pearl' US contract to upgrade avionics of J-8-11s for China, 1987 (since cancelled).

'Pipe Down' Combined US/UK operating trials, October 1957.

'Plainfare/Vittles' Substitute name for the Berlin Air Lift, formerly code-named 'Carter Paterson'.

'Post Mortem' Victors' evaluation of German early-warning radar systems, 25 June, 1945.

'Proud Deep' Strikes by aircraft of the US Navy against supply storage areas, coastal interdiction points and airfields in Vietnam, late 1972.

'Redwing' Test drop of atomic bombs over Bikini atoll, May 1956.

'Ring' Coordinated attacks on Stalingrad front launched on 10 January 1943.

'Robinson' RAF dusk attack on Schneider

works at Le Creusot, 17 October, 1942.

'Rob Roy' Air operation carried out by Dakotas of No 46 Group with Short Stirlings and HP Halifaxes of No 38 Group to drop fresh supplies to Allied armies on the ground 6– 10 June 1944.

'Rolling Thunder' Air offensive to force North Vietnam to negotiate. Begun 18 March 1965.

'Rot' Red. German code-name for the Battle of France.

'Rumpelkammer' German attacks on Great Britain using flying bombs, begun June 1944.

'Salvo' Israeli Aircraft Industry reconstruction programme of Mirage aircraft, 1969 onwards.

'Seelöwe' Sealion. Proposed German invasion of the British Isles, 1940.

'Shed Light' Visual target assistance scheme, parallel with Operation 'Gunboat'.

'Shingle' Fifth Army troops landing at Anzio under Allied air cover, 22 January 1944.

'Silverplate' Atomic bomb attack on Hiroshima, 6 August 1945.

'Slugger' Heavy US air attacks against North Vietnam begun February 1971.

'Starkey' RAF attacks on targets in Pas de Calais area simultaneously with simulated raid by troops on Boulogne, 9 September 1943.

'Steel Tiger' US operation using aerial gunships in South Laos, 1965.

'Steinbock' Ibex. The 'Little Blitz', 447 sorties against London, which opened on 21 January 1944.

'Strangle' Road/rail interdiction operation in Italy, beginning 19 March 1944, lasting to May.

'Subject' Flare-drops over enemy night bombers by RAF aircraft to facilitate interception. Tested over Britain during spring and summer 1942 but abandoned in October.

'Surprise Package' Operations with modified gunships by US in Vietnam, 1965.

'Swamp' RAF concentration of aircraft for 48hr search of an area where U-boat sighting reported. First flown 15 October 1943.

'Taifun' Typhoon. German offensive by 2nd

Panzer Army on Russian Front.

'Taxable' Diversionary pre-'Overlord' RAF attack of 5/6 June 1944 in Pas de Calais area.

'Thunderbolt' (1) Luftwaffe air cover for warships during Operation 'Cerberus', 12 February 1942. (2) Israeli operation to free Entebbe hostages, 27 June 1976.

'Thunderclap' Proposed heavy air attacks on Berlin and Dresden.

'Tidal Wave' US bombing attack on Ploesti oilfields, 1 August 1943.

'Titanic I/II/IV' Diversionary pre-'Overlord' RAF attacks of 5/6 June 1944.

'Torch' Allied invasion of North Africa, 1942.

'Vapour' British operation to intercept and destroy flying bombs before launch, 1944.

'Varsity' Airborne landing accompanying Operation 'Plunder', the ground assault. The largest single airborne operation ever. Carried out by the US 17th and British 6th Airborne Divisions, the former with 610 tugs and 906 gliders (chiefly C-47s and CG-4As respectively). Troop Carrier Groups 435, 436, 437 and 439 participated.

'Velvetta' Kanovica (Czechoslovakia) to Ramat David AFB (Israel) ferry operation, 1948. Associated with Operation 'Balak' (q.v.).

'Venerable' Attack by US and French ground forces on Gironde following napalm raid by Eighth Air Force and shelling, 15 April 1945.

'Warden' Post-Gulf War surveillance by RAF/US flights from bases in Turkey to enforce declared 'No-Fly Zone' over Iraq.

'Weserübung Nord' Weser Crossing North. German invasion of Norway.

'Weserübung Süd' Weser Crossing South. German invasion of Denmark.

'Zeppelin' German plan to fly agents to Moscow to assassinate Stalin.

'Zipper' Planned Allied landing on west coast of Malaya near Morib but mounted as an exercise after Japanese surrender on 14 August 1945 with Spitfires of Nos 11 and 17 Squadrons flying from HMS *Smiter* and *Trumpeter*.

'Zitadelle' Citadel. German spring offensive on Kursk salient launched, after several postponements, 9 May 1943.

bombers 2,300 tons of high explosive. At the end of April 1945 casualties amounted to 7,889 killed or presumed killed from a total enlistment of 14,414.

India possessed an air force from 1932, but its first complete squadron was not formed until 1938. A large expansion scheme began in 1939 and the IAF first went into action in 1943 on the Burma Front. In recognition of its outstanding service thus begun and later widened to cover many theatres, including Arakan and service with the 3rd TAF, it became the Royal Indian Air Force in March 1945.

Although acquiring a Blériot XI monoplane, *Britannia*, in 1913 and thus laying foundations, a New Zealand air arm did not materialize until the Air Corps was set up in 1923. It was termed the New Zealand Permanent Air Force in the same year, becoming the RNZAF in 1934. Its strength in 1939 was about 1,800 men, rising to over 45,000 in 1944. It served in many theatres.

Steps were taken to found an air arm for Rhodesia in 1936 with the creation of an air section of the Permanent Staff Corps, and in 1939 an offer was made to bring the unit up to squadron strength. Thus No 237 Squadron was operationally attached to RAF Middle East Command, to be followed by No 44 Squadron with Avro Lancasters and No 266 with Typhoons, both in Europe. The separate Rhodesian Air Askari Corps performed labour and guard duties.

The history of the South African Air Force began in 1914 when the Air Corps was formed. Later to become No 26 (SA) Squadron, this operated first over German South-West Africa. The foundation of the SAAF followed a British gift of 100 aeroplanes in 1920 and a five-year expansion scheme was initiated in 1936. In 1939 the force began its participation in WWII, at first in the campaign in Italian East Africa.

Concrete Dibber A bomb measuring 8ft in length and weighing 1,200lb, of which 800lb was the warhead which was designed to deny the use of runways to an enemy. First used by Israel at the beginning of the 1967 Six-Day War, it had eight rockets attached to the body, four designed to fire forward and retard the fall immediately after release, while a drogue changed the missile's trajectory from horizontal to vertical, thus permitting the escape of the delivering aircraft from the area of the blast. The remaining four rockets would then ignite and drive the bomb into the concrete.

Condor Legion The popular name for the units sent by Nazi Germany during 1936 to support General Franco's Nationalist forces in the Spanish Civil War in November. It was manned by 4,500 volunteers, hence its alternative name, the German Volunteer Corps. The first aircraft consisted of three Staffeln of Ju 52/3m bombers, three Staffeln of He 51 fighters and two reconnaissance Staffeln, one each of He 70s and He 45s, together with nine He 5 seaplanes and one He 70 floatplane. Later more modern types were substituted, including He 111Es, Do 17Es and Ju 86s operated by Kampfgruppe K/88, plus three units with Ju 87A/Bs and Hs 123 dive bombers. Some twelve Do 17Fs, a number of He 70s and a few Hs 126s were also to arrive, but perhaps the most outstanding equipment change was that involving J/88 biplane fighters for twelve Messerschmitt Bf 109Bs in 1938. The commander of the Legion was Generalmajor Hugo Sperrle, who in the 1920s had enjoyed connections with the Lipetsk training centre in Soviet Russia, while his Chief of Staff was Obstlt Wolfram Freiherr von Richthofen, a cousin of Manfred who had commanded Jagdgeschwader 1 in WWI.

The first major air operation in Spain to be made with German support was that which enabled General Franco to overcome the blockade of the Straits of Gibraltar, on the Moroccan side of which lay the army essential to support his cause. The audacious plan to move these men, partly with the help of an airlift (see CHRONOLOGY, 1936) was successful not only because of the German transport machines but also because of the planning by Franco's air force chief, General 'Prologo' Alfredo Kindelan, who had originated the idea of such an operation.

The Condor Legion was theoretically under Franco's direct control, an arrangement which at first encouraged him to make some uncharacteristically swift moves, but communications problems soon made liaison impossible and Sperrle was granted permission to deal direct with General Emilio Mola commanding the northern troops and his Chief of Staff, General Jorge Vigon Suerodiaz, so that the German officer was to note in his diary on 24 March 1937, 'We are practically in charge of the entire business without any of the responsibility.'

However, by December 1938 it was clear to many that a larger European war was not far distant, and operations by the Condor Legion ceased. Von Richthofen, who had now succeeded his leader in Spain, was recalled, eventually to command the dive bombers of Fliegerkorps VII in Poland, France, the Baltic and Russia before finally becoming responsible for Luftflotte 2 in the Mediterranean with the rank of Generalfeldmarschall in 1943. Meanwhile in February 1939 Sperrle was appointed commander of Luftflotte 3, covering south-west Germany and later, with Luftflotte 2, to be involved in the Battle of Britain. Both men would draw on their experience of modern warfare gained in Spain while contributing to the successes there, so that it was left to Hitler to sum up the achievement of his Condor Legion when, at a dinner in 1942, he was to comment, 'The intervention of the German General von Richthofen and the bombs his squadrons rained from the heavens decided the issue.'

Contour-chasing A term coined for the practice developed on the Western Front during WWI of flying very low and following the contours of the terrain in order to remain out of sight for as long as possible before making an attack on a ground target. Later known as 'hedge-hopping', contour flying continues to be practised with the aid of electronic devices as a means of avoiding detection by radar.

'Cookie' The popular name for the RAF's 4,000lb cylindrical, high-capacity bomb used during WWII.

Corkscrew An evasive manoeuvre adopted by bombers to change their position both in elevation and azimuth which made the task of the intercepting night-fighters virtually impossible.

Corpo Aereo Italiano (CAI) The Italian Air Corps was a unit of Mussolini's Regia Aeronautica which was assembled in Belgium from mid-September 1940 for the purpose of attacking targets in Britain. It consisted of 80 BR.20 bombers and 50 Fiat CR.42 and 48 G.50 fighters. The first sortie took place at night on 25 October, the target being Ramsgate. A larger attack was that of 11 November directed against Harwich at about 1330 hrs when some fifteen of the raiders were accounted for by intercepting Hurricanes of Nos 17, 46 and 257 Squadrons RAF.

Cross A basic form of national insignia chiefly associated with Germany, the first form being the Cross Patée, or Iron Cross (sometimes erroneously termed a Maltese Cross) which was used as an aircraft marking from the first weeks of WWI, often on a rectangular white field. A white border was substituted with the adoption of dark camouflage schemes during 1916–17. In January 1918 this marking was replaced by a Balkenkreuz or 'wooden cross' with straight arms, as before in black picked out with white. A similar marking, combined with a swastika on the vertical members of the tail unit, was retained by the Nazi Party, to be finally replaced after 1945 by the Luftwaffe of West Germany with a marking similar to that of 1914. Bulgaria, Hungary, Portugal, Romania, Slovakia, the Spanish Nationalists and Switzerland have all included varying types of cross in their national markings from time to time.

'Crossbow' The Allied code-name for defensive measures adopted against flying bomb attacks on the British Isles. See Flying Bombs.

Croydon An aerodrome in Surrey, England, the western half of which was used as an RFC base from 1915, initially by No 19 Reserve Squadron, to intercept enemy raiders. Nos 29 and 40 Training Squadrons were later based there until 1920, the Duke of York (later HM King George VI) being

among the pupils. By 1939 both this and the National Aircraft Factory (q.v.) in the eastern half ('Waddon Aerodrome') had been united and it was used as a fighter station and later an RAF transport base until 1945.

CRU The abbreviation for Civilian Repair Units, an organization set up in Great Britain in 1938 and later transferred to the Ministry of Aircraft Production. Intended to take battle-damaged aircraft from RAF salvage units, they were responsible for 38 per cent of all machines returned to service in 1940.

C-Stoff Methyl alcohol: 30 per cent hydrazine hydrate, 57 per cent methyl alcohol and 13 per cent water.

'Cub' The NATO code-name for the Antonov An-12 paratroop and freight transport, huge numbers of which were used by many of the Eastern Bloc countries. Four-engined and capable of taking 100 fully armed men, it was evolved from the An-10 airliner and was capable of operating from non-paved surfaces. The aircraft could also be fitted with skis. Some had a rear defensive gun position.

Curtiss Among the first US aircraft manufacturers, this company's JN-2 and JN-3 aircraft were used from the early days by the US Army. Also manufactured were the Hawk fighters (the firm's first all-metal monoplanes) of the 1930s onwards and, during WWII, the successors to this design, the P-40 ,Tomahawk, Kittyhawk and Warhawk. See also C-46.

'Cyclamen' See Flares.

D- (1) The designation adopted by Germany during WWI, indicating Doppeldecker, for single-place, single-engine, armed biplanes – hence Albatros D.I, Fokker D.VIII, etc. Three competitions were organized at Adlershof in January–February, May–June and October 1918 to select further aircraft in this category, with fighter evaluation flights by front-line pilots at the same venue in July. (2) (D-Series) The designation for the USN non-rigid airship type ordered in 1919.

It was an improved version of the C-Series.

Dackelbauch Dachshund-belly. The Luftwaffe term for the plywood long-range fuel tank for Messerschmitt 110D-ls.

Dagger Embargoed Mirage 5Js, known as Neshers, were constructed in Israel from 1973 and when they were phased out of service with the Israeli Defence Force/Air Force most of the surviving examples of the type were reworked for export and became known as Daggers. The majority were purchased by Argentina and were the so-called 'Mirages' encountered during the Falklands War.

Daisy Cutter An anti-personnel weapon used by the US Marine Corps during WWII. It consisted of a 100lb HE bomb wrapped with belts of 0.30in calibre machine-gun ammunition.

Dambusters The name commonly used for No 617 Squadron RAF in recognition of their bombing of the Ruhr dams in 1943, a fact recorded in their badge and motto 'Après Moi le Deluge'. See Bombing, 'Chastise'.

Darky A system whereby aircraft fitted with R/T over the UK could acquire a positional fix, first introduced in Bomber Command, 1940. It consisted of simple TR9D high-frequency transmitter/receivers working on 6,440Hz with a useful range of some ten miles. These were operated on the ground by WAAFs and in the air by the crew. The procedure was extended to include operation by selected ROC posts in October 1942. Gatwick, Surrey, was the venue for part of the trials.

Dassault Marcel, founder of Avions Marcel Dassault after the end of WWII, having previously existed as the Marcel Bloch organization, builders of the MB.151–155 fighter series from 1937 which reached its peak in the MB.152 although insufficient numbers of these aircraft were available. The renamed Dassault company was responsible for a whole dynasty of military aircraft, beginning with the Ouragan fighter-bomber and followed by the Mystère and Super-Mystère

Above: Dassault Mirage 400 No 01 takes off on a demonstration flight at Farnborough in 1986. (Author)

series. Avions Marcel Dassault merged with Breguet in 1972 to become Dassault-Breguet.

'Dave' The WWII Allied code-name for the Nakajima E8N floatplane of the Japanese Navy. It was used for light reconnaissance from aircraft tenders, battleships and cruisers from 1935, seeing service against the Chinese almost at once. It was phased out during the first year of Japan's participation in WWII, but not before it had seen occasional service in the new and unintended role of dive-bomber.

DC-2 A twin-motor Douglas transport aircraft used by the United States in that form and also as a bomber development known as the B-18. This first entered service with the USAAC in 1936, some also being operated during WWII by the Royal Canadian Air Force. The type was also licence-built in the Soviet Union as the Li-2 (q.v.).

DC-3 See C-47.

DC-4 See C-54.

DCON The abbreviation for the 1990s UK Regional Air Operations Centre Duty Controller (Duty Controller, Operations North). See UKADR.

Death ray A secondary field of investigation carried out in parallel with the first serious investigations into radar in Great Britain during 1934 based on the principle of the harmful effects of an electromagnetic field. Trials said to have been carried out by the Royal Navy were not successful. See Radar.

Decca Examples of the operational Decca 72 Doppler radar are included in the avionics installed in, for example, the British Aerospace Harrier and the Panavia Tornado.

Decoy airfields and targets Areas laid out to represent nearby airfields and act as decoy targets for bombers. Many of these included dummy aircraft, flarepaths etc in addition to buildings. Electric power came from a generator manned by a corporal and aircraftman in a deep bunker and 'runways' ran across hedges and open ditches in the hope of snagging any enemy attempting to land, while trees were cut to about 4ft in height for the same purpose. Decoy targets in WWII could take the form of deliberately lit fires designed to attract raiders' bombs, particularly at night.

Defence White Paper That published in Great Britain in 1957 was of particular significance since it envisaged a relatively speedy run-down of the country's defences over the coming five years and placing an increasing reliance on the United States, despite the fact that, at the time, the American system of warning was different from its British counterpart with the result that mutual employment was not immediately possible. In addition, much consternation centred about the fact that the Paper marked the expectation that manned military aircraft would vanish from operational use with relative swiftness and that, in their stead, missiles would be used, so that manned aircraft such as the English Electric Lightning and the bombers which were its contemporaries would be the last to see service. The result of so many ill-founded conclusions was that enormous sums spent on development before the new policy were never really recouped and the harmful effects on several parts of the British military aircraft industry were more or less permanent.

Defender The military version of the Britten-Norman Islander, equipped with underwing strong points for offensive stores to enable it to be used for counter-insurgency work and ground attack. The aircraft can also drop parachutists or be employed as a light troop transport, for medevac work and for 'sky-shouting'.

Defoliation Also called 'defoliantization'. The chemical stripping of trees of foliage with a view to denying an enemy shelter or cover. Although this form of aerial warfare is commonly associated with the United States, it was first undertaken by the RAF using Auster aircraft and Dragonfly helicopters over Malaya in 1950. Later, during 1962–70 in Vietnam, the USAF sprayed vast areas of the terrain with Agent Orange, a chemical made from a mixture of dichlorophenoxacetic and trichlonophenoxyacetic acids, about fifty million gallons being used. It is said to have created many new plant mutations as well as, from its half-life survival in human tissue, causing cancers, abortions and malformations among both the enemy and the chemical's users.

Degaussing ring A magnetically energized ring measuring 49ft 9in in diameter, fitted in Britain to Wellington bombers and in Germany to Junkers Ju 52/3ms to sweep by detonation magnetic sea mines. Known by the codename 'DW 1' (Directional Wireless 1) to the RAF and conceived by Lt-Cdr A. S. Bolt RN, the device was first tested in P2518 during January 1940, flown by

Sqn Ldr H. A. I. Purvis. With the ring energized at first by a Ford V8 car engine, the aircraft had to be flown without a magnetic compass at very low level. Twelve Wellingtons were subsequently modified by the Rollason Aircraft Co. of Croydon Airport, Surrey, in 'D' hangar as late as 1942. Later versions had their rings energized with the aid of 900kW generators producing a current of 500v which were driven by de Havilland Gipsy Six aero-motors, while the coils within the rings were of increased turns of thinner aluminium strip, so that the installation was greatly lightened. These aircraft were designated DW1 Mk II.

De Havilland A British aircraft company founded by Captain Sir Geoffrey de Havilland, who was responsible for such WWI military types as the Airco D.H.1, D.H.2, D.H.4, D.H.5, D.H.6, D.H.9, D.H.9A and D.H.10. Foremost of the de Havilland types produced during WWII, and an aircraft which also saw service with a vast number of other countries, was the wooden Mosquito, which ran to many variants used for reconnaissance and bombing and as fighters. The name Tsetse was proposed, but not adopted, for the Mk XVIII multi-role Coastal Command fighter. Later came the Hornet, said to be the fastest piston-engine machine in the world. Post-war departures into the field of jet-propelled military aircraft produced the Vampire series, including the Sea Vampire and the associated Venom (which also includ-

ed a naval version). The Sea Vixen followed, the second production version of this aircraft being exhibited at Farnborough in 1957 with its armament of four 30mm Aden guns augmented by four de Havilland Firestreak guided missiles, these marking a new line of production for the organization. De Havilland were absorbed into the Hawker Siddeley Group in 1964.

De Havilland Canada Formed in 1947 from the former de Havilland assembly plant, this company was responsible, after the design and production of the successful DHC-1 Chipmunk trainer, for such types as the DHC-2 Beaver, DHC-3 Otter, DHC-4 Caribou and DHC-5 Buffalo, all of which had military utility. The organization was purchased by the Canadian Government in 1972.

Depth charge Conventional naval depth charges, fitted with tail fins etc, were used against submarines from a very early period of military aviation, but until the late summer of 1942 they suffered from the fact that they had to be set to detonate far below a target, which would be submerging after being spotted by an aircraft. At this time charges began to be fitted with shallow-firing pistols which detonated around a submarine in the act of diving instead of below it. Coupled with the introduction of Torpex fillings, attacks with depth charges resulted in an increased number of successes henceforth.

Above: Wellingtons such as HX682 seen here were fitted with a magnetically-energized de-gaussing ring, an early method of dealing with magnetic sea mines introduced in 1940. Later, German Ju 52/3ms were similarly fitted. (Bruce Robertson collection)

British Aircraft Depth Charges in WWII

Type	Total wt Filling	Length x diameter
Mk VII	450lb Amatol	63in x 18in
Mk VIII	250lb Amatol	39in x 11in 1941
Mk XI	272lb Torpex	55in x 11in 1942

The final weapon, re-designated the Mk 11, was still in use by helicopters during the Falklands War, following which it began to be replaced by homing ordnance.

Destroyer Classification introduced in WWII in Germany for aircraft that would at once be long-range, twin-engine fighters and have the performance of single-motor interceptors. To see production and service use in this Zerstörer category was the Messerschmitt Bf 110, Bf 210 and Bf 410, The first Zerstörergeschwader was formed in 1938 with the Bf 110.

Deterrent The concept after WWII that the use of nuclear weapons, usually delivered by aircraft or missile, would inflict an unacceptable degree of damage on an aggressor if used in a retaliatory attack.

Detling An RAF station in Kent established in 1915 for Home Defence use, serving chiefly as an Auxiliary Air Force and Coastal Command base between the wars and participating after the Battle of Britain as a fighter station responsible for some of the Rhubarb attacks over occupied France. The station was reduced to Care and Maintenance status on 1 January 1945. The first occasion it had been relegated in this manner had been in December 1920, when it reverted to agricultural land following brief use by the RNAS and the RFC, the latter employing it as a landing ground for Sopwith Camels of No 143 Squadron attempting night interception, and it was not until the promotion of the RAF Expansion Schemes between the world wars that it was again used as an airfield. The general public probably first became aware of its existence as a result of its participation in the 1939 Empire Air Day display, when a crowd

numbering 15,000 attended, the principal attraction being the Avro Ansons with which 'Kent's own' No 500 Squadron had been equipped, sporting a newly acquired coat of 'shadow shading' (as disruptive camouflage was called at the time).

Dewoitine A French aircraft manufacturer flourishing between 1923 and 1941, responsible for the design and construction of two significant service fighters, the D.510 and the D.520. The first of these in one form or another was flown by both the newly-independent Armée de l'Air from 1 July 1935 and the French Navy. Turkey, Lithuania, China, Japan, the Soviet Union and Spain all flew the type, some examples of which remained in use until well after its rather primitive appearance with a large, faired, fixed undercarriage marked it as being obsolete and the D.520 was in use at home. This latter, a potential rival of the contemporary Hurricane and Spitfire, was altogether excellent but unfortunately available in only limited numbers in May and June 1940.

DFS The initials of Deutsches Forschungsinstitut für Segelflug, the German Gliding Research Institute. It was employed throughout WWII in an increasing number of investigative programmes, one of these culminating in the high-altitude DFS 54 and the rocket-propelled DFS 228, ultimately intended for reconnaissance (q.v.) in the manner of the Lockheed U-2 of later years. The DFS 230, originally developed for meteorological research, was pressed into service as a troop and cargo glider whose forward movement could be assisted by a group of three specially developed rockets delivering 1,202lb, 1,650lb or 2,205lb thrust according to type. Production was completed in 1941.

Although undeservedly forgotten, this Hans Jacobs-designed type is of significance in the history of air warfare in that it was used to carry out the first assault by glider-borne troops in history, the capture during WWII of the Belgian fort of Eben-Emael on 10 May 1940. The first version was flight-tested by the diminutive and lightweight Flugkapitän Hanna Reitsch (q.v.), the tug on this occasion being a Junkers Ju 52/3m.

In 1937, after trials in which the design was tested with progressively heavier loads, culminating in one of equivalent weight to eight fully armed troops, it was demonstrated to a group of senior officers with troops being disembarked after a series of towing displays, the result being the placing of an immediate production order for DFS 230As. The next significant design was the DFS 331 cargo glider, which existed only in prototype form, followed by the research DFS 332. See Troop Gliders.

DFW Joint companies trading as Deutsche Flugzeug Werke produced the DFW C.V reconnaissance, artillery cooperation and infantry contact aircraft towards the end of 1916, which proved so successful that examples were still in service on the Italian Front up to the end of 1918. Although of independent design, it owed much to the Albatros two-seaters.

DIANE The abbreviation for Digital Integrated Attack Navigation Equipment, a combination of two radar systems, the Norden APQ-92 search set and the APQ-88 for target tracking, plus an APN-141 for terrain-following in addition to inertial and Doppler navigational systems, the whole linked to a flight control system and a Litton ASQ-61 digital computer. Thus equipped, an aircraft can fly over any terrain by night or day, deliver an attack and return to base without any crew intervention or guidance or outside visual reference. See Intruder, Radar.

'Dick' Little known is the fact that Japan briefly operated twenty examples of the Seversky 2PA-B3, a two-seat fighter known as the Navy Type S, or A8V1 and code-named as stated by the Allies during WWII. By this time, however, the type had been withdrawn from service after being flown throughout the closing period of the war against China.

Digibus An alphanumeric multiplex link system for the HUD and laser rangefinders of an aircraft's avionics system.

'Dinah' The Allied code-name for the Japanese Mitsubishi Ki-46, a very cleanly designed two-seat reconnaissance aircraft of WWII which was also available for use as an interceptor and ground-attack fighter. Also designated Army Type 100 Command Reconnaissance Plane Model 3, a small number saw service with the Japanese Navy and were regularly operated over northern Australia from bases in Timor. The aircraft was also to attract the attention of the Germans, who attempted to negotiate a manufacturing licence for the type.

Dinort An extension rod fitted to the nose of a free-fall bomb to detonate it just above ground level and thus maximize the blast effect. German.

Dirigible A steerable lighter-than-air vehicle, of either rigid or non-rigid type. Airships of this kind were used, chiefly for coastal patrol, by the Royal Navy during WWI and by the US Navy from 1915 into WWII. The former service adopted rigid airships with the R.9 at the end of 1916, and this type of vessel continued to be used after the end of hostilities, and, with the Admiralty abandoning airships in December 1919, the survivors of the fleet were passed to the RAF in much the same way as Army airships were passed to the RNAS in November 1913. German military airships were used by both the Army and the Navy during WWI, wooden-framed rigids of Schütte-Lanz design and metal-framed Zeppelins. See Parasite.

Dive bomber An aircraft which delivered its load at the end of a dive, thus pin-pointing a specific target. In this way accuracy against a small target such as a ship was increased since judgements concerning speed and wind, necessary for conventional bombing, were eliminated. Although the use of Sopwith Camels is reported by the RAF in Russia during 1919 for this work, the first true dive bombers were the US Navy Curtiss and Boeing fighter-bombers used from 1929, and it was a demonstration seen by Ernst Udet of Curtiss Helldivers at Cleveland, Ohio, that resulted in an order during 1933 for the German Ju 87 'Stuka' series, the progenitor of which was the Swedish-built Junkers K47 of 1928. Backed by propaganda, the dive bomber was seen before and during the opening months of WWII as

the ultimate weapon, against which no adequate defence existed, but the attempt to repeat the success the Ju 87 had enjoyed in Europe during the Battle of Britain proved them to be vulnerable against disciplined opposition. Meanwhile the Royal Navy operated its Blackburn Skuas, which had dive bombing potential, and the Hawker Henley was at first conceived for this role, as was, in the United States, the Vultee Vengeance of 1942. In Germany the belief in dive bombers persisted throughout WWII, and the Junkers Ju 88 and even the Heinkel He 177 were expected to have this capability.

'Diver' The Allied code-name for the German FZG-76. See Flying Bombs, Observer Corps.

DN-1 The designation (Dirigible, Navy, No. 1) for the USS *Connecticut* non-rigid airship delivered in December 1916. Later known as 'A-type'.

'Doc' The Allied code-name for the Messerschmitt Bf 110 erroneously believed to have been adopted for use by the Japanese Navy.

'Dodge' The code-name for the operation to repatriate released prisoners-of-war to the United Kingdom during 1945–46, converted Stirling bombers being among the aircraft used.

Dogfight A term first used during WWI but remaining in vogue during WWII to describe a daylight aerial battle between numbers of aircraft, particularly after formations had been broken up and there was a tendency for individual combats to emerge.

'Domino' The method used to jam German Y-Verfahren (q.v.) navigational radio beams. See 'Benito'.

Doodlebug (1) The name for the first McDonnell design. Produced in 1929, it was biplane with a 110hp Warner radial engine and a very low stalling speed by virtue of being fitted with flaps and slotted leading edges to the wings. (2) The popular name for the WWII German FZG-76 (V-1) flying bomb. It was coined by pilots of a New Zealand fighter squadron who claimed that the note emitted by the weapon was similar to the buzz of the harm-

less insect of that name resident in their homeland. See Flying Bombs.

Doppler A type of airborne radar (q.v.) used to determine information on moving objects. Unlike pulse radar, which emits intermittent signals, those of Doppler radar are sent out in a continuous stream at a constant frequency. When this signal is reflected by a moving object, the return frequency is higher if the target is moving towards the transmitter and lower if the object is moving away.

'Doris' The Allied code-name for the Mitsubishi B-97 medium bomber, a type which was unknown at the time the name was awarded but was nevertheless believed to exist. In fact it never existed. It should not be confused with the Japanese aircraft code-named 'Sally', which, although being in fact the Mitsubishi Ki-21 (at one time code-named 'Jane') was described in WWII publications as the 'Mitsubishi OB-97'.

Dornier A German aircraft company formed by Claude Dornier in 1922 which at first concentrated on flying boats before graduating to airliners, one design for which was modified to become the Dornier 17 bomber on the formation of the Luftwaffe. Known in the early days of WWII as the 'Flying Pencil' from its slim fuselage, the Do 17 was followed into service by the Do 215 and 217, and the company was later responsible for the remarkable Dornier Do 335 tandem-motor fighter which did not enter service because of the end of hostilities. Military types produced since 1945 include the excellent Dornier 28 series which, although designed for civilian purposes, is used for liaison work by the present Luftwaffe and five of which were hastily converted for ground attack by the Katanganese Government against the Congolese during the rebellion of 1960-61. The name Dornier is also associated with the Zeppelin cantilever metal biplane designed to participate in the 1918 Fighter Evaluation when it was placed second to the winning Fokker D.VII. Known both as the Dornier D-1 and as the Zeppelin D-1, it made its first flight on 4 June 1918 and could be powered by a 160hp Mercedes, a

Above: The Dornier 17 existed in many forms, of which this, the Do 17P, was the photographic reconnaissance version introduced into the Luftwaffe in 1938 and equipped with continuous-strip cameras of types Rb 10/18, Rb 20/30 and Rb 50/30 in addition to a hand-held camera. (Author's collection)

195hp Benz IIIb or a 185hp BMW IIIb motor driving a 2.7m wooden airscrew. It also carried a drop tank under the fuselage and was armed with two fixed machine guns. The maximum speed was 124mph and, of the seven built, two were sent to the United States for evaluation by the Army and Navy.

Dornier 335 See Göppingen Gö 9.

Dornier 435 A staggered two-seat development of the above with a widened fuselage, powered by two 1,750hp Jumo 213s. Length was increased by 13.7in and the wing area increased to 482 sq ft. Only a mock-up was built.

Dornier 635 A projected version of the Do 335 consisting of two such machines joined by a rectangular cen-tre-section and powered by four 1,800hp DB 603 motors. This long-range variant was never built.

Dornier MTC II This 1981 'mini tele-copter' relied on a coaxial, contra-rotating dual rotor for its lift and was unmanned, being an electronic equip-ment-carrying surveillance platform for Army or Navy use. With a two-hour duration, it was controlled at first via cable from a ground-based console and later by radio.

'Dot' The Allied code-name for the Japanese Yokosuka D4Y Naval Carrier Bomber Suisei (Comet). Largely forgot-ten is the fact that the type passed into the history of air warfare from its use in the final kamikaze attack off Okinawa on 15 August 1945 when eleven such aircraft were led by Admiral Ugaki. The type was also coded 'Judy', a name by which it is probably better known.

Douglas A United States aircraft man-ufacturer founded in 1920, soon com-ing to fame with the construction of its World Cruiser aircraft of 1924 and later for the design of the DC-2 and DC-3 (C-47) aircraft as well as a series of fighters and bombers during and after WWII, including the A-20 Havoc, A-26 Invader and A-4 Skyhawk. The organization merged with that of McDonnell in 1967 to become McDonnell Douglas.

Dover Three military aerodromes existed in the area, at Guston Road, at St Margaret's and on Swingate Downs. From the historical viewpoint the lat-ter pair are of significance, the first being one of the bases retained for aircraft to set alight petrol pumped on to the surface of the English Channel if a German invasion fleet had put to sea in 1940. A Westland Lysander was earmarked for the work in this case. It was from Swingate Downs that Nos 2, 3, 4 and 5 Squadrons RFC flew across the Channel to Amiens after the outbreak of WWI between 13 and 15 August 1914. Aircraft flown by this, the air contingent of the British Expedition-ary Force, were B.E.2As, B.E.8s and Blériot Monoplanes. A granite column now marks the spot.

Dr A WWI period German abbreviation of the designation 'Dreidecker' or tri-plane. The most famous German aircraft of the time to have this configuration was the Fokker Dr.I, often described as being a copy of the Sopwith Triplane although this is untrue. However, fourteen triplane designs from German and Austrian designers appeared following the inspection of a captured Sopwith in July 1917.

Draken (Dragon) The name for the Swedish Saab-35 double-delta fighter which first flew in October 1955. There were seven variants, some of which were to see service with the Danish and Finnish Air Forces in addition to that of Sweden. The armament comprised a pair of 30mm can-

Above: Douglas A-20 Havocs, of which this is an A-20G model, were fighter versions, distinguished by their 'solid' noses housing the armament. In service circa 1942, this was the most formidable version, having a devastating nose armament of four 20mm cannon, a dorsal turret and a heavier bomb load than that of its predecessors. (Bruce Robertson collection)

Above: A three-seat attack bomber resembling the Douglas Havoc, the A-26 (later B-26) Invader was first delivered in December 1943. It was one of the few types entirely designed, developed and delivered during WWII. Many remained with various arms thirty years later, being used in Korea and in Vietnam, for attacks on the Ho Chi Minh trail. This is A-26B 41-39144. (Bruce Robertson collection)

non and four Sidewinder air-to-air missiles.

Drone Remotely controlled, unmanned gunnery target aircraft, either specially constructed or adapted obsolete fighters.

Durandal A type of high-explosive anti-runway bomb used by some of the Western Allies. Also the name of a French jet of the 1950s.

Dzus A fastener consisting of a screw-type disc within a panel periphery. Closure is assured if the gate of the head is turned to line up with markings on the surrounding collar.

E- (1) German prefix of the WWI period indicating Eindecker or monoplane. It is perhaps more generally associated with the Fokker E.III, from the series which ran from E.I to E.V. The last-mentioned was a parasol-wing type later to be redesignated the Fokker D.VIII and sometimes called the 'flying razor' from its small frontal area and the subsequent difficulty in observing it head-on. (2) The British Air Ministry designation for aircraft specifications of an experimental nature. An example is that describing the Gloster E.28/39, issued for the first Allied turbojet aircraft to fly, the Gloster Whittle. (3) (E-Series) The designation for a single non-rigid USN airship adopted in 1920.

E-1B The Grumman Tracer, an airborne early warning aircraft based on the S-2 Tracker and C-1A Trader designs which made its first flight in March 1957. A high-wing monoplane with a dorsal-mounted, lozenge-shape radome, it was distinguished by having three fins, unlike the single fin and rudder of the earlier pair, and was capable of operating from carriers. Endurance was 7hr. Eighty-eight examples were delivered from February 1958 for use by the US Navy.

E-2A The Grumman E-2 Hawkeye began to replace the E-1B during 1965–66, and from this was developed the E-2A with its circular radome disc for operation from the larger carriers. The C-2 Greyhound was a COD (q.v.) development of the standard type. The initial flight of the prototype

took place in October 1960 and deliveries commenced four years later. Endurance was 8hr and the maximum speed 300mph.

E-3 Known as the Boeing Sentry, this jet Airborne Warning and Control System (AWACS, q.v.), based on the Boeing airliner concepts, is manned by a crew of seventeen and first flew in the form of a pair of development machines (EC-137Ds) in February 1972, two pre-production E-3As following in 1975. The first twenty-four aircraft subsequently delivered as E-3As were later modified to A-3B standard, while a final ten were E-3Cs. NATO was to receive eighteen of the type by April 1985, while Saudi Arabia took delivery of five, with CFM56 engines instead of TF33-PW100 turbofans, between August 1985 and March 1987.

E-4B Boeing Airborne National Command Post aircraft with a range of 6,000 miles, used by the US Air Force and based on the 747 airliner.

EA- (1) The designation used by the US Navy for electronics countermeasures aircraft. See ECM. (2) The abbreviation used by the RAF in both world wars for enemy aircraft.

EA-6B A four-seat, all-weather shipboard electronic countermeasures aircraft for the US Navy based on the Grumman A-6 Intruder. The prototype of the EA-6B (Prowler) first flew on 25 May 1968, being in turn developed from the two-seat EA-6A also used for electronic countermeasures, the chief change in the new version being a 40in 'stretch' in the forward fuselage to accommodate new crew members responsible for the operation of the electronics, much of which were stowed in external fuselage and wing pods fitted with small windmills to operate their own generators in much the same manner that fuel pumps were powered on aircraft of the WWI period. EA-6Bs were introduced into the Vietnam War by US Marine Corps Squadron VMCJ-2, flying in the vicinity of Da Nang, in July 1972. The type remained in service over the battle zone until the final withdrawal in 1975.

EAP Experimental Aircraft Programme. A British Aerospace project of the 1980s designed to bring together all important new technologies and integrate them into a single high-performance warplane. Production of the greater part of the airframe was by British Aerospace, although some parts, including the port wing and some control surfaces, were contributed by Aeritalia and West Germany's MBB while the power unit came from Turbo-Union, an international consortium comprising Rolls-Royce, Motoren und Turbinen-Union (MTU) of West Germany and Fiat.

Eastchurch A historic military aerodrome in Kent which offered flying instruction for naval officers as early as November 1910 and before WWI came under Admiralty control as HMS *Pembroke II*. It served as the base for a variety of naval aircraft throughout the following conflict, being used for, among other duties, the attempted interception of enemy raiders. After 1918 the 600-acre site was used by both services, although it remained primarily a naval station, and it became a base for No 59 Squadron's Bristol Blenheims in 1940, following which it saw Fairey Battles and Spitfires until 1941, when it was taken over by Technical Training Command (which in fact made little use of it). The next claim to fame for the station came when its aircraft covered the actions over Dieppe in 1942, and it served as a base for rocket firing instruction in 1944. Eastchurch housed an Aircrew Reselection Centre in the closing months of WWII, and this work continued until August 1946, following which, after a period of Care and Maintenance by the RAF, the site was used as an open prison from 1950.

EC-121 The Lockheed Warning Star electronic reconnaissance, early warning and communications aircraft employed by the USAF, USN and Indian Navy in the civilian Constellation airframe. The type was also used as a transport and as the R70-1 from 1945, while the conventional camera-equipped surveillance variant was first used in 1962. That employed for electronic early warning patrols was equipped with ventral and vertical dor-

Above: The British Aerospace Experimental Aircraft Programme (EAP) demonstrator stands behind an example of its powerplant, the RB.199 turbofan. (BAe)

sal fairings for the housing of equipment, only one aircraft, a WV-2E appearing in 1957, being fitted with a large disc radome.

ECM See Electronic countermeasures.

Electronic countermeasures Techniques intended to minimize the result of an enemy's use of electronic tracking equipment and facilitating jamming and confusion in an enemy radar system by means of false echoes. See Chaff, Window. The term may also embrace the construction of aircraft to such a design as to minimize their electronic signatures, or from materials likely to do this. See Stealth.

'Edna' The Allied code-name for the Japanese Mansyu Ki-71, an experimental Army tactical reconnaissance type. This was an advanced version of the Mitsubishi Ki-51 ground-attack and tactical reconnaissance type, fitted with a more powerful motor, a retractable undercarriage and twin

20mm cannon in place of the 7.7mm guns of the original. Despite the seeming advantages that the redesigned aircraft offered, it was not put into production.

EF-111 The General Dynamics F-111 aircraft fitted with the Electrical Fox Tactical Jamming System (TJS) as well as ALQ-99 stand-off/escort jamming systems in the weapons bays and an internal ALQ-13 self-protection ECM system. See Electronic Countermeasures, F-111.

Ejection seats As the speed of military aircraft increased there was a decreasing chance of the pilot relying on his physical ability alone to bale out, so that it became clear that some type of mechanical assistance was called for. The first ejection seats fitted to a warplane were those of the Heinkel 219 Uhu (Owl) (q.v.), which entered service in April 1943, and at some unrecorded time between that date and the end of the war in Europe the first escape with

the aid of such a seat was made by the pilot of a Heinkel 280. This was quickly followed by a Swedish pilot escaping from a J.21R. The first ejection seat escape for which complete data is available was made on 24 July 1946 when an experimental ejection was made from a Gloster Meteor travelling at 320mph at an altitude of 8,000ft by Bernard Lynch. This was followed by others at up to 420mph and 30,000ft. The seat was a Martin-Baker, of a type which was fully in use by the RAF by 1954. It was succeeded by the Mk 4, adopted by twenty-eight nations, with which it was possible to eject from ground level with the aid of sensing equipment which delayed the opening of the main parachute until deceleration of the seat was recorded, when a Duplex drogue gun fired the static time release mechanism. Fully automatic 'zero-zero' seats were later evolved. The first US flyer to eject in an emergency, was Lt J. L. Fruin USN, who successfully did so at about 575mph from a McDonnell F2H-1

Banshee over South Carolina on 9 August 1949. NATO aircraft equipped with an ejection seat are marked with a red equilateral triangle beneath the cockpit edge.

EKA-3E The designation of the Douglas Skywarrior, an air refuelling tanker aircraft and electronic counter-measures platform capable of some 600mph and a range of 2,000 miles, used by the US Navy Reserve around 1980.

EL-73 The reported designation of the Panavia Tornado's EW system developed by AEG-Telefunken and Elettronica. It is reported to be an internally mounted jamming system.

EL/M-2001B Elta bombing and navigational equipment carried in the nose of the majority of IAI Kfirs, although some are reported to be equipped with the more advanced EL/M-2021, a system similar, but reportedly superior, to the Mirage III's Cyrano system.

ELAS The ELAS 106 electrical fuse, combined with the ENT 106 type (both chosen for their increased sensitivity), was fitted to later variants of the German FZG-76 flying bombs with increased range.

Elettronica Member of the electronics team which produced, under licence, the navigation and terrain-following radar system fitted to the Panavia Tornado. Other members of this European consortium are Ferranti, FIAR, Marconi and Siemens.

Elint Electronic intelligence on the location, volume, direction and type of electronic devices used by an enemy.
Elta See EL/M-2001B.

Embraer A joint aircraft manufacturer formed during 1969 in Brazil, the state holding 51 per cent and private enterprise 49 per cent, the full title being Empresa Brasileira de Aeronautica SA. The organization took over the government-sponsored CTA and was later responsible for the licence-production of the Aermacchi 326 military jet trainer and the indigenous Tucano light attack aircraft and trainer. The Tucano was accepted as a trainer by the RAF, first flying to this service's standard on 14 February 1986, following which the first Shorts-built variant flew on 30 December. Production versions from Belfast started to be delivered on 1 September 1988. The Tucano was also manufactured for the Kenyan Air Force, which placed an initial order for fifteen.

Emerson A manufacturer of light-weight radar, including the 140lb APQ-159 I/J-band target acquisition and tracking system. Capable of identifying targets at a maximum range of 23nm, this system is included among the avionics of the Northrop F-5E Tiger II used by the US Air Force and Navy plus the air forces of Brazil, Chile, Ethiopia, Indonesia, Iran, Jordan, Kenya, Malaysia, Mexico, Morocco, Saudi Arabia, Singapore, South Korea, Sudan, Switzerland, Taiwan, Thailand, Tunisia, and Yemen.

'Emily' The Allied code-name for the Japanese Kawanishi H8K Navy Type 2 four-motor flying boat, on the original of which design work was begun in 1938. This, the Type 1, was in service by the beginning of 1942 and is of interest in that its defensive armament included a 20mm cannon in the front and rear turrets. Further variants were the Type 3 and the transport version, the H8K2-L. One of the outstanding aircraft of WWII, the 'Emily' had a span some 12ft greater than that of the Short Sunderland. See Kawanishi.

Empire Air Armament School Originally based at RAF Manby, this was amalgamated with the Empire Flying School from Hullavington in June 1949 to become the Royal Air Force College.

England Geschwader The unofficial description of Kagohl 3, a German unit equipped with Gotha G.IV bombers for daylight and night attacks on British targets during WWI. Its first sortie was made against Folkestone on Friday 17 May 1917 using the six 110lb bombs per aircraft generally carried owing to the long distances that had to be flown, and a landing to refuel was customarily made near the Belgian coast before the final leg of the journey was embarked on. However, the delivery of a maximum bomb load of 1,100lb was possible. The first aircraft of the unit to be brought down was that destroyed from a formation of twenty-two attacking Sheerness. A total of 15.8 tons of bombs was dropped during the main attacks of 1917, resulting in 346 deaths and 866 injuries. The last major attack made by the unit was that of the night of 5–6 December 1917, by which time it had been redesignated Bombengeschwader OHL, abbreviated to Bogohl 3.

English Electric (later BAC) Canberra This aircraft is important in that it was the first jet bomber produced in Britain, and the first to be used by the RAF. The first prototype, VN799, flew on 19 May 1949 when it was seen as a two-seat radar bomber, but after the construction of a fifth prototype, XV165, it was to enter service as the three-seat B.2 with No 101 Squadron, replacing Avro Lincolns. Large orders were subsequently placed, some Canberras being exported to Australia, Rhodesia and Venezuela, while in the United States it was produced as the Martin B-57. The next variant was the B.5 for target-marking, but only the prototype VX185 was built before the B.6 appeared with more powerful motors and wing fuel tanks in 1954, and from this resulted the B(I).6 intruder for the 2nd Tactical Air Force with a gun-pack in the bomb bay and underwing pylons. This was followed in 1956 by the ground-attack B(I).8, identified by an off set crew canopy; this mark was exported to Peru, Venezuela and New Zealand, the last designating it the B(I).12. Rocket-armed B.6s for the RAF were introduced as the B.15 and 16, differing only in their avionics, while India received some 66 B(I).8s there known as B(I).58 models. Other overseas users were the RAAF, operating B.20s largely with Australian Avon 109 motors. Later from the Martin B-57B with its fixed wing-guns and rotating bomb doors, and the dual-control B-57Cs were evolved the high altitude reconnaissance RB-57D and RB-57E bombers and target tugs. In the RAF reconnaissance versions of the Canberra ran between the PR.3 and PR.9, typical being the PR.7 with six 36in F.52 cameras and a vertical 6in F.49, or alternatively four 20in F.52s and a 6in F.49.

Above: Canberra B.20 A84-227 of the Royal Australian Air Force. (Author's collection)

English Electric (later BAC) Lightning
The first British-designed aircraft capable of Mach 2 Its introduction and early service career were surrounded by strong security measures. One of the world's outstanding fighters, it was based on the P.1A that first flew on 4 August 1954. No 74 Squadron RAF received the first production examples (F.1) in 1960, and these were followed by F.1As fitted for flight refuelling and the F.2 and F.3 which introduced the square-topped fin. On 17 April 1964 the first Mk 6 flew, being a developed Mk 3 with reduced sweep to the outer wings and a ventral fuel and weapons pack plus overwing fuel tanks. There followed operational trainer versions, the T.4 and T.5, with side-by-side cockpit seats. Export variants were sold to Saudi Arabia and

Above: The English Electric Lightning, entering service in 1960, brought to the RAF and later such overseas forces as that of Saudi Arabia the ability to intercept in all weathers coupled with supersonic performance. This is XS894/'F', an example of the final F.6 version, flown by No 5 Squadron in 1968. (Bruce Robertson collection)

Kuwait. The standard armament of combat versions consisted of twin Aden 30mm cannon, (none on the F.3 variant) plus two Firestreak or Red Top missiles or forty-four 2in rockets according to the mission pack, and externally stowed 1,000lb HE, retard or incendiary bombs, with provision for eighteen 68mm rockets.

Enigma A German cypher machine in use during WWII, breaking ('Ultra') the codes of which gave the British fore-knowledge of enemy plans to assist in countering attacks.

ENT See ELAS.

Ericson The Ericson UAP 1023 (PS-46/A) radar is an advanced pulse-Doppler set with a range in excess of 26 miles in look-down mode operated on medium-PRF transmissions. Low-PRF transmissions are used for look-up operation. It has been fitted to the Saab JA37 Viggen fighter.

Erprobungsgruppe The term used in the Luftwaffe of WWII for a unit charged with the operational evaluation of an aircraft type. Thus Test Group 210 was allegedly formed to look into the matter of Messerschmitt Me 210 evaluation. Experimental groups of this nature nevertheless made operational sorties, and Erp 210, for example, equipped with Messerschmitt Bf 109s and 110s, was responsible for the raid on Croydon Aerodrome at 1855 hours on 15 August 1940, losing its commander, Swiss-born Hpt Walter Rubensdorffer, in the attack.

Erprobungsstelle German term for experimental station such as established at Rechlin in 1934.

Escadrille The title given to a French fighting unit subordinate to a Groupe and Escadre and approximating to an RAF squadron. An Escadre took the same place in the chain of command occupied before 1 April 1933 by a regiment.

Etendard A Dassault-Breguet design, the Etendard IV was accepted by the Aéronavale (French Naval Air Arm) for service aboard the aircraft carriers *Clémenceau* and *Foch*, and these were replaced by a redesign, the Super Etendard, the first equipping Flottille 11F aboard *Foch* from 4 December 1978. The first order for the type from abroad was for fourteen to be operated from the Argentine carrier *25 de Mayo*, and these were to see service in the Falklands War. Others later went to Iraq on lease for use against Iran during 1983, their first sortie being against the Kharg Island oil terminal on 28 March that year.

Etrich A German aircraft designer who produced his first machine in 1909. This and those which followed had a characteristic bird-like outline in plan view so that they were quickly dubbed Tauben (Doves). A military two-seater of this type was produced by Rumpler in 1912, and a number were in service at the outbreak of WWI two years later, when the type quickly proved its value as a reconnaissance machine and for bombing, Paris being among the earliest targets. Dr Etrich's design began to be copied by a large number of manufacturers after his break with the Rumpler company, so that the name 'Taube' became for a time synonymous with 'enemy aircraft', but, undemanding a machine as it was to fly, its military potential was limited since its manoeuvrability was limited, so much so that Etrich's Tauben were decreasingly encountered by the spring of 1915. It was flown without armament except for any rifles, duck-guns or side-arms the crew happened to carry.

Euler A German manufacturer of military aircraft with works at Frankfurt from the outbreak of WWI. Its first designs, such as the B.I, with its tricycle landing gear, and the B.II, seemingly copied from LVG, met with little success so that the firm soon began construction of the Rumpler Tauben, although later a trainer was built under licence from LVG and a whole series of experimental and fighter aircraft were produced either in prototype form alone or in limited numbers. Among these was a copy of the French Nieuport 11C (Euler was one of several firms requested by the government to explore this field), three triplanes and a so-called quadruplane, although the horizontal surfaces of the latter were in fact full-span ailerons.

European Fighter Aircraft (EFA) (Eurofighter 2000) A fighter designed and produced by the aircraft industries of Great Britain, Germany, Spain and Italy at a cost estimated at the beginning of January 1990 to be £22bn, at which time it was also announced that the production of 800 aircraft was envisaged, 250 of these going to the RAF at a cost of about £8bn following the projected first flight of the prototype in 1997–98. The EFA would be among the most spectacular and advanced fighters ever seen with a manufacturing share-out analyzed as 33 per cent each British and German, 21 per cent Italian and 13 per cent Spanish. The maximum speed is stated to be in excess of Mach 1.8, equivalent to some 1,370mph, carrying air-to-air and air-to-ground guided weapons. Advanced avionics enable the pilot to have the initial advantage over an enemy and to have less exacting duties to perform. The distribution of airframe construction has been described as follows: rear fuselage, Spain and Italy; fuselage centre-section and vertical tail, Germany; canopy, foreplanes and nose-cone (containing Ferranti avionics), Britain; port wing, Italy; starboard wing, Britain. The outline specification of the EFA is: span 35ft 5in; length 47ft 7in; combat radius 290–345 miles; armament comprising internally mounted 27mm cannon, plus missiles, according to mission, mounted on fifteen external strongpoints. See EAP.

'Eva' The Allied code-name (also 'Eve') issued for the Japanese Mitsubishi Ohtori long-range communications aircraft. This was in fact civil, but was erroneously believed to be a bomber.

EWS The abbreviation for Early Warning System, radar to give advanced warning of intruding enemy aircraft likely to carry out an attack. One of the first aircraft fitted to carry out surveillance of this type was the Douglas EA-1 Skyraider. The concept of EWS has to some extent been replaced by that of AWACS (q.v.).

Executive Flight Detachment A joint Army and Navy unit for the air transportation of the President of the United States of America and other VIPs. A lesser-known, military responsibility of this Detachment is its retention for the emergency evacuation of key Washington personnel.

Exercises Known at one time in the United States as 'wargames', these are carried out at least annually by most of the world's major air forces to give experience to aircrews and personnel under simulated wartime conditions, the concept being based on that of traditional Army and Fleet manoeuvres. Since the end of WWII a tendency has emerged to conduct exercises involving groups of countries in a defence federation (for example, NATO) rather than arrange them on a national basis,

Exocet The much-publicized French-designed AM.39 anti-ship guided missile which first came into prominence in the Falklands War when it was employed in attacks on ships. After launching, a speed of some 700mph is reached in 2.5 seconds and guidance is designed on a basis of a two-axis radar which searches the horizontal plane only so that it skims about 50ft above the surface of the water with the aid of a radio altimeter and is thus more difficult to destroy than missiles which climb before losing height. The range and bearing of the target having been fed into the missile's memory before firing, its search radar takes over in the vicinity of the target and the missile locks on and penetrates the outer plating of a vessel before exploding the 364lb warhead. During the Falklands conflict Argentine Navy Super Etendards fitted with Thompson-CSF radar and Singer-Kearfott navigational and weapon-aiming systems tended to carry a single M39 under the starboard wing, balanced by a fuel tank on the opposite side.

'Exodus' The repatriation by air of former prisoners-of-war from the Continent to Britain after WWII, carried out in April, May and June 1945.

Expansion scheme Various expansion schemes for the RAF were launched between the two world wars, those designated 'C' and 'D' calling not only for new personnel but also for massive production contracts for interim aircraft from the industry. Expansion Scheme 'E', which finally caught the public's imagination, provided for increased training facilities, bringing the total number of Flying Training Schools to eleven in 1936. The Royal Air Force Volunteer Reserve was formed at the same time, providing 310 pilots by 1939 in addition to a vast number of new tradesmen.

Expeditionary Force – China A United States Marine Corps force assigned to China in 1927–28. Its VF-10M (VF-3M redesignated) flew nine of the ten new Boeing FB-1s which had been delivered between 1 and 22 December 1925.

Experimental Stealth – Tactical The full name for the XST project of the US Defense Advanced Research Projects Agency (DARPA) circa 1984 which resulted in entirely new military aircraft designs such as the F-117A Nighthawk. See Stealth.

F- (1) The role designation for fighters used as a prefix to the mark number for RAF aircraft and adopted in 1942. Thus Spitfire Mk XIVs became F.14s etc. Fighter-bombers were designated 'FB'. (2) A similar designation adopted by the US Air Force and US Navy in 1947, replacing the former 'P' (for 'Pursuit') used by the US Army Air Corps and Army Air Forces. (3) (F-Series) The US Navy designation for a single non-rigid airship adopted in 1920. See E-Series.

F2F A Grumman single-seat US Navy fighter. The F2F-1 was the US Navy's first carrier-based type to have a retractable undercarriage and enclosed cockpit, deliveries beginning in early 1935 to VF-2B on USS *Lexington*. The aircraft was powered by a 650hp Pratt and Whitney radial motor.

F-4 The McDonnell Douglas Phantom two-seat fleet defence intercepter developed for the USN and later adopted by the USAF as the F-4C, entering service in December 1960 and 1963 respectively. There followed the RF-4C reconnaissance version, the 'D' and 'E' models with progressively updated armament and avionics, and by the 'G' and 'J' variants with uprated engines. The Royal Navy later adopted the F-4K and the RAF the F-4M, both powered by Rolls-Royce RB.168 Speys. Other versions were widely exported including to West Germany, Iran, Japan, South Korea, Israel, Turkey, Spain and Egypt.

F4F The Grumman Wildcat carrier-based fighter of WWII. A single-seat monoplane ordered on 28 July 1936, the aircraft made its first flight on 2 September two years later, the first deliveries being made to VF-4 on USS *Ranger* and VF-7 on USS *Wasp* in 1940, the same year that the 81 examples ordered by France were taken over by the Royal Navy and given the name Martlet. The introduction of escort carriers by the United States promoted the development of the final FM-2 version of the design, this having a more powerful motor, a taller fin and rudder and a lightened airframe permitting operation from the shorter decks of the new vessels. Although having an inferior performance to the Japanese Zero, the Wildcat's rugged construction and heavier armament ensured that the two met on roughly equal terms.

F-5 The Northrop 'Freedom Fighter', of which the F-5A was a single-seater and the 'B' variant a twin-seat version. This US design first flew in July 1959 and variants were exported to Ethiopia, Greece, Iran, South Korea, South Vietnam, and Turkey, while Canadian CF-5A/Bs were purchased by the Netherlands as NF-5A/Bs and similar SF-5A/Bs were assembled in Spain.

F6F A Grumman design based on the F4F (q.v.), serving with both the US Navy and the Royal Navy as the Hellcat. The first operational use was by VF-5 flying from USS *Yorktown* on 31 August 1943, and the type was eventually credited with a total of 4,947 enemy aircraft destroyed. The F6F remained in service long enough to see action in the Korean War.

F-8 The US Navy's Ling-Temco-Vought Crusader first flew as the XF8U-1 on 25 March 1955 and was significant in being a supersonic carrier-borne fighter with a variable-incidence wing, the angle of which could be increased to reduce the landing speed without the aircraft assuming an exaggerated nose-up attitude. The first deliveries of F8U-1s (F-8As) were made to VF-32 aboard USS *Saratoga* in March 1957, and this mark was followed by the F8U-1E which boasted a limited all-weather capability. The final production version was the F-8E of 1961 which incorporated APQ-94 search and fire-control radar.

F-14 The Grumman F-14 Tomcat first flew in 1971 and was a variable-geometry, twin-seat air superiority fighter fitted with all-moving twin fins and rudders. Capable of a maximum speed of Mach 2.34 at height, it was difficult to stall with the wings fully forward, while with full sweep the angle of attack of the nose could be raised to 90° or depressed to 45°. Armed with Phoenix, Sparrow or Sidewinder missiles and carrying radar capable of simultaneously tracking a number of targets, the F-14 could be operated from ultra-short landing strips and also be catapult-launched from carriers.

F-15 The McDonnell Douglas F-15 Eagle single-seat air-superiority fighter was capable in its first form of reaching Mach 2.7 and first flew on 26 February 1979. The second major production version was the F-15C, the 444th airframe produced in 1980 seeing this variant and the two-seat F-15D begin to replace the earlier versions so that, by the beginning of 1980, 900 of an expected 1,488 examples had been delivered, including 392 dual-control F-15Es fitted from 1980 with Low Altitude Navigation and Targeting Infra-Red for Night (LANTIRN) equipment. Apart from those operated by the US Air Force, 47 F-15Cs and fifteen F-15Ds were exported to Saudi Arabia, while 173 F-15Fs were licence-built as F-15Js in Japan, which also purchased 187. Meanwhile Israel received 51 F-15A, B and C versions. The advent of the F-15E, which first flew on 11 December 1986, meant that the Eagle

was redesignated an air-to-air and air-to-ground fighter, for the former role retaining the 20mm six-barrel rotary cannon, plus a maximum of eight air-to-air missiles (AIM-7s and 9s or 120s), and for the attack role various bomb loads, combined with APG-70 radar, upgraded avionics and fly-by-wire control.

F-16 The basic concept of this small and agile General Dynamics fighter go back as far as 1972, when several US aircraft manufacturers were invited to submit proposals for lightweight fighters. After evaluation in competition with a similar design submitted by Northrop, the General Dynamics machine was selected, chiefly because large overseas markets seemed to be available. The initial example of the F-16 first flew in January 1974 and five months later the type was selected by a number of NATO countries – Belgium, Denmark, the Nether-

Above: The F-16, of which this is an early 'A' model in 'rear shadow finish', was described on its introduction in 1978 as 'a General Dynamics aircraft, small, lightweight, agile and difficult to see'. It represented the latest state of the art in aerodynamic structure, fire control systems and avionics, including multi-role Doppler radar with a 'look-down' capability. (Bruce Robertson collection)

lands and Norway – to replace their F-104 Lockheed Starfighters.

The technology incorporated in the design immediately showed in the aircraft's appearance, with the wings blended into the fuselage contours, thus, combined with the lift given by the swept strakes at each side of the nose, not only saving weight but increasing overall lift at high angles of attack and at the same time reducing drag at transonic speeds.

Similar care went into the cockpit and instrument panel layout so that pilot fatigue was reduced as well as offering an optimum outside view. Although first seen as a defensive air superiority fighter, the F-16 proved capable of speedy adaptation to ground-attack duties as a tactical fighter, although this meant that the original armament of AIM-9 missiles on wing-tip mountings had to be augmented by a wide variety of stores disposed about the airframe. Delivery of these was assisted by a good range of avionics, and the F-16 benefited also from a low radar signature and a high degree of manoeuvrability. It was not long before the F-16 attracted the attention of other potential purchasers abroad, including Australia, Canada, Iran, Israel and Turkey, although for political reasons not all of these placed orders.

The F-16's maximum speed with two Sidewinders (q.v.) was claimed to be Mach 1.95 at 36,000ft, fixed armament consisting of a General Electric 20mm multi-barrel cannon with 500 rounds (operating on the Gatling gun principle) in the port wing fairing.

F-18 The design of the McDonnell-Douglas Hornet strike fighter may be traced back to the Northrop YF-17, which is of interest since this was the type that alone rivalled the F-16 (q.v.) as a lightweight fighter. However, the US Navy called for a developed and heavier version of the YF-17. In point of fact the Navy's demand placed Northrop in something of a quandary since this company lacked experience in the design of maritime aircraft. A solution was found in the decision to make the Hornet a joint McDonnell-Douglas/Northrop project, the latter taking responsibility for a variant with a lowered tare weight, fixed wings, a lightened undercarriage and addition-

al stores provision while the former drew on its long experience in satisfying maritime aircraft demands for the navalised version.

The resultant Hornet flew for the first time on 15 November 1978, but so stringent were the design demands that the prototype was followed by no fewer than ten trials machines, these being used to incorporate structural modifications and the mass of changes deemed necessary as tests proceeded. Not that the F-18 fell short of expectations at any point in its trials: many of the changes called for arose from the Marine Corps' interest in the F-18 as a replacement for its F-4 (q.v.).

The influence of McDonnell became clearer as work progressed. The F-18 owed much to Northrop's P.530 Cobra project of 1960, but this was now interpreted in the light of the modern materials which were available and composites were used extensively throughout, metal being employed chiefly for the load-bearing areas.

Avionics equipment has been claimed to be the most advanced of any military aircraft in the world. Three multi-purpose displays in addition to a head-up display (HUD) for the pilot replaced much conventional instrumentation, and although the original air-to-air armament was a pair of Sidewinder (q.v.) missiles, there were finally twenty weapon combinations available, plus the capability to deliver tactical atomic weapons.

Early in the development of the F-18, interest was expressed by the air forces of Australia, Canada and Spain, which now operate the type.

F-22 A designation relating to the Lockheed Martin 645, a design for a tactical fighter, the proposals for which were invited in September 1985. Both Lockheed and Northrop eventually produced a pair of prototypes each (the YF-22 and the YF-23 respectively), and these were the subjects of ground-based avionics trials during 1990. Pratt & Whitney and General Electric engines were also the subject of an evaluation programme, begun in September 1983, and finally the first flights took place in May 1997 after some twelve months' delay–the result of no fewer than three consecutive budget cut-backs.

Meanwhile, in 1993 demands had to be met for equipment with air-to-ground armament with guided missiles, a call that meant a partial re-design of the types' weapons bay and the adoption of fresh avionics, while the US Navy also showed interest in the type being adapted as a maritime variant (the 'A/F-22X'), although this project was later abandoned. Simultaneously Lockheed announced plans to adapt the design as a two-seat naval strike/attack fighter.

The standard armament proposed for the F-22 included the long-barrelled M61A-2 20mm cannon with its hinged muzzle cover, 480 rounds of ammunition being carried in three internal weapons bays. In addition to these a wide variety of missiles was catered for, including AIM-9 Sidewinder in the main weapons bay and on external weapons racks.

Despite the lengthy gestation period which has marked the progress of the F-22, typical results encountered worldwide with modern aircraft, plans are formulated for the first 33 examples of the type to be delivered in November 2004; the last of a total procurement of 428 are expected eight years later.

F-47 See P-47.

F-51 See P-51.

F-80 The first US operational jet fighter, the Lockheed Shooting Star first flew in March 1946. Based on ideas laid dawn in 1941, it was revised in 1943 with the arrival of a British Whittle jet engine in the United States. By January 1945 a pair were operating under combat conditions in Italy, although it was not until the Korean War that F-80s saw service in numbers, the first claim of a MiG-15 being made on 8 November 1950.

F-84 The Republic Thunderjet first flew in prototype form in 1946, although a long delay followed before it entered service with a large number of NATO air forces. Developments included the F-84F Thunderstreak fighter and the RF-84F Thunderflash reconnaissance aircraft. The armament including twenty-four 5in rockets, while a nuclear capability and LABS (loop-bombing) were claimed for

Above: North American F-86 Sabres of No 459 Squadron Royal Canadian Air Force at the Coronation Review of Commonwealth air forces, Odiham, 1953. (N. W. Cruwys)

the former, which could make use of a RATO 4,000lb boost system fitted as a jettisonable collar under the fuselage.

F-86 The North American Sabre swept-wing fighter was among the most successful of the early US jets. It first flew in October 1947 and many hundreds were eventually ordered. In the Korean War the F-86E appeared with a powered 'flying tail' and the F-86F followed with an extended leading edge to the wings. Later the F-86D 'dog nose' Sabre entered service with the new concept of gunless collision-course interception directed by radar and autopilot.

F-100 The North American Super Sabre was first delivered in November 1953, a fighter-bomber variant with an uprated engine being produced later. Denmark, France, Nationalist China and Turkey all flew the type – an achievement for a design that had initially suffered problems with the inertia coupling between yaw and roll axes so that the wings and fin had to be lengthened.

F-104 The Lockheed F-104 Starfighter was a fighter, fighter-bomber, interceptor and multi-mission aircraft which first flew in February 1954. In Europe the more powerful F-104G was jointly produced by Belgium, West Germany, Italy and Holland for multi-mission duties. The Starfighter also saw service in Japan, Pakistan, Turkey and Canada, and Italy later adopted the even more powerful F-104S variant.

F-105 The Republic F-105 Thunderchief supersonic fighter first flew on 22 October 1955, and production versions, chiefly of the F-105D variant, were to see much service in the Vietnam War. It was the largest single-seat combat aircraft in history, hence its popular name – 'the Thud'. A small number were updated to 'T-stick II' standard with a large dorsal fairing from cockpit to fin, and about 30 were converted to twin-seat configuration with Wild Weasel radar, Westinghouse jammers and external Goodyear chaff pods.

F-111 The world's first variable-geometry warplane, this General Dynamics design was at first plagued with design problems, chiefly with the engines and intakes. The F-111D had simplified avionics, while the F-111K version was

due to be supplied to the RAF after the cancellation of the TSR-2 programme (although in the event it never materialized). All versions had an ejectable crew module. The fighter version also saw service with the Royal Australian Air Force, and a bomber variant, the FB-111A was produced for the US Strategic Air Command. See EF-111.

F-117 See Stealth.

FAA Although Britain's naval air arm had been widely known as the Fleet Air Arm at least since 1924 when the title indicated the Fleet Air Arm of the Royal Air Force, the Admiralty did not have direct control over sea-going aircraft, and such strange arrangements existed as that whereby aircraft were maintained by RAF fitters and riggers, piloted by a member of the RAF and crewed by a RN officer observer plus a naval rating as the air gunner. Meanwhile the Admiralty continued to make strenuous efforts to regain control of its air arm.

By 1935 many regarded the political position evolving in Europe as certain to lead to another war, and the latest attempt by the Navy to gain control of the Fleet Air Arm was this time led by the First Sea Lord, Admiral Chatfield. As had happened in the past, the question went to arbitration, but the result on this occasion was a report issued to the Cabinet by Sir Thomas Inskip in July 1937 which recommended that the Admiralty should henceforth have full control of the FAA (which would be known as the Air Branch of the Royal Navy but unofficially continue to be called by the long-applied name). This was accepted, and an announcement in the House of Commons stated that the change would take place within two years, that all personnel would be naval and that the Admiralty would have its own shore stations for the first time since the days of the old RNAS, the first of these being Donibristle, Eastleigh, Evanton, Ford, Hatston, Lee-on-Solent, St Merryn and Worthy Down.

Organization and training had to some extent to be re-created and occasionally whole stations had to be constructed, so that to assist in the mammoth task a post for a Fifth Sea Lord with full responsibility for naval matters was created. Meanwhile the strength of the service stood at a little over 217 aircraft in fifteen squadrons, although this was an improvement on

the figures for January 1924 when the new *Hermes* and converted *Eagle* carriers had been commissioned, the aircraft strength then being a mere 78 machines in thirteen Flights. Clearly the task of, in effect, creating a new service was impossible to complete in the two years left before the outbreak of WWII, but great advances were made and on 3 September 1939 a strength of 500 machines had been reached.

The quiet period of the 'Phoney War' that had been utilized for training abruptly ended on 10 April 1940 when the Germans invaded Norway, and HMS *Furious*, with two squadrons of Swordfish, accompanied the Home Fleet into Norwegian waters. However, vast numbers of the enemy, snow and fog forced a British withdrawal, which was covered by the FAA. Soon the Battle of Britain loomed, and a number of naval pilot volunteers were temporarily attached the RAF.

The next action to focus public attention of the FAA was the successful attack on the Italian Fleet in Taranto harbour. This, carried out by Swordfish aircraft, changed the course of the war when Cdr Kiggell with observer Janvrin dropped the first flares while his assistant Charles Lamb

saw over 1,000 shells explode round the first machine.

Subsequent actions in which the FAA participated included Operation 'Torch' in 1942, the Salerno landings a year later and of course Operation 'Overlord'; but there was still work for the nine-year old FAA in other theatres of war, and in November 1944 the British Pacific Fleet was formed, its four armoured carriers now equipped with Corsairs, Hellcats, Avengers and Fireflies, all monoplanes in contrast with the biplanes with which the service had entered the war. The targets for the new aircraft were different, too, and included the oil refineries in Sumatra and the installations at Palembang.

It was during the contraction of the service after 1945 that the first Hawker Sea Furies were adopted as strike fighters in 1947, a year after the name 'Fleet Air Arm' was officially replaced by 'Naval Aviation', and soon aircraft of the Royal Navy were involved in fighting terrorists in Malaya. This was followed by the Korean War that lasted until 1953, when the title 'Fleet Air Arm' was officially re-adopted.

Fighting was to break about once more with the Suez Crisis, which saw

Above: Obsolete when WWII started, having been based on a design originating from six years earlier, the open-cockpit Swordfish biplane offered only hardship to its crew. It nevertheless outlived its replacements, taking part in the attack on Taranto and the sinking of the *Bismarck* among other actions. (P. A. Cooksley)

the first use of the angled deck and mirror landing sights, steam catapults and a new type of arrester gear, and the first operational use of the radar-equipped all-weather Sea Venom fighter and Whirlwind helicopter, the latter type fitted with 'dipping sonar' as submarine hunters. Soon swept-wing fighters were adopted in the form of Supermarine Scimitars, as were Sea Vixens equipped with such guided weapons as Firestreak, and Wessex helicopters for general duties.

The closing years of the 1960s found the Fleet Air Arm with Mach 2 McDonnell Douglas Phantoms, Buccaneers and AEW Gannets soon to be joined by Westland Sea Kings and Lynx helicopters. During the Falklands conflict of 1982 the Sea Harrier VSTOL aircraft operated with distinction,

aided by ski-jump take-off ramps. A new chapter had opened for the Fleet Air Arm of the Royal Navy.

'Fagot' The NATO code-name for the Soviet MiG-15, the prototype of which first flew on 2 July 1947, production machines being powered by an RD-45, a virtual copy of the Rolls-Royce Nene. Produced under licence by Poland and Czechoslovakia, the type also served with the air forces of Bulgaria, China, Hungary, North Korea and Romania.

Fairchild A US aircraft manufacturer which sprang from the Kreider-Reisner organization in 1930. At first it tended to be associated with light aircraft pressed into military service, the Fairchild Argus (otherwise the F-24) and the Cornell trainer being two

examples associated with WWII, but the adoption by the US Air Force in 1950 of the C-119 tactical troop and cargo transport with its distinctive twin-boom configuration marked a step forward for the organization's output. This type served also with Marine units in Korea, designated the R4Q Packet.

Fairey A British manufacturer of military aircraft, known for the Fairey Battle bomber with which the RAF's AASF went to France in 1939. Subsequent types included the Fulmar two-seat fighter, which re-established the company's association with the Royal Navy, enjoyed during the interwar years by the Fairey Flycatcher fleet fighter, IIID and F, Seal and of course Swordfish. This association was con-

FLYING BOMB

There was nothing new in the idea of a flying bomb – experiments in unmanned flight may be traced back to those conducted by Sir Hiram Maxim in 1891 – but the application of the principle to an offensive weapon was first made during WWI by Professor A. M. Low, who was asked to develop a radio-controlled aeroplane for attacks against heavily defended targets. It quickly became known at the 'AT', indicating 'Aerial Target', a title designed to hide its real purpose. The result was a shoulder-wing monoplane powered by an uncowled 50hp Gnome rotary motor, but this interfered so greatly with the radio guidance system that the project was abandoned in October 1916 after perhaps six had been assembled.

A new flying bomb was developed at Farnborough during the following year, jointly designed by Geoffrey de Havilland and H. P. Folland, powered by a 35hp horizontally opposed engine and made from low-grade materials. However, its début in March was inauspicious as it lacked any certain lateral control, and nothing more was heard of the idea of a flying bomb in England until one was produced by the Sopwith company. Once more powered by a 35hp motor, this was a biplane, but it was so damaged during erection at Feltham that work was discontinued.

Meanwhile, similar trials had been conducted in the United States, where in 1916 the Curtiss-built Hewitt-Sperry radio-controlled biplane, fitted with a 300lb warhead, was claimed to be capable of a range of 50

miles with the aid of its 40hp motor. It was also in America that there appeared, two years later, the nearest concept to the German V-I, the Kettering Aerial Torpedo, which had an all-up weight of 530lb, including a 180lb warhead and a range only slightly less than that of the Curtiss.

In Britain, experiments with the radio control thought indispensable for such weapons continued after the Armistice of 1918, and two years later a standard Bristol F.2B flew under radio control at Farnborough, although a human pilot was aboard as a precaution against the device running amok. Seven years were to pass before the lessons learned in these trials were put to practical use in a properly designed flying bomb. Known as the Larynx, this was fitted with the equivalent of a warhead weighing 250lb and proved its ability when set to fly an accurate course off Devon, Cornwall and Somerset. Five were built and sent for operational tests with No 84 Squadron RAF at their base at Shaibah, Iraq. Of this set, one was lost in launching, three came to premature ends owing to problems with engines and fuel systems and the final one was seemingly launched without trouble but was afterwards lost without trace.

With experiments such as these so much to the fore, it is surprising that in Germany proposals for a flying bomb made to the Reichsluftfahrtministerium by Paul Schmidt in 1934 were at first snubbed, but a generous grant was quickly forthcoming for the development of a pulse-jet motor for use with such a weapon, and as a result Britain was quite aware of the strenuous efforts to produce a reliable flying bomb made by Nazi Germany

as early as October 1939 – before, let it be said, official sanction was given by the RLM scientific committee on 19 June 1942 to accord the development programme for such a weapon the highest priority. The overall responsibility for the coordination of the project fell to Fieseler Werke of Kassel, with the result that the world's first operational flying bomb – which would become popularly known by its propaganda description 'V-1' (Vergeltungswaffe Eins, or First Revenge Weapon) – was officially designated the Fieseler Fi 103, or, in an attempt to confuse Allied Intelligence, Flakzielgerät (anti-aircraft target apparatus), a deception conceived along the same lines as the old British 'AT' ruse. Not unnaturally, the German experimental station at Peenemünde was chosen for the development of the new device, it being here that on Christmas Eve 1942 the first launch of a powered flying bomb was made after some weeks of test-drops from the underside of a four-motor Focke-Wulf FW 200.

By June 1943 the project, now officially described as 'very hopeful', was taken a positive step further with the establishment at Zempin of the headquarters of Lehr und Erprobungskommando Wachtel (named after Max Wachtel, its commander) to carry out the development that was to hone the device as an offensive weapon, and after six weeks the first so-called Flak Regiment responsible for the actual launchings from France was set up.

The missiles so far were development specimens so that work made slow progress. A severe set-back was suffered as a result of the RAF's massive attack on Peenemünde – Operation 'Hydra' (q.v.) – forcing a move ▶

Above: The Fairey Barracuda, introduced into service in 1940, was an attempt to replace the aged Swordfish and Albacore biplanes used by the Royal Navy. In fact they did more, remaining in service for some two years and being described as 'ASV sophistication exemplified'. They first saw action during the Salerno landings and later took part in attacks on the German battleship *Tirpitz*. (Bruce Robertson collection)

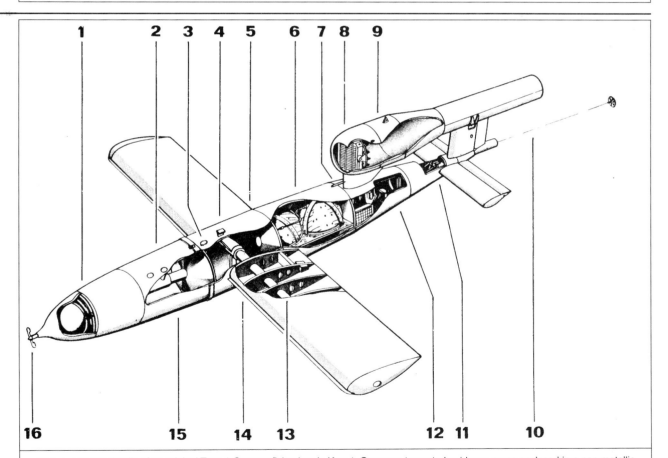

Above: Internal details of an original Type 1 German flying bomb. Key: 1. Compass to control guidance gyros enclosed in a non-metallic (wooden) sphere. 2. Twin fuse pockets in horizontal main fuse. 3. Fuel filler cap. 4. Lifting lug. 5. Fuel tank. 6. Wire-bound compressed air spheres for pneumatic control motors. 7. Ram tube. 8. Jet motor flanked by mixing venturis. 9. Combustion chamber. 10. 400ft aerial for ranging transmitter (some). 11. Pneumatic motors for operation of controls. 12. Battery, fuel and guidance controls. 13. Wooden ribs (some were metal) on tubular metal spar. 14. Cable cutter (optional, one of two forms). 15. Warhead. 16. Air log to determine length of flight. (Author)

tinued during WWII and afterwards by such types as the Firefly and Gannet.

Fairey Queen See Queen.

Falcon The US Hughes AIM-26 (Nuclear Falcon) and AIM-4 air-to-air missile. In the early 1970s these, which had a range of about five or six miles at a speed of Mach 2.5, were the standard armament for many Canadian, Swedish, Swiss and US fighters, those outside the country of origin being licence-built by Saab-Scania. The AIM-26A had a nuclear warhead and the AIM-4D/H had an improved close-range performance.

'Fantan' A Chinese redesign of the Soviet MiG-19, designated Nanchang A-5C. Export versions, known as Q-5

IIIs, were purchased by Pakistan in 1990. See 'Farmer'.

'Farmer' The NATO code-name for three versions of the Soviet MiG-19, 'Farmer-A' being the original version fitted with a Mikulin AM-5, which was succeeded by the 'Farmer-B' with a more powerful AM-9b motor and AI radar. This was followed by the 'Farmer-C', similar but armed with later-model cannon. The final version, the MiG-19PM, had its guns removed and pylons fitted for early beam-riding air-to-air 'Alkali' missiles. Large numbers of the original variants armed with NR-30 cannon and K-13A 'Atoll' missiles were purchased as F-6s from the Chinese factory at Shenyang by Pakistan. See 'Fantan'.

Farnborough The Hampshire base of the Royal Aircraft Factory and later the Royal Aircraft Establishment, now the DEA, the foundations of which were laid with the move of the Army Balloon School and factory from Aldershot in 1902. After the design and construction of warplanes during WWI was abandoned, the station became the base for much military and experimental development.

FAW Alternatively F(AW), the designation given to denote an all-weather fighter type.

Fenders Protective barriers for aircraft to deflect and cut barrage balloon cables.

FGA British type designation indicat-

FLYING BOMB

▶ of the tests to Brüsterort. Meanwhile the preparation of intricate concrete launching sites in the Cherbourg area went ahead, and from these is was anticipated that attacks on targets in the British Isles would begin around Christmas 1943. A series of delays in fact prevented this, not least those occasioned by a number of Allied assaults in the vicinity of the sites, causing the hurried construction of simpler launching ramps with log and earth barriers to protect the new weapons.

Now identified by the code-word 'Kirschkern' (Cherrystone), the V-1 had evolved into a comprehensive weapon, a few of which were capable of carrying a ranging transmitter or taking propaganda leaflets (q.v.) to be scattered by the explosion of the 1,870lb warhead from their external cardboard box. Poison gas could be carried as an alternative to the explosive, although this facility was never used.

The opening flying bomb attacks took place on 13 June 1944 when ten were launched. Only four reaching the English coast, but these were sufficient to trigger the code-word 'Diver', setting into motion long-planned defensive measures. The first pair to be spotted were those seen by Mr F. C. Marsh, an auxiliary coastguard at Folkestone who logged them as 'two aircraft with lighted cockpits coming from the French coast in a north-westerly direction' and by personnel manning ROC Post M2 at the end of the same harbour, who correctly identified and reported the intruders at 0406 hrs. One was

to land near Gravesend, while the other carried on to fall on a railway viaduct at Bethnal Green, claiming the lives of six people and blocking all the lines out of Liverpool Street.

These opening assaults were inauspicious, and they were followed by a lull in future operations until 15 June, when at 2318 hrs the order was given to 'Open fire on

Target 42' and the first of the 150 or so to be sent off in the next twenty-four hours was winging its way to London. But, until almost the end of the flying bomb campaign, many lives were to be saved because of the fact that warning of the final dive was given by the motor cutting-out – due to a design oversight, later corrected, whereby the fuel was

Above: A flying bomb over southern England, 1944.

ing Fighter (Ground Attack), changed in recent years to FA.

Fiat See Aeritalia.

FIDO Fog Dispersal Investigation Operation, a British fog-dispersal system for airfields used during WWII. It depended on petrol (initially coke) burnt in vaporizing pits, giving maximum heat and minimum vapour. FIDO layouts existed at Bradwell Bay, Carnaby, Downham Market, St Eval, Fiskerton, Foulsham, Graveley, Hartford Bridge, Ludford Magna, Manston, Melbourne, Metheringham, Sturgate, Tuddenham and Woodbridge in Britain, and at Epinoy and in the Aleutians abroad.

Fighter An aircraft evolved from the original 'scout' of WWI and intended at first primarily as an interceptor. From the type evolved the specialist escort and night fighters of later years.

Fighter-bomber A fighter aircraft capable of being used additionally as a light bomber and designated 'FB'. The role was later absorbed by specialist ground-attack machines.

'Fighter Night' The code-name for a British WWII system whereby day fighters were used to make patrols above certain altitudes, the pilots being ordered to shoot at any aircraft with more than one engine. The system was introduced in November 1940.

Finland The first air combat of the Russo-Finnish war took place on 1 December 1939 when Eino Luuk-kanen, flying a Fokker D.XXI, shot down a Tupolev SB-2 bomber. No further encounters took place until 6 January, when seven Ilyushin DB-3 bombers were encountered, all being claimed shot down and six falling to the guns of Jorma Sarvanto. Such actions indicated the poor training of Soviet aircrew first used in the campaign.

'Firedog' See Code-names.

Firestreak A British air-to-air, clear-weather, infra-red homing missile, originally of de Havilland design. The first of its type, it was adopted by the RAF for Gloster Javelin and Lightning fighters and by the FAA for its Sea Vixens. The original name was Blue Jay.

splashed away from the feed pipe as the nose dropped, starving the Argus Rohr pulse-jet at the critical moment. The RAF code-word 'Fickle' indicated weather allowing fighters intercepting V-1s full freedom of action, while 'Flabby' described medium weather allowing chases over the gun-belt to the balloon line.

Both the United States Navy and the Soviet Union experimented with flying bombs, the American JB-2 ('Loon') closely resembling the German weapon. The Soviets also tested air-launched variants powered by twin pulse-jets. See V-1.

Above: An experimental Soviet twin-jet flying bomb, differing from the German prototype in having twin fins and rudders. (Via Piotr Butowski)

'Fishbed' The NATO code-name for the Soviet MiG-21 day fighter which became one of the most common interceptors in Warsaw Pact countries. Armed with 30mm cannon and a pair of 'Atoll' missiles, it was also exported to over 30 countries including Cuba, Czechoslovakia, Finland, East Germany, Hungary, Indonesia, Iraq, Poland, Romania, the United Arab Republic and the former Yugoslavia as well as being constructed for the Indian Air Force by Hindustan Aeronautics. Variants were coded from 'Fishbed-A' to 'Fishbed-N'.

'Fishpot' The NATO code-name for the Soviet Sukhoi Su-9, constructed as an experiment in limited commonality of parts so that the design shared some major components with the Sukhoi Su-7B 'Fitter'. An one stage the nose centre-body was moved forward to produce a two-shock air intake and leave room for an enlarged AI radar. The armament was four 'Alkali' beam-riding, air-to-air missiles.

'Fitter' The NATO code-name for the Soviet Sukhoi Su-7A/B single-seat ground-attack fighter. A fuselage similar to that of the Su-9 was married to a swept wing with a leading-edge angle of 62° instead of the 57° of the Su-9. The type entered service about 1955 and was armed with a pair of 30mm cannon. It saw service with the air forces of Egypt, Cuba, India, Syria, Hungary, Iraq and North Vietnam.

'Flagon' The NATO code-name for the Soviet Su-15 and 21 fighter developed from the Su-11 (which it strongly resembled), the first version ('Flagon-A') entering service in 1969. A STOL version ('Flagon-B') was powered by direct-lift engines ahead of the main propulsion units and had extended outboard wing panels, giving a double-delta appearance.

Flak WWII slang for anti-aircraft fire.

Flakhelfer Youths of 14 or 15 years of age recruited to help man German anti-aircraft guns towards the end of WWII.

Flaming onions A WWI and early WWII term for a type of anti-aircraft fire.

Flares The British 'Cyclamen' project of late 1940 envisaged a night fighter towing a flare to illuminate an enemy aircraft for an accompanying 'killer' machine.

'Flashlight' The NATO code-name for the Soviet Yakovlev Yak-25, an early two-seat reconnaissance and tactical strike FAW aircraft, believed to have first been flown early in 1953. Vaguely

FRANCE

The practical foundations of French military aviation may be said to have been laid in 1908 with the Wrights' agreement that their biplanes be manufactured in France for the fledgeling aviation element of the Sapper Corps. As no flying schools existed, the responsibility for training pilots fell to the emergent aircraft industry, producing in the main Blériot and Borel monoplanes, Henry and Maurice Farmans, Sommers, Nieuports, Voisins and Wrights for the service which was to be created as a semi-independent arm with effect from 22 October 1910 following an Order in Council creating the Aéronautique Militaire. However, as will be clear, the variety of types was a handicap to the development of an efficient service, the 6th Army Corps alone being equipped with seven different types of machine. Nevertheless, attempts to place the organization on a proper military footing continued, and in March 1912 the service was divided into three independent Groups with headquarters at Versailles, Reims and Lyon, so that two years later mobilization for WWI found France with a front-line strength of 21 Escadrilles and a total of 132 military machines, not including reserves. By the time the Battle of Verdun opened in February 1916 this strength had risen to 1,149.

By the time of the Armistice of 1918 France was operating the most formidable air arm on the continent, with a strength of 3,222 front-line machines backed by considerable reserves, a state of affairs that had been achieved through the prodigious efforts of the industry which at one time, a few months before, had been manufacturing warplanes at a rate of 100 a day. To fly these aircraft there were more than 12,000 trained aircrew from a total strength of 127,630 officers and men, some of whom were to be responsible for the pioneering and long-range ventures that marked the immediate post-war years. Meanwhile an extensive reorganization and an extensive renumbering of escadrilles was taking place.

Although a steady re-equipment with new types was to take place throughout the post-war years, the Aéronautique Militaire was still wedded to the Army until the fateful year of 1933, when new doctrines were adopted to meet both the changing political situation in Europe and advances in aviation, with the result that total independence was achieved by a decree of 1 April establishing the new Armée de l'Air with effect from 2 July 1934. Two years later a logistical restructuring of the service's divisions was begun and escadres were substituted for the old air regiments, each composed of two (later three) groupes of wings, these being subdivided into escadrilles. In theory, all this looked modern and progressive, but in practice it proved cumbersome, coming as it did in parallel with problems springing from the nationalization of the aircraft industry from August 1936 following the election of the Left-leaning Popular Front government. This severely restricted the production of military aircraft.

By the outbreak of WWII in 1939 many of these restrictions were being overcome and some useful aircraft types were beginning to appear, but in such small numbers as the result of political doctrine that orders were placed in the United States for such types as the Curtiss Hawk 75, Martin 167, Douglas DB-7 and Consolidated B-24, the last having only just flown in prototype form. From Italy, Caproni Ca.313s and Nardi FN.305s were ordered. However, few of these designs, except for the Curtiss machines, had been delivered before the French air arm was defeated in 1940. The numerical strength on 10 May consisted of 1,501 front-line machines, of which 784 were fighters. There was a small naval air element based on the carrier *Béarn* and the support ship *Commandant Teste* and on warships and vessels of the coastal force. For the next two years two French air forces existed, one fighting for the Allies, the other for Vichy France (l'Armée de l'Air d'Armistice), while the Aéronavale became almost entirely shore-based following the British destruction of the French fleet.

Following the defeat of Nazi Germany, Western Union, the forerunner of NATO, purchased a wide range of aircraft types for a new Aéronavale, while a new Armée de l'Air was equipped with British machines. The production of several ex-German designs was begun at home by an industry that largely

similar in appearance to the French Vautour, it was the first Soviet warplane to carry both radar and operator, the set being stowed in the large nose. A night-fighter version also existed. See 'Mangrove'.

Flechette A steel dart which was sharpened at one end after the fashion of a pencil and measured some 5in long and 5/16in diameter. The rear two-thirds was milled to form a cruciform cross-section and act as fins. Used in the opening stages of WWI. An alternative form existed utilizing a steel shank on to which a brass tail was pressed.

Flensburg German airborne radar designed to detect the British 'Monica' tail warning device and thus guide interceptors.

Flight A sub-division of a British squadron, usually designated 'A' , 'B',

and 'C' and consisting of three aeroplanes each and their crews. Before WWII some squadrons were organized on a two-Flight basis, operating six machines each.

Flight refuelling See In-flight refuelling.

'Flower' An RAF WWII operation consisting of a patrol above an enemy night fighter base intended to keep the majority of the aircraft on the ground and to intercept any attempting take-off.

FMA IA-58B See Pucará.

Focke-Wulf A German aircraft manufacturer best-known for three WWII designs, the four-motor maritime patrol FW 200 Condor; the FW 189 'Owl' (q.v.); and the FW 190 fighter, which first entered service in March 1942 with II/JG 26 and ran to 55 versions (see list).

It was 1924 when the first designs to the Focke-Wulf formula began to appear, these being characterized by their bulky appearance. It was not until seven years later that the company's aircraft assumed a more conventional look, a change coinciding with the employment of Kurt Tank at the Bremen plant. Tank's first design was for a sports and training biplane, the FW 44, but this was swiftly followed by a high-wing monoplane, the FW 56 Stösser, which was quickly adopted by the Luftwaffe as a trainer and also exported as a light bomber. There followed the twin-motor FW 58 Weihe military communications and light transport type, the FW 187 Falke twin-engine, single-seat fighter, the unconventional twin-boom FW 189 and, marking a complete change from earlier established norms, the FW 190 and the FW 191 medium bomber.

remained in the groupings created by the 1936 nationalization.

The formation of NATO saw the Armée de l'Air re-equipping with new products of that industry and responsible for two arms of the strategic nuclear deterrent, the Groupement de Missiles Strategiques (GMS) and the Forces Aériennes Strategiques (FAS), while the Army was supported from 1954 by the ALAT, l'Aviation Légère de l'Armée de Terre to provide an airborne observation and communications arm.

Above: A preserved example of the Dewoitine D.520 fighter, this being No 408. (Author's collection)

Above: During WWII the Luftwaffe began equipping itself with the formidable Focke-Wulf 190 in the autumn of 1941 and its success was proved by the fifty-four variants, including trainers, that were to appear in the following years. This is an early A-1 model being prepared for a post-production test flight. (Bruce Robertson collection)

Although this last appeared in 1939, the next Focke-Wulf product in numerical sequence, the FW 200 Condor, dated from 1936. It was originally intended as an airliner, so that it was not until September three years later that ten pre-production Condors, specially strengthened as unarmed transports, were delivered to the military, and it was from these that the five-man armed maritime versions were evolved, the first being encountered as early as April 1940.

Development work resulting in the FW 190, officially known (but seldom referred to) as the Würger (Butcher Bird or Shrike), began in the last quarter of 1937, setting a design trend which was to be followed internationally for the next decade. The first operational encounters were made over the French coast four years later. The prototype had first flown from Bremen on 1 June 1939, it being unique in having a ducted fan spinner to reduce drag, although this was later discarded. The second prototype emerged in October, the original 1,550hp BMW 139 radial motor being replaced by the heavier BMW 801 giving 1,660hp.

FW 190A Variants

A-0	Pre-production machines for evaluation.
A-1	Initial 102 aircraft for operational testing.
A-2	Wing span increased by 190.5mm (7½in)
A-3	Improved armament.
A-3/U1	Fighter-bomber version with MG FF guns replaced by bomb racks.
A-3/U3	Increased weight and improved speed.
A-3/U4	Reconnaissance fighter.
A-3/U7	Fighter-bomber with MG FFs replaced.
A-4	MW50 fuel injection system.
A-4/Trop	With filters and rack for 250kg (550lb) bomb.
A-4/U1	Twin MG 151s plus a pair of bomb racks.
A-4/U3	Ground-support fighter. Became the FW 190F-1.
A-4/U8	Long-range fighter-bomber with drop tanks.
A-4/R6	No MW50. Fitted with rocket tubes.
A-5	Length increased by 152.5mm (6in).
A-5/U2	Night fighter.
A-5/U3	Ground support fighter.
A-5/U8	Long-range fighter-bomber.
A-5/U9	Twin MG 151s, plus two MG 131s.
A-5/U10	Became the FW 190A-6.
A-5/U11	Heavy fighter. Became the FW 190A-8/R1 and F-8/R3.
A-5/U12	Heavy fighter. Became the FW 190A-6/R1 and A-8/R1.
A-5/U13	Long range fighter-bomber. Became the FW 190G-3.
A-5/U14	Experimental torpedo fighter.
A-5/U15	Special torpedo fighter. Only three built.
A-5/U16	Special bomber-destroyer with 30mm MK 108 guns.
A-5/U17	Became the FW 190F-3.
A-5/R6	Fitted with WGr 21cm rocket tubes.
A-6	Airframe lightened.
A-6/R1	Heavy fighter with eight guns.
A-6/R2	Fighter-bomber version of A-6.
A-6/R3	Heavy fighter project.
A-6/R4	GM 1 fitted.
A-6/R6	Fitted with WGr 21-cm rocket tubes.
A-7	Modified armament and strengthened undercarriage.
A-7/R1	Heavy fighter.

A-7/R2 30mm Mk 108 guns out board.
A-7/R3 Provision for single drop tank.
A-7/R6 Increased gross weight.
A-8 Increased internal tankage.
A-8/U1 Trainer. Became the FW 190S-8.
A-8/U11 Fighter-bomber.
A-8/R1 Twin MG 151s in underwing packs.
A-8/R2 GM 1 version with increased gross weight.
A-8/R3 Ground support version. Believed project only.
A-8/R7 Assault fighter.
A-8/R8 Assault fighter with modi fied armament.
A-8/R11 All-weather fighter.
A-8/R12 Projected version with modi fied armament.
A-9 Engine change.
A-9/R8 Assault fighter project.
A-9/R11 All-weather fighter with turbo-supercharger.
A-9/R12 All-weather fighter project.
A-10 Long-range escort fighter.

The ultimate development of the FW 190 series lay in the Focke-Wulf Ta 152 design, the initial prefix being that of Dipl Ing Kurt Tank in recognition of his work on the FW 190. The chief variants of the new fighter were as follows:

A-1, A-2 Projects similar to the FW 190D with four MG 151/20 cannon and Fu G 24 radio.
B Jumo 213E-1 motor and engine-mounted MK 108 can non.
B-1 Project only.
B-2 Project only.
B-3 Armoured ground-attack variant.
B-4 Heavy fighter.
B-4/R1 Version with standard arma ment.
B-4/R2 Armed with three MK 108s and two MG 151/20s.
B-5 Armed with three MK 108s only.
B-5/R11 All-weather variant.
C-O DB 603L engine and one Mk 108 with four MG 151/20s.
C-1 Production model.
C-1/R14 Fighter-bomber.
C-2 As C-1 with improved radio.
C-3 MK 108 replaced by MK 103.
C-4 Project with WGr 21 rocket tubes.
E-1 Photo-reconnaissance version with various cameras.
E-1/R1 Variant with oblique cameras.
E-2 High-altitude version with H-series wing.
H High-altitude fighter. Pressure cabin and new wing.
H-1 Production version. Only ten completed.
H-10 High-altitude reconnaissance fighter.
R-2 Long-range version of H.
S-1 Tandem twin-seat trainer.

Fokker A Dutch aircraft manufacturer producing designs for Germany during WWI, including monoplane scouts (fitted with a synchronized machine gun, one was the cause of the 'Fokker Scourge' of late 1915 and early 1916); the famous Triplane; biplanes which culminated in the Fokker D.VII, produced in sufficient numbers to equip 42 Jastas in 1918; and the 'Flying

Above: During the later years of WWI the Imperial German Air Force flew the formidable Fokker D.VII. Its success was marked by a special clause in the Armistice agreement demanding the surrender of all examples extant. D.VIIs were also flown by air forces of Holland and the Dutch East Indies and were innovative in having a steel-tube fuselage. (A. E. Jessop)

Above: Although the Fokker Dr.1 Triplane is traditionally associated with Manfred von Richthofen, it was used by a number of Staffeln from August 1917. Less fast than its contemporaries, it was extremely manoeuvrable, with an ability to 'hang on the prop' and pepper an adversary. The twin guns could be fired independently. This view shows well the streaked dope scheme of the period. (Author's collection)

Razor', the parasol-wing Fokker D.VIII of WWI's closing months.

Foster mounting See S.E.5.

'Foxbat' The NATO code-name for the MiG-25 Soviet all-weather interceptor which first appeared in 1967, differing from previous designs in that the wings were shoulder-mounted and twin fins and rudders were fitted. The underwing armament consisted of four AA-6 ('Acrid') air-to-air missiles (two radar-guided and two infra-red seeking).

'Frances' The Allied code-name for the Japanese Yokosuka P1Y1 Ginga (Milky Way) twin-engine medium bomber and night fighter of WWII. It enjoyed a combat life of some six months but was well designed and well respected.

'Frank' The Allied code-name for WWII Japanese Nakajima Ki-84 Hayate (Gale) fighter. A superb fighter which outclassed even the P-51. This was the second application of the name, the previous one having been to the fictional Mitsubishi TK-4 special twin-motor fighter that was at one time alternatively known by the code-name 'Harry'.

Freccia See G.50.

'Fred' At one time during WWII it was believed that the German Focke Wulf FW 190A-5 (q.v.) had entered operational service with the Japanese Army Air Force. This was not the case, but this code-name was nevertheless issued by the Allied High Command.

'Fresco' The NATO code-name for the MiG-17 development of the MiG-15. The aircraft entered service during 1953 with the Soviet Air Force and member forces of the Warsaw Pact. Several variants were identified, including the MiG-17F 'Fresco-C' with afterburning. Armament consisted of cannon combined with either two 550lb bombs on external racks or rockets. It was built in China as the Shenyang F-4. See N-23, N-37.

Freya A German WWII radar installation for long-range detection installed as part of the ground-based system of 'boxes' across Western Europe, one such set being used each for general surveillance in company with a pair of Würzburg sets.

Fritz-X The general name for the German Ruhrstahl/Kramer X missile of WWII. It consisted of a PC 1400 bomb warhead fitted to a controlled, free-fall weapon intended for attacks on armoured ships and was fitted with plain cruciform fins forming the pivotal aerodynamic points which were radio controlled via the Kehl/Strassburg system, the signals being received by an antenna contained in the tail shroud. Early models had been developed for control by a simple direct-current system via five miles of twin wire unwound from bobbins in the missile's tail, but to relieve the strain on manufacturing industry this system was discontinued. Notable achievements were the sinking of the Italian battleship *Roma* and seriously damaging the British battleship HMS *Warspite*.

'Front Line' Deep-penetration bombing trials carried out by the RAF and USAAF during 1946–47 using the incomplete U-boat pens at Farge, near Bremen, as targets.

Fuel–air explosive (FAE) A contemporary mixture bomb creating a detonation equal to 10 atmospheres, useful for destroying minefields and underground complexes.

'Fu-Go' Balloon bombs used by Japan during WWII in retaliation for the bombing on 18 April 1942 of Tokyo by sixteen B-25s. The intention was to use favourable winds to carry the unmanned, 32.8ft diameter silk and tissue paper balloons to the United States and there drop a selection of 5kg or 12kg incendiary or 15kg anti-personnel bombs using an automatic device activated when all sandbags dropped for altitude adjustment by auto-barometric sensing were exhausted. The first of a total of 9,300 Fu-Go balloons was launched on 3 November 1944. It was discovered with its load intact in the Pacific Ocean, off California, after a journey of 5,965 miles and about 60 hours after leaving its launching station, one of three on Honshu. Manufacture, spread throughout Japan, was carried out by schoolchildren, who glued together the silk and paper envelopes. By no means all such weapons were unsuccessful, and lives were lost as a result of their use. The campaign was halted in March 1945.

'**Fulcrum**' The NATO code-name for the MiG-29 Soviet fighter which first flew in 1977, the first deliveries being made six years later. Several variants were identified: the 'Fulcrum-A' single-seater, the 'Fulcrum-B' (MiG-29UB) combat trainer, and the 'Fulcrum-C', which had additional avionics carried in an enlarged fairing aft of the cockpit. Armament was a single 30mm cannon, four AA-10 'Alamo-A' semi-active, radar-guided and 'Alamo-B' IR-homing medium-range missiles, plus two AA-11 'Archer' close-combat IR missiles. Bombs and rocket pods could also be carried.

Funryu A series of Japanese Navy guided missiles of WWII. Type 1 was radio-controlled, Types 2 and 4 by radar. None was proceeded with.

G (1) A suffix applied to serial numbers of RAF aircraft during WWII, as '/G', indicating that an armed guard was necessary. (2) Generally written as 'g', the gravitational pull on an airframe during manoeuvres, the prefix numeral indicating the increase over normal 'g'.

G- (G-Series) The designation for three differing types of non-rigid airship operated by the US Navy, the first from 1919, the second sixteen years later and the final variant as part of the expansion programme of 1942. These last continued in use until 1959.

G.50 Italy's Fiat Freccia (Arrow) fighter, a low-wing monoplane powered by a radial motor that made its début in the Spanish Civil War, later figuring prominently in North African operations in WWII. The closed cockpit of the early models was disliked by the pilots and was discarded on later versions, to which wheel fairings were added for the retractable undercarriage. The initial letter of the designation indicated the designer, Giuseppe Gabrielli.

G.91 A Fiat design which won the NATO strike-fighter competition early in the 1950s, the first flight of the prototype following in April 1956. Deliveries commenced two years later, some being supplied to the West German Luftwaffe before licence-production was begun for other nations

by Dornier. A small number of these were later passed to Portugal. Last flown 1990.

G.222 A Fiat-designed tactical military transport developed for the Italian Air Force. The first flight of the prototype took place in 1970. A high-wing design powered by twin General Electric T64-P-4C turboprops, it was capable of being rapidly loaded with heavy equipment via twin rear doors.

'**Gainful**' Properly designated SA-6, this was a medium weight, rocket-propelled Soviet surface-to-air missile measuring some 20ft in length and normally deployed from a triple mobile launcher.

'**Galosh**' A Soviet surface-to-air missile measuring over 60ft long, introduced primarily as part of the Moscow defences. With a range of several hundreds of miles, it was intended to be deployed against enemy ballistic missiles.

'**Gander**' The Allied code-name for the only Japanese transport glider to be met in combat during WWII, based on the Ki-59 light transport aircraft and fitted with a hinged nose section and entry ramp so that the 20 troops for which accommodation was provided could be quickly embarked.

'**Ganef**' A mobile Soviet surface-to-air missile, also designated SA-4, introduced in 1967. Powered by a ramjet similar in concept to that which powered German WWII flying bombs (q.v.), it was assisted into the air by means of four rockets which were later jettisoned. The missile was guided by radio and radar, and the range was about 40 miles.

'**Gardening**' The WWII RAF term for laying sea mines by means of aircraft.

Gas Poison gas was first used in warfare of the twentieth century on Thursday 22 April 1915 and promoted a retaliatory attack by French bombers against the chemical factory at Ludwigshafen on 26 May following. This method of killing or incapacitating enemy troops was later copied by the Allies, and during the years of the uneasy peace between the two world

wars it was regarded as the most likely means of waging warfare in any future conflict. All the major countries of the world experimented with it during the period, including Great Britain, which included simulated measures in the Air Exercises immediately before 1939. Trials with sprays and bombs were made, the latter seemingly the most promising. That such tests were justified seemed apparent in 1935 when Italy used mustard gas against defenceless Abyssinians.

Defence against the use of gas on civilians then became a preoccupation of all governments, extending to the inclusion, in Britain, of suitably protected decontamination squads as part of Air Raid Precautions (later called Civil Defence), and gas masks were issued to the entire population. Although gas was not employed by any of the belligerents in WWII, RAF aircraft were earmarked to use mustard gas against the invading German troops expected in 1940.

The best-known form of gas distribution has been by means of bombs, spraying only being suitable from low level, and a variation of the former method, known to have existed in the German armoury, consisted of combined gas/high explosive bombs (Gasbrisanzbomben), percussion fused and with a large explosive content and a gas capacity which, although small, was sufficient to incapacitate survivors. These weapons were identified, in the manner of normal gas bombs, by means of coloured crosses: yellow for the blister-inducing mustard gas, a vapour that slowly evaporated from an oily liquid smelling of garlic; white for incapacitating tear gas; and green for the highly lethal phosgene, the musty, hay-smelling vapour from which attacked the lungs. Lewisite was another deadly gas, completing an array of poison vapours that could be used in warfare and representing a threat that was taken sufficiently seriously in 1940 that RAF aircraft were marked with a rectangular yellow-green patch of sensitive paint that changed colour in a poisonous atmosphere and thus gave warning of the presence of gas. Britain stored 105,000 gas bombs of all types during WWII.

Nerve gases were perfected by the Germans in 1943 with the intention of using them against the Russians, and although these were not employed, a new line of development for similar weapons was established, culminating in the deadly 'VX'" gas of the years immediately following the end of WWII. It has been alleged that mustard gas was used against Iraq by Iran in April 1988. Chemical warfare cloaks continued poison gas trials today.

Gatwick A civil airport near Horley, Surrey, which first came into use in August 1930. Its military potential after the outbreak of WWII was slight although it had become the base for various short-stay squadrons including some responsible for early Rhubarbs (q.v.), and for anti-aircraft and army cooperation units. However, it served as the base for no fewer than four RAF Mustang squadrons during Operation 'Jubilee' (q.v.) and for two employed for spotting in support of naval guns aimed at coastal targets during Operation 'Overlord'. Its chief claim to a place in the history of air warfare is its choice as a site for Darkie (q.v.) homing beacons in use from October 1943.

Gee A radio aid to navigation employed by the RAF bombers in WWII. It had a range of about 350 miles and was used for target identifi-cation, employing ground transmitters and an airborne receiver. It was origi-nally intended to be of use for night bombing, but it proved too inaccurate for all but the most modest ranges. It was first used in August 1941, and a year later same 80 per cent of the RAF's bombing force was equipped with it. A significant example of the use of this equipment as a navigation-al aid was seen on the night of 25 June 1942 when a force of 960 aircraft attacked Bremen even though the city was covered in cloud, the bombers being led by aircraft using Gee. A chart enabled time to be converted into dis-tance, and thus the position of the air-craft could be fixed. G-H, for blind bombing, employed Gee equipment in conjunction with an airborne transmit-ter-receiver and two ground stations as beacons. This has been sometimes described as 'Oboe in reverse'.

General Dynamics A major US group founded as Electro Dynamics in 1880. Its aviation connections dated from 1908, and the acquisition of a number of important military aircraft manufac-turers followed. These included Consolidated, Dayton-Wright, Gallaudet, Thomas (later Thomas Morse) and Vultee. Perhaps the best-remembered warplanes from General Dynamics as the twentieth century drew to its close were the F-111 fighter-bomber and the F-16 fighter.

'George' The Allied code-name for the WWII Japanese Kawanishi N1K1-J Shiden (Violet Lightning) naval fighter. It was evaluated in 1943 after a trial period attended by a number of engine and undercarriage problems, although when it finally entered service at the end of 1944 it proved to be an out-standing machine. Nevertheless, pro-duction had been handicapped by the attentions of US B-29s and it entered service with only three Kokutais. However, it proved capable of meeting Allied fighter aircraft on equal terms.

Geschwader See Staffel.

Gigant (Giant) The German Messerschmitt Me 321 and 323, the first being a massive, high-wing, monoplane glider with a span of 180ft 5½in on which design work began as early as 1940, the prototype making its first flight a year later in March. The crew consisted of the pilot alone, who found the work of controlling the glid-er physically demanding since there were no power-assisted controls. Loading was facilitated either via con-ventional side doors or the clamshell

---

GERMANY

The foundations of military flying in Germany were laid in October 1912 when a determination to keep in the forefront of aviation was supported by large govern-ment grants, so that entry into WWI was made with both the Army and Navy operating airships and heavier-than-air machines in strategic and tactical roles. It is true that the collection of 246 warplanes Germany pos-sessed was a heterogeneous one, but once conflict had been joined a period of develop-ment saw the evolution of Jagdstaffeln (Jastas), the special fighting units of 1916 which were pre-dated by the establishment in 1915 of the first Kampfstaffel, or battle squadrons. Emphasis on these and the work of airships has tended to give the inaccurate impression that most of the activities of the Military Aviation Service were concentrated on the Western Front. That this is not so is shown by German participation on the Italian Front and in the Dardanelles, where the first warplane arrived in April 1915, as well as on the Russian Front, although here it is true that participation was confined largely to reconnaissance and bombing missions. All this was to vanish in November 1918 when the Armistice was signed, demolishing the Military Aviation Service and surrendering to the Allies, largely for destruction, 15,000 air-craft, including 4,050 suitable for front-line service.

Apart from a very small number of scout (fighter) aircraft attached to little-publicized Polizei units, Germany now had no military air force, but there still existed a small Defence Ministry (Reichswehrministerium) in Berlin, and its chief began to form a small internal aviation section in 1921. Two years later an agreement was signed with the Soviet Government for the provision of train-ing facilities at Lipetsk for pilots, observers and mechanics and a little later a large num-ber of sports flying clubs sprang up, giving pilot instruction at first with the aid of gliders and later in powered aircraft. By 1929 these clubs could boast a total membership of more than 50,000. In parallel with these arrangements, a school was founded in Germany to instruct young boys as glider pilots, the most promising candidates gradu-ating to powered machines.

Germany was still prevented from manu-facturing warplanes, but a large number of aircraft types began to appear in sports or civilian guise which were clearly designs capable of adaptation to military purposes. At the same time glances were cast abroad for suitable machines, so that what was in effect the first design from which the Ju 87 would be developed made its maiden flight in Sweden. Slowly and by such means as these a new Luftwaffe was built up. After Hitler seized power on the death of Hindenburg in August 1934, General Milch was entrusted with the task of forming a new Air Ministry. The scene was now set for the official announcement in March 1935 that Germany now possessed a new Air Force, a target being set for aircraft production to reach 4,021 machines six months later. Plans were also laid for the 30 or so factories which con-stituted the aircraft industry to begin produc-

nose. Rocket-assisted take-off was sometimes employed for loaded aircraft, and in the 321B version, on which large-diameter wheels replaced the earlier bogie undercarriage, armament was provided and the crew increased to three. The Me 323 was a powered version of the aircraft fitted with six Gnome Rhône 14N radial motors. Its undercarriage reverted to the bogie type of the early glider, and the defensive armament was retained. This was increased in the Me 323D variant, which had a crew of five. The 323 was capable of transporting 130 armed troops on two decks and first entered operational service in late 1942, being used mainly in North Africa and Sicily.

Glider bomb An unmanned glider fitted with a warhead, released some distance from the target and guided with the aid of radio signals from a parent aircraft. An example during WWII was the Blohm und Voss Bv 246 (earlier known as the Bv 226) Hagelkorn (Hailstone), ordered into production in 1943 before lapsing unused, only to see official interest reawakened when it was seen that they might be launched to ride British radio signals intended to guide Allied bombers. Many were employed in a series of fur-

ther tests in 1944, launched from Focke-Wulf FW 190G-8s. (q.v.) The United States used its GB-1 glider bomb only once, against Cologne in April 1944.

In effect, glider bombs were the precursors of the stand-off bomb and had a strong relationship to such as the Henschel Hs 293, a powered glider fitted with a Walter 109-507B rocket fuelled by a mixture of T-Stoff (high test hydrogen peroxide) and Z-Stoff (sodium permanganate), which gave about ten seconds' thrust. The first of these was designed as early as 1940 and code-named FZ 21, although the first recorded use of the Hs 293 was not until 25 April 1943 when the missiles were launched from Dornier Do 217E-5s of II/KG 100 against vessels in the Bay of Biscay – without result. On 27 April, however, the first success was recorded with the sinking of the corvette HMS *Egret*. A large number of developments of the Hs 293 were designed, though not all entered operational service. The guidance system of some was electro-optical, based on television cameras within the missiles themselves. All were subsonic, although one, the Hs 293A-2 Zitterrochen (Torpedo Fish) was designed to attain Mach 1.5.

Gliders To Germany must go credit for the establishment of a new form of air warfare, namely the transportation of troops by gliders. The foundations were laid innocently enough in 1932 with the design of a glider with high aspect ratio wings for meteorological research, but the potential of such a machine was not lost on Ernst Udet, who conceived the wider use, and the first box-like DFS 230, capable of taking eight fully armed men, was demonstrated in 1937, the glider being towed by the ubiquitous Junkers 52/3m. The following year was to see the foundation of a small glider assault command responsible for the development of the idea.

The advantages of such a glider-borne force were many. Army commanders were given a new and flexible dimension, allowing the landing of soldiers under conditions impossible for parachute forces, placing them by day or by night at almost any given spot and leaving an enemy guessing until the final moment where this might be. In addition, using a 'remote release' technique, an approach could be made in complete silence from many miles distant, and time would permit the evolution of unpowered aircraft capable of taking medium guns, heavy supplies and light transport – all impossible to drop near to special objectives

---

tion of more modern types which would figure in World War II that was still four years distant. The civil conflict in Spain fortuitously provided an opportunity to test these under operational conditions, as well as giving many aircrews battle experience by means of service with the Condor Legion (q.v.).

The operational balance of the Luftwaffe was well established between transport, trainer, army cooperation, fighter and bomber aircraft, although the lessons of WWI had been learned perhaps too well with regard to the last, for there persisted a tendency to see the bomber arm almost exclusively as a tactical one, with the result that, in August 1939, of the 1,157 bombers constituting the total of 2,928 warplanes available (but not necessarily serviceable), none could be classified as strategic bombers.

During the years that followed, attempts to rectify this situation were made, and hasty attempts to develop suitable types met with some success. There is no question that some excellent fighting aircraft for other purposes were produced, but a tendency emerged to concentrate on increasingly

advanced designs as the war situation swung in favour of the Allies, and a large number of projects had been examined at the expense of proven developments in an attempt to snatch victory from the jaws of defeat.

The 1945 division of Germany into West and East sectors gave rise to the existence of two air forces, that of the Federal Republic being established in 1956. For a considerable time this force operated exclusively warplanes of US manufacture, the prevailing high rate of defence expenditure and low rate of inflation resulting in excellent equipment and the steady introduction of new weapons. A year later came the creation of the Marineflieger or Naval Air Arm, to conduct shore-based attack, fighter, reconnaissance, anti-submarine and search and rescue sorties, and to these two services was added the Heeresflieger or Army Air Corps, operating over 500 helicopters in army cooperation, communication and observation duties. A major programme of re-equipment and modernization was initiated, to be completed at the end of the 1970s, by which time some

2,100 aircraft were operated by the three services, which now had a manpower of more than 100,000.

The air force of the remainder of the divided Germany was served by the East's Luftstreitkräfte (LSK) which formed, with the Soviet Union's 16th Air Army, the first line of the air strength of the Warsaw Pact. The force began to be formed in 1950, before international treaty officially permitted Germany to possess any warplanes. In a way history was repeating itself in that this force was at first known as the Volkspolizei-Luft (People's Air Police) or VP-L. It became the LSK in 1956 and was eventually one of the largest of the Pact's air forces, unique in falling directly under Soviet command. The equipment was very largely of Soviet origin, the exceptions being a small number of Czechoslovakian and Polish jet trainers.

The two German air forces began the difficult task of integration with the reunification of Germany which took effect from 3 October 1990.

in support of parachute troops. Moreover, the latter were, unlike glider-borne men, at their most vulnerable during the first few minutes of landing, having to free themselves of their harness, collect equipment and form into units as quickly as possible, as well as being at the mercy of the wind during a drop which could scatter them and extend their deployment time even further. It was realized that gliders, too, suffered from a number of disadvantages. Their successful use required that local air superiority be enjoyed, since they were unable to defend themselves, particularly under tow. Furthermore, the terrain surrounding a target should not be too rough or closely wooded.

Nevertheless, for the final period of about eighteen months of peace remaining in Europe, the development of troop gliders and the training of pilots and soldiers went ahead with some priority, and on 10 May 1940 the training was put into practice. The target was the Belgian fortress of Eben-Emael, occupying a strategic position on the Albert Canal, and the operation was initiated at 0435 hrs at the airfields of Cologne-Ostheim and Cologne-Butzweilerhof when a total of 45 (some sources quote 41) Ju 52/3ms took off, each with a DFS 230 glider containing eight men in tow. The plan was simply to land a part of the force on top of the garrison, trapping the men inside, while troops from ten other gliders landed behind the three bridges over the canal, intent on capturing them and thus preventing their destruction. The glider force was divided into four sections, the main one intended to consist of eleven gliders, of which only nine had survived to make a landing. Even though depleted, the Germans managed to hold the position until the arrival of ground forces by 0700 hrs on the following day. Six men from the section were killed and twenty wounded of the total of 72.

It was clear to many that the new form of air warfare had came to stay. Only forty-three days later Winston Churchill suggested to his Chiefs of Staff that a similar British airborne force be formed, adding, 'Pray let me have a note from the War Office on the subject'. Events moved swiftly, and on 24 June Maj John Rock, a regular sapper, was ordered to create such a force.

He was appointed GSOI Airborne Forces at Ringway (now Manchester Airport), with the rank of Lieutenant-Colonel, his original equipment by the end of October consisting of a pair of Slingsby sailplanes towed by Avro 504s of WWI vintage. By the end of the following April the number of sailplanes had increased to five and had been augmented by a specially designed troop glider, the GAL (General Aircraft Ltd) Hotspur, capable of taking eight armed men and in its original form having a span of 61ft 10in (later reduced by 16 feet for the Mk II).

While these events were unfolding in Britain, Germany was to take troop gliders into action for a second time, now as part of the invasion of Crete (Operation 'Merkur'). A total of 490 Ju 53/3ms took off from primitive air strips near Athens, the bulk with 6,000 paratroops but 100 towing the same number of DFS gliders again, 53 of which were used in the initial assault attempting to land near Maleme airfield. Part of this section was given the task of capturing the town of Canea.

Meanwhile in the United States, troop gliders were being designed in great profusion, although this country was not destined to use them on the same scale as their British and German counterparts. Only one design, the Waco CG-4A, would see operational use. Production of the Hadrian (as the Waco was known), the Hotspur (soon earmarked entirely for training) and the first British operational glider, the Horsa, was distributed around scattered centres, largely among furniture manufacturers.

The new British glider, meeting Specification 26/40, was designed by the Airspeed company of Christchurch and was a 28-seater which had a wide door for the loading such small vehicles as motorcycles and motorcycle combinations. Production commenced in 1941. Aside from two examples termed Horsa 'B', seen as experimental glider-bombers capable of lifting a maximum of 8,000lb of offensive hardware, there were two variants of the type. The Mk I, rather unsatisfactorily, had to have its tail and rear fuselage removed to extract its load, but despite this it saw use during the invasion of Sicily and on D-Day. The Mk II had a hinged nose. For training purposes these 88ft span aircraft were

generally towed by Whitley Mk Vs at the end of a 33/8in thick cable.

Meanwhile a new transport glider was being introduced by the Germans – the twin-boom Gotha Go 242. This aircraft entered large-scale service for transport work with six special glider units in 1942, the towing aircraft in some cases being Heinkel 111Z five-motor tugs formed from combining of two Heinkel 111H airframes. Various rocket-assisted take-off methods were tried for this glider, which was first used in the Middle East and also saw service on the Eastern Front. However, perhaps the most impressive of military gliders was the British General Aircraft Hamilcar, designed to carry alternatively 60 troops, a 7-ton Tetrarch IV or Locust tank, two Bren Gun carriers, a 25pdr gun and tractor, Bailey bridge parts or, distributed between three Hamilcars, parts for HD10/HD14 bulldozers. It had a load capability of 7.8 tons, and the tugs for this glider were usually HP Halifax bombers.

Augmented by the US Hadrian, all the British operational gliders were used at the time of the D-Day landings to liberate the continent of Europe. This operation also saw the solution of such problems as the retrieving of gliders that remained airworthy by the 'snatch' method, a low-flying tug such as a DC-3 seizing the suspended towrope of a glider without the necessity of landing.

The summer of 1944 represented the zenith of glider development and use in Europe. Yugoslavia did develop an indigenous glider, a pod-and-boom type designed by Ivo Sostaric, in the early 1950s. It was not adopted by the Army, although it could lift a Jeep and its crew or a small field gun, or accommodate twelve armed men. Elsewhere troop glider units lingered on only briefly and then quickly vanished, their place in air warfare being taken by helicopters – which could extract men it had dropped. See Code-names.

GLO The British WWII abbreviation for Ground Liaison Officer, an RAF officer working with an Army unit to oversee cooperation with units providing air support.

Gloster A British aircraft manufacturer which was founded in 1917 and came to prominence six years later with the adoption of the Grebe as the RAF's standard fighter. In 1935 the last fighter to the old formula was produced in the shape of the Gladiator, which bridged the gap between the open cockpit, two-gun biplanes of an earlier age and the multi-gun monoplanes with retractable landing gear that were to come. It lasted sufficiently long in service to be used over Norway and Malta in the war, despite being technically obsolete by that time.

Glosters were later significant in being the constructors of the first British jet-propelled (q.v.) aircraft, the E.28/39, built to the design of Frank Carter and powered by an engine designed by Flt Lt Whittle. Clearly con-

Above: Gloster Gladiators were introduced into service in 1937 and are thus regarded by some as the last of the biplane fighters. They saw limited service in WWII, including the legendary episode when they constituted the sole defence of Malta. (Author's collection)

Above: An Armstrong Whitworth-produced Gloster Meteor NF.11 two-seat night fighter of 1950. (Armstrong Whitworth)

ceived as a fighter (original drawings show space provisionally allocated for guns) and bearing a certain resemblance to the Gloster F.5/34s of 1937–38, the Gloster Whittle (as the jet has been occasionally called) made it maiden flight on 15 May 1941. W4041/G was followed by W4046 but the latter was destroyed in a crash, leaving the former to be exhibited to the public after the end of the war, at Britain's Aircraft Exhibition held on the bombed site of John Lewis's store in Oxford Street in June 1945, and later placed on permanent display in the South Kensington Science Museum.

Although experience gained from these two machines was incorporated, the idea of an operational jet fighter pre-dated the E.28/39 and a new aircraft, named the Meteor and powered by twin turbojets, was first flown in prototype form as EE210/G on 12 January 1944. The first operational Mk Is were issued to No 616 Squadron RAF six months later, just in time to be used for the interception of flying bombs (q.v.). So successful was this Gloster aircraft (in which pilots were at first forbidden to cross the English Channel for reasons of security) that a total of eighteen versions were produced, together with 33 sub-variants for export. See Javelin.

'Goa' A Soviet surface-to-air missile also known as the SA-3, first seen to be in service in 1964. Measuring 20ft in length and powered by a two-stage solid-fuel rocket motor, it was used chiefly for the defence of sensitive installations and ocean-going vessels. Guidance was by means of radar homing.

Goeben A German battlecruiser which was at the centre of a unique 2,000mile air operation in 1917. Turkey joined the Central Powers a few months after the outbreak of war in 1914 as the best way of ensuring protection against a Russian threat to the Bosphorus, and *Goeben* was used to lead a Turkish fleet across the Black Sea in preparation for an attack on the Russian ports. Since its continued presence remained a threat to both Russian and British vessels in the Aegean, it was decided to fly out a Handley Page O/100 bomber from England in an attempt to destroy it. Preparations for the flight were completed by mid-May 1917 and a crew consisting of Sqn Cdr Savory (pilot), Flt Lt McClelland RN, Lt Rawlings RNVR, CPO Adams and Ldg Mech Cramack was selected. The take-off for the first leg of the journey was made from Manston en route for Paris at 1030 hrs on 23 May. After delays caused by

GREAT BRITAIN

In November 1911 a sub-committee of the Committee of Imperial Defence under the chairmanship of Lord Haldane was appointed to consider the development of military aviation. This recommended the establishment of an air arm with separate Naval and Military Wings, plus a joint Central Flying School; as a result the RFC, constituted by Royal Warrant the following year, absorbed the former Air Battalion of the Royal Engineers. This Military Wing and School (opened in August) fell under the direct control of the War Office, the Naval Wing being independently controlled by the Admiralty. The Naval Wing was renamed the Royal Naval Air Service on 1 July 1914, and a month later both services were involved in WWI. There was little standardization, and Nos 2, 3, 4 and 5 Squadrons, equipped with a motley collection of aeroplanes, left Swingate Downs, Dover, for Amiens between 13 and 15 August.

The four years of war which followed saw great developments in weapons and tactics as specialist aircraft became available. In 1918 the RFC and RNAS were amalgamated to form the Royal Air Force, and that this was an independent service owed much to the influence of General Smuts, a South African officer who had fought against Britain during the Second Boer War which had ended only sixteen years earlier.

In common with those of many other countries, the British air force participated in

a number of long-distance proving flights in the post-war years as engines became more reliable. Meanwhile the service shrank in size but gained in efficiency until the deteriorating political situation in Europe triggered a number of Expansion Schemes, popularly and not inaccurately known as 'panic measures'. These were, however, sufficient to see that the RAF entered the Second World War on a par with the rest of Western Europe, although too 'lean' for comfort, with some of its bombers redolent of earlier design thinking and biplane fighters having only recently been replaced by monoplanes. Scheme 'M' (in force in September 1939) had resulted in a numerical strength of 173,958 personnel, with a total of 9,349 aircraft, 3,550 of which were regarded as first-line.

The RAF's advances during 1939–45 were due less to changes in aircraft design philosophies than to progress based on firmly laid foundations and the perfection of operational techniques made possible by advances in industrial technology, including those of engine power. Thus such forward steps as that taken in the dying days of peace to standardize on the eight-gun fighter, the introduction of interception techniques aided by radar, bombers defended with the aid of power-operated turrets and steps to introduce four-motor bombers had all laid the foundations on which to base new technologies such as the use of high-explosive bombs of a power hitherto undreamed of (see 'Grand Slam'), the supplementing of conventional light bombers with rocket-armed fighters and airborne interception (AI)

radar for night fighting. All these developments would ensure that the RAF took its place in the forefront of the world's air forces.

Clearly, by the end of WWII in 1945 a transition had to be made in the means of powering of fighters since those with piston motors had reached the limit of their development. The conversion of the RAF to a jet force began smoothly, first with fighters and a few years later in the field of strategic bombers. Although the strength of 55,000 aircraft (8,395 of them first-line), with 173,958 personnel, was soon allowed to decline, another expansion programme was initiated in March 1951, and although the period was one when much of the equipment was of an interim nature, future developments would ensure that the RAF would eventually became an all-jet force using guided missiles, with an efficient air-refuelling organization, flying V-bombers with a stand-off capability and thus making a major contribution to nuclear deterrence.

The modern RAF became a European force after the government decision to relinquish bases 'east of Suez', with the tasks of supporting the Army, carrying out strategic bombing of a wide range of enemy targets, and defending the United Kingdom. The various Commands at home were re-grouped to form only two, Strike and Support, the latter having absorbed Training Command in 1977, However, in practice the new policy meant a much wider commitment than such parameters would seem to indicate, since virtually all the RAF's aircraft were assigned to NATO. ►

poor weather, Mudros was finally reached on 7 June.

The earlier proposal for a torpedo attack was discarded owing to the belief that *Goeben* may have been protected by nets and booms, and, after examining the possibility of attacking with 500lb bombs with 2½-second fuses to create underwater damage, it was decided that 112lb bombs would be used. The date of the attack was set as 3 July, in the evening. Unfortunately, hot winds caused the engines to overheat and the sortie had to be postponed until 5 July, but now a burst tyre caused another cancellation. The next selected date was three days later, but this again had to be delayed until the following day because of poor weather.

Leaving Marsh aerodrome at 0847 hrs, Cdr Savory found the target area at five minutes before midnight and set course for the harbour where both *Goeben* and the cruiser *Breslau* lay. The bay was circled three times to make sure of the target, and the first bombs were released from 800ft, falling to the starboard side of the cruiser and causing a fire. The second salvo of the total of eight bombs dropped was considered to have included a direct hit. Then, having bombed another ship, *General*, regarded as being the German headquarters, with 112pdrs, as well as the Turkish War Office, Savory set course for home, having spent some 35 minutes over the target area.

Exactly what was achieved by this attack – because of the distances involved it was regarded at the time in much the same light as the Vulcan attacks on Port Stanley in 1982 – is now a subject for debate. The German press claimed that *Goeben* was undamaged but that a submarine had been sunk, although a British agent, described as of 'doubtful reliability', reported 29 killed and five wounded plus a destroyer and transport sunk, adding that the cruiser had escaped, as had the Turkish War Office, a neighbouring bookshop having been hit instead. What is known with certainty is that *Goeben* survived the war and continued in service with the Turkish Navy as *Yavuz Sultan Selim*, being finally decommissioned as late as 1960.

Göppingen Gö 9 A design for a German aircraft patented and built by Dornier in 1937 which had a tractor airscrew at the front and a pusher to the rear. Trials with this type supplied data on which the Dornier Do 335 (q.v.) Pfeil (Arrow) of similar layout was based. Although a small number of these had been produced by

Above: An RAF Vickers Victoria V troop-carrier K2797 over Heliopolis. This type participated in the evacuation from Kabul between 12 December 1928 and 25 February 1929 – the first major air-lift in history. (Author's collection)

the time of the German collapse, none reached operational fighter units.

Gosport An aerodrome in Hampshire, four miles west of Portsmouth. The land was acquired in November 1913 and preparatory work began in February 1914. Its historic claim in the field of air warfare lies in the establishment there of Major Smith-Barry's Special School of Flying in August 1917, the new type of pilot instruction practised there quickly becoming known as the 'Gosport System'. It was soon to be copied throughout the world's air force schools, doing away with the earlier haphazard methods, and its philosophy was summed up as follows: 'The object is not to prevent flyers from getting into difficulties or dangers, but to show them how to get out of them satisfactorily'. Gosport was finally closed in May 1956.

Gotha An almost legendary twin-engine bomber type of WWI, the term being inaccurately applied to all large enemy aircraft of the period. Best known were the G.III, G.IV and G.V versions, which shared the greater part of offensive sorties from 1917, the latter pair being significant in that they were fitted with a rearward-firing defensive armament. Gothaer Waggonfabrik AG was dissolved in 1919 but re-established in 1933, and it went on to produce warplanes for the Luftwaffe, including the Go 242 twin-boom transport glider and the Go 244 powered version. The company was also responsible for a number of other projects, not all of which achieved production status chiefly because of their late appearance.

GR An RAF role-designation indicating an aircraft type intended for Ground Attack/Reconnaissance.

'Grace' The Allied code-name for the Japanese WWII Aichi B7A2 carrier-borne attack bomber. Known to the Japanese as the Ryusei (Shooting Star), it was a large, single-engine type, completed in prototype form in May 1942. A number of improved versions followed, but its entry into service was restricted after the Funakata production plant was gutted by fire following an earthquake in May 1945. However, two Kokutais were equipped with it.

Grain Also known as Port Victoria, this was a British Admiralty station on the marshy Isle of Grain in Kent. It was commissioned on 30 December 1912 and proved useful for experimental work because of its remote location. Among the trials carried out at Grain were those of 1917 with a new design known as the Grain Kitten, a miniature aircraft with a span of only 18ft intended to be carried by destroyers and other small naval vessels. This was not a success, largely on account of the ABC Gnat motor giving only 35hp. The station was finally closed in 1924.

Gran Chaco A minor war between Paraguay and Bolivia waged between 1932 and 1935 which saw the first use in combat of some of the post-1919 designs of minor warplanes.

'Grand Slam' The 22,000lb, 25ft long deep-penetration or 'earthquake' bomb of WWII accommodated by Avro Lancaster bombers which had their bomb bay and lower fuselage cut away for the purpose. These aircraft were designated Mk I (Specials) and were first used in an attack by No 617 Squadron on the Bielefeld Viaduct on 14 March 1945. The first test-drop had taken place on 13 March.

GREAT BRITAIN

▶ The lessons learned as long ago as the Korean and Suez conflicts were drawn upon for the efficient service rendered by the RAF to the Coalition Force's mobilization for the Gulf War in 1991, where the modernity of the RAF was once more demonstrated by, for example, its 'brushfire' high-speed deployment and its first operational use of laser-guided bombs.

The close of the century found the RAF equipped for a changing type of warfare, with a higher reliance on technology than ever before, the vast numbers of aircraft associated with WWII no longer necessary. Among these fundamental alterations were the 'hard kill' and 'soft kill' methods associated with the now primary necessity of quickly destroying an enemy's radar system, the first calling for a weapons system to attack and destroy such installations and the second for specially designed aircraft to jam all counter-air radars and prevent them detecting bombers. Naturally, such reliance on electronics called for a vast increase in the numbers of airborne technicians. The new brevets 'AT' and 'FC' (Fighter Controller) signify this change, the latter being surveillance and weapon control specialists while the former fall into three categories, Communications Technician, Display Technician and Radar Technician.

Equivalent RAF Commissioned Ranks, 1918–19 and Present-Day

1.4.18–1.10.19	Current
Second Lieutenant	Pilot Officer
Lieutenant	Flying Officer
Captain	Flight Lieutenant
Major	Squadron Leader
Lieutenant-Colonel	Wing Commander
Colonel	Group Captain
Brigadier-General	Air Commodore
Major-General	Air Vice-Marshal
Lieutenant-General	Air Marshal
General	Air Chief Marshal
	Marshall of the RAF

General officers' uniforms and insignia were in practice the same as for the regular Army and all uniforms were khaki (replaced by sky blue after October 1919 and later by RAF blue) with fawn braid on the tunic cuffs, this having a narrow inner band of light blue, all being surmounted by a gilt eagle and crown. The peaks of caps were black patent leather and the wide, black headbands had a single, vertical, bright metal bar at each side of the central badge to denote First and Second Lieutenants, two each side for those of Captains. The peaks of field officers' caps were intended to have a single row of oak leaves while the caps of cadets had a white headband. Trade badges of airmen – such as those of 1st Class Air Mechanics (now Leading Aircraftman) and the original Wireless Operator insignia showing a fist gripping representations of lightning – were red. Buttons bore the familiar eagle surmounted by a crown but differed from subsequent practice in having the periphery edged with a rope design, indicating the service's naval origins.

The cap badges of officers differed little from those of the contemporary uniform, but those worn by mechanics consisted of a woven design formed by a vertical oval containing the eagle in flight, the whole surmounted by a crown, all in red on a black cloth background. Cap badges of NCOs were similar but in gilt wire with the details of the crown picked out in colour.

Above: Fairchild A-10s, officially known as Thunderbolt IIs but colloquially as 'Warthogs' due to their ugly lines, were intended as single-seat close support/anti-tank bombers and for this role the pilots were protected by a an armoured 'bath' capable of resisting all but groundfire of the heaviest calibre. (Author's collection)

'Granite' ROC procedure using flares to warn aircraft likely to fly into high ground. See Observer Corps.

'Grapple' The code-name for an operation between March and September 1957 to test the effectiveness of the British nuclear deterrent, using Malden Island, some 400 miles from the Christmas Island base, as the target. The aircraft used were eight Vickers Valiants of No 49 Squadron (formerly 'C' Flight, No 138 Squadron) specially modified, with tail cameras and given a coat of anti-flash white. Their crews were issued with protective clothing, shields and filters. The first bomb, dropped on 15 May, weighed 10,000lb and in its 'Blue Danube' casing was released at 600mph from 45,000ft, to detonate 35,000ft lower. Seven other bombs were dropped, and two were detonated in balloons.

Green Spot Fire An RAF marker used during WWII which burnt with a reduced ground pattern (although a high intensity) so that it could be used on small targets and as a route marker to guide a bomber force.

Greif (Griffon) The name adopted in Germany for the Heinkel He 177 four-motor bomber.

'Griffon' The code-name adopted by NATO for the Soviet SA-5, a 50ft long surface-to-air missile intended for the long-range destruction of an enemy aircraft and powered by a two-stage rocket motor. It was fitted for radar-homing and was wrongly regarded by some as having an anti-missile capability.

Also the name of a Rolls-Royce 2,000hp liquid-cooled engine developed during WWII and used to power such aircraft as the Spitfire XII intended to combat Fw190s, which in 1942 had been pressed into use as low-level fighter-bombers.

Ground attack aircraft A development of the 'trench fighter' of WWI via the idea of fighter-bombers of the next major conflict, having a more rugged construction for the work. The Hawker Typhoon, armed with rockets, and the Australian Commonwealth Boomerang may be counted as among the first modern examples, although these were at first introduced as conventional fighters. The A-10 'Warthogs' and Su-25 (see 'Fitter') carried the idea into the closing years of the twentieth century.

Grumman An important US aircraft manufacturer established in 1930, the foundations originating with the Loening organization. The traditional association of the Grumman Aircraft Engineering Corporation of Bethpage, New York, with naval aircraft was

Above: The Grumman Avenger first flew in action in June 1942 at the Battle of Midway, but such was its excellence as a torpedo-bomber that derivatives of the original design were still in service after 1945, among them being seven-seat transports and the 3U and 3M versions for target-towing and special night operations respectively. (Bruce Robertson collection)

Above: From an historical viewpoint the Grumman F4F is of interest in that it served with the United States Navy and Marine Corps as the Wildcat and, as here (where JX822 carries a 1,000lb bomb), with the Royal Navy as the Martlet. It was a contemporary of the Zero: the performance of the Japanese aircraft was superior, but the Grumman was capable of giving a good account of itself due to its sturdy construction and better armament. (Bruce Robertson collection)

Above: Resembling the Grumman F4F from which it was developed, the F6F Hellcat was the result of advice from battle-hardened pilots and a study of European air fighting reports, with the result that, once in service from 1944, the type was credited with 4,947 combat victories by carrier-borne examples alone. This F6F-5 is seen post-WWII. (Bruce Robertson collection)

established by the signing of a contract dated 2 April 1931 authorizing the company to construct the prototype of a new fighter, then designated the XFF-l. This success was something of a business coup because hitherto the youthful manufacturer had experience only in the construction of sets of floats to permit the conversion of landplanes to seaplane configuration. The FF-1 was a carrier-borne fighter aircraft fitted with a retractable undercarriage, something of an innovation for the time. Designs that followed were mainly intended for maritime use and included a number of amphibians, but the organization is perhaps best remembered for its Avenger design of WWII. Subsequent types included the twin-engine F7F Tigercat and the single-engine F8F Bearcat, both carrier-based fighters, followed after the end of the war by the F9F Panther and its swept-wing development the Cougar. A diversion from the company's traditional role of designing naval aircraft was the OV-1 Mohawk STOL observation machine for the US Army in 1959, and Grumman's naval associations were continued to the end of the twentieth century with the F-14 Tomcat (q.v.).

Gruppe See Staffel.

G-suits Aircrew suits laced with pipework to exert pressure on the wearer's body in high-speed manoeuvres, thus preventing 'black-outs' caused by a flow of blood from the brain. They were first used in mid-1944.

'Guideline' The NATO name for Soviet SA-2 used in mid 1950s by majority of Warsaw Pact forces. Reported to be 20ft long and have a range of 22 miles with the aid of a liquid fuel rocket motor boosted by solid fuel rockets for launching, it had radio command and was still being developed as late as 1969 when some sources stated that it could carry a nuclear warhead.

'Guild' The Soviet SA-1 mobile SAM missile with a dual-thrust solid fuel rocket. Introduced in 1960 as a replacement for 'Guideline', it was some 40ft long and was developed over a considerable period.

Gulf War On 2 August 1990 Iraq invaded Kuwait and within some four hours troops had entered Kuwait City, about 60 miles distant. As the first steps were taken to gather an international force to oppose the Iraqi move, and with the aid of a massive airlift, the 82nd US Airborne Division was dispatched to northern Saudi Arabia, along whose borders Iraq massed large armoured formations four days later.

There was a risk that a pre-emptive strike might be launched against the US concentration of equipment, using aircraft of French and Russian design with which the Iraqi Air Force was largely equipped. The Iraqi crews had gained valuable experience in the Iraq-Iran War, although their lack of aggression in this conflict had been noted. Even so, the threat was taken seriously in the West. The air arms of the Coalition air forces were the finest of their type, and patrols were mounted over the whole twenty-four hours, with the support of AWACS machines and in-flight refuelling (q.v.).

In the New Year there began a 38-day series of intensive air attacks against military installations, 'Scud' missile-launching sites and Iraqi Army formations using, in some cases, weapons hitherto untried under operational conditions, and after 100 hours of ground fighting the advance of the Coalition ground forces was halted and a cease-fire ordered which allowed the escape of many Iraqi army units and their equipment. About 110,000 air sorties were flown and 88,500 tons of bombs dropped, 7,400 tons of these being precision-guided weapons. A total of 44 Coalition aircraft were lost.

Gun Bus The popular name for two aircraft of the WWI period. One was Sopwith design originally produced for the Greek government in 1913 as the Hydro Biplane Type S. From this was quickly developed the landplane Gun Bus. A more powerful version fol-

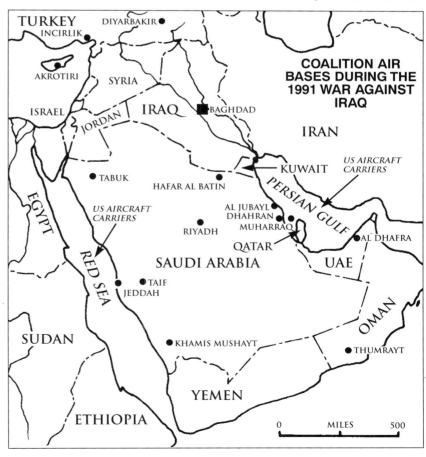

lowed, specially constructed for the Royal Navy, first as a two-seat fighter and later as a bomber with an elongated nacelle. The name was also used to describe the Vickers FB.5, a development of the 1914 FB.4. Like the Sopwith, this was a pusher, with the gunner seated in front of the pilot. The type began to be delivered to the RFC in mid-December 1914, the first to reach France joining No 2 Squadron at the beginning of the following February. In all, six RFC units were thus equipped. A single armoured variant was also constructed.

Guns Although as early as 1910 the United States Army had experimented with the possibility of mounting a gun on an aircraft, the general concept of flying machines was that they would be used in warfare for little more than scouting, so that the first decisions to arm aircraft were made at operational unit level in WWI when crews took aloft such weapons as bricks to fling through an opponent's propeller arc, grapples and duck guns, although on 27 November 1913 a Grahame-White biplane had flown at Wisley with a Lewis gun fixed to its undercarriage, followed a year later by a Short floatplane with a 1pdr Vickers gun. When machine guns began to be fitted to scout aeroplanes, the latter became in effect the first fighter types.

The way in which this was done at first presented difficulties since it was dangerous to fire through one's own airscrew, and although fitting the blades with deflectors and, later, methods of synchronising the action of the gun by the passing blade were tested in the field, the solution that generally found favour with the RFC only was to arm pusher aircraft with a forward-firing gun and so give a clear field of fire. Alternatively, guns were fitted at an angle to the centreline of a machine so that there was no risk of damage to a tractor airscrew. Meanwhile the generally accepted method of defending bombers was by the employment of a gunner, at first with several weapons points disposed round his cockpit and a single (later twin) gun. The weapon was mounted in a traversing ring, France at first using the Nieuport type although the British Scarff ring later became near-universal. However, in the developing

field of fighters the introduction of means of synchronizing the gun's action with the passage of an airscrew blade revolutionized both armament and aircraft design.

The usual calibre of the machine guns that could now be rigidly fixed to fire forward was that of contemporary rifles, although Britain had experimented with 37mm quick-firing guns on D.H.4s and F.E.2bs, an idea that was revived for the Westland F.29/27 after the war when the accepted armament of the final years of the conflict – two machine guns – was regarded as sufficient for new designs of the period. Bomber defence methods, too, remained unaltered, but the Le Prieur rockets introduced for use against observation balloons had been discarded, along with the explosive darts, 16lb incendiaries and light bombs for attacking Zeppelins.

Guns of all types had been aimed by means of ring-and-bead sights, but it was not long before Britain introduced the Norman vane-sight, a semi-automatic device for free guns. This was abandoned only when the increased speed of aircraft made it inefficient. Also there was the Aldis sight for fixed armament, and later came the reflector sight (q.v.), which enabled a target to be aligned in a projected circle of light. Increased speeds were to prove a problem for gunners protecting bombers, so these crewmen were protected first by 'lobster shell' hoods and then manually operated transparent cupolas. These were in turn succeeded by the power-operated turret, al-

though some nations, including Germany, continued to favour open positions protected by windshields. The basic pattern of transparent, enclosed defensive gun positions for bombers was then virtually set, and although changes in equipment such as the introduction of 0.5in calibre guns took place when the United States entered the war and operational experiments with remotely controlled barbettes were conducted, the next major step forward was to come with the adoption of radar detection and gun-laying, the British Boulton Paul Type 'D' tail turret fitted to late-production Avro Lancasters and Avro Lincolns being an example.

As war in Europe became seemingly inevitable, attempts were made to increase fighter armament, so that while some countries supplemented machine guns with one or more cannon, Britain alone doubled the four guns originally specified for its new fighters, banishing the synchronised fuselage-mounted weapons that had endured for so long. This was possible because the problem of outboard-mounted wing guns freezing was partially overcome.

In part due to the United States' isolationist policies, fighter armament in that country had not made as much progress as in Europe, so that some of the machines procured by the French Purchasing Commission were armed with four or six 0.303in guns or a mix of 0.303in and 0.50in guns, although exploration in fresh directions was being made for such types as the Bell

Representative Periods: Total Weights of Fire (Single-Seaters)

Date(s)	Aircraft	Weight of fire (lb/min)	Gun(s)
1915	Vickers F.B.5	9.5	1 x Lewis
1917	RAF S.E.5	37.5	1 x Lewis, 1 x Vickers
	Sopwith F.1 Camel	40.0	2 x Vickers
1918	Sopwith 5F.1 Dolphin	75.0	1 x Lewis, 2 x Vickers
1931–37	Gloster SS.19	110.0	2 x Lewis, 2 x Vickers
	Gloster Gladiator	165.0	4 x Brownings
1939–45	Messerschmitt 109E-2	290.0	2 x MG 17, 2 x MG FF cannon
	Supermarine Spitfire V	420.0	4 x Brownings, 2 x 20 Hispano cannon
	Focke-Wulf 190A-3	610.0	2 x MG 17, 2 x MG 151 cannon
1985–95	Rafale B	1,515.6*	1 x GIAT 791B cannon
	Fairchild A-10	6,384.0*	1 x GE GAU-87A cannon

*Selective rate of fire set at maximum.

Airacobra, which was armed with twin machine guns and a 37mm cannon firing through the airscrew boss.

After adopting cannon in 1940, Britain took the bold step of using such armament alone, introducing the four 20mm Hispano cannon of the Hurricane IIC, to be continued as standard on subsequent types, and later the twin 40-mm Vickers 'S' anti-tank guns of the IID. Similar thinking for anti-tank work in Germany created the Ju 87G. It was only a short step from heavy weapons such as these to the adoption of various rocket armament, British and US aircraft thus equipped doing tremendous damage during the liberation of France in 1944. In effect these weapons were the precursors of present-day air-launched missiles.

The development of larger aircraft guns continued, with the introduction of such deadly weapons as the 57mm cannon for the Mosquito XVIII and the 75mm weapon installed in some North American Mitchell B-25Gs, developments echoed by Germany's 20ft BK 7.5 gun carried by the Hs 129B-3.

Meanwhile, in the East, Japan was travelling along much the same road as the rest of the world, although here the tendency had long been to follow much the same line of reasoning as the US as to the number of fighter guns, although weapons of slightly greater calibre were in use. Nevertheless, as the war progressed, vigorous steps were taken to develop 20mm, 37mm and 40mm cannon alongside increasingly heavy machine guns, as well as guided missiles, reflecting the new age of guns and armament that was to come.

After the war the development of the machine gun was in a sense given fresh impetus by the United States' adoption of a new weapon based on an old principle, the Gatling gun, with its seven-barrel 30mm General Electric GAU-8/A, able to fire its 1,170 rounds at the rate of 70 a second – a punch far heavier than that of the RAF's 30mm Aden or the Armée de l'Air's DEFA 533 revolver cannon adopted as the twentieth century entered its final decades.

Any list of famous guns of the century must include the German 7.9mm Parabellum of WWI, which was a lightened Maxim working on the recoil system, firing 650–750rpm, and the

British and US mainstay, the 0.303in gas-operated Lewis (q.v.), the Mk 2 version of which, introduced in 1915, fired at 550rpm. Twenty-five years later the Browning M2 0.5in recoil-operated, 800rpm gun could be fitted in both wings and turrets and the similarly operated Mk 2 for turrets alone was of 0.303in calibre, firing at 500rpm. The final decades of the century saw the 20mm Oerlikon Swiss auto-cannon; the British Aden development of the German Mauser 30mm, a belt-fed five-chamber revolver operated by a recoil piston and gas introduced in 1950 and firing at 1,200–1,400rpm; the US M61A1, an electrically operated 20mm cannon for helicopters with five chambers and six revolving barrels, giving a combined 6,000rpm; and the US 20mm auto-cannon, one of the M-50 series, operating with the aid of an electric primer.

Ammunition may be divided into three general types: armour-piercing, with a hardened steel core covered by softer metal for rifling grooves; tracer, with a lead tip and containing a firework-like compound to take fire in flight; and incendiary, designed to penetrate and burn with its chemical content igniting on impact.

Gunship Developed by the United States during the war in Vietnam, gunships were at first modified transport aircraft fitted with an armament of machine guns or cannon to fire through side window openings and thus bring to bear a heavy concentration of fire on any chosen target, delivering what was in effect the aviation equivalent of a naval broadside. Such adapted aircraft were given the designation 'AC' followed by the normal type number. Later the idea was extended to heavy helicopters.

'Gus' The Allied code-name for the 'Nakajima AT-27' twin-motor fighter. The existence of the type during WWII was based on inaccurate intelligence reports, and such a type never in fact existed.

'Gwen' The Allied code-name for the Japanese Mitsubishi Ki-21-IIb heavy bomber which was later renamed 'Sally III'. It was adopted as part of the modernization programme for the Imperial Japanese Army, for which, although twin-engined, it was the first heavy bomber, making its maiden flight in December 1936. Two versions existed, of which the IIb was the heavier, re-engined version with a superior performance. Both were to see operational service, with a total of eleven Sentais.

H2S Self-contained S-band (10mm) airborne radar in service with the RAF from January 1943. It could be used for target identification and for ground mapping, bombers thus fitted

Above: The fairing over the ventral H2S scanner on an Avro Lancaster. (Author)

being identified by their prominent ventral scanner fairing. The device, which gave a crude picture of the terrain below, could be easily 'confused' by other radar returns over large built-up areas, but it had the advantage that it could not be jammed, although this was balanced by the Germans' use after March 1944 of the airborne 'Naxos' aid to interception so that night fighters could home directly on to a bomber's H2S signals. In July 1944 the similar 'Korfu' ground-based system was introduced, and use of H2S was restricted.

H2X A US development of H2S working on X-band (3cm) and popularly known as 'Micky'.

H-3 See Sea King,

H-19 See S-55.

Haddock Force An RAF bombing force assembled on two airfields near Arles to bomb targets in Italy, which was expected to declare war on Britain immediately. When this took place, Wellington bombers of No 99 Squadron were prevented from taking off on 11 May 1940 by French lorries deliberately blocking the runways (opinions differed as to whether such raids had been authorized). Meanwhile Whitleys of Nos 10, 51, 58, 77 and 102 Squadrons departed for the Channel Islands, there to refuel before attacking northern Italy. Having done so and been dispatched, all but thirteen were forced back by storms and severe icing encountered over the Alps. Bad weather hindered a sortie out of Salon, only a few aircraft finding the target, and the French collapse prevented further operations.

Above: The Handley Page Halifax was one of Britain's WWII trio of four-motor bombers, the others being the Short Stirling and Avro Lancaster. Little-known, however, is that the type was also used by Coastal Command, as a glider tug, for paratroop dropping, weather reconnaissance, on radio counter-measures sorties and on espionage Special Duties operations. (Author's collection)

Hailstone See Glider bomb

Halifax One of the RAF's three four-motor bomber types in service during WWII, the first variants being powered by Rolls-Royce Merlin liquid-cooled engines and the final variants by Bristol Hercules radials. The prototype was first flown on 25 October 1939 and the first operational Halifax sortie took place on the night of 10–11 March 1941 against Le Havre, the aircraft's daylight début being made on 30 June against Kiel. Six variants achieved squadron service, the maximum bomb load of the type being 13,000lb.

Halton The RAF apprentice fitters, training establishment at Halton Park, originally known as the Boy's Depot and part of the Royal Flying Corps. After the formation of the RAF, the first specially constructed buildings were completed in January 1922 and the scope of the course was eventually widened to embrace instruction for fitters rather than mechanics ('Boy Entrants').

Hamel See Parachute.

Hamilcar Built by General Aircraft, this heavy transport troop glider (q.v.), also used for tanks or cargo, was the largest of its type in service by the Allies during WWII and was constructed almost entirely of wood. It first flew with C. Hughensden at the controls on 27 March 1942 after trials with a half-scale model. Halifax aircraft were the usual tugs for the Hamilcar, the load of which could optionally consist of:

Military equipment
Tetrarch Mk IV tank.
Locust tank (US).
Two Bren gun carriers.
Three Rota trailers.
Two armoured scout cars.
17pdr anti-tank gun and towing vehicle.
25pdr gun with towing vehicle.
Bofors self-propelled gun.
Jeep with universal carrier and batteries.
Bailey bridge equipment.
48 ammunition and equipment panniers.

Construction equipment
D4 tractor and angledozer
Scraper and Fordson tractor-Grader
H.D.10 Bulldozer (in three gliders).
H.D.14 Bulldozer (in three gliders).

Hampden An RAF twin-motor medium bomber introduced into squadron service three years before the outbreak of war in 1939. It was known as the 'Flying Suitcase' from its fuselage shape (one that under active service conditions was to prevent crew movement) or the 'Panhandle' from its boom-like rear fuselage. It was powered by Bristol Pegasus engines, and a version fitted with H-type Napier Daggers was known as the Hereford. The aircraft is usually recorded as never having been used on operations, but a published claim was made by a pilot in 1943 to have flown one on several sorties against Italian targets, including Naples.

Handley Page A British aircraft manufacturer founded in 1909 which came to prominence as a producer of warplanes with the 0/100 of 1916, the first really successful heavy bomber, which was followed two years later by the 0/400 then the larger V/1500 design. After a spell constructing civil airliners, the Heyford from the company was the RAF's final biplane bomber, followed by the shoulder-wing Harrow bomber-transport and the Hampden (q.v.) and the Halifax (q.v.) four-motor type. After the war the company produced the Victor, one of the RAF's three V-bombers and the Hastings long-range troop transport.

Hardened steel shelter A protective building which by both its robust construction and shape is designed to accommodate one or two aircraft and protect them from all but a direct hit from modern weapons. Buildings of this nature are used by selected front-line units of many of the world's airforces.

HARM The US AGM-88 High-Speed Anti-Radiation Missile, an 800lb weapon with a range of eleven miles that can be pre-programmed to attack known sites. Fitted with a seeker head homing on emitting enemy radars, it saw widespread use during the Gulf War (q.v.). It could only be launched from outboard stations and was carried on LAU-118 rails.

Harmonize To align the fixed guns of a fighter aircraft to produce a convergent pattern of fire at a given range. During WWII this was usually reckoned to be 250yds for 0.303in machine guns and 700yds for cannon in the RAF, although there were lots of variations.

Above: The external appearance of production Handley Page Hampden bombers differed only from the prototype seen here in that the nose contours were modified. With a maximum bomb load of 4,000lb and a range of 1,885 miles, the aircraft was much used by the RAF in the early part of WWII, although it was unpopular with its crews because of its cramped accommodation. (Author's collection)

Harpoon An extended-range maritime reconnaissance aircraft, the PV-2, which entered operational service before the close of WWII, was constructed by the Lockheed Corporation and was based on the Lockheed PV-1 Ventura, which was in turn derived from the pre-WWII Lockheed Lodestar civilian aircraft.

Harpoon Sea skimming anti-ship missile. The US equivalent to the Excocet. The McDonnell Douglas AGM-84 Harpoon has a 488lb warhead and a range of at least 30 miles.

Harrier A British Hawker Siddeley VTOL design which was developed from the the P.1127 Kestrel, when it was powered by the then new Bristol Siddeley Pegasus vectored thrust turbofan, and made its first flight, tethered, in October 1960. Four years later nine Kestrels were constructed, for trial use by a tripartite German/British/US squadron. RAF production versions were fitted with a more powerful engine and sent to No 1 Squadron, thus becoming the first VTOL fighter to enter service anywhere in the world. The engine of the RAF machine was a 19,200lb Rolls-Royce Pegasus vectored turbofan giving a maximum speed of nearly Mach 1; the external loads consisting of up to 5,000lb of rockets, bombs, mines and 30mm cannon pods. Later developments were the United States' McDonnell Douglas AV-8B and the Sea Harrier, of which latter 29 of the FRS.2 (Fighter, Reconnaissance, Strike) version joined the Royal Navy in 1993. The Sea Harrier's radar is the GEC-Ferranti Blue Vixen, and its armament can include AIM-120 AMRAAM air-to-air missiles capable of striking a small, fast and low target up to 30 miles distant, beyond visual range.

Hart A British Hawker biplane design produced as a two-seat, single engine day bomber during the inter-war years. From it was developed a lengthy series of related warplanes which were used both at home and by foreign air forces in numbers. Some 700 of all types were built, including the Osprey carrier-borne reconnaissance aircraft and the Demon two-seat fighter. The prototype Hart first flew in June 1928

Above: Britain's successful pioneering of vertical take-off fixed-wing aircraft has revolutionized some aspects of air war. Here a McDonnell Douglas AV-8B of the US Marines, based on the RAF's Harrier aircraft, hovers on its efflux. (Dr F. Leach)

Above: The Hawker Tempest, which leapt to the notice of the British public following its successful use in countering attacks by flying bombs in 1944, remained in RAF use until the arrival of Vampire jets in 1949. These F.6 models are seen with No 6 Squadron stationed in the Canal Zone during that year. (Via L. J. Dickson)

and derivatives were still in service in minor roles in September 1939. There was some variation in powerplants among the six British models, but for most the engine was a 525hp Rolls-Royce Kestrel. Radial-engined versions equipped some overseas air forces.

Havoc The name adopted for the fighter version of the Douglas DB-7 family of aircraft during WWII. Originally ordered as bombers by France, some of these aircraft were diverted to Britain and were used as to night fighters, as were the remainder of the diverted batch. Two versions were operated by the RAF, the Mk I, powered by two Pratt & Whitney Twin Wasps and armed with eight 0.303in fixed machine guns, and the Mk II, with Double Cyclone engines and a modified fin and rudder and armed with twelve nose guns. A night intruder version also existed, while the US Ninth and Fifteenth Air Forces later operated the A-20/P-70 Havoc. See Turbinlite.

Hawker A British aircraft manufacturing company formed as a successor to the Sopwith organization after WWI and soon specializing in warplanes, of which the first was the Hornbill of 1925. Among others, the Horsley, Hornet and Woodcock followed, the last also being produced in Denmark as the Danecock; later came the series of Hart (q.v.) biplanes and the related Fury fighter, the first RAF machine to exceed 200mph. After the introduction of the Fury II with its superior rate

Above: Among the first of the new generation of RAF fighters armed with rockets was the Hawker Typhoon, such as EK497, seen here when serving with A&AEE. An early model, indicated by the framed hood which was later to give way to a moulded canopy, this example was later shot down in error in a 'friendly fire' incident while serving with No 183 Squadron. (BAe via Bruce Robertson)

of climb, biplanes were succeeded by the illustrious Hurricane (q.v.), Typhoon and Tempest of WWII. Hawker's entry into the field of jet fighters was signalled by the Sea Hawk and Hunter before the company merged into the Hawker Siddeley Group in 1960, by which time development work on the Harrier (q.v.) was proceeding.

Hawker Siddeley Aviation An airframe design, development and manufacturing subsidiary of the Hawker Siddeley Group created by the merger of 1960 and responsible for development work in the field of VTOL and for that of the (formerly Blackburn) Buccaneer.

Hawker Siddeley Dynamics A guided weapons subsidiary of the Hawker Siddeley Group (q.v.) responsible for such missiles as Blue Steel, Firestreak, Red Top, Sea Dart and Seaslug.

Hawkinge An RAF station near Folkestone, Kent, used for military purposes from 1915, permanent buildings being erected in 1916. The chief role of the site was as No 12 Aircraft Acceptance Park until the Armistice. A fighter station during the inter-war period, it was similarly used during part of WWII, although a Coastal Command element for which it was also a base participated in Operation 'Channel Stop' before D-day. The status of Hawkinge was reduced to Care and Maintenance at the end of 1945 and the airfield was eventually used for various civilian purposes.

HB WWII RAF designation denoting Heavy Bomber.

HB(N) WWII RAF designation denoting Heavy Bomber (Night).

HE British abbreviation for high explosive.

Heinkel He51 The final German biplane fighter. Also usefully employed as a ground attack aircraft in its C-1 version, it was used from November 1936 in the Spanish Civil War by the Condor Legion, having first flown in May 1933. It was at first the subject of clandestine design, only 75 being initially ordered, but such was the state of the warplane industry in Germany at this time that manufacture had to be subcontracted before the first were issued to JG 2 'Richthofen'. Later some 30 were ordered by the Spanish Nationalists. A small number were still in use in September 1939, including the 38 Heinkel 51B-2 floatplanes built for operations from cruisers.

Heinkel He111 A German medium bomber that was the mainstay of the Luftwaffe in WWII. It entered service in late 1936, early models having a stepped-down nose incorporated in the A, B and D versions and differing

Above: The mainstay of the Luftwaffe bombing force throughout WWII was the Heinkel 111. The He 111P variant seen here introduced the ventral gondola for a prone defensive gunner in early 1939. A torpedo-bomber version existed in the form of the He 111H-6, while the He 111Z glider tug comprised two coupled machines. Late in WWII modified aircraft of this type were used to air-launch V-1 flying bombs when the ground launching sites had fallen to the Allied advance. (Author's collection)

from the later variants, which were characterized by a multi-piece glazed nose. It was used in Spain by K/88 from 9 March 1937 and a series of improved models was steadily introduced, the He 111P being the main variant when WWII broke out. Torpedo-bomber, reconnaissance and V-1 launching models existed, the armament of later variants being increased and the dorsal gunner's position replaced by a turret. Perhaps the most bizarre modification to the airframe was that which created the He 111Z, consisting of two twin-engine machines joined by a single wing centre-section mounting a fifth engine. This type was used a glider tug. The internal bomb load of the standard machine, of which some 7,000 were produced, was 4,410lb.

Heinkel He115 A German Luftwaffe twin-motor floatplane which first flew in 1936 but was flown throughout the greater part of WWII and was one of the best seaplanes used by any of the combatants. It proved significantly successful during the Norwegian campaign of 1940.

Heinkel He162 Known as the Salamander, or popularly as the Volksjäger (People's Fighter), the He 162 was introduced as a 'last ditch' effort in the hope of reversing the certain defeat that faced Nazi Germany in late 1944. It was a single-seater with a dorsal-mounted jet engine exhausting between twin fins and rudders, and 275 of various types had been produced by VE-Day, with 800 more under construction. The armament was either two 30mm Rheinmetall Mk 108 cannon or two 20mm Mauser MG151/20 guns. A Mistel role, with the fighter mounted atop a Ju 288, was projected. The maximum speed of this machine, which was unstable in flight, was 522mph at 19,700ft.

Heinkel He177 A German six-seat heavy bomber and missile carrier known as the Greif (Griffon) and powered by two 2,950-hp DB610A-1 motors each consisting of two coupled powerplants, thus giving the appearance of a twin-engine machine. The type was issued to a number of operational units, but its service career was bedevilled by engine overheating prob-

lems so that aircrews quickly dubbed it 'The Flaming Coffin'. It was nevertheless used in combat, for ocean patrol, over the Russian Front and also over Britain in Operation 'Steinbock'. The maximum internal load of free-fall bombs was 13,200-lb, and, surprisingly for an aircraft with a maximum loaded weight of 68,343lb and a span of a little over 103ft, the original specification had called for a design capable of making dive-bombing attacks. The maximum speed was just over 300mph.

Helix' The NATO code-name for the Soviet Kamov Ka-27 helicopter. It bore strong resemblance to the Ka-25 but it was greater in length, had slightly larger diameter rotors than its predecessor and was powered by larger motors. The 'Helix-A' was the anti-submarine model, the 'Helix-B' being the naval infantry assault transport and the 'C' the SAR version. This last had search radar and an antenna in a radome under the nose, and other electronics, plus a rescue hoist above the cabin door on the port side.

Helmore See Turbinlite.

Hendon (1) An RAF Fairey-designed heavy bomber used only by No 38 Squadron and a Flight of No 115, the first being equipped with the type between 20 November 1936 and 9 July 1937. Only fourteen examples were constructed, No 38 Squadron at different times receiving them all. It was a twin-engine monoplane, the striking appearance of which was enhanced by its dark overall scheme of 'Nivo', and it boasted such features as a glazed forward defensive position and an enclosed cockpit. (2) An aerodrome at Colindale, North London, established by Grahame-White with the purchase of 207 acres of farmland in 1910 on which to establish his 'London Aerodrome' (at the time only the third flying field in the country). The field and shed were requisitioned at the outbreak of war in 1914 when it became a Royal Naval Air Station, three Belfast-truss hangars being built in the following year. Claud Grahame-White briefly becoming a Flight Commander in that service. After the war, the first RAF 'Tournament' (later Pageant) was held there in 1920, and it

was officially bought by the government five years later, the station becoming a base for the (later Royal) Auxiliary Air Force in 1927. The air displays became an annual event. In 1940 the station became an air transport base, and seventeen years later the final powered take-off from the site was made before the resident Metropolitan Communications Squadron departed for Northolt. The land was sold to the local authorities in 1970.

Henschel 293 See Glider bomb.

Heyford An RAF Handley Page biplane night bomber which first flew in prototype form in June 1930, the first aircraft entering service with No 99 Squadron three years later. Three variants were developed, some having open crew accommodation. A total of eight home-based units received the type, which, although relegated to second-line duties by such introductions as the Vickers Wellington, was still retained in a training role when WWII broke out. The maximum speed was 142mph and the bomb load 2,800lb.

HF A British type designation indicating a high-altitude fighter.

'Highball' A special spherical bouncing mine intended to sink the German battleship *Tirpitz*. The idea was suggested by Dr Barnes Wallis. It was intended that a pair of mines be carried in tandem in the open and enlarged bomb bay of a Mosquito aircraft, and tests were made with this type over Loch Striven, chosen for its remote location. In late August 1943 nine of No 618 Squadron's aircraft were loaded with the new weapons with orders to drop them unrotated, not on the battleship for which they had been developed but on selected U-boat pens. This operation was no sooner announced than it was unexpectedly cancelled, and the aircraft were placed in storage while further trials were made, again over Loch Striven. These gave improved results, and an operation was envisaged in which the mines, now dropped rotating, would be rolled into railway tunnels and detonate inside.

The Squadron was assembled to resume training at Wick in October while a number of the new mines were ordered from Vickers and tests were made with a ram air turbine on the starboard side of the Mosquitos, now powered by Merlin 25s, to increase the efficiency of the drive system. In fact, all the investigations came to naught, although some thought was given to using the lessons learned to permit 'Highball' operations by carrier-borne Mosquitos in the Far East. A new training phase for No 618 was begun to prepare it for anti-shipping work, but the Squadron was ordered to be disbanded on 29 June 1945.

During 1944 the United States had shown interest in 'Highball', and a Martin B-25 Mitchell and B-26 Marauder were both modified to take four such weapons, but these, like their British counterparts, were never used operationally.

Hiroshima A Japanese city destroyed by an atomic bomb on 6 August 1945 (q.v.). The US bomber crew were Col P. W. Tibbets, Capt R. Lewis, Maj D. van Kirk, Maj T. Ferebee, M/Sgt W, Dezenbury, T/Sgt R. Caron, S/Sgt J. A. Stiborik, Sgt J. Nelson and Sgt R. Shumard.

Hispano cannon For the beginnings of this weapon it is necessary to go back to 1916 when Guynemer (see 'Aces') suggested that single-seat scouts could be fitted with shell-firing guns both for attacks on U-boats off the Flanders coast and for long-range combat. The idea caught the imagination of Swiss engineer Marc Birkigt (see Hispano engines), and he modified a 37mm Puteaux gun, a weapon that had been experimentally used by a Voisin unit in 1915, shortening the barrel at a cost to muzzle velocity, and also allowing the pilot to perform single-handed loading in flight. This was flexibly mounted between the cylinder blocks of a geared Hispano-Suiza V-8 engine by means of a recoil spring and hydraulic recoil brake, and test versions were fitted to a number of SPAD scouts. Guynemer was credited with

HELICOPTERS

Although the first concept of such flying machines is attributed to Leonardo da Vinci as long ago as 1490, credit for the idea of the helicopter as a battlefield observation platform to supplement balloons must go to Germany, which produced an electric-powered rotor-craft during WWI. Focke-Wulf produced the twin-rotor FW 61 that first flew on 26 June 1936, and twenty examples of a military version, the Fa 223, were built soon afterwards, establishing a lead that was soon challenged by Igor Sikorsky, who produced his successful VS-300 in America during 1939. The VS-300 was rapidly developed to become the Sikorsky R-4 (the first rotorcraft to serve with the US and British armed forces), an evaluation example of which, the YR-4B, made the world's first deck landing with such a machine on board the USS Bunker Hill on 6 May 1943. Six months later the R-6 first flew, a type bearing a strong resemblance to its predecessor, the R-5, which as the four-seat S-51 was rapidly adopted for military flying and first served for such purposes in Korea.

By now Sikorsky was not alone as a designer of helicopters, and 1945 saw the introduction of the historic Bell 47, which, with its simple construction, transparent crew compartment and easy maintenance, was eminently suitable for war work, so much so that it was adopted as the H-13 by the US Army and as the HTL by the Marine Corps. Later redesigned as the HTL/HUL-1 Ranger, it was adopted by the US Navy for training and utility work. This type continued to be produced under licence by Agusta in Italy,

Kawasaki in Japan and Westland in Britain after the Bell line closed in 1962.

On 7 November 1949 Sikorsky's S-55 first flew, and it proved such a significant design that it was quickly added to inventories of the US Air Force, Army, Navy and Marine Corps, as well as being adopted by Britain, France and Japan, these countries also producing licence-built models. However, Sikorsky's departure from his native Russia had by no means robbed the Soviet Union of skilled helicopter designers, and in 1953 Mikhail Mil produced his second design, the Mi-4. As the 'Hound', this was soon to adopted for military use as a gunship, for anti-submarine work and for general purposes, a derivative, the Mi-14 ('Haze') being employed for maritime work.

Meanwhile, Sikorsky's design department had not been idle, and in 1954 it produced the S-58, its answer to the US Navy's specification for a new helicopter with increased range for anti-submarine work. Later adopted for all the US services, it was soon being built in Britain as the Westland Wessex, re-engined with twin Bristol Siddeley Gnome turboshafts. The US Navy developed the S-58 as a hunter/killer duo for ASW operations, one of each pair equipped with dipping sonar and the other armed with torpedoes. As a transport, the S-58 could carry up to sixteen troops.

While large-rotor machines such as this were emerging, it was also clear that a niche existed for lighter types, and although none of these reached the simplicity of the unpowered German Focke Achgelis rotorkite intended to be flown from submarines for observation while cruising on the surface, the British Army adopted the Saunders-Roe Skeeter for light observation. This was in turn replaced by the Westland Scout, which the Royal Navy adopted for shipboard work as the Wasp, a design that had emerged from the same P.531 private venture. In the meantime, following inspiration drawn from the Bell 47, France was to develop a whole series of Alouette helicopters, the third, produced over a period of twenty years, being used for light attack work armed with machine guns, cannon and anti-tank missiles.

At the opposite end of the design spectrum, twin-rotor helicopters were soon being designed for the warlike purposes for which their relative heavy lifting potential seemed to make them ideal. One of the first such was the RAF's Bristol Belvedere, its later opposite numbers including the Piasecki HUP-1 Retriever, an ancestor of the famous Boeing Vertol and one of a whole series of twin-rotor designs widely used in the 1950s. Another twin-rotor design was the Piasecki H-21 Shawnee, known by the West German Army as the 'Flying Banana' from its high ground angle forward and the sharply canted rear assembly. Meanwhile Nikolai Kamov was examining solutions to the problems of heavy-lifting machines in parallel with his successful co-axial rotor designs.

The Algerian war for independence was to become the proving ground for the large scale use of military helicopters. One design among many that are associated with the Vietnam conflict is the Bell UH-1, a turbine-powered utility machine that flew first in prototype form on 22 October 1956. Deliveries of the type, at first termed the HU, commenced three years later, these being the first turbine-powered aircraft of any type ordered by the US Army, where it was affectionately known as the 'Huey' from the initials of its original designation. The Huey proved invaluable for performing a wide number of roles, including troop transport, aerovac, gunship and ►

the destruction of an enemy aircraft at a range of 200yds with one such gun in July 1917.

With the end of the First World War, interest in the idea lapsed until the mid-1930s, when the Paris Hispano factory introduced its *'Moteur-Canon'* aero-engine with a 20mm shell firing through the propeller boss. The spur-gear reduction chain was raised to permit the gun to be aligned with the airscrew centre, the recoil being catered for by a rear buffer at the opposite end of the engine.

In France the immediate appeal of the device was made clear by its adoption for several fighters under design. These included twelve Dewoitine D.501s and derivatives such as the D.51 which saw service after 1932. Engine/gun combinations similar to the 12Xcrs 20mm *'Moteur-Canon'* were later incorporated in at least seven other French fighter designs, including some which saw service in the opening months of the Second World War.

Hispano thus being firmly established in the armament field, Britain applied for, and was granted, a licence to produce the gun alone, and the BSA factory at Sparkbrook delivered the first of the 582 A2 Hispano cannon it was to produce during the Second World War on 12 April 1940, while a factory was specially built at Grantham early in the conflict to pro-

duce this weapon. The cannon was fitted, one in each wing, to some Spitfire Is in 1940, but troubles with the feed were experienced and the design was rapidly eclipsed. Later models were installed in fighters such as the Tempest and Meteor.

Hispano engines The foundations of Hispano-Suiza Fabrica de Automoviles SA, eventually with its head office at Avenida de Jose Antonio, Madrid, and its aero-engine works at Carretera de Ribas No 279, Barcelona, were laid about the turn of the century when Swiss engineer Marc Birkigt began the production of motor vehicles. He quickly achieved notoriety in 1901

Above: The development of the Bell AH-1 HueyCobra was based on a realization of the importance of helicopters early in the Korean War and several derivatives resulted, all sharing the provision of a gunner behind the pilot with a forward-firing barbette under his control in addition to air-to-surface missiles. (Bruce Robertson collection)

with his Castro car, the Spanish connection being reflected three years later by SA Hispano-Suiza opening a Paris office and factory to market its cars.

With the outbreak of the First World War Birkigt investigated aero-engine production, his Hispano V-8 representing about half the specific weight (then about 5lb) of existing liquid-cooled motors by means of an overall lightening process, resulting in the 150hp 8Aa which powered the first SPAD scouts and the early British S.E.5

design. Large-scale production of this and its 180, 200, 215 and 220hp successors was met not only at the Paris factory, but also by thirteen other firms in France.

The war years also saw the grant of licences for the manufacture of Hispano engines in the United States, Italy and Russia in addition to limited production in Barcelona, so that Birkigt's power units became associated with a wide diversity of warplanes, from the S.E.5a to the Vickers Vimy, via the SPAD 12 and 13, Sopwith

Dolphin, Caudron R.11 and Bristol R.2B. Meanwhile Wolseley in Britain undertook Hispano engine production, their own versions being known as the Python, Adder and Viper.

Some twenty years later and a new world war found Hispano entering aircraft production when Hispano Aviacion manufactured the HS-42 and HA-43 advanced trainers for Franco's Spain, although these were powered by the Armstrong Siddeley Cheetah radial motor. The company's modest aircraft output, now under the guidance of

HELICOPTERS

▶ search and rescue. Indeed, so suitably did the UH-1 carry out the Army's requirements that a more powerful variant, the UH-1H, was produced.

But, despite growing competition, Sikorsky was never far from the vanguard of helicopter evolution, and this was proved in 1961 by the adoption of the new S-61 Sea King, the prototype of which had made its first flight in early March 1959. This design was innovative in that the fuselage formed a sealed, boat-like hull, the outrigger floats containing the retractable wheels so that the design was completely amphibious, making it suitable for hunter/killer duties. Its dipping sonar was complemented by a Doppler search radar installation and radar altimeter, the actual 'killing' being performed with the aid of homing torpedoes and depth charges up to a maximum weight of 840lb. A Russian response emerged in the form of the Mi-8 ('Hip-E'), which could be used also in a gunship capacity. The US Army still found a need in other fields for light, direct-lift aircraft, and the Light Observation Helicopter (LOH) competition of 1965 was won by the tadpole-like Hughes OH-6A Cayuse.

Two years later the ubiquitous S-61 was the subject of a fresh field of investigation which had seemed impossible a decade before – in-flight refuelling. This was successfully demonstrated in July 1967 when, with the aid of nine refuelling rendezvous, a non-stop crossing of the Atlantic was accomplished. It was not long before the technique was applied to military versions of the helicopter, although problems had first to be overcome arising from the dissimilar speeds of the aircraft involved. Meanwhile other developments were taking place, including the adoption of the Jet Ranger for the US Army and the entry into

Above: The modern instrumentation of a Westland Sea King HAS.5. (Royal Navy)

Professor Willi Messerschmitt, continued into the military jet age in 1955 with the C.10-C ground attack/trainer, though once again the engines (twin turbojets) were not of Hispano design.

'Hook' The NATO code-name for the Soviet Mi-6, the largest helicopter in service until the introduction of the Mi-12. The Mi-6 represented a decisive technical step forward when it first flew in 1957. It proved to be the fastest machine of its time, also pioneering heavy flying crane work with

the aid of lifting stub wings to lessen the rotor load in forward flight. It carried a crew of five, and one helicopter, piloted by Boris Galitski, established a record 62-mile closed-circuit flight at 211.36mph on 26 August 1964. The operational range was 900 miles.

'Hormone' The NATO code-name for the Russian Kamov Ka-25 helicopter. A total of nearly 500 Ka-25s were delivered before production terminated in 1975, these being of three versions. The 'Hormone-A' was a five-seater for

anti-submarine work, admirably suited for use from small ship platforms, equipped with 'Big Bulge' search radar, a 'Tie Rod' optronic sensor, sonobuoys and either dunking sonar or towed MAD. There was also the 'Hormone-B' missile-support helicopter, with a data link for mid-course guidance update of long-range anti-ship missiles, and the 'Hormone-C', an SAR/utility variant carrying a winch.

Hornchurch A historic RAF station established in 1915 and known at first

Above: A US Air Force Sikorsky HH-3E helicopter. (Author)

production of the Soviet Mi-8 ('Hip'), which latter was subsequently to serve with some twenty countries, including member nations of the Warsaw Pact. It was about this time, too, that there emerged a pair of heavy-lift helicopters, the Mi-10 ('Harke') and Sikorsky's S-64/CH-54 SkyCrane.

A fresh line of development involved the technique of using twin rotors which were no longer separate and independent (as with, for

example, the early H-21), but intermeshed or contra-rotated on a common shaft. This enabled fuselage length to be reduced. Among the types to benefit from this development was the Kamov Ka-25 ('Hormone'), the Russian Navy's standard ASW helicopter for many years which was employed aboard carriers, cruisers and destroyers in two forms, the 'Hormone-A' for submarine hunting and the 'Hormone-B' with missile-guidance radar.

But perhaps the greatest advance of all was that seen in 1961 when, at the Tushino Air Display, half a dozen Mi-6s, then the largest helicopters in the world, each disgorged a 26,000lb payload of troops, artillery, missiles and vehicles. European military helicopter design was meanwhile forging ahead, one example being the Sud Aviation Super Frelon, adopted by the Aéronavale chiefly for anti-submarine duties. ▶

as Suttons Farm, when it was used as a base for B.E.2cs intended to intercept airship raiders. The B.E.s were augmented by S.E.5as when the enemy began daylight operations with aeroplanes. Despite its return to agriculture in 1919, the land was used for a permanent aerodrome from 1928, when the new name was officially adopted, its role being chiefly that of a fighter station as part of London's defences. This brought it much atten-

tion from the Luftwaffe in WWII. Transferred to Technical Training Command post-war it was relegated to Care and Maintenance in 1947 and was finally closed on 1 July 1962.

Horsa A British Airspeed-designed WWII troop glider, one prototype of which made its first flight, towed by a Whitley bomber, from the Great West Aerodrome (later to become part of London's Heathrow Airport). With a

wingspan greater than that of the Wellington bomber. It was totally of wood construction and had a capacity for 25 fully armed troops. The first operational use was during the invasion of Sicily in 1943, and the type featured in large numbers in the operations following the Allied invasion of Europe on 6 June 1944. See Troop gliders.

Hotchkiss An early French 8mm free-mounted machine gun with a 25-round

HELICOPTERS

▶ However, despite such advances as these, the helicopter remained a potential victim of accurate ground fire despite the provision of facilities to defend itself such as machine guns and rockets. The United States tackled the problem in a different manner, redesigning the Bell UH-1 in the form of the AH-1 HueyCobra gunship, with the AH-1J SeaCobra for overwater operations. The Cobra 2000, a designation indicating the company's envisaged use of the basic design into the following century, appeared later, armed with 20mm cannon, rockets, laser fire control and night vision sensors.

As was the case with fixed-wing aircraft, helicopters had been evolved to fill specified roles, but an attempt to combine the two most potent of these, the assault machine and the gunship, was seemingly made in the early 1970s with the Mi-24. This not only had a potential eight-man capacity, but also massive firepower combining guns, rockets and cannon. The nose gun of the 'Hind-D' was of 0.50in with four barrels, 20mm gun on later models, while the two-man crew was protected.

Meanwhile the US Army was making an attempt to evolve the 'ultimate' Advanced Attack Helicopter (AAH), with an airframe giving a low radar signature, its powerplant emitting diffuse exhaust gases (thus reducing the risk of missiles locking on to the infra-red heat source), and a fuel tank and rotor blades capable of absorbing hits by 23mm shells. Other innovations as the century closed included combat ranges extended to perhaps 155 miles armed with 20mm or 30mm cannon, plus new missiles of greater range and air-to-air capability, forward-looking infra-red sensors and crews wearing visors giving flight information. Thus equipped, the gunner was able to deal with simultaneous targets in two ways, either by

merely looking at them, allowing the helmet-linked sights to lock on, or by designating a thermal imager to do this. Other equipment included a digital mapping system (undetectable by radar), electronic countermeasures, a radar warning system and chaff and flare dispensers.

DASH unmanned anti-submarine rotor-craft drones, such as the Canadair CL-227, were among other developments, as were sophisticated concepts such as the Bell XV-15, which had stub aerofoils carrying swivelling rotors at the tips, permitting re-alignment for conventional forward flight.

Above: A detail view of a Soviet Mi-8 helicopter, showing, forward of the fixed undercarriage, one of the several launchers for 55mm unguided rockets that make up the bulk of the armament, suspended from six hardpoints. In addition a 12.7mm machine gun is carried in the nose. (Author's collection)

Above: A Hucks mobile engine starter. (Author's collection)

drum. later replaced by the Lewis (q.v.).

'Hound' The NATO code-name for the Soviet Mi-4 utility helicopter that first flew in May 1952 before entering large-scale production. Three variants existed, the 'Hound-A', a version used by Czechoslovakia with clamshell doors for bulky loads, including military vehicles, being the best-known.

Hucks Starter A semi-universally mounted shaft, chain-driven from the engine of the mobile chassis on which the whole was mounted, which engaged a dog on an airscrew hub, rotating this to start an aero-engine. It was used during WWI and later, and it is said to have been developed by pioneer aviator C. B. Hucks

HUD Head-Up Display. A system wherein an aircraft's performance or

Above: The shaft of a Hucks starter, engaged in the airscrew dog of an Avro 504K. (Author)

Above: A Lockheed Hudson, showing the distinctive flap-guides at the trailing edges of the wings. (Author's collection)

attack information is projected on to a transparent screen in the forward line of sight of its pilot.

Hudson A military version of the Lockheed 14 Super Electra used by the RAF during WWII as a maritime general reconnaissance aircraft. Two hundred were ordered by the British Purchasing Commission in June 1938, initial deliveries arriving by sea without turrets (which were fitted at Liverpool) on 15 February 1939. A total of 800 were finally employed, in six variants. Early Hudsons were powered by a pair of 1,100hp Wright Cyclone GR-1820-G 102A radial motors, later changed to 1,200hp Pratt and Whitney Twin Wasp S3C4-Gs. The bomb load was 750lb, later increased to 1,000lb, and the maximum speed of the final Mk VI was 284mph at 15,000ft.

'Hunger' The operational code-name for the RAF air transport of rice for starving inhabitants of southern Burma during 1945–46.

Hurricane A British fighter aircraft designed by Sydney Camm and built by the Hawker Aircraft Company. It was first conceived as the 'Fury Monoplane' of October 1934, and after the decision had been taken to exchange the Goshawk engine for the new Rolls-Royce PV12 motor (later to become the Merlin), a prototype was ordered on 21 February 1935, this making its maiden flight on 6 November. An official contract for 600 was placed in June 1936, increased to 1,000 in November 1938. The first RAF squadron to be equipped with the Mk1 was No 111 in December 1937, and some of this version, with fabric-covered wings, were still in use during the Battle of France and not entirely replaced by the time of the Battle of Britain, in which the aircraft's girder-like construction proved capable of absorbing great punishment. Subsequent variants were armed with twelve instead of eight machine guns, four 20mm cannon, two underslung Vickers "S" guns or eight 60lb rockets, and were used as fighter-bombers. It was September 1944 before the last of the 12,780 built in Britain was delivered. An additional 1,451 were constructed in Canada, designated Mks X, XI, XII and XIIA.

'Hurricane' The British code-name for a series of bombing attacks on German targets during WWII which were intended to emphasize the overwhelming superiority of the Allied Air Forces. The policy was summed up in the 'Hurricane Directive' issued on 13 October 1944, and the first of the series ('Hurricane 1') was intended to achieve the virtual destruction of the industrial Ruhr, the first actual sortie being carried out against Duisburg on 14 October 1944 and involving 1,013 RAF bombers operating in daylight with a fighter escort. Later that day 1,251 bombers of the US Eighth Air Force, with an escort of 749 fighters, raided Cologne, again during daylight, while after dark 1,005 RAF bombers again visited Duisburg.

Hustler The US B-58 supersonic strategic bomber which made its first flight in 1958. A Convair design, it was capable of a maximum speed of Mach 2.1 at 70,000ft, although it was later to be used in a low-level role. Capable of taking five nuclear or stand-off bombs, or alternatively air-to-surface missiles, it had a maximum range of 2,000 miles and could be fitted with rocket-powered BLU-2/B-2 or MB-1C underfuselage pods for weapons and fuel. Fatigue, operational suitability and high costs limited the Hustlers to a life of only nine years, the two Bomb Wings equipped with it having their aircraft withdrawn on 31 January 1970.

HVAR The abbreviation denoting High-Velocity Aircraft Rocket.

'Hydra' The operational code-name for the attack carried out by the RAF on 18 August 1943 on the German experimental base at Peenemünde, intended to kill as many as possible of the 8,000 technicians and scientists employed there, chiefly on the development of V-1 flying bombs and V-2 rockets. It was delivered by three waves of 600 aircraft dropping almost 600 tons of high explosive in 30 minutes. Five days later work at the station was transferred to the underground centre at Kohnstein. See Flying bomb.

Hydrogen bomb A nuclear fusion weapon achieving its explosive effect from uniting the very light atoms of deuterium and tritium versions of hydrogen, the fusion being obtained under considerable heat, to create which a fission device provides the trigger. The principle is therefore dif-

ferent from that of the atom bomb (q.v.) which is a nuclear fission weapon. See Neutron bomb.

I.A.R.80 The only indigenous fighter designed and produced in quantity by Romania during WWII. The Romanians built the PZL P.24 under licence in 1937, and the new fighter, which first flew towards the end of 1938, was an ingenious combination of some of the major parts of the earlier type, with a new forward fuselage, centre-section and wing. The armament of the early models, first produced in 1941, consisted of four 7.7mm machine guns and two 20mm MG FF Oerlikon cannon, although these were later replaced by Mauser MG 151s. A pair of external bomb racks was fitted to the I.A.R.80 of the home defence units that first received the type in early 1942. Production ceased in the spring of 1944 to make way for Messerschmitt 109Gs when some 120 of the indigenous type had been manufactured. The engine was a single 940hp Gnome-Rhône 14K fourteen-cylinder radial, giving a maximum speed of 317mph at 13,000ft.

IFF Identification, Friend or Foe. A radio transponder sending out a continuous coded signal indicating a friendly aircraft.

'Igloo White' US operations in 1967 against the infiltration network known as the Ho Chi Minh Trail, air-dropping

seismic and acoustic sensors to detect traffic and transmit their presence back to the Infiltration Center at Nakhon Phanom. Aircraft involved included the EC-121R radio-relay version of the Lockheed Constellation.

Igo The general designation for Japanese air-to-ground guided missiles initiated for the Army by Koku Hombu during the mid-years of WWII. These included the Mitsubishi Igo-1-A, a part-wood, rocket-engined monoplane to be dropped by a Ki-67; the smaller Igo-1-B, designed by Kawasaki and test-dropped by a Ki-48-II; and the Igo-1-C, designed by the Tokyo Imperial University, intended to home on the shock waves of a warship's guns.

Il-2 The 'Ilyusha', as the type was known to the Soviet soldier, was the first military aircraft from the Ilyushin design bureau and one of Sergei Ilyushin's earliest machines. It was a single-motor, low wing monoplane, and the first were single-seaters although later models had a gunner. The type was used throughout WWII for ground attack, the two versions frequently operating at low altitude in pairs without fighter escort, or in formations of ten with escort at about 1,000ft altitude. Armed with four fixed machine guns and two fixed forward-firing 23mm cannon, the aircraft proved of great value in destroying enemy AFVs, its crew being protected

Above: The Ilyushin Il-2m Shturmovik was among the most successful military aircraft in the world, so successful in fact that Soviet Russia maintained the largest production run in history, an output of 1,200 per month resulting in an estimated 40,000 being built. It was originally designed as a single-seater, and its true potential as a close-support machine was only fully realized when a second crew member was accommodated. Armament consisted of either bombs or rockets. (Bruce Robertson collection)

by heavy armour. Eight 55lb rockets could be carried under the wings, and these weapons proved their value in such actions as that when the Luftwaffe attempted to relieve the trapped 16th Army at Staraya early in 1942. The Il-2 was widely known as the 'Shturmovik', although the term was not a type-description but more correctly described all Soviet ground-attack and assault aircraft.

Ilmen A Russian lake near which 100,000 German troops were trapped in February 1942. Attempts to relieve them took the form of the first major airlift in history. Ground forces eventually managed to reach them by 19 May, by which date a total of 33,086 sorties had been flown in, bringing 64,844 tons of supplies and 30,500

troops, part of the relief force being transported in gliders.

Ilya Mourometz An important design by Igor Sikorsky which was based on the earlier giant Bolshi (Great) and Russki Vityaz (Russian Knight) designs. It first flew in 1913 and was named after the tenth-century Russian folk-hero. Powered by four engines, two of 132hp and two of 140hp, it made a pioneering long-distance flight from St Petersburg to Kiev in 1914 and was later experimentally converted to a floatplane.

An order for ten from the Central Board of the General Staff resulted in the deliveries being concentrated into a single operational unit, the Eskadra Vozdushnykh Korablei (Squadron of Flying Ships), and these aircraft were

equipped with a defensive armament of three machine guns. The first operational mission was flown only six weeks after the formation of the unit, Capt Gorskoff's aircraft dropping 600lb of bombs; in another notable mission, in the summer of 1915, Capt Ivan Baschko's IM (as the type was universally called) was credited with the destruction of a train in Prjevorsk railway station. Meanwhile production was accelerated and some examples were even fitted with self-sealing fuel tanks.

Fresh variants began to appear, including the smaller and lighter Type V that entered service during the winter of 1915 and was capable of a greater maximum speed and an improved ceiling. EVK units began to be regarded as élite. The Type D was characterized by its large glazed nose,

---

INDIA AND BURMA

Both Britain and the United States having national interests in this theatre, it was two years into WWII before a firm operational programme was agreed upon, one of the first moves being the provision of facilities at Rangoon from April 1941 for Lend-Lease goods to China to be sent to the Burmese capital for trans-shipment along the Burma Road, despite a savage Japanese offensive employing 100,000 men (which was finally halted at Shingbwiyang by the monsoon in May 1942).

Eight weeks earlier the US 7th Heavy Bombardment and 51st Fighter Groups had been assembled in the India-Burma theatre, equipped in the main with seven B-17s and 10 P-40s. However, further Japanese successes gave impetus to the establishment of air transport operations between India and China.

Following this, October saw the formation of the India Air Task Force, composed of the 7th Bomb Group (Heavy) now expanded to four squadrons, the 341st Bomb Group (Medium) with three squadrons, and two squadrons of the 51st Fighter Group, a total of 99 aircraft. To this was added a China Air Task Force made up of 98 aircraft, composed of four fighter squadrons and one of medium bombers and together these two Forces made up the operational arm of the Tenth Air Force, committed, with its total of 197 machines to the defence of the Hump route.

During this period a steady build-up of Allied air strength was begun, the progress of which is shown in the following table:

	Oct 1942	Dec 1943
Fighters	63	141
Medium bombers	9	37
Heavy bombers	16	48
Transports	48	267
Photo-reconnaissance	13	10

On the wider canvas, this progress was to be reflected by the results of the Quebec Conference of September 1943, attended by both President Roosevelt and Winston Churchill, for it was to create the South-East Asia Command for the British/American prosecution of the war in Asia, the air forces of the two nations having co-equal status with surface forces and operating under a unified Eastern Air Command. This had its headquarters at Calcutta and exercised control over all RAF and AAF units assigned to the air war over Burma and the defence of bases in Bengal and Assam. It consisted of:

No 222 (Coastal) Group RAF A general reconnaissance group based in South-East Asia.
Air Transport Command The India–Burma–China division was controlled directly from Washington with coordination of CBI agencies commanded by US Army Air Forces, India-Burma.
20th Bomber Command Also controlled directly from Washington, this force was available for attacks on selected targets in South-East Asia.

Fourteenth Air Force Not integrated in the larger air arm, this force was directly responsible to the theatre commander until 24 October 1944, when command was passed to China.

It is important to note the events which had gone before in order to understand the magnitude of establishing such a Command, and to do this it is necessary to go back to the Japanese assault on Rangoon, which began in December 1941 and lasted throughout the following January and February. In Burma, the RAF at the time could only muster three Hurricane fighter squadrons, with support from the 21 P-40s of the AVG, the total of serviceable aircraft from the two never amounting to more than 45. Plans to augment these proved impossible due to the speed of the enemy advance following air attacks frequently consisting of up to 70 bombers protected by escorts of some 30 fighters each, so that from such attacks the RAF and Col Chennault's AVG were finally able to claim a total of 137 victories, but despite such successes it was clear that a withdrawal of the ground forces was unavoidable, and this the air arms covered before themselves retreating to Magwe, there only to be pounded by the enemy so that by March 1942, all that remained of Allied air power in southern Burma were six Blenheims, eleven Hurricanes that were later withdrawn to Akyab and three P-40s which were later retired to Lashio. Nevertheless, on such reverses as these the EAC was formed as earlier outlined.

It operated in the face of enemy air activity which reached a peak during March, April and May 1944 when 2,700 sorties were

and the final model of the *Ilya Mourometz* was the largest and heaviest of all, the Type Ye-2, which was defended by eight gun positions – a small increase over the seven of the penultimate Ye-1. Such monsters as these were not easy to fly, and pilots were chosen as much for their physique as for their airmanship. Constant pressure was needed for the control column, and it was common practice to send the entire crew aft as a prelude to landing.

By the time of the Revolution, the Kerenski government had halted production, but about 80 had been delivered, divided equally between operations and training. Some 30 are reported to have been destroyed by their crews at Vinnitsa to prevent their capture by the advancing Germans at the

beginning of 1918, while the remainder of the EVK squadrons slowly disintegrated as the country slipped deeper into anarchy.

Impala See MB.326.

Imphal Capital of Manipur state in India, close to the border with Burma to which a massive airlift involving 18,300 tons of supplies and 12,622 reinforcements was flown between 1 April and 23 June 1944. More than 10,000 wounded were evacuated by the Allies using both bombers and transport aircraft.

Incendiary devices Free-fall missiles to set targets alight. The earliest took the form of crude conical bombs wound with impregnated 'rope' to pro-

vide the necessary flammable substance. They were used during WWI, but were eventually replaced by weapons the content of which was chiefly thermite, a mixture of iron oxide and aluminium powder which, when ignited, becomes incandescent. Other contents have been magnesium, petrol/rubber and jellied oil or petrol. Added later were oil bombs, heavy cylindrical missiles containing oil and other flammable substances. On impact, these bombs burst and scattered the contents for a distance of several yards.

The larger incendiary bomb measured about 18in in length and was a little over 2lb in weight, sufficient to penetrate the average roof. Many thousands could be carried by an attacking force, an example of the type of chaos

observed or plotted, from which 309 aircraft were to be confirmed lost either on the ground or in air combat, but although Japanese activity by no means lessened thereafter, its intensity did, in part due to a lack of reconnaissance. Countering this state of affairs was an increase in Allied sorties, which were concentrated at first on enemy airfields, the attacks being most sustained in Operation 'Eruption' on 3/4 November 1944. In this 49 B-29s, 28 B-24s and 156 P-47s and P-38s took part, while diversionary attacks were made on six airfields by B-25s, Mosquitos, Spitfires, P-47s and P-38s of the Tenth Air Force and No 221 Group.

Meanwhile operations over the Hump continued, since this was the route on which China depended for the supply of its war material. The scale of the effort is indicated in a comparison of the tonnage transported, rising from a mere 100 tons in early 1942 to 12,641 two years later. The initial operations here had been conducted by the Tenth Air Force, but it quickly became clear that a separate command was called for which was not involved in combat, so that an India-China Wing, ATC, was activated, assuming control on 1 December 1942. At about the same time a new and similar supply route was envisaged to provide support for the ground armies in the northern Burma campaign. This too, became the responsibility of the heavily committed Tenth Air Force after the road was formally opened on 28 January 1945, so that troop and cargo aircraft began flying at an operational rate of 220hr each per month, placing a burden of 150 to 200 flying hours per month on pilots and 300 hours on radio operators.

Meanwhile Bomber Command operations in India were not neglected, China acting as a staging base for the 20th's B-29s flying from their main base in the Calcutta area, and in a nine-month period ending in March 1945 twenty-six primary targets were attacked in 1,070 sorties which saw the dropping of 4,664.5 tons of HE bombs, plus 670 mines, on railheads, oil refineries, harbour installations, supply dumps and railway bridges. Naturally, operations of such magnitude had themselves to be supplied, so here again the Hump came into its own, B-29s and C-46s flying in 14,517 tons of fuel and supplies to the Tenth's North China bases.

Mention has been made of the handicap suffered by the Japanese because of the lack of adequate reconnaissance, and that the AAF and RAF realized the vital nature of this is illustrated by the importance placed on such sorties, due in part to the prevailing lack of intelligence from ground sources. Since the maintenance of air superiority depended on a knowledge of Japanese dispositions and strength, daily coverage had to be made of airfields within 1,200 miles of the Allied base area – as many as 80 had to be photographed daily. Similarly, all railways and important roads in Burma and Siam were photographed, as well as the Bangkok–Singapore railway to a point south of the Malayan frontier, to give information on the condition of bridges and the use of the railway and also a count of rolling stock, and this, combined with the results of survey photography, gave the necessary information to produce accurate maps. In addition, battle area photographic coverage was

made of the territory over which the Fourteenth Army and 15th Corps campaigns were to be carried out, well in advance of ground operations, thus providing commanders with reliable information on essential geographic features. Enemy anti-shipping operations were monitored as well, a daily count being made of coastal shipping and barge movements. In this way just under sixty per cent of all Burma had been mapped by May 1944 – an area of 152,000 square miles, three times the size of England – and by January 1945 354,000 prints per month were being delivered to air and ground forces.

Anti-submarine and general reconnaissance operations were almost entirely the preserve of the RAF, and between 15 December 1943 and 1 June 1945 a total of 5,848 sorties were flown, including those directed to the laying of 1,078 mines. The areas to be covered were vast and included the Indian approaches, the Mozambique Channel, the Gulf of Aden and the Bay of Bengal.

A little-known aspect of the India-Burma air campaigns concerns the number of agents who were dropped behind Japanese lines by parachute and in some cases supplied thereafter entirely by air. In northern Burma, for example, an army of 5,000 to 10,000 Kachin rangers operated. They were equipped with radios and by this means supplied the Tenth Air Force with specific target information on hundreds of Japanese supply points. Similar work in Burma and Siam was exclusively the responsibility of the RAF.

caused by their use being the fire raid on 7 August 1940 by the Luftwaffe: 613 canisters of incendiaries were dropped on London and 31,000 fire-fighters, regular and volunteer, had to be mustered to deal with the situation, which involved 2,500 individual fires, six of them officially described as 'con-flagrations' and sixteen merely 'large'. These were blown by a westerly wind, although such fires always create their own gigantic updraught and therefore an artificial fanning of the fires. Some incendiary bombs have also contained an explosive charge intended to kill those tackling the immediate blaze created.

An alternative device in use at the time by the RAF was the incendiary leaf, code-named 'Razzle'. Intended at first to be dropped on German forests, it consisted of two strips of celluloid, some 3in in length, between which was sandwiched a small piece of phospho-rus wrapped in wet cotton wool. Packed moist, about 450 to a canister, these were dropped via a chute, to ignite on the ground after naturally drying out. A larger type was known as 'Decker'.

Other artificial fire-raising devices have included the incendiary bullet of WWI (see Buckingham) and, from the same period, the Ranken Dart. This lat-ter consisted of tube about 5½in long and weighing 13oz, filled with an explosive designed to send back a shower of sparks to ignite a mixture of air and the hydrogen escaping from

IN-FLIGHT REFUELLING

The first successful refuelling of an aircraft in flight from another aircraft in order to increase its duration or range took place on 27 June 1923 over San Diego when a D.H.4 of the US Army Air Corps made repeated refu-ellings of a second machine of the same type flown by Lts L. H. Smith and J. P. Richer, enabling them to remain aloft for four days, thereby establishing a world endurance record. Although there are reports of a second such feat over a Kelly Field carnival on 18 November, the next authenticated case took place in the same year when two Frenchmen, succeeded in passing twelve gallons of fuel in five minutes at 10,000ft over Le Bourget. Six years later the US Army again demonstrated the technique using two Douglas-built C-1 tanker biplanes to pass over 5,000 gallons to the Fokker C-2 trimotor piloted by Maj Carl Spaatz, enabling the monoplane to stay in the air for 553 hours. To achieve this 223 ren-dezvous were made, between 50 and 90 gal-lons being passed on each occasion. This achievement was rivalled in the same year, 1929, by the Americans Jackson and O'Brian, who stayed aloft for 420 hours between 6 and 24 July in a Curtiss Robin light monoplane over St Louis. However, for each such demon-stration crude equipment had to be put togeth-er and the first manual contact had to be made with the aid of a trailing line towed by one aircraft, calling for great flying skills.

The first similar attempts made in Britain were those by long-distance flyer Alan Cobham, following the American pattern and accomplished using two D.H.9s in 1932. More ambitious trials were undertaken the next year, again using a D.H.9, this time to replen-ish the tanks of a Handley Page W.10 trans-port biplane. However, one of the first practical tests of flight refuelling was to come in 1934 when Cobham and Sqn Ldr Helmore (q.v.) attempted a non-stop flight to India using an Airspeed Courier; once more the tanker was the reliable Handley Page W.10 G-ABMR. The two men took off from Portsmouth on 24 September, having taken on board 275 gal-lons into overload cabin tanks, but all came to naught: the provision of a series of RAF tankers along the route was unused, not due to any fault in the refuelling system or organi-zation but from the breakage of a throttle lever in the Courier so that a forced landing had to be made at Malta, the first rendezvous point out from England. A spin-off from this abortive attempt was the association formed with A. Hessel Tiltman, who was to remain the con-sulting engineer for the British development of refuelling in flight for the next twelve years. The techniques embraced such advances as the evolution of the principles of aligning the tanker and receiving aircraft in 1935 as well as the development of improved equipment. The year also saw the grant of a patent for similar work conducted by Flt Lt R. L. R. Atcherly, of Schneider Trophy fame.

Interest in the new technique was still divided between the RAF and civil flying. The aviation world was witnessing the increasing popularity of long-distance passenger flights, and the formation of the British firm Flight Refuelling, enjoying the benefits of having Atcherly's patents assigned to them, came as no surprise. It was supported by Imperial Airways, which was then looking into the problems associated with operating its Short Empire flying boats that were being consid-ered for work over the Atlantic. G-ADUV Cambria was chosen for the tests, the tanker now being the Armstrong Whitworth 23 proto-type (a forerunner of the Whitley bomber) in the trials over Hamble begun on 20 January 1938. New equipment which had been spe-cially designed in the light of increasing expe-rience meant that the trials, some of which had to be made under weather conditions that included rain, cloud and fog, were deemed a success.

The new tankers, capable of better speeds than the Handley Page W.10s, had been acquired in 1937 and included an H.P.51, but both this and the A.W.23 were rendered obsolete for the work in the spring of 1939 by the acquisition of three Handley Page Harrows, G-AFRG, G-AFRH and G-AFRL, the first pair being sent to Hattie's Camp (later Gander) in Newfoundland and the third to Rineanna, later Shannon. All were capable of carrying 900 gallons of transfer-able fuel and represented a great improve-ment over the Vickers Virginias that Imperial's directors had witnessed giving a demonstra-tion in 1933.

The flying boat service across the Atlantic was the first large project involving flight refuelling, Imperial Airways' G-AFCU Cabot and G-AFUV Caribou making a total of sixteen crossings between Hythe and Montreal during August and September 1939. The preliminaries had begun in May, when 'FCU, flown by Capt Parker, was suc-cessfully attended by a tanker on the 24th, while FCV was similarly refuelled in the air on 3 July. Nine days later this boat was cleared for take-off at 50,500lb and landing at 48,000lb, so that on 5 August Capt Kelly Rogers inaugurated the new weekly service from Southampton, calling at Foynes and then being refuelled after take-off for New York via Botwood and Montreal. Eight such crossings were made each way, ending with Cabot's eastern flight on 30 September, refu-elling having successfully taken place on the 15th when it was required. Each transfer took only eight minutes, 800 gallons being passed in that time, between three and seven min-utes additionally being taken by the two air-craft making contact and linking the hose. It was decided to double the service in 1940 with extra boats so that the whole summer season could be served.

As we have seen, the foundations of in-flight refuelling had been laid in the United States and much of the pioneer work per-fected in Great Britain, but it was at about

the fabric of an airship which the dart was expected to pierce. This it did with the aid of a cast iron nose. It was supported during its fall from an interceptor flying some 60ft above by a small rubber parachute. These darts were released from cases containing fifty, and the charge was ignited by the opening of three sprung arms which also prevented a total penetration of the fabric. The resultant tug from the iron nose pulled an internal wire and ignited the contents.

Independent Bombing Force The British Independent Force was formed towards the end of WWI to enable bombing attacks to be carried out against strategic targets without weakening the RAF's commitment to actions on the Western Front. It was originally intended to consist of 100 squadrons, but only nine were ever formed. These dropped 543 tons of bombs between 6 June and 11 November 1918, losing 352 aircraft in so doing.

Indo-Pakistan conflicts War broke out between the two nations early in September 1965 as the result of conflicting territorial claims, and proved the Indian Air Force to be numerically superior, although, against this, that of Pakistan was able to hold its own on account, it was said, of superior training. The Pakistanis made particularly effective use of Sidewinder missiles launched from F-86 Sabres, 73 victories being claimed by this method and with conventional guns. Further clash-

this time that an interest began to be taken by France. Air France Transatlantique decided to apply the technique in 1940 to their own air mail service, using Farman 2284 four-engine machines, but the war situation caused the whole enterprise to collapse when the Farmans were captured by the Germans. The specially stressed British boats which had performed so well across the Atlantic were destroyed in a Narvik fjord while impressed for communications service with the Royal Navy. Soon after this Flight Refuelling's facility at Ford was destroyed by enemy action and the Air Ministry officially decided that future development work should be suspended.

It was 1944 before interest was reawakened in the system, when the RAF was investigating means to bomb Japan using Lancasters and Lincolns which, it was calculated, were capable of taking a bomb load comparable with that of the US B-29 over an equivalent range if refuelled 1,000 miles from their take-off point. The plan envisaged building these types as either bombers or tankers with the aid of conversion kits, enabling machines to be adapted in a very short space of time depending on operational requirements. Tests were begun in the early part of 1945, only to be rendered unnecessary by the Japanese collapse following the dropping of the two atomic bombs.

In 1946 developments enabled radar to be used to supplement the radios previously used to aid the rendezvous of the two aircraft, tanker and receiver, calibrated 'blips' on a 'Rebecca' indicator showing the relative position of the two, their distance apart and the necessity to turn to port or starboard. Tests next year over the English Channel were successful at altitudes as great as 20,000ft using Lancasters for both roles.

Until now the method of catching the tanker's hose had been by hand, and later by rocket line and grapple, but this was inappropriate for military aircraft so a new method was evolved whereby the tanker trailed its

hose with a drogue at the end, so designed that it remained steady in the airstream, and into this a fixed probe on the receiver was aligned and driven, the actual coupling being automatic for the fuel to be passed and then simply broken as the first aircraft pulled away. In the United States this was retained

only by the US Navy, Air Force fighters adopting the boom-receptacle system, while in time the 'Buddy' method was evolved wherein one aircraft could replenish the tanks of another of the same type. Even helicopters were ultimately capable of being refuelled in flight.

Above: Gloster Javelin FAW.9 XH890 of No 23 Squadron RAF showing its very pronounced in-flight refuelling probe. (Author's collection)

Above: A Handley Page Victor K.2 tanker releases a pair of Phantom jet fighters, having refuelled both simultaneously in flight. (Author)

es followed in the wake of hostilities that broke out on 3 December 1971, in which Pakistani F-104As were to meet India's Soviet-designed MiG-21s in combat for the first time.

Infra-red homing A method wherein a homing device used for the guidance of air-to-air missiles seeks the hottest spot within its range, always assumed to be the jet efflux of a target, and homes on to this. Although missiles using this method had a tendency to perform poorly at low altitude or under tropical conditions, it was adopted for the early generation such as the British Firestreak and US Sidewinder from which the target was ideally assumed to be retreating, but those of a later generation such as the · British Red Top and US 'all-aspect'

Sidewinder were developed to be effective even if the target was approaching.

Insertion The introduction, by helicopter, of troops.

Instrument panel The earliest examples of these consisted of panels produced as separate fittings with all the instruments regarded as essential already in place. Smith's Instruments produced a standard panel with an altimeter, an rpm counter, a turn and bank indicator, a clock and air speed and climb indicators which weighed 7½lb and was available with either black or white dial faces, while a simpler one was produced by Elliotts with a clock, an altimeter and rpm and ASI dials. In Britain the RAF's Gloster

Gladiators, introduced into service in 1937 but designed in 1934, first incorporated a standard central panel featuring turn and bank, rate of climb and directional gyro indicators with an artificial horizon, altimeter and ASI, and this was only supplanted by technological advances in navigation and fire control with electronic assistance. See HUD.

Interceptor A development of the basic concept of a fighter aircraft with the design emphasis on speed and rate of climb, and although all fighters used in one form or another for interception have tended to be loosely classified as such, only a relatively small number of designs have been truly of this category. Examples from WWII must include the Messerschmitt Me

ISRAEL

Established with the founding of the State of Israel in 1948, the Chel Ha'Avir (q.v.) is responsible for the operation of nearly all the country's warplanes, having rapidly built up experience from continued conflict with its Arab neighbours to become one of the best-

trained and equipped air forces in the east. The first types flown were redundant British, German and US aircraft from WWII, during which a large number of its personnel had gained battle experience. French aircraft were ordered during the 1950s and 1960s, but a major change in equipment took place in 1967 when, following the Six Day War, France placed an embargo on continued supplies of aircraft and other war materials, with the result that new types tended to be of US design.

But, almost unnoticed, Israel was by this time establishing its own aircraft industry, the first steps towards which were taken by the formation of the Bedek Aircraft organization in 1953. This was intended to concentrate on maintenance and repair, but, renamed Israel Aircraft Industries, it turned to manufacture, at first of licence-built aircraft and later of its own designs such as the Kfir C-2. See Near East.

Above: A de Havilland Mosquito in the insignia of the Israeli Defence Force/Air Force. (Author's collection)

163 Komet, while those immediately post-war included such types as the Gloster Javelin (q.v.) and the Lockheed F-104. The modern category labelled 'air superiority fighters' would properly include interceptors.

Interdiction A policy wherein bombing attacks are confined to targets of considerable military or industrial importance, thus reducing the likely number of civilian casualties caused by blanket, area bombing. It is necessary that such a policy is confined to conflicts with an enemy of a reasonable standard of sophistication and operates under conditions of air superiority.

Interrupter gear An appliance allowing the fixed, forward guns of an aircraft to fire through the arc swept by the airscrew disc of a propeller-driven machine without damaging the blades. Before 1914 both Franz Schneider of LVG and Raymond Saulnier of Morane-Saulnier had looked for solutions to the problem, the trials made by the latter proving a frustration due to faulty ammunition so that steel deflector plates fastened to the airscrew blades were adopted as a compromise, Roland Garros flew a scout thus fitted and accounted for five victims in three weeks before being himself brought down and the secret discovered. The enemy attempted to copy the idea but with little success, possibly due to the use of steel-jacketed ammunition so that Fokker engineers then resorted to the pre-1914 idea and perfected the interrupter gear which was first fitted to an E.1 monoplane. The first victory with the system was achieved on 1 August 1915.

Intrepid One of the seven tethered balloons built by Thaddeus S. C. Lowe which were at the disposal of the Federal American forces at the end of 1861 and were used for observing Confederate troop movements during the Civil War of 1861–65. It was first used above Maryland on 8 December 1861 with Col W. F. Small as sketching officer, and was therefore the precursor of observation balloons and powered reconnaissance aircraft in subsequent conflicts.

Intruder (1) Night operations flown over the airfields of an enemy to intercept returning aircraft, the first such being made by the RAF during June 1940. The enemy mounted similar sorties until October 1941, when Hitler personally ordered their suspension in order that the achievements of the Luftwaffe in the field of night interception at home could be seen by the civil population, thereby maintaining morale. (2) The name adopted for the US Grumman A-6, an aircraft design based on experience gained in the Korean War for use by the Navy and Marine Corps for all-weather (q.v.) long-range, low-level attack work, capable of being accommodated on aircraft carriers and lifting a heavy armament load. The Grumman design was selected from the submissions to a competition held in 1957, the prototype making its first appearance three years later and proving to be a two-seater capable of Mach 0.95. Part of its 18,000lb armament was carried in a recessed weapons bay . Later, the aircraft flew with the aid of the Digital Integrated Attack/ Navigation Equipment (see DIANE), which not only guided the aircraft to its target, but also automatically delivered the load. The four-seat ECM & EW variant, the EA-6A developed for the Marine Corps, first flew in 1963.

Invader A three-seat, twin-engine attack bomber constructed by the Douglas Aircraft Corporation which was almost unique among warplanes in that it was one of the few participating aircraft which was conceived, designed, developed and used in substantial numbers all within the duration of WWII. It seemed that its career

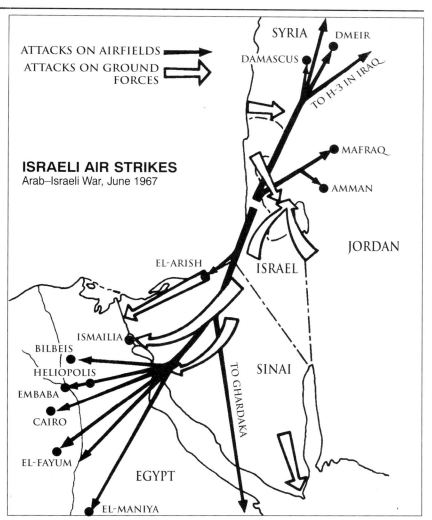

ATTACKS ON AIRFIELDS

ATTACKS ON GROUND FORCES

ISRAELI AIR STRIKES
Arab–Israeli War, June 1967

SYRIA
DMEIR
DAMASCUS
TO H-3 IN IRAQ
MAFRAQ
AMMAN
JORDAN
ISRAEL
EL-ARISH
ISMAILIA
BILBEIS
HELIOPOLIS
EMBABA
CAIRO
SINAI
TO GHARDAKA
EL-FAYUM
EGYPT
EL-MANIYA

was over by 1945, yet in fact use was made of it in both the Korean and Vietnam conflicts, so that by 1963 a re-manufacturing programme had to be initiated to meet the demand, twenty-two years after the first flight of the original. Other claims to fame include the fact that it was the first bomber ever to have wings designed around a NACA laminar flow airfoil and the first to have double-slotted flaps. It also shared, with the B-29, the distinction of having early remote-control turrets. It was also unusual in that it was known under a number of designa-

tions. Beginning as the A-26, it became the B-26 and JD-1. Rebuilt variants were B-26Ks, which were in turn redesignated A-26As. FA-26 described the reconnaissance version, while the JD was a target tug.

Invisible aircraft Laying aside the attempt towards the end of the twentieth century to design a warplane that was 'invisible' to electronic detection, i.e. stealth (q.v.) designs with a low radar signature, there have been odd attempts to produce aircraft difficult to see with the naked eye. Probably the

earliest was a Taube in 1912 which was entirely covered in transparent sheeting. This may well have been the source of unauthenticated British Press reports in 1940 describing a similarly covered Junkers 88 with 'virtually silent' motors. Soviet trials on these lines had lasted into the 1930s.

Iran In August 1935 the Nirou havai Shahanshahiye ceased to be part of the Iranian Army and became independent under the Ministry of War, the other two services building up their own air arms, but it was not until 1970 that a

ITALY

When Capt Piazza reconnoitred the Turkish positions during the war in Tripolitania on 11 October 1911, he was flying a Blériot monoplane that was part of a recently established air force made up of nine aero-

planes and two airships. From these small beginnings, Italy entered WWI beside the Allies on 24 May 1915 with twelve Squadriglia, and when the war ended the Aeronautica del Regio Esercito (Royal Army Air Service) had grown to a total of 1,800 aircraft. Its founding strength of thirty-one pilots eight years previously had flourished to make such names as Baracca, Piccio and Calabria world-renowned.

Italian government was by a constitutional monarchy until 1922, when events following the formation of the first fascist group as an anti-Bolshevist organization led to the Congress to install Mussolini as premier and dictator, and following this the Air Service – which had scarcely developed as a peacetime force over the previous four years – was replaced by the independent Regia

Above: Production of the Fiat G.50bis Falco commenced in 1940. One of Italy's first monoplane fighters, it was said to have been conceived for participation in the Spanish Civil War. (Author's collection)

massive build-up was begun, partly triggered by the British withdrawal from east of Suez and partly due to the concern resulting from the Soviet Union's use of Umm Qasr in Iraq as a base. Coupled with these events was the involvement of Iranian forces in the trouble spots which erupted in the Kurdish rebellion against the Iraqi government, in Baluchistan and in South Yemen. However, the declaration of an Islamic republic by the Ayatollah Khomeini resulted in a massive cancellation of orders for military equipment although the final position of the air arm was placed in some doubt by the coincidental outbreak of war with Iraq.

Iraq The Iraqi Air Force sprang from a necessity to replace the RAF element in that country, where it had been involved in a system of policing or peace-keeping since the end of WWI. It followed that British influence would be to the forefront of the establishment of the Iraqi Air Force proper in 1931. The first officers of the new arm (which was established as part of the Army) were trained in Britain, while RAF officers and NCOs were seconded as instructors and the equipment was British.

This influence persisted well after the war, Hawker Hunter jets being the final examples of the British influence before the country was declared a socialist state in 1958. Thenceforth strong ties with the Soviet Union meant that the greater part of the air force's equipment would come from that source. A period followed when this was relaxed and such types as helicopters were ordered from France, and until 1975 the force was involved in protracted actions against Kurdish

---

Aeronautica the following year, enjoying the same status as the Army and Navy. The force was supported by an active military aircraft industry based on the engineering progress made with that for automobiles.

In addition there came into existence the Army Reconnaissance units and the Naval Aviation Corps, which included the Naval Co-operation units, all three services falling under the direct control of the Air Minister.

The first operational duties which fell to the reconstituted air service were actions against rebellious tribes in Libya and East Africa, work that had the result of hastening the development of such types as the Caproni 101 and 133 bomber-transports and the assembly of general-purpose aircraft such as the Meridionali Ro-1, all this against a background of such policies as that for total war outlined in General Giulio Douhet's book *Command of the Air*, published in 1921.

The Regia Aeronautica's first experience of war was that resulting from Mussolini's imperial ambitions, begun by the annexation of Abyssinia in 1935. The opening phase of this campaign on 3 October saw light ▶

Above: Cant Z.501 bomber-reconnaissance flying boats such as this patrolled the long Italian seaboard before the outbreak of WWII following which they performed early operational duties. (Author's collection)

separatists. Soviet ties were renewed in 1977 with the negotiation of a further arms agreement.

The Gulf War (q.v.) found Iraq with a substantial air force that included a ground attack section made up of MiGs and Sukhois, plus some French Mirage F.1EQs, while the small bombing force was composed of sixteen Tu-16 'Badgers' plus some Su-24 'Fencers'. However, the Iraqi Air Force failed to distinguish itself in the brief conflict.

'Iron Hand' US defence-suppression sorties during the Vietnam War, primarily flown by Vought A-7E Corsair II aircraft with AGM-45A 'Shrike' missiles (q.v.).

Isonzo An offensive launched in October 1917 by the Austro-Hungarian forces with German support and strong air participation and evolving into the Twelfth Battle of Isonzo which forced an Italian retreat to Caporetto. The air war significance of this engagement is that it represented the peak of

involvement in the war by the Austro-Hungarian air arm.

Iwo Jima A Japanese-occupied island in the Pacific for the assault on which during WWII the carrier aircraft strikes on Tokyo were a preliminary. Task Force 58 launched 2,761 sorties despite bad weather, destroying about 200 enemy aircraft on the ground or in the air in the process. The USAAF launched the first sortie of a seven-month bombardment of Iwo Jima on 10 August 1944 and aircraft from fifteen carriers of Task Force 38 made widespread raids on the island and its neighbours between 31 August and 24 September, claiming 1,000 Japanese aircraft destroyed in the process. A landing was made by the US 4th and 5th Marine Divisions on 19 February 1945 (Operation 'Detachment') .

J A designation prefix indicating Jaktflygplan (fighter aircraft) by the Svenska Flvgvapnets (Swedish Air Force) since the introduction of the J1 FVM Phoenix 6 in 1919

J-1 Jastreb (Hawk). A SOKO-constructed single-seat, low-wing, jet-propelled, light attack aircraft in service with the former Yugoslav Air Force (Jugoslovensko Ratno Vazduhoplovstvo) since 1968, representing an attempt to meet service requirements with the products of a national industry and thus draw less on those of the Soviet Union and the United States as had been done after the end of WWII. The armament consisted of three 12.7mm machine guns in the nose and there were eight underwing attachment points for external offensive stores. The powerplant was a Rolls-Royce 531 Viper turbojet, the maximum speed was about 500mph and the aircraft had a range of up to 850 miles.

J21 A twin-boom, Saab-built fighter used in two versions by the Royal Swedish Air Force, the first being powered by a Daimler Benz DB 605B driving a pusher propeller. It first flew in 1943. In service during 1945–51, the J21A was followed into service in 1949 by the turbojet-propelled J21RA, pow-

ITALY

tanks and infantry with modern weapons supported by 320 aircraft, chiefly the ubiquitous Caproni 101 reconnaissance bomber-transports. These were joined by Caproni Ca.111s, 133s and Savoia SM.81s as well as some Romeo Ro-1s, plus eight Squadriglie flying two-seat Ro.37s and Fiat CR.20 single-seaters. What followed was an inglorious page in the history of Italian military aviation, with unopposed fighters being directed to make ground attacks against defenceless troops and the crews of the trimotors finding themselves ordered to carry out 'offensive reconnaissance' which often called for the use of mustard gas (q.v.).

The year 1936 saw the Abyssinian campaign draw to its close, but in July that year the Spanish Civil War provided another opportunity for Mussolini's air force to extend the experience of its personnel, the Italian dictator favouring the Nationalist cause. The first supporting units arrived on 4 August, the pilots bringing Fiat CR.32 fighters to begin the Avia Legionaria's Spanish participation. Ultimately Italy would contribute 730 warplanes. Meanwhile an Italian Air Mission comprising Regia Aeronautica officers went to China in 1937.

On 10 June 1940 Italy declared war on Britain and France, by which time her front-line strength of operational aircraft was 1,796 of a total of 3,296. It was a relatively large force, but it had fallen behind general European standards largely because of a lack of engines of suitable power. However, large commands were scattered around the Mediterranean and at home, and the first strike by the Italian air arm was that directed against Malta on 11 June. Others followed against French bases at home and abroad. Soon Greece was to be invaded, the first day of this attempt, 28 October, seeing 283 aircraft committed against the 92 found by the defenders.

Aside from two abortive attempts by the CAI (q.v.) to participate in the daylight fighting after the Battle of Britain, the Regia Aeronautica was steadily worn down for the remainder of its participation in WWII, its last action in East Africa beginning on 19 January 1941, although a large force of Italian air transports, with a number from the Luftwaffe, was gathered in Sicily during April 1943 to supply Axis forces in Tunisia, a partly successful operation which had to be dealt with by the Allied Operation 'Flax'. However, the year was to see the unexpected collapse of Italy, her unconditional surrender being announced on 8 September of the same year. Henceforth her military aircraft were to fly in support of the Allies.

Italy's membership of NATO found the Aeronautica Militare Italiana (AMI) forming a major part of the Organization's 5th Allied Tactical Air Force, with overall responsibility for operations carried out by the Army and Navy. The AMI itself had three commands, for air defence, air transport (combined with rescue) and training, and although the end of the 1970s found Italian military spending reduced, the previous decade had seen L2,365bn allocated for re-equipment over a ten-year period.

For operational purposes, Italy is divided into three areas or regions, these replacing the earlier Air Brigades that were in turn based on US Wings. These were divided into three Gruppi or squadrons, each consisting of 16 to 25 aircraft plus reserves. These units were therefore larger than their present equivalents, which have only 12 to 18 machines each. Nineteen such units are specifically assigned to NATO and all are largely equipped with warplanes of US design. The air arm of the Italian Navy, the Marinavia, is not responsible for anti-submarine operations, this work falling to the AMI. The former is therefore entirely a missile-armed helicopter force, while the Army's Aviazione Leggera dell'Esercito (ALE) combines a large force of rotary-wing aircraft with fixed-wing types devoted to anti-tank, assault, medium-lift and observation duties.

ered by a DH Goblin II, the prototype having made its first flight in March 1947. About 300 of the first model and 60 of the latter were supplied. This was the only airframe in the world to be fitted with both types of propulsion, although the later type was envisaged from the first. The armament of the J21RA consisted of one 20mm Bofors cannon and four Bofors 13.23mm machine guns, which could be augmented by a belly pod with eight further machine guns. The J21R ground-attack variant could carry ten 8cm or 10cm or five 18cm anti-tank rockets.

J22 The German invasion of Poland in 1939 found the Swedish Flygvapnet with a strength of only 140 aircraft, so that when an embargo was placed on the supply of fighters from the United States and those ordered from Italy proved insufficient, an emergency programme was introduced to design an indigenous fighter. The result was the FFVS J22, designed around the STWC3-G radial motor (a copy of the Pratt &

Whitney SC3-G Twin Wasp), which first flew on 1 September 1942, the first production example entering service on 23 November the following year. The airframe was mainly steel tube and the covering ply, while the armament consisted of two 7.9mm machine guns and two of 13.2mm calibre. The J-22B was armed with four 13.2mm machine guns. The type was in service until 1949 and the designation prefix 'FFVS' indicated Flyforvaltningens Verkstad (Air Board Workshop), an organization created expressly for the production of the fighter.

J29 See Tunnen.

J32 See Lansen.

J35 See Draken.

J37 See Viggen.

J39 See Grippen

Jabo An abbreviation of the German Jagdbomber (fighter-bomber).

'Jack' The Allied code-name for the WWII Japanese Navy Mitsubishi J2M Raiden (Thunderbolt) fighter. The first flight of the prototype took place on 20 March 1942 when it was clear that undercarriage retraction problems had to be overcome and the Kasei 13 engine replaced. Production difficulties were encountered after orders were placed, and these continued after the first examples were accepted for service in 1943. A variety of engines were fitted, the J2M5 aircraft powered by the Mk 4U-4 Kasei 26a giving the best maximum speed of 382mph. The armament of this model consisted of four 20mm cannon mounted in the wings.

Jagderfaust See Climbing attacks.

Jagdgeschwader A German fighter unit composed of Gruppen and Staffeln (q.v.).

Jagdgruppe A German fighter unit, usually three, sometimes four, rarely five in number, composed of three Staffeln and a Stab.

Above: Designed as a bomber-transport, the Savoia Marchetti SM.82 held a number of world records. In 1939 it flew 8,037.97 miles in 56.5hrs at 143mph. (Author's collection)

Jagdverband A German fighter unit.

Jaguar (1) The unofficial name of the Messerschmitt 162, a fast, three-seat, twin-motor bomber resembling the Messerschmitt 110 from which it differed most obviously in having a glazed nose. It first flew in 1937 but, despite reports of sightings in 1940, never entered production. (2) See SEPECAT Jaguar.

'Jake' The Allied code-name for Japanese Aichi E13A naval reconnaissance seaplane, a low-wing cabin monoplane accepted for production in December 1940, the intention being to operate the type from cruisers and seaplane tenders. Powered by a single Mitsubishi Kinsei 43 radial motor, the aircraft was later employed for a wide number of tasks, including kamikaze (q.v.) attacks late in WWII. Three versions were manufactured, the E13A-1 variant being capable of a maximum speed of 234mph.

'Jane' The original Allied code-name for the WWII Mitsubishi Ki-21 heavy bomber, two prototypes of which were produced to meet an Army specification in December 1936, the last of the three subsequently built becoming a service trials aircraft before a production order was placed in November 1937. Although all early aircraft delivered were used as bombers, a shortage of transports during the Chinese campaign forced the adaptation of some 'Janes' for this role, and in one or the other the type became one of the best-known enemy aircraft in the Pacific theatre. The code-name 'Sally' was adopted after the discovery that the earlier name was that of Gen MacArthur's wife! Two versions of this twin-motor bomber were produced, the Ia and the IIb, the latter giving the best performance with a maximum speed of 302mph with a 1,653lb bomb load.

'Janice' The A-5 version of the Luftwaffe's Junkers Ju 88 (q.v.) was erroneously believed to be operated by Capt Tokugawa. Attempts were soon made to acquire other aircraft types, together with suitable technicians, from Britain and Germany but above all from France, then regarded as the cradle of the new science of flying. Six years after the return of the two Europe-trained officers, a second new design, and Japan's first operational machine, a floatplane developed by 1/Lt Chikuhei Nakajima in conjunction with Kishichi Magoshi, was built.

JAPAN

The foundations of the Japanese military air service were laid during 1910, not in its country of origin but in Europe, where Army officers Yoshitoshi Tokugawa learned to fly in France and Kumazo Hino in Germany. Their courses complete, the pair returned to their own country at the end of the year, taking with them a Henry Farman biplane and a Grade monoplane, and when these were flown for the first time, on 19 December, none would have realized that they were the precursors of a new military arm in the country. Neither would it have been possible to guess that, about a year later, an industry, too, would be established, for it was then that there emerged from the Army balloon workshop at Nakano, near Tokyo, a new version of the Henry Farman which had been designed

Above: The Mitsubishi Ki-46-IV Army reconnaissance bomber Model 3, which was powered by two supercharged Ha-112-II Ru motors. It was code-named 'Dinah' by the Allies during WWII. (Author's collection)

by the Japanese Army during WWII, so this code-name was bestowed on it by the Allies.

Jasta A contraction of the German Jagdstaffel or fighting squadron. The first, which made its initial operational sortie in September 1916, was Jasta 2, quickly re-named Jasta Boelcke after that officer's death on 28 October of the same year.

JATO Jet-Assisted Take-Off, developed from RATOG (Rocket-Assisted Take-Off Gear, a method of helping a heavily laden warplane into the air.

Javelin A British all-weather fighter which first flew in prototype (WD804) form on 26 November 1951 at Moreton Valence. It was the first twin-jet, two-seat delta-wing fighter in the world, being designed to have a very high performance, possess a long endurance and be capable of intercepting at great altitude and speed. The third prototype (WT827), which first flew on 7 March 1953, was the first to be fitted with the armament of four 30mm Aden cannon as well as various types of radar. The first production aircraft (FAW.1 XA544) flew on 22 July 1954. Seven variants followed with various engines, improved armament (including Firestreak missiles) and better radar. The aircraft was capable of exceeding Mach 1 in a shallow dive.

'Jean' The Allied WWII code-name for the Japanese Yokosuka B4Y carrier-borne attack biplane, the prototype of which first flew in late 1935. After seeing action in the war with China, the type was relegated to secondary duties. Used for torpedo training after 1940, it never took the major part in air operations imagined by the Allies, only 205 being built. Its maximum speed was 173mph and its offensive load 1,102lb. Production versions differed from the prototypes in that the gunner was now accommodated in a glazed position, leaving the pilot in the open.

The name of the first of this pair of designers was to pass into history, for it was the Nakajima organization founded on 6 December 1917 by the designer of the seaplane, now partnered by Seibei Kawanishi, that was soon to enter independent production, financed by the wealthy Mitsui family. Alongside were two other manufacturers, Kawasaki and Mitsubishi, although both were merely new departments of the established engineering firms of those names. In the meantime young technicians were studying in the United States and to a lesser extent Europe, perhaps with the foreknowledge that the Japanese Army and Navy must eventually break free from dependence on foreign companies for their equipment; despite the advances made, many Western manufacturers were seeking markets in the east for their redundant warplane designs after 1918 (the Spad S.13 was adopted as the standard Army fighter, and the Nieuport 24C went into production by Nakajima). The different attitudes between the two hemispheres was plain, for while Europe and America saw the aeroplane as being a means of transport, Japan saw it essentially from a military viewpoint.

The two decades following the end of WWI were a time of great industrial activity, spearheaded in 1918 by Kawasaki Jukogyo KK founding a subsidiary, Kawasaki Kokuki Kogyo KK, exclusively for the manufacture of air- ▶

Above: A Nakajima Ki-44-IIb Army Type 2 in the Philippines with a pair of drop tanks under the centre-section inboard and aft of the undercarriage. Beyond are a pair of Kawasaki Ki-45 Toryu heavy fighters. (Author's collection)

'Jerry' The Allied code-name for the Japanese version of the Heinkel He 112B-0, of which twelve were purchased for the Navy to use as fighters with the designation A7He1. They were not employed during WWII but saw action in the Sino-Japanese conflict. An order for thirty had originally been placed, the first being delivered in the spring of 1938, but the balance were impressed by the Luftwaffe. The maximum speed of this monoplane was 317mph and the armament consisted of a pair of synchronized 7.9mm machine guns and two 20mm cannon in the wings.

Jet propulsion It is commonly believed that this method of powering an aerial craft is a phenomenon of the twentieth century, but in fact it was suggested as long ago as 1784 by the Frenchmen Miolan and Janinet, who constructed a Mongolfier type balloon designed to be propelled by jets of hot air. However, an examination of the associated problems leading to the first practical jet aircraft were those conducted in Germany and Italy.

Initial steps in the former were taken when Heinkel employed Dr Hans Joachim Pabst von Ohain and assistant Max Hahn in 1936 and allowed the pair to continue experiments begun at Göttingen University. Bench-running the HeS 1 demonstration turbojet was possible in September 1937, and after a time successful flight tests were made with an improved model of the engine under a Heinkel 118. It was decided to fit a further development (the HeS 3) into a Heinkel 178, and with this a short hop along the runway was made on 24 August 1939.

Three days later there followed the first true flight, with Flugkapitän Erich Warsitz, at the controls and despite the undercarriage refusing to retract and the ingestion of a bird stopping the engine so that a power-off landing had to be made, this was declared a success, the date proving significant since it was exactly one year later that the Italian Caproni-Campini CC.1 made its first flight, having been developed in collaboration with Secondo Campini who had been experimenting for same years with jet propulsion.

The concept of the CC.1 was cruder than its German counterpart since for the aircraft to become airborne a normal aero-motor was used before a switch was made to jet propulsion in

---

JAPAN

▶ frames and parts, while Mitsubishi Jukogyo KK did the same by separating its aviation department from its main division to concentrate on heavy aircraft and their engines. The period also saw smaller manufacturers gather round these nuclei and gradually specialize. Thus Kawanishi concentrated on naval machines from 1928, while Tachikawa Hikoki KK became one of the chief builders of transport aircraft, all taking encouragement from the competition between the two armed forces for increasingly advanced warplanes. Yet, strangely, all this escaped the attention of the West, where even 'informed' observers dismissed Japanese military aviation as being of little merit, equipped with foreign machines or flagrant copies of them. However, in April 1916 the Yokosuka Kokutai of the Naval Air Corps had been founded, followed by the Sasebo Kokutai in March two years later, while the Army Air Corps was founded on 1 May 1925 with a status equal to that of the Artillery, Cavalry or Infantry.

Eight years later found the Army Air Division in the process of modernization in the light of experience gained in limited conflicts in the late 1920s and early 1930s which fitted it better for waging the war against China that flared in 1937. The greater part of the action was borne by the better-equipped Navy, and it was this force that took Japan into WWII with its pre-emptive attempt to destroy the US Fleet in Pearl Harbor on 7 December 1941, although it was to the Army, attended by its air arm, that success came over the following nine months. The war was then largely one of attrition, with mounting losses in New Guinea, as Army aircraft, although still able

Above: A Mitsubishi A6M5a Zero fighter of the Japanese Navy. (Bruce Robertson)

flight, but the behaviour of the machine was sufficiently encouraging for the larger CC.2 to be constructed, a design that still relied on an ordinary piston engine although in this instance only to drive the compressor. The CC.2 having successfully flown on 1 December 1941, a flight of 168 miles was attempted between Milan and the Guidonia Research Station near Rome, with a stop en route at Pisa. Piloted by Col Mario de Bernardi, who had distinguished himself in the 1926 Schneider Contest, the 2¼hr flight was made at an average speed of 168mph, Capt Pedace of the Regia Aeronautica acting as observer and a bag of mail being taken as freight.

Both of these pioneering attempts to evolve a new form of reaction propulsion were made in complete ignorance

of similar investigations being made in Britain by Frank Whittle. He had filed patents for such a propulsion system in 1930, but a lack of funds prevented the flight of an aircraft powered by this means taking place until 15 May 1941, when the first of the two Gloster E.28/39s (W4041 and W4046) made its maiden flight from Cranwell, Lincolnshire. The pilot was P. E. G. Sayer and the motor fitted at the time was an 860lb s.t. Power Jets W.1.

As might be expected, bearing in mind the political atmosphere during which the design for this aircraft was drawn up, an examination of the original drawings reveals that provision was made for armament to be fitted in the lower part of the E.28/39's nose, and although this never went beyond the drawing board it was inevitable

that warplanes using the new form of propulsion would be quickly developed. Thus Germany's Messerschmitt Me 262 made its first flight in prototype form on 18 July 1942 using a pair of BMW 109-004A-0 motors for the first time, previous air trials having been made with the aid of a piston engine since the jets were not ready. Meanwhile Glosters had not been idle, and, an official specification for a single-seat fighter with twin jet motors having been written around the company's proposals for a fighter, the first flight of such a type took place on 5 March 1943, DG206/G being powered by two de Havilland H.1 engines and piloted by Michael Daunt.

When the Me 262 entered service towards the end of 1944 its appearance alarmed the Allies. The 527mph

to inflict considerable punishment, began to show their age. The Navy fared rather better at first until its losses — comparatively light up till that time — rose sharply with the Battle of Midway, and it was something of an admission of defeat when kamikaze tactics were resorted to as WWII drew to its close. The end of the war saw not only the surrender of the once-proud air arms' equipment marked with the green crosses of capitulation, but also the collapse of the Japanese aircraft industry.

It fell to the United States to re-establish the country's air arm along lines acceptable

to the victors, the first step being to set up National Security and Safety forces equipped with light aircraft in August 1952. From these, two years later, was evolved the Japanese Air Self-Defence Force, its first North American F-86F Sabres arriving in December 1955. Initially these were used for training, but in the following October they equipped the JASDF's first tactical fighter unit. A five-year Defence Build-up Programme calling for 1,300 machines operated by 33 squadrons was initiated in the following year, but in fact a total of only 1,127 aircraft and seventeen operational units was attained.

Even so, the events of the closing years of the 1950s established the form of the postwar Japanese air arm with its organization based on the US pattern and operating warplanes of American design, some of which were built under licence by a re-established aviation industry. This system has largely continued via a series of five-year development programmes, despite increasingly stri-

dent demands for a more independent defence policy.

In addition to the JASDF there also exist the air arms of the Army and the Navy, the first, known as the JGSDF, having been set up in 1954 with US assistance. It is now predominantly a helicopter force, although some light fixed-wing aircraft and transports are operated. This force is divided into Regional Commands with subordinate District Commands each consisting of a minimum of two squadrons, although there are, in practice, frequently more. The Navy operates its own Maritime Self-Defence Force (JMSDF), which is an anti-submarine arm largely assigned to the Fleet and organized under the Fleet headquarters and the subordinate Air Command or Koku-Shuhdan. Once again the foundation was of US origin in 1956, the organization being based on the American system. Both these air services have their own training and instructional facilities, that of the Navy being the larger.

Japanese Warplane and Engine Manufacturers during WWII

Aichi Kokuki KK	Aichi Aircraft Company Ltd
Fuji Hikoki KK	Fuji Aeroplane Company Ltd
Hitachi Kokuki KK	Hitachi Aircraft Company Ltd
Ishikawajima Koku Kogyo KK	Ishikawajima Aircraft Industries Ltd
Kawanishi Kokuki KK	Kawanishi Aircraft Company Ltd
Kawasaki Kokuki Kogyo KK	Kawanishi Aircraft Engineering Ltd
Kyushu Hikoki KK	Kyushu Aeroplane Company Ltd
Mansyu Hikoki Seizo KK	Manchurian Aeroplane Manufacturing Company
Mitsubishi Jukogyo KK	Mitsubishi Heavy Industries Ltd
Nakajima Hikoki KK	Nakajima Aeroplane Company
Nippon Hikoki KK	Japan Aeroplane Company Ltd
Nippon Kokusai Koko Kogyo KK	Japan International Air Industries
Showa Hokoki KK	Showa Aeroplane Company Ltd
Tachikawa Hikoki KK	Tachikawa Aeroplane Company Ltd

Above: The Gloster E.28/39 prototype, W4041/G, taking off from Farnborough. It carries a ventral camera and experimental fins on the tailplane. (Author's collection)

fighter with its heavy armament of 30mm cannon and rockets might well have brought a halt to the US daylight bombing campaign which was a necessary preliminary to the liberation of the continent begun in June 1944. But it entered service to late to do so and Allied air superiority was such that it could not achieve any decisive results.

Other countries, too, could foresee the value in the military applications of jet propulsion. The first US jet aircraft was the Bell XP-59A Airacomet, which made its initial flight on 1 October 1942 powered by twin General Electric I-16 motors (based on samples of the Whittle W.1X gas turbines supplied by Great Britain that year), the pilot on this auspicious occasion being Robert M. Stanley and the venue Muroc, California. The maximum speed of the Airacomet was 413mph. Only 50 were built and used for jet training, thus leaving the way clear for the Lockheed F-80 Shooting Star to become the first US operational fighter, the prototype of which was powered by a de Havilland Goblin turbojet and later a General Electric J33.

Japan was also giving priority to the development of a jet-powered warplane, and, although resembling the Me 262, the Kikka (Orange Blossom) naval aircraft, which, powered by two 1,047lb s.t. Ne-20 engines, first flew on the day the atomic bomb hit Hiroshima, was an entirely indigenous design by the Nakajima company, con-

structed on a farm after many of the suitable factory buildings had been destroyed by Allied bombing. The armament was to be a pair of 30mm cannon, but an unarmed reconnaissance two-seater was also to be built, this and the single-seat attack bomber being early examples designed from the start to utilize jet propulsion for aircraft other than fighters. Meanwhile attempts to build a jet engine in the Soviet Union were soon to be immensely accelerated by the presentation to that country of details and specimens of British engines in the belief that a political millennium was about to dawn, and designs based on this information were fitted to modified forms of existing aircraft.

The speeds at which it was anticipated future air operations would be conducted brought both new advantages and new problems, among the former being that sorties of shorter duration in aircraft with relatively simple controls would benefit those who flew them: crews would suffer a lower level of fatigue than had been common during the war, and it was then believed that the likelihood of jet bombers being intercepted would be reduced, so that, when flying in all but a tactical role, the potential strain imposed under anti-aircraft fire would be less severe. Even so, the reverse of the benefits indicated that smaller crews on such bomber types as the English Electric Canberra would

require duties to be performed with increased rapidity and accuracy.

Greater still were the changes that jet propulsion would create in terms of warplane design, and nowhere was this to be seen more clearly than in the British decision to adopt an entirely new class of bombers, popularly known as the 'V force'. The changes were most clearly to be seen in the Handley Page Victor, which had its Rolls-Royce Sapphire motors completely buried in the contours of the root of the thick wing section. Allied to such changes as these was the ability of such a force of jet bombers to deliver sophisticated weapons such as the Blue Steel missile.

It is important here to touch on a completely different application of jet propulsion to military aircraft, the socalled 'prop-jet' system in which the turbo unit is so designed that it not only offers thrust in the manner of a normal jet engine but also turns a propeller via the turbine shaft. The advantages of this type of powerplant for some forms of military aircraft use is obvious, since it preserves the aerodynamics normally associated with conventional propeller-driven designs, allowing a reasonably powerful motor or even a coupled pair in a relatively small airframe.

Finally, mention must be made of the crudest and simplest form of aircraft jet propulsion, the ram-jet. Its very simplicity – it involves no more

Above: The Messerschmitt 262 was the first jet-propelled aircraft in the world to see operational service. This example is an A-2a model. Werk Nr 112372, formerly of JG 7. It became VK893 during British examination and eventually 8482M for preservation. (Author)

than a controlled thrust of air, mixed with fuel, compressed and ignited by a residual flame after an initial assisted take-off – makes for not only speed and cheapness of production, but also for expendability.

'Jill' The Allied code-name for the WWII Japanese Nakajima B6N carrier-borne attack bomber monoplane, the Tenzan (Heavenly Mountain) intended to replace the earlier B5N. It had its early flight trials in 1941, these highlighting major defects in the tail design so that the vertical members had to be re-aligned to compensate for the considerable propeller torque. Progress was further slowed by the decision to cease manufacture of the Mamoru radial engine, and after 135 aircraft had been delivered with this power unit subsequent machines were fitted with the Kasei 25. The 'Jill' saw considerable service during the concluding two years of the war in the East, and although normally a three-seater a large number were flown solo for early kamikaze (q.v.) attacks in the Okinawa region. The maximum speed was 299mph, while the defensive armament consisted of two 7.7mm machine guns, one on a free mounting and the other firing through a ventral tunnel.

'Jim Crow' An RAF Fighter Command patrol along the British coast. These patrols were instituted in 1940 to intercept enemy aircraft attempting to make 'sneak' attacks and to provide early warning of any invasion attempts.

JN-4 See Curtiss.

'Joe' The Allied code-name for a WWII Japanese aircraft which never existed. The fictional machine was believed to be a single-seat fighter, the TK-19.

'Joyce' The Tachikawa Ki-54 (Allied code-name 'Hickory') was a Japanese trainer for the Army, both advanced and operational, as well as a transport, but it was never a light bomber, yet frequent misidentifications led the Allies in WWII to believe that such a type had been developed from it. Such was the conviction that the code-name 'Joyce' was allocated to the supposed aircraft.

'Judy' The Allied code name for the Japanese Navy's Yokosuka D4Y1-C/D4Y2-C, a reconnaissance type operated from aircraft carriers, and the related D4Y bomber, both being known to the Japanese as Suisei (Comet). Now undeservedly little-remembered, this aesthetically-pleasing monoplane was inspired by Japanese tests with a German Heinkel He 118 in 1938 and was sufficiently successful eventually to be operated from eleven carriers as well as by a number of shore stations. Its final use

on operations may be traced to a kamikaze (q.v.) mission by eleven aircraft, each armed with a high-explosive 1,764lb load, led by Admiral Ugaki off Okinawa on 15 August 1945 (see 'Jill'). The maximum speed of the ultimate D4Y4 was 350mph.

'Julia' Frequent misidentification of the Kawasaki Ki-48 ('Lily' to the Allies) caused the allocation of this code-name to what was erroneously believed to be a Kawasaki heavy bomber, a mistake to which weight was added by intelligence reports of the 'Lily' being developed for new duties.

'June' A further example of a WWII code-name being allocated by the Allies to a non-existent type, this time because of the misidentification of the 'Jake' (q.v.), the Aichi E13A naval reconnaissance seaplane. Intelligence even went as far as to state that the 'June' was a version of the Aichi D3A ('Val') with floats substituted for its wheeled undercarriage!

Junkers In December 1915, the maiden flight took place of the Junkers J.1 Blechesel or 'Tin Donkey', a type which derived its name from its all-metal construction. It was the first aircraft of this kind in the world, its designer, Dr Hugo Junkers, having employed thin iron sheet for his creation. Only one J.1 was built, but corrugated dural construction, introduced for the J.4 of 1917, was to be used for a series of successful all-metal airliners produced by the Junkers organization during the years between the two world wars.

Junkers 52/3m The original Junkers Ju 52 was a single-engined all-metal type embodying the method of construction successfully employed for the Junkers J.1 and the designation is frequently (but wrongly) applied to the three-motor transport, the number of engines being the reason for the suffix. A prototype of the Ju 52/3m first flew in April 1932, and most of the production models were 15–17-seat passenger airliners until the introduction of the bomber version. This was

designated the 3mg3e, the defensive armament including a gunner's 'dustbin' on the port undercarriage fairing, and 450 were delivered in 1936. They were used mostly as transports for the Condor Legion (q.v.) in Spain, supporting the Nationalist forces. Having prominently featured in the German show of strength during the Austrian Anschluss in March 1938, the type, virtually unused as a bomber by the Luftwaffe, formed the greater part of the German military air transport force during WWII, operating in the early Blitzkrieg campaigns as well as in the invasion of Crete and at Stalingrad. It was also used in various sundry roles, for example the sweeping of magnetic mines, fitted with an ener-

gized hoop similar to that mounted on RAF Wellington bombers (see Degaussing), as a glider tug and as a floatplane, as well as an early test-bed for a number of turbojets. The maximum speed was 168mph and the offensive load of the bomber version was 3,307lb. A payload of 4,067lb could be lifted by the transport model.

Junkers 87 The first model of the so-called Stuka (q.v.) dive-bomber flew in the late spring of 1935 from Dessau, powered by a 640hp Rolls-Royce Kestrel V liquid-cooled engine. This aircraft was destroyed in a crash, and the second prototype, powered by a 610hp Junkers Jumo 210A, was delivered to Rechlin in 1936. This more

Above: A Junkers Ju 52/3m, showing its corrugated metal construction. (Author)

Above: A Junkers Ju 87D, the precursors of which (particularly the B variant), enjoyed a reputation for invincibility at the beginning of WWII. (Author)

strongly resembled the production versions with a trousered undercarriage, dive brakes and provision for a main external bomb load that swung the missile clear of the airscrew arc in the dive. Three similar Ju 87A-1s went to Germany's StG 162 in December 1937 for operational evaluation during the Spanish Civil War.

In WWII the type was regarded almost as the ultimate weapon against which no defence existed, and although much of this belief was the result of skilled propaganda, it seemed justified by its use against lightly defended targets and the inadequately disciplined air forces it met in the early days. However, the Ju 87's reputation was disproved when employed in the Battle of Britain, and after early losses it was relegated to lesser duties during 1940, by which time the 'Jericho trumpets' or screamers fitted to the undercarriage fairings to heighten the psychological effect of the already noisy dive had been discarded for aerodynamic reasons.

The type in use during this time was the Ju 87B, identified by the flat upper line to the glazing of the crew compartment, but in the spring of 1940, a new, re-engined variant, the Ju 87D, was designed, with a sloping line to the gunner's position and more refined cowl contours, and this version was used with some success on the Eastern Front and in the Western Desert, chiefly in support of artillery. Similar in general appearance to this version was the Ju 87G, which was fitted with a pair of underwing 37mm cannon pods. Casualty evacuation and glider tug models also existed. The fastest variant was the Ju 87D-7 with a maximum speed of 248mph, its bomb load being 3,968lb. A total 5,709 of all versions of the Ju 87 is believed to have been built.

Ju 87 Variants

A-0	Ten pre-production aircraft with modified wing leading edges.
A-1	Limited production with Jumo 210Da motor.
A-2	Broader-bladed airscrew fitted.
B-0	Ten pre-production models with revised canopy.
B-1	Production version with Jumo 211Da motor.
B-1/U1	Re-designated B-1.
B-1/U2	Production model with new radio.
B-1/U3	As U2 but with additional armour.
B-1/U4	Service modification with ski undercarriage.
B-1/Trop	Tropicalized version of B-1.
B-2	Jumo 211Da motor and modified undercarriage.
B-2/U1	Redesignated B-2.
B-2/U2	Revised radio equipment.
B-2/U3	As U2 but with additional armour.
B-2/U4	Modification of U1 with ski undercarriage.
C-0	Pre-production carrier-borne version.
C-1	As C-0 but with folding wings and jettisonable under-carriage.
D-1	Jumo 211J, VS11 propeller and strengthened under-carriage.
D-1/Trop	Tropicalized version of D-1.
D-2	Strengthened tailwheel and glider hook fitted.

D-3	Ground attack version with additional armour.	H-3	Unarmed trainer variant of D-3.
D-3Ag	Overwing pannier for carriage of agents.	H-4	Believed further trainer variant.
D-4	Project for torpedo bombing.	H-5	As H-3 but based on D-5.
D-5	Increased wingspan and jettisonable undercarriage.	H-6	Believed further trainer variant.
D-6	Project only. Based on D-5.	H-7/8	Unarmed versions of D-7/8.
D-7	D-3 with Jumo 211P motor and two 20mm MG151/20 machine guns.	R-1	Long-range anti-ship version of B-2 with extra radio.
D-8	D-5 conversion to D-7 standard.	R-2	Strengthened R-1 with revised fuel system.
D-E	Project only.	R-2/Trop	Modifications to produce a ropicalized version of R-2.
D-F	Project with Jumo 213 motor and oversize tyres.	R-3	As R-1 but with improved equipment.
G-1	Anti-tank version of D-3 with 37mm Flak 18 cannon.	R-4	Factory version of R-/Trop.
G-2	As G-1 but based on D-5.	187	Projected revision of design with Jumo 213 motor.
H-1	Pilot trainer with rear armament deleted.		
H-2	Believed crew trainer version of H-1.		

Junkers 88 This mid-wing, twin-motor bomber was used by the Luftwaffe throughout WWII in a variety of roles, including reconnaissance, night fighting (constituting nearly the whole of that force), ground attack and torpedo-bombing, as a turbojet test-bed and as the lower component of the Mistel (q.v.) combination. Historically, a machine of this type was the last enemy aircraft to be brought down over Great Britain, a Ju 88G-6 of 13/NJG 3 falling near Pocklington aerodrome, Yorkshire, on 3 March 1945.

K-Class The designation for non-rigid US Navy airships operating along the extensive coasts of the United States during WWII, a total of 135 of this class being flown by twelve squadrons from fifteen bases during 1942–43. This type was also the first non-rigid to cross the Atlantic Ocean, K-101, 112, 123 and 130 doing so between South Weymouth, Massachusetts, and

Above: Alongside the Heinkel 111, the Junkers Ju 88 constituted part of Germany's bomber force throughout WWII, as well as being the basis of night fighter, reconnaissance and pilotless bombing variants, while the type also acted as a test-bed for early jet engines and rocket launchers. It first entered service in early 1940. The final days of the war saw the introduction of the improved Ju 188. Seen here a Ju 88A-5 Werke Nr 6073, captured after landing in error at Chivenor. Its German code marking had been M2+MK, but on capture the aircraft became HM509. (Bruce Robertson collection)

the Azores in 58 hours. The gas capacity of the K-Class vessels was 425,000 cu ft, their range 2,000 miles and their maximum speed 75mph. Twelve men formed the crew of each.

Kabul The capital of Afghanistan which was the target for one of the first RAF attacks after the end of WWI when a single Handley Page V/1500 bomber raided it on 24 May 1919.

Kamikaze (Divine Wind). Although this term has since 1945 become associated with Japanese aerial suicide attacks, the name originally referred to the great typhoon that saved the country from the threat of the superior invading force from Kublai Khan's Mongols in 1281 and the choice of the term for sorties such as those first flown in any strength in 1944 indicates the faith placed in such missions

wresting final victory for Japan after a stunning series of US successes on land, sea and in the air.

Examples of attacks of this kind can be traced back to the assault on Pearl Harbor, during and after which individual pilots, fanatically determined or flying hopelessly damaged aircraft, deliberately sacrificed themselves, but it was not until after the Battle of the Philippines that the Special Attack Group (Tokkotai) was formed. The participants were commanded by Vice-Admiral Ugaki and their uniform had seven buttons decorated with three petals of cherry blossom and an anchor on the sleeve indicating a naval unit. The immediate objective of the unit was to disable or destroy American carriers providing protection at Leyte Gulf and thus enhance the likelihood of an Imperial Navy victory in the subsequent surface engagement.

At first various conventional aircraft were flown solo for suicide attacks of this nature, and it was not until September that the first specially designed machines were completed. Known to the Allies as 'Baka', these were Yokosuka MXY7 Ohka ('Cherry Blossom') aircraft and which differed from earlier machines flown on kamikaze missions in that while the latter had flown to the target under their own power, these were taken to it by a 'mother' aircraft and only flew on their own rocket engine after being released in the target area.

Every unit of the air services was to provide a certain number of volunteers for the Group, and, after acceptance, the majority continued with their normal duties for a time until directed to special training, supported in the meantime by great publicity, extra rations and privileged treatment

Above: A Yokosuka MXY7 Ohka Model 11 suicide flying bomb ('Baka'). This particular specimen was captured by US forces on Kadena airfield, Okinawa, in 1945. (Edward T. Maloney)

for their families. It was men such as these who made the most successful kamikaze attack of WWII during the six days leading up to the invasion of Luzon in the Lingayen Gulf on 9 January 1945. Less than 100 suicide aircraft were involved, but they achieved 34 hits on Allied vessels, sinking one escort carrier and damaging four others.

Attacks of this kind reached a peak during the Okinawa (q.v.) campaign, 335 such sorties being launched, for example, on 6 April, outnumbering the conventional warplanes employed. In total 1,900 suicide aircraft are stated to have been dispatched during the three-month campaign. The rationale behind sorties of this nature may be found in the Shinto teaching that death in battle is a warrior's guarantee of entry into heaven. See Kawanishi.

Kamov A Soviet design bureau presided over by Nikolai Kamov and specializing in helicopters, of which the best-known military example is probably the Ka-25 'Hormone' (q.v.).

Kampfgeschwader See Staffel.

'Kangaroo' The NATO code-name for a Russian air-to-ground missile measuring some 50ft in length, of comparatively simple design but reportedly capable of being fitted with a nuclear warhead. It was particularly associated in the West with the Tu-95 'Bear' (q.v.) bomber.

'Kate' (1) The Allied code-name for the Japanese WWII Nakajima B5N carrier-borne attack monoplane, best-remembered as being one of the types involved in the attack on Pearl Harbor on 7 December 1941, in which 144 of the type participated. The prototype made its first flight in January 1937 and production was commenced the following November. The aircraft's first operations, flying from both carriers and land bases, took place during the Sino-Japanese War, and battle experience was incorporated in a re-engined variant, the B5N2, which first flew in December 1939. It was a three-seater, and the maximum speed of the later model was 235mph. (2) 'Kate 61' the code was applied to the Mitsubishi B5M attack bomber, at one time known as

the 'Mabel', a type more conventionally constructed than the above and conceived along the same lines. It was at first favoured by the Imperial Navy, but production was terminated after 129 had been delivered and it served in only small numbers during the Pacific War, operating from land bases. The maximum speed was 237mph.

Kawanishi A Japanese manufacturer of warplanes during the period between the two world wars, specializing in such as the E5K1 reconnaissance floatplane of the early 1930s and the four-motor H6K1. An excursion into fighter design produced the Ki-4 and Ki-61, but the most significant of the company's products in the Pacific War were the four-engined H6K and H8K 'Emily' (q.v.) high-wing flying boats, both of which proved outstanding. An unbuilt suicide bomb designed by Ogawa and Tani was the Baika (Plum Blossom).

Kawasaki A Japanese industrial group, formed after WWI, which was responsible for a number of warplanes for the Army during the interwar years, including the Ki-10 fighter, the prototype of which was completed in 1935. The Ki-32 single-motor light bomber, a monoplane with a fixed undercarriage that first entered service in 1938, was still in front-line use in December 1941 and was significant in that it was the last bomber type used by the Army to have a liquid-cooled motor. It played a major part in operations against Hong Kong. Later designs included the Ki-45 Toryu (Dragon Slayer) twin-engine night fighter, conceived originally also for ground attack. In the former role it was the only type available during the closing months of WWII. After the war the company produced a number of licence-built American military types.

'Kelt' The NATO code-name for a Soviet air-to-surface anti-shipping missile developed from the 'Kennel' (q.v.). Measuring about 30ft in length, it was powered by a liquid-fuel rocket motor and had a range of some 100 miles. It entered service towards the end of the 1960s, carried by 'Badger' (q.v.) bombers.

Kenley An RAF aerodrome near Purley, Surrey, which was established in 1917 on part of Kenley Common as No 7 Aircraft Acceptance Park (AAP) by Lt-Col Conway Jenkins, who lived a short distance away. Although its designated role was that of accepting and delivering warplanes to operational units, the ferry pilots were also expected to intercept enemy aircraft with whatever armed types were available. Temporarily the base of No 1 (Communications) Squadron, providing a shuttle service to Paris in 1919, Kenley became a fighter station during the interwar years, towards the close of which period it was enlarged in area.

The home station of No 615 Squadron of the (then) Auxiliary Air Force, Kenley was still a fighter base during 1940, when it was heavily bombed on several occasions, most significantly at 1315 hrs on Sunday 18 August. In subsequent years its fighters took part in 'Circus' and 'Ramrod' (q.v.) operations. In 1945 the station was transferred to Transport Command, and it was officially closed on 1 May 1959.

'Kennel' The NATO code-name for a 30ft long Soviet anti-shipping missile associated with the 'Badger' (q.v.) bomber type. Its range has been stated to have been no more than 50 miles and the missile is said to have had radio guidance.

Kette A basic Luftwaffe flight formation made up of three aircraft, usually flown in 'vic' formation, consisting of a leader and two Kettenhunde (Chained Dogs).

Kettering Torpedo A pioneering US attempt to construct a flying bomb (q.v.).

KG An abbreviation associated with the Luftwaffe indicating a Kampfgeschwader (Bomber Wing). Such a unit was made up of a total of 106 aircraft from a Stab and three Gruppen, each of which was constituted from three Staffeln and a Stab (q.v.). A Geschwader was indicated by a letter/number combination carried on the sides of aircraft aft of the Balkenkreuz; thus KG 1 was coded 'V4', KG 2 'U5', KG 3 'SK' etc. Some

Kampfgeschwader also had unofficial names, KG 1 and 2 being known as the 'Hindenberg' and 'Holzhammer' (Wooden Hammer) Geschwader respectively. The code system was introduced during the winter of 1938/39 and was followed throughout WWII.

KG 200 Founded early in 1942 as 2 Staffel Versuchsverband Ob.d.L. with its headquarters at Berlin-Rangsdorf, I/KG 200 was the Luftwaffe's spy squadron. It was later expanded to many Staffeln within the Gruppe and was commanded by Obstlt Werner Baumbach, with Lt Paulus as the parachute expert.

Specialization in this role was necessary since the main work of the Gruppe was operating clandestine night missions to drop agents and saboteurs over Iran, Iraq and the Caucasus, operating from Simferopol; over southern Russia from Romania; over Egypt, Transjordan and Libya from Kalamaki and Athens; over Italy from Bergamo; over Tunisia, Algeria and Morocco from Marseilles; over the Balkans from Neustadt; and of course over the Western Front. Planned but not carried out was a long-distance operation to India calling for the establishment of a chain of refuelling stops.

A variety of different aircraft types were used for such sorties, which eventually delivered over 600 male and female agents into enemy territory. Focke-Wulf 200s and Fieseler Storchs represented the extremes of designs employed, but between these fell the normal Luftwaffe equipment such as the Ju 88, 188, 252 and 290 with, perhaps inevitably, the Heinkel 111 and the Savoia SM.79. More unusual aircraft types included captured B-17s (given the cover name of Dornier Do 200s) and B-24s.

The work of KG 200 was only partly espionage as the following summary shows:

I/KG200   Air transport-connected 1 Staffel. Long-range with movement of operations, intelligence and sabotage

2 Staffel   Operations in agents combat zone

3 Staffel   Personnel replacement and training II/KG200 Pathfinders, radar jamming

and Mistel (q.v.) operations

III/KG200   Intended to use torpedo-armed FW 190s but not issued with aircraft due to trial problems

IV/KG200   Training

Khe Sanh A jungle base in Vietnam defended from January 1968 until the following June by a well-equipped US Marine garrison kept supplied entirely by aircraft of the RVNAF, USAF, USMC and USN which flew in ammunition and food during the longest siege of the war. The aircraft also provided area and close support while harrying enemy supply lines, B-52s dropping up to 70,000lb of high explosive. Helicopters and fixed-wing aircraft also flew out the sick and wounded. The US Navy aircraft involved in interdiction sorties with bombs, guns and rockets came from five carriers specially deployed.

'Kipper' The NATO code-name for a Soviet air-to-surface missile believed to have been some 30ft long, turbojet-propelled and with a range estimated as 100 miles. It is said to have seen little operational service.

'Kipper' patrol A patrol flown by RAF fighters based on the English East Coast to protect fishing fleets in the North Sea that were allegedly being targeted by Luftwaffe aircraft in 1940.

'Kitchen' The NATO code-name for a Soviet anti-shipping missile measuring a little less than 40ft in length and having a liquid-fuel rocket motor. It was observed carried by 'Blinder' bombers.

Kite The use of the kite for observation dates from about the turn of the century. Early kites were semi-experimental, being used to lift a man to a sufficient altitude to observe enemy movements, the deployment of guns etc. The British Army conducted trials with two types, both consisting of teams of kites. One was the Baden-Powell pattern, the other the more complex Cody Man-Lifting Kite Team, introduced by 'Colonel' Sam Cody. This was made up of three lifting kites topped by a pilot kite; below these was a larger carrier kite, directly beneath which was suspended a trolley to keep

the basket for the observer on an even keel.

Kite balloon A captive observation balloon, so-called because of its combination of both kite and balloon principles, being oblong in shape and having a stabilizing tail. Cruisers of several of the world's navies were equipped with kite-balloons, although they are generally associated with land operations, particularly on the Western Front during WWI. The basic concept was devised in 1893, and the Germans particularly made use of them, for observing the results of gunfire as well as directing it. The Caquot balloon (q.v.) was an improved type developed by France. See Balloons.

Kittyhawk The name adopted for Curtiss P-40D/E single-seat fighter-bombers developed from the P-40A/B/C Tomahawk, significant in being the last of the American Curtiss types to be used in WWII by the RAF, which employed it exclusively in the Mediterranean theatre, first in the Western Desert and then in Sicily and Italy. In addition, more than 3,000 were delivered to Commonwealth air forces, including the RAAF and RNZAF, which used them in the Pacific area. The first converted to carry a 250lb bomb under each wing and one of 500lb under the fuselage were those of the RAF operating in the Western Desert in June 1942, on occasion operating in conjunction with Douglas Bostons. The armament consisted of six 0.50in machine guns, and the maximum speed was 346mph.

'Knickebein' (Bent Leg). A WWII Luftwaffe code-name for a radio navigational aid and bombing device consisting of a beam directed by a ground station over a target along which bombers flew until meeting a second radio beam intercepting this over the target. The initial advantage of the system was eventually broken by countermeasures that at first jammed and later deflected it so that the intersection was encountered over open country where the bombs were wasted.

Knife A 30in serrated blade under tailskid of Nesterov's Morane G in 1914, used to slash enemy balloons and airships.

Komet See Messerschmitt 163.

Kondor Legion See Condor Legion.

Kopfring A raised steel ring fitted to the nose of a free-fall bomb to prevent over-deep ground penetration so that the blast of the explosion takes place over a wider surface area than would otherwise be the case.

Korean War The conflict which opened with the Communist North Korean forces invading the UN-aided South on 25 June 1950, thus providing the first aerial confrontations after the end of WWII and the first in which jet aircraft met in combat (although there was at first a shortage of jet-propelled aircraft for the United Nations, so that large quantities of ex-WWII P-51 Mustang fighters were returned to service). Later the principal jets involved were the Russian MiG-15, with a maximum speed of 665mph, and the American F-80, F-84 and F-86 Sabre, the later capable of a maximum of 670mph. The Sabre's armament comprised six 0.50in machine guns and later four 20mm cannon compared with the single 37mm fuselage-mounted cannon and two 23mm wing cannon of the MiG.

'Kurt' The German code-name for a copy of the British bouncing bomb used against the Ruhr dams in Operation 'Chastise' (q.v.). Drawings of the copy weapon were dated 20 May 1943 – three days after the British attack – and included a proposal that the bombs be rocket-boosted.

Küstenfliegergruppe Abbreviated as KuFlGr, this was the Luftwaffe's Coastal Reconnaissance Wing in WWII.

Kut-el-Amara A town on the River Tigris defended by the British 6th Division which was besieged from 4 December 1915 until 15 April 1916 and supplied entirely by air during that time. The airlift failed. See CHRONOLOGY.

Kuwait A Middle Eastern country which sprang to the world's headlines as a result of its invasion in 1990 by Iraq, which in turn triggered the Gulf War (q.v.). The reason for the attempted annexation was the drop in oil prices during 1990 coupled with over-production, placing a severe economic strain on the Iraqis, who saw the possibility of acquiring the Rumalia oilfield as being particularly inviting.

The Kuwaiti Air Force is responsible for all military aviation in the country and had been expanded as a result of a seven-year programme introduced in May 1973. The traditionally close ties to the country enjoyed by Britain had resulted in a 1960 mission set up to advise on the establishment of a modern air arm from the heterogeneous collection of transports and light aircraft supplied mainly from British sources during the 1950s. At that time

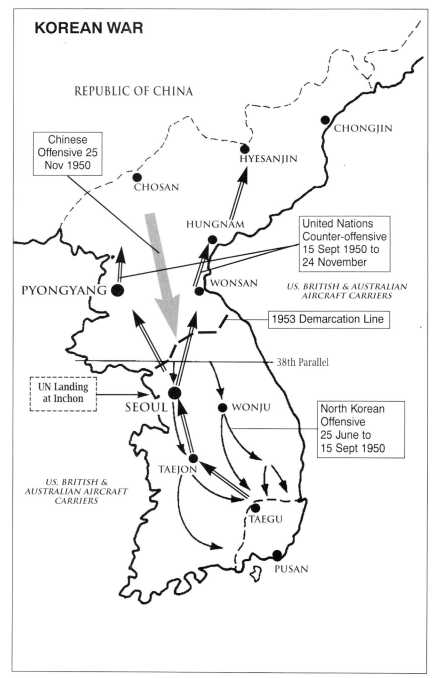

KOREAN WAR

REPUBLIC OF CHINA

CHONGJIN

Chinese Offensive 25 Nov 1950

HYESANJIN

CHOSAN

CHOSAN

HUNGNAM

United Nations Counter-offensive 15 Sept 1950 to 24 November

PYONGYANG

WONSAN

US, BRITISH & AUSTRALIAN AIRCRAFT CARRIERS

1953 Demarcation Line

UN Landing at Inchon

38th Parallel

SEOUL

WONJU

North Korean Offensive 25 June to 15 Sept 1950

TAEJON

US, BRITISH & AUSTRALIAN AIRCRAFT CARRIERS

TAEGU

PUSAN

the country's Security Department had been responsible for the acquisition of aircraft, the earliest modern examples being Jet Provost T.51s – the KAF's first armed machines – and Hunters. These in turn were replaced by Lightnings in 1968, and a number of Strikemasters were added over the next few years.

More modern equipment took the form of eighteen Mirage F.1CKs to replace the Lightnings and 36 Skyhawks armed with Sidewinders. Puma and Gazelle helicopters for assault and observation followed, thirty of the latter making up the strength of two squadrons, one flying HOT-armed machines. The last warplanes for the KAF delivered before the Iraqi invasion were the twelve Hawk T Mk 64s, operated beside the Strikemasters in an advanced weapons training role but also available for light strike duties.

L-band radar A combination of defence and radar techniques first introduced for Great Britain in 1954 from the United States under the latter's Military Aid Program. This gave additional information, at the same time overcoming many of the imperfections associated with manual plotting on the sector table. It combined data covering both early warning and tactical interception on a single display, thus reducing the time in which interceptions could be ordered, in turn making it possible that these could be made at greater range.

L-Class The type designation for 132 small non-rigid airships used by the US Navy during WWII, their primary duties being the shadowing of enemy submarines and escorting convoys. The design is of historical significance for being the first non-rigid to make an Atlantic crossing. Six of the type achieved this in 1944, including K-101, 112, 123 and 130, the group being ordered to Port Lyautey in French Morocco, there to operate with the 14th Squadron. The route was from South Weymouth, Massachusetts, via Newfoundland and the Azores, and the journey was completed in 58 hours. The first of the class had been ordered in 1937, to be used for experiments and training.

LAM Long Aerial Mine. Code-named 'Mutton', this British weapon, used on a limited scale during WWII, consisted of an explosive device at the end of a long cable. Batches were 'sown' in the path of enemy night bombers by such RAF machines as the Harrows of No 93 Squadron, operating from Middle Wallop, which carried the small devices in the bomb-bays of the twenty specially modified aircraft. The measures were not regarded as successful and the unit was disbanded on 22 November 1941, although tests were continued by its Coltishall detachment (redesignated No 1458 Flight) two days later. Nevertheless, interceptions had been accomplished after the first operational sortie, using the HP Harrow aircraft with which the Squadron was first equipped, on 7 October, and the first encounter with the enemy had taken place on the 26th when Harrow K6994 released three LAMs, only to have them explode against the side of the aircraft. On 22 December two mines were released from Harrow K6993 flown by Flt Lt Burke in the path of a pair of enemy bombers, one of which was claimed destroyed. Other trials by this unit included the experimental towing of a barrage balloon with an explosive device attached into the path of enemy bombers with the aid of a Wellington. Only one sortie was made (on 3 April), using T2906, but without result. Japan used similar 66lb LAMs, and the Germans used a 22lb device on a 4mm, 600ft cable by night from 1943 and a 500pdr on 550, 600 or 1,200ft cables by day. All these weapons were anticipated by Kazakov's 1915 trailed anchor with explosive flukes.

Lancaster The British Avro four-motor bomber of WWII powered by Rolls-Royce Merlins or Bristol Hercules radials. Based on the twin-engined Avro Manchester, the prototype Lancaster (BT308) first flew on 9 January 1941 and was known as the Manchester III, even retaining the triple fins of the original. It was not until the maiden flight of the second prototype, DG585, on 13 May that the aircraft's appearance resembled the production versions. L7527, the first production aircraft, flew on 31 October. No 44

Squadron was supplied with BT308, now modified, for service evaluation, and the unit converted to Lancasters in early 1942. The same squadron made the first operational sortie with the type on 17 April, accompanied by Lancasters of No 97 Squadron (converted almost simultaneously), in a low-level daylight attack on the MAN (Maschinenfabrik Augsburg-Nürnberg Aktiengesellschaft) diesel factory at Augsburg.

Subsequent employment of the type found it taking part in the first Pathfinder (q.v.) operation (by No 83 Squadron, against Flensburg on 18–19 August 1942), converted to carry the 12,000lb 'Tallboy' and 22,000-lb deep-penetration 'Grand Slam' bombs and the bouncing bomb of Operation 'Chastise' (q.v.), appearing as an ASR aircraft equipped with an airborne lifeboat and in special radar-jamming versions. In all, 7,366 Lancasters were built, including 422 in Canada, and the last was retired from service on 15 October 1956.

Experiments with Lancasters included a pair (SW244 and HK541) being fitted with 1,200-gallon 'saddle' tanks in an attempt to extend the range of the FE version, and two (LL780 and RF268) being equipped with remotely controlled cannon barbettes (q.v.) in tail and dorsal positions.

Principal Lancaster Production Variants

Mk I	Original version, some of which were modified post-war with faired-over turrets for PRU work and designated PR.I.
Mk I (Special)	Mk I converted to take 8,000lb, 12,000lb or 22,000lb bombs.
Mk I(FE)	Aircraft introduced for use by 'Tiger Force' in Far East.
Mk II	Version powered by Bristol Hercules VI radial motors. Some aircraft had bulged bomb bays.
Mk III	Version powered by Packard-built Merlin 28, 38 or 224 engines.
Mk VI	Version powered by Merlin 87s driving four-blade airscrews. Used for radar-jamming, with nose and dorsal turrets deleted.

Mk VII   Final production version. Nash and Thompson dorsal turrets replaced by relocated Martin turrets.

Mk X   Canadian production version of Mk I but with Packard built Merlins.

Lansen The name adopted for the Swedish Saab J32 ground-attack fighter, the A32A version of which entered service in 1955. The prototype of the all-weather and night-fighter J32B first flew on 7 January 1957 and production versions entered service eighteen months later. The J32B was powered by a turbojet giving improved performance and was equipped with an increased armament of four 30mm fuselage-mounted cannon, Sidewinder missiles and a total of 38 75mm unguided Bofors missiles in two underwing pods, all monitored by a Saab S6 all-weather fire control system. A two-seater, the Lansen had a maximum speed of 627mph and a range in excess of 2,000 miles.

Laos See Royal Laotian Air Force.

Laser guidance A method of directing bombs accurately on to their target which first attracted wide attention by its use in the Gulf War (q.v.), the RAF first using the Pave Spike system ten days after the opening of hostilities. Laser guidance was developed under the Paveway programme in answer to needs of the Vietnam War, and, first used in April 1965, was adapted for six types of conventional bombs. Requiring no modifications to either airframe or the carrier aircraft's electrical systems, the conversion calls only for the fitting of a guidance system to the nose of the bomb in a universally jointed free housing, enlarged fins and an annular tail ring.

The system is based on a silicon detector array which is divided into four quadrants which send signals to the guidance computer and in turn drive the four control fins, the sensor being pointed at the target which is illuminated by the attacking aircraft. Development of the system assumed new potential with the introduction of the Pave III with microprocessor control and flip-out wings, making it suit-able for use at low altitudes. Other systems include the French SAMP and Matra methods, compatible with Ferranti and Hughes designators. See Low-altitude targeting.

'Laura' The Allied code name for the Japanese Navy's WWII Aichi E11A night reconnaissance seaplane. The specification was drawn up in 1936 and called for a seaplane capable of operation from cruisers and battle-ships, and the first flight of the pro-totype took place in June the next year. A total of seventeen had been built by 1940. The maximum speed was 135mph and the range 1,200 miles.

LC (Leuchtcylindrische) Parachute flares (q.v.), as in the German LC50.

Leaflets Propaganda or information sheets dropped by most nations from aerial vehicles from the earliest days of warfare, such operations at the beginning of WWII being officially code-named 'Nickels' in the RAF. Crude early methods of sending bundles of paper down flare chutes, there to be scattered by the slipstream, were later superseded by enclosing large quantities in harmless bomb-shaped casings which were opened during the drop by the automatic detonation of an explosive cord. Leaflets were even carried by German flying bombs (q.v.) contained in cardboard boxes, the first known use of this method of distribution taking place on 28 August 1944 at Madams Court Farm, Frinsted, near Maidstone, Kent.

Leigh Light A powerful battery-operated searchlight devised by Wg Cdr H. de V. Leigh and adopted for some RAF Coastal Command Wellingtons and later Liberator Vs and VIs for nocturnal anti-submarine duties. The first use of the device was by a Wellington of No 172 Squadron on the night of 3/4 June 1942, the first successful sinking with the aid of such a light being made on 6 July. Although the cupola housing the light was at first raised and lowered by means of a block and tackle through the former ventral defensive position, this crude method was later replaced by hand-pumped hydraulic power.

Lewis An American manufacturer of machine guns, Col Isaac N. Lewis set up a factory to produce his own drum-fed designs before 1914 in Belgium. Parallel belt-fed developments in Britain and France were, respectively, the Vickers 0.303 and Hotchkiss, variants of the Maxim infantry machine gun. See Guns.

LF An RAF role designation prefix introduced during WWII indicating Low-Altitude Fighter.

LFG A German aircraft builder (Luftfahrzeus Gesellschaft) created on the basis of an earlier company set up by Krupps, adopting the registered name 'Roland' for its products, which were at first made at Adlershof and then at Charlottenburg after the first plant was destroyed by a fire on 6 September 1916 allegedly started by British agents. Types participating in WWI included the Roland C.II 'Walfisch' reconnaissance two-seater and the D.II, IIa, VIa and VIb single-seat scouts.

LG (Lehrgeschwader). Instructional/ Operational Development Group (German).

Li-2 A licence-built version of the Douglas DC-2 (q.v.) constructed in the Soviet Union by the Lisunov design bureau. The type was in use by the Soviet Union from the closing years of WWII.

Liberator The name adopted for the Consolidated B-24 (q.v.), the first example of which was delivered by air across the Atlantic in March 1941.

Libya A Near East air arm now designated the Libyan Republic Air Force but founded on the Royal Libyan Air Force, created in 1959, when its equipment was only four aircraft, two Egyptian Gomhourias for primary training and a pair of ex-RAF Austers. From 1963 the United States supplied warplanes to Libya, but four years later both Britain and the US were asked to withdraw from the bases in use as staging posts, although the former continued to meet aircraft orders until 1969, when the country was declared a republic. Henceforth French warplanes tended to be favoured.

In October 1973, when relations had deteriorated with Egypt, the Soviet Union was asked to supply arms, although French and Italian materïel continued to be forthcoming during the 1970s. A small, separate air arm, consisting of observation and general liaison types, is operated by the Army.

Liechtenstein A series of airborne interception (AI) radars employed by the Luftwaffe in WWII, primarily for night fighters. The series included the pioneer FuG 202 Liechtenstein BC, which enabled crews to 'see' a target at distances between 3,500 and 6,100yds, the image being registered as a 'blip' on a pair of screens, although this proved particularly taxing on the eyesight of the operators and a maximum of 30min continuous operation only was acceptable. The operating wavelength was 490MHz, and aircraft thus equipped were distinguished by prominent double pairs of dipoles mounted on the nose. These effectively reduced the top speed by 25mph but are reported not to have affected handling. The system was first introduced early in 1942.

Light-assisted landing See Mirror deck-landing system.

Light fighters When the Hindustan HJT-16 entered service in its native India it was at once significant in being one of the few light fighters to be operationally accepted, but attempts to produce a warplane at once economical in terms of its weight, size and complexity can be traced back to WWI, when two designs for the RNAS, the Grain and Eastchurch Kittens, underwent trials. Both powered by 30/35hp ABC Gnat engines, they were intended to operate from destroyers and small naval craft, and the former, with a span of only some 18ft and weighing only 520lb, was capable of taking a Lewis gun and enough fuel for three hours' endurance at a speed of 88mph.

The BAT Bantam was something over twice this weight. Powered by an ABC Wasp radial, it showed an astonishing performance for the 1918–19 period when it flew briefly before being converted for sports flying, but it was quickly eclipsed with the appearance of the monoplane HP.21 and Vickers Vireo, both of which, together with the contemporary Avro Avocet, were designed with an especially keen regard to minimizing weight and dimensions. In 1928 the Blackburn Lincock returned to biplane configuration and proved capable of challenging machines about double its power. Two metal versions of the Mk III (the Mk I was of wooden construction) went to Japan and two to China. The armament was a pair of Vickers machine guns and a radio was carried. It is to France, however, that one must look for light fighters of the 1930s, examples being the Caudron Cyclone, with a 20mm cannon in each wing, and the Mureaux 190. The Italian Romeo Ro.41 once more favoured biplane design and a radial motor.

During WWII the United States was active in this field of design, producing the cannon-armed Bell XP-77, which reputedly had a top speed of some 400mph, while a little later attempts were made to produce a lightened version of the Mustang in the Merlin-powered XP-51F, which was such a totally new concept that, as well as being 1,600lb lighter than the standard model, none of its parts were interchangeable with the standard machine.

The last years of Nazi Germany were to see several light fighters, expendable and non-expendable, including the Bachem 349 Natter (q.v.), the Messerschmitt 163 (q.v.) and the Heinkel 162 (q.v.), while there was even a projected Arado design with provision for a prone pilot. Post-war, specialist lightweight fighters appeared, for example the miniature McDonnell XF-85. A jet powered by a Westinghouse J-34, it spanned just 21ft 11½in and was intended to act as a protective parasite (q.v.), air-launched by the B-36. Perhaps best known of all was the British Folland Midge, from which was developed the similar Gnat, so long associated with the *Yellowjacks* and their successors the *Red Arrows*. These aircraft,officially classified as trainers, were nevertheless first designed as fighters, and as such saw operational service in India where they were produced under licence by Hindustan Aeronautics, later to be responsible for the HJT-16 described earlier.

Lightning (1) See English Electric Lightning. (2) The Lockheed P-38 twin-boom fighter first appeared in prototype form in 1939 and immediately caught the imagination with a flight from March Field to New York of 7hr 2min with only two refuelling stops en route – an astonishing performance at the time. It was to go on to be developed into a number of variants as a long-range interceptor and escort fighter after the first production aircraft was delivered on 8 June 1941. Unusual features for the period included a tricycle undercarriage and turbo-supercharged Allison engines. These were not fitted to the 143 ordered for the RAF in March 1940, so that this variant became known in the factory as 'the castrated P-38'. When the first pair (AF105 and AF106) were tested at Boscombe Down the type was rejected and the aircraft handed back to the US as P-322s. A subsequent order for 524 Lightning Mk IIs in August 1942 was cancelled. Nevertheless, Lightnings were to go on to operate world-wide in US Army Air Force service. The maximum speed of the P-38M variant was 360mph; the armament comprised one 20mm cannon and four 0.50in machine guns, with provision for either bombs or rockets.

Lignum vitae A West Indian wood that assumes extreme hardness after exposure to the air. It was used for the starter-shaft thrust bearings of Rolls-Royce Merlin engines.

'Lily' The Allied code-name for the Japanese Kawasaki Ki-48 twin-motor light bomber which was intended to duplicate the performance characteristics of the Soviet Tu-2 met with during the Sino-Japanese War. Design work was begun in January 1938, one of the four prototypes first being available in July of the following year. Production versions reached operational units before the autumn of 1940 following a delay while tail flutter was eradicated, and the type later became one of the Army's most important aircraft, flying on a number of Fronts including Burma, Malaya, New Guinea and the Netherlands East Indies. However, in combat with Allied aircraft it proved to be underarmed. The maximum speed of the Ki-48-IIb was 314mph and the bomb load, 1,746lb.

Above: The Avro Lincoln was the final RAF piston-engine bomber, and although entering service too late to take part in WWII was used in action against terrorists in Malaya. It was originally to be known as the Lancaster IV or V according to variant. (L. J. Dickson)

Lincoln An Avro-designed bomber originally intended to be known as the Lancaster IV and owing much to the earlier design, of which it may be regarded as a 'stretched' version. Entering squadron service too late to take part in the European war, the type was earmarked for operation by 'Tiger Force' assembled to bomb targets in Japan, but it was unable to do so before the end of Japanese resistance. It saw action during the Malayan Emergency and in Kenya, (now flying with the dorsal turret deleted) against Mau Mau terrorists. It was the RAF's final piston-engine bomber, and it was also operated by the Royal Australian and Argentine Air Forces, by the latter until 1965. The maximum speed was 319mph, and a bomb load of 11 tons could be carried over a range of about 1,400 miles.

Ling-Temco-Vought A US company, the military aviation association of which resulted from the acquisition of Chance Vought in 1961 during the production of the F-8 Crusader (q.v.), and later the A-7 Corsair II attack aircraft. Guided missiles also form

part of the organization's weapons interests.

Lioré et Olivier A French warplane manufacturer established in March 1912 which leapt to prominence during the closing years of the 1920s with the LeO 20 heavy bomber (better known under in civilian guise as the LeO 21 'Golden Ray') and later with the 1936, four-man LeO 451 medium bomber. A total of 484 of the latter had been ordered by May 1940, 132 having been received of which 54 were with operational units. The actions of greatest historical significance involving the type were those of 11 May against the Albert Canal bridges, and that against occupied Sedan four days later when bombs were dropped from below 2,600ft in order to ensure accuracy. The maximum speed of this type was 292mph, it range 1,530 miles and its bomb load, 4,470lb.

Lisunov See Li-2.

'Liz' The Allied code-name for the Japanese Navy's Nakajima G5N Shinzan (Mountain Recess) experimen-

tal attack bomber of WWII. A four-motor monoplane, it was based on the American DC-4E prototype which had been purchased for Japan Air lines but secretly handed over to Nakajima to be dismantled and studied, in ignorance of the fact that it had been rejected by US airlines. The resultant long-range machine retained all but the tail and fuselage of the DC, had a glazed nose and was fitted with a bomb bay, but after six prototypes had been built it proved unsuccessful. Two of the aircraft were produced to an improved standard (G5N2), and this aircraft had a maximum speed of 261mph, a range of 2,647 miles and a normal bomb load of 4,409lb.

Lockheed A US aircraft manufacturer producing the Model 414 Hudson for the RAF immediately before the Second World War, the design being followed by the Ventura and Harpoon and eventually, post-war, the P2V Neptune, a land-based maritime-patrol type like its predecessors and a mainstay of the US Navy for fifteen years. The other design for which the company is remembered during the war

Above: The introduction of the Lockheed F-104 resulted in a whole family of similar fighters flown by a large number of nations, although only those equipping the Pakistani air arm were ever used in combat, during border disputes with India. It was first flown in prototype form at the beginning of 1954, publicity declaring that, so sharp were the wings, ground crews were protected against the leading edges by felt covers! The armament of this Mach 2 multi-mission strike fighter consisted of Sidewinder missiles and a 20mm six-barrel cannon. (Author's collection)

Above: Twin-boom layouts were regarded as novel when the first Lockheed P-38s entered Air Corps service in 1941. These were powered by Allison motors, the export of which was prohibited, so that the first of the 143 ordered by Britain gave a poor performance with the replacement powerplants and the order was cancelled. Even so, the United States' Lightnings rendered yeoman service until 1945, the final versions being capable of carrying 4,000lb of bombs or ten rockets. (Bruce Robertson collection)

Above: A US 'Loon' flying bomb is experimentally launched from the submarine USS *Carbonero* (SS-337) on 19 May 1949. (US Navy)

years is the twin-boom P-38 Lightning.

The introduction of jet propulsion saw Lockheed early in the field with the Shooting Star, which made its first flight in 1944 and lasted in service long enough to see action in the Korean War. Experience with jet fighters in that conflict led to the design of the Model 83 Starfighter, operated by a large number of NATO nations.

Meanwhile the mighty Hercules ('Fat Albert' in the RAF) transport was designed, incorporating in 1954 a number of new and bold features including a pressurized fuselage combined with full-section rear doors capable of being opened in flight, turboprop engines and a bogie-type landing gear. According to the role for which the Hercules was intended – the aircraft was officially described as a 'multi-role' transport – a defensive armament could include 'Gatlings', grenade dispensers or rockets. Other heavy-lifters from Lockheed were to include two strategic transports, the C-141 Starlifter and the Model 500 Galaxy, while the US Navy adopted the carrier-based, four-seat S-3 Viking for anti-submarine work at the end of 1973.

The end of the 1950s had seen the adoption of a strange glider-like machine designated the U-2 and allegedly intended for atmospheric research until the truth was revealed on 1 May 1960 when one such machine, in the charge of CIA pilot Gary Powers, was shot down while conducting a reconnaissance flight over Soviet territory at an altitude far in excess of its announced maximum of 55,000ft. Before the aircraft's relegation to roles less likely to promote international incidents, U-2s were also brought down over China and Cuba. However, Lockheed remained in the strategic reconnaissance field with the design of the A-11 'Blackbird' family.

Lodestar A Lockheed-designed, twin Pratt & Whitney engined transport, the final development in the Lockheed 10, 12 and 14 series which first flew in September 1939 before being operated as the C-56 by the USA Army Air Force, US Navy and RAF, the latter operating the US-designated C-56, C-59 and C-60 as the Lodestar I, Ia and II respectively. These were flown by Nos 162, 173, 216 and 267 Squadrons in the Middle East. An air ambulance version also existed. The maximum speed was 272mph and the range 1,890 miles.

Loening An aeronautical engineering company formed in the United States during 1918 by Grover C. Loening who, despite having added to his experience as an aviation engineer with the Wrights, was a champion of the mono-plane in an age dominated by the biplane. Asked to produce a warplane which would outperform the Bristol Fighter, he designed the M-8, which incorporated such novel features as a shoulder wing attached to the upper longerons, thus giving a wide view to the pilot and an extensive field of fire to the gunner, lifting struts bracing the wing to the lower longerons, and ailerons at the wing tips. The same general principles were followed for the Loening seaplanes and perpetuated in the M-81 two-seat fighter, a small order for which was forthcoming from the US Navy, which required them for observation. Although a small number of Loening monoplanes were sold to the Army, business considerations meant a capitulation to the biplane school and Loening designs for the services in the 1920s included the OL-2 OL-4, OL-6, OL-8, OL-9 and XHL-1 biplane amphibians with a single float under the fuselage.

'Louise' (Also 'Loise'). The Allied code name for the Japanese Mitsubishi Ki-2-1, a twin-engine light bomber operated by the Army. This saw service during the Sino-Japanese War and although obsolete by WWII was erroneously believed still to be in service – hence a code-name was allocated.

Long Aerial Mine See LAM.

Longhorn A Maurice Farman design used chiefly as a trainer by France and Great Britain during WWI with a prominent 'tea tray' elevator in front of the pilot which gave the type its name. Cecil Lewis remembers it as 'docile and well behaved. It climbed at forty-five, flew level at sixty and settled down like a kite when landing.' A small number of Longhorns were flying against the enemy in Mesopotamia at least up until 7 September 1915, and the two serviceable examples from the four at Basra made useful reconnaissance flights at much the same time. The name of this aeroplane and that of the Shorthorn are said to derive from the French remark that they were 'Les vaches méchaniques!'

Loon The name applied to the US version of the German FZG-76 flying bomb (q.v.).

'Lorna' The Allied code-name for the WWII Japanese twin-engine Kyushu Q1W Tokai (Eastern Star) Navy patrol bomber. A three-seater, this design was demanded quickly by the authorities, who added that it must also be capable of dive bombing. Thus it was in much the same category as the Junkers 88 (q.v.), which it resembled. The prototype was completed in September 1943, production commencing the following spring. However, only a small number were built of the standard Q1W1, which was all-metal, the mixed-construction W1W2 or the all-wood four-seater Q1W1-K, the sum total of all variants being a mere 153 by August 1945. All those serving with operational units were used for anti-submarine convoy

protection. The maximum speed was 200mph and the bomb load was 551lb, carried externally.

Low-Altitude Targeting Properly Low-Altitude Navigation and Targeting Infra-Red for Night (LANTIRN), the aiming of a bomb whereby a target is illuminated with a laser which reflects the radiation to the homing head, which then measures the angle between the longitudinal axis of the missile and the missile-target line, thereupon automatically guiding the missile to the centre spot of the target.

Low-Cost Missile Properly Low Cost Advanced Technology Missile (LOCATM). A concept from Rockwell International for a missile carried in packs of three, four or six, with a triangular, low-drag cross-section giving a generally low radar signature, and fitted with folding control surfaces.

Low-Cost Dispenser Properly Low Cost, Low Altitude Dispenser (LOCLAD). An airborne weapons dispenser system which offers day/night targeting over ranges up to 20 miles and from altitudes down to 100ft. Several variants have been developed

or are under development, including REVISE (Research Vehicle for In-flight Submunition Ejection), MANTIS Man-in-the-loop Tactical Interdiction System), AUTIS (Autonomous Tactical Interdiction System) and LOCPOD (Low-Cost, Powered, Off-boresight Dispenser).

Luftwaffe Literally Air Force, and applicable to the German air arms of either WWII or the present. See Germany.

'Luke' The Allied WWII code-name for the Japanese Naval Mitsubishi J4M Senden (Flashing Lightning) experimental fighter. This was seen as a twin-boom type with a pusher airscrew between in the rear of a central nacelle. Although it never progressed beyond the design stage, its maximum speed was estimated at 437mph, with an armament consisting of one 30mm and two 20mm cannon, all in the nose.

LVG (Luft-Verkehrs Gesellschaft) A German aircraft manufacturer originally accommodated in the former Parseval airship shed, Berlin, until it was burnt down in 1914. The company at first producing machines under

Above: A late-production LVG C.VI of 1917 comes into land. This aircraft was used not only on the Western Front but also, in its earlier form, in Palestine. (Author)

licence, the first original design being the LVG B.I, which was judged a suitable warplane for the new air arm in June 1914. This was followed by the B.II, an unarmed, two-seat scout, reconnaissance type and trainer. The LVG C.II, which appeared in 1915, was the first of a series of reconnaissance two-seaters which figured prominently on the Western Front throughout WWI, and the series continued with the C.V and C.VI, both being significant in having ply-covered fuselages.

Lynx The name of a helicopter type constructed in Britain by Westland and in France by Aérospatiale. The prototype first flew on 21 March 1971 and naval production versions were capable of carrying anti-submarine torpedoes. An outstanding agility is coupled with sufficient avionics and flight systems to make it easily one-man operable, even in bad weather. Early orders were received from Argentina, Brazil and the Netherlands.

Lysander A British two-seat army cooperation monoplane high-wing which made its first flight on 15 June 1936, deliveries beginning in June 1938. It was, in effect, an early STOL machine by virtue of its wing slats and automatic, slotted flaps. Although its primary duty was artillery spotting, it passed into history as the type used to supply the beleaguered British defenders of Calais in May–June 1940. It was also pressed into use in other roles, for example as a target-tug, for air–sea rescue and for the nocturnal insertion of agents into German-occupied Europe although only a small number were used for this specialized work and the role of the Lysander in 'spy-dropping' has been much exaggerated since.

LZ Prefix of Luftschiffbau Zeppelin for the 130 Zeppelins built from LZ1 of 1900 to LZ130 Graf Zeppelin II that first flew 1938. See Zeppelin.

Maccabeem 'The Hammers' (Hebrew) The early Israeli 69th Squadron consisting of three B-17s.

Macchi See Aermacchi.

MAD Magnetic Anomaly Detector. A short-range device capable of detect-ing the presence of a submerged submarine due to the slight variation of the earth's magnetic field caused by its presence. Aircraft thus fitted are identifiable by the tube-like 'sting' protruding from the rear of the fuselage.

'Mahmoud' An RAF Bomber Support Group operation flown by Fighter Command during WWII using Mosquito aircraft fitted with rearward-facing radar. These flew alongside bomber streams or, alternatively, to known German night-fighter rendezvous. On detecting the presence of the enemy in either of these roles, the Mosquitos would, with the assistance of their radar, make a 360-degree turn and the target would then be subjected to a rear attack.

'Mail' The NATO code-name for the Soviet Beriev Be-12 Tchaika maritime reconnaissance (q.v.) amphibian in service circa 1975. It was based on the earlier Be-6 'Madge', which it replaced, but incorporated an advanced hull design. Range was in the region of 3,000 miles and the maximum speed approximately 340mph.

'Mallow' The NATO code-name for the Beriev Be-10, the predecessor of the foregoing. Also a maritime reconnaissance twin-jet flying boat, it entered service in 1961, carrying anti-shipping missiles under the wings, and its hull design incorporated a number of advanced features. The maximum speed was 570mph and the range was estimated at 4,000 miles.

Manchester A British WWII Avro-designed bomber powered by twin Rolls-Royce Vulture inline motors, the prototype (L7246) making its first flight on 25 July 1939. A second aircraft (L7247) first flew on 26 May 1940 and deliveries to squadrons commenced to No 207 in November. The Manchester's first operation was an attack on Brest on the night of 24–25 February 1941, its last that on the night of 25–26 June 1942, following which the aircraft was withdrawn from service, chiefly because of the unreliability of its engines, which had been insufficiently developed before being adopted for the type. Manchester Is had triple fins, but the central fin was deleted from, and rudders of increased area were fitted to, tailplanes increased by 11ft in span on the Mk IA. Rumours abounded that airflow buffeting induced by the dorsal turret in certain positions tended to damage the early central fins. The top speed was 265mph and the range 1,200 miles, with a maximum bomb load of 10,350lb.

Mandrel A WWII British system for swamping German early warning radar by radio transmissions.

'Mangrove' The NATO code-name for the trainer version of the Yak-25 'Flashlight' (q.v.) all-weather twin-seat fighter. It retained the excessive anhedral of the fighter variant, necessitating wing-tip wheels.

'Manna' Operation 'Manna' was carried out by the RAF during April and May 1945 using bombers to drop food and other supplies to the Dutch, who were in danger of starving. The operation was arranged with the occupying German forces.

Marauder The US Martin (q.v.) B-26 medium bomber, the prototype of which made its first flight in November 1940. Production versions appeared in 1941. In its early days the type was viewed with caution as it was alleged to present handling difficulties, particularly when landing. This was not so, and the aircraft went on to establish itself in the South West Pacific from April 1942 and later in Europe. Speed had been particularly stressed in the original specification issued on 25 January 1939, and to this end as streamlined a fuselage as possible was designed, and the popular press at once termed the B-26 'The Flying Torpedo'. Less polite names included 'The Flying Prostitute' ('no visible means of support'), an allusion to the seemingly inadequate wing span of 65ft (which was later increased to 71ft on the B-26C), and 'Widow Maker', from its 'hot' reputation. The type served with the USAAF, the South African Air Force and the RAF, the last using it particularly in the campaigns in Sicily, Sardinia and Italy. The maximum speed of the B-26G (Marauder III in the RAF) was 305mph, range was 1,200 miles and the bomb load was 4,000lb.

Maritime reconnaissance The use of aircraft for sea patrol, particularly in order to discover submarines, was begun during WWI, landplanes, flying boats and lighter-than-air craft being used for this although occasionally unsuitable machines had to be used, calculated more to intimidate by their presence than to be capable of any hostile action. Reconnaissance in its purest sense, such as that carried out to shadow elements of the German High Seas Fleet at the Battle of Jutland in May/June 1916 must also be included. All these activities established a sphere of warfare that continued with little variation into WWII, after which specially designed aircraft types such as the Lockheed P2V Neptune appeared.

As new designs were evolved and jet-propulsion was adopted, progressively longer ranges and duration became possible. Increasingly sophisticated devices were introduced, including MAD (q.v.) and autolycus equipment, the latter being capable over short distances of detecting diesel fumes from a submarine either submerged using its snorkel or having recently dived. Perhaps, however, the greatest advance in ASW equipment has been the appearance of sonar buoys, which, dropped into the sea with the aid of parachutes, transmit their audio findings back to the parent aircraft. Modern offensive stores include depth charges and homing torpedoes. The duties of maritime reconnaissance should not be confused with those of spotting for gunfire to aid a friendly surface vessel.

Marker See Target-indicator.

Martel A joint French (Matra) and British (Hawker Siddeley) air-to-surface missile (Missile Anti-Radar and Television) introduced in the closing late 1960s and early 1970s for use by such aircraft as the Atlantique, Buccaneer, Jaguar, Mirage and Nimrod. Measuring only some 12ft in length, it was fitted with a solid-fuel rocket motor and in its British form employed television guidance from the launching aircraft even after the latter was no longer aligned on the target. French versions homed on a target's radar emissions. Range was in the region of 40 miles and a high-explosive warhead was carried.

Martin A US aircraft manufacturer which first came to prominence in the military sphere with the manufacture at the end of WWI of the MB-1 twin-engined biplane bomber, which remained in US service for several years. An updated variant, the NBS-1, was followed by the MO-1 single-motor observation monoplane and the MS-1, a floatplane with folding wings for submarine stowage; both the latter were used by the US Navy. The company concentrated on the development of the dive bomber (q.v.) throughout the 1920s and, following the B-10 concept for a twin-engine, all-metal, mid-wing, record-breaking monoplane bomber, evolved the B-26 Marauder (q.v.). This was followed by other medium bombers until a move to flying boats was marked by the Mars and Mariner designs. The years following WWII saw Martin turn to licence-production of the British Canberra as the B-57.

'Mascot' The NATO code-name for the Soviet Ilyushin Il-28U, the training variant of the Il-28 'Beagle' (q.v.) bomber.

Master bomber A technique first employed by the RAF on the night of 7 August 1943 wherein the marking of a target (in this case Peenemünde) was aided by radio instructions from a leading aircraft and relayed to the main force. This method of control was still being employed by the time of the D-day landings in June 1944.

Matra Engins Matra is a major French manufacturer of aircraft armament, including rockets such as the Martel (q.v.) anti-ship missile and the Magic air-to-air missile, together with associated equipment such as pods and launchers.

'Max' (1) A German thin-cased, WWII general-purpose bomb weighing 5,500lb. (2) The NATO code-name for the Soviet Yak-18 standard trainer in use since 1946. It was a low-wing monoplane with tandem seats and a retractable undercarriage, later versions having a tricycle landing gear. A single-seat version officially designated the Yak-18P was code-named 'Moose'.

MB.326 This Aermacchi two-seat trainer first flew in prototype form on 10 December 1957. The ground-attack variant is known as the MB.326A. The first machines were delivered to the Italian Air Force in October 1960, and orders were later received from Argentina, Australia (where it was built under licence as the MB.326H), Bolivia, Brazil, Dubai, Ghana (MB.326F), South Africa (where it was also built under licence, as the single seat light attack MB.326K or Impala 1), Togo, Tunisia (MB.326B), Zaire and Zambia. The maximum speed was 540mph on internal fuel and the range 290 miles. Armament could consist of two optional 7.7mm fuselage guns, with six underwing points for machine guns or reconnaissance pods, rockets or bombs to a maximum of 2,000lb (a load doubled on later variants).

McDonnell A US aircraft manufacturer founded in 1939, its first major warplane project being experimental work on the twin-engined high-altitude XP-67. Subsequent products included the FH-1 Phantom, the US Navy's first carrier-borne jet, and the F2H Banshee. Excursions into other fields resulted in the KDH-1 Katydid target drone (q.v.).

McDonnell Douglas A company founded as a result of a merger of the above and the Douglas (q.v.) Corporation in 1967, simultaneously assuming responsibility for the current design, the F-4 Phantom (q.v.) and later introducing the F-15 (q.v.) air superiority fighter. The company also took out a licence for the manufacture of the Harrier (q.v.) 'jump-jet' in the US.

Meacon A device used during WWII to re-transmit German navigational beacon signals in order to give false bearings.

Messerschmitt A German aircraft manufacturer established at Bamberg in Bavaria in 1925. It began collaborating with Bayerische Flugzeugwerk of Augsburg two years later, hence the letters 'Bf' in aircraft designations after that date, and a year later Dipl Ing (Professor) Willy Messerschmitt, who had founded the former organization, became one of the company managers. Although an expert of long experience with glider designs, he readily turned to powered aircraft.

Among the company's most outstanding creations was the Bf 109E. Known as the 'Emil' from its designation suffix, the type was the Luftwaffe's standard single-seat fighter at the outbreak of WWII, the initial prototype having first flown in September 1935. It was in turn based on the earlier Bf 109B, forty of which had been delivered to Jagdgruppe 88 of the Condor Legion and seen service in the Spanish Civil War. The maximum speed of the 109E was 354mph and its armament consisted of two 20mm cannon and two synchronized 7.9mm machine guns.

Variants of the Bf 109E Series

E-0   Pre-production machines for evaluation.
E-1   First production model.
E-1/B   Fighter-bomber variant.
E-3   DB 601A motor replaced by DB 601Aa.
E-4   MG FF cannon in airscrew hub deleted.
E-4/B   Fighter-bomber variant.
E-4/N   Night fighter with DB 601N engine.
E-4/Trop Version for use in North Africa.
E-5   Reconnaissance model with twin MG 17 guns.
E-6   As E-5 version but with DB 601N motor.
E-7   Provision for drop tank.
E-7/Trop Air filters and a new, pointed spinner fitted.
E-7/U2 Armoured low-level model of E-7.
E-7/Z   GM1 supercharging.
E-8   Reconnaissance fighter with DB 601E motor.
E-9   Similar to E-8 but with RB50/30 camera.
T-O   Ten pre-production carrier versions.
T-1   Sixty production shipboard fighters.
T-2   De-navalized version with DB 601N motor.

Via the Bf 109F, which first dispensed with the earlier characteristic, square-cut wing tips, the externally similar Bf 109G, popularly known as the

Above: The spinner of later Messerschmitt Bf 109s (this is that of an E-4) still bore testimony to the cannon firing through the airscrew hub of earlier versions. (Author)

Above: The backbone of the Luftwaffe fighter force in the early days of WWII consisted of Messerschmitt Bf 109Es, immediately identified by their square-cut wing tips. This preserved example is an E-4 model which was flown by Lt Wolfgang Teumer at the end of the Battle of Britain. (Author)

Above: A Messerschmitt Bf 110 of I /ZG 52's Geschwader Stab over the English Channel some time in 1940. (Author's collection)

'Gustav', entered service towards the end of 1942, and with a more powerful Daimler-Benz engine carried an armament of a single engine-mounted 20mm cannon, two synchronized 13mm machine guns and a pair of underwing 20mm cannon. The maximum speed was 387mph. A number of variants of the basic 109 airframe followed, including the Bf 109/N, produced for night interception and distinguished by the transparent dome over its Naxos 'Z' antenna aft of the cockpit.

Such a successful airframe was the subject of a number of variations and experimental modifications, among the more unusual being the Bf 109Z, the suffix indicating 'Zwilling' or 'twin'. This consisted of a pair of standard airframes of the F-series which were joined in much the same manner as the North American P-82 Twin Mustang. The German design anticipated the P-82 by a number of years, being completed in 1942, although it was never flown. The pilot would have been accommodated in the port fuselage and the armament would have been five MK 108 cannon, although in the planned Bf 109Z-2 this was reduced to only a pair of guns in order that a bomb load of about 2,205lb might be carried. The designations Z-3

and Z-4 were reserved for, respectively, versions of the Z-1 and Z-2 powered by Jumo 213 motors. An even more revolutionary variation of the Bf 109 airframe was the 109TL, a projected jet-propelled version investigated in 1943.

A contemporary design was the Bf 110 twin-engine two-seater, which met with only limited success although a night fighter version was developed, and from this were evolved the Me 210 and Me 410 Hornisse two-seat medium-range fighters, the 'Bf' prefix being now no longer applied. However, perhaps the most bizarre Messerschmitt design of the period was the Me 163 Komet, the only WWII fighter powered by a rocket motor to see service. The fuel for this aircraft was high test hydrogen peroxide (T-Stoff), using calcium permanganate as a catalyst, but as this tended to clog the jets, giving variable thrust, hydrazine hydrate and methyl alcohol as a catalyst were substituted (C-Stoff). A prototype was completed by May 1942 and the first operational evaluation models were delivered to 1/JG 400 at the end of June 1944. Komets of this and the second Staffel, formed in July, made their first interception on 16 August, meeting B-17 bombers, but the type was to prove an incalculable machine, highly

dangerous to those flying it, and accidents were frequent, usually taking the form of explosions of residual fuel while landing. About 370 were completed, their maximum speed being 590mph, carrying an armament of two 30mm cannon with provision for twenty-four R4M unguided rockets under the wings.

Of much of greater historic importance was the Me 262, the world's first turbojet aircraft to be used in warfare. The prototype made its first flight on 4 April 1941, powered by piston engines in order to determine the type's flight characteristics since turbojets had been given low priority. The first flight with turbojets installed was made on 25 November 1941, a training programme for pilots being started exactly three years later. Operational models of the Schwalbe (Swallow) were purely interceptors, but, allegedly on Hitler's personal orders, the type was adapted as the Me 262A-2a attack bomber and re-named Sturmvogel (Stormbird). It was used in this role against Allied forces following the opening of Operation 'Overlord', troops reporting the phenomenon of its bombs seemingly travelling backwards after release, although a much-favoured tactic was to release bombs at some 3,000ft, having dived at about

Above: German Messerschmitt 410s were also operated and built under licence by Hungary. Those of the Luftwaffe made their first sorties over the British Isles in September 1942. (Author)

Above: Messerschmitt 163B Komet Werke Nr 191454 on display in Green Park, London, soon after the end of hostilities in Europe. (Author)

30 degrees from 12,000ft higher. Several versions were produced, including radar-equipped night fighters and four interestingly modified with single, nose-mounted 50mm MK 114 cannon for attacks on bombers. The barrels of these weapons projected about 7ft forward of the fuselage. About 500 of the total of the 1,433 Me 262s manufactured were destroyed in Allied bombing attacks before delivery, a high proportion being Me 262A-1as which had a maximum speed of 536mph and were armed with four 30mm nose-mounted MK 108 cannon and twenty-four 5cm R4M air-to-air rockets.

Undoubtedly the largest Messerschmitt products of WWII were the Me 321 and 323 Gigants (q.v.).

Meteor See Gloster.

Midway A decisive air and sea battle of WWII which opened on 4 June 1942. For the preceding six months the Imperial Japanese Navy under Admirals Yamamoto and Nagumo had carried before it all British, Dutch and US resistance, and gaining control of the tiny Midway atoll, 1,300 miles WNW of Pearl Harbor, would bring

with it control of the Pacific. To this end a total of six carriers, two of them intended for diversionary attacks, approached the island at the beginning of June, and the historic day began with a dawn strike. The Americans could muster 314 aircraft, 232 carrier-borne, against the Japanese 254, but this first action cost the US Marine Corps 28 machines. The day also saw a mixed American force of B-17, dive and torpedo bombers attack the Japanese Fleet at a cost of seventeen machines, although in mid-morning aircraft from the carriers *Enterprise* and *Yorktown* fatally damaged *Akagi*, *Kaga* and *Soryu*, leaving only *Hiryu* to launch a retaliatory attack with dive and torpedo bombers. These aircraft seriously damaged *Yorktown*, which was finally sunk by torpedoes three days later. Earlier, only six of 35 Douglas Devastators had returned from an attack on the Japanese vessels, but other US dive bombers sank *Hiryu*, so that with the loss of all four carriers in the immediate area the Japanese abandoned the operation for Midway.

MiG-3 A Soviet piston-engine, single-seat fighter of WWII, the second design

from the Mikoyan-Gurevich bureau, based on the open-cockpit MiG-1, of which 2,100 were built after a design period of only three months. The MiG-3 first flew in 1941 and was accepted by operational units towards the end of the year. Several thousand were constructed before their limited manoeuvrability resulted in their relegation to tactical reconnaissance duties before they were phased out from front-line service by the end of 1943. The maximum speed was 407mph and an armament of two 7.62mm ShKAS and one 12.7mm Beresin BS machine gun was carried, with provision for six RS-82 underwing rockets or up to 450lb of bombs.

MiG-9 The first Soviet turbojet-powered fighter, the type made its first flight on 24 April 1946, partially based on captured German data and powered by two motors slung under the forward fuselage. Production was not completed until February 1949. Known to the West by the NATO codename 'Fargo', this well-designed single-seater had a maximum speed of 559mph and carried an armament of one 37mm and twin 23mm Nudelmann cannon in the nose.

Above: Making its first flight in the spring of 1941 and in production for only about seven months, the MiG-3 was of mixed wood and metal construction and was introduced as a more refined replacement for the MiG-1, features of the later machine being a more powerful engine, a sliding hood, increased dihedral, a new airscrew and additional tankage. Despite increases in armament, however, the MiG-3 fared badly at the hands of German pilots and by 1942 had been relegated to armed reconnaissance and close support duties. (IWM Rus 19721)

MiG-15 The West knew nothing of the existence of MiG's first operational jet, nor of the fact that it was only put into production after the naive gift of a suitable engine from Britain, until Allied fighters found themselves confronted by this swept-wing single-seater during the Korean War. The aircraft was at first armed with twin cannon (later increased to three) and in one form or another 8,000 MiGs of this type were delivered in the Soviet Union alone over a five-year period. A substantial number were also produced in satellite countries, principally Poland. Drop tanks were standard equipment, as was simple AI radar on the night fighter model, but in the Soviet Union the type began to be phased out in 1954. However, four years later it began to enter production in China,

Above: The existence of the MiG-15 was unknown in the West until it was encountered by Allied pilots over Korea, problems of finding a suitable power unit having been overcome by the presentation of details of the Nene jet engine by Britain's Socialist government. Armed at first with one 30mm Type N cannon on the starboard side and a 23mm Type NS on the port, it was a formidable opponent, being capable of a maximum speed of 668mph. (Author)

and the 'Fagot', to quote its NATO code-name, was still common, either in the fighter or trainer (UTI) form, as late as 1975. The maximum speed of the original version, which had first flown on 30 December 1947, was 668mph, later bettered by 16mph in the improved 15bis.

MiG-17 Differing little in external appearance from the earlier design although a completely new concept, the 'Fresco' was classified as a single-seat fighter with limited all-weather capability. Its single 5,952lb s.t. Klimov jet engine gave the aircraft a maximum speed of 711mph without external stores, making it very far from being merely an improved model of the MiG-15 as was at first erroneously believed in the West.

The prototype first flew in January 1950, the first service delivery being received two years later, and the aircraft soon proved to be a steady gun platform, having been designed from the first to be rid of the tendency shown by the MiG-15 to snake and pitch when fire was opened. The armament was similar, albeit using improved weapons, and was augmented with underwing stores including overload tanks, bombs, various air-to-ground missiles and packs of eight 55mm air-to-air missiles.

Production figures are believed to have well exceeded 5,000, including the 1,000 exported by China, and the type equipped some 22 air forces before it began to be replaced in the 1970s.

MiG-19 Bearing a strong resemblance to the MiG-17 but with a less tubby profile and without the high-set tailplane of this design, the MiG-19 first flew on 18 September 1953, five prototypes of the new fighter having already been ordered.

It was not only in terms of aerodynamics that the MiG-19 differed from its predecessor, for while the latter had only a single engine of 5,005lb s.t., the 'Farmer' (as the new MiG was known in the West) was powered by twin 4,410lb s.t. Milkuin jets with afterburning, both contained within the fuselage and served by a single nose intake – an arrangement that brought the Soviet Union into the supersonic field and immediately

resulted in the design being put into large-scale production. The numbers of MiG-19s produced ultimately bettered the totals achieved for the MiG-15 and -17.

The armament originally comprised no more than that carried by the two earlier types, but after some 500 MiG-19s had been delivered, the -19S was introduced, having a ventral air brake and three new NR-30 guns, one in each wing root and one under the starboard side of the nose. The improvement programme continued, eventually resulting in the MiG-19F which had an upgraded and more powerful engine (the RD-9), raising the top speed from Mach 1.1 to Mach 1.3.

The total production of all variants has been estimated as exceeding 10,000, the type being flown also by Poland, China, Czechoslovakia and Pakistan. All could carry K-13A 'Atoll' air-to-air missiles (based on the West's Sidewinders) on underwing pylons in addition to 551lb of other offensive weapons.

MiG-21 Finally throwing off the last vestiges of the chunky contours of the earlier MiG jets, this single-seat, limited all-weather, multi-role jet, which first flew in 1955, was to run to an astonishing fourteen basic versions, plus a multitude of variants from China (called F-8s), making it among the most widely used aircraft of its type in the world – as much due to its cost-effectiveness as to its operational efficiency. Known to NATO as 'Fishbed', it served in the air forces of India, Egypt, Afghanistan, Bangladesh, Cuba, Bulgaria, Finland, Algeria, North Korea, Iraq and Syria, in addition to a number of Eastern European countries then regarded as Soviet satellites and of course the Soviet Union itself.

In 1973 the MiG-21SMT was introduced. This had new avionics equipment which gave the distinctive curved line to the dorsal spine, a feature that also distinguished the multi-role MiG-21bis.

MiG-23 With a maximum speed of Mach 2.2, this Mikoyan single-seater (known to NATO as 'Flogger') first entered service in 1971 and existed in two versions, the attack model known as the -23B and the dedicated all-weather interceptor designated the

23S. The design marked Mikoyan's first excursion into the field of swing-wings. These gave the type a distinctive plan, having notched leading edges at maximum sweep. There was a leading-edge droop on the outer sections of the mainplanes, a folding ventral fin and a complex undercarriage to save space when the landing gear was retracted into the fuselage.

Armament consisted of a single 23mm GSh-23 twin-barrelled cannon under the fuselage and twin AA-7 medium-range air-to-air missiles on hardpoints under the inboard, fixed wing surfaces. There was a belly hardpoint or provision for a pair of AA-8 air-to-air missiles.

'Floggers' saw service with the air arms of not only the USSR but also Algeria, Bulgaria, Czechoslovakia, Egypt, Ethiopia and Libya.

MiG-25 It is perhaps surprising that the MiG 'Foxbat' (as it was known in NATO circles) could trace its ancestry back to about 1957 – the time when the MiG-19 'Farmer' was attracting world attention as a relatively new type in service. However, there is little doubt that the concept of the MiG-25 was influenced by the atmosphere of the arms race then gripping both East and West, in particular by reports of the United States' Mach 3-capable Lockheed A-11, a strategic reconnaissance type with a strike capability. Equally, there is little doubt that certain design parallels between the new MiG when it appeared and the American NA-5 indicate that the former had inspired the latter.

To meet these design requirements it had been necessary for the 'Foxbat' to be constructed largely from fabricated steel sections, with the fuel tanks, otherwise prone to leakage with temperature changes, from steel sheet. The two afterburning Tumansky R-12s produced 27,000lb s.t. and gave the aircraft a Mach 3 capability at high altitude, but at low speeds a considerable nose-up attitude was called for. Manoeuvrability suffered, the MiG-25 being derisively termed a 'straight-line' machine.

Used by Algeria and Libya in addition to the USSR, 'Foxbat-A', the interceptor version, was armed with two AA-6 radar-guided air-to-air missiles and two AA-6 infra-reds, plus a belly-mounted gun-pack, while 'Foxbat-B' was the reconnaissance version and is said to have been used for regular sorties over Israel between 1971 and 1975.

MiG-27 Simply expressed, this tactical attack fighter may be described as a MiG-23 with a redesigned front fuselage, the slimmer nose made possible by disposing of the radar (although simple ranging radar was retained), thus giving an improved view for the pilot who now occupied a raised seat. The Tumansky R-29B afterburning turbofan gave the 'Flogger-D' Mach 1.6 capability

It was not until 1981 that the West identified a variant of this type which, although officially designated MiG-27M, was soon to be given the NATO identity 'Flogger-J'. Differences between the true 27M and the earlier

version were chiefly that the former had a wider nose with a lip at the top covering a window for radar range-finding while below was a blister with a further window for laser target identification. It was built under licence in India as the Bahadur (Valiant).

Some 830 aircraft of both types were delivered. The armament of the MiG-27M consisted of two gun pods carried on underwing pylons which permitted the barrels to be depressed to deal with ground targets, while that of the MiG-27 included a six-barrel 23mm Gatling-type gun in an underbelly pack and five pylons for external stores which could include nuclear weapons.

There also existed the so-called 'Flogger-F' and '-H', but these were more accurately members of the MiG-23 series.

MiG-29 A single-seat counter-air fighter with a full dual-role capability, enabling it to be used also as an attack fighter. It entered Soviet service at the beginning of 1985, whereupon NATO immediately bestowed upon it the code-name 'Fulcrum'; at a later date, when the MiG-29 was adopted by India, it became known as the Baaz, or Eagle.

The MiG-29 is a twin-engined design with its pair of Isotov RD-13 turbofans (11,240lb s.t.) 'buried' within the fuselage. The airframe weight was kept as low as possible by manufacturing some seven per cent (by weight) of the structure from composites, while equipment included large pulse-Doppler look-down/shoot-down radar with only search-while-scan capability rather than the infinitely more complex track-while-scan.

MISTEL COMBINATIONS

In WWII the theory of using a large aircraft to lift a smaller one and thus increase the latter's range was not new, experiments having been carried out on 17 May 1916 whereby a Felixstowe flying boat took off carrying a Bristol Scout intended to be used for intercepting Zeppelins. A separation was made over Harwich, allowing the smaller aircraft to land at Martlesham Heath. However, despite the success of these trials, the idea was not to be repeated until adopted for civilian purposes by the Mayo composite of flying boat *Maia* bearing seaplane *Mercury* in 1938, and it was left to Nazi Germany to adapt the idea to landplanes.

In fact it was 1941 when Flugkapitän Siegfried Holzbauer, Junkers' test-pilot, suggested the idea, adding that it could be modified, not so much to lift a light aircraft with the aid of a larger one as to use redundant aircraft as flying bombs, controlled from a smaller machine carried above. The pilot of this would be in no danger of crashing with the type selected for the lower component (a Junkers 88) since he would be able to fly his unmanned charge to the target area, select the target and aim the larger machine, and then, separating some distance away, return to base. No method of controlling of the lower machine was envisaged after the two had parted.

Almost a year was to pass before the suggestion, at first coldly received, was given consideration, so that it was 1942 before the first steps were taken by Fritz Stamer of the German Research Institute for Gliding – generally known as the DFS, or Deutsche Forschnungsinstitut für Siegelflug – using either Klemm 35s or Focke Wulf 56 Stössers mounted on a framework or trestle of light struts above DFS 230 gliders. It was not long before a series of successful flights ending in safe separations indicated the feasibility of the system – which had rapidly earned the nickname 'Huckepack' (Pick-a-back) – although a strong school of opinion existed favouring air-towed offensive loads. However, the new combinations gained the notice of the Luftwaffe's technical department, which went a stage further and authorized the continuation of the tests, this time using Messerschmitt 109E fighters as the upper component, still above the ubiquitous DFS 230 glider.

There then followed a protracted experimental period using this composite, until in July 1942 permission was given for a Junkers Ju 88A-4 to be substituted for the glider, and at the same time the original upper component was exchanged for a Messerschmitt Bf 109F-4 (marked with the call-sign CI+MX), the promise shown by the trials to date seeming to justify such a combination. When the trials had been completed in October, fifteen such composites, known as Mistel (Mistletoe) types, were on order, the general code-name of the project now adopted being 'Beethoven Gerät' although aircrews preferred the reference to

the parasitic plant or else knew the combinations as 'Vater und Sohn' (Father and Son). Much detailed research had gone into development to this point, such problems as suitable coupling links, explosive or mechanical, having to be investigated.

Investigations into a suitable explosive charge for the lower component had resulted in a 7,715lb warhead of the hollow-charge type containing 3,800lb of a high explosive made up of 70 per cent Hexogon and 30 per cent TNT, the impact fuse for this being automatically primed three seconds after the separation of the pair. Tests with the first warheads were made also during 1943 using the former French battleships *Oran* and *Océan* as targets. Developing the guidance, control and fitting systems had been delegated jointly to DFS, Junkers and Past, the latter developing the control gear in cooperation with DFS. The controls and throttles of the Ju 88 were actuated from the smaller aircraft and worked by automatic pilot once separation was effected, the bomber being held in a shallow, 15-degree dive. Meanwhile DFS alone was responsible for devising a cradle for the upper machine. One of the problems that had to be overcome concerned the single stay supporting the rear of the fighter. This was spring-loaded, so there was for a time a danger of its rebounding and striking the fighter once the main attachment points had been simultaneously released, and an arrester clip was designed for the stay to prevent this.

By April 1944, when the final warhead tests had been completed, a small unit designated 2/KG 101, commanded by Hpt Horst

Above: Known in the West by the reporting name 'Fulcrum', the MiG-29 first entered service in 1985, variants soon going to the Czech Air Force (here illustrated) and to India, where the name Baaz (Eagle) was adopted. Although it is a land-based, twin-jet, single-seat counter-air fighter, among the four versions developed beyond the basic design may be included a two-seat combat trainer, a variation for deck landing trials and one fitted with fly-by-wire. Doppler look down/shoot down, search-while-scan radar is carried and the type is reported to be aerodynamically incapable of entering a flat spin. (Bruce Robertson collection)

Rudat, was formed to carry out aiming instruction using the Mistel S1 trainer versions of operational Mistel 1s off the Danish coasts. At much the same time discussions were finalized as to suitable targets for the Mistel, major naval anchorages being largely discarded because the war situation placed them at the extreme range of the aircraft. However, since the Allies' D-day landings forced the deployment of 2/KG 101 to St Dizier, it was from here that the first sortie with five of the type was made on the night of 24–25 June 1944. Landing the combinations was considered impracticable (tyre bursts had proved to be a problem during the development programme, when the bomber undercarriages had to be strengthened), so that one Mistel of the formation had to be jettisoned, but it was claimed that the remaining four all hit ships, the first being released by Fdw Saalfed. Although escorted, this mission had been made at night because the combinations were regarded as vulnerable, but the darkness proved the undoing of this sortie since the ships hit were later claimed to be among a number that had been deliberately sunk as parts of a Mulberry harbour. Little operational damage was done therefore, but, ignorant of all this, the Staffel of KG 101 responsible was withdrawn and placed under the command of KG 200 to await its next assignment.

This was not long in coming, taking the form of an abortive attack on shipping in the English Channel on the night of 9–10 August 1944. It was during this sortie that one Mistel crashed near Andover, Hampshire, with a massive explosion which destroyed all but

the smallest evidence of the way in which it had been caused. Now the idea of attacking naval centres was reconsidered. The British Fleet at Scapa Flow was selected as a target, and a number of reconnaissance flights were mounted in preparation, but before the sixty Mistels earmarked for the operation could be mustered the Fleet dispersed: in the intervening time the battleship *Tirpitz* had been sunk, and, this threat to Atlantic convoys no longer present, the Royal Navy was going about other duties. The Germans, however, had no knowledge of this development and 2/KG 101, now augmented and redesignated III/KG 66, sent five Mistels against Scapa in October. Three crashed and the remaining pair failed to locate the target.

In November the operating unit was once more redesignated, this time as II/KG 200, and a move was made to the east to prepare for Operation 'Eisenhammer', an attack on Soviet power stations scheduled for 1 February 1945. This was never carried out. Henceforth the weapon tended to be used for specialist attacks on various important bridges over rivers as widely separated as the Rhine and the Oder. Experience would show that, once released, there was no guarantee that the explosive-carrying component would hit its target, and as WWII drew to is close DFS was investigating the possibility of guiding it by means of a wire link or by television.

Operational Mistel Combinations

Type	Upper component	Lower component	Remarks
Mistel 1	Me 109F-4	Ju 88A-4	80 reported built
Mistel 2	FW 190A-6 or F-8	Ju 88G-1	125 built
Mistel 3	FW 190A-3	Ju 88A-4	Proposed only
Mistel 3B*	FW 190A-8	Ju 88H-4	Did not enter service
Mistel 3C	FW 190F-8	Ju 88G-10	Reported proposed only
Mistel 4	Me 262	Ju 287	Reported proposed only
Mistel 5	He 162 or E377A or Ju 268	Arado or Me 262	Reported proposed only

*Described as a Führungsmaschine in which the upper component could be released to provide protection for the lower.

Other undesignated combinations: Ta 152H/Ju 88 G-7; Ar 234C/Fi 103; Ar 234C-3/E.377; He 162/Ar E.377; Do 217K V3/DFS 228 for reconnaissance; Ta 154/FW 190 for attack; Si 204/Lippisch DM-1 for research.

In the main listing Ju 188s could be, and sometimes were, substituted for Ju 88s. The E.377 was described as pilotless mid-wing monoplane without control surfaces, with a modified standard bomb forming the warhead.

Among the most interesting features of the MiG-29's electronics is an aiming device which allows the aircraft to approach a target without giving detectable radio/radar signals.

The design paid special attention to aerodynamic potential, so that the aircraft enjoys what has been described as 'super-manoeuvrability'. This includes a disinclination to enter a normal spin, it being claimed that the aircraft will recover unaided if the controls are released, and an alleged refusal to go into a flat spin.

Several operational versions of the MiG-29 have been produced, among them one known as 'Fulcrum-C', with a deeply curved decking to the rear fuselage to house additional or re-sited equipment, and the 'Fulcrum-D' which, with narrow-chord rudders, folding outer wings, an arrester hook and extended wings with tips having an increased chord, was used for deck-landing and ski-jump take-off trials from the carrier *Tbilisi*.

The armament of the standard version of this formidable machine is a basic 30mm gun in the port side wing root fairing and six medium-range missiles carried on three pylons under each wing, with alternative provision for the heavier R-60 missiles, bombs or rockets on the attack variant. The maximum speed is Mach 2.3.

MiG-31 Although the Lockheed A-11 was reportedly capable of Mach 3 in the dread days of the late 1950s, the final intelligence exposing the fact that such reports were strongly reinforced by propaganda, not to say panic, would have been greeted with relief in Soviet circles when it became clear that the MiG-25 'Foxbat' was equally incapable of achieving this, its 'never-exceed' combat speed being no more than an estimated Mach 2.8. It was as much to remedy this performance shortfall that the MiG-31 was developed from the basic MiG-25 concept, promptly dubbed 'Foxhound' in the West.

The first requirement was that the airframe of the new fighter should be strengthened with a view to allowing supersonic speed at low altitude, and to this end also a pair of Tumansky turbojets were installed which, with afterburning, could deliver 30,865lb s.t. The avionics, too, were improved,

and for the first time in a Soviet interceptor gave a look-down/shoot-down and multiple target engagement capability as well as counter-measures dispensers and infra-red search/track sensors.

Deliveries of the new MiG-31 from the Gorkiy airframe factory commenced during the first half of 1983, Western intelligence reports soon confirming that there had been no change to a light alloy structure for the MiG-31, the MiG-25's steel construction being retained. A tandem cockpit accommodated both a pilot and a weapons operator under a common canopy.

The weapons systems included four semi-active radar homing air-to-air missiles under the fuselage in pairs and on a single pylon under each wing, augmented by a heavy-calibre, fixed, forward-firing gun in the starboard side of the lower fuselage. The maximum speed of the 'Foxhound' has been estimated as Mach 2.4, and about 170 of the type had been delivered to operational units by 1990.

MiG-33 This new Mikoyan design is a redesigned version of the MiG-29 (q.v.), specifically of the M/ME version, and is an advanced tactical fighter for the control of upper airspace. It is also employed for naval high-altitude precision control and as a ground attack aircraft.

Fitted with fly-by-wire controls, the first of six prototype MiG-33s flew on 25 April 1986, although it was not until the development programme was well advanced in February 1992 that production Klimov RD-33 turbofans were fitted. This gave the aircraft a maximum speed in excess of Mach 2.2 (only marginally less than the declared speed of the MiG-29 at high altitude) over a minimum estimated range of 820 miles when carrying a warload of six air-to-air and air-to-surface missiles on outrigger underwing pylons and three external fuel tanks.

Mil A Soviet helicopter design bureau headed by Mikhail L. Mil and responsible for a number of military designs, including those known by the NATO code-names 'Harke', 'Hip' and 'Hound'.

Miles A British aircraft manufacturer based at Reading, Berkshire, which is

chiefly remembered for such trainer designs as the Magister, Master and Martinet although historically significant for its Hoopla flying bomb (q.v.) and M.23 fighter. The latter was evolved against an envisaged shortage of other fighters after the Battle of France, and the first M.20 (AX834) was designed, built and flown in nine weeks and two days to specification F.19/40. As many parts as possible from the Master trainer were incorporated, and eventually a variant was built (U-0228) to meet specification N.1/41 for the Royal Navy. Both versions had fixed undercarriages in order to eliminate the need for hydraulics and boasted such (then) revolutionary features as a 'bubble' hood. A brief specification of the type in service configuration makes an interesting comparison with those of its contemporary single-seaters, the maximum speed being 333mph and the armament eight wing-mounted 0.303in machine guns.

Mines (1) Long Aerial Mines. See LAM. (2) Parachute or Land Mines. Explosive weapons, 470 of which were dropped on British land targets during WWII. Based on standard sea mines, they had coarsely-woven dark green canopies and dark blue bodies. The Type 'C', measuring 8ft 8in long and containing 1,500lb of HE, was common. (3) Sea Mines. Anti-shipping explosive devices dropped by aircraft into sea lanes by many warring nations. Those used by the Germans during WWII weighed about 1,100lb and could not be dropped into water less than 7ft deep since the fusing would thereby cause premature detonation. The first sea mines laid by aircraft were those sown in the Baltic during 1916.

Mirage F.1 A Dassault-Breguet multimission fighter produced as a replacement for the Mirage III family. A development contract was placed in February 1964, and the result was the prototype F.2 twin-seater, which made its first flight in June 1964, to be followed at the end of the year by the smaller F.1 single-seater. Although the F.1 prototype was lost in a crash, three pre-production examples were ordered, the first making its maiden flight in March 1969. The high-lift design of the F.1 gave a short take-off and landing capability. Equipment included the Thompson-CSF Cyrano IV radar, which had an extended range and permitted interception at all altitudes, even low down, where targets could be visually selected by the pilot who could then monitor matters via his HUD (q.v.), while tracking and firing the missiles was carried out automatically. The F.1 was ordered by Ecuador, Egypt, Greece, Iraq, Kuwait, Libya, Morocco, South Africa, and Spain in addition to France. The maximum speed was 1,450mph and the armament two 30mm DEFA 553 cannon with the alternatives of a pair of air-to-air missiles of either R.550 Magic, R.530 or Super R.530, or AIM-9 Sidewinders in varying combinations with rocket launchers, pods or bombs.

Mirage III A French delta-wing supersonic fighter which first flew in prototype form in November 1956. In October 1958 it became the first European aircraft to fly at twice the speed of sound (Mach 2) and it was regarded as one of the most successful military aircraft of the period, seeing service with such air forces as Argentina, Australia, Brazil, Egypt, France, Israel, Lebanon, Libya, Pakistan, South Africa, Spain, Switzerland and Venezuela. The maximum speed of the IIIE was 1,460mph and the armament consisted of two 30mm DEFA cannon with one AS.30 air-to-surface missile or an equivalent weight of bombs for the ground-attack version. Other variants included all-weather and reconnaissance models and an austere variant, the Mirage 5 (q.v.).

Mirage IV A scaled-up version of the Mirage III designed to meet official French requirements for a supersonic attack bomber capable of delivering nuclear weapons. The prototype first flew on 17 June 1959, and this was followed by three pre-production prototypes, the first of which took to the air on 12 October 1961. Fifty examples were ordered for delivery during 1964–65, a further twelve being ordered later, and these were intended to maintain France's independent nuclear deterrent until the year 2000. A 60-kiloton, free-fall nuclear bomb was carried in a belly recess. The maximum sustained speed was 1,222mph.

Mirage 5 An austere version of the Mirage III (q.v.), stripped of sophisticated electronics and take-off rocket assistance and intended for use by developing countries. The maximum speed was 1,385mph, the range was 1,500 miles and the armament comprised two 30mm cannon and a maximum of 8,000lb of externally stowed bombs, rockets or missiles. A development, the Milan, was basically a Mirage 5 with retractable foreplanes to reduce the landing speed.

Mirage G.8 The production variant of the Mirage G variable-geometry fighter-bomber. A two-seater which first flew in November 1967, it was powered by twin SNECMA Atar 9K turbojets. The maximum speed has been given as about 2,000mph and the range 2,000 miles.

Mirage 2000 A Dassault aircraft which was selected for service use on 18 December 1975. It was first intended as an air superiority and interceptor fighter although it was later to prove of use in the reconnaissance, close support and low-altitude attack roles, being an aircraft that gave a low radar signature and good manoeuvrability with a reasonable range. The reduced number of control surfaces limited the risk of battle damage.

The 2000 was quickly accepted for the *Armée de l'Air* as an all-weather defensive fighter, the first of the 372 examples that were to be delivered by the end of 1994 going to *Escadron de Chasse 212* ('Les Cigognes') in 1984. In the space of three years all the units at Dijon (No 2 Wing) were flying Mirage 2000s, and in 1988 No 5 was taking the type, although these differed from the earlier examples in being powered by M53-P2 jet engines, giving increased thrust; they also had a new radar system, giving an improved interception capability with the two Super 530D radar-guided missiles, two heat-seeking Magic 2s and pair of DEFA 30mm cannon.

Meanwhile export models were purchased to equip the Indian Air Force, where the 49 aircraft were known as Vajras (Divine Thunder), although the procurement of MiG-29s caused plans to licence-build the Mirage 2000 in that country to be shelved. The 2000 was also sold to Abu Dhabi, Egypt, Greece and Peru.

Meanwhile France was about to procure 112 Mirage 2000Ns for its air force's strike/attack arm. These were two-seaters, similar to the 2000B trainer but equipped with Antelope 5 ground-mapping and automatic terrain-following radar and capable of all-weather performance. On 9 March 1979 a new Mirage made its first flight, the phenomenally expensive 4000, which externally seemed little more than an enlarged 2000. It was reputedly funded by Saudi Arabia, but no orders were received for this aircraft from either nation.

The maximum speed of the Mirage 2000 is Mach 2.2; at low level, carrying eight 550lb bombs and two missiles, it can reach 690mph without afterburning.

Mirror deck-landing system An automatic deck-landing device for aircraft carriers, intended to replace the traditional 'batsman' to guide landing aircraft. It was developed by Cdr H. C. N. Goodhart and consisted of a series of white lights mounted horizontally at the after end of a carrier's flight deck, so aligned as to shine forward and converge their beams on a concave mirror and form a single point of light. To either side of this were mounted arms carrying coloured lamps, and, by keeping these in line with the reflected centre of white light while landing, a pilot was assured that his approach was being maintained at the correct angle. He was thus prevented from looking down at the instrument display giving the approach speed, so this was represented on the windscreen of the aircraft by a HUD (q.v.) consisting of a series of colour-coded lamps. The vital mirror for the convergent lights was set on a gyro mounting which maintained it at a constant angle to both the vessel and the horizon. Trials of this system were made on HMS *Illustrious* and HMS *Indomitable* before it was publicly announced on 15 March 1954.

Missiles Aimed explosive devices of various types, air-to-air, air-to-surface, ASV, ASW and surface-to-air; surface-to-surface weapons are beyond the scope of the present volume.

The idea of such weapons had been suggested by Dr Wilhelm von Siemens as early as October 1914 and flight tests were made in the following January with gliders controlled by electric signals sent by fine copper wires unrolled from a spool. One of the first, which was tried out in August 1916, took the form of a monoplane designed to split and release a torpedo. The culmination of these tests was the No 7 SSW torpedo-glider. It flew over 4.5 miles at 2,936ft on 2 August 1918, but the wires broke and ended the trial, although plans existed to introduce ASMs operated from bombers at the time of the Armistice. The Allies had developed similar missiles by this time, but none was intended for airborne launch.

During WWII, the German missile programme concentrated on air-to-surface missiles, and in January 1940 Dr Herbert Wagner joined the Henschel organization to develop an air-launched sea skimmer. This consisted basically of a standard free-fall bomb with wings, simple solenoid-driven ailerons and an electric screw-jack actuating the elevators. Early Hs 293 missiles were dropped over Karlshagen in the spring of 1940. On 27 August 1943, 30 miles west of Vigo, Spain, HMS *Egret* became the first victim of an air-launched missile (from a Dornier 217E-5 of II/KG 100).

By the 1950s both wire and radio guidance had been discarded in favour of infra-red and semi-active radar homing. In the latter the missile followed the launcher's signals reflected from the target. High-impulse solid-fuel motors (such as those used for the US Hughes AIM-4 Falcon) and glass-fibre construction ushered new developments at the close of the century. See Vickers, Mistel combinations.

Mitchell See B-25.

Mitsubishi A Japanese industrial group which entered aviation in the early 1920s, at first building European designs before graduating to such indigenous types as the Type 10 carrier fighter, adopted by the Imperial Navy, as well as several other fighters and bombers, some of them for the Army. The most significant Mitsubishi aircraft of WWII was the A6M Reisen (Zero fighter), known at first to the Allies by the code-names 'Ray' and 'Ben' and finally as 'Zeke', for which a preliminary specification was issued

on 19 May 1937. This was revised in October in the light of experience gained from Chinese combat reports, and the prototype first flew on 1 April 1939. After acceptance by the Navy of fifteen A6M2s for operational trials, a production order was placed. The aircraft were in service by the time of the attack on Pearl Harbor, and the type continued to feature in almost every Pacific naval/air battle of WWII. The A6M3, with a two-speed supercharger, appeared in mid-1942, and this was in turn superseded by the A6M5 and A6M8 models, the maximum speed of the latter being 356mph. The armament comprised two synchronized 13.2mm machine guns and a 20mm cannon in each wing.

An example of modern Japanese military aircraft design appeared in 1975 when in March the first examples of the Mitsubishi FST-2 began to be delivered to units of the JASDF. This was a swept-wing, single-seat, close-support fighter-bomber resembling the European Jaguar. It was powered by two Ishikawajima-Harima TF40-801 A turbojets (R-R/Turboméca Adour 102s), which gave a maximum speed (clean) of Mach 1.6, and its armament consisted of a 20mm M-61 cannon under the port side of the nose, plus provision for two ASM-1 anti-ship missiles, four Sidewinders or an equivalent weight of bombs. Sixty-eight of these aircraft had been manufactured when production ceased in 1979.

Molotov Bread Basket A WWII HE bomb with incendiary sub-munitions.

'Monika' The name for the Luftwaffe's WWII 2,200lb 'G' (George) mine.

'Moonshine' The British code-name for operations during WWII originally carried out by Defiants of No 515 Squadron fitted with special equipment designed to jam enemy radar systems.

'Moose' The NATO code-name for Soviet Yak-11 two-seat intermediate trainer in use by a large number of Warsaw Pact countries in the first half of the 1970s. The type could be fitted with a machine gun, and practice bombs could be carried.

Morane-Saulnier A French aircraft

manufacturer producing a number of successful warplanes at the beginning of WWI, including the Morane-Saulnier Type 'L' two-seat parasol reconnaissance monoplane and the associated single-seater, one of which (3253), in service with the RNAS, passed into history when it was used to shoot down Zeppelin LZ37 in the early morning of 7 June 1915. Military aircraft continued to be produced by this manufacturer throughout the years between the two World Wars. culminating in the MS.406. This was the production version of the MS.405, the second prototype of which had been sent for official trials in June 1937, and an order was placed later in the year.

The first unit to be equipped with the new monoplane was GC I/6, and by July 1939 a number of escadres were operating the type, their duties also embracing reconnaissance and army cooperation. Although it was intended from the spring of 1940 to phase the type out of service in favour of more modern fighters, many were still in use at the time of the French collapse and the aircraft was retained by the Vichy Air Force. The maximum speed of the MS.406 was 281mph and the armament consisted of one 20mm Hispano-Suiza HS 9 or HS 404 cannon firing through the airscrew spinner and a 7.5mm MAC 1934 machine gun in each wing. The manufacturers ceased operations on the fall of France, resuming manufacture with the MS.760 basic jet trainer for the Armée de l'Air during the 1950s before passing out of existence.

Mosquito See de Havilland.

'Moss' The NATO code-name for the Soviet Tu-114 maritime reconnaissance and early-warning development of the 'Cleat' airliner of 1957.

'Mouse' See 'Max'.

'Moujik' The NATO code-name for the Su-7UTI twin-seat trainer developed from the Sukhoi Su-7B fighter known in the West as 'Fitter' (qv).

MRCA Multi-Role Combat Aircraft. An attempt to meet the need for a military aircraft capable of performing a wide range of duties, such as bombing, fighting, ground-attack and reconnaissance. The designation was first coined for the Panavia P.01 from which the Panavia MRCA Tornado was developed.

MSFU See Shipborne aircraft (2).

MTC See Dornier MTC II.
Mustang See P-51.

'Mutton' The British code-name for the sowing of aerial mines by Handley Page Harrow aircraft. See LAM.

mV The abbreviation for mit Verzogerungszunder, a German term common during WWII indicating a delayed-action fuse.

Mya-4 The Soviet Union's Myasischev bomber. See 'Bison'.

Mystère A series of warplanes produced by the French Dassault manufacturer, the Mystère II single-seat fighter-bomber which first flew on 23 February 1951 being basically the earlier Ouragan fighter design fitted with swept wings. Eight prototypes following during 1952–53 introducing new armament, and two later, adopting the first French gas turbine for a military aircraft. A total of 180 were built, 156 of them for France and the remainder for Israel, although these were never delivered. The Mystère was the first swept-wing military aircraft to be produced in Western Europe and the first to be dived (on 28 October 1952) at a speed greater than that of sound. The maximum speed was 658mph and the armament finally two 30mm Hispano 603 cannon, replacing four of 20mm calibre.

There followed the Mystère IV, also a fighter-bomber, with a new, thinner wing, and although strongly resembling the foregoing it was in fact a totally different design. It first flew on 28 September 1952, production versions being adopted by France, Israel and India. A total of 425 were constructed. A night-fighter variant was also produced, the IVN, together with the supersonic IVB. Mystère IVAs saw active service during the Suez Crisis of 1956. The maximum speed was 696mph and the armament consisted of two 30mm DEFA 551 cannon. As with the Mystère II, provision was made for underwing loads of rockets or bombs.

Developed from the Mystère IVB, the Super Mystère first flew on 2 March 1955 and was also a fighter-bomber, as well as being the first European fighter to enter service or production capable of supersonic level flight. In addition to those operated by the Armée de l'Air, twenty were flown by Israel. The maximum speed was 686mph, two fuselage-mounted 30mm cannon were carried and provision for thirty-five SNEB 68mm rockets and their Matra launcher was made.

N A suffix indicating a naval item, used by Great Britain during WWI. Thus 520lb high-explosive bombs with a light sheet steel case could be described as 'Mk 1/N, Light Case'.

N-23 A Soviet 23mm cannon, two of which were carried, with 80 rounds each, in the port wing root of MiG-17F 'Frescos' (q.v.).

N-37 A Soviet 37mm cannon, a single one with 40 rounds being carried in the starboard nose of the MiG-17. See NR-30.

N-bomb A type of weapon reported by Lord Cherwell as being held in reserve for use if the Allied invasion of Europe failed. The bombs were said to contain 'spores' carried in 'ordinary incendiary containers' weighing 4lb, and there was 'no known cure and no effective prophylaxis for their effect'. Cherwell added: 'Half a dozen Lancaster bombers could [have] carried enough, if spread even[ly], to kill anyone within a square mile and to render it uninhabitable thereafter.' Three weeks before Operation 'Overlord' Churchill had minuted: 'We have ordered a half-million [N] bombs from America for use should this mode of warfare be employed against us.'

Nachtjagdgeschwader Luftwaffe WWII Night Fighter (q.v.) Group.

Nagasaki The Japanese city on which the second operational atomic bomb (q.v.) was dropped, on 9 August 1945. Out of a population of 173,000, about 38,000 were killed outright and 21,000 injured.

Nager-Rolz The German manufacturer of the world's first portable helicopter.

Each of its twin rotor blades was driven by an 8hp motor with its own small airscrew, thus giving torqueless drive. After the appearance of the first model, the NR 54 V2, in 1941, four were ordered for development in the military field. The project was not proceeded with, however, and the reason has never been satisfactorily explained.

Nakajima One of three companies which commenced aircraft production in Japan soon after WWI, at first concentrating on the licence-construction of British and French designs. Its first indigenous product was a trainer, the Nakajima Type 5, and this was quickly followed by a carrier-borne fighter, the A2N1, although the firm's most important types were the B4Y1 fighter for the Navy, the B5N1 strike aircraft, which was to see service in the Pacific war, and the Ki-27 for the Army, all developed towards the end of the 1930s. Other significant warplanes from Nakajima included the four-motor G5N Shenzan (Mountain Recess), based on the Douglas DC-4E, the single-float A6M2-N fighter float-plane and the B6N Tenzan (Heavenly Mountain) single-engine, three-seat torpedo bomber. Japan's first jet-powered aircraft the Kikka or Orange Blossom (q.v.) was also produced by this organization, which ceased aircraft production with the end of WWII.

Nanchang A Chinese aircraft manufacturer responsible for, among other types, the J-12, an ambitious swept-wing fighter project, later abandoned but of military significance in that it was a re-worked MiG-19 'Farmer' (q.v.), for which manufacturing rights were agreed in 1958. Less than two years later Moscow and Peking were locked in an ideological dispute, and the Shenyang National Aircraft Factory developed the J-6 – Jianjiji (Fighter Aircraft) No 6 – from the Soviet fighter after the withdrawal of some 1,400 Russian advisers. The prototype first flew in December 1961. Aircraft for service with the Chinese Air Force were largely dedicated to the attack role and designated Q-5 IIIs, those for the Navy being Q-5 III PLAs; export models were A-5Cs and used by Pakistan. The builder's name is taken from its location in the province of Jiangxi.

Napalm 'Class C Fire Bombs' containing a gel of aviation spirit, paraffin and phosphorous and available from the second half of 1944. The substance, the name for which is derived from the words naphtha and palm oil, is enclosed in special bomb casings or aircraft drop tanks. When ignited it sticks to objects and living creatures while burning fiercely. Unstable once mixed, it has to be used immediately. It was developed from petrol bombs first used by the United States over Guadalcanal on 14 January 1943.

Narrow beam radar A radar beam which oscillates round a target, thus making escape virtually impossible, and having locked on can be used for the guidance of missiles. Other anti-aircraft measures can be employed with the assistance of such a beam when it is used to survey an area.

'Nate' The Allied code-name for the Japanese Nakajima Ki-27 Army fighter, a single-motor interceptor with a fixed undercarriage first used operationally during the Sino-Japanese War which opened on 2 July 1937. The prototype first flew in mid-October the previous year. Classified as a light fighter, the aircraft was later relegated to advanced trainer duties, although an improved version was designed in 1940 after problems arose with the Ki-43 intended to replace it. The maximum speed of the standard model was 290mph and the armament comprised two synchronized 7.7mm Type 89 machine guns.

National air competitions That experience and data gained by Britain as a result of her successful participation in the Schneider Trophy contests between 1921 and 1931 was called upon in the design of the Spitfire fighter is part of military aviation's folklore, but it is also true that the competitions between the two world conflicts were of use in the advancement of warplane design, providing test facilities and design experience for airframes and engines. Thus it was not entirely coincidental that the Gloster floatplane entry for 1925 was of military origin, as were aircraft entered later by Italy and the United States.

Similarly, the US National Air Races between 1921 and 1923 saw entries of Curtiss CR-3 floatplanes, originally designated in their landplane form as CF-1 fighters, as well as Curtiss 18T triplane interceptors, while in the Pulitzer Trophy race of 1923 R2C landplane racers owed much to the Navy's CR-1s and the Army's R-6 fighters.

National Aircraft Factory No 1 and the Aircraft Disposal Company The momentous events of 1918 are recorded in the history books, but few if any of the latter tell of the creation in Britain that year of what was in effect a miniature nationalized aircraft industry.

Above: Armstrong Whitworth F.K.8 fuselages awaiting customers in the sheds of the Aircraft Disposal Company, Waddon. (Author's collection)

The spring of 1917 found the Royal Flying Corps with a total of 108 squadrons. The War Office was soon to issue a recommendation that this be increased to 200, and Cabinet approval was granted on 2 July. The decision presented the Ministry of Munitions with a problem of massive proportions if the demand for such an immense number of aircraft was to be met, and it was not until October that measures were announced to solve it. Three new aircraft works, to be known as National Aircraft Factories, were to be established, at Waddon, near Croydon, Surrey, at Aintree, Liverpool, and at Richmond in Surrey. In the event, only the first of these, designated NAF No 1, was ever established in the manner which was foreseen. NAF No 2 eventually emerged at Heaton Chapel, Stockport, in a converted factory taken over while under construction, while work on the factory at Richmond was never begun.

The Armistice brought the need for NAF No 1 to an abrupt end, and the factory was closed on 31 December 1918, having turned out some 270 de Havilland D.H.9s and associated equipment. However, peace brought the Ministry of Munitions a set of problems that had not been envisaged by the planners, since it was faced with the disposal of huge stocks of both used and unused materials, airframes, engines, spares, components and accessories. Urgent steps were taken to find storage for this material, and following a period during which stock was sold off in a haphazard manner and at bargain prices, the Aircraft Disposal Company was set up to regulate the sale. Handley Page was its sole agent. The airfield quickly assumed the status of an international aviation centre with the joining of Beddington and Waddon Aerodromes into Croydon Airport. ADC took on the task of aircraft manufacture, its products including the ADC.1, a modified Martinsyde F-4 single-seat scout.

The company ceased trading in 1930 and its buildings were taken over for other purposes. Some of them remain in existence today.

NATO North Atlantic Treaty Organization. A multinational military alliance founded in April 1949 and comprising Belgium, Canada, Denmark, France, Great Britain, Iceland, Italy, Luxembourg, the Netherlands, Norway, Portugal and the United States. These were joined by Greece and Turkey in 1952 and West Germany in 1955 (and the entire country after unification). Control headquarters was at first based in Paris, and later in Brussels, and was divided into a pair of commands, Allied Command Atlantic (ACLANT), controlling some 300 aircraft, plus those contributed by the carrier-borne force of the US Navy; and Supreme Headquarters Allied Powers in Europe (SHAPE). Its sub-commands were AFCENT (q.v.), AFNORTH (q.v.) and AFSOUTH (q.v.). All this had been based on the original Western European Union (WEU), founded in March 1948, which comprised Belgium, France, Great Britain, Luxembourg and the Netherlands.

Natter (Viper). The name adopted for the German Bachem Ba 349, a semi-expendable, vertically launched, piloted interception missile conceived in 1944. The first pilotless launching was made on 23 February 1945, and one with a pilot (Lothar Siebert) took place at the end of the month. Although this was not successful and the pilot was killed, twenty such aircraft were constructed although none was ever used operationally. Launches were made via a 70ft vertical tower with the aid of an HWK 109-509B rocket motor assisted by four external auxiliary units developing an extra thrust of 1,000lb each for six seconds, giving an initial rate of climb of 37,000ft/min. The maximum speed of the Ba 349 was 497mph and the armament consisted of twenty-four R4M rockets in the nose.

Naxos A German airborne interception radar, developed to use transmissions from British H2S (q.v.) radar to guide intercepting fighters. The range was in the region of 40 miles and it was first used operationally in January 1944, some 1,500 night fighters being thus equipped.

NDAC Northern Defence Affairs Committee. An organization within NATO (q.v.) for the formulation of policy, operating via the Ministers of Defence of member countries.

Near East This term was, until 1945 a commonplace description for those countries clustered on the eastern shores of the Mediterranean, and was sometimes taken to include south-west Asia and even the Balkan peninsula, but present-day terminology tends to include this important area under the wider heading of the Middle East. However, the strategic importance of the Near East is immediately apparent when it is realized that it stands on the fringes of some of the world's largest oilfields.

The region was dominated after the end of WWII by the emergence of the State of Israel (q.v.), with its well-organized air arm, and, from 1 February 1958, by the political union of Egypt and Syria to form the United Arab Republic (UAR), a term which was perpetuated by Egypt until 2 September 1971 although it effectively ceased to exist with the political coup in Syria on 28 September 1961. Both Egypt and Syria, operating Soviet aircraft, were involved in the Yom Kippur War of 1973 with a total of 720 machines, 400 from Egypt (plus 200 in store) and 320 from Syria, despite having lost many warplanes in the Six Day War, also with Israel, in 1967.

The Lebanon, whose Force Aérienne Libanaise alone operates the country's military aircraft, saw little action in these operations and took only a minor part in the civil war of the mid-1970s. The force flew, in the main, French machines, which were taken on charge to replace the modern founding equipment of six British Hunter F.6 jets supplied as the 1950s drew to their close. The history of Israel's air arm and its associated industry is dealt with elsewhere, but a neighbouring force, established only a little later, is the Royal Jordanian Air Force, the Al Quwwat Aljawwiya Almalakiya, which originated as the communications and logistics arm of the Arab Legion, its equipment a single DH Rapide biplane! Six years later, Jordan received its first jets, nine Vampires, and as if to mark this step into modernity the former designation ALAF (Arab Legion Air Force) was abandoned in favour of RJAF (Royal Jordanian Air Force). British aircraft continued to be the primary equipment, its Hunters seeing their first combat during the Six Day War, not only engaging Israeli fighters but also flying from their base at Mafraq to attack targets at Netanya.

Although from a geographical viewpoint an occupant of the Near East's fringe, Iraq is important if only in being the third-largest oil exporter in the area. It became a socialist state after 1958, when close ties with the Soviet Union were forged, thus breaking the ties with Britain with regard to aviation equipment that had existed previously. Links with the Soviets were strengthened in 1977 with the negotiation of fresh arms deals and invitations to arms advisers to monitor and control the build-up of Iraqi forces, and the latter were technically well-placed for their participation in the war with Iran which broke out on 24 September 1980 after a period of simmering border disputes. Although the resulting conflict lasted a number of years, during which allegations of the use of gas (q.v.) were proven, the Iranian air arm did not distinguish itself. The latter had originally been formed as an independent service as the Nirou Havai Shahanshahive Iran, or Imperial Iranian Air Force, in 1955, following which the Army and Navy formed their own air arms. These three services assumed large proportions following the British withdrawal from east of Suez in 1970 .

Saudi Arabia is another oil giant of the Near East, and this country, in addition to granting financial assistance for the modernization of Egypt's and Jordan's armed services, at one time rapidly built up its own air defences into a highly efficient organization with the purchase of British equipment, later augmented by aircraft of US design. The beginnings of the Royal Saudi Air Force were laid during the 1920s, but by 1933 the air arm was still operating only nine aircraft. British advisers were replaced by Italians until 1950, when a new mission from the former secured the acquisition of some Tiger Moths and Ansons. Although the United States strengthened its influence via the Mutual Defence Assistance Program, British influence persisted and Strikemasters and Lightnings were purchased, although the latter were eventually superseded by F-15s (q.v.).

The Libyan Republic Air Force was established in 1959 as the Royal Libyan Air Force, equipped largely with donated ex-RAF Austers, to which US T-33s and C-47s were added in 1963, but four years later both countries were requested to withdraw from their internal bases. The United States still supplied F-5s (q.v.) while Britain prepared to meet orders for a complete air defence system, including radar and missiles, but all were summarily cancelled in 1970 following a military coup after the country had been declared a republic in the previous year. Orders for aircraft were now placed in France.

Some 400 missions were flown by Egypt during the October 1973 war with Israel. Pakistan had supplied the Egyptians with training facilities and many of the aircrews for this conflict. Relations between Egypt and Israel deteriorated once again to become four days of open warfare in July five years later, and a US embargo resulted in Egyptian Air Force equipment thereafter becoming largely of Soviet origin, in return for which free access to bases was granted in much the same way as concessions had been granted to Britain before 1967. Some Italian and Yugoslav aircraft types were also taken on strength, search and rescue helicopters augmenting the small force belonging to the Army.

Other countries which may be regarded as falling within eastern Mediterranean territory include Greece and Turkey, members of NATO (q.v.) from 1952.

'Nell' The Allied code-name for the Japanese Mitsubishi G3M twin-motor naval attack bomber, intended to be land-based and to operate in support of naval units. The prototype first flew in April 1934 and was fitted with a Junkers-type 'double wing', although corrugation was abandoned on production models. Three versions were eventually built. Thirty-four examples of the G3M1 were delivered during 1936–37 before this mark was replaced by the G3M2, with rearranged and improved defensive armament. This variant was responsible for sinking HMS *Prince of Wales* and HMS *Repulse* in December 1941. The final version, production of which terminated in the same year, was the re-engined G3M3. This mark had a maximum speed of 258mph, with an offensive load of either a 1,764lb torpedo or an equivalent external weight of bombs, over a range of 3,871 miles.

Netheravon A site in Hampshire, 4½ miles south of Upavon on the present A345, where the Royal Flying Corps' six squadrons, HQ Flight, Aircraft Park and a detachment of the Kite Section were gathered throughout June 1914 at a Camp of Concentration for training, lectures, discussions, trials and experiments to explore the potential of military flying. The Camp dispersed on 2 July, with the units returning to their own bases there to make preparations for the Army's annual summer manoeuvres.

Neutron bomb A tactical fission weapon confining heat and blast to a small area but capable of penetrating thick earth or armour with neutron and gamma rays over a larger one. US production was postponed in 1978 but resumed in 1981.

Neutron kill Radiation resulting from a nuclear explosion which neutralizes the warhead of an attacking missile.

Nieuport A French aircraft manufacturer established in 1910 by Eduard de Nieuport and producing of a range of semi-sesquiplane single- and two-seat military biplanes used by Belgium, Britain, France and the United States throughout WWI. The best-known and most successful of these aircraft were the Nieuport 11 Bébé and Nieuport 17. The Nieuport 28, favoured by the US Army, abandoned the earlier wing configuration in favour of conventional biplane construction. All were designed by Gustave Delage. Nieuport warplanes were also built in Britain by the Nieuport and General Aircraft Company of Langton Road, Cricklewood. This concern went on to produce its own designs after the end of WWI, including the Nighthawk, which saw RAF service, and the Nightjar, in service with the Royal Navy during 1922–24.

Nimrod An RAF maritime reconnaissance aircraft introduced to replace the Avro Shackleton. It was based on the de Havilland Comet design (thus making it the world's first jet-powered aircraft for such duties), the external changes being the addition of a MAD

Above: Although a French design, examples of the various Nieuport scouts were also used by Britain and Imperial Russia during WWI. Among the later aircraft was this Nieuport 27, a type which abandoned the rectangular rudder traditionally associated with these fighters, although the older wing form was retained. The armament consisted of the twin synchronized guns associated with scouts of the period. (Author's collection)

(q.v.) tail, a redesigned fin and a weapons bay in a new fuselage with a 'peanut' cross-section. Rolls-Royce Spey 250 two-shaft turbofans replaced the civil type's Avons. The first flight of the aerodynamic prototype took place on 23 May 1967, and that of the first production aircraft on 28 June 1968. The two versions for ocean patrol were the MR.1, first delivered on 2 October 1969, and the MR.2 of 1977 with Searchwater radar, increased 'computerization' and a new acoustic processing system coupled to Barra sonobuoys. A crew of twelve was carried, and stores could include A/S torpedoes, mines, depth charges and conventional or nuclear bombs, plus air-to-surface missiles on underwing pylons. The maximum speed was 575mph (economical transit speed 490mph) and the endurance twelve hours over a range in excess of 5,500 miles. The Nimrod R.1 was a version specially developed for electronic reconnaissance, sensing, recording and emitting electromagnetic fields.

NORAD North American Air Defence Command was operated jointly by the United States and Canada, covering surface-to-air missile units, aircraft interception, radar and communications systems. No longer exists.

Noratlas The Nord (q.v.) N.2501 twin-boom military transport produced in France and Germany and also flown by the Portuguese and Israeli Air Forces. The prototype flew on 10 September 1949 and the first production aircraft on 24 October 1952. The maximum speed was 270mph and the aircraft had a range of 930 miles. The N.2502 had Turboméca Palas turbojet boosters at each wing tip.

Nord Nord Aviation was a French aircraft manufacturer founded in 1936 and later merged with Sud Aviation to become Aérospatiale.

'Norm' The Allied code-name for Japanese Kawanishi E15K Shiun (Violet Cloud) single-engine reconnaissance seaplane. It was designed on the principle of a single central float with retractable outriggers under the wing tips, the prototype first flying on 5 December 1941. The type entered production for the Imperial Navy, this being terminated in February 1944 after only nine production aircraft had been built. It was eventually found to be necessary to fix the stabilizing floats and make provision to jettison the large central float, although this failed to operate in practice. The maximum speed was 291mph, range 2,000 miles and the offensive armament load 640lb.

'Norma' The Allied code-name for the bomber version (erroneously believed to exist) of the Mitsubishi C5M ('Babs') reconnaissance monoplane.

North American Rockwell A US company brought about through the merger of the North American and Rockwell Standard organizations. The former is remembered for such WWII warplane designs as the B-25 Mitchell (q.v.) bomber and the P-51 (q.v.) Mustang

Above: The North American P-51 Mustang became one of the foremost US fighters of WWII, but these were powered by a Rolls-Royce Merlin engine. The early models ordered by Britain were Allison-powered. They gave their best at low level, so were relegated to army cooperation work as shown in the photograph. (Bruce Robertson collection)

fighter (F-51 after 1947), the F-86 Sabre (q.v.) and the F-100 (q.v.) Super Sabre. These were followed by aircraft intended for new roles such as the OV-10 Bronco (for counter-insurgency work) and the A-5 Vigilante (q.v.) Navy bomber and reconnaissance aircraft.

Northolt An RAF station north of London, opened on 1 March 1915 and named after the local railway station. It first served as a base for aircraft intended to intercept German airship raiders. From 1916 the Fairey company used it for test flying, and soon many American and some Russian pilots trained there. After WWI it became the home of the South Eastern Communications Flight and some civil flying took place. In January 1938 the first operational Hurricanes were received there by No 111 Squadron. The station acted as a fighter base throughout WWII, after which it remained an RAF airfield, its Polish connections recalled by a memorial in Western Avenue.

Above: An important US WWII type was the twin-boom, three-seat Northrop P-61 Black Widow, designed for night fighting. The armament consisted of four fixed 20mm cannon firing forward plus a remotely controlled dorsal barbette with four 0.5in machine guns. It was used both in Europe and over the Pacific. The Reporter, a two-seat strategic reconnaissance model, also existed. (Author's collection)

Above: A Northrop F-5 'Freedom Fighter' rolls to show its distinctive shape and Sidewinder missiles over Edwards Air Force Base, California, in 1959. (Northrop)

Northrop A US aircraft manufacturer, the first military aircraft from which was the A-17 used by Britain, Canada and US forces into the early years of WWII. Its most important wartime aircraft was probably the P-61 Black Widow night fighter. Among its significant designs of the 1950s was the F-5A/B 'Freedom Fighter' (q.v.).

North Weald An RAF station in Essex dating from 1916 as a base for airship interceptors, its most famous victim being the Zeppelin L31, brought down at Potters Bar on 1 October that year. After a period of neglect after WWI the station was reconstructed and used as a fighter base from 1927 and throughout WWII. Post-war it hosted Vampire, Meteor and Hunter squadrons. From 1960 the station was used for gliders and light aircraft and in August 1979 it was sold to the local authority.

NR-30 A Soviet 30mm aircraft cannon. When fitted to the MiG-19 'Farmer' (q.v.) this weapon proved so much more powerful than earlier armament that double skins of stainless steel

were introduced to the adjacent fuselage areas to protect them from the muzzle blast.

Nuclear weapon A general term used to describe both the nuclear fission atomic bomb (q.v.) and the nuclear fusion hydrogen bomb (q.v.).

O The designation prefix used by the US Army and Air Force to indicate aircraft intended for tactical reconnaissance and observation, an example being the Cessna O-1 Bird Dog which won a design competition for such types in 1950.

O/100 The designation of a Handley Page heavy bomber designed to meet an Admiralty specification issued for a twin-engine sea patrol biplane in December 1914 on the advice of Commodore Murray Sueter when he was Director of the Air Department. The prototype – which was unusual in initially having an enclosed crew cabin – first flew at Hendon on 18 December 1915 and deliveries of production versions began to the Fifth Naval Wing at Dunkirk the following

November. Power was provided by either two 250hp Rolls-Royce Eagle II or two 300hp Sunbeam Cossack motors. On 1 January 1917 the third aircraft being ferried to France fell into enemy hands due to a navigational error while. The first operations were conducted during daylight, but night sorties, generally by single aircraft, were carried out later. Forty-six of the type were built, one being used to attack the battlecruiser *Goeben* (q.v.). The maximum speed was 85mph, and the offensive load sixteen 112lb bombs.

O/400 A Handley Page bomber based on the O/100 with the fuel tanks transferred from the elongated nacelles to the fuselage and powered by two Rolls-Royce Eagle VIII motors. It began to appear in quantity in the spring of 1918 and was used in numbers for night operations against targets in the Rhineland and Saar during the last three months of WWI. Fifteen hundred were ordered from the Standard Aircraft Corporation by the United States Government, but none saw action. The maximum speed was

Above: F5417, one of a small number of Handley Page O/400 bombers manufactured by National Aircraft Factory No I but assembled at Cricklewood. (Bruce Robertson)

97mph and the offensive load was sixteen 112lb bombs, three of 550lb or one of l,650lb.

'Oak' The Allied code-name for the WWII Japanese Navy Kyushu K10W1 intermediate trainer, a licence-built version of the North American NA-16 acquired in 1937. One hundred and seventy-six were built, the final 150 by Nippon Hikoki from November 1942.

'Oboe' Introduced in December 1942, this RAF ground-controlled radar system of target-marking and blind bombing used one station to indicate the track and another to indicate the target point. Each transmitted radio pulses which were boosted by the aircraft's equipment and then, to give extended range, re-transmitted. The aircraft flew along an arc which passed over the target and was at a constant range from the transmitter ('the cat'), deviations from this being signalled from the station as dots or dashes indicating right or left respectively. The second station ('the mouse'), about 100 miles from 'the cat', transmitted the release signal. The system operated over a range of some 270 miles with bombers flying at about 28,000ft. Below, the system was affected by the earth's curvature. 'Oboe' was correctly known as the 'Type 9000 Precision Bombing System'.

Odiham An RAF station six miles ESE of Basingstoke established following an aerial survey of 1926 and opened on 18 October 1937. Two years later it was among the first aerodromes to have concrete runways. From here flew part of the heavy-lift Chinook helicopter force in the Falklands War of 1982.

Oerlikon A Swiss-designed 20mm cannon used over a long period as the armament for a number of aircraft types, the first British example probably being Hurricane I L1750, so equipped in April 1938 after investigations into the feasibility of the project during 1938. These weapons carried 60 rounds per gun and one was slung under each wing. On 13 August 1940 a machine of this type and armed in this way was credited with destroying a Dornier 17 while undergoing evaluation with No 151 Squadron.

Oil bomb An incendiary bomb (q.v.) carrying its own flammable materials, Those used by the Luftwaffe in WWII

OBSERVER CORPS

Thursday 11 July 1991 had no special significance for the majority, but for a few the date was memorable for it saw an official statement by the British Home Secretary that the Royal Observer Corps was to be disbanded. No doubt for many this merely served to provoke surprise that the Corps still existed, but in fact it had done so in one form or another for some 77 years, gathering in the process a wealth of proud tradition.

With the outbreak of war in 1914 and the threat of airship raids, a system of reporting was devised whereby the police were instructed to telephone to the Admiralty, then in charge of defence, reports of raiders sighted within a 60-mile radius of London. In 1915 the area was extended to cover East Anglia and Oxfordshire, running as far as Northamptonshire and the Isle of Wight in other directions.

In 1916, when this proved unsatisfactory, air defence was taken over by the War Office and cordons of military observers were organized thirty miles around vulnerable areas, and two years later this system was augmented by reporting posts manned by Special Constables. At the same time all units of the London Air Defence Area (LADA), of which the Metropolitan Observation Service formed the core, were amalgamated, with scattered Posts reporting enemy movements by telephone to a central Operations Room. In 1918 this organization lapsed. It was reviewed by the Committee for Imperial Defence in 1921, although only for an area south of a line from Portland Bill to the Wash. Thus were established the beginnings of Britain's WWII defences, which were by no means assembled at the last minute as is sometimes claimed.

In August 1924 experiments with a series of Posts between the Romney Marshes and Tonbridge, connected to an Operations Room at Cranbrook, Kent, resulted in the foundation the following year of an Observer Corps under that name, and the new organization took part in the annual air exercises during September. Its original Groups were No 1, with its Headquarters at Maidstone and comprising 27 Posts, and No 2, with 16 Posts centred at Horsham. Its members, still Special Constables, performed their duties in civilian clothes but with a police brassard marked 'Observer Corps' in red and worn on the upper arm, a lapel badge depicting an Elizabethan coast watcher, and the dark blue beret that was to become the mark of the Corps.

By 1931 Europe's deteriorating political atmosphere resulted in the system being extended to cover the greater part of the country, and new Operations Rooms were established to which each Post (identified by a number), joined to its neighbour and forming a Cluster (identified by a letter) of three or four, was connected by Army field telephone. Aircraft tracks were laid with the help of coloured plastic counters on the gridded map of the Operations Rooms' Main Tables.

The Corps was called out for war service on 24 August 1939 and thereafter its installations were continuously manned, day and night, for some five years, the only major change in plotting procedure being that original reports of sightings as 'aircraft' or 'bomber' were replaced

were thin-skinned cylinders filled with a variety of volatile substances, but chiefly oil, which were scattered and set alight on impact.

'Omar' The Allied code-name for a fictitious Japanese twin-engine fighter believed to be designated the Suzukaze 20.

'On the deck' A slang expression prevalent in military aviation circles during WWII and indicative of very low flying.

Operation names Code titles for military operations intended to hide their true purpose from an enemy. See Code-names.

Organic air power A term indicating air assets intergral with a surface or maritime force.

'Oscar' The Allied code-name for the Japanese Nakajima Ki-43 Hayabusa (Peregrine Falcon) single-seat fighter on which design work was begun in December 1937. The first prototype flew in January 1939. Ten were ordered later for service evaluation, differing from the three prototypes in having, among other changes, all-round vision canopies. In service the

aircraft was to prove a formidable enemy, and it remained in use after obsolescence for kamikaze (q.v.) missions. The Ki-43-II had a smaller wing span than the Ki-43-I, which was also operated by the Royal Thai Air Force during WWII. Post-war a small number were flown by the Indonesian People's Security Force and the Armée de l'Air in Indo-China. The maximum speed of the Ki-43-IIIa was 358mph.

Osprey A Hawker-built carrier-borne spotter and reconnaissance biplane based on the classic Hart (q.v.) design and operated during 1932–1939 by the Royal Navy. A floatplane version also existed, for operation from battleships and cruisers.

Osterov The scene of a WWII battle on the Russian Front on 6 July 1941 employing the newly devised Soviet tank–air liaison system wherein an air officer travelling in a tank with an advancing ground force could direct close-support attacks on enemy armour.

Ouragan A French turbojet fighter-bomber which first flew in prototype form on 28 February 1949 as a private venture by the Dassault (formerly

Marcel Bloch) factory. The first production model appeared in June 1951 and the type entered service with the Armée de l'Air, Indian Air Force (which knew them as Toofanis) and Israeli Air Force. The Ouragan (Hurricane) proved to be highly manoeuvrable in flight and cheap to produce, its maximum speed being 580mph and its armament four Hispano 404 cannon with an offensive load of either 2,200lb of bombs or sixteen rockets.

oV The abbreviation for ohne Verzogerung (bomb fuse without time delay mechanism). German.

'Overlord' The code-name for the Allied operation to liberate Europe begun on 6 June 1944. The invasion was launched at dawn, preceded by a night attack by 1,000 bombers dropping 5,000 tons of bombs on ten selected targets including the coastal batteries between Cherbourg and Le Havre. Day bombers, including those of the US Eighth Air Force, used 1,000pdrs on similar targets and fortifications as well as employing their heavy anti-personnel bombs and a new, lighter variety which exploded in the air with a strong downwards blast effect. A total of 13,743 aircraft commenced the day's 14,674 sorties, as

by type names. These were recorded alongside a track on a plaque, giving number, altitude and strength. Posts, manned in pairs, had a section of the corresponding Main Table map on the base of their Micklethwait instrument in order to give this data.

The first Greater London reports for the Battle of Britain (q.v.) were those of 15 August 1940 during an enemy strike at the fighter station that had been Croydon Airport (q.v.). Over the next few weeks and months the Corps proved its value, to mark which HM King George VI granted the title 'Royal Observer Corps' on 11 April 1941. In that year women were introduced into the Corps for Operations Room duty. Two classes of Observer existed now, whether men or women, 'A', who were paid for a 48-hour week of six eight hour days, and 'B', who served as unpaid volunteers.

June 1942 saw the appointment of a new Commandant, Air Commodore Ambler, who introduced new training, a system of ranks and RAF blue battledress. An earlier attempt to introduce uniforms had been unsuccessful, since the dark one-piece overalls were of such

poor quality that they had to be worn over ordinary clothing which the dye stained if wet.

Long Range Boards were now added to Operations Rooms, making possible the decentralization of public air raid warnings, while the growing speed of aircraft was reflected in the adoption of plotting clocks with double the former number of segments (thus, for example, 'stale' tracks could be easily identified). Other innovations were the adoption of 'Totter', a method for 69 selected Posts to attract the attention of fighters to the presence of raiders flying below 1,000ft (difficult for radar) by means of parachute flares launched from a Schermuly Type 'A' projector, and measures ('Granite') similarly to give warning to aircraft likely to fly into high ground, as well as the priority call 'Rats' to give warning of the former. Gaps in Cluster layout were also filled by the introduction of satellite Posts, single-manned.

The penultimate year of WWII was eventful for the ROC, seeing the first of its members sailing with the Allied invasion fleets after D-Day. This sprang from the concern of

the C-in-C Allied Air Forces at the number of aircraft shot down by 'friendly' fire, and as a result the 'Seaborne' scheme was devised whereby ROC personnel sailed in Allied vessels to advise gun crews. All were volunteers and wore an appropriate sleeve identification which they were permitted to retain on their uniforms after the end of the war.

Another event which marked 1944 for the Royal Observer Corps was the introduction by the enemy of unmanned flying bombs (q.v.), 'V-1s', 'Doodlebugs' or 'P-planes' to the majority but code-named 'Divers' to the Allies. The first of these was correctly identified and reported by the duty crew of Post M ('Mike') 2 of No 1 Group at 0406 hrs on 13 June. It crashed twelve minutes later near Gravesend, the first of 6,725 weapons of this type to approach the south coast of the United Kingdom. The event is appropriately commemorated by the civilian tie worn by former members of the Group, bearing its number and small representations of flying bombs. Many of the bombs accounted for during this period by fighters were directed by controllers working directly from Corps plotting ▶

follows: heavy bombers, 3,467; medium bombers 1,645; fighters 5,409; transports 2,355; and gliders 867. Immediately before the opening of the attack all Allied aircraft were marked with equal-width black and white identification bands round the fuselage and across the wing chord (contemporary reports that these were alternatively applied in red or blue and white have never been confirmed by subsequent research). A total of 100 sorties is estimated to have been flown by the Luftwaffe up to midnight on 6–7 June, when 15,000 American with 7,900 British and Canadian airborne troops were deployed.

Overseas Commands At the peak of WWII the RAF organization of these Commands differed from those at home in that they contained elements of units which would be grouped separately according to their specialized function. Thus, for example, Middle East Command combined Army Cooperation, Balloon, Bomber, Fighter and General Reconnaissance squadrons, as well as repair and maintenance facilities, with those for flying and operational training. Organization was 'elastic', under subordinate Air Headquarters, Wings and Groups, in

such a way that re-grouping was possible to meet strategic situations both internally and in relation to other Commands.

Overstrand See Boulton Paul Overstrand.

Owl (1) The name adopted for the US Navy's Curtiss E-1, also known as the AX-1. This was a modified version of the A-1 pusher flying boat of 1911 with a retractable undercarriage. Its maximum speed was 60mph. (2) The Luftwaffe's WWII Focke-Wulf FW 189 twin-boom, three-seat reconnaissance and close support aircraft which first flew in July 1938. Delivery of production versions began in September 1940. It rendered especially meritorious service on the Eastern Front. It also served with the Slovak, Romanian, Bulgarian and Hungarian Air Forces. The maximum speed was 217mph and the range 410 miles. (3) The twin-engine Heinkel 219 night fighter, which first flew on 15 November 1942. Only some 250 were built, but the type was significant in having a nosewheel undercarriage and in being the first operational aircraft to feature an ejector seat. The maximum speed

was 416mph and the maximum range 1,200 miles.

P- (1) The designation prefix used by the USAAC and USAAF indicating a 'Pursuit' aircraft. During 1947 this was replaced by 'F' (Fighter). (2) Also adopted from 1923, the letter 'P' was used by the US Navy to indicate 'Patrol' or maritime reconnaissance aircraft. USN extensions were PB (Patrol Bomber) and PTB (Patrol Torpedo Bomber).

P-26 A Boeing fighter aircraft, the first all-metal type adopted by the USAAC, deliveries of which began in 1933. The 'Peashooter', as it was affectionately called, was armed with either one 0.30in and one 0.50in machine gun or two of the former, plus 200lb of bombs on external racks. Powered by a single Pratt & Whitney radial motor giving a speed of 235mph, it had a fixed undercarriage and by the outbreak of WWII had been relegated to mechanic training, although of the 136 produced some had been exported and those to China were used against Japan in the late 1930s. Those in the Philippines made their last operational sortie on 9 December 1941.

OBSERVER CORPS

tables, and in some areas civilian air raid 'alerts' also emanated from this source.

The Luftwaffe's final effort involving the Corps was that of March 1945, following which the air war over Britain ceased. The work of the ROC now took the form of assisting the RAF during the closing months of WWII, at the end of which the Corps was rather arbitrarily stood down. Officially this took place on 30 June 1945, but in fact the order 'Cease plotting' was given at 1700 hrs on Saturday 12 May. In 1940 there had been 26,000 Observers serving part time, the total being 28,000 manning more than 1,000 Posts and Operations Rooms. The peak strength was 33,000 in 1941, which was maintained throughout WWII.

It seemed that this was the end of Britain's Royal Observer Corps, but less than two years later, in January 1947, it was re-formed under the command of Air Commodore the Earl of Brandon and re-

enrolment and fresh recruiting began. The activities of the Corps following its re-formation ran very much along wartime lines, although it was always actively experimenting with new and improved ways to increase its efficiency. Some of these, such as direct communication with fighters from ROC Operations Rooms, were not adopted, but one which was involved the replacement of its maps, formerly based on the British Modified Grid along with those of the RAF, by the 'Georef' system in 1950, a reference method applicable to the whole of the world's surface which gave a rectangular grid in place of the former square one.

Until now the function of the Corps had always been primarily to track aircraft seen or heard over Britain and to alert RAF Fighter Command Operations Rooms appropriately, but with effect from 15 June 1955 a change of role was to take place, brought about by the belief that any future war involving the United Kingdom would be nuclear. To this end the ROC now became a reporting body for nuclear fall-out, with its Operations Rooms re-located deep underground and equipped with highly sophisticated instruments for the new work.

The work remained the responsibility of the Corps until the defence cuts associated with the dissolution of the Warsaw Pact and other changes in Eastern Europe significantly reduced the threat of nuclear attack on Britain. As a result, the announcement of the dissolution of the Corps in July 1991 meant that its part-time members left at the end of September, its full time officers becoming redundant in the spring of 1992. With their departure, the Royal Observer Corps passed into history.

Similar defence organizations existed in several parts of the world, including Nazi Germany, the United States, New Zealand and Australia.

The Australian Corps was organized along similar lines to the ROC, the Volunteer Air Observers' Corps (VAOC) dividing Australia into six areas, No 1 (Victoria and Tasmania), No 2 (New South Wales), No 3 (Queensland), No 4 (North Queensland), No 5 (Western Australia) and No 6 (South Australia), with a total of some 2,800 Posts, these areas being divided into sub-sectors, each with its own Control Room.

P-38 See Lightning.

P-47 The Republic Thunderbolt of WWII. The aircraft was at first constructed with a conventional hood, but the 'D' model introduced a teardrop canopy and cut-down rear fuselage. Capable of carrying bombs and rockets externally, it was dubbed 'The Jug' (Juggernaut).

P-51 The North American Mustang of WWII. Allison-powered examples lacked performance at altitude, so that not until Rolls-Royce Merlins were fitted did the design justify itself. The cockpit area was modified in a similar fashion to that of the P-47 (q.v.). The aircraft, which had a maximum range of over 1,000 miles with external tanks, was revived as the Cavalier Mustang in 1967, powered by a turbo-prop Turbo III for co-in (q.v.) work. Mk I AM106 was tested with twin Vickers 'S' cannon in 1943.

PAC Parachute and cable. A British anti-aircraft device first used in 1940, consisting of a container fired into the path of enemy bombers to release a small parachute with a length of steel cable and another suspended below. In another form, two 8ft parachutes connected by 1,500ft, 3.5-ton cable could be released by barrage balloons on impact.

Parabellum A German machine gun in use during WWII. There were two main types, the 7.92mm LMG.08 and the LMG.08/15.

Parachute Crews of observation balloons at the outbreak of WWI were provided with Spencer-type free-fall (i.e. ripcord-operated) parachutes which were little more than the earlier showman's variety. Retired engineer E. R. Calthrop developed the 'Guardian Angel' parachute, a sound although not free-fall design, tested from 7,000ft in May 1914. It relied on the action of the wind on the folds of silk to open. The Irvin, pulled from its pack by a small auxiliary canopy, was an improvement.

The war ended without any parachutes being used by the British airmen in France, except for a number of black Calthrop canopies ordered for spy-dropping and by observers in kite balloons, although in September 1918 test-drops were made from an S.E.5a and a Snipe. Germany began to issue parachutes to her pilots in the middle of the year, France and Italy having developed escape parachutes some eight months earlier. A search of official files finds no evidence to support the calumny that General Trenchard (not then the dominant figure he later became) was personally opposed to the use of parachutes, the reason for the lack of such equipment being due to no single officer but rather to technical ignorance at War Office level. Nevertheless, large-scale parachute production was undertaken in Britain towards the end of WWI, the Tower Ballroom, Blackpool, being turned into a massive workshop for the purpose. The first parachute supply drop to troops took place at Hamel in July 1918, pilots being trained and the dropping gear devised by Captain Wackett. Only a few German fliers actually used parachutes, and then only towards the end of the war, until wider adoption occurred about 1923.

Developments in more recent years have resulted in the use of massive canopies for the dropping of road vehicles; ribbon and braking parachutes; and the individual rectangular Strato-Star 5-cell and Strato-Cloud 7-cell military para-glider designs.

Parachute flare A pyrotechnic device suspended from a parachute to illumi-

Above: The 'Jug' ('Juggernaut') or Republic P-47 first entered US service in the spring of 1942, the final example (now boasting a 'teardrop' hood) appearing three years later. In the meantime the aircraft's eight Colt-Browning 0.5in guns in the wings, augmented by the ability to deliver an external load of 2,500lb of rockets or bombs, made it a weapon much hated by the enemy. After the end of WWII it was used by a wide spectrum of the world's air forces well into the 1950s. (L. J. Dickson)

nate an area of ground for the purpose of military observation, target-marking, assisting navigation or photography.

Parachute forces Two years before the announcement in 1936 that the Soviet Union was planning to spend the equivalent of £148m on her armed forces, the Red Army formed the first paratroop division in the world.

Shocked contemporary writers commented on the new strategy, which could deploy '1,000 men or more carrying machine guns', and, as if to give emphasis to this, during the summer of 1937 the Soviet armed forces gave the largest display of paratroops ever, using a huge number of ANT-6 G-2 four-engined transports to drop about 30 men each. The method of exit was crude, since the parachutists had to

emerge from the dorsal defensive position and crawl forward along the open fuselage and then await the signal to jump from an NCO in the front gun position. This was obeyed when the troops hurled themselves off the trailing edge of the wing centre-section.

However, it is to Italy that credit for the idea of parachute troops must go, a special experimental unit being

PARASITE AIRCRAFT

The carriage of a fixed-wing aircraft by an aerostat or aeroplane evolved for two purposes: (a) to lift an aeroplane intended to intercept, with the advantage of altitude, a sighted enemy; and (b) to provide a measure of personal protection to a military airship. An early experiment for the former purpose was carried out in Britain during August 1915 when B.E.2c 989 was carried aloft under an SS type airship envelope, the combination being the brainchild of Cdr N. F. Usborne and Lt-Cdr de Courcy W. P. Ireland and known as an 'airship-plane'.

The control gear was to prove troublesome and the first real flight trials were not made until 21 February 1916, crewed by the inventors who saw the device as a possible answer to the problem of the Zeppelin. This particular experiment was not to prove the answer for at some 4,000ft the aeroplane was prematurely released, and, falling inverted, threw out Ireland, to crash, killing Usborne, in the railway goods yard at Strood station.

The idea of an airship carrying a parasite aeroplane was revived, this time to defend its aerostat, in Germany, and on 26 January 1918 an Albatros D.III was successfully launched from Naval Airship L35. These trials were echoed in Britain during 1918 when Sopwith 2.F1 Camel N6622 or N6814 was slung from a special horizontal surface beneath the keel of airship R.23, the upper wing of the aeroplane neatly fitting to this, secured by a quick-release through the upper centre-section cut-out. The first launch was made with the controls locked and a dummy pilot on board. There followed a live drop when Lt R. E. Keys of No 212 Squadron found no difficulty in starting the engine after diving away, later making an uneventful landing at Pulham.

However, by this time the need for developing such experiments had passed, and it was not until 1925 that Britain revived the idea of launching parasite aircraft from aerostats. This time the trials were conducted

with the aid of Rigid Airship R.33, originally operated by the Royal Navy but now serving with the RAF, the aeroplane being the lightweight de Havilland D.H.53 Humming Bird J7325 fitted with the rudder of J7326. The only monoplanes used anywhere in the world for such trials, seven of these had been ordered for communications in the previous year. For the new experiments the D.H.53 was fitted with a complex cabane of steel tubing to incorporate the grab mechanism intended to engage the airship's 'trapeze', and, using this, the pilot, Sqn Ldr R. A. de Haga Haig, accomplished a successful launch on 13 October 1925, the aeroplane being released at some 5,000ft over Norfolk without power and the engine started by diving away. Haig then climbed to the same altitude as the airship, intending to hook on to the gear, but when this was attempted the airship proved slower than the aeroplane so that the gear swung upwards about the hook and the airscrew fouled the airship's suspension wires, breaking off part of one blade. The pilot released again immediately and made a successful dead-stick landing.

It was probably this event which resulted in a delay until towards the end of the year before further trials took place, when J7325 reappeared now fitted with the Farnborough-designed grab gear extended to incorporate an airscrew guard, and on 4 December a successful launch and re-engagement were made. During the following year the British experiments were taken a stage further with the modification of a pair of standard service fighters for continued investigations, Gloster Grebes J7400 and J7385 being slung, as before, from the keel of R.33. Their biplane structure was stabilized by diagonal struts, and special provision was made to start the aircraft's Jaguar motors with the aid of a Bristol gas starter within the airship connected via flexible tubing to the fighters. On 21 October 1926 this combination of aeroplanes and aerostat took off from Pulham, having on board two RAE pilots, Fg Off R. L. Ragg and Fg Off C. Mackenzie-Richards, the first making a successful separation at an altitude of

2,500ft, diving for about 100ft and then levelling off and turning back to base. Slightly higher, the second Grebe was then released after some problems starting the fighter's engine, and the Grebe was flown to Cardington without incident.

There were to be no further British experiments with parasite aircraft, successful though these had been. Three years previously the US Army had become actively interested in the subject of parasite fighters, but the first practical trials comparable to those in Britain were to be made by the US Navy. As a preliminary, on 3 July 1929 Lt A. W. 'Jake' Gordon made a cautious approach to airship ZR-3 *Los Angeles* flying at 78mph in his adapted Vought UO-1 biplane and in a few moments made the US Navy's first successful engagement with an airship in flight. A programme of trials was planned, the intention being to include ZR-4 *Akron* due to be commissioned on 23 June four years hence, so for pilot familiarization six Consolidated N2Y-1s (A8600–A8605), service versions of the two-seat Fleet I trainers, were purchased by the Navy in the meantime. For the new airship, soon to be joined by ZR-5 *Macon*, it was decided to use a small carrier fighter, the Curtiss F9C-1 Sparrowhawk, the first being sent after normal flight trials to Lakehurst where, fitted with a new and experimental hook-on gear, a successful engagement with *Los Angeles* was made on 27 October 1931.

Six production examples of the improved F9C-2 Sparrowhawk were now ordered, and the first made its initial hook-on to *Akron* on 29 June 1932. The five others were delivered the following September. The trials included a twenty-four-hour cruise on 14 July 1932, when 104 hook-ons and drops were made. The vessel was lost on 4 April 1933, but the detachment responsible for these experiments, now termed the HTA or Heavier-Than-Air unit, was quickly transferred to ZR-5 *Macon* after commissioning on 23 June, and the new programme included participation in exercises with the Pacific Fleet off the Californian and Mexican coasts. By this time the Sparrowhawks were operating without

formed using Salvatore parachutes in November 1927. The United States, looking into the same idea, used Irvin static-line canopies the following year. In 1936 the German Maj Inmann created a trial paratroop formation at Stendal, Bavaria, which was still functioning in 1937, (it was expanded to twelve companies in 1938) and the first shock troops to be operationally used were those dropped by some 299

Ju 52s over Rotterdam in the early hours of 10 May 1940, each aircraft carrying eighteen men. These were followed by others dropped during the afternoon four days later, this time supported by a force of 86 Heinkel 111 bombers.

The pattern seemed set for future invasions, so that after the British withdrawal from Dunkirk and a German invasion of the country

seemed inevitable once the Luftwaffe had won the Battle of Britain (q.v.), special opposition forces were formed, the LDV (Local Defence Volunteers), as they were first called, later becoming Britain's Home Guard. These would have been expected to stem the advance of highly trained men, specially equipped with radio, entrenching equipment, folding bicycles etc. in addition to normal infantry armament

---

undercarriages and with belly tanks, depending entirely on their hooks for launch and recovery. During this year also the need was felt for the diminutive fighters to be augmented by a pair of utility and training aircraft, and for this Waco XJW-1s 9521 and 9522 were selected and equipped with hook-on gear so that they too could be drawn up into the airship's hangar.

With the coming of summer, a new and intensive trials procedure was introduced by a new airship captain, and *Macon* began regularly to carry the maximum number of aircraft, using radio direction-finding and a new radio homing device which permitted the aircraft to operate out of sight of the airship's control officer. By the autumn the airship may be said to have been developing into an aeri-

al aircraft carrier, but all came to an abrupt end on 12 February 1935 when, off Point Sur, California, *Macon* was lost with four F9C-2s aboard.

This turn of events effectively closed all experiments with parasite aircraft, and plans

to construct a 900ft airship, the ZRCV, with a gas capacity of 10,000,000 cu ft and capable of accommodating nine dive bombers, were dropped. In 1942 the US Chief of Naval Operations suggested the revival of the idea, but a cool response ended such notions.

The World's Parasite Fighter Trials

Aircraft used	Airship used	Country	First use
B.E.2c	SS-type	GB	21 Feb 1916
Albatros D.III	L35	Germany	26 Jan 1918
Sopwith 2F.1	R.23	GB	1918
D.H.53	R.33	GB	19 Oct 1925
Gloster Grebe	R.33	GB	21 Oct 1926
Vought UO-1	ZR-3	USA	3 July 1929
Curtiss XF-9C	ZR-3	USA	17 Oct 1931
Curtiss F-9C	ZR-4	USA	29 June 1932
Curtiss F-9C	ZR-5	USA	1933

Above: The US *Akron*, otherwise the Goodyear-Zeppelin ZR-4, was used in the parasite trials. She was a rigid airship chiefly of duralumin construction which was designed by K. Arnstein and made its first flight on 23 September 1931, having been laid down in October 1928. Power came from eight 570hp Maybach VL2s. (Author's collection)

and wearing one-piece overalls with leather covers over standard Wehrmacht steel helmets.

The greatest use of German paratroops during this period was, however, to be seen during the invasion of Crete, when 6,000 such men together with other airborne infantry were recklessly flung at Maleme airfield during Operation 'Merkur' on 20 May 1941, their profligate use also resulting in heavy losses when many were dropped from too low an altitude. Britain and the United States had not been slow in forming similar forces, those of the former opening their first school at Ringway, Manchester, on 21 June 1940 for training and experimentation with both paratroops and gliders. Trials of mass drops were begun on 21 July 1941 with 500 men of No 2 Commando from Knutsford using Whitley bombers, each 'stick' of men being commanded by a sergeant and dropping through a hole in the fuselage floor.

Men had been prepared for the new role earlier, and the first British paratroop action had already taken place on 10 February 1941 when, in Operation 'Colossus' (q.v.), eight Whitleys had been specially flown out from Mildenhall at dusk on the 7th for Malta, each on this occasion with a 'stick' of five men, with a total of five officers, detailed to destroy the Tragino aqueduct in southern Italy which carried water to Taranto, Brindisi and Bari. In fact the operation would make little difference to the progress of the war, but the men of 'X' Troop (as the detachment was termed) were being sent to prove an ideal, namely that the new paratroop force was the equal of, or indeed superior to, similar forces on the continent. The greater part of the operation went according to plan. The first aircraft had arrived over the dropping zone some twelve minutes late, at 2142 hrs on the 10th, and at 0032 the detonator for the approximately 1,000lb of gun-cotton on a 60-minute fuse ruptured the viaduct and sent thousands of gallons of water cascading into the river valley.

The Parachute Regiment, all members of which were under 6ft 2in tall, aged between 22 and 32 and weighing no more than 196lb, was formed on 1 August 1942.

American paratroops made the longest-range airborne invasion in military history on 8 November 1942 by flying 1,500 miles in Douglas C-47s (q.v.) from England to take part in the assault on Oran, and three days later British parachute troops left England to land at Maison Blanche, Algeria, successfully capturing the aerodrome at Bône the following day. The first operational use of Japanese paratroops took place on 11 January 1942 when three companies were dropped from 'Nell' transports to capture, after a few hours' fighting, Menado airfield on the Celebes Island.

On 6 June 1944 the greatest ever use of parachute troops was seen during the Allied invasion of Normandy when, together with glider-borne infantry, a force of 7,900 British and Canadian airborne men with 15,000 Americans was dropped behind the coastal defence belt to attack special objectives. Later, the dropping of parachute infantry on 17 September in an effort to end the war before the onset of winter has passed into history. This took the form of drops, combined with landings of glider troops, at Grave, Nijmegen and Arnhem for the purpose of capturing vital bridges and thus to allow the passage of Allied land forces straight into northern Germany through Holland. Although the first pair of objectives were taken, bad weather prevented support from the air in the region of Arnhem, and the presence of enemy armoured units meant that the men of the Parachute Regiment (part of the 1st Allied Airborne Army consisting of two US and one British division, with the Polish Parachute Brigade) were forced to withdraw over the Rhine by night on 25 September, having sustained 7,000 casualties during a lengthy stand against great odds.

The most successful of the Allies' large-scale airborne operations during WWII was that which, including gliders, was mounted the following year in the early hours of 24 March in collaboration with the waterborne crossing of the Rhine, with the object of uniting Montgomery's four bridgeheads into a single 30-mile salient.

All the men involved in the long-distance Operation 'Colossus' referred to earlier were captured, although there had been plans to evacuate them

with the aid of the submarine *Triumph*. This underlined the problem facing all parachute forces, namely that they, being lightly armed, must either fight their own way out of enemy territory or quickly be supported either by advancing friendly forces or by air supply drops. Helicopters are often the solution, this type of transport affording a means of both access and evacuation. However, it is likely that, for special operations, the silent entry of highly trained specialists will still be the surest way of achieving the required objectives for a long time to come.

Parasol wing A monoplane with its wing set above the fuselage. The most historically important example was the Morane Type L, a two-seater of 1913 ordered by the French Army. A version modified as a single-seater was flown in small numbers by the RNAS, 3253 being used by Flt Sub-Lt R. A. J. Warneford to destroy the first Zeppelin in the air when LZ37 was brought down over Bruges on 7 June 1915.

'Party lights' See Tiger Moth

'Pat' The Allied code-name for the WWII Japanese Tachikawa Ki-74. Designed early in 1939, this twin-engine, long-range reconnaissance aircraft, originally described as a fighter, was not put into production (as a long-distance stratospheric bomber), so that the envisaged non-stop flights from Japan to Germany never took place. When the aircraft's true role was discovered, the code-name was changed to 'Patsy'. It carried a crew of five in a pressurized cabin, and a bomb load of 2,200lb. The maximum speed was 350mph.

Pathfinders A force of bomber aircraft manned by experienced and proficient crews which could be used to lead the greater force to its target, introduced by the Luftwaffe as early as 1940. The British equivalent was formed on 15 August 1941, the specialist squadrons coming under the overall command of the peace-time distinguished pilot and navigator Wg Cdr (later Air Vice-Marshal) D. C. T. Bennett. The RAF force was redesignated No 8 (Pathfinder) Group on 8 January 1943 and comprised nineteen squadrons by 1945. The original squadrons, all aircrew members of which were volunteers (automatically promoted one rank on acceptance), were Nos 7 (Stirling), 35 (Halifax), 83 (Lancaster) and 156 (Wellington). The headquarters of the force was at Wyton, with Oakington as a second base and two satellite stations at Gravely and Warboys. The distinguishing badge was a gilt eagle worn on the flap of the left upper breast pocket of uniforms of No 1 Dress, and unofficially on battledress.

'Patsy' See 'Pat'.

'Paul' The Allied code-name for the WWII Japanese twin-float, two-seat, single motor Aichi E16A seaplane, the prototype of which was completed in May 1942. The first production versions of the Zuiun (Auspicious Cloud), as it was called, appeared for use in the naval reconnaissance role in August 1943, these early aircraft having less powerful radial motors than those of later models. The last aircraft were used in kamikaze (q.v.) missions in the Okinawa theatre. A total of 252 of two variants were manufactured, the last having a maximum speed of 270mph, a range of 730 miles and an external bomb load of 550lb.

PC The abbreviation for the WWII German Panzerbombe-Cylindrisch, or armour-piercing bomb.

Pe-2 A Soviet Petlyakov light bomber, also used for reconnaissance and training, which saw service throughout WWII and was one of the outstanding aircraft of the period. The prototype, originally intended to be for a twin-motor, high-altitude fighter, first flew in 1939, its speed resulting in its being difficult to intercept. Some models were fitted with underwing dive brakes. The maximum speed was some 330mph, with a bomb load of up to 2,205lb over a range of 740 miles.

Pe-8 A WWII Soviet four-motor heavy bomber with a crew of nine, the prototype (ANT-42) making its maiden flight on 27 December 1936. Production continued until 1944. Several versions appeared, differing chiefly in the powerplants, liquid-cooled, diesel or radial

motors being fitted. The maximum speed of the radial-engine variant was 280mph over a range of 2,500 miles, and a bomb load of 11,600lb could be carried. The first news of the type in action to reach the West described its appearance at Oran, but only a few hundred were built, although an example visited Britain in June 1942, bringing Mr Molotov before he went on to the United States, and from there taking him directly back to the USSR.

Pegasus A loose or free barrage balloon.

'Peggy' The Allied code-name for Japan's best bomber of the Pacific War, the Mitsubishi Ki-67 Hiryu (Flying Dragon). A comparatively small twin-engine aircraft, it commenced service trials during 1943, when 100 were earmarked for modification as torpedo bombers, in which role the type first saw combat, off Formosa in October the following year. A total of nine variants appeared, not only fitted with various motors but also as fighters and glider tugs. A projected transport version was abandoned. The maximum speed was 334mph and, with an offensive load of 1,102lb, the range was 1,740 miles. A total of nearly 700 were built, including some intended for suicide missions.

Penetration aid A device that enables a hostile bomber to try to create a diversionary track from its own radar and thus confuse defending systems. See Quail.

Perimeter radar Correctly Perimeter Acquisition Radar, this is a unit of communications equipment, computer and radar, intended for use against missiles, often within a larger anti-ballistic system. Using phased array radar (q.v.) it is possible to track several missiles simultaneously and also indicate the likely target. The operational range is in the region of 1,000 miles.

'Perry' The Allied code-name for Japan's Kawasaki Ki-10 Army fighter biplane, the design of which was begun in 1934. The aircraft saw the greatest part of its service use during the war with China, few being retained after the outbreak of WWII. Four variants were produced, the final version

to see combat being the Ki-10-II of 1937 which was distinguished by a new, cantilever undercarriage. Its maximum speed was 276mph and it was armed with a pair of synchronized 7.7mm machine guns on the cowling A total of 280 were built, plus 300 of the earlier Ki-10-I.

'Pete' The name by which the Japanese Mitsubishi F1M central-float observation seaplane was known to the Allies during WWII. Powered by a single radial motor, the F1M2 was the second of the two versions constructed, this having a slightly increased dihedral, a cleaner and longer cowling, and increased fin and rudder areas. Over 500 of each variant were delivered throughout the Pacific War, despite the first prototype being completed as early as 1936. The maximum speed of the final version was 230mph and an offensive load of 550lb could be carried externally.

Peto A small, Parnall-built, two-seat biplane reconnaissance seaplane, built mainly from stainless steel and designed to be carried by the Royal Navy submarine *M2*, which was eventually lost on 26 January 1932 off Star Point, Weymouth, allegedly because of the misinterpretation of an order to open the hangar doors. Two prototypes of the Peto were built, one (N181) powered by a Bristol Lucifer IV engine and the other (N182) by an AW Mongoose, both of 135hp. N181, rebuilt after sustaining damage, was re-numbered N255 and was the Peto lost in the *M2*. Further orders cancelled. The maximum speed of the Peto was 113mph and it had an endurance of 2hr.

Phased array A radar system which differs from the conventional form in having the single, mechanically swept beam replaced by a very large number of fixed beams, thus enabling several targets to be tracked simultaneously. Thus the phased array system is an essential part of perimeter radar (q.v.).

Phosgene A gas (q.v.) used in chemical warfare which is normally colourless but, once released, sometimes becomes visible as a white cloud due to the condensation of water vapour in the atmosphere, at the same time giving off a pungent odour similar to musty hay. Apart from being a tear gas, it also causes coughing as it attacks the air cells in the lungs, acting as an irritant so that they fill with an inflammatory liquid which obstructs the passage of oxygen into the bloodstream, resulting in death.

Phosphorbrandbombe The German term for a phosphorous incendiary bomb (q.v.). The device was also used by the British from 1915 and consisted of a bomb fitted with a time-fuse set to explode in mid-air after being dropped from an aircraft. On detonation it rained a burning substance in the form of a spray over an area of about half a square mile.

Photography The use of sketches prepared by an observer in the basket of a balloon was rapidly replaced by the use of photography. Special cameras for use from powered aircraft were introduced by all the major combatants by the time of WWI, so that it was possible for the first pictures of enemy positions to be taken by the RFC in September 1914. With hand-held oblique or fixed vertical cameras the process was slow at first, since plates were yet to be succeeded by roll-films and the former had to be individually changed. Even so, in the final complete month of British air operations in France, 23,000 negatives were exposed and 650,000 prints issued. Much of Britain's pioneer work in this field had been carried out by the Army's Experimental Photographic Section under the direction of Lt J. T. C. Moore-Brabazon (later Lord Brabazon of Tara), and an attempt to develop plates in the air was even made.

Nine years earlier, in 1909, a Dr Neubronner had experimented with the use of pigeons for this work in war, fitting each with a tiny carrier with a good lens strapped to a small breastplate, although lengthy training was required to accustom the birds to the additional weight. The identity of the positions photographed could be roughly calculated from the known speed of the bird.

Throughout the period between the two world wars the science of photographic reconnaissance was rapidly developed, its initial use being extended from supplying information for operations by ground troops to gathering wider intelligence as the speed and range of aircraft increased By September 1939 the world's major nations all had special units for this work. The RAF's Photographic Reconnaissance Unit flew a variety of aircraft, especially specialist unarmed Spitfires, for deep-penetration work; equally, clandestine photographic missions were carried out over each other's territory by both Britain and Germany before the outbreak of hostilities.

The value of the work for war purposes may be judged from the fact that it was largely as a result of photographic reconnaissance that the secrets of V-1 flying bombs (q.v.) were discovered; its magnitude is indicated by the fact that by mid-1944 the entire coastline of the continent, from Denmark to Bordeaux, had been recorded on film, making known the position of every fortification, gun emplacement, post, communications centre, operations room and barracks.

'Pine' The Allied code-name for the WWII Japanese Mitsubishi K3M crew-trainer. This was a four-seat, high-wing, single-engined monoplane ordered by both the Army and Navy, but its chief claim to listing as a warplane comes from the use of modified K3M3-L variants as utility transports. The maximum speed was 146mph and the range 497 miles. Some 625 were built.

Plotters Personnel employed in an Operations Room laying tracks on a horizontal or vertical map to show the courses of aircraft over a geographical area.

'Ploughman' An attack made by Mosquitos of the RAF's Pathfinder (q.v.) Force during WWII, dropping a single bomb on each of four targets as a diversionary tactic.

Poison gas See Gas.

Polikarpov A Soviet design bureau which flourished in the closing years of the 1930s and those following, producing a number of outstanding warplane designs, including the Po-2 utility biplane and the I-16 monoplane fighter which received its baptism of fire as the 'Rata' (q.v.) in the Spanish Civil War.

Pomeroy British explosive machine gun ammunition introduced by John Pomeroy, an Australian engineer, but developed by Cdr F. A. Brock RN. An order for half a million bullets of this kind was placed in May 1915 and the first were accepted that summer. In February 1917 a more sensitive version known as the PSA Mk II was introduced.

'Post Mortem' One of a series of simulated attacks by RAF Bomber Command on targets in Germany, conducted during June and July 1945 for the purpose of evaluating the former enemy radar.

Potez A French aircraft manufacturer established under that name in 1920, its chief claim to historical recognition being the design and construction of the twin-motor, two/three seat 630/631 monoplane in fighter, light-bomber, army cooperation and reconnaissance versions for the Armée de l'Air from the spring of 1938. It also attracted considerable foreign interest, and several orders for the P.633 light bomber version were placed. The Czechoslovakian Avia company took out a licence to build the three-seat fighter P.636 variant, while China ordered four P.631s. The maximum speed of the long-range fighter variant was 275mph. Armament consisted of two forward-firing 20mm Hispano-Suiza HS-9 cannon and six 7.5mm MAC 1934 machine guns, with a pair of similar weapons flexibly mounted in the rear cockpit.

Pre-emptive strike An attack made without warning on a potential enemy seemingly in a hostile position, Historically, one of the most successful was that made against the nations of the Arab Federation by Israel in June 1967, triggering the Six Day War.

Presentation aircraft A warplane financed by public subscription. Aircraft of this type were usually marked with the name of the donor, which might be a wealthy citizen, an industrial organization or a geographical area. Whether such practice actually augmented the flow of military aircraft from factories already working to maximum capacity is doubtful. This opinion was published in a British aviation magazine in 1940 and it generated intense opposition, but the existence of photographs of the same aircraft with a number of different identities has never been satisfactorily explained. Even so, such considerations ignore psychological effects: contributions to presentation funds enabled the wider public to feel that they were involved in practical participation.

Prieur Properly Bristol-Prieur, this was two-seat monoplane designed by M. Pierre Prieur, Bristol's Chief Instructor, in 1911. The military version had a wing span extended by 3ft 10in and is significant because of its use during the following year at Hendon in connection with some of the earliest experiments in aviation wireless. The maximum speed was 68mph.

Projects During the second half of the century a number of projects were undertaken, particularly in the United States, with the object of improving

the striking potential and performance of various warplanes.
The following list is selective:
'Agile Eagle' Replacement of wing-leading edge flaps of the McDonnell F-4E Phantom by slats to improve combat manoeuvrability. A modification introduced to overcome disadvantages when meeting MiG-17s.
'Black Curtain' Israeli programme to upgrade the Mirage fighter, resulting in the design of the IAI Kfir in 1975.
'Bullet' Development of the RF-8 Crusader high-speed photographic reconnaissance aircraft in 1956.
'Dart Board' Pilot safety measures for the Convair F-106A, including supersonic ejection seat and thermal flash hood necessary in conjunction with use of Genie missile,* 1963.
'Grindstone' Addition of 2.75in folding fin rockets to armament of F-104 Lockheed Starfighter in 1961.
'Gunval' Fitting of 20mm cannon to a small number of F-86 Sabres.
'Harvey' Development of the F-117 stealth aircraft, 1973.
'Look Alike' Introduction of acrylic aluminium paint scheme and fitting

new multiple ejector racks under fuselage of Republic F-104 Thunderchief.
'Six Shooter' Armament of Convair F-106 Delta Dart improved by replacing Genie* missiles by M61A1 six-barrel cannon.
'Tom Tom' Boeing ETB-29A Superfortress tested with an EF-84B Thunderjet close-towed from each wing tip ('Aerial Tip-Tow').
'Wild Goose' Addition of an infra-red search/track ball above nose of Convair F-106 Delta Dart, 1960.
*An Air-2A unguided rocket missile with a 1.5-kiloton nuclear warhead capable of reaching Mach 3 ten miles after having been fired, and designed to explode in the midst of an enemy aircraft formation.

Propaganda leaflets See Leaflets.

Prototype codes A system of allocating British aircraft manufacturers an identification letter to be used as a prefix to the company type designation of new designs, and carried in that manner on the aircraft. Thus the first Westland G.4/31 general-purpose

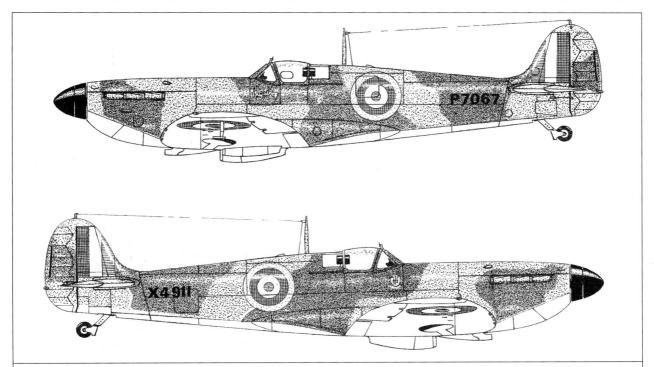

Above: Examples of WWII 'presentation' fighters. The upper Spitfire was subscribed for by Hastings, Sussex, the name of the town being carried under the windscreen; the lower is Bournemouth's X4911, the first of a pair. Both appeared in 1940 and had camouflage patterns differing in detail. (Author's collection)

and torpedo monoplane of 1932 was marked 'P7' and the Miles M.20 N1/41 of 1942 'U-0228'.

The alphabetical system fell into disuse on 1 January 1948 and was replaced by the 'G' system wherein firms were awarded identification numbers, these being preceded by that letter and having the company designation as a suffix. The three parts of these Class B registrations were separated by hyphens; thus the the 171st provisional registration by Supermarine, an Attacker for the Pakistani Navy (R4001) was 'G-15-171'. This system also fell into disuse in the 1950s. See table, right:

Pup The unofficial but widely used name of a British single-seat biplane 'scout' produced by the Sopwith Aircraft Company (q.v.) during WWI. It was easy to fly, despite its rotary engine. The maximum speed was about 104mph, while the armament was a synchronized Lewis gun.

Quail A US diversionary missile carried by a B-52 bomber. Fired ahead of the launching aircraft, it gave a similar radar signature, thus deceiving defensive radar.

Queen An early British radio-controlled target aircraft, converted from the Fairey IIIF floatplane.

Queen Bee A radio-controlled target version of the de Havilland Tiger Moth biplane used with both wheeled and float undercarriages for gunnery practice with live ammunition. It was first flown on 5 January 1935 and the final example was delivered by the Scottish Aviation Company during 1942. A total of 320 aircraft were built, 100 by Scottish Aviation and the balance by the parent firm at their Hatfield factory. The type was regarded as expendable and when used as a target was always flown over the sea. It differed from the Tiger Moth trainer in being constructed entirely of wood, with a ply-covered fuselage. An aircraft of this type was demonstrated to HM King George VI when he visited the Fleet in June 1938. Maximum speed was 109mph.

Queen Wasp An Airspeed-designed radio-controlled biplane meeting

PROTOTYPE CODES

Company name	Original system	'G' system
Armstrong Whitworth	A	G-1
Blackburn	B	G-2
Boulton Paul	C	G-3
Portsmouth Aviation	–	G-4
de Havilland	E	G-5
Fairey	F	G-6
Gloster	G	G-7
Handley Page	H	G-8
Hawker	I	G-9
Parnall	J	–
Reid and Sigrist	–	G-10
Avro	K	G-11
Saro	L	G-12
Short	M	G-14
Supermarine	N	G-15
Vickers	O	G-16
Westland	P	G-17
Bristol	R	G-18
Heston	S	G-19
General Aircraft	T	G-20
Miles	U	G-21
Airspeed	V	G-22
Weir	W	–
Percival	X	G-23
Cunliffe-Owen	Y	G-24
Auster	Z	G-25
Slingsby	–	G-26
English Electric	–	G-27
Scottish Aviation	–	G-31

Specification Q.32/35, produced in both a landplane version (prototype K8887) and with twin floats (prototype K8888). Sixty-five were ordered, the first, P5441, flying on 29 March 1940, and the next, P5442, on 18 May. The type was used for catapult trials from HMS *Pegasus*, and the public debut of the type was at the RAF Display at Hendon in June 1937. The maximum speed was 170mph, the floatplane version being 10mph slower.

R The designation prefix 'A-' (q.v.), applied to attack aircraft of the United States Navy, was given this additional prefix (thus 'RA-') to indicate a reconnaissance version of the attack type. Also prefix for bombers on reconnaissance duty and initial for rotary wing helicopters USAAF/USAF 1941–47.

Radar beam riding A missile-guidance system chiefly used for surface-to-air work wherein a beam directed at a target aircraft, having locked on, provides a track along which a rocket may be launched.

Radio Among the first wireless telegraphy signals between an aircraft in flight and the ground were made using the British airship *Gamma* during the 1912 Army Manoeuvres. No 4 Squadron had a receiver for communication with aircraft in France during 1914. Later, when wireless came into wider use, an enemy would attempt to jam transmissions over the Western Front. After WWI a programme of concentrated trials of radio telephony (i.e. transmitting speech) was carried out at Biggin Hill, Kent. In 1918 the RAF had 600 radio-equipped aircraft.

Radio command guidance A method of guiding missiles either directly by radio or by transmitted control guidance commands from an operator who (usually) had also launched it.

Radio direction-finding The fixing of an aircraft's position by the use of radio signals converging on it from two or three ground stations.

Radome The (usually) streamlined cover over an aeroplane's radar antenna. This was particularly prominent in the ventral position of Avro Lancaster and Lincoln aircraft.

RAF (1) Royal Air Force. See Great Britain. (2) Royal Aircraft Factory. A British experimental station in Hampshire, founded on the transfer of the Royal Engineers' Balloon Factory from Chatham in 1907, partly to facilitate the construction of an airship. It was also the site of the early trials made by Samuel Cody and, later, that of the first Royal Flying Corps Workshop. Such famous squadrons as No 4 were later established there. The term 'factory' came from its responsibilities for designing and constructing its own warplanes, the earliest being such types as the B.E. series, and later the R.E.8 and S.E.5 and 5a scouts. Following the establishment of the Royal Air Force, the factory was re-named the Royal Aircraft Establishment, becoming responsible for research into a wide spectrum of aviation subjects.

Ramenskoye See Zhukovsky.

Ramming Although cases are recorded throughout the history of air warfare of pilots deliberately ramming an opponent to bring about his destruction, a propeller-driven aircraft specially designed to achieve this was proposed by Phillip & Powis (Miles) in early 1939, the machine being specially strengthened with steel reinforcement, a cockpit set well back and an automatic ejection mechanism for the pilot. A decision not to proceed with the idea was taken in early August that year. Naxi Germany also examined a similar idea of a *Ramjaeger* as did Northrop in the United States with their *Ramfighter*.

Rapier A surface-to-air missile used by the RAF and British Army, intended for use against low-flying aircraft. It is powered by a single-stage solid-fuel rocket, fitted with an HE warhead and controlled by radio-command guidance.

Rata (Rat) The name by which the Soviet Polikarpov I-16 monoplane

fighter was known when participating in the Spanish Civil War.

RATOG Rocket Assisted Take-Off Gear, fitted to various aircraft from the WWII period to give flying speed over a shortened take-off run. Its ultimate development at the end of the century was the Zero Length Rocket Launcher.

'Razzling' The distribution from an aircraft of incendiary leaves. Each was made up of a pair of celluloid strips some 3in long with a small piece of phosphorous wrapped in wet cotton wool between. On drying out these would take fire, perhaps several hours after having been dropped. The Razzle leaves were stored in water, about 450 to a canister, and dropped from the aircraft via a special chute.

Reconnaissance The foundations of aerial reconnaissance may be said to have been laid before the advent of powered aircraft, when, with the realization that the mere altitude extend-

RADAR

Originally known as 'radio location', this method of finding the range and direction of an aircraft in flight is based on the principle of ultra-high frequency radio waves being interrupted by the machine and thus reflected by it back to the transmitting source, indicating its presence. The name 'radar' was a US anagram for 'radio detecting and ranging'.

Electronic detection had been developed in Britain by Dr Watson-Watt, and the first aircraft successfully detected by this method is said to have been a Handley Page Heyford bomber over Salisbury Plain. Such was the proven value of the system that in order to create an industry manufacturing the all-important cathode-ray tubes the British government launched a campaign to develop and popularize television.

The first British experiments were begun in May 1935 at Orfordness with the aid of a Westland Wallace aircraft flying at a predetermined altitude on a set course at a prearranged time, but these were moved to Bawdsey in February 1936 after the purchase of the site by the Air Ministry for £24,000. In the same year work began on Britain's defensive radar chain.

Such electronic assistance reduced the necessity of constant patrols so that the defending fighters could be committed to battle economically and with maximum results.

The night attacks which followed these daylight sorties placed a greater reliance on radar for the defenders, and AI (airborne interception) radar, which could be carried by defensive fighters, was developed. This functioned in association with GCI (ground controlled interception), relying on a ground controller choosing a specific raider as target and vectoring a fighter under his control on to an interception course to a position about three miles short of the target, where the fighter's AI radar would take over. The radar operator on board the aircraft would direct the pilot to within range, when the attack would be completed. Detractors were vocal in the early days, claiming that such a device indicated the planning of an entirely defensive war. It is true that by January 1943 no offensive systems had been delivered, except for a small number of gun control sets for naval vessels and other sets for anti-submarine work.

The period when electronic warfare was being developed under battle conditions in Europe was also one when the United States remained at peace, with the result that urgent steps were taken in the USA to hasten the formation of an Aircraft Warning Service, using Signal Corps equipment and personnel – an

enormous task given to the size of the geographical area to be covered. Much of the development work which was to follow was based on the foundations laid in November 1938 and concentrated on perfecting a scanning system that was officially announced as having advantages over 'the best sound locator', it being possible to feed the data on an aircraft's movement directly into standard M-4 and M-7 gun directors. The final range of the new sets was 120,000yds, and they could thus be used for a pioneer early warning GCI system.

While the British term for the new electronic measures was 'radio-location', in the United States the Signal Corps had opted for 'RPF' (radio position-finding), but, whatever name was used, an important step in unifying British and US research and development was taken when an independent agency was established on 27 June 1940. In July a Microwave Committee, headed by Dr Alfred Loomis, was set up to examine the possibility of such waves in radio location, and the research on both sides of the Atlantic was combined after an agreement between the respective governments that same year. October 12 saw a meeting between representatives of the Microwave Committee and a British Technical Mission under Sir Henry Tizard, following which the United States undertook to look further into the use of AI equipment and also investigate a ▶

ed the range of an observer's field of view, tethered balloons took aloft officers skilled in preparing pencil sketches of what could be seen beyond enemy positions with the aid of binoculars. It naturally fell to aeroplanes to be used for similar work – and they had the added advantage of mobility. Indeed, that this was seen as the primary function of early powered aircraft may be seen in the designation of early fighters as 'scouts': they were expected to perform in the air much

the same types of duties as had been delegated to sections of the cavalry in earlier conflicts.

Following the outbreak of WWI, continuous British reconnaissance during the retreat from Mons proved of immense value to General Headquarters, and Sir John French's staff were kept informed both of the position of the advancing Germans and of that of the British rearguard, although the system was troubled by the impossibility of communicating

with an airborne observer. Until the introduction of wireless, air-to-ground communication had to be made with the aid of weighted bags marked with coloured streamers. As the war progressed, specialized two-seat aircraft were devised purely for reconnaissance.

This practice, now augmented by photography (q.v.), marked the attainment of the art throughout the period between the two world wars, and the months immediately preceding the

RADAR

▶ microwave position-finder for anti-aircraft control.

Practically every radar set developed thereafter consisted of the following major parts (although detail design varied from system to system):

1. A *modulator*, the function of which was to take power from the main supply source, be it an electrical line, batteries or a generator, and form it into suitable voltage pulses to drive the radio-frequency oscillator in bursts of radio-frequency oscillations, these being perhaps only a millionth of a second in duration.

2. The *radio-frequency oscillator*, being a vacuum tube or tubes designed to oscillate at the desired frequency and give bursts of radio-frequency power when connected to the modulator. Since this, as already outlined, is turned on for such brief bursts, a power of some hundreds of kilowatts must be generated. It followed, therefore, that practical equipment had to run at powers many thousands of times greater than was thought possible only a few years previously, a factor that caused the original Microwave Committee to proceed into such a speculative field with great caution at first.

3. The *antenna*, or aerial, posed some of the most difficult problems in the early days of radar development since it was necessary for it to conform to a number of requirements, the chief of which were:

(i) that its function must be directional in order to concentrate the radio energy in a clearly defined beam and thus illustrate the direction taken by detected objects (e.g. aircraft in flight);

(ii) that the entire generated power output must be concentrated into the beam, thereby ensuring the very highest efficiency with none of the power leaking off into 'side lobes' and various directions which could be confusing

and possibly have fatal results; and

(iii) that the antenna must be capable of being scanned or directed from one fixed point to another with great accuracy (for example, if mounted in a moving object such as an aircraft it must be stabilized to the extent that such scanning is possible without absorbing the motions of the aircraft).

The antenna proper could be of several different types, including that which may be described as being constructed on the 'searchlight principle', whereby the loosely directional energy is caught by a parabolic reflector and concentrated by the concave surface into a beam – the principle on which a modern satellite dish is constructed. Alternatively the antenna may take the form of a number of miniature aerials or dipoles, phased and spaced in order to concentrate the energy in a single direction; this arrangement is particularly applicable to large aircraft profiles. The size of either is important in that the greater the dimensions, the sharper the beam for any given wavelength. A modified version of the parabolic reflector form, it was discovered, could be greater in one direction, thus giving a fan-shaped beam, which was sharper in one dimension.

Scanning, already mentioned, is the sweeping of an area by mechanical means, calling for a structure that must be capable of movement both in elevation and azimuth. In some cases it is only necessary to scan a small area and electrical scanning, not calling for movement of the entire structure, is possible, but mechanical methods could be rotated only at between one and twenty rpm, and since the fading of a signal on a cathode-ray tube is almost immediate, giving only a series of dots instead of an illuminated map or picture, special screens had to be developed to hold the glow for a time after the passing of the swept signal.

4. A further problem to be overcome was that of perfecting a *receiver*. Nearly all radars worked on the superheterodyne principle, calling for the production of low-power radio

signals close to the frequency of those received and comparing these with the latter, making an intermediate frequency, while displaying the information by means of an indicator posed several problems, not the least of which was ensuring that the receiver was not burnt out by the massive bursts of energy generated by the transmitter.

5. A radar *indicator* presented the information in the best form adapted to the set. Almost all consisted of one or more cathode-ray tubes, these giving, if no signals were being received, a single, bright, 'time base' line across the tube, the distance along that line representing the elapsed time after an outgoing pulse. A returning echo would give a 'blip' or break on that line at the point corresponding to the time taken for the signal to return, and the position of that 'blip' indicated the distance of the reflected object. An alternative tube was that known as a PPI (plan position indicator), where the time base starts at the centre of the tube's diameter and moves radially, rotating in synchronization with the antenna. The returning signal, instead of giving a 'blip', momentarily intensifies its brilliance, causing a map-like image on the screen.

Japan, having radar at least from 1942, tended to reserve it for home defence, while other forms included the Luftwaffe's SN-2 Liechtenstein used by night fighters and the British 'Gee' (q.v.) and 'Oboe' (q.v.) systems. Developments include Doppler radar, especially useful in providing information on moving objects, since this sends out a continuous stream of constant-frequency signals which are reflected back at a higher frequency from an object moving towards a transmitter and at a lower frequency if it is moving away, the 'Doppler effect' being the apparent difference between the frequency at source and that on its reading by an observer (the so-called 'train through a station' effect). British trials from May 1940 to 1942 were centred around Worth Matravers and Langton on the Isle of Purbeck. See Tracking radar.

outbreak of WWII saw both the major combatants flying clandestine missions. The Luftwaffe, however, had been taking a fresh look at the requirements of the work and in 1940 evolved an idea for a rocket-propelled sailplane for reconnaissance which would operate at an altitude giving immunity from interception. The exigencies of war prevented practical work from being done until three years later, and then the DFS 228 appeared. It was a relatively clean,

mid-wing monoplane with a span of almost 58ft which was intended to be carried aloft as the upper unit of a composite aircraft or towed to an altitude of some 33,000ft and released, the rocket motor then being relied on to increase the operating altitude by a further 22,000ft. Thereafter height would be maintained by bursts of power over a period of about three-quarters of an hour, during which the machine would have flown over the target area, a glide begun to some

40,000ft and photographs taken with the aid of infra-red cameras. The altitude could then be depended upon to facilitate the aircraft gliding back to base, perhaps with the aid of thermals as with sailplaning, whereupon a landing would be made on retractable skids. Three prototypes of the DFS were built, chiefly of wood construction, and a batch of ten was ordered. However, no powered flights were ever made, and the end of the war terminated the programme. More conventional German reconnaissance developments during WWII were the Junkers Ju 86P and R machines which, with diesel engines and pressure cabins and carrying only a light armament, severely challenged the Allied defences.

As the DFS project demonstrated, the key to successful reconnaissance was altitude, and this was the way in which, for example, photographs were obtained in preparation for the German invasion of the Soviet Union. However, despite steady improvements in the development of infra-red photography, flying at altitude in itself brought difficulties since there was no solution to the problem of vapour trails encountered at between 27,000 and 40,000ft (depending on the temperature and humidity encountered). These gave a highly visible indication of the presence of an intruder, although it is true that such trails would also give warning of intercepting fighters to reconnaissance crews.

During WWI Russia had been quick to realize the advantages of reconnaissance, but the size of the fighting front had required the adoption of *Ilya Mourometz*-type aircraft with a specialist crew of two observers, enabling penetrations 150 miles behind enemy lines to be made. Even so, the experience gained in this field was wasted by the later Soviet Union, only about one in every twenty warplanes being suitable for reconnaissance by the time of the outbreak of the 1941 war with Germany. Rapid steps had to be taken to rectify the situation, using converted single-engine fighters for army support and once again adapted bombers for long-distance work.

In the USAAF F-3s (A-20s), F-7 (B-24s), F-9s (B-17s) and F-13s (B-29s) were used for reconnaissance during WWII, but perhaps the most numeri-

Above: Radar antennae on the nose of a Messerschmitt Bf 110. (Author)

Above: A German Fk.I 122 hand-held reconnaissance camera of 1915. (Author's collection)

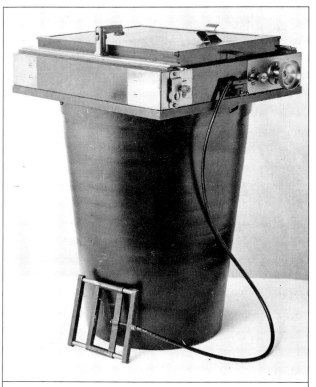

Above: A remotely controlled vertical plate reconnaissance camera of WWI vintage. (Author's collection)

cally significant type used for the work were the 1,000 or so specially modified P-38 Lightnings. They also used PR Spitfires and Mustangs. Japan employed such converted bombers as Mitsubishi Ki-46 'Dinahs' (q.v.), which had a performance that gave an equality with likely interceptors when stripped of their armament.

In Britain much pioneer work was accomplished by Sidney Cotton in the two months before WWII flying his blue-painted, camera-equipped Lockheed 12A over Germany, and some of the tactics learned were applied to the RAF's wartime PRU (Photographic Reconnaissance Unit; PDU until July 1940) which chiefly operated Spitfires at first, later augmented by Hurricanes, Beaufighters and Mosquitos. A type little-remembered for such work was the US-built Martin 167, known to the RAF as the Maryland, one of which, flying from its base on Malta, was responsible for ascertaining the position of the Italian Fleet lying in the harbour at Taranto before the historic attack on the five

battleships, fourteen cruisers and 27 destroyers there by FAA Swordfish on 11 November 1940.

The addition of Mosquito aircraft to the RAF's reconnaissance force immediately added long-awaited range to photographic sorties, so that it became possible to fly a 2,000-mile reciprocal course at some 380mph. This speed was almost equalled by the PR Spitfire Mk IV, the range of which was extended by the 'D' section of the wing leading edges being used to store extra fuel. Among the most notable achievements of the RAF's Photographic Reconnaissance Unit must be included the watch maintained on enemy radar, the confirmation of the existence of flying bombs and the mapping of special targets, including the experimental base at Peenemünde and the Ruhr dams.

Alas, as in 1919, the carefully nurtured science of reconnaissance was allowed swiftly to disappear by all nations after 1945, and converted bombers began to be pressed into service once more. The United States, for

example, was using the Convair RB-36 and Boeing RB-47, sometimes carrying up to seven cameras and thus capable of photographing close to 480 square miles in three hours. The inadequacy of the resources was soon to be shown during the Korean War, when the enemy tended to move at night: photography under such conditions had never been properly explored.

To meet the problems associated with the 'Cold War', the United States began the development of a new type of aircraft for such work in 1954, and the prototype Lockheed U-2 flew for the first time the following year. The most celebrated incident in the aircraft's career was the loss, while on a spy mission over the Soviet Union, of a U-2 flown by Capt Garry Powers. The aircraft was shot down, allegedly by a SAM, near Sverdlovsk on 1 May 1960. That lost over China on 9 September two years later was, it was claimed, one of a pair sold to Nationalist China in 1960, although eight fell to Chinese defences following the Nanching nuclear tests of September 1962. It is interesting to note that these aircraft reflected the sailplane concept of the German DFS 228 twenty years earlier, with glider-like wings and lightweight construction.

Reconnaissance towards the end of the twentieth century might be defined as being of four types: normal surveillance; emitter location, in which the defences are forced to switch on their tracking radar and thus reveal its location; imaging, including normal and infra-red photography; and radar scanning. Modern reconnaissance aircraft carry a wide variety of optical cameras and ultra-violet sensors, plus the infra-red and radar sensors already described, and this equipment is accommodated either in fuselage extensions or in 'bolt-on' pods measuring about 25ft in length. These pods are of different types for medium/high-level work and for multi-role reconnaissance, and film capacity must be sufficient for 200 miles' coverage in the case of low-level sorties, allowing for a 60 per cent overlap. Just as demanding are the requirements for high-altitude work: the Lockheed SR-71, the successor of the U-2, carried equipment that enabled the aircraft to photograph 60,000 square miles in a single hour. See also Remotely piloted vehicles.

Red Dean A British air-to-air missile with a semi-active homing guidance system operating on continuous-wave transmission. It was developed during the mid-1950s. Never entered operational service.

Red Top A British air-to-air missile (see Sea Vixen).

Red spot fire A German target indicator of WWII which burnt with a very high intensity although with a reduced ground pattern so that, in quantity, it could be used to guide bombers not only to the smaller targets but also along the route to a target area.

Red Hebe A development of the Red Dean (q.v.) missile, fitted with an infra-red target-seeking device.

Reflector gun sight An optical sight which allowed the gunner/pilot to alter his position without any error of deflection arising so that it was only

necessary to watch the target as the reticule appeared to be superimposed on it. Early models such as the N-3 and the first N-6 type were of only single reticule design, however, and a error as high as 25 per cent could result in beam shots. The three-ring N-8 allowed much more accuracy, and sights in this series were used for the free guns of WWII B-17, B-24 and B-26 bombers. The N-3 was originally the standard sight for such fighters as the P-38, P-47 and P-51, although by the time the P-38J-10 was introduced it had to be replaced as it could not be accommodated behind the redesigned windscreen and the Lynn Instrument Company's L-3 was therefore adopted. Meanwhile the successful British Mk II was adopted as superior to the standard N-3 for P-47s; this was later replaced by the generally similar Mk VIII in late 1943. P-51Ds carried the improved N-9.

Reichsluftfahrtministerium German Air Ministry (WWII).

Remotely piloted vehicle A low-cost, short-range, unmanned aircraft capable of taking photographs of the ground, either optically or outside the visible spectrum. Designed to be operated at low altitude, they are difficult to shoot down. They are also suitable for use in high-speed passes to confirm information gained by conventional reconnaissance.

Republic A US aircraft manufacturer formed from the Seversky organization in 1940, its first major warplane design being the P-47 (q.v.) of WWII. The company was also responsible for the XF-12 Rainbow, a reconnaissance aircraft of which only two were built. Its first jet-propelled fighter design was the F-84A, B, and G Thunderjet, which was followed by the F-84F Thunderstreak and RF-84F Thunderflash (q.v.) and in turn by the F-105 Thunderchief (q.v.).

Rescue The British air–sea rescue service – probably the first of its type in the world to be properly organized – began in WWI with a system of directing trawlers, merchant ships and naval vessels to the spots where aircraft were known to have been forced down in the Channel, an ever-present possi-

bility in the days of unreliable engines. Along certain parts of the French and English coasts special launches were gradually introduced for such work. With the return of peace this service was run down, but the need for such boats was recognized by the RNLI and in 1930 the *Sir William Hilary*, a vessel of 25 tons displacement and capable of 17 knots, was based at Dover.

Meanwhile, for some years prior to 1939 the RAF had maintained a small number of tenders for various duties including those connected with bombing practice, and in May 1940, with these craft as a basis, the beginnings of a new service were officially laid, the first boats operating chiefly around Dover.

There is no doubt that, at this time, the Luftwaffe was better organized in this regard, mooring special floats in the Channel where downed aircrews could find shelter, medical supplies, warmth and food while being assured of eventual rescue by the tenders which regularly patrolled the floats (later copied by Great Britain), while Heinkel He 115B and He 59B floatplanes and Dornier Do 18G flying boats were all used to snatch airmen from the sea.

The RAF during this time was building up its own rescue service with specially designed launches from such yards as British Power Boats, Thornycroft, Walton Thames and Vosper, while such aircraft as Spitfires, Lysanders and Walrus flying boats were used, soon to be augmented by twin-motor types such as Wellingtons, Hudsons and Warwicks, some carrying external lifeboats to be dropped by clusters of parachutes.

These measures were copied by a variety of nations until the necessity for such a large and complex rescue service evaporated with the end of WWII. Since then, peacetime work has increasingly fallen to helicopters.

Retard bombs 'Parachute mines' (see Mines) of WWII were probably among the first weapons to come into this category, those dropped by the Germans being identified by their coarse, green parachutes, but modern air attack systems demanding the low-level delivery of perhaps 1,000lb bombs with improved accuracy have required that these be fitted with one or more small conventional canopies or balloon parachutes. These slow the rate at which the bombs fall. An alternative method of applying deceleration is to employ automatically opening retard fins which, when fully open, are perpendicular to the airstream. An example of the latter is the US Snakeye bomb, the retarders of which flick open almost immediately once the weapon is released from the aircraft.

RF- The designation applied to the reconnaissance (q.v.) development of a fighter aircraft by the US Air Force, US Navy and US Marine Corps.

'Rhubarb' The WWII RAF code-name for a small-scale harassing operation by fighters using cloud cover.

'Rivers' The original code name for X-system radio navigational beams during WWII.

RLM Reichsluftfahrtministerium (q.v.).

'Roadstead' The WWII RAF code-name for an operation in unison with fighter escorted bombers (including Hurri-bombers) in diving or low-level attacks on ships whether in harbour or at sea.

Rockets Armament of this type was first used in WWI and consisted of little more than the traditional form with a sheet-metal warhead, the stabilizing rod running through eyes on the interplane struts of aircraft in groups of four or five missiles per side. Mounted at an upward angle of 15 degrees, they proved effective in destroying balloons. The Belgians and the Italians used them on a small scale, the Germans hardly at all. Such weapons fell into disuse after the war except in the Soviet Union, where B S Petropavlovskii developed a type with a welded steel body, a windmill nose fuse and four fins, with an offset nozzle to impart spin to the flight. A powder warhead and propellant were fitted. Air trials made in April 1936 resulted in orders for two subsonic types, the 51lb, 5.2in diameter RS-132 measuring some 37in long and the 15lb, 3.23in diameter RS-82 which was 34in in length. Both were used in WWII together with a third, the RS-75, all of which formed the basis for the supersonic RS-182,

TR-190 and ARS-212 developed after 1950.

The foundations of British WWII rockets were laid as early as 1934 using cordite propellants for a 3in type first fired from a Beaufighter in October 1941, and standard heads were developed of 60lb semi-AP and 25lb types. The 6in head of the first was identified by having one red and one white band, both of ½in width, and one 1in broad band of mid-green; the 12in head of the second was identified by two ½in white bands. Total lengths were 74in and 66½in respectively.

United States rocket technology in WWII owed much to British development, eventually evolving into the 38.2lb, 4.5-inch subsonic 'M' of 1943 used by the Air Force and the Navy. Later a wide range of rocket types was introduced, the most significant being the 5in HVAR or 'Holy Moses' and the 11.75in 'Tiny Tim', the latter over 10ft long and carrying a 150lb charge.

Nazi Germany introduced the Nebelwerfer artillery rocket adapted for air-borne use in several sizes, no version proving particularly effective against bombers and it was eventually discarded as the huge launcher seriously affected the interceptor's performance. The Rz73 Fohn used for ground attack had no such problems, and this was complemented late in WWII by the supersonic 3.5kg, 5mm air to-air R4/M, the eight fins of which unfolded in flight. Ultimately 400 R4/M rockets could be fired per minute with the aid of a belt feed. The American 'Mighty Mouse' owed much to this German weapon.

'Rodeo' A WWII RAF fighter sweep intended to entice the Luftwaffe into battle.

Rotor kite A rotary-winged aircraft of the autogyro type, the best-known warplane version of which was the Focke Achgelis Fa 330 Bachstelze (Water Wagtail) of WWII. This was intended to be stowed in and flown from a U-boat, the forward motion of which maintained rotation and therefore lift. The elevated position of the single crew-man enabled him to observe likely convoy targets and send his report to the U-boat by means of a telephone line. Should an emergency

abandonment be necessary, an ingenious device jettisoned the rotor, which, flying upwards, pulled out a parachute, enabling the pilot to release himself and make a normal descent. These kites were chiefly employed from Type IX U-boats, probably from mid-1942.

Royal Aircraft Factory See RAF.

Royal Flying Corps See Great Britain.

Royal Laboratory This establishment was responsible for the design of several British air bombs during the 1914–18 war, including the 100lb weapon, a high-blast bomb with a thin skin for use against 'soft' targets. Another type weighed 112lb: with a low blast effect, this had good penetration and was useful against buildings and the like. For similar work there was also the 230pdr, which was introduced in 1917 at a time when aircraft design had advanced sufficiently to take the weight, while the SN 1650 was introduced in 1918 for bombing industrial targets, remaining part of the armoury of the RAF well into the 1920s but never being used in action.

Royal Laotian Air Force Founded in 1954 as the air arm of the French-influenced ANL (Armée Nationale Laotienne) with nine Morane-Saulnier MS500 Criquets (Fieseler Storchs), this force changed its title soon after the country gained independence. From that time its equipment was largely of US origin and included Cessna U-17s, C-123K Providers, T-6 Texans, Sikorsky UH-34 helicopters and a Super Helio.

Royal Naval Air Service See Great Britain.

Royal Observer Corps See Observer Corps.

RPV See Remotely piloted vehicle.

'Ruffians' The later code-name for X-system navigational beams, originally called 'Rivers' (q.v.).

'Rüpelkammer' The German code-name for operational attacks on Britain by means of V-1 flying bombs (q.v.) which opened on 13 June 1944.

Above: A Scarff ring mounting for the rear gunner of a Bristol F.2b Fighter. The fuselage here is uncovered, showing the woven seat for the pilot, for whose forward gun an Aldis sight is fitted. (Author)

S-51 A military Westland-Sikorsky helicopter which first flew in prototype form in February 1946 and later entered service with the US Air Force as the H-5, the US Navy as the HO2S-1 and the RAF and RN as the Dragonfly. The first Westland-built example was WF308, delivered in 1950. A four-seater for communications and casualty evacuation, it had a maximum speed of 103mph and a range of 310 miles. The last British examples were those serving with the Far East Air Force, which were withdrawn in 1956.

S-55 A military Westland-Sikorsky helicopter which first flew in prototype form on 15 August 1953 and was used by the US Air Force as the H-19 Chickasaw, the US Navy as the HO4S-1, the US Marine Corps as the HRS-1 and the RAF as the Whirlwind. In the RAF, deliveries commenced with XD179 in 1955. The type was also licence-built by Mitsubishi in Japan. The maximum speed of this search and rescue/light transport machine was 110mph, the range being 470 miles.

S-58 A military Westland-Sikorsky helicopter designed to meet a US Navy requirement for anti-submarine work, the first flight taking place in March 1954. It was eventually to enter service with the US Navy as the SH-34 Seabat, the US Army as the CH-34 Choctaw, the US Marine Corps as the UH-34D Seahorse and also the RAF and RN, the last using some 150 HAS.1s. The type, named Wessex in British service, was also employed as a Commando assault helicopter and was used by the Royal Australian Navy, Ghana and Brunei. Dipping sonar was among the equipment carried by anti-submarine versions, with rocket or missile armament. The maximum speed was 130mph and the range 600 miles.

S-61 A military Westland-Sikorsky anti-submarine helicopter which first flew on 11 March 1959, deliveries to the US Navy commencing two years later as the SH-3A Sea King. Other countries to use the type included Britain, Egypt, Germany and Norway. Several versions were produced, and equipment carried included dipping sonar, Doppler navigation gear, search radar and an automatic piloting and weapons system. The maximum speed was 166mph and the range 625 miles.

SA-2 See 'Guideline'.

SA-3 See 'Goa'.

SA-4 See 'Ganef'.

SA-5 See 'Griffin'.

SA-6 See 'Gainful'.

Saab-32 See Lansen.

Saab-35 See Draken.

Saab-37 See Viggen.

Saab-39 See Gripen.

Sabre See F-86.

Salamander See Heinkel 162.

'Sally' The Allied code-name for Japanese Mitsubishi Ki-21 heavy bomber of WWII. Formerly known as 'Jane', it was adopted in August 1938 as part of a modernization programme and used in many Far East theatres, proving to be comparable with the best machines in the West. The maximum speed of the improved Ki-21IIb model – at one time believed to be a completely new design and provisionally coded 'Gwen – was 302mph and the range 1,680 miles. The bomb load was 2,200lb.

Samolyot Zvyeno (Aircraft Nest). Soviet air-launching (q.v.) trials.

Satellite airfield A service base subservient to a nearby larger one and having less comprehensive facilities. This type of airfield proved useful for the accommodation of detachments and as a diversionary base when conditions at the main station were problematic.

S-Bo A German free-fall weapon, also known as a Sägebombe or saw bomb, consisting of a 400m weighted steel cable intended to destroy high-tension power lines.

Scarff ring A manual free gun mounting invented by WO Scarff during WWI. No 6 pattern was still in use by the RAF in the late 1930s.

Schräge Musik A WWII German cannon installation fitted to some night fighters (for example, Bf 110Gs and He 219s) in which the weapons were positioned behind the cockpit, angled forwards and upwards to enable enemy bombers to be raked with fire as the fighter passed beneath.

Schweinfurt The site of ball-bearings factories subjected to two heavy attacks during WWII. The first took place on 17 August 1943 and was made by 363 B-17s, of which 60 (plus others too badly damaged to return from North Africa) were lost. After dark, RAF Bomber Command carried out the first night precision bombing with the aid of radio instructions by a Master Bomber, one of the earliest uses of this technique. Another attack against Schweinfurt was made by the US Eighth Air Force on 14 October

Above: The cockpit and upper Lewis gun of an S.E.5a, probably at an armament school in 1918. (Author's collection)

1943, the 291 B-17s involved (of which 28 were lost) having an escort of P-47s for part of the way as did the earlier raid (q.v.).

Scimitar A Supermarine single-seat, carrier-borne strike fighter also having a fighter-reconnaissance capability which was first delivered to the Royal Navy in June 1958. The armament consisted of four 30mm Aden cannon in the fuselage and provision for Sidewinder air-to-air missiles, bombs or unguided rockets on wing pylons. Power was supplied by a pair of Rolls-Royce Avon 202 single-shaft turbojets, their installation being a novel one at the time.

Carrier trials were conducted with the first production version (XD210) aboard HMS *Ark Royal* in April 1956 and the type was seen as a dramatic improvement on the Sea Hawk. The first batch then ordered exceeded 100 machines, but in fact only 76 Scimitars were finally delivered. They were to prove popular and reliable machines. In design terms they had a certain air of technical novelty, including an area-ruled fuselage (which gave the aircraft a 'waist' in plan view), 'dog-tooth' leading edges to the wings, blown flaps and the Royal Navy's first experience of power-operated controls. Surprisingly, Scimitars were not fitted with radar, although a camera pack

SEA HAWK

could be added via an interchangeable nose.

The first operational squadron to receive the type was 803 NAS, this being formed at Lossiemouth in June 1958 and later embarked on HMS *Ark Royal*. The Scimitar was withdrawn from service in 1965.

'Scimitar' was also the name of an Armstrong Whitworth biplane fighter which first appeared in 1934. It was powered by a Panther XI radial engine, and in addition to a pair of prototypes three aircraft were flown by the Norwegian Air Force, numbered 405, 406 and 407. They were still being utilised as trainers in 1939 and the last one was not broken up for scrap until 1958.

S.E.5 A single-seat fighter designed by the Royal Aircraft Factory (q.v.) in 1916, the first example being received by No 56 Squadron RFC in March of the following year. Like its equally successful successor, the S.E.5a, it was armed with a single synchronized Vickers gun and a Lewis gun mounted on the upper centre-section. This latter employed a Foster mounting, a device which allowed the gun to be drawn down on a curved rail in order to change the ammunition drum and fire over the airscrew arc. It was perfected by Sgt Foster and Capt H. A. Cooper of No 11 Squadron RFC. Some 2,000 S.E.5/5as were built, including a small number in the United States. The aircraft's maximum speed with a 200hp Wolseley W.4a Viper fitted was 117.5mph.

Seacat A surface-to-air, ship-based, short-range missile, with limited surface-to-surface potential, capable of being operated in conjunction with a large number of guidance systems and having a high-explosive warhead. Produced by Shorts for the Royal Navy.

Sea Dart A shipboard surface-to-air missile (with a surface-to-surface capability) adopted by the Royal Navy in 1972. Powered by a ram-jet, assisted in the first stage by a solid-fuel rocket, it is homed by semi-active radar.

Seafire The shipboard version of the Spitfire fighter, adopted in 1941. The original aircraft, designated Seafire IB, were modified Spitfire VBs, some having clipped wings and prominent trop-

ical filters slung under the nose. The Mk IIC followed, being generally similar to the IB but with a type 'C' wing. The first sorties were flown during Operation 'Torch' by 801 and 807 Naval Air Squadrons, four more units receiving the type before the end of 1942. Although the aircraft was generally regarded as successful, Seafire undercarriages lacked the strength required for carrier work. The maximum speed of the Mk III was 353mph and the armament comprised two 20mm cannon and four 0.303in machine guns in the wings.

Sea Harrier Despite Britain's pioneering of practical 'jump-jets', the seemingly logical step of operating V/STOL Harriers from carrier decks escaped examination until February 1967, when the first trials were made with a Harrier from the deck of HMS *Hermes* in the English Channel. The success of these trials resulted in further investigations, leading to the approval of a fully navalised Harrier in May 1975, the first such aircraft making its maiden flight at Dunsfold on 20 August the following year.

The new variant included a radically changed forward fuselage with a 'bullet' nose, atop which was a cockpit raised to improve the pilot's view, while internal equipment now incorporated a fresh nav-attack system, more advanced avionics and a new weapons system and autopilot. The engine was an improved Pegasus 104.

It had been envisaged that the new Sea Harrier would be assigned an exclusively defensive role, but it soon became clear that such would not realise the aircraft's full potential, which could clearly also embrace strike and reconnaissance capabilities – hence the production aircraft's designation FRS.1.

The first front-line squadron to operate Sea Harriers was 800 NAS in April 1980, and this unit took its machines on board HMS *Hermes* in June the following year; 802 NAS was re-formed on 26 February 1982 and later embarked in HMS *Invincible*. These two squadrons 'blooded' the type with distinction during the Falklands War of 1982, their duties including low-level strikes against shipping and air bases in addition to interception.

Sea Hawk The first jet-propelled fighter design to emerge from the Hawker factory, and one of the many new and often revolutionary types that were ushered in by this new method of aircraft propulsion, was the P.1040, and this was adapted as the Sea Hawk.

The new production naval fighter had much in common with its predecessor, including the split orifice for the single Nene engine, a layout that released internal space for a fuel tank of copious proportions. Three prototypes were ordered, the first making its maiden flight on 31 August 1948, but it was not until November 1951 that the first truly navalised production machine made its début. The wing span had been increased from the original 36ft 6in to an overall 39ft and the area of the tailplane, too, had been increased, while the cockpit canopy had been modified. The later characteristic 'acorn' fairing at the junction of vertical and horizontal tail surfaces was still to come, in 1953.

The F.2 was not to appear until 60 F.1s had been produced by Armstrong Whitworth, the new variant incorporating powered ailerons, and after 40 of these had been delivered by the same Coventry firm the F.3 entered manufacture with strengthened wings capable of carrying two 500lb 'iron' bombs. The Sea Hawk F(GA).4 was the final version – the FB.5 and F(GA).6 were retrospective modifications of the F.3 and F(GA).4 respectively – which first flew in 1954 and was intended for the close-support role.

Sea Hawks saw service with twelve front-line RN squadrons, half that number seeing action in the operations against Egypt during the Suez Crisis of 1956. In addition three squadrons of the RNVR were equipped with the type, as were a pair of training units.

The standard armament of the Sea Hawk consisted of four fixed 20mm guns under the nose, and, in addition to the bomb load already described, underwing pylons could carry ten rocket projectiles or drop tanks. In 1956–57 22 export Mk 50s (F.6s) were supplied to the Royal Netherlands Navy; 34 Mk 100s (F(GA).6s) and 34 Mk 101 night fighters went to the West German *Kriegsmarine* and later 74 Sea Hawks were supplied to the Indian Navy, these last serving until 1977 aboard the carrier *Vikrant* and ashore.

Sea King See S-61

Sea Skua A British anti-ship missile introduced in 1982 and carried by Royal Navy Lynx helicopters.

Seaslug A medium range ship-to-air anti-aircraft missile carried by 'County' class destroyers of the Royal Navy. It was powered by a solid-propellant rocket with four wrap-around solid-propellant boosters which were automatically jettisoned as they burned out. Guidance was by beam-riding.

Sea Vixen A de Havilland two-seat, carrier-borne, all-weather fighter, this large twin-boom aircraft first flew in prototype form (as the D.H.110) on 26 September 1951 and was eventually accepted as a replacement for the smaller Sea Venom, although the original plan was that it would enter service also with the RAF as an advanced night fighter. In the event, its place was taken by the Gloster Javelin in the RAF. The airframe was re-engined with a pair of Rolls-Royce Avon Series 200s, and the first semi-navalised version flew on 20 June 1955, the delay since the appearance of the prototype being due to official indecision following the disintegration of a D.H.110 over Farnborough.

Time-consuming modifications deemed necessary included an 'all-flying' tail, increased wing chord outboard of the boundary layer fences and a reduction in the fin area, the curious offset cockpit and the 'buried' accommodation to starboard lit by a transparent roof hatch.

After 92 FAW.1s had been delivered, the FAW.2 was introduced. This had a considerably increased range, thanks to extra tankage in the tail booms, and a completely new armament system which permitted all-aspect collision-course interceptions.

The offensive armament included provision for four Firestreak air-to-air missiles on the FAW.1 or four Red Tops on the FAW.2, on wing pylons. On the outer wing pylons, 150 gallons of fuel in drop tanks, 1,000lb of 'iron' bombs or four air-to-surface Bullpup missiles could be carried, while unused accommodation in a pair of flip-out boxes under the cock-pit floor could take 28 folding-fin aircraft rockets. The last Sea Vixens were withdrawn from service in 1971.

Seawolf A high-speed, close-range anti-aircraft missile carried by Royal Navy frigates, guided by fully automatic radar control.

Searchlights Powerful lights for illuminating aircraft in flight first appeared before WWI, although originally they were seen principally as aids to maritime warfare. However by 1914, this attitude had changed and they were seen as useful both for illuminating aircraft and for battlefield signalling.

Naturally there were problems moving such a large piece of equipment, and in Britain a modified Napier motor-car appeared for Army use in 1911. The same year a similar vehicle, based on a Renault chassis, was introduced into the French Army to take the standard Harle light, which, having its own four-wheel carriage, could be easily off-loaded or moved as required. Italy, on the other hand, while utilizing farm carts for the actual movement of her searchlights, evolved special generator vehicles based on the Fiat 18BL to serve the lights.

In Britain, perhaps the most unusual employment of searchlights was that calling for them to be mounted on the upper decks of a small number of boarded-up, grey-painted trams that would patrol streets after dark, their operators keeping in touch with headquarters by means of an Army field telephone which could be plugged into sockets fixed to alternate tram-standards en route. Each anti-aircraft gun had a pair of attendant lights either of this type or fixed.

During the period between the two world wars searchlights became increasingly large, although British lights, either lorry-mounted or on individual eight-wheel caterpillar tracks, were never of great size, being generally 36in in diameter and giving 210 million candlepower. In contrast the Germans mostly used the large 150cm Flakscheinwerfer 37 light, the final examples being SLC radar-controlled.

Second strike An indication of the capacity of a nation to mount a second attack of a nuclear nature against an aggressor once the latter's own attack has been determined as imminent.

SEPECAT Jaguar An Anglo-French fighter-bomber developed from the Breguet Br.121 by the two countries who were also responsible for joint manufacture under the supervision of the specially founded SEPECAT (Société Européenne de Production de l'Avion ECAT) organization. Orders were also procured from Ecuador, India, Nigeria and Oman. Its first operational use was in the Central Africa, and developments continued with the trial fitting of LLTV (Low-Light Television) for night attacks and fly-by-wire. Indian-assembled versions are fitted with the Ferranti COMED map and electronic display. Powered by twin Rolls-Royce Turboméca Adour Mk 881 turbofans, the aircraft has a maximum speed of 1,065mph while the armament consists of two 30mm Aden or DEFA cannon with provision for 10,500lb of external stores.

'S' Gun See Vickers 'S' Gun.

Sherut Avir The Israeli Air Service, established in November 1947 and later organized into three squadrons, 'Galilee' (Galil) based at Yavneel, 'Tel Aviv' at Sde Dov and 'Negev' at Dorot and Niram (later Ekron). The service disbanded on 27 May 1948 with formation of Chel Ha'Avir (q.v.).

Shipborne aircraft The place was the North Sea, the time 1308 hrs and the date 31 May 1916 when a two-seat seaplane took off and headed north. Ten minutes later the pilot, Flt Cdr Rutland, accompanied by Assistant Paymaster Trewin acting as observer, reported back to HMS *Engadine* that the enemy had been sighted. He had approached low down as visibility was poor, at the same time making his aircraft a target for every gun on the three German cruisers and several destroyers which were below. Despite this, Short 184 seaplane 8359 returned unscathed from the first such sortie to be made in battle.

Launching aircraft from naval vessels was still relatively new at this time though it had been anticipated in the United States successfully in 1910, with the RN making similar trials three

Above: Two basic versions of the SEPECAT Jaguar, the GR.1 and T.2, were put into production for the RAF in 1970, the first for ground-attack and reconnaissance and the second for training. The first GR.1 was delivered three years later, having the distinguishing nose profile and fin-mounted electronic support measures fairing as seen here. The formidable armament of twin cannon under the fuselage could be augmented with external stores, including 600lb cluster bombs. The aircraft gave distinguished service during the Gulf War. (Author's collection)

years later from the old cruiser HMS *Hermes*, converted with a flying deck from which seaplanes had to take off with the aid of a trolley. In 1914 several ships were adapted for this work, including the former Cunard liner *Campania*, which was capable of taking ten seaplanes. Others would follow, including HMS *Ben-my-Chree*, probably the most famous of all. However, from a historical viewpoint, pride of place must go to HMS *Ark Royal* (later *Pegasus*, 6,900 tons), which, although conceived as a merchant vessel when laid down on 7 November 1913, was built from the first as a seaplane carrier for ten aircraft.

One of the first indications of the value of carriers took place in the Gulf of Xeros, where on 12 August 1915 a Short 184 seaplane from *Ben-my-Chree* flown by Flt Cdr Edmonds sank an enemy ship with a Whitehead torpedo, descending to only 15ft at a distance of 300yds to do so. The result of such an action was not lost on naval planners, and September 1918 saw the commissioning of the 15,750-ton HMS *Argus* (formerly the liner *Conte Rosso*), the first flush-deck vessel. Thus by degrees was evolved what is currently regarded as the accepted aircraft carrier, a large open deck occupying the entire length of the ship and the

greater part of its width, with an 'island' superstructure to the starboard side (on a small number of Japanese carriers it was to port) and with measures to prevent the overrun of landing aircraft such as athwartships arrester wires. The years of WWII were also to see the proliferation of such devices as catapults and RATOG (q.v.).

At the beginning of WWII Britain had a total of 115 catapult aircraft on warships and 225 on aircraft carriers, an increase of only some 125 over the number carried by the Grand Fleet in November 1918. The Royal Navy had eight carriers in commission with a total displacement of 126,000 tons, plus seven described as 'building and authorized' with a total displacement of 138,000 tons, thus presenting a picture unrivalled in Europe: France, with a single elderly carrier, was the only other country operating such a type. Elsewhere, Japan possessed no fewer than eleven aircraft carriers at the end of 1939, totalling 147,000 tons, while the United States had five vessels with a total displacement of 120,000 tons plus two representing 35,000 tons.

The strength of what was, relatively speaking, a new branch of naval/air warfare was not long in being demonstrated. On 11 November 1940 Swordfish aircraft of the Royal Navy

crippled the powerful Italian Fleet while it lay in Taranto harbour. The aircraft had been specially fitted with long-range tanks in the aft cockpit normally occupied by a third crew member in order to fly the 180 miles which lay between HMS *Illustrious* and the target. Twelve aircraft made up the first strike force, taking off at 2030 hrs, followed by eight (eventually nine) an hour later, the actual attack, led by Lt Cdr Williamson, being made through the balloon barrage at 1200 hrs. The squadrons involved were 813, 815, 819 and 824 NAS, the first and last having been temporarily transferred from HMS *Eagle*.

Realization of Japan's carrier potential came sharply to the West on Sunday 7 December 1941 when, without warning, a force of 350 bombers, torpedo aircraft and fighters of the First Koko Kantai attacked the US naval base at Pearl Harbor. They flew from six aircraft carriers and succeeded in doing great harm, sinking the battleship *Arizona* and damaging *Nevada*, *Oklahoma*, *West Virginia*, *Maryland*, *Pennsylvania* and *Tennessee*. Ten other ships were sunk or damaged; 188 US aircraft were destroyed, against 29 Japanese.

From 1942 aircraft carriers replaced battleships as the principal fighting vessels. The introduction of

Above: An F-9F fighter lands on the US carrier *Bon Homme Richard* during the Korean War. (US Navy)

jet aircraft required new technologies such as the angled deck (permitting overshooting aircraft to continue uninterrupted and not have their progress halted by the system of nets and barriers previously relied on), the mirror landing aid and the steam catapult. Of the six aircraft carriers added to the strength of the Royal Navy, *Albion* and *Bulwark* were eventually to be converted to Commando ships, but in February 1966 the British government announced that no new carriers were to be laid down to replace the four survivors, after the disappearance of which only *Ark Royal* (44,000 tons) would remain. The Royal Australian, Canadian and Indian Navies had one light carrier each, as did the Argentine, Brazilian and Royal Netherlands Navies while France built two new ships, *Clémenceau* and *Foch* (each 22,000 tons). The United States was at the same time maintaining a total of 25, fifteen of them attack carriers, including the nuclear-powered, 75,000-ton *Enterprise*.

With the passage of time, the superficial appearance of aircraft carriers changed little, but certain modified designs were commissioned, among

Above: HMS *Exeter*'s Westland Lynx helicopter, with folded rotor blades and rear fuselage, is carried on the vessel's after landing pad. (Author)

SOPWITH

them light carriers equipped with large quantities of electronic gear for the detection of submarines and helicopter carriers for use in amphibious assaults. Britain did in fact commission three new light carriers (*Invincible* class), and, equipped with a 'ski-jump' for the operation of Harrier V/STOL aircraft, the design showed its value in the 1982 Falklands War. Spain and Italy now operate carriers with a similar capability.

What seemed to be the ultimate in aircraft carriers appeared in 1990 as the USS *George Washington*, a vessel displacing 100,000 tons and capable of accommodating nine squadrons for a total of 80 fixed-wing aircraft plus helicopters. See 'Ski-jump'.

Short 38 A British single-engine, two-seat, pusher aircraft which was experimentally equipped with both wireless and armament before WWI. It was also the first aeroplane to take off from a ship under way, Lt Rumney flying one from a platform fitted over the bows of HMS *Africa* in December 1911.

Short take-off and landing See STOL.

Shrike A US air-to-surface missile designed by Texas Instruments specifically for attacks on enemy radar, using the emissions for homing on to the installation. Adopted by the US Navy in 1964, it carried a high-explosive warhead, had a solid-propellant rocket and had a range of some two miles. It was subsequently adopted by the US Air Force and by Israel.

Sidewinder Otherwise designated AIM-9, this air-to-air missile was first introduced for the forces of the United States and her allies in 1956 as the Sidewinder 1A. Homing by infra-red, it had a range of about half a mile when fired directly at a target in good visibility. The Sidewinder 1C, with a range of roughly two miles, used semi-active radar homing, unlike the later Sidewinder 1D which, solid-fuelled and with a range in excess of two miles, employed wide-angle infra-red homing. The name is taken from a species of snake.

Six-Day War A pre-emptive air strike by Israel at dawn on 5 June 1967 saw Mystères and Mirages attacking radar installations and airfields in Sinai. Mirages and Super Mystères were used for attacks against Cairo, the Suez Canal and the Nile Delta bases, and southern Egypt was hit by Vautours. Israeli aircraft later attacked bases in Jordan, Syria and Iraq. By noon 100 Arab aircraft were claimed destroyed, the claims at the end of the day being 240 Egyptian, 45 Syrian, sixteen Jordanian and seven Iraqi. Israeli losses were stated to be twenty machines.

'Ski-jump' The upward-sloping foredeck of an aircraft carrier which assists heavily laden aircraft into the air. This device, invented by Lt Cdr D. Taylor, gives an advantage similar to that enjoyed by a vessel steaming into a Force 7 wind.

Skip-bombing A technique developed to improve on the results of poor bombing attacks by B-17s against Japanese vessels evacuating Guadalcanal. It was first employed at low level on the moonlit night of 23 October 1942, again by US B-17s.

SKC Searchlight control radar ('Elsie'). See Searchlights.

'Slick' bomb A simple low-drag, free-fall weapon.

Slip wing During WWII the experimental Hillson FH.40 used a Hawker Hurricane with an additional strut-mounted biplane wing which was jettisoned when sufficient altitude had been gained despite its exceptional all-up weight.

'Smart' bomb A bomb relying on laser, infra-red or electro-optical guidance, sending back pictures of the target to a launcher who locks the weapon on to the image. In Vietnam Walleye bombs of this type were extensively used by the United States. They were released some ten miles from the target, thus reducing the vulnerability of the launching aircraft.

Snowflake An illuminating rocket flare used by the Royal Observer Corps in WWII to show fighters and AA guns the position of low-flying raiders and, later, flying bombs (q.v.). Also used by the Royal Navy whilst hunting U-boats. It was known by the code-name 'Totter'.

SOKO A state-owned aircraft factory at Mostar in the former Yugoslavia. Amongst the aircraft it produced was the piston-engined P-2 Kraguj light attack aircraft which entered service with the Jugoslovensko Ratno Vazduhoplovstvo in 1968. The aircraft had a short take-off capability of less than 120yds, and its armament consisted of two forward-firing 7.7mm machine guns in the wings and an assortment of stores on underwing strongpoints. The maximum speed of the Kraguj was 183mph and the range 495 miles.

Somme The scene of a major offensive launched by British and French ground forces on 1 July 1916. This was preceded by extensive air operations in which the Anglo-French air arms used 386 machines (138 of them fighting scouts) concentrated to relieve the pressure on Verdun and including D.H.2s, F.E.2bs and Nieuport 11s. At the same time the enemy employed a total of 129 aircraft (nineteen of them fighters). As a result of the Allied superiority, German observation balloons and reconnaissance aircraft were prevented from gaining a picture of the unfolding events. Aircraft were also used to aid accurate shooting by the artillery, while patrols sealed off the battle zone and contact patrols were carried out (though with limited success at first). On the German side, the experience gained was to result in the formation of Jagdstaffeln each made up of fourteen machines (from October these were chiefly the new Albatros D.IIs, which were superior to their Allied counterparts) in an attempt to wrest local air superiority over areas of intense ground activity.

Sonar See MAD.

Sopley An RAF station in Dorset originally known as 02G, surveyed for radar use in September 1940 for connection with RAF Warmwell (q.v.). By 1947 it was one of only 26 radar stations left and in 1955 it was equipped with the new high-power, long-range Type 80 radar.

Sopwith A British manufacturer of military aircraft founded before WWI, its products including, in addition to

Above: The Sopwith Camel is perhaps the most famous aircraft of WWI, being responsible for 1,294 victories in combat, a total greater than that of any other machine of the period. This is an F.1 model; the 2F.1 differed chiefly in having a dismountable rear fuselage, steel centre-section struts and a Lewis gun on the upper wing. Both types could carry a light load of bombs. (E. T. Maloney)

the ubiquitous Camel F.1 and 2F.1, the Cuckoo, Dolphin, Pup, Salamander, Snipe, 1½-Strutter, Triplane and Tabloid designs. No subsequent types were produced as the firm went into voluntary liquidation in 1921, being succeeded by H. G. Hawker Engineering Ltd,

An air arm is only as potent as the industry which supports it, and to illustrate this there follows a list detailing manufacturers contracted to build Sopwith warplanes during the period 1914–1919 (some of the contracts were cancelled without any aircraft having been built, chiefly because of the cessation of hostilities):

Great Britain
Air Navigation Company, Addlestone, Surrey
Arrol-Johnson, Dumfries, Scotland
Barclay, Curle & Co. Whiteinch, Glasgow
William Beardmore & Co. Ltd, Dalmuir, Scotland
Blackburn Aeroplane & Motor Company, Roundhay Road, Leeds
Boulton & Paul Ltd, Riverside Works, Norwich
British Caudron Company Ltd, Broadway, Cricklewood, London

Clayton & Shuttleworth Ltd, Stamp End Works, Lincoln
Coventry Ordnance Works Ltd, Coventry
William Cubitt & Co, Ham
Darracq Motor Engineering Co. Ltd, Townmead Road, Fulham
Fairey Aviation Co. Ltd, Clayton Road, Hayes, Middlesex
Fairfield Shipbuilding & Engineering Co. Ltd, Govan, Glasgow
Grahame-White Aviation Co. Ltd, Hendon, London
Hooper & Co, Chelsea, London
Kingsbury Aviation Co. Ltd, Kingsbury, Surrey
Mann, Egerton & Co. Ltd, Prince of Wales Road, Norwich
Marsh, Jones & Cribb Ltd, Leeds
Morgan & Co. Ltd, Leighton Buzzard, Bedfordshire
D. Napier & Son Ltd, Acton, London
Nieuport & General Aircraft Co. Ltd, Langdon and Temple Roads, London
Oakley Ltd, Ilford, Essex
Palladium Autocars Ltd, London
Parnall & Sons Ltd, Mivart Street, Eastville, Bristol
Pegler & Co. Ltd, Doncaster
Portholme Aerodrome Ltd, Huntingdon

Robey & Co, Lincoln
Ruston Proctor, Lincoln
Frederick Sage & Co. Ltd, Peterborough
Standard Motor Co. Ltd, Coventry
Vickers Ltd, Crayford, Dartford and Weybridge
Wells Aviation Co. Ltd, Elystan Street and Whitehead's Grove, Chelsea
Westland Aircraft Works, Yeovil, Somerset
Whitehead Aircraft Co., Feltham, Middlesex
Wolseley Motors Ltd, Adderley Park, Birmingham

France
Amiot-SECM, Colombes, Seine
Bessoneau, Angers
Hanriot, Billancourt, Seine
Liorė et Olivier, Levallois-Perret
REP, St Alban, Seine
Sarazan Frères, Puteau.

Russia
Duks, St Petersburg
Lebedev (VA), Novoi Derevnii, St Petersburg.

Sound mirrors The airship attacks against targets in Great Britain during the First World War by no means took the defences by surprise, although preparations to meet the threat were by and large apathetic at first since it was generally believed that the raiding Zeppelin was the ultimate weapon against which no defence was possible. However, by the second year of the conflict a more positive attitude had been adopted by the authorities and steps were taken to evaluate a means of locating raiders other than visually. Professor T. Mather and J. T. Irving of the City & Guilds Engineering College reasoned that the range at which the approach of enemy aircraft could be heard might be extended beyond that possible with the human ear by means of so-called 'sound mirrors'.

The first of these trials took the form of the excavation of a parabolic reflector 16ft in diameter in the face of a chalk quarry at Bimbury Manor Farm at Detling. It received sound waves captured by a centrally mounted stethoscope, and the best results of tests conducted in July 1915 showed that the note of a B.E.2c's engine could be picked up 2½ minutes before becoming audible to the unaided ear, the greatest distance at which this proved possible being 10½ miles from the coast. Encouraged by this, Professor Mather suggested continuing the trials with a movable, concrete-lined acoustic saucer set clear of trees, it being conjectured that, with its aid, detection of the increasingly familiar measured throb of a Zeppelin's motors would be possible at a range of twenty miles. No record has survived detailing whether such detection was ever attained, but it is known that trials with smaller devices at Farnborough, the Central Flying School at Upavon

and Capel proved insufficiently hopeful for the Royal Naval Air Service, responsible for the air-defence of the country, to continue them.

This seemed to be the end of the investigations, but records dated some eighteen months later indicate that a fresh look at the problem of detecting approaching aircraft by sound was being taken, whether by Mather or the Munitions Inventions Department is uncertain. A fixed sound mirror, 15ft in diameter and faced with concrete, was cut into the face of a chalk cliff at Fan Bay, between St Margaret's and Dover. The sound waves from the sides of this were picked up by a universally mounted 3ft trumpet at the centre, connected to stethoscopes graduated to show the bearing and direction of the sound. The focal point of the alignment of this device was mid-way between Calais and Dunkirk, and the trumpet, later doubled, was eventually replaced by resonators. Successful results from the Fan Bay mirror were reported during the night attack of 1 October 1917, when twelve Gotha G.Vs, later to drop bombs on London, were detected while still about twelve miles out over the Channel.

Investigations into the audible detection of aircraft by other means were, however, being conducted, and with the increasing successes enjoyed by the defences in combating air raids over England sound mirrors no longer received first priority. Some continued interest in the scheme resulted in the construction of a parabolic sound mirror of concrete in the vicinity of Dover. It was only 4ft in diameter and was set in a cast iron mounting which allowed movement in azimuth and elevation. A

similar mirror was set up at Joss Gap, near Broadstairs, Kent, together with another movable disc, this time measuring 12ft 6in in diameter, which was working by May 1918. Yet another, 20ft across, made from plywood and equipped with several microphones, was set up below the cliffs but was not ready for trials until 8 September that year, when it is reported as having detected a B.E.2e fifteen miles away and flying at an altitude of 3,000ft. All these were located in Kent, but similar trials were taking place elsewhere in England to cover enemy approaches across the North Sea. Two which still survive were located at Redcar and Boulby Cliff, their apparent purpose being to protect the Teesside factory at Skinningrove, the only steel plant in Britain to make high explosives at a time when there was a critical shortage of TNT. During the period when these Cleveland discs were erected – about 1916 – there were factories nearby producing a significant amount of mustard gas.

With the end of WWI, and in the light of the success of work developing more conventional sound locators, trials with sound mirrors were abandoned. They were revived in the mid-1920s by the Army Acoustic Section, and several differing designs were constructed, some as small as 15ft across. Two others measuring 25ft in diameter were set up at Greatstone, near Lydd, together with one of 30ft west of Hythe and another of 20ft at Lympne. Nevertheless, large as these were, they did not compare with the vast concrete wall, 26ft high and 200ft in length, constructed near Lydd, with which protracted trials were carried out under all weather conditions. The best results with these devices indicated that the sound of a twin-motor aircraft could be picked up at a range of slightly over 20 miles with relative ease, but it was impossible to eliminate other sounds, obtain accurate bearings or assess numbers, so although sound mirrors were used during the air exercises in 1934, the work was abandoned the following year in the light of the successful first trials with what was at the time known by the cover-name 'radio location' (radar).

This, it might be thought, was the end of the story, but surprisingly the idea was revived in a series of emergency trials which Post Office engi-

Above: A surviving sound mirror at Kilnsea, Spurn Point, near the mouth of the River Humber, where it was intended to give warning of raiders approaching Hull. (C. S. Parker)

neers were to undertake in 1943 in case it became necessary to reactivate the system of sound mirrors should the enemy find means of jamming Britain's defensive radar, although whether these envisaged discs, walls or a third form, slab reflectors, is not clear. Perhaps the last sound mirror to be constructed was 'Il Widna' (The Ear), erected on Malta during 1936. It took the form of a concave wall 30ft high and 200ft long, and it was claimed that with its aid aircraft taking

off from Sicily, 60 miles to the north, could be heard.

Officially, several types of sound mirror existed. It is important to note that a degree of interpretation of the plans by builders resulted – in some, even design discrepancies – but these nevertheless fell into three broad categories. Dish mirrors were a type particularly associated with Yorkshire, and from these the variants known as bowl mirrors were developed. Dish mirrors have also been described as Coast

Watchers and as Track Plotting Mirrors. Disc mirrors differed from the foregoing vertical type in being no more than concave concrete discs laid flush into the earth's surface in twin rows, spaced at three miles and individually separated by half-mile (later one-mile) intervals. These mirrors were also known as Listening Wells. The third and final type of sound mirror, and one which was adopted after the disc type ceased to be favoured in about 1934, was that already described as being in the form

SOUTH AMERICA

Of the eleven air forces dominating this region, that of Colombia was established as the air arm of the Army in April 1922, at much the same time that the Navy set up a flying-boat flight. It was not until 1943 that the Fuerza Aérea Colombiana took a separate identity, accepting US military aid in the form of Thunderbolts, B-17s and Mitchells five years later, before graduating to jets in March 1954, a single fighter squadron being formed with F-86 Sabres. These were replaced in 1970 by Mirages, operated both as fighters and fighter-bombers. A single squadron of B-26 Invaders represented the bomber arm until they were partially replaced by Lockheed AT-33s with underwing racks. While much of the FAC's time is occupied with internal security matters, coastal patrols on both the Atlantic and Pacific seaboards, at first made by Catalinas, were later carried out by Twin Otters, while Beavers and Hercules transports were reserved for communication and logistics work.

The Fuerza Aérea Argentina came into world prominence during the Falklands War, the indigenous IA.58 Pucará particularly achieving fame, but the origins of this service may be traced back to September 1922 with the setting up of a flying school using aircraft of French design. However, the really formative years were those after 1918, when an Italian aviation mission arrived with six Ansaldo fighters and four Caproni bombers. A French mission two years later contributed Dewoitine fighters and Breguet reconnaissance types. At the end of WWII 100 Fiat G.55 fighters brought the fighter arm up to date, and the bomber arm was modernized with the acquisition of 20 Lancasters and Lincolns. Much attention was paid to the transport arm – essential for such a vast country – with DC-2s, Bristol Freighters, Doves and Valettas being taken on charge.

Above: During the Falklands war one of the mainstays of Argentina's air force was the FMA IA.58 Pucará. This is a captured example. The prototype made its first flight in 1969, production models being intended for armed support, counter insurgency work and reconnaissance. The two-man crew was protected against ground fire by an armoured floor, the pilot also by the windscreen. (RNAS Museum)

of a 150–200ft curved wall, microphones mounted in a trench in front of this picking up the sound of approaching aircraft. This type was generally known as the Sentry.

Spad A French aircraft manufacturer of 19 Rue des Entrepreneurs, Paris, the name of which was an anagram from the full title of the organization – Société pour Aviation et ses Dérives. The company produced a range of aircraft during WWI which saw service with British, French and US air arms. The best known of these were the Spad S.7, the S.XI two-seater and the S.13, the first being also manufactured in the United Kingdom. The company combined with the Blériot organization in 1921.

Sparrow An air-to-air missile more correctly described as the Raytheon AIM-7E which was the standard armament for the McDonnell Douglas F-4 (q.v.) Phantom and is for a number other aircraft. It employed semi-active radar homing for guidance under a wide spectrum of weather conditions and was driven by a solid-fuel rocket motor, giving a maximum speed of around Mach 3 over a range of up to 35 miles and carrying a high-explosive warhead. The AIM-7F model was carried by F-14 and F-15 (q.v.) fighters.

Spitfire A British fighter design developed by R. J. Mitchell for the Supermarine organization, the prototype

Gloster Meteor fighters were later adopted. The FAA is slightly younger than the naval Comando de Aviacion, while the modest Army Aviation Command (Comando de Aviacion del Ejercito) operated largely rotary-wing types.

The Fuerza Aérea Boliviana, formed as a Corps of the Army in 1924 operating mainly French and Dutch military aircraft, is now chiefly a counter-insurgency force operating US designs. Four F-86 Sabres constituted the fighter arm in the 1960s and were later replaced by more modern types. A strong military transport force forms the greater part of the FAB, which is hardly surprising for a country covering 415,000 square miles.

The Fuerza Aérea del Peru is one of the best-equipped in Latin America, and there are additionally both Army and naval elements. With a mixture of French and British aircraft, the service was established with the assistance of France in 1919 and a separate maritime section was set up five years later, the two being combined in 1929. The first jets were received in the form of F-86F Sabres, followed later by Canberra bombers and Hunter and Mirage fighters devoted to the strike role, while the maritime element has lately concentrated on helicopters although retaining some fixed-wing types for ocean patrol.

North of this country lies Ecuador, protected by the Fuerza Aérea Ecuatoriana, one of Latin America's most modern air forces. It was formed with Italian aid in 1920 as a corps of the Army, and in subsequent years passed through much the same phases of equipment as its neighbours, leaping ahead in the 1970s when increased defence spending permitted the purchase of the first Jaguar aircraft to operate in the region, flying alongside Israeli Kfir fighter-bombers. Relatively small Army and naval elements are also maintained.

The largest area of South America, is the 3¼ million square miles of Brazil, the 600 or so aircraft of its Forca Aérea Brasileira ▶

Above: An Argentine Skyhawk pilot at the time of the Falklands War. The victory symbol under the cockpit indicates a British Type 42 destroyer with the date '12.5.82'. Records mention no such loss on that date. (Author's collection)

Above: Perhaps the most famous aircraft of all time, the Spitfire flew first in 1936, production running to twenty-two versions, the later ones exchanging their Merlin engines for Griffons and the original rifle-calibre machine guns for cannon, rockets and the ability to carry 1,000lb of bombs. The aircraft's performance made immense strides, and one variant or another served with a huge spectrum of the world's air forces, particularly after the end of WWII. The preserved Mk VC shown here carries No 310 (Czechoslovak) Squadron, codes. (R. W. Cranham)

SOUTH AMERICA

▶ making it one of the larger air forces in the world. The country is divided into six regional air commands, all based on the naval air foundations laid in 1913 and the French-established Army element of October 1918. The latter, now an autonomous force, operates a very large transport group supported by liaison, reconnaissance and attack elements, only a single unit being entirely reserved for interception duties, but the equipment is modern throughout, and is partly supported by an indigenous industry.

Neighbouring Venezuela is protected by the variety of widely gathered modern aircraft of its Fuerza Aérea Venezolana. This air arm dates from April 1920, although little official interest was taken until its re-establishment, under Italian influence, in the late 1930s. In the post-1945 period its equipment was dominated by ex-WWII US designs until an ambitious modernization brought the first Vampire and later Venom jets in 1950. Progress was maintained by the FAV, with the emphasis partially on transport and reconnaissance. There is also a naval element. Nearby Guyana (formerly British Guiana) operates the Guyana Defence Force Air Command, largely a liaison, transport and policing force.

Situated in the centre of South America lies the small country of Uruguay. The Fuerza Aérea Uruguaya, although established under French and Italian influence as long ago as 1916 and expanded throughout the 1920s when it could boast the possession of a small naval air element, has undergone little recent expansion and has continued to favour US designs, with the emphasis on liaison and transport. The Fuerza Aérea del Paraguay has been described as flying entirely second-line aircraft since the establishment of its air service in the early 1930s as part of its army, then locked in combat with Bolivia, but in recent years a small helicopter force has been founded to support the Navy.

Above: Canberra B-102 of the Fuerza Aérea Argentina.

(K5054) first flying at Eastleigh, Southampton, on 5 March 1936. A total of 23,000 production versions followed, many variants having a variety of armament replacing the eight machine guns of the first models, which were powered by the Rolls-Royce Merlin engines until supplanted by the Rolls-Royce Griffon. Other design changes wrought by Joseph Smith (who was responsible for the development of the design after Mitchell's death), included the introduction of a tear-drop cockpit canopy. Fighter, fighter-bomber and photographic reconnaissance (q.v.) versions were produced, many having a maximum speed in excess of 400mph. The Spitfire was used by a wide variety of air forces during and after WWII, and it served in most theatres.

SR.A/1 A single-seat jet-fighter flying boat, the only machine of its type ever designed, nicknamed 'The Squirt'. This Saunders-Roe aircraft showed no potential and was not proceeded with as it offered no advantages over conventional carrier-borne fighters. Three machines were produced at Cowes, Isle of Wight, the first, TG263, making its maiden flight on 16 July 1947 piloted by Geoffrey Tyson. This was followed by TG267, and the third boat was TG271, which was lost on 12 August 1949. Power came from a pair of Metropolitan-Vickers F2/4 Beryl axial-flow jets. The maximum speed was 512mph and the armament four Hispano V cannon.

Staffel A Luftwaffe flying formation with a nominal strength of nine aircraft, i.e. three or four Ketten or two or three Schwarme, roughly corresponding to a Flight in the RAF. During WWII this strength rose on occasion to sixteen machines. With three Staffeln to a Gruppe (approximating to an RAF squadron), making a nominal strength of 27 machines, a total of three Gruppen plus a Stab normally constituted a Geschwader (similar to an RAF Wing).

Stealth aircraft There are several ways in which the presence of an aircraft may be detected, and means of overcoming these for military purposes have occupied the minds of scientists almost from the pioneering days. The first of these is obviously by sight, and, in emulation of nature, the application of a concealing or at least disruptive camouflage has led to attempts either to break up the recognizable shape of an aeroplane or to cause it to blend into its background or surroundings. Alternative methods to make a warplane 'invisible' have involved covering the airframe with a transparent material, or applying dull grey paint overall to render the aircraft more difficult to see.

Detection by sound is another way in which the presence of an aeroplane is revealed, and while little could be done about reducing this in the days of the universal piston engine, jet propulsion allowed some modification of the noise emitted by the efflux since this is caused by the interaction of the

hot exhaust gases with the surrounding air. Careful attention to the design of jetpipes can speed the mixture of the two and lessen noise by several decibels without imposing the penalty of reduced thrust. Such methods can never eliminate the problem, however. Similarly, while infra-red emission can be lowered, this too cannot be completely eradicated.

Revelation by such methods apart, detecting the signature of an object subjected to electromagnetic radiation directed at it (radar) is now the most common technological means of confirming the presence of an aircraft. For long it seemed that there was no way of escaping this, other than by flying low and thus approaching beneath the field swept by the microwaves. In fact belief in the infallibility of radar was completely in error since James Clerk Maxwell, a Scottish scientist working about a century ago and thus long before the day of the powered flying machine, had developed a set of mathematical formulae, later refined in Germany and Russia, which indicated that certain geometrical configurations could scatter or deflect electromagnetic waves. It was this principle that was incorporated in an aircraft specification from the deputy director of Lockheed's Advanced Development Projects Department to produce a new type of military aeroplane as long ago as 1974, the work being based on experience gained in the evolution of the SR-71 Blackbird design of 1960. Trials with two test models proved the concept highly successful, and in con-

Above: The Saunders-Roe SR.A/1 prototype TG263, which first flew in 1947. The hood seen here was a replacement for the original 'tear-drop' canopy. (Author's collection)

sequence Lockheed embarked on a full-scale development programme which would eventually result in the F-117. Before this goal was reached each panel and component had to be individually blueprinted and matched with suitable radar-absorbent material, although the wider emphasis of the design was rather to deflect investigative radiation away from its source. Meanwhile a separate programme looked into the problem of masking the aircraft's exhaust.

The F-117 was eventually to materialize as the world's first operational 'stealth' combat aircraft. No prototypes were assembled, development work being instead carried out on the first five flight-test vehicles. These proved to be not the smoothly contoured and blended airframes expected, but probably the most angular machines ever to exist. The first aircraft made its maiden flight on 18 June 1981, this and all the following flight trials being carried out only during the hours of daylight. Nevertheless, the F-117 had become unofficially known as the Nighthawk or Black Jet.

On 15 October 1979 the US Air Force formed the 4450th Squadron for operational evaluation of the new

Above: The Northrop B-2 'stealth' bomber. (Northrop)

'stealth' type at the suitably remote Tonopah station, a former atomic weapons support facility which lay in a desolate location far from prying eyes. The decision to form three 'stealth' squadrons, of which the 4451st Test Squadron was the first, was soon to impose accommodation problems. A designation change dated 5 October 1989 gave existence to the new 417th, 418th and 419th TF (Tactical Fighter) Squadrons, the 417th becoming a TFTS (Tactical Fighter Test) unit, all subordinate to the 37th TF Wing.

There now remained the question of how the 'stealth' concept was to fit into operational policy, and official declarations on this point were shrouded in secrecy. The first stated that the role was to 'penetrate a dense threat environment with a high degree of survivability, in order to attack high-value targets with extreme accuracy'. Later it seemed that this announcement might be advantageously 'clarified' by a further statement that the purpose of the F-117 was 'to serve as a force multiplier, increasing the survivability and effectiveness of conventional forces' – in other words the Nighthawk was seen as a 'back-up' type for the immediate future, since by now the new 'stealth' fighter had been accepted for operational use.

The first demonstration of the aircraft's capabilities was inauspicious. On 20 December 1989, during Operation 'Just Cause' a pair of F-117s each dropped a 2,000lb bomb near the barracks of Manuel Noriega's Panamanian Defence Force at Rio Hato. In fact the bombs landed in a field adjacent to the supposed target, and the Air Force deemed it necessary to issue a statement that the intention of the attack had been to 'stun and confuse', a remark that triggered much speculation among the uninformed as to the value of the new aircraft.

Nevertheless, a start had been made. There was no reason to doubt the significance of the stealth fighter concept a little over a year later when the F-117 was used to deliver the first manned attack in Operation 'Desert Storm': using 2,000lb laser-guided bombs, the aircraft attacked the communications centre of the Iraqi Ministry of Defence in central Baghdad during the night of 17 January 1991,

flying from Saudi Arabia and flight-refuelling en route. Operations of like kind were to be carried out for the following six weeks, the aircraft approaching undetected to strike at selected targets with laser-guided ordnance.

Fighters may be depended upon to attract more attention than bombers from the laity, and the severe geometric appearance of the F-117 set fresh standards in 'stealth' technology. However, another design, this time a bomber, made its first flight on 17 July 1989. This was Northrop's B-2, serial 82-1066, and when it lifted off from Palmdale's runway for a two-hour series of handling tests before setting down at Edwards AFB the significant differences in appearance compared to the F-117 caused much comment. Here was a design closely based on the age-old concept of a 'flying wing' which was smoothly contoured at the centre but making no concessions to blending in the angular flying surfaces. It had four non-afterburning General Electric F118-GE-100 turbofans with curved intakes to shield the tell-tale compressor faces from radar energy, and shallow exhaust channels were arranged to blow back the gases across a section of the wing upper surface coated with carbon, thus dissipating heat and therefore reducing the bomber's infra-red signature. Offensive stores were carried in two weapons bays side by side under the main fuselage, each able to accommodate a CSRL (Common Strategic Rotary Launcher) capable of taking either B61 free-fall nuclear weapons or eight SRAM-11 nuclear missiles. The main attack sensor in the nose was a Hughes LPI (Low Probability of Intercept), a radar facility capable of detecting targets by means of very short and highly directed beams so that ground sensors were presented with little to detect and therefore adding to the B-2's 'stealthiness'. All this was contained in an aircraft capable of a 7,500-mile range which with in-flight refuelling could be extended to global proportions.

Like the earlier Nighthawk, the new 'stealth' bomber had a pronounced sweep of no less than 55 degrees to the leading edge of the flying surfaces, the trailing edges of which gave the aircraft a unique 'double-M' planform.

There were no vertical surfaces, control in this dimension being by means of four-section control surfaces embodying a split-drag rudder and elevon on each outboard panel and a pair of further elevons on each inboard surface. Two-man flight crews were expected to operate the type, accommodation being provided from the outset for a third member, all sitting on ACES-11 ejection seats which would fire the occupants through frangible roof panels.

It came as no surprise when there emerged from Russia, in the first half of 1993, details of 'Object I.42' – a 'stealth' fighter. With a superficial resemblance to the US F-22, this was a product of the Mikoyan design team and was in fact one of a pair, the Mongofunktsionalniy Istrebityl (multi-role fighter) and in fact the true 'Object I.42'. A second aircraft, the Mongofunktsionalniy Dalniy Perekhyatchik, or long-range multi-role interceptor, was a development which never proceeded: an airframe was constructed, but the powerplant was unreliable from a stealth viewpoint. Both types were seen as embodying new but unspecified radar-absorbent materials.

Differing from its US counterparts, 'Object I.42' had been designed to have directional control by means of conventional (and very probably fly-by-wire) rudders on vertical fins and to have leading-edge flaps, inboard flaperons and normal ailerons or perhaps elevons on the trailing edge of the wings, together with horizontal tail stabilators. Twin engines are known to have provided power, deeply buried within a smoothly contoured fuselage similar in appearance to that of the B-2 but with a raised cabin of conventional form, the whole blended into the inner wing panels and liberally covered in radar-absorbent materials. The individual cost of such an aircraft was estimated to be £30m, compared with the equivalent of £250m stated to be that for the B-2 – figures which seem to indicate that a vigorous sales campaign for 'Object I.42' would make wide-scale 'stealth' aircraft production relatively cheap!

STOL A term applied to a military aircraft designed to operate from a runway of reduced length. An example long in service is the Lockheed C-130 Hercules.

Stormovik (Shturmovik). See Il-2.

SVVS Sovietskii Voenno – Vozdushnie Sili (Soviet Military Aviation Forces). The original collective name for the air commands of the Union, made up of the Aviatsiya Dalnyevo Deistviya (Long-Range Aviation), the Isrebit-elnaya Aviatsiya P-VO Strany (Protective Air Defence), the Frontovaya Aviatsiya (Frontal Aviation), the Voennatransport naya Aviatsiya (Transport Command) and the Aviatsiya Veonnomorskova Flota (Naval Aviation).

Sunderland This flying boat was the military development of the civil 'C' Class Empire boat produced by Short Brothers and represented a major improvement over the slow biplanes such as the Singapore III it was to replace for long-range reconnaissance and anti-submarine patrol. The first Sunderlands were delivered in 1938, these going to No 230 Squadron at Singapore and No 210 at Pembroke Dock, but only three squadrons of Coastal Command were fully equipped with the type by September 1939. Soon

SOVIET UNION

The foundations on which the mighty Soviet Air Force were laid may be traced back to the motley collection of types, at first having a strongly French influence, that made up the air arm of Czar Nicholas II's Russia, although it is a matter of history that this was in small measure augmented by the aircraft sent to assist the White Russians by the RAF after WWI. Events springing from the October Revolution of 1917 by no means established a stable government, however, and it was in part the precarious nature of the new administration, with revolts in the Caucasus and the Ukraine necessitating the use of aircraft, coupled with open war with China in 1929 that set the pattern of the next decade as a formative one. Efforts to make the people air-minded were made with the formation of the Society of Friends of the Red Air Fleet, long-distance flights with an eye to their propaganda value and huge public parachute (q.v.) displays. It was not long before the VVS set up a significant bomber force, at first with such types as the TB-1 and later with the TB-3.

These years also witnessed the design and construction of massive bomber/transports. This work was instrumental in establishing an internal industry, so that there was no reliance on outside sources for military aircraft when Nazi Germany invaded in 1941. Such types as the La-7, Yak-1 and Yak-9 quickly gained a notoriety far beyond Soviet frontiers and dispelled the image of quaint fighting machines given by the appearance of such types as the I-16 in the Spanish Civil War.

Even so, warplane design technology was inferior to that in the West, and this tended to hamper Soviet entry into the field of jet propulsion after the German defeat until assistance came from an unexpected quarter in the complete revelation of British jet engine experience by the newly elected British Labour government, which believed that a world-wide Socialist brotherhood had dawned. Suspicious of the intentions of the United States, Communist Russia immediately set about modernizing and enlarging its air arm to become one of the mightiest in the world. Strictly speaking, there was no 'Soviet Air Force' with all military aviation under a single command, the various elements being controlled independently and in concert with the similar arms of Warsaw Pact member countries.

The numerically well-placed Soviet forces found themselves in good stead by the

Above: Representative of the Soviet WWII fighter arm, the LaGG-3 had a resemblance to Western designs. (Author's collection)

after the outbreak of war two machines (of Nos 204 and 228 Squadrons) were able to rescue between them all thirty-four members of the torpedoed *Kensington Court*, a tramp steamer discovered sinking off the Isles of Scilly. From June of the following year No 228 Squadron was operating the type over the Mediterranean, and by the next spring

No 95 Squadron was operating Sunderlands over the South Atlantic.

The Mk II was introduced towards the end of 1941 and at first resembled the Mk I externally, but later examples were to appear with a pointed, power-operated dorsal turret replacing the manual beam guns. The Mk III had the new defensive armament as standard, earning the aircraft the nickname 'The

Flying Porcupine' in *Luftwaffe* circles; it also had an improved planing bottom and frequently sported an array of twenty ASV Mk II aerials on the rear fuselage.

The first three Sunderland versions had been powered by Bristol Pegasus XVIII radial motors, but with the arrival of the Mk V Pratt & Whitney Twin Wasps were substituted. Examples of

---

1950s, not only as a result of the inauguration of a crash programme to develop nuclear weapons, but also because of an improvement in the technological quality of the equipment developed to deliver them. The once-restricted sphere of operations was extended, even as far as the Indian Ocean, a development some 'experts' in the West at one time refused to acknowledge, giving scant praise to the capabilities of such warplanes as the MiG-21 and the Tu-126. In addition to such potential as this, one of the Soviet air commands, the VTA, closely associated with paratroop forces, was taking delivery of very long-range transport helicopters and such impressive aircraft as the Antonov An-22, giving a global airlift capability.

If the emphasis of Soviet air planning seemed to be on deterrence, the defence organization was equally potent, the PVO

command being sub-divided into one section responsible for manned interception and the other for anti-ballistic missile measures. The naval air arm was not neglected, the Soviets having no fewer than sixteen vessels capable of taking aircraft as long ago as the late 1970s. This period saw the emergence, after a troubled gestation period, of the Yak-36 VSTOL single-seater. Meanwhile the land-based component was operating with such heavy long-distance types as the 'Bear' (q.v.), 'Blinder' and 'Badger'.

Then suddenly, as the world moved towards the final decade of the twentieth century, the Communist bloc took on a new political complexion, affecting the military climate of the Union in a manner undreamed of even six months earlier. What the future holds must depend on the results of the political manoeuvring that must develop and recede for many

years to come, but, short of the re-establishment of a politically united union of all the Russias, in the strict understanding of the term, the Soviet Air Force has now gone for good. See SVVS.

The RAF's Hurricane Wing in the Soviet Union

After the German attack on the Soviet Union which opened on 22 June 1941 (Operation 'Barbarossa'), it was decided that two RAF squadrons, Nos 81 (Sqn Ldr A. Hartwell Rook) and 134 (Sqn Ldr A. Garforth Miller), both equipped with Hawker Hurricane fighters, should be sent to support the Soviets as No 151 Wing, commanded by Wg Cdr H. N. G. Ramsbottom-Isherwood. Consequently ground crews embarked on the *Llanstephan Castle* and pilots and aircraft on the carrier HMS *Argus* sailing from Liverpool on 12 ▶

Above: Following a surprise appearance over Berlin, the new Ilyushin Il-28, known to the West as the 'Beagle', made its official début at the 1950 May Day Parade. (Author's collection)

Above: Britain's Short Sunderlands are rightly regarded as the finest flying boats ever built, entering service in 1938 and being still in use sixteen years later. Throughout WWII they were used for ocean patrol, not only over home waters but also over the Mediter-ranean, over the Pacific, in the Middle and Far East and off Africa and Iceland. The Mk V was capable of carrying a bomb load of 2,000lb. (RNZAF)

SOVIET UNION

▶ August, the total manpower of the Wing being 550 of all ranks, with 24 aircraft. These should have been armed with twelve machine guns apiece, but at first they carried only six in order to reduce weight, and when landfall was made on 7 September all were flown off. Course was set for Vaenga, some seventeen miles from Murmansk, where there was an airfield which consisted of a large plateau of rolled sand fringed with silver birches and was to be shared with a Soviet bomber unit.

The Wing was declared operational on 12 September and the first sortie was made the same day to intercept a Luftwaffe Henschel 126 reconnaissance aircraft which was escorted by five Finnish Bf 109Es. Three of the Messerschmitts were claimed destroyed, the first of a grand total of sixteen victories confirmed, with four probables and seven damaged, during the five weeks before 28

October, when No 134 Squadron was ordered to hand over its fighters to the Soviets and return to England. A month later the same fate befell No 81's aircraft, both units of the Wing eventually equipping the 72nd Regiment of the Red Naval Air Fleet. In RAF service, these Hurricanes, some of which were still fitted with air-intake filters for tropical service, were marked with a two-digit numeral aft of the Soviet-style national marking on the fuselage and a two-letter code forward, the first of these being that of the standard RAF system. Aircraft Z5227 was 'FE-53' and Z5159 'GV-55'.

Operationally, the aircraft's duties had evolved in such a way that No 81 Squadron had been concerned with interception and No 134 chiefly with bomber escort, and in order to extend the range at which operations could be conducted an advanced landing ground known as 'Afrikanda' was adopted. Meanwhile the personnel of both units were simultaneously employed in the training of Soviet pilots in preparation for the eventual hand-over (which had been envisaged from an early stage).

this variant, now redesignated MR.5, participated as transports in the Berlin Air Lift, landing on the Havelsee, while the post-war period also found these boats operating over Korea from Japanese bases, over Greenland and against terrorists in Malaya. The Sunderland also saw service in the French Navy and the RNZAF for patrol duties over territorial waters.

The final RAF Sunderland sortie was made from Singapore on 15 May 1959, the last home-based squadrons (Nos 201 and 230) having stood down at Pembroke Dock in January two years earlier.

T- US trainer designation.

TA (1) The WWII abbreviation for Target Area. (2) The US designation suffix for the three-motor 'Atlantic' transport based on the Fokker F.VII that was accepted in 1927 and joined the Marine Corps a year later. Since the designation conflicted with that for torpedo aircraft, it was changed to 'RA' (multi-engine transport) soon afterwards.

'Tallboy' The official name for the RAF's 12,000lb high-explosive bomb used in WWII.

Target-indicator A pyrotechnic device dropped to mark a target for following bombers.

Taube (Dove). A German reconnaissance monoplane of bird-like planform, based on an Etrich glider design. The type was widely constructed and modified under licence, and the name became a generic term for any German warplane of the WWI period. None was armed. One, flown by Lt Pluschow, was the sole type flown in defence of Kiaochow, the German colony in China, during August–November 1914, one was used during the Battle of Tannenburg and another dropped a small load of bombs on Paris. A variety of motors of about 100hp were fitted to the aircraft. An all-steel variant was known as the Stahltaube.

TG The designation for the US Naval Aircraft Factory three-float gunnery trainer of 1922. Five variants existed, identified as TG-2s to TG-6s.

Thomas Morse A US aircraft corporation formed on 31 January 1917 by the merger of the Thomas Morse Aeroplane Company of Bath, New York and the Morse Chaw Company of Ithaca, New York. The organization is best remembered for its Thomas-Morse S-4 biplane scout trainer, which, powered at first by a Gnome B9 rotary motor and in later variants by a Le Rhone C-9, superficially resembled the Sopwith Camel in exterior appearance. The ultimate variant was the T-M S-4E, which had sharply tapered wings of unequal span. The later MB.22, known to the US Air Service as the R-5, was a high-wing monoplane.

Thunderbolt See P-47.

Thunderbolt II See A-10

Thunderchief See F-105.

Thunderjet See F-84.

Thunderflash See RF-84

'Tiger Force' The RAF Lancaster, Lincoln B.1 and B.2 bomber force assembled for attacks on Japan in 1945 but which was never deployed due to the sudden ending of the war in the Far East, where operational conditions called for a new paint scheme consisting of entirely white upper surfaces and black undersurfaces. Six hundred of these bombers were in the process of being fitted for in-flight refuelling (q.v.), while an equal number of Lancasters were prepared to act as tankers.

Tiger Moth A British, de Havilland-designed biplane trainer, a number of which were modified as single-seat attack aircraft for anticipated use against German troops establishing bridge-heads in England following the expected invasion of the country in 1940. For this work 1,500 sets of bomb racks were produced by the parent company in very short time. These each took eight 20lb bombs and could be fitted beneath the fuselage immediately under the rear cockpit. The initial trials of this emergency measure (code-named 'Party Lights') were conducted by Maj Hereward de Havilland, and, had these machines been used in action, sorties would have been carried out by pilots of the de Havilland Flying School.

'Tojo' The Allied code-name for the WWII Japanese Nakajima Ki-44 Shoki (Devil-Queller) single-seat fighter, the prototype of which first flew in August 1940. The aircraft was found to be quite successful despite a heavy wing loading, although the poor forward view while taxying, caused by the massive radial engine, came in for unfavourable comment. The type was accepted for operational service in September 1942, when it proved the fastest fighter available to Japan. Three variants eventually existed, differing chiefly in engine type and armament, that of the Ki-44-IIIb consisting of two 20mm Ho-5 cannon in the fuselage and a pair of 37mm H-203 cannon in the wings. The maximum speed of the Ki-44-IIb was 376mph.

'Tony' The Allied code-name for the WWII Japanese single-seat Kawasaki Ki-61 Hien (Swallow). This type, which resembled a European design more

than its contemporaries in having tapered wings of high aspect ratio and a liquid-cooled motor, first flew in December 1941. There were eleven further prototypes and pre-production models, so that the aircraft was not accepted for operational service until the end of 1942. The first theatre of war in which it was encountered was New Guinea, where extended supply lines prompted the design of a simplified version, the Ki-61-I KAIc. In all, three variants were produced, although its engine trouble and production problems were never completely overcome. The fastest model was the Ki-61-II KAIa, capable of 379mph. This version was armed with a pair of 20mm Ho-5 cannon in the fuselage and two 12.7mm Ho-103 machine guns in the wings.

'Tillie' The Allied code-name for the projected WWII Japanese Yokosuka H7Y experimental 12-Shi flying boat.

Tornado A multi-role military aircraft (MRCA) produced by a consortium originally consisting of Britain, France, Germany, Holland and Canada, although the final pair withdrew on 26 March 1969. The aircraft was designed to meet seven major roles – close air support, battlefield interdiction, counter-air strike, naval strike, reconnaissance, air superiority and interdiction/air defence – the demands of this combination being met by the provision of a variable-geometry wing. When the first machine (D9591) made is initial flight on 14 August 1974, it rapidly became clear that here was a type which was destined to become a key operational aircraft for the remainder of the century and beyond. The RAF ordered 385, Germany taking 322 and Italy 100. A dual-control trainer followed in 1975, one of a total of nine prototypes delivered in order that simultaneous trials of armament, avionics, engine and handling could take place.

Control is by means of two large, all-moving 'tailerons', assisted for pitch and roll with the wings either in their unswept or intermediate positions at low speed by means of a normal fin and rudder, plus spoilers on the upper surfaces of the wings, all operated by means of a 'fly by wire' system. The engines are two Turbo-

Above: The Panavia Tornado prototype 03 here wears the colours of the nations involved in its development – Germany, Italy and Britain. Fitted with a complex variety of electronics and a fly-by-wire capability, and having the ability to take a wide variety of weapons systems, the type is among the most formidable military aircraft in service at the turn of the century. The Royal Saudi Air Force took delivery of their first example in 1986. The Tornado saw extensive combat against Iraq during the Gulf War of 1991, with the British, Italian and Saudi air forces. (BAe)

Union RB.199-34R three-spool turbofans, produced by a consortium comprising Rolls-Royce, Germany's MTU organisation and Fiat of Italy.

The standard internal armament was specified as a pair of 27mm Mauser high-velocity cannon suitable for either air-to-air or air-to-ground use, augmented by a very large spectrum of rockets, missiles and laser-guided or 'iron' bombs of many types. Accommodation is provided for a pilot and navigator in a tandem cockpit fitted with Martin-Baker Mk 10A zero-zero ejection seats, and the maximum speed is stated as being Mach 2.2 at medium and high altitude.

The name 'Tornado' was also adopted for a single-seat, single-engine fighter aircraft developed to replace the Hawker Hurricane. It was armed with twelve wing-mounted rifle-calibre machine guns and powered by a Rolls-Royce Vulture V with provision for a number of other engines, including the Bristol Centaurus. In fact only two prototypes were built, the first flying on 6 October 1939, but the aircraft may be regarded as heralding the Hawker Tempest, which gave good service during the Second World War.

Torpedoes Air-dropped torpedoes were based from the first on naval types strengthened to withstand the shock of impact on the water, but they carried more explosive in relation to their weight and travelled at higher speeds. Among the earliest trials were those conducted with a 14in weapon from Short floatplane 121 in July 1914, these forming the basis for the adoption of the 18in Whitehead, the Mk VIII weighing 1,423lb, containing 400lb of high explosive and capable of 42kts over a range of 2,000yds, and the shortened Mk IX of about 1,000-lb. WWII developments included the introduction in Britain of air tails, outrigger fins on a horizontal after surface ensuring a straight and level drop on the release of the cable from a tensioning drum, the standard method of dropping. Fixed-wing aircraft have always tended to carry a single torpedo, an exception being the twin weapons carried by the Heinkel He 111H-6 and modern ASW aicraft, although more than one torpedo may be carried by helicopters, the modern method of delivery ensuring a steady release from low altitude.

Toss-bombing A technique introduced about 1956 whereby a bombing aircraft runs in at as low an altitude as possible in order to minimize risk of radar detection, pulling up into a half-loop just short of the target. The bomb is released at such an angle that it falls on to the target in a semi-parabolic trajectory, allowing the aircraft to escape from the vicinity before detonation. Toss-bombing also obviates the problem of bombs striking each other during their fall and exploding beneath the aircraft which has released them.

'Totter' See Snowflake.

Torching A dangerous technique of 'dumping' fuel into an aircraft's jet efflux and using re-heat. This leaves a long, trailing flame, burning away perhaps 1,500lbs of fuel in a few minutes. It was used briefly at air shows by Australian F-111s, but was soon halted.

Towed fighter Both Britain and the United States conducted trials of this method of conserving a fighter's fuel, the former using four Gloster-built Hurricanes from Staverton, Gloucestershire, around January 1942. These aircraft were fitted with Malcolm hydraulic towing attachments under each wing, these taking a 'Y' towing bridle connected to a Wellington tug. The fighter would take off under its own power and the trailing cable would be grabbed by the Wellington. The pilot of the Hurricane then throttled back and shut off the engine to maintain tension. Similar trials in the United States are known to have featured a Curtiss SB2C Helldiver tug and Grumman J4F Widgeon amphibian. The desire to extend the range of a fighter aircraft by conserving its fuel led to other RAF tests with a Hawker Hurricane lifted on to a Consolidated Liberator. See also Mistel, Parasite aircraft.

Tracer Pyrotechnic ammunition leaving a visible trail as an aid to aiming a machine gun.

Tracking radar Also known as narrow-beam radar, this is designed to lock on to targets and follow them while a secondary beam oscillates round the target, making escape difficult. It is used by aircraft for missile guidance and by anti-aircraft guns.

Triplane An aircraft constructed with either staggered or unstaggered sets of three wings, one above the other, The layout was confined almost entirely to military aircraft of WWI, the best-known examples among the fighting scouts being the Fokker Dr.l and the Sopwith Triplane. Others included the Armstrong Whitworth F.K.6 and the Austin, Nieuport, Sopwith Snark, Hippo, Albatros and Pfalz single-seat triplanes, while larger multi-engine versions included the Bristol Braemar, the Sopwith Cobham and the Italian Caproni Ca.42 bomber.

'Trixie' German Ju 52/3m transports were erroneously believed to be in service with the Japanese forces during WWII and were thus allocated this code-name by the Allies.

'Trudy' The WWII Allied code-name allocated to the Focke-Wulf FW 200, which was erroneously believed to be in service with the Japanese Navy.

TSR-2 A British bomber designed to meet Operational Requirement 339 for the RAF on 1 January 1959, the original design responsibility going to Vickers-Armstrong, shared with English Electric. Nine pre-production models were ordered eight months later, followed by a requirement for eleven more in June 1963. The first example, XR219 made its maiden flight from Boscombe Down on 27 September 1964 and was then identified as a tactical strike and reconnaissance machine – hence the designation. Sophisticated electronic equipment made the TSR-2 the most potent military aircraft in the world, with a supersonic performance at low altitude and capable of speeds in excess of Mach 2 at altitude. It had a STOL capability and was equipped to operate away from main base facilities. Perhaps for political reasons, the programme was cancelled in April 1965

Above: With its Fokker opposite number, the supreme example of the triplane configuration of WWI was the Sopwith Triplane, this one being contract-built by Clayton & Shuttleworth and serving with No 1 (Naval) Squadron. (Author's collection)

Above: TSR-2 XR219 turns for a landing approach, showing its modern lines and bogie undercarriage. (BAC)

Above: TSR-2 XR222 was preserved but relegated to exhibition use, as seen here at Cranfield. (Author)

and no aircraft entered service. Of those built after XR219, XR220 was not flown, becoming 7933M; XR221 was broken up; XR222 was preserved; and XR223–227 were not completed.

Tu-20 See 'Bear'.

Turbinlite At first taking the name of its originator, Gp Capt Helmore, the Turbinlite was a 2,700 million candle-power GEC searchlight mounted in the nose of 31 modified RAF Douglas Havoc I night fighters with AI radar in 1941. Batteries were carried in the bomb bay and the aircraft were unarmed, their role being to illuminate a target while an accompanying Hurricane fighter was responsible for the actual attack. No 532 Squadron RAF first operated Turbinlite Havocs on 22 October 1941, following which a total of 39 Havoc IIs were similarly modified before the development of centimetric radar rendered them obsolete. The first to operate with No 534 Squadron (coded 'W' and former-ly No 1457 Flight) were BK882/'A', its light battery-powered only, and AW393/'B', carrying both batteries and a dynamo. Squadrons flying Turbinlite Havocs were Nos 530 to 539 inclusive. No 532 participated in Operation 'Subject' with non-Turbin-lite aircraft.

Turbofan A gas turbine in which air is ducted from the tips of the fan blades to bypass the main turbine. This is mixed with the jet efflux to give very high propulsive efficiency.

Turbojet A gas turbine engine which produces a high-velocity jet efflux.

Turboprop A gas turbine engine which, via a gearbox, drives a power take-off shaft.

U- The designation adopted by the US Air Force to indicate a utility fixed-wing aircraft. An additional use for the designation has been to conceal the true function of a type, e.g. U-2 (q.v.).

U-2 A Lockheed design for a high-altitude reconnaissance type which entered US service in 1954 but first leapt to the public eye when one was brought down by an SA-2 missile on 1 May 1960 while on a mission over the Soviet Union. The pilot, Garry Powers, was taken prisoner and tried for spying, The anticipated route had been from Peshawar in Pakistan to Bodø in Norway and the intention to photograph rocket sites in the Sverdlovsk area from 70,000ft. Two MiG fighters had been scrambled earlier in an attempted interception, one allegedly being brought down by a SAM intended for the U-2. A number of these machines were also used for weather flights, although those which were sold to Nationalist China were undoubtedly used for reconnaissance missions, one at least being shot down while undertaking such work. The U-2 was essentially a powered sailplane, so extreme lightness was chief aim at the design stage, and those used on photographic sorties were finished with a matt black dope consisting of millions of micro-

UNITED STATES

Seven years before the outbreak of WWI and less than four after the Wright brothers had first flown, the United States established on 1 August 1907 an Aeronautical Division of the Army's Signal Corps, this being renamed the Aviation Section on 18 July 1914. The country did not enter the world conflict until 1917, and it is small wonder that by this time only 1,000 warplanes could be mustered, few if any of them suited to battle conditions. A supporting industry scarcely existed on any scale, so American pilots on the Western Front were to fly almost exclusively French machines. By 11 November 1918 528 American-built DH4s were in France and 33 had been lost in action on the Western Front. The only US types to fly in action during the period being the Curtiss JN-4s used in support of the Army during General Pershing's Mexican Expedition of 1916.

By the end of WWI, however, US military aviation had been firmly established, a fact confirmed by the creation of the Army Air Service. Still subordinate to the Army, this was to be the cause of heated argument in the years immediately following when moves were tentatively made to establish an independent air force. The compromise was the creation of an Army Air Corps (q.v.) in the mid-1920s.

Something of the isolationist policy adopted by the United States in the inter-war years appears to have affected warplane design during the same period, since although some outstanding types were to enter service, it has to be said that few rivalled European aircraft, a fact confirmed by the swift relegation to either training roles or less demanding theatres of war of the machines ordered by various purchasing commissions in the closing years of the 1930s and undelivered by the time of the German advance across Europe. On the entry of the US into WWII some of the lessons experienced by the RAF, for example those associated with massed daylight bombing, had to be re-learned. Nevertheless, the Eighth and Fifteenth Air Forces were developed into a formidable fighting arm in Europe, and by 1944 the USAAF could boast a strength of nearly 2.5 million men. This was to diminish to 300,000 just three years later, but the influence of the force now spread throughout the world. Some thirty years later uniformed personnel totalled some 570,000, plus about 100,000 each representing the Air National Guard at home and the Air Force Reserve, all trained to operate the sophisticated weaponry which became available during the South-East Asia campaigns of the late 1960s and the opening years of the 1970s.

In 1910 the newly appointed officer in charge of naval aviation commissioned Glenn Curtiss to design and construct a pair of naval aeroplanes, the first taking to the air on 1 July 1911. The service had two qualified pilots at the time, Lts Ellyson and Rogers, and from these small beginnings seven pilots and five aircraft were available to participate in the Mexican campaign of 1916. A Naval Flying Corps, with 150 officers and 350 men, was created in August two years later. In the following April, 54 aircraft are stated to have been available, a number that had grown to 2,107, plus fifteen airships by 1918.

The end of WWI inevitably saw a reduction in the size of the Corps, but with the development of the aircraft carrier the naval air force was finally declared a component of the Fleet. Twenty years later the Naval Expansion Act legislated for the acquisition of a minimum of 3,000 aircraft (not all of them combat types), a total that had grown to 5,233, with eight carriers in commission, by the time of the Japanese attack on Pearl Harbor in December 1941.

Thereafter US naval elements tended to be grouped into the Atlantic and Pacific theatres until post-WWII cut-backs reduced the size of the force by some 50 per cent. Even so, the US Navy was to see action in the Korean, Vietnam and Gulf Wars, the last, especially, indicating the importance of swiftly deployed shipborne (q.v.) air forces with modern weapons at their disposal.

scopic balls to combat the reflections of intercepting radar.

U-502 The first German submarine to be sunk by an aircraft equipped with a Leigh Light (q.v.), the action taking place on 6 July 1942 in the Bay of Biscay, where the submarine was encountered making for its home port after operations in the Caribbean. This was one of ten successes claimed by No 172 Squadron RAF flying Vickers Wellingtons equipped with airborne searchlights. The pilot on this historic occasion was P Off W. B. Howell, an American volunteer who was to transfer to the US Navy in December. No 172 was the first unit to be equipped with Leigh Lights. Other squadrons detailed to hunt U-boats with Leigh Light Wellingtons were Nos 179, 612, 407, 304, the first at one time flying Warwicks. Nos 210 and 202 with Catalinas were also equipped, as were Nos 53, 120, 206, 220, 224 and 547 with Liberators.

UE Unit Establishment. A WWII RAF term introduced to cover and replace the former designations IE (Initial Establishment: the number of aircraft a squadron was expected to have available for operations) and IR (Initial Reserve: the number of machines a squadron was allowed to hold in reserve).

'Ultra' A term employed throughout WWII and the following years to describe the British system of breaking German 'Enigma' communication codes (produced by an encyphering machine), using cryptanalysis. This first proved its value during the air fighting over the British Isles in the summer of 1940, so that the Air Officer Commanding-in-Chief at Fighter Command had prior knowledge of the Luftwaffe's plans. The machine used for this work had been developed in Holland, the patent being bought by a German manufacturer in 1923. One fell into Polish hands en route to the German Legation in Warsaw and the information was passed on to Britain.

USAAC United States Army Air Corps The new title, adopted on 2 July 1926, for the former US Army Air Service which had been created on 24 May 1918.

USAAF United States Army Air Forces, created on 20 June 1941.

USAF United States Air Force. A totally independent service with similar status to the Army and Navy, created on 18 September 1947, its major Commands being SAC (Strategic Air Command), TAC (Tactical Air Command), ADCOM (Aerospace Defense Command), MAC (Military Airlift Command), USAFE (USAF Europe), PACAF (Pacific Air Forces) and AAC (Alaskan Air Command), supported by ATC (Air Training Command), AFSC (Air Force Systems Command), AFLC (Air Force Logistics Command), AFCS (Air Force Communications Service) and AU (Air University).

US Eighth Air Force Bases in Britain, June 1944

No	Base	Aircraft
1	Abbotts Ripton	
2	Alconbury	B-17
3	Atcham	P-47
4	Attlebridge	B-24
5	Bassingbourn	B-17
6	Bodney	P-47
7	Bottisham	P-47
8	Bovingdon	B-17
9	Boxted	P-47
10	Brampton Grange	
11	Bungay	B-24
12	Bushey Hall	
13	Bury St Edmunds	B-17
14	Cheddington	B-24
15	Chelveston	B-17
16	Debach	B-24

Above: B-17G 232083 of the 730th Bomber Squadron, 452nd Bomber Group, at Digby. (Author's collection)

17	Debden	P-51
18	Deenethorpe	B-17
19	Deopham Green	B-17
20	Duxford	P-47
21	East Wretham	P-47
22	Elveden Hall	
23	Eye	B-24
24	Fowlmere	P-51
25	Framlingham	B-17
26	Glatton	B-17
27	Goxhill	P-38, P-51
28	Grafton Underwood	B-17
29	Great Ashfield	B-17
30	Halesworth	B-24
31	Hardwick	B-24
32	Harrington	B-24
33	Hethel	B-24
34	High Wycombe	
35	Hitcham	
36	Honington	P-38
37	Horham	B-17
38	Horsham St Faith	B-24
39	Ketteringham Hall	
40	Kimbolton	B-17
41	King's Cliffe	P-38
42	Knettishall	B-17
43	Lavenham	B-17
44	Leiston	P-51
45	Martlesham Heath	P-47
46	Mendlesham	B-24
47	Metfield	B-24
48	Molesworth	B-17
49	Mount Farm	F-5, Spitfire
50	Neaton	
51	North Pickenham	B-24
52	Nuthampstead	B-17
53	Old Buckenham	B-24
54	Oulton	B-17
55	Podington	B-17
56	Polebrook	B-17
57	Rackheath	B-24
58	Rattlesden	B-17
59	Raydon	P-47
60	Ridgewell	B-17
61	Seething	B-24
62	Shipdham	B-24
63	Snetterton Heath	B-17
64	Steeple Morden	P-51
65	Sudbury	B-24
66	Thorpe Abbotts	B-17
67	Thurleigh	B-17
68	Tibenham	B-24
69	Troston	
70	Wattisham	P-38
71	Watton	B-17, B-24, Mosquito
72	Wendling	B-24
73	Wormingford	P-38

US EIGHTH AIR FORCE BASES IN BRITAIN, JUNE 1944

Above: The dorsal Martin turret with twin 0.50in machine guns in a Consolidated B-24. (Author's collection)

Luftwaffe Interceptions of Eighth Air Force Missions, March–December 1944

	Days on which interceptions were made	Number of Bombing sorties flown
March	11	1,530
April	9	2,010
May	10	3,070
June	3	570
July	8	1,080
August	7	830
September	5	1,890
October	4	420
November	4	1,870
December	3	830

V- A US Navy designation adopted in 1962 to indicate a STOVL aircraft type.

V-1 See Flying bomb.

Valiant The first of the three British V-bombers to enter service, No 138 Squadron, based at Gaydon, Warwickshire, being equipped with the type in 1955. The first operations by the four-jet Vickers design were carried out during the Anglo-French dispute with Egypt in October–November 1956 when the type, based at Luqa, Malta, dropped normal HE bombs. A Valiant from No 49 Squadron was the first British aircraft to drop an operational atomic bomb (q.v.), over Maralinga, South Australia, on 11 October 1956.

Variable-geometry A reference to a warplane designed with the ability to vary the sweep of its wings during flight, permitting a low angle for take-off and slow flight or landing and a greater one for high speed. An early example was the Grumman XF10F jet fighter, but only one of these was built.

Variable incidence The ability of a warplane to change the angle of inci-dence of its flying surfaces in flight. The Vought F-8 Crusader carrier fighter had this facility for its wings and the McDonnell Douglas F-15 fighter, among others, for its tailplane. In the case of the former, a selection of two positive angles (which varied according to the sub-type) was possible with the wing pivoted at its main spar, and when this angle was raised to the maximum, ailerons, flaps and dogtooth wing leading edges all automatically drooped to 20 degrees.

VCP An abbreviation for Visual Control Post. These were used by the British Army towards the end of WWII, set up by advanced troops to direct strike aircraft held on 'cab rank' duty to specific targets.

Very A flare or smoke cartridge used for pyrotechnic signalling when fired by hand from a 1.5in bore Very pistol. The name is taken from that of the inventor, S. W. Very.

V-Force V-bombers, the name being based on the delta/swept-wing planform of the aircraft, the Avro Vulcan, Vickers Valiant and Handley Page Victor were selected from six types prepared to Specification B.35/46, which, among other demands, called for a bomber with a still-air range of 5,000 miles and an over-target altitude of 50,000ft, a blind-bombing capability with the aid of H2S, high manoeuvrability and the ability to deliver a 10,000lb nuclear device. All this was based in part on OR (Operational Requirement) 229 of 1947, originally calling for a minimum speed of 500kts at 45,000ft and a still-air range of 3,500 miles, envisaging a four-jet Avro Lincoln replacement.

It was coincidental that the entry of the Vulcan into service should take place at the same time as the successful trial detonation of the Yellow Sun (q.v.) atomic weapon, the destructive power of which was said to equal the total of all the high explosive dropped by the RAF in WWII. These free-fall bombs, together with the later Blue Steel stand-off weapons, formed Britain's nuclear deterrent until 1968, when the role was assumed by four Royal Navy nuclear-powered submarines each carrying sixteen Polaris A3 missiles. The bombers, 140 of which were available at the end of 1962, were initially distinguished by an all-white, anti-flash paint scheme with national markings of reduced colour intensity and were camouflaged for low level during 1962–63.

The organization of the deterrent meant that, depending on the prevailing political climate, a striking force representing 80 per cent of the available aircraft were ready for dispatch within twelve hours, although each station had to maintain a number of bombers at fifteen minutes' readiness. The survival of the force and its striking power depended on the aircraft becoming airborne in the minimum time, so that during periods when a Quick Reaction Alert (QRA) was declared, machines at their Operational Readiness Platforms (ORPs) were held on stand-by with crews already aboard.

After the deterrent responsibility was assumed by the Royal Navy, the RAF's V-Force, now totally composed of Vulcan bombers, took on a low-level role for penetration below an enemy's radar. The offensive loads would now have been conventional high-explosive free-fall bombs.

The original ten top-class airfields for bombers capable of delivering a nuclear weapon in response to a similar attack being made on the country consisted at first of 9,000ft runways with hardstandings and taxyways but were later improved with the provision of Operational Readiness Platforms (ORPs) each capable of taking four aircraft. In this way the original QRA time of four minutes was cut to less than two, thus ensuring that all aircraft could be in the air before a pre-emptive ICBM strike had its effect. These airfields were Coningsby (Vulcan), Cottesmore (Victor), Finningley (Vulcan/Victor), Gaydon (Valiant/Victor), Honington (Valiant/Victor), Marham (Valiant), Scampton (Vulcan), Waddington (Vulcan), Wittering (Valiant/Victor) and Wyton (Valiant). In addition, 26 dispersal airfields were upgraded to Class 1 standard and the squadrons at the ten permanent bases were rotated around these (as well as to airfields overseas) so that the location of the V-Force could not be predicted by a potential enemy: Aldergrove, Bedford, Boscombe Down, Brawdy, Burtonwood, Cranwell, Elvington, Filton, Kemble, Kinloss, Leeming, Leconfield, Leuchars, Llanbedr, Lossiemouth, Lyneham, Machrihanish, Manston, Middleton St George, Pershore, Prestwick, St Mawgan, Shawbury, Tarrant Rushton, Valley and Yeovilton.

Vickers A British aircraft and arms manufacturer, the first notable aeroplane from which was the Gun Bus fighting scout of 1915, a type of pusher design in order to give a clear field of fire for the front-mounted gun. By the end of WWI the firm was producing the very different Vimy bomber, a huge aircraft for its day intended to carry the war deep into Germany. Too late to see operational service, it was to become the RAF's standard heavy bomber, remaining in use, although ultimately as a trainer, until 1931. Meanwhile work was proceeding on such designs as the Vildebeest torpedo bomber, two squadrons of which survived in Singapore to meet the Japanese threat in 1941.

Based on knowledge thus gained, the design team turned to troop carriers, the Vernon serving from 1921 until superseded five years later by the 22-man Victoria, which was in turn replaced in 1934 by the Valentia development. The Wellesley single-engine monoplane bomber of 1935 introduced the new geodetic construction, perfected in the Wellington bomber of WWII and the subsequent Warwick transport and general reconnaissance aircraft. The final Vickers design for a military type to be adopted before the company was merged into the British Aircraft Corporation in 1960 was the Valiant (q.v.) V-bomber.

In 1928 Vickers had acquired Supermarine and was thus responsible for the continued output of that organization under its separate name, including the development of the Spitfire, Seafire, Attacker, Swift and Scimitar.

Vickers 'K' Gun Vickers machine guns were all based on the Maxim design, the patents of which were purchased by Vickers in 1892. All the new weapons had a slower rate of fire than the original's 600rds/min, and the British Army's 0.303in weapon was no exception. The 'K' gun was little more than a lightened version of this, shorn of its water jacket, and formed the flexibly mounted defensive armament for most of the RAF's 1930s-designed types in service in the early days of the Second World War. It was sometimes described as the Vickers gas-operated gun from the fact that it came from a whole family of similar weapons in which, expressed simply, gases from a fired round also caused the barrel to recoil, the empty cartridge case to be extracted and the belt moved to bring a fresh round into the breech. Vickers redesigned this action utilising shallower, and therefore lighter, breech cases.

Vickers 'S' Gun A 40-mm cannon fitted externally to British Hawker Hurricane (q.v.) IIDs for anti-tank attacks during WWII and also experimentally to the P-51 (q.v.) Mustang.

Victor A Handley Page design produced as part of Britain's V-bomber programme. Significant for its crescent wing and high-set tailplane, the prototype first flew on Christmas Eve 1952 and three years later the aircraft was declared to be capable of flying at just under Mach 1. The first examples were delivered to No 232 Squadron at Gaydon, Warwickshire, on 28 November 1957. The design was later adapted to serve as an in-flight refu-

Above: Saab Viggen '02' makes a landing approach, September 1972. (Author)

6373

Above: Until the production of the Panavia Tornado, the Saab 37 Viggen was the most advanced combat aircraft ever to be produced in Europe. A canard design with a 400sq ft wing area, it had a STOL capability and was available in five versions, of which the AJ, a single-seat all-weather attack variant, is illustrated. The aircraft, which could fly at Mach 2, first entered service in 1971. External stores could be carried on seven (optionally nine) pylons. (Author's collection)

elling tanker, and a strategic reconnaissance version, the Victor SR.2, also existed.

'Viffing' An acronym for vectoring in forward flight, a tactical manoeuvre adopted by Harrier pilots in which an enemy in pursuit was surprised as a Harrier altered direction vertically by the use of the appropriate jet thrust, rising out of the firing line and allowing the enemy to overshoot, thus placing him in a disadvantageous position.

Viggen The Swedish Saab J37 canard multi-role combat aircraft, which first flew on 8 February 1967. The configuration of the aircraft gave excellent STOL (q.v.) capability, enabling it to operate if necessary from runways on roads 500yds in length. Equipment in all five versions included a head-up display for the pilot, automatic throttle/speed control for approach, no-flare autopilot landing and thrust reversal, making the Viggen in its time one of the most advanced warplanes in the world. The chief versions were the AJ all-weather attack fighter, the JA all-weather fighter, the SF armed photo-reconnaissance version, the SH for armed maritime reconnaissance aircraft and the SK two-seat tandem conversion trainer. The maximum theoretical speed (clean) was 1,320mph and the range over 600 miles. The armament included a 30mm Oerlikon KCA cannon and a maximum of 13,200lb of offensive stores, or Rb.27, Rb.28 or Rb.324 missiles on external pylons.

Vought A US aircraft manufacturer which, as Lewis & Vought, delivered its first military aircraft to the Navy in 1918. This was the VE-7, an advanced biplane trainer designed in response to a call from the Aircraft Production Board to break away from the custom of relying on modified European types. The machine was produced in large numbers after the end of the First World War, a large-scale production programme being entered into in the early 1920s, when the company became known as the Chance Vought Corporation, perpetuating the name of its founder Chance M. Vought.

This association with maritime requirements was still evident into the 1930s, when the US Navy adopted the new SBU scout bomber for carrier operations. The SBU was to be Vought's last naval biplane, since the next design was the SB2U, an all-metal, low-wing, carrier-based scout and dive-bomber with a Pratt & Whitney radial motor and the crew of two accommodated under a long transparent canopy. Designed by R. B. Beisel, this was known as the Vindicator in the USN and as the Vought-Sikorsky Chesapeake in the RAF during the Second World War. A number were also delivered to France, these falling into Nazi hands in 1940; it has been alleged, but never confirmed, that a small number were used by the enemy for attacks on Dover in the same year.

Wartime Vought designs, again used by both the US and Britain,

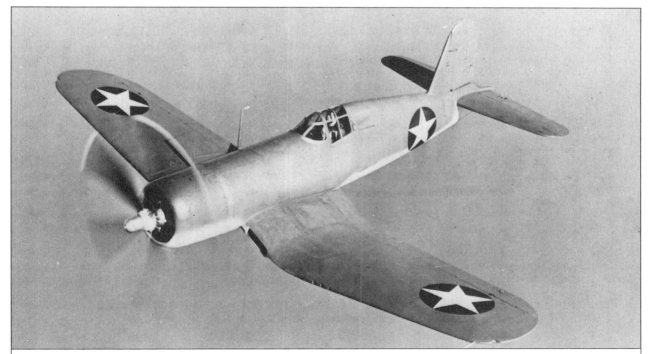

Above: The first Vought F4U-1 Corsair single-seat carrier-borne fighters (as shown here) were delivered in October 1942 and, serving with the US and Royal Navies, proved to be among the greatest combat aircraft in history. The aircraft's maximum speed in its ultimate F4U-5N form was 470mph at 26,800ft, this in part being due to its powerful engine, driving the largest propeller ever fitted to a fighter. It was still in use in the Korean conflict, armed with cannon and used in the AU-1 version as an attack bomber with a warload of 4,000lb. In addition, photographic reconnaissance and an 'N' version for night interception, with wing pods carrying APS-4 or -6 radar, existed.
(Bruce Robertson collection)

included the Kingfisher, an alternative to the variant with a wheeled undercarriage having a novel (but not unique) central float beneath the fuselage with smaller outriggers for lateral balance, while a contemporary flown by the Royal Navy, the US Navy and France's *Aéronavale* was the Corsair, a single-seat, carrier-based fighter with distinctive cranked wings. The F4U Corsair was introduced in 1942, and the last example was not rolled off the production line until ten years later.

The field of jet propulsion found Vought making use of the mass of German aeronautical research available after the end of the Second World War, the result being the Cutlass fighter, with its almost constant chord wings with elevon control and a sweepback of 38 degrees, armed with four fixed 20mm forward-firing guns and provision for a quartet of missiles. The highly advanced A-7 Corsair II, suitable for ground support or hi-lo-hi and hi-lo-lo-hi ground attacks with a

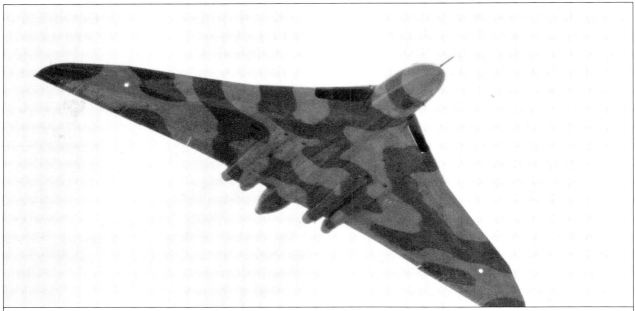

Above: The final representatives of the RAF's V-bomber force were the Vulcans which, when they were part of the British nuclear deterrent, were finished entirely in anti-flash white with national markings of reduced intensity. (F. Wood)

Above: When responsibility for the nuclear deterrent passed to the Royal Navy, Vulcans took on a low-level role and an overall disruptive camouflage scheme was applied. (F. Wood)

huge variety of stores to a maximum load of 3,000lb, is still in service at the end of the century.

Vulcan Probably the best-known of Britain's three V-bomber designs, the delta-winged Avro Vulcan first flew in prototype form on 30 August 1953, the first production model following in February 1955. A later model featured a wing with a compound taper on the leading edge – the so-called 'double delta'. The first operational squadron to receive the type was No 83 at Waddington in the summer of 1957, although the aircraft had leapt to public prominence the previous year with a flight to Australia taking only 23hr 9min. The Vulcan formed the backbone of Britain's nuclear deterrent and was later adapted for low-level work. The SR.2 strategic reconnaissance variant appeared in 1973. See V-Force.

WAAF See Women's Auxiliary Air Force.

Walleye A US air-to-surface missile employing television guidance. This Martin-built weapon, introduced in 1969, was fitted with a high-explosive warhead and was intended for use against hard-surface targets.

Warmwell An RAF fighter station in Dorset at which were based, among other units, Nos 152 and 609 Squadrons in 1940. From March 1944 it operated Lockheed P-38 Lightnings of the US Ninth Tactical Air Force. Air–sea rescue Walrus amphibians were also based there. See Sopley.

Wasp Subsequently known as a Westland helicopter design, the type originally emanated from Saunders Roe and made its first flight on 20 July 1958. It was adopted for the British Army as the Scout in 1960, this variant differing in that a skid undercarriage was fitted, and by the RN two years later. The type was also used by the navies of Brazil, the Netherlands, New Zealand and South Africa. Two Mk 44 anti-submarine torpedoes could be carried, the maximum speed was 131mph and the range was 270 miles.

WASP Women's Airforce Service Pilots. With its headquarters at New Castle Army Air Base near Wilmington, Delaware, this US service was created in 1941 for non-combatant home duties in order to free men for other work and at its peak reached a total of 1,074 pilots, who had to have flown a minimum of 500 hours before volunteering. On 1 January 1942, twelve months before the service was disbanded, the grand total of hours flown by its members was 3,000,000.

Wellington See Vickers.

Wessex The Westland-built version of the Sikorsky S-58 (q.v.) helicopter, some 150 being used for anti-submarine work by the RN. The first, HAS.1 version was replaced by the HAS.3, unofficially known as 'The Camel' because of its radar hump, while about 100 HAS.5s were used for Commando assault work. The type was also used by Australia, Brunei and Ghana. The armament could include two torpedoes for HAS (Helicopter, Anti-Submarine) use. The maximum speed was 121mph and the range 390 miles.

Westland A British aircraft manufacturer originating from Petters Engineering of Yeovil in April 1914. Early warplanes included the N.16 and 17 floatplanes, the Wagtail single-seat reconnaissance biplane and the two-seat Weasel, which were followed by the revolutionary high-wing Wizard fighter design and the heavily-armed COW gun fighter. The first types to be ordered in large numbers, however, were the Wallace and Wapiti of the mid-1930s, and the end of the decade saw the emergence of the Lysander, originally intended for army cooperation work and distinguished by its early form of STOL, made possible by its slotted flaps. Westland's WWII fighter designs were, first, the single-seat, twin-motor Whirlwind, a carefully guarded secret despite the enemy's being in possession of full details. Used as a 'Whirlibomber' on cross-

Above: Westland Lysander 'A' of No 26 (RM) Squadron takes off from St Margaret's Bay, Dover, where it was kept in 1940 to set alight, with phosphorus bombs, petrol pumped on to the sea had a German invasion been attempted. (A. E. Jessop)

Above: AS-11 missiles carried by a Westland Scout AH.1 helicopter. (Author)

Left: Royal Navy Westland Sea King HAS.5 ZA136(51) leads another of the same type off the coast of Cornwall. (Author)

Channel 'Rhubarb' (q.v.) operations, it was issued only to Nos 137 and 263 Squadrons. Later came the high-altitude Welkin fighter. After WWII the company built the Wyvern before it tended to specialize in helicopters.

West Malling A 47-acre RAF station in Kent, opened for private use in 1930 although, as Kings Hill, it had been a Second Class landing field during WWI. Officially taken over as a station headquarters for No 26 (Army Co-operation) Squadron with Lysanders and No 51 Wing on 8 June 1940, it operated as a fighter station (No 141 Squadron Defiants) from 12 June. After the virtual destruction of No 141 in July, West Malling continued to operate as a satellite of Kenley (q.v.). Several attacks by the Luftwaffe were suffered during August–October 1940. Turbinlite (q.v.) Havocs and their attendant Hurricanes, and Beaufighters and Eighth Air Force (q.v.) Thunderbolts were among later types here, with the rare Vultee Vengeance in 1946. Post-WWII residents included No 500's Meteors and No 25's Vampires. Closed for operations in August 1964, West Malling was re-opened for two years for the US Navy, but the site was finally purchased by Kent County Council in 1970.

Wettererkundungs Weather reconnaissance (German).

White Russia The possessor of a small air force, evolved to combat the spread of Communism following the October Revolution. Fierce fighting followed the opening of the Dardanelles after the 1918 Armistice and large numbers of British, American and French troops were sent to the area. These were supported by the RAF, and in addition a special squadron equipped with D.H.9s was formed to patrol the Black and Caspian Seas. In 1919 one Flight each of the same type, D.H.4s, D.H.9s and Sopwith Camels (some of which were earmarked as dive-bombers) was sent to support General Deakin's Army waging an offensive campaign in the valley of the Don.

Wiking (Viking). The name adopted for the Blohm und Voss Bv 222 (q.v.) flying boat.

Wild Weasel The US Air Force's F-4G version of the McDonnell Phantom which carried specialized electronics for defence suppression operations in addition to a mixed armament load such as AGM-88 HARM, AGM-78 Standard, AGM-65 Maverick and AGM-

45 Shrike. Similarly configured F-105 Thunderchiefs were also known by this name and predated the Phantom in this role.

Willows E. T. Willows of Cardiff was a pioneer airship pilot and designer who completed his first dirigible in June 1905 (Willows Airship No l). This was followed by the more advanced No 2 of November 1909 and by No 3, which was a reconstruction of No 2, a year later. From a viewpoint of air warfare, his next vessel was of interest in that it was purchased by the Admiralty in September 1912 and, as a two-seater adapted for instructional purposes, became Admiralty No 2. It was still in service in July two years later when it appeared over the Fleet at the Spithead Naval Review. Seemingly not allocated an Admiralty number, Willows No 5 dated from 1913 and was used for training at Hendon (q.v.). This had a little over twice the gas capacity of the others and was capable of a maximum speed of 38mph.

Wimbledon Common An emergency landing ground established in 1915 as part of the belt of RFC defensive aerodromes around London from which two B.E.2c aircraft each could ascend to protect the capital against airship raiders. The others were Beddington (q.v.), Blackheath, Enfield, Eynsford, Northolt and Woodcock Field at East Horden. Similar RNAS sites were at Chelmsford and Maidstone.

'Window' Metallic reflective foil strips dropped by aircraft to confuse defensive radar (including that of night fighters), which 'saw' it as vast numbers of aircraft due to the huge number of echoes given off. It was known as Düppel in Germany. See Chaff.

Winkton An RAF Advanced Landing Ground in Dorset in use from early 1944 due to its proximity to Sopley (q.v.). In the preliminaries to D-Day operations it acted as a base for the US Ninth Air Force's 404th Fighter Group operating the 506th, 507th and 508th Fighter Squadrons equipped with P-47 (q.v.) Thunderbolts. Most of these, which totalled about fifty machines, were used in the subsequent Operation 'Overlord', although the sta-

tion was closed in the following July. The unit was commanded by Col Carrol W. McColpin, a former member of the RAF's Eagle Squadron.

Women's Auxiliary Air Force This was formed by Royal Warrant on 28 June 1939 and was intended to be an integral part of the RAF, becoming part of the Armed Forces of the Crown on 10 April 1941. Prior to the formation of the WAAF there had existed Royal Air Force Companies of the Auxiliary Territorial Service (ATS), which had been formed in July 1938. The WAAF on formation had a total strength of 1,740 of all ranks, growing to a peak of 181,835 in 1943, the total in June 1944 being slightly reduced to 174,406 and 153,000 a year later. During WWII the Service suffered 611 casualties, 187 killed, four missing and 420 wounded. On 1 February 1949 it was renamed the Women's Royal Air Force and given permanent peacetime status, and rank designation identical to that of the RAF replaced the earlier structure, so that former Section Officers were now known as Flying Officers, Flight Officers as Flight

Above: Willows' first successful airship, 'Willow II', as it appeared in 1910. (Author's collection)

Lieutenants etc. This 'new' name had in fact already been used for the WWI counterpart of the WAAF, a Service constituted on 1 April 1918 from the former Women's Royal Flying Corps. The latter had not been formed until mid-1917 but before disbandment on 1 April 1920 had reached a maximum strength of 25,000 all ranks.

Wood meal A constituent of HE bombs combined, for example, with petrol in the core of German oil bombs (q.v.), also containing a mixture of charcoal with magnesium powder and 125kg of TNT, and with aluminium powder alone in 'L' type 1,000kg 'Hermann' bombs to double the blast effect.

Wotan A beam transmitter of which two types existed (designated Wotan I and II), associated with the WWII Luftwaffe's X-Verfahren (q.v.) VHF-beam precision bombing aid.

W/T Lettering indicating Wireless Telegraphy on various parts of WWII and early RAF aircraft indicating electrical bonding to each other. Although it continued in use after the introduction of radio telephony it had by then strictly become an anachronism.

Wyvern First flown on 12 December 1946 and entering production in 1950, the Westland W.35 resulted from specification N.11/44 for a carrier-borne, single-seat attack fighter capable of carrying a torpedo. It was unique in being powered by an Armstrong Siddeley Python turboprop motor. A total of 132 production versions were built, equipping four FAA squadrons. The production aircraft had a maximum speed of 440mph with a range of 900 miles, carrying external stores which could include the equivalent weight of a torpedo in either bombs, mines or depth charges. The fixed armament was four wing-mounted 20mm Hispano V cannon, while launchers under the folding wings took sixteen 60lb rockets.

X- A designation prefix used by the United States to denote research aircraft, not necessarily prototypes 1948 to date. It is often used before an index of the role-function; for example, XB would indicate an experimental or prototype bomber.

X-1 An early WWII German guided missile also known as Fritz-X, one of a series of weapons which depended for control on tail-mounted spoilers – a relatively cheap method requiring little power to operate. The radio link used the Kehi/Strassburg system with the aerial contained in the cylindrical tail shroud. Wire-link control was also developed, using two bobbins and five miles of twin wires, but this was later discontinued. In action X-1s, carrying tail flares to assist in guidance, were flown chiefly from Dornier 217Ks. They were first used on 29 August 1943 over the Mediterranean. Plans existed to produce 750 X-1 missiles per month.

X-4 A WWII Luftwaffe air-to-air missile which was developed between April and August 1944 with a performance which made it suitable for use with such aircraft as the Messerschmitt 262, although early test-firings were made from a Focke-Wulf 190 (q.v.) – the first on 11 August – Junkers 88Gs and Junkers 388s. Promising though these were, Allied bombing prevented the manufacture of sufficient rocket motors, and although 1,000 airframes were produced the missile never went into production.

X-7 A WWII German missile known as the Rotkappchen (Red Riding Hood) which was originally designed for use by ground troops against Soviet tanks and only used operationally for a limited period in January 1945 as the control system was not fully developed. It is included here because of a proposal that it be adapted for air-to-air use, but the maximum speed available from the WASAG 109-506 solid diglycol motor – 224mph – would seem to have made it inadequate for that role.

X-29A A Grumman aircraft developed for the USAF Flight Dynamics Laboratory fitted with a forward-swept wing (FSW) in 1977. The potential advantages of a fighter designed along such lines include a lower stalling speed, improved low-speed manoeuvrability, and a weight-saving of up to 30 per cent compared with conventional types, as well as a good STOL (q.v.) and landing capability without the need for high-lift devices or vectored thrust.

X-31 Used for one of the most important of a number of experiments conducted to investigate Enhanced Fighter Manoeuvrability (as the trials programme was called), the single-seat Rockwell/MBB X-31 was scheduled to fly in 1990, it later being joined by a second example. The object of the X-31 design was to develop aerodynamics that would give combat advantage by means of breaking the so-called 'stall barrier', thus allowing short-range dog-fighting with the aid of high angles of attack.

The resultant unarmed aircraft approximated closely in appearance to modern design trends, so that it superficially resembled the British Aerospace EAP, being a canard with a compound delta wing and foreplanes well forward on the nose. It was powered by a thrust-vectoring General Electric F404-GE-400 turbofan, giving a maximum speed of Mach 0.9

X-Gerät X-equipment carried in aircraft for the reception of X-Verfahren (q.v.) precision bombing signals. It was used by the world's first pathfinder force, the WWII Luftwaffe's Kampfgruppe 100, and proved difficult to jam effectively until the opening months of 1941.

XST (Experimental Stealth Project). Believed to be an alternative designation to the CSIRS (Covert Survivable In-Weather Reconnaissance Strike Aircraft), along which guidelines the F-117 stealth (q.v.) project was developed.

X-Verfahren X-system. A WWII German VHF multi-beam precision bombing system.

Y-Service RAF Radio interception branch functioning during WWII.

Y Station A wireless listening position set up to monitor enemy transmissions, the first being established by the Admiralty in 1915 with the intention of providing an early warning system for advance information of potential airship attacks on targets in Britain. Proving highly efficient for this, and also for listening to U-boat surface transmissions, they were, with X and Z Stations, soon extended down the length of the eastern coastline of England and Scotland and along the

English south coast. A total of 32 such stations were set up. In modified form, the system existed into the early 1920s, although then only protecting the south and south-east of England, while three remained in Scotland with a new one established on the west coast of Ireland. These stations, not all of which were sited on the coast, operated on wavelengths between 300 and 600m, giving a nautical range of from 45 to 250 miles. Some could also operate on the 1,000m band, that at Poldhui on the extreme south-western tip of England having a range in excess of 1,000 miles. All reports were transmitted to the Admiralty in London. Mention has been made of some similar stations in France during WWI.

Y-Verfahren Y-System. A WWII German VHF single-beam precision bombing and range-measuring system, not to be confused with X-Verhabner which employed multi-beams.

Yak-3 A Soviet single-seat fighter powered by a liquid-cooled engine which made its first flight in July 1943, based on the earlier Yak-1 and finally developed into the Yak-9. Around 37,000 of all versions were built, including the intermediate Yak-7. The maximum speed of the final version was 370mph, with a range of about 550 miles. The armament varied, some having a single 20mm ShVAK gun above the cowling, offset to port, a 12.7mm gun in each wing and provision for 220lb of bombs. The type also saw service with North Korea.

Yak-15 The Soviet Union's first jet fighter, which first flew on 24 April 1946, based in a modified Yak-9 airframe. It saw limited service in the closing years of the 1940s and only about 200 were constructed, retaining many of the earlier type's features including a tailwheel. It was succeeded in service by the MiG-15 which had a nosewheel undercarriage and other improvements. Some 1,500 were built, and they were given the NATO codename 'Feather'. The maximum speed of the Yak-15 was 503mph and that of the Yak-17 516mph, with ranges of 370 and 460 miles respectively.

Yak-23 A Soviet jet day fighter which first flew in the summer of 1947 and

was code-named 'Flora' by NATO. Although bearing a superficial resemblance to the foregoing, it was a completely different design with a pressurized cockpit and an ejector seat. It was widely used by Warsaw Pact countries and had a maximum speed of 550mph and a range of some 870 miles. The armament was a pair of 23mm Nudelmann-Richter NR-23 cannon mounted under the jet intake.

Yak-25 See 'Flashlight'.

Yellow bands Wide areas of colour carried by German aircraft as a recognition marking on the rear fuselage of warplanes operating on the Eastern Front during WWII.

Yellow Sun A thermonuclear weapon issued to the RAF V-Force (q.v.) which had been developed after earlier trials off Christmas Island. It was deployed for use by Valiant bombers during the Cuban Missile Crisis of 1962 but later replaced by Type WE.177 free-fall nuclear bombs, which remained in service until the 1990s.

Young Airmen's League The Bournemouth Young Airmen's League anticipated the Air Defence Cadet Corps of 1938, being founded by Charles W. Longman in about March 1927, and although never becoming a national organization it flourished locally for many years. Members were boys between the ages of 13 and 15 years who were air-minded. They were taught the principles of flight and aircraft construction with the aid of a model of 4ft span and received disciplinary training along the lines of the Boy Scouts.

In 1928 they were reported to be building an airframe with an 18ft wing span for rigging instruction and in 1929 were negotiating with the Air Ministry for the purchase of a full-size aircraft for the same purpose. The Headquarters of the League was 'The Cottage', 28 Wimborne Road, Bournemouth, the home of Mr Longman, who was then a chauffeur but had served in the RAF. The membership at the time comprised about forty boys, who paid an enrolment fee of sixpence and afterwards a weekly subscription of threepence. They wore a uniform consisting of grey flannel shorts and a blue double-breasted

blazer with brass buttons and rank badges as appropriate, together with a peaked cap.

Ypres The centre of the Allied offensive at Passchendaele of 1917 and significant for the degree to which Corps units were protected by air action, although in general the offensive proved disastrous with heavy losses aggravated by conditions of heavy rain and poor visibility. On 11 September Capitaine Georges Marie Ludovic Jules Guynemer was lost on the French side and Kurt Wolff on the German, and the epic air engagement of WWI took place on 23 September when Werner Voss was killed after a protracted struggle. The Third Battle of Ypres drew to its close in November and saw Sopwith (q.v.) Camels and D.H.5 aircraft engaged in ground attack.

Z Station See Y Station.

'Zeke' A Japanese single-seat fighter of WWII, officially termed the Mitsubishi A6M or Navy Type 0, a designation which resulted in its well-known name 'Zero', although it was code-named 'Zeke' by the Allies. It was latterly used as a fighter-bomber and even in a kamikaze (q.v.) role, although the prototype, designed to an exacting Navy specification by Jiro Horikoshi, was, when it first flew on 1 April 1939, seen as a pure carrier aircraft and had manually folding wing tips. After some design adjustments, including reinforcement of the rear wing spar, production was commenced and over 500 were in service in time for the Pacific war, the type spearheading the attack on Pearl Harbor. Lack of collaboration between Allied intelligence departments resulted in the temporary allocation of the code-names 'Ray', 'Ben' and 'Hap', the last being at first reserved for 'Zekes' with square, clipped wing tips as these were believed to be a new type. Four main versions, differing in engines or armament, appeared. The maximum speed of the final A6M8 model was 356mph, with a range in excess of 1,000 miles. It was armed with two 13.2mm Type 3 machine guns and two 20mm Type 99 cannon, all in the wings.

ZELL A Soviet concept using a Zero-Length-Launcher to assist into the air heavily laden SM-30 – Mig-19 'Farmer' (q.v.) – fighter aircraft accepted by the High Command in April 1955. Due to the 4.5g involved in take-offs, the fuselage was specially strengthened, as were the wing spars and fuel tanks, while twin fins were substituted for the original one of similar area. Thrust to catapult the aircraft was provided by a pair of PRD-22 RATOG (q.v.) units under the rear fuselage, sending the aircraft up the launcher, which was made mobile by mounting it on a YaAZ-210 trailer. Some 80,000lb of acceleration was produced in 2.5 seconds, this being some five times the weight of the aircraft, which was sent away at a maximum angle of 30 degrees.

After the successful first launch, a test programme was begun, the seventh launch, made on 3 June 1957, seeing the fighter carrying a pair of external 200-gallon drop tanks. In the final demonstration the aircraft reached an altitude of 32,800ft in 66 seconds. However, attempts to land the aircraft within a restricted space (1,300ft being stated in the requirement) proved difficult. The trials included a system whereby the pilot was expected to engage a ground line with the undercarriage and decelerate with the aid of automatically deployed canopies; a method similar to that traditionally used on aircraft carriers was also tried Although the general concept was regarded as practicable under operational conditions, it was finally abandoned.

Zeppelin The name generally refers to German airships before and during the period of WWI, but it is also associated with the Zeppelin-Lindau (Dornier from 1922, when it ceased to be a subsidiary of the larger organization) and Zeppelin-Staaken multi-engine seaplane and 'Giant' bomber series. Although the last was a large aircraft used for attacks by the German Navy on Eastern Front targets among others, the all-metal cantilever Zeppelin-Lindau D.I scout is probably the more technically interesting. Although submitted for evaluation by Western Front pilots, its performance proved disappointing and it was not proceeded with. Nevertheless, two were taken to the United States after 1918, one each for examination and testing by the Army and Navy. Construction was of dural, with the forward two-thirds of the wing built up of web ribs and full-depth spars, all metal-covered – a practice which later became commonplace. The rear third consisted of metal ribs butted to the rear spar, the covering of this section being fabric. The upper wing was held in place by

Above: Nothing less than 'Zeppelin hysteria' had gripped Britain by the outbreak of WWI, airships being seen (partly because of propaganda) as the ultimate weapon against which there was no defence. Thus the name became a generic term for all enemy airships. On the other hand, these vulnerable monsters were operated by cold, frightened and often lost crews. Typical of these airships was the German Army's LZ25, which, having made its first flight on 29 July 1914, was destroyed on 8 October when British aircraft bombed its shed at Düsseldorf. (Bruce Robertson collection)

four bolts fitted to the ends of the rigid centre-section struts, eliminating the need for bracing wires, and the lower wing was fastened directly to the bottom longerons with a further set of six bolts. Sheet metal covering was plain material, not corrugated in the manner of Junkers practice, and a jettisonable fuel tank was carried under the fuselage. The maximum speed was given as 124mph and the armament consisted of twin synchronized Spandau guns.

Zhukovsky A test and experimental centre located about 35 miles southeast of Moscow with the longest runway in the world, extending for about ten miles, with a second that is only slightly shorter. It is named after Nikolai Jegorovich Zhukovsky, regarded by many, including Lenin, as the founder of Soviet aviation. He established the Central Hydrodynamic Institute nearby, the present complex being set up in 1922. This station accommodates the Air Force Test and Experimental Centre (NII-VVS) for testing combat aircraft and guidance systems, the Gramov Flight Research Institute (LII) and the body formerly known as the All-Union Institute for Aviation Material (VIAM). Ramenskoye is the name by which the centre used to be known in the West, particularly the United States, although this in fact is the name of the nearest rail link.

'Zion' Countermeasures taken between 1600hrs on 5 September and 0100hrs on 6 September 1947 against the threatened bombing of London with Tiger Moth aircraft by Jewish terrorists. Anti-aircraft guns were alerted, No 11 Group Fighter Command maintained patrols, operations rooms were manned and Nos 1 and 2 Groups ROC stood-to 267 officers and observers at four hours' notice. The attack was prevented at the last moment when arrests were made in Paris.

Zitterrochen (Torpedo Fish). A German air-to-ground missile produced in 1942. A Henschel design, it was a monoplane with thin wings, triangular in planform with a pair of underslung rockets, and a cylindrical fuselage resembling that of the V-1 flying bomb (q.v.). The tailplane was carried below ventral fin, while control was by means of spoilers on the trailing edges of the wings instead of conventional ailerons. Although production was expected, the work was cancelled by the RLM (q.v.). The anticipated speed was in the region of Mach 1.5.

Z-rockets Also known as Z-guns, these British anti-aircraft weapons were introduced to support conventional heavy AA batteries in 1942 and were manned by units of the Home Guard. A battery consisted of 8 x 8 (i.e. sixty-four) projectors mounted on a revolving platform manned by two gunners situated one each side of the rails to launch the 5ft long projectiles. Gunner No 1 was in charge of aiming and firing while No 2 set the elevation and loading. The order to fire came from the Command Post to which the launcher was connected, together with a radar installation. Crews were specially trained by the Royal Artillery at cliff-top sites such as those at Frinton-on-Sea, Essex, and Southsea, Hampshire, before being deployed to defend major cities such as London and Bristol The batteries were retained into the period of flying bomb attacks. The range of the weapon was 10,000ft, later improved to 12–15,000ft.

Zwicky A mobile 350-gallon aircraft refuelling tender adopted by the RAF in 1937 and still in use at the outbreak of WWII. They could be found mounted on six-wheel Albion, Crossley or Morris CD chassis and had the facility to serve three fighter aircraft simultaneously, thus ensuring a swift turnaround.

Zwilling German for 'twin', and used to designate machine guns coupled in pairs during WWII, indicated by the addition of the suffix 'Z' to the type designation (for example, MG 81Z).

Above: An RAF Zwicky refuelling tanker on an Albion AM463 chassis. Adopted in 1937, the triple boom facilitated attention to three aircraft simultaneously. Capacity was 350 gallons. (Author)

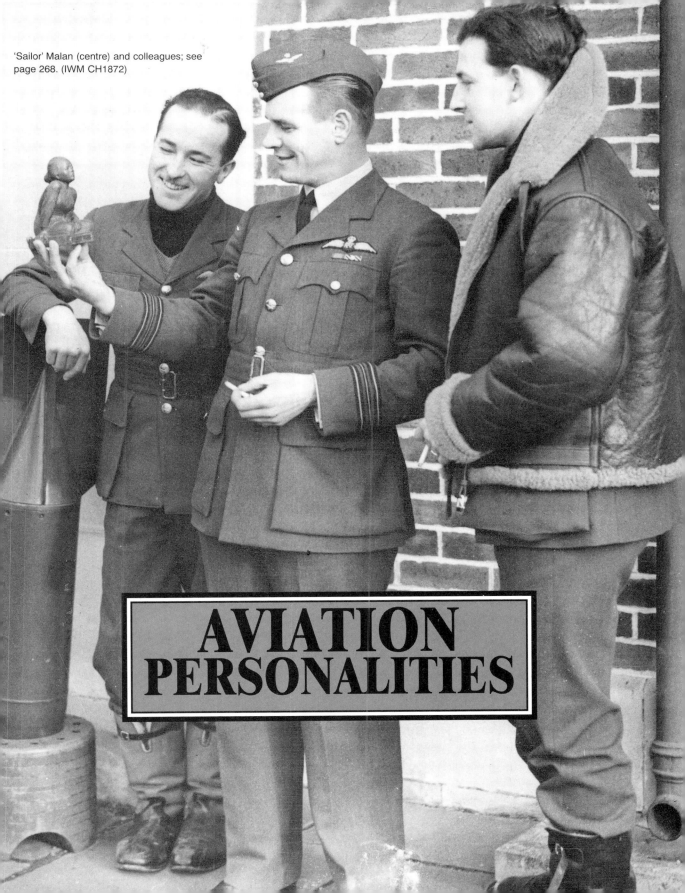

'Sailor' Malan (centre) and colleagues; see page 268. (IWM CH1872)

AVIATION PERSONALITIES

Arnold, General H. H. (1886–1950)

General 'Hap' Arnold was not only an early American military air pioneer but a famous air commander. During the active years of WWII he headed the US Army Air Force and, as a five-star general, he became the first head of the independent US Air Force in 1947.

Henry Harley Arnold was born in 1886 at Gladwyne, Pennsylvania. After passing through West Point he was commissioned in the Infantry during 1907. Widening his interests, he took flying lessons at the Wright Brothers' school, receiving his pilot's certificate in 1911. Transferring to the Aviation Section of the Signal Corps, he rose steadily in rank to become Assistant Director of the Air Service during WWI. Between the wars Arnold commanded the 1st Wing of the US Army Air Corps and when war came again he proved to be a strong advocate of the heavy bomber force; he was also forceful in facilitating the supply of aircraft to the Allies under Lend/Lease. His book *The Flying Game* was first published in 1936 and his famous work *Global Mission* appeared only shortly before he died on 15 January 1950. The Arnold Engineering Center of the USAF, named after him, activated on 1 January 1950, is deemed to be the largest complex of wind tunnels, test cells, simulation chambers and ranges in the world.

Bader, Douglas (1910–1982)

Group Captain Sir Douglas Robert Steuart Bader was universally known as 'Tin Legs' after a flying accident which robbed him of both of these limbs. His father was killed in WWI and the boy was brought up by his mother until she was married again, to a clergyman. Always an energetic youth, excelling at school cricket and football, Douglas joined the RAF as soon as he was able to and received his commission as a Pilot Officer in 1930, his interest in flying having been triggered by a childhood visit to an uncle who was the first Adjutant of the RAF College at Cranwell.

Posted to No 23 Squadron at Kenley, which was equipped with Gloster Gamecocks, the young man proved to have a natural aptitude for flying and he was chosen for the squadron's aerobatic team for the 1932 Hendon Air Display, but on 14

Above: Lord Brabazon of Tara. (MoD)

December 1931 he suffered the crash that nearly cost him his life while giving a spontaneous aerobatic display at Woodley near Reading, his injuries being such that he was not expected to live.

However, a fighting determination to survive pulled him through, despite his having two artificial legs henceforth. However, he had to leave the RAF, which he was not to re-join until the outbreak of war in 1939. He served with No 12 Group during the Battle of Britain and ardently supported Leigh Mallory's 'Big Wing' tactics.

In August 1941 Bader was shot down, taken prisoner and confined in Stalag Luft III, his two attempts to escape (once a replacement leg had been dropped by the RAF) and his policy of baiting his captors being viewed with mixed feelings by his fellow prisoners.

He later worked for Shell before retirement, during which he brought hope and self-esteem to many disabled people. He died from a heart attack in 1982.

Brabazon of Tara, Lord (1884–1964)

John Theodore Cuthbert Moore-Brabazon, a great sportsman and yachting enthusiast, was also a pioneer motorist and aviator, who went on to play an important role in British civil aviation. Born on 8 February

1884, Moore-Brabazon was educated at Harrow and Trinity College, Cambridge, where he took up ballooning. Turning to aeroplanes in 1909, he won the *Daily Mail* £1,000 prize for the first circular flight of one mile. The following year, on 8 March, he qualified for the first pilot's certificate awarded by the Royal Aero Club.

Joining the Royal Flying Corps in 1914, he was directed to experimental work on wireless telegraphy. Later he pioneered photographic reconnaissance in the Corps, devised the first practical aerial camera and attained the rank of Lieutenant-Colonel. Entering Parliament post-WWI, he continued his interest in aviation, becoming Chairman of the Air Registration Board and, in 1935, President of the Royal Aeronautical Society. He succeeded Lord Beaverbrook as Minister of Aircraft Production in 1941 and in 1943 he presided over the Civil Aviation Committee on Post-war Transport which became known as the 'Brabazon Committee'. Created a peer in 1942, Lord Brabazon of Tara PC GBE MC died in May 1964.

Camm, Sir Sydney (1893–1966)
While Sir Sydney Camm CBE FRAeS is remembered chiefly as the designer of the Hawker Hurricane, the main RAF fighter involved in the Battle of Britain, it should also be realized that the preceding Hart and Fury series were to his design. These aircraft, with their many variants (Audax, Hind, Osprey, Nimrod, etc) provided the mainstay of the RAF in the 1930s. They were also widely exported, enabling Hawker to expand and open plants that were vital to the production of the Hurricane, Typhoon and Tempest of WWII.

Born in 1893, Sydney Camm joined Martin & Handasyde (later Martinsyde) in 1914, but not until 1918 did he start on design work. In 1923 he joined H. G. Hawker Engineering, being made their Chief Designer two years later and becoming a Director in 1935. Post-war the Sea Fury was produced under his guidance, followed by the Sea Hawk and Hunter jet fighters. After being knighted in 1953 for his services to aviation, he became President of the Royal Aeronautical Society while remaining with Hawker as their Chief Engineer. Thus for 35 years he directed a series

of major designs that went into large-scale production. He died 12 March 1966.

Caproni, Count Gianni (1886–1957)
A famed Italian aircraft designer and manufacturer, Dr Gianni Caproni, later Count of Taliedo, was born at Massine Trentino on 3 July 1886 and died on 27 October 1957. From 1908, when he founded the Societa Italiana Caproni, he held many patents in aircraft construction and built up his works at Taliedo near Milan to become Italy's major aircraft manufacturer. His Scuola Aviazione Caproni became Italy's first established flying school.

During WWI his firm was noted for its production of a series of large bombers that came to be used by Italian, French and American flying services. His Ca.46 design was selected for mass production in the United States in 1918, but it was too late for service. Between the wars a series of commercial, bombing and training aircraft were produced, as well as seaplanes from Monte Calino on Lake Iseo. In connection with S. Campini, experimenting in reaction propulsion, the Caproni-Campini CC.l first flew in August 1940 powered by ducted fan propulsion but, with the improved CC.2, the propulsion system could not be developed beyond the research stage. The lack of orders following the intensive production of bombers and transports during WWII led to bankruptcy in 1950. As the Caproni complex comprised some 20 plants, some subsidiaries managed limited production for a short period.

Chadwick, Roy (1893–1947)
The fact that Roy Chadwick CBE FRAeS is chiefly remembered as head of the design team that produced the famous Avro Lancaster bomber of WWII has eclipsed his contribution to aviation in WWI and between the wars. Born in 1893, he was 19 years old when (Edwin) Alliott Verdon Verdon-Roe

Above: Roy Chadwick (left), with Avro test pilot Bill Thorn. (Bruce Robertson collection)

gave him the job of draughting out the Avro 500. Early in WWI he became Avro's chief draughtsman and contributed greatly to the development of the Avro 504 trainer series that was built in its thousands.

Chadwick contributed to most of the Avro designs in the interwar years, but not until the Anson did production go into thousands. In addition to his major work on the Avro Manchester and Lancaster, he was intimately involved in the modification of Lancasters for the famous dams raid in May 1943. An intuitive designer with great enthusiasm and energy, he would see his designs through to the post-test flight stage. It was in the course of this dedication to his profession that he lost his life. On 23 August 1947 he accompanied the firm's test pilot 'Bill' Thorn and two technicians on a test flight of the Avro Tudor II prototype G-AGSU. This aircraft crashed at Woodford, killing all the occupants.

Cobham, Sir Alan (1894–1973)

Few airmen have made such a long and varied contribution to aviation as Alan John Cobham. A talented and resourceful airman, he served three years in France during WWI and was commissioned in the RFC in 1917. Turning to civil aviation post-war, he had piloted 10,000 passengers by 1920. He then concentrated on aerial survey work and in 1921 inaugurated a Spanish airline to Morocco. He flew continuously with such highlights as a record London–Belgrade flight in one day of 1923, winning the King's Cup Air Race 1924, flying to the Cape and back in 1925 and flying to Australia and back the following year. These achievements brought him an AFC and a knighthood (KBE). He then headed the first flying boat expedition around the African continent and promoted the Through Africa Air Route scheme.

During the 1930s Sir Alan organized air displays throughout Britain. From 1936 he devoted much time to experimental work, furthering his vision of world-wide airways by devising means of flight refuelling. Much of his WWII service was devoted to this concept, which was proved post-war when his probe and drogue air-to-air refuelling was adopted by the US Air Force, the US Navy and the RAF. He became Chairman of Alan Cobham Aviation and Bournemouth Airport and Director of Flight Refueling Inc (USA). Sir Alan, born on 6 May 1894, died in 1973.

Cody, S. F. (1861–1913)

An American who became a British citizen in 1909, Samuel Franklin Cody was the most flamboyant of the early air pioneers, who achieved a number of 'firsts' in British aviation. Born in 1861 of Irish stock, Cody grew up in farming in Texas. Horse dealing brought him to England, where, in 1899, he started experimenting with man-lifting kites which caught the interest of the military. Later, as an instructor at Aldershot, he became involved with Britain's first dirigible, the *Nulli Secundus*, and early aeroplane projects. A biplane of his construction made the first officially recognized aeroplane flight in Britain on 16 October 1908 at Farnborough. In flying this aircraft from Laffan's Plain to Dongo Hill on 14 May 1909 he made the first British aeroplane flight of over a mile. He took his wife up in this biplane the following month, Mrs Cody thus becoming the first lady to fly in an aeroplane in Britain. In the first British military trials at Larkhill in

Above: 'Colonel' Samuel Franklin Cody, photographed probably in front of his 'Cathedral' design. (Bruce Robertson collection)

Above: Glenn Curtiss at the controls of the *Silver Dart* aircraft. (Bruce Robertson collection)

August 1912 Cody, flying another biplane of his design, won the speed competition. Although his designs, which included a monoplane, were not suitable for production, he actively continued to experiment until 7 August 1913 when he and his passenger, W. H. B. Evans, fell to their deaths after a structural failure of their Cody machine over Farnborough.

Curtiss, Glenn 1878–1930

Glenn Curtiss was an early American air pioneer who in 1908 received the *Scientific American* award for the first public flight of 1 kilometre. That same year, mounting his June Bug biplane on floats, he introduced the seaplane, then known as a hydroplane, to America; later he demonstrated the use of such craft to the US Navy. He is also credited with introducing practical aileron control in 1911.

Born in New York in May 1878, Glenn Curtiss had an engineering bent. From a small bicycle business he progressed to building cars, and an order for powering an early aeroplane project brought him into the aero-engine field. In 1907 he joined Dr Alexander Graham Bell, inventor of the telephone, with others, in the Aerial Experimental Association at Halifax, Nova Scotia. During 1909 he was flying a biplane of his own design in French contests.

Returning to America, he built up a business in aircraft design and production. During WWI his JN-4 (Curtiss Jenny), built in its thousands, became the standard American trainer. Both Curtiss aeroplanes and flying boats were supplied to the RNAS. In cooperation with the US Navy, his NC-4 flying boat was in 1919 the first aircraft to fly across the Atlantic. By these suc-

cesses the Curtiss Aeroplanes and Motors Corporation of Buffalo, Hammondsport, New York, was firmly established.

de Havilland, Sir Geoffrey (1882– 1965)

The name de Havilland is among the most famous of aircraft designers. Geoffrey de Havilland, born on 27 July 1882, was by 1910 designing his own aircraft and its engine and teaching himself to fly. Selling his aircraft for £400 to Farnborough, where he found employment, he played a major part in the Royal Aircraft Factory B.E.2, B.E.8, R.E.1, R.E.7, S.E.1 and S.E.2 designs.

Leaving Government service in 1914 to become chief designer and test pilot for the Aircraft Manufacturing Company (Airco), he designed their D.H.1 before joining the RFC. Since Captain de Havilland was

Above: Capt Sir Geoffrey de Havilland (left) in May 1955 with Duke of Edinburgh. (Hawker Siddeley)

deemed more useful as a designer, he returned to AMC, from which his WWI designs D.H.4, D.H.6 and D.H.9 were produced in their thousands.

His de Havilland Aircraft Company was formed in 1920 and a series of successful designs ensued, among them the famous Moth series first flown by him 22 February 1925. During the interwar years single-, twin-, tri- and four-engine airliners were produced. The Rapide became a standard feeder liner and the Tiger Moth a standard trainer, and subsidiary companies were opened in Australia, Canada and New Zealand to build DH designs. Managing a vast complex, he chose his staff with care. A team under R. E. Bishop designed the famous Mosquito of WWII, and in 1943, with design D.H.100, the jet age was entered with the Vampire, first flown by his son Geoffrey. Knighted in 1944, Sir

Geoffrey de Havilland OM CBE AFC died on 21 May 1965 shortly after the company name disappeared in the Hawker Siddeley merger.

Doolittle, James (1896–1993)

Lt-Gen James Doolittle, air commander and company executive, won fame for pioneering and proving flights. Outstanding among these was the first US coast-to-coast flight in a single day, made on 4 September 1922, and winning for America the 1925 Schneider Trophy Contest at an average speed of 232.57mph. In 1927, as a famed aerobat, he was credited with becoming the first pilot to execute an outside loop.

Born in California on 14 December 1896, Doolittle joined the US Army to fly when America entered WWI in 1917. During most of the 1930s he was a civilian pilot, but he re-joined the Army Air Corps in its period of

expansion. After the Pearl Harbor attack he planned a spectacular retaliation that was launched on 18 April 1942 when he led a special unit of B-25 Mitchell bombers on take-off from the carrier USS *Hornet* to bomb Tokyo and fly on to land in free China. This well-publicized operation has tended to obscure his series of achievements both before and after. He was later appointed to form the US Twelfth Air Force and subsequently commanded the Fifteenth in Italy and the Eighth in Britain. Post-war he became a director of Shell. His awards include the American Congressional Medal of Honor and an honorary KCB. He died in September 1993.

Dornier, Dr Claude (1884–1969)

A pioneer of metal construction of aircraft and an early aeroplane designer, Claude Dornier founded the

Above: Lt-Gen James Doolittle (left), with Lt Batten, in front of a Curtiss P-1 Hawk. (Bruce Robertson collection)

famous and long-standing aircraft manufacturing firm that bears his name. He was born at Kempten in Bavaria during 1884 and worked first at a steel works. His connection with aircraft came in 1910 on joining the experimental design office of Luftschiffbau Zeppelin. In his initial involvement with airships he designed and patented a revolving airship hangar.

Dornier's first all-metal aeroplane was conceived in 1911, but it was in 1914, when Count Zeppelin instituted Zeppelin-Werke Lindau to produce giant seaplanes, that a series of Dornier designs began to evolve. Post-war, benefiting from this experience, he founded Dornier Metallbauten at Friedrichshafen on Lake Constance in 1922, but transferred main production to the Swiss side of the lake in 1926. A series of flying boats ensued, some designs also being built in Italy, Holland, Japan and Spain. In size they culminated with the Dornier Do X, the 12-engine flying boat (the world's largest) that first flew 29 July 1929. The German works expanded from 1933, with branch factories joining in the production of the Do 17 series of bombers and various experimental designs throughout WWII. Post-war Dornier operated technical offices in Madrid, designing the Do 25 for the Spanish Air Ministry. A following Do 27 general-purpose aircraft, first fabricated in Spain, was produced in Germany where once again Dornier aircraft production flourished from the 1950s. Claude Dornier died in 1969.

Douglas, Donald W. (1892–1981)

Douglas has been a name in aviation over many years and still is today, not least for the DC-3 Dakota built not only in large numbers but used commercially and by air forces for a period of over 50 years.

Donald Wills Douglas, born in 1892, studied aeronautical engineering and in 1915 was chief engineer to the Wright-Martin Company. For a brief period, 1916–17, he was chief civilian aircraft engineer to the US Signal Corps. When war came in 1917 he joined the then separate Glenn L. Martin Company, where he designed bombers that were adopted by the US Army Air Corps.

Forming his own Douglas Aircraft Company in 1920, he produced the Cloudster, the first aircraft to carry more than its own weight in payload. It was the Douglas World Cruisers that, by circling the earth, first brought fame to his name. A series of designs followed before he evolved his

Above: Air Chief Marshal Sir Hugh Dowding GCB GCVO CMG, at the age of forty in 1922 when holding the rank of Air Commodore. (Bruce Robertson collection)

Douglas Commercial series, of which the DC-3 airliner and troop transport became the most famous, followed by the DC-4 and progressive designs to the DC-7, the fastest piston-engine airliner. The series continues with the DC-8, 9 and 10 jet airliners.

In 1967 the Douglas Company merged with the McDonnell Company to form McDonnell Douglas, of which D. W. Douglas became chairman. He died early in 1981, aged 88.

Douhet, Gen Giulio (1869–1930)

It was the publication of Gen Douhet's *Il Domino dell'Aria* (*The Command of the Air*) in 1921 that established him as the world famous exponent of air power. Perhaps his most striking dictum was that wars could be won by strategic air attack alone. Ridiculed in some military circles, his views nevertheless had a marked effect on military aviation in the 1930s. The Luftwaffe subscribed to his doctrine and the French adopted multi-seat fighters largely through his concepts on their operation.

Born at Caserta in 1869, Douhet is said to have seen the need for air supremacy as early as 1909. From 1912, when commanding one of Italy's first air units, he agitated for a strong air arm. Proclaiming his views in late 1915, after Italy had joined in the European conflict, led to his being court-martialled the following year. However, the disastrous retreat at Caporetto late in 1917, showing the superiority of the Austro-Hungarian air arm, led to Douhet's views being vindicated. Reinstated and promoted to general, he became head of the Italian Army Air Service in 1918. He continued to endorse his theories in further writings until his death in 1930.

Dowding, Lord (1882–1970)

Air Chief Marshal Lord Dowding of Bentley Priory, GCB GCVO CMG, will be remembered as the Commander-in-Chief of RAF Fighter Command during the Battle of Britain in 1940, but his greatest contribution to the defence of Britain was in his feat of organization and resolution that preceded the battle. Born on 24 April 1882, Hugh Dowding joined the Royal Artillery in 1900 and the Royal Flying Corps in 1914. In the course of his service he

had the experience of commanding a squadron (No 16).

In 1929 Dowding was appointed to command Fighting Area 1929-30 and went on to become Air Council Member for Research and Development. With this experience he went on to be the first commander of the newly formed Fighter Command in 1936. Under his leadership a reporting and control network was set up using a combination of electronic detection devices and visual reporting that stood the test of battle. When dissipation of his squadrons was threatened by the needs of the battle for France, he stood firm for the needs of his command. Although events were to show his sound foresight, he was criticized in political circles. Later in 1940 he was sent to the Ministry of Aircraft Production post in America and he retired from the RAF two years later. He died in 1970.

Duke, Neville (1922–)

Of all the famous test pilots, Neville Frederick Duke DSO OBE DFC** AFC is the most outstanding as an air ace of WWII, a test pilot of early jet aircraft and the holder of a world record flight.

Neville Duke was born at Tonbridge, Kent, on 11 January 1922. At 18 he joined the RAF, making his first flight on 20 August 1940 in Tiger Moth N6790. Serving first in No 92 Squadron at Biggin Hill, Duke then went to North Africa to fly Tomahawks with No 112 Squadron and was able to re-join his original squadron in North Africa. Later he took over command of No 145 Squadron and in the course of WWII shot down 28 enemy aircraft.

In the immediate post-war years Duke served in the RAF High Speed Flight and at the Empire Test Pilots' School. During 1948 he left the RAF to become a test pilot with Hawker Aircraft and the following year made record London–Rome and London–Karachi flights. When becoming Hawker's chief test pilot in 1951 he was also commanding No 615 Squadron of the Royal Auxiliary Air Force. He played a significant part in the development of the Hawker Hunter and with a special Mk 3 established a world speed record of 727mph on 7 September 1953. Later he became a technical adviser and consultant test pilot, having set up his own company.

Eaker, Gen Ira (1896–1987)

A tough, cigar-smoking bomber commander, Eaker was the leader of the Eighth Air Force's VIII Bomber Command in 1942 and in 1943 took command of the whole Force, plus all US Army personnel in Britain. An advocate of leading from the front, he took part in air incursions over enemy-held territory on more than one occasion.

Born in Texas on 13 April 1896, Eaker was first commissioned in the US Army in 1917 and qualified as a pilot in 1918. During 1919-22 he served in the Philippines. Studying while serving in the US in following years, he took a degree in journalism and became a writer and lecturer on air matters. In 1941 he was commanding the 20th Pursuit Group; his appointment to the Eighth Air Force in England followed.

When at the end of 1943 Mediterranean Allied Air Forces was formed, Eaker was appointed to command. His final service appointment was as Chief of the US Air Staff. Post-war he became Vice-President of Hughes Tool Company, which had aviation interests, and, being still a journalist, he wrote on defence matters in a newspaper column for eighteen years. Lt-Gen Ira Clarence Eaker who had US and many foreign decorations and was an honorary KBE and CBE, died in early August 1987 aged 91.

Eckener, Dr Hugo (1868–1954)

The German engineer Dr Hugo Eckener, a critic of the early Zeppelins, was invited by Count Zeppelin in 1906 to cooperate with him. From Zeppelin LZ3 onwards Eckener was available to the Count as a consultant, airship test pilot, air and ground crew training organizer and public relations manager. On his own account, he became flight director of DELAG (Deutsche Luftschiffahrts-Aktien Gesellschaft), whose aim was to provide a network of passenger-carrying airships using Zeppelins.

When war came in August 1914 the German Army and Navy had already taken delivery of thirteen and three Zeppelins respectively. Experience showed that the Navy had a greater need than the Army for such craft, and Eckener was directed to improve the range, lifting power and speed of naval

Above: Sir George Edwards OM CBE FRS BSc CEng DL. (Bruce Robertson collection)

1945 he was their chief designer and responsible for the Viscount and Vanguard airliners as well as for the Valiant, the first of the jet V-bombers for the RAF.

While noted for his gas-turbine airliners post-war, his wartime work involved development of the Wellington and Warwick, and in particular his dedicated efforts over the Christmas period of 1939 preparing Wellingtons for magnetic mine destruction. From as early as 1943 he was concerned with the 'Wellington airliner' project, the VC-l (Vickers Commercial No 1), which emerged as the Viking that served in British European Airways and foreign airlines as well as with the Royal Flight.

Among Sir George's many awards are the British Gold Medal for Aeronautics and the Daniel Guggenheim and Air League Founders' Medals. His many appointments in later years have included Pro-Chancellor of the University of Surrey 1964–79 and then its Chancellor Emeritus.

Fairey, Sir Richard (1887–1956)

Founder in 1915 of the Fairey Aviation Company and remaining its Chairman and Managing Director, Sir Richard Fairey was one of the outstanding personalities in British aviation, His firm, renowned for its shipborne aircraft, produced from 1917 the Fairey III series that, together with the Fairey Flycatcher, became the mainstay of the Fleet Air Arm in its early days. In 1931 he opened a subsidiary company, Avions Fairey, in Belgium. During WWII Fairey designs were in use by the RAF and RN, notably the Battle, Fulmar, Barracuda and Firefly, while the Swordfish was the only British biplane to remain operational throughout the war.

Born on 5 May 1887, Charles Richard Fairey's first influence on aviation came as manager of the Blair Atholl Aeroplane Syndicate in 1913, then as Short Brothers' chief engineer 1913–15. With his own company he tried aero-engine and propeller design and introduced various devices, including camber-changing and amphibian gear. He also devoted time to the general benefit of aviation as Chairman of the Society of British Aircraft Constructors and a member of the Aeronautical Research Committee in

Zeppelins. By the 1920s he was regarded as the world's greatest authority on lighter-than-air craft. In 1924 he captained LZ126, which became the US Navy's ZR-3 *Los Angeles*, across the Atlantic. Later he captained the most famous of all airships, LZ127 *Graf Zeppelin*. He remained in Germany during WWII but went to America in 1947 as a consultant to Goodyear. When in 1952 Germany tried to revive interest in airships, Dr Eckener, then 84, was convinced that such craft could not com-

pete against the aeroplane. He died on 14 August 1954.

Edwards, Sir George (1908–)

An eminent aircraft designer and company director, Sir George Robert Edwards OM CBE FRS BSc CEng DL was for twelve years (1963–75) Chairman of the British Aircraft Corporation. Born on 9 July 1908 at Highams Park, Essex, he joined Vickers-Armstrong, after graduating at London University, to become their experimental section manager during World War II. By late

the 1920s. During WWII, from 1942 to 1945 he was Director-General of the British Air Commission in Washington. Before WWII ended his firm was already in the missile field, and it had produced helicopters before Sir Richard died on 30 September 1956.

Farman, Henry (1874–1958)

Henry Farman and his two brothers were among the world's earliest aircraft builders. They had already made their name in the field of motoring and motorcycling when they turned to aviation in 1906. Henry's aviation fame dates from 1908, when he made a series of record flights, including the first aeroplane flight between two cities, Châlons and Reims, a distance of 27km, on 30 October that year.

Born on 28 May 1874, and a British subject who later took French citizenship, Henry became a trained engineer. Both he and his brother Maurice became noted for a series of pusher biplanes that went into large-scale production before and during WWI. Their factory, established at Billancourt in 1912, produced their joint designs during WWI and a civil version of their bomber of 1918 became France's first airliner.

The brother Richard, associated with the company, faded from aviation and Maurice founded a Farman car factory in 1920 which was active until 1931. Henry continued to design and direct the Farman aero interests until 1936 when, under the French aircraft industry nationalization, Farman merged with Hanriot to become the Société Nationale de Constructions Aéronautiques du Centre. After WWII Henry Farman founded and was first president of the Association des Amis du Musée de l'Air. He died on 21 July 1958.

Although the adopted spelling of his Christian name was French, in his personal circle he favoured the English form given by his parents.

Fedden, Sir Roy (1885–1973)

Alfred Hubert Roy Fedden, born on 6 June 1885, became one of the world's greatest experts on piston-aero engines. In 1920 he founded the Bristol Aeroplane Company's Engine Division and then became responsible for the design and development of Bristol engines until 1942. During that time he brought Bristol engines to such eminence that not only were they used in aircraft throughout the world, but they were also produced under licence by eighteen firms in seventeen different countries.

Educated at Bristol colleges, Roy Fedden first worked as a draughtsman for Brazil Straker & Company in 1906–08, becoming works manager in 1909–14 and then Technical Director and Chief Engineer. During WWI the firm made 1,450 aero engines of Renault, Gnome and Rolls-Royce design, plus six prototype engines of 200 and 300hp to Fedden's designs.

At the Bristol Aeroplane Company his development of sleeve-valve radial engines contributed greatly to Britain's lead in this field. After a disagreement with the firm's management he retired in 1942. For the rest of the war he

Above: Sir Richard Fairey MBE Hon FRAeS Hon FIAeS. (Bruce Robertson collection)

Above: Sir Roy Fedden (left) in front of a Vickers Vespa powered by a Bristol Pegasus engine of his design. To his left is Captain Uwins and then R. K. Pierson. (Bruce Robertson collection)

became Technical Adviser to the Minister of Aircraft Production. He was knighted in 1942. Sir Roy Fedden MBE DSc, member of several learned societies, had the distinction of twice becoming President of the Royal Aeronautical Society (1938–41 and 1944–45). He died at his home in Wales on 21 November 1973.

Fokker, Anthony (1890–1939)

A flamboyant Dutchman, with a flair for original design and having business acumen, Anthony Herman Gerard Fokker, an aviation pioneer, set up aircraft factories in Holland, Germany and America. Although he died at a relatively young age, his name is still borne by commercial aircraft types flying today.

Born in Java 6 April 1890, Fokker became interested in aviation as a schoolboy in Holland and by 1911 was flying machines of his own design. The following year he established a factory. Having sold aircraft to the German Army, he opened a flying school and factory at Schwerin. His light monoplanes, for which his firm devised an interrupter gear to permit forward fire through the propeller arc, gave Germany air superiority over the Allies

in 1915–16 in a period that became known as the 'Fokker Scourge'. A series of fighters ensued, including a manoeuvrable triplane and notably the Fokker D.VII biplane of 1918, quantities of which Fokker smuggled to Holland for export. With the proceeds he set up the Netherlands Fokker Works at Amsterdam. There he produced civil and military aircraft that had a world-wide market.

Realizing the potential of his firm's designs in America, Fokker made a series of visits to the United States in the 1920s. There he established plants that, although separate from his Dutch

Above: Anthony G. Fokker in front of his D-9 design at McCook Field, USA (Bruce Robertson collection)

factory, used their constructional techniques. His American interests were
taken over by General Motors in 1930
and he went into semi-retirement, taking up yachting. He died on 23
December 1939 at Murray Hill
Hospital, New York.

Foulis, Gen Benjamin (1879–67)

Gen Foulis, a pioneer airman who
became the first pilot to become
Chief of the US Army Air Corps, has
been described as the link between
the Wright Brothers and the astro-
nauts. He was born on 9 December
1879 at Washington, Connecticut,
where he was buried in April 1967.
After joining the US Army and serving
in the ranks, he was commissioned in
the field in 1901; his assignment to
aviation duties came in 1908. In the
course of flying the US Army's only
aeroplane in 1910, Foulis devised the
first efficient seat belt and experimented with wireless telegraphy from
aeroplanes.

During the 1916 US military operations against Pancho Villa in Mexico,
Foulis, then a captain, took command
of the 1st Aero Squadron engaged on
reconnaissance during the campaign.
During WWI he went to France in
October as a brigadier-general to take
charge of US Air Service administration, and for a period he was Chief of
Air Service for the American
Expeditionary Force.

Foulis was Chief of the US Army Air
Corps in 1931-35 when the Corps
struggle started for a separate identity. He was at the forefront of those
pressing for large bombers as instruments of air power. After his retirement in 1935 his influence on air
power continued through his series of
lecture tours lasting up to 1964.

Galland, Adolf (1912–1996)

At the age of 29 General Adolf Galland
became the Luftwaffe's General der
Jagdflieger in 1941. By then he had
amassed experience as a fighter
leader. He was born in Westphalia on
19 March 1912. Showing an interest in
aviation from an early age, he was
accepted for training by a commercial
air transport firm in 1932. With
German rearmament he joined the
Luftwaffe, but in spite of his fighter
training he was forced to operate in
the ground attack role, first in Spain

Above: Adolf Galland is seen here at the height of his WWII career, after which he
was to become a personal friend of his former opponent, Stanford Tuck, and also acted
as an adviser for the film *The Battle of Britain*. (Bruce Robertson collection)

Above: As he warms up the engine of his P-51 Mustang, Capt Don Gentile, a flight leader in an Eighth Air Force fighter group, receives a wave from a colleague. (IWM)

and then in the 1939 Polish campaign. His persistence in obtaining a transfer to fighters led to a posting to JG 26, with which unit he he achieved his first victory, a Belgian Hurricane on 12 May 1940.

Galland's leadership and grasp of air tactics led to his command of III Gruppe of JG 26 during the Battle of Britain. With rapid promotion he controlled fighter operations on the Eastern Front, Balkan and Mediterranean regions as well as organizing fighter cover for the German warships breaking out of Brest to sail to Germany via the English Channel.

Fated to fall out over air policy matters with Hitler and Göring, Galland was relieved of his overall fighter control. He then led an élite unit flying the Me 262 jet fighter, during which he was badly injured. By this time he was credited with 104 personal air combat victories. Released as a prisoner-of-war in 1947 he went to South America as adviser to the Argentine Air Force. Returning to Germany in 1955, he joined Air Lloyd, later to become its Chairman. He died in February 1996.

Gentile, Don S. (1920–1951)

One of America's most famous fighter pilots, Don Salvatore Gentile, born to Italian parents in Ohio on 6 December 1920, had the distinction of flying pre-war, serving in both the RAF and USAAF in wartime and becoming a test pilot in the USAF post-war. As a keen pilot and owner of an Arrow Sports biplane, he sought to join the US Army Air Corps but was not accepted. Going to an RAF Recruiting Office, he eventually found his way into No 71 (Eagle) Squadron, but due to his exceptional flying ability he was transferred to train others.

Following a reprimand for a 'beat-up' of a dog racing track, he was taken off training and sent to No 133 (Eagle) Squadron RAF, which became the 336th Fighter Squadron USAAF in September 1942. The unit's Spitfires were soon replaced by P-47 Thunderbolts. Gentile's score rose steadily and he became the first American in the European theatre to exceed Rickenbacker's legendary 26 victories of WWI. Sent home to rest, he returned to operations to finish the war with 36 victories.

Gentile remained in the USAAF and became a test pilot at Wright-Patterson Field. On 28 January 1951, after starting on a routine training flight in a Lockheed T-33, the aircraft had a flame-out, stalled and crashed in a wood, killing Gentile.

Gray, Colin (1914–1995)

As in WWI, so in WWII a number of fighter aces came from Commonwealth countries. The leading fighter pilot from New Zealand in WWII was Gp Capt Colin Falkland Gray DSO DFC**. He was one of twin brothers born on 9 November 1914 in Christchurch. His brother Ken, whom he followed into the RAF, was awarded the DFC on bombing operations and died 1 May 1940 when his Whitley, on a cross-country flight to pick up his brother, hit a hill in fog.

Colin first served with No 54 Squadron, flying Spitfires over France and Belgium during May 1940. This was followed by intensive operations during the Battle of Britain and then on offensive fighter sweeps. In mid-1941 he became a flight commander in No 1 Squadron, flying Hurricanes, and later in the year was given command of No 616 Squadron. After a period on staff duties at HQ No 9 Group, he took

Above: Colin Gray with his Spitfire IX, which bears a squadron leader's pennant painted on the nose. (IWM CNA1133)

'refresher' periods with operational squadrons prior to the command of No 81 Squadron in North Africa, leading to the command of No 322 Wing. Returning to England, he ended his third operational tour on VE-Day, 8 May 1945, having flown 633 hours, mainly on operations, and scoring 27½ confirmed victories plus a number of probables.

Remaining in the RAF, where he reached the rank of Group Captain in 1954, he retired in 1961 to return to New Zealand. He died, aged 80, in August 1995.

Hafner, Raoul (1905–1981)

An Austrian, born in 1905, Raoul Hafner produced his first rotorcraft in 1927 while studying in Vienna. Reading of progress being made in Britain on vertical flight, he came to that country in 1932 to work on problems of cyclic pitch control. Then, using the Martin-Baker factory, he built his AR.III Gyroplane, a vertical lift autogyro with variable-incidence rotor blades, first flown in February 1937.

Hafner presaged the assault helicopter concept years before its time, and he planned to meet Air Ministry Specification A.22/38 for an army cooperation gyroplane. Prototypes for the latter were under construction by Short Brothers when war came and Hafner was interned as an alien. Following representations on his behalf he was permitted to take British citizenship and he worked for the Ministry of Aircraft Production on Rotachute and Rotaplane projects. Post-war, appointed Chief Designer (Helicopters) with Bristol, he designed the Sycamore, the first British production helicopter to obtain a Certificate of Airworthiness. Under his direction the Belvedere, Britain's first twin-rotor helicopter, evolved. From 1960 to 1969 he was technical Director (Research) of Westland Aircraft at Yeovil. He was lost accidentally, early in 1981 when he disappeared from his yacht.

Harris, Sir Arthur (1892–1984)

Arthur Travers Harris who, as related below, had a varied RAF career, will be remembered as Commander-in-Chief of RAF Bomber Command from 1942 until 1945. His forceful policy of bombing as a means of winning the war, to which end he mounted a continuous campaign against the major towns of the Third Reich, involved at times raids by a thousand or more aircraft.

Born on 18 April 1892 at Cheltenham, Harris joined the 1st Rhodesian Regiment in 1914 and returned to England the next year to join the Royal Flying Corps, wherein he became a squadron commander. After service throughout WWI he served in India, Iraq and Egypt during the 1920s. He was appointed Deputy Director of Plans at the Air Ministry 1934–37, then followed his first association with Bomber Command as AOC No 4 (Bomber) Group. In 1938 he headed an RAF delegation to the United States and Canada. When war was declared in September 1939 he took command of No 5 (Bomber) Group before becoming Deputy Chief of the Air Staff and heading another delegation to America.

Retiring from the RAF at the end of 1945, he became managing director of the South African Marine Corporation for five years. Marshal of the Royal Air Force Sir Arthur Harris, GCB OBE AFC and holder of various foreign decorations, died in 1984.

Ilyushin, S. V. (1894–1977)

Sergei Vladimirovich Ilyushin became one of Russia's leading designers. His aircraft were produced in their tens of thousands. As a student in the early 1920s at the Zhukovski Military Academy, he designed gliders. His first appointment was to the Scientific Technical Committee of the Military Air Forces Administration concerned with advocating the specifications to which aircraft were designed. His personal achievements later in this office were the CKB-55 and 57 ground attack prototypes, which, in their developed form, became the famous Shturmovik:

Above: Marshal of the Royal Air Force Sir Arthur Harris Bt GCB OBE AFC when holding the rank of Air Marshal in 1941. (Bruce Robertson collection)

when he headed his own design bureau this became the Il-2 and was reckoned to be one of the war-winning factors in the Russian armoury.

Turning in 1943 to transport aircraft design, his bureau produced the Il-12 and Il-14, enabling Aeroflot to provide a Soviet airline network; moreover, these airliners were widely exported. Russia's first turboprop airliner, the Il-18, paralleled the Bristol Britannia and his Il-28 provided the backbone of the Soviet bomber force in the 1950s.

Ilyushin designs, by his successors, continued in his name in the transport field. When he retired he held the rank of Engineer-General in the Soviet Forces and had been awarded the Order of Lenin and nominated a Hero of Socialist Labour.

Junkers, Professor Hugo (1859–1935)
An aircraft designer famed for his welded metal airframe construction and research into diesel propulsion, Hugo Junkers was a scientist specializing in thermodynamics, in which

sphere he was the founder of a gas heating company in Germany. He was born in 1859, but it was not until he was 50 years of age that his interests turned to aviation. During 1915 he produced the first of a series of metal monoplanes for the German Army, and at his Dessau factory the Junkers Flugzeugwerke produced some 300 aircraft during WWI, 227 of them being Junkers armoured biplanes.

Post-war Hugo Junkers turned to building civil aircraft, using also a base in Sweden to avoid restrictions imposed by the Allies. His rugged metal monoplanes became early 'bush' aircraft in Scandinavia and in North and South America. His firm's designs culminated, during his lifetime, from the single-engined Ju 52, the three-engined Ju 52/3m, which was built in its thousands, equipping airlines and becoming the Luftwaffe's main transport aircraft. His Jumo diesel aero-engine was widely exported. However, by this time the liberal-minded Hugo was regarded as politically unreliable by the Nazis. He was retired from office in 1933 and died on 3 February 1935, on his 75th birthday. The factory that he had established continued to grow and in 1944, with 140,000 employees, it was deemed the largest in the world.

Kamov, N. (1902–1973)
Nikolai Ilyich Kamov, born in Siberia 1902, became one of the noted Russian helicopter designers whose competence resulted in a Soviet design bureau being set up in his name. His early studies at the Tomsk Technical Institute had concerned locomotive design. In 1928, after qualifying as a pilot, he worked on experimental marine aircraft. His first association with rotary-winged aircraft came in 1929 when involved with developing a Russian version of the Cierva C-8 autogyro. Later he had his own design bureau, but the development of vertical lift aircraft was abandoned when Russia was attacked in 1941.

In 1945, under a new Kamov bureau, he concentrated his ideas for helicopters employing twin coaxial contra-rotating rotors. This method was first successfully applied to his Ka-8 design for an ultra-light helicopter that became dubbed 'the flying motorbike'. While the Ka-8s built were

Above: 'Sailor' Malan (right) and a colleague admire a wooden Javanese carving presented to him by W. A. de Vos as a Christmas present. Malan held the rank of Squadron Leader at the time. (IWM CH1872)

Above: Hans Joachim Marseille, victor in 158 engagements, is seen here in the Western Desert. (Bruce Robertson collection)

purely trials aircraft and the following Ka-10 in 1952 had only limited production, his two-seat utility Ka-15 went into series production for the Soviet Navy and Aeroflot. His stretched version, the Ka-18 in 1956, allowed a further passenger to be carried. With his coaxial rotor system well proven, he designed the Ka-25 as a standard anti-submarine helicopter for the Soviet Navy and a passenger version ensued. The Ka-26 of the 1960s introduced twin engines to the rotor system to produce a utility and agricultural helicopter for wide use in the USSR and export. Kamov died near Moscow in 1973, but his bureau continued to produce designs in his name.

Malan, A. G. 'Sailor' (1910–1963)

Group Captain Adolph Gysbert Malan DSO* DFC*, Legion d'Honneur, Czech

War Cross and Croix de Guerre of both Belgium and France, was a born leader and one of the earliest air aces of WWII. His nickname 'Sailor' resulted from his earlier service in the Merchant Marine. A South African, he joined the RAF in 1936 and after training flew Gauntlets with No 74 (Tiger) Squadron, whose Spitfires he was destined to lead in the Battle of Britain.

Realizing the inadequacy of the prescribed Fighter Command set formation attacks, he introduced the paired section and finger-four formation with such success that it suppressed the criticism that at first was levelled from above. Leadership was his forte, but on his own account he shot down 27 enemy aircraft by day and two by night during the Battle of Britain. Later he commanded the Biggin Hill Wing and then that station, which precluded further operations.

By then he had scored 32 victories, placing him third in the British Commonwealth listing, but it is more for his influence on RAF air fighting tactics that he is remembered.

Returning to his native South Africa post-war, he took up farming, which he later left for politics, taking an anti-apartheid stand in collaboration with other ex-servicemen. He died in 1963 at the age of 52.

Marseille, Hans Joachim (1919–1942)

In his book *The First and the Last*, Generalleutnant Adolf Galland wrote that Marseille was the unrivalled virtuoso of the fighter pilots of WWII and that his achievements had previously been regarded as impossible and were never exceeded after his death. While some German pilots were to gain higher scores than Marseille's 158 victories in 382 sorties, his score was the highest for a pilot pitted exclusively against British Commonwealth (RAF, RAAF and SAAF) personnel.

Marseille's initiation to air fighting came during the Battle of Britain, in which he obtained seven victories flying a Bf 109E. This experience served him well when, in April 1941, he was sent with JG 27 to North Africa, where he became the 'scourge of the desert air'. He realized that the British fighters were capable of very tight turns, so his favourite tactic was to dive, fire and zoom away. In his seventeen months in North Africa he accounted for a succession of Hurricanes, Tomahawks, Kittyhawks and, later, Spitfires. In his 158 confirmed victories, mainly flying the Bf 109F, only four were other than fighters, viz. two Baltimores, a Blenheim and a Maryland.

Born on 13 December 1919 the son of a senior German officer, he rebelled against authority in his early flying years. By the time he died, in a baling-out accident on 30 September 1942 in a new Bf 109G, he had risen to the rank of Hauptmann and been awarded the Knight's Cross with Oakleaves, Swords and Diamonds.

McCudden VC, J. T. B. (1895–1918)

James Thomas Byford McCudden VC DSO* MC* MM probably knew more about the airframe and engine of the aircraft he flew than any other fighter ace. Born on 28 March 1895 into a military family, he enlisted as a bugler in the Royal Engineers in 1910. Transferring to the Royal Flying Corps in 1913, he was an Air Mechanic First Class when war came in 1914, taking him to France with No 3 Squadron RFC. Flying at times during 1915 as an observer, he gained some piloting experience and was sent to England early in 1916 for flying training.

In mid-1916 he was posted to No 20 Squadron flying F.E.2ds, from which he transferred to No 29 Squadron flying D.H.2s. After gaining a few air combat victories he went to Joyce Green and later Dover as an air fighting instructor. After a further spell at the Front flying Pups, he again returned to England, but briefly as he was appointed a flight commander in No 56 Squadron. His victory log then stood at seven, but by the time he left this S.E.5a-equipped squadron, six months later, he had 57 victories to his credit.

It was while returning from another spell of Home Establishment, to take command of No 60 Squadron at the Front, that he met his end. He took off from Aux-le-Château aerodrome on 9 July 1918 but the engine of his S.E.5a failed, causing the aircraft to stall and bring an end to a magnificent fighting career.

Messerschmitt, Wilhelm (1898–1978)

Wilhelm ('Willy') Messerschmitt, born at Frankfurt in 1898, helped to shape the industrialization of German aircraft production, in which nearly 50,000 aircraft produced were to his designs. While still a minor he designed his first aircraft in 1916, and he was still studying in 1923 when he founded Flugzeugbau Messerschmitt. Merging his company with Bayerische Flugzeugwerke four years later, he became the firm's design chief. After building sailplanes, he turned to powered aircraft, including some of all-metal construction. His Bf 108 cabin monoplane of 1934 had a wide market, and the following Bf 109 became the Luftwaffe's standard fighter with some 35,000 eventually built, the largest production figure for any fight-

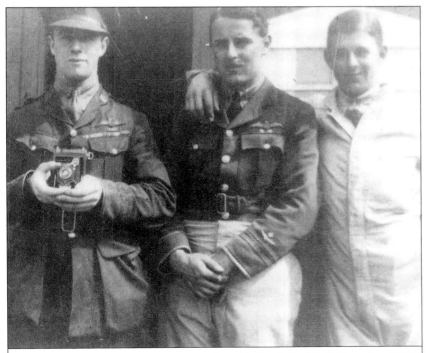

Above: James McCudden, a keen photographer, with friends Capt G. C. Maxwell and Lt E. L. Zinc. (Bruce Robertson collection)

Above: 'Willy' Messerschmitt. (Bruce Robertson collection)

Above: R. J. Mitchell (left) with Bert Hinkler (behind), about to depart for the Schneider Trophy Contest at Baltimore in 1925. (Bruce Robertson collection)

er type. In 1938 the firm became Messerschmitt AG.

During WWII his Bf 110, Me 210 and Me 410 had more limited success, but the Me 262 was the first production jet to become operational. His Me 321 Gigant, with a useful load of 22 tons, was the largest glider and landplane in the world.

Post-war Messerschmitt designed prefabricated houses. Wilhelm returned to aviation in 1952 by designing for Hispano in Spain and then moved to Egypt. From 1956 he worked for Bölkow and Heinkel and in 1973 became honorary chairman of Messerschmitt-Bölkow-Blohm. He died in September 1978.

Mikoyan, Artem (1905–1970)

Probably the most famous of all Russian designers, Artem Ivanovich Mikoyan is remembered in particular for the initial series of Russian jet fighters, loosely known as Migs but more correctly as MiGs, from the design bureau of Mikoyan and Gurevich. The latter, Mikhail Gurevich, a talented mathematician, joined Mikoyan in 1938 tasked with producing a high-altitude fighter.

Mikoyan, born in 1905, went through military academy before joining the design team of Polikarpov in the 1930s. When teamed with Gurevich their initial MiG-l design, developed into the MiG-3, gave Russia one of the finest fighters in the world when the country was attacked in 1941. By the end of 1942 over 3,000 had been built. Design work continued on single- and twin-engine fighters.

Post-war, benefiting from captured German equipment, the MiG bureau produced a version of the Messerschmitt Me 262. Their more original work resulted in the MiG-15, 17 and 19 single-seat jet fighters that were built in their thousands and armed most East European countries for two decades. With the following MiG-21 and subsequent designs, MiGs became the most widely used jet fighters.

Engineer Col-Gen Mikoyan, Hero of Socialist Labour and holder of the Order of Lenin, died on 9 December 1970.

Mil, Mikhail (1903–1970)

Like his compatriot helicopter designer Kamov, Mikhail Leontovich Mil, who was to became Russia's leading helicopter designer, first had experience of autogyros. Born in Siberia in 1903, he graduated from the Tomsk Institute to become in 1936 Kamov's deputy. When war came in 1941 he did field service with the First Autogyro Artillery Communications Squadron and later worked on rotary wing stability and control. In 1945 he was appointed to head the Soviet Union's Rotating Wing Scientific Research Laboratory.

The first design to be placed in production by the Mil bureau, set up in 1947, proved a great success. The Mi-1 light helicopter, and its twin-turbine Mi-2 development, captured world helicopter records for altitude, speed and distance, going into large-scale production in Russia and Poland for home use and export. The following Mi-4, rivalling the Sikorsky S-55 series in the West, progressed into the 25-seat Mi-8. In 1965 the Mi-6 heavy-lift transport helicopter went into large-scale production, followed by the specialist Mi-10 flying crane. This series culminated with the Mi-28, the world's largest helicopter.

By the mid-1960s it could be said that more Mils had been built, and were in service, than any other designs of helicopter throughout the world. The designs continued from the bureau in the Mil name, but Mikhail Mil died near Moscow on 31 January 1970.

Mitchell, R. J. (1895–1937)

An aircraft designer who died at the early age of 42, Reginald Joseph Mitchell made his mark on British aviation in his short span of life and will be remembered as the designer of one of the most famous fighters of all time – the Supermarine Spitfire. Had he lived it is certain that he would have been knighted.

Born in 1895, R. J. Mitchell, after an apprenticeship, started work in 1916 with the Supermarine Aviation Works. He soon became involved with design work for the Sea Lion flying boat series being produced for the Schneider Trophy Contest. While continuing with flying boat design, he soon realized that floatplanes stood the best chance in the maritime Schneider event. Under his guidance the Supermarine S.4, S.5 and S.6 series evolved, winning successive contests and the Schneider Trophy outright in 1931; moreover, the S.6B achieved a world speed record that year.

It was his high-speed aircraft experience that Mitchell put into meeting an Air Ministry Specification for an interceptor fighter from which the Spitfire evolved. At this period Mitchell had his time divided to meet another specification for a four-engine bomber. During this time he became gravely ill and an operation was only partially successful. Nevertheless, he now learned to fly, making his first solo in G-ABEK on 1 July 1934. He succumbed to cancer 11 June 1937, having lived to see the proving of the prototype Spitfire.

Mitchell, Brig-Gen William (1879– 1936)

An air strategist who forcibly demonstrated his views on air power, Gen Mitchell is now regarded as one of the principal architects of American air power. He was born in Nice 29 December 1879 during a French Riviera sojourn by his parents. The Spanish-American War of 1898 induced him to enlist and, as a senator's son, he was soon commissioned, electing to serve in the US Signal

Above: Brig-Gen William Mitchell, photographed in about 1922. (Author's collection)

Corps. Transferring to the Corps' Aviation Section in 1916, he received training at the Curtiss Flying School. With the American Expeditionary Force in France, he rose to become Chief of the Air Service Army Group and had at one period a force of 1,500 aircraft under his operational control.

After WWI, conscious of the lack of appreciation of air power by the Army and Navy in the United States, he agitated for a separate air arm divorced from their control. In his capacity as Assistant Chief of Air Service he aptly demonstrated the vulnerability of warships in bombing experiments carried out against captured German, and obsolete American, warships during 1921. An outspoken tirade against the military traditionalists led to his sus-

Above: Werner Mölders in the cockpit of his Messerschmitt Bf 109.
(Bruce Robertson collection)

pension from duty by sentence of a court martial. Electing to resign his commission, he continued his campaign outside the Service until he died of heart failure 20 February 1936.

Mölders, Werner (1913-1941)

The most influential German fighter leader in the early years of WWII was Werner Mölders, who, by 1936, was a Leutnant in the Luftwaffe instructing in fighting tactics. His operational experience began with the fighter group J 88 of the Legion Condor flying He 51 biplanes, taking over from Adolf Galland. His fourteen victories in the Spanish Civil War made him the most successful fighter pilot of the Legion, but it was his qualities of leadership that brought him the rank of Hauptmann at the age of 25.

From September 1939 he was in action on the Western Front with JG 53, shooting down the occasional French Curtiss Hawk and RAF Hurricane. During the Battle of France his score rose quickly to 23, but he was himself shot down and taken prisoner by the French. Released after the armistice with France, he was promoted Major to lead JG 51 during the Battle of Britain and later on the Eastern Front. In July 1941 he was appointed Inspector of the Luftwaffe's fighters and again promoted and decorated.

With his personal victory log standing at 115 (68 on the Western Front and 33 on the Eastern Front), he died on 22 November 1941 in an He 111 while on the way to attend Ernst Udet's funeral at Hitler's request.

Nesterov, P. N. (1887-1914)

Petr Nikolaevich Nesterov, born in February 1887 at Nizhni Novgorod (now Gorki), was Russia's first air hero. As a measure of the esteem in which he was held the town of Sholkiv, in the Lvov region, was renamed Nesterov in his honour. Having an early interest in aviation and attempting to build a monoplane while serving in the artillery of the Imperial Russian Army, he was selected for officer pilot training in October 1911 and gained his pilot's certificate on 12 September 1912. By May 1913 he was commanding the XI Corps Air Squadron near Kiev.

When stunting with a Russian-built (Dux) Nieuport Type 4 monoplane on 27 August 1913 he became the first man to loop-the-loop, for which he was initially reproved for endangering government property. This was soon recognized as a unique feat, his career was unaffected and promotion to Staff Captain ensued. Soon after the outbreak of WWI, on 26 August 1914, he was at an airfield in Galicia when it was attacked by three enemy aircraft led by the Austrian Baron von Rosenthal. Taking off in an unarmed Morane Type M monoplane, Nesterov rammed Rosenthal's aeroplane and both men fell to their deaths. This was Russia's first air battle casualty and the first case ever of aircraft ramming in air warfare.

Park, Sir Keith (1892-1975)

Air Chief Marshal Sir Keith Rodney Park GCB KBE MC DFC MA (Oxon), born in New Zealand 15 June 1892 the son of a professor, had the most exacting RAF air commands in WWII. Joining the Army in 1914, he transferred to the RFC in 1917 and remained in the RAF post-war. With other aspiring leaders – Sholto-Douglas, Peirse and Portal – he was a 1922 RAF Staff College entrant, after which he was appointed to Air Staff (Operations) duties in RAF Middle East. Back in England, he commanded No 111 (Fighter) Squadron in 1927-29 before promotion and a series of staff appointments.

As Air Officer Commanding No 11 Group, with its fighter stations in south-east England, he bore the brunt of the Luftwaffe's onslaught in the 1940 Battle of Britain. His brilliant handling of the squadrons under his control was a major factor in the victory achieved. Sent to oversee training at the close of 1940, he was recalled for operational duties, first to command the air defences of the beleaguered island of Malta in 1942 and then as AOC Middle East in 1944. Finally he was appointed Allied Air Commander-in-Chief South-East Asia in February 1945. Retiring to his New Zealand homeland, he died on 6 February 1975.

Platz, Reinhold (1886-1966)

Reinhold Platz, born at Cottbus in Brandenburg on 16 January 1886, was a first-class welder and a good 'rule of thumb' designer who, in serving Anthony Fokker, contributed to both the design and the construction of Fokker aircraft for twenty of their formative years.

Above: Air Chief Marshal Sir Keith Park during the Battle of Britain, when he commanded No 11 Group Fighter Command. (Author's collection)

Platz, who had learnt autogenous welding in 1904, became highly skilled and instructed in the technique in Russia, Switzerland and Germany. In 1912 he offered his services to Fokker, who used metal construction in his 'Spin' series of aeroplanes. When Martin Kreutzer, the firm's chief engineer, was killed test-flying a Fokker D.I biplane, Platz was appointed in his place. The following year he became manager of the Schwerin works, employing some 1,600 people. Combining management with design, Platz played an important part in

Fokker Dr.I triplane, D.VII biplane and D.VIII monoplane production.

Proving to Fokker that he had intuitive ability to design as well as being a skilled engineer, he remained the head of the Fokker design team until 1931, when designers with a more scientific approach to design and construction took over. Platz then left the company. While there have been published reports that Platz was badly treated by Fokker (though not by Platz himself), the firm's manager at the time stated, when these allegations were made, that Platz had no reason

professionally or financially to be discontented.

Porte, J. C. (1884–1919)

Born on 24 February 1884 in County Cork, John Cyril Porte CMG entered the Royal Navy as a cadet in 1898 and opted for the submarine branch. Possibly it was the hardships of early submarine service that led to him contracting pulmonary tuberculosis, to which he succumbed 22 October 1919.

From 1908, when involved in the building of a glider, he took an active interest in aeronautics and two years later he became airborne in a Santos Dumont Demoiselle of his own making. Invalided out of the Navy in 1911, he became Technical Director of the British Deperdussin Company and in 1913 test pilot for White and Thompson, who held rights for producing Curtiss flying boats. Through meeting Glenn Curtiss, Porte was given the chance to make the first Atlantic crossing by air in a Curtiss craft. This attempt was thwarted by war in 1914, when Porte immediately returned to Britain, re-joined the Navy and was given command of RNAS Hendon. Meeting the Director of the Air Department, he interested Admiralty sources in acquiring Curtiss flying boats for maritime patrolling. By the time these were arriving, Porte had been given command of RNAS Felixstowe. There he redesigned the Curtiss' hulls had the craft re-engined, leading to the successful F.2A and F.3 flying boats produced for anti-submarine patrolling in 1916–18. Larger flying boats were produced under his direction and to his designs, and he was also involved in various methods of flying boat construction and maritime operational techniques. He has been rightly dubbed 'The father of the British flying boat'.

Reitsch, Hanna (1912–1979)

A renowned pilot and possibly the world's most outstanding glider pilot with many gliding records, Hanna Reitsch became the first female test pilot and the first woman to fly helicopters and jet aircraft.

She was born in Silesia in 1912, and as a medical student aspired to be a flying missionary doctor. Taking the opportunity to fly in her homeland, she made her first gliding record flight in 1934. With the expansion of the German aircraft industry she became a test pilot with powered aircraft and experienced several crashes. She became the first woman to be awarded the Iron Cross First and Second Class. In the course of her work, holding the rank of Flugkapitän, she flew the Me 163 rocket-powered aircraft and, because of her small stature, she was the only pilot to fly a modified V-1 flying bomb.

She had a stormy meeting with Göring and was with Hitler shortly before his suicide. Ill when Berlin fell to the Russians, she defied her doctor to make the last flights from the German capital, ferrying out wounded German soldiers. Continuing flying post-war, she achieved her final glid-

Above: Hanna Reitsch, who was to achieve a final gliding record after having turned sixty years of age. (DAeC via E. R. Hooton)

Above: Manfred von Richthofen in the centre of (left to right) Festner, Schaefer, his brother Lothar von Richthofen and Kurt Wolff. (IWM Q42262)

ing record while in her sixties. She died in August 1979.

Richthofen, Manfred von (1892-1918)

Rittmeister Manfred Freiherr von Richthofen achieved such fame as the highest scoring fighter pilot of WWI that his name is better known than those of most of the military leaders of his time. Born on 2 May 1892 in Silesia, he indulged as a child in local sports and became a proficient marksman. A keen horseman with military cadet school training, he followed his father into the cavalry. When war came in 1914 he was a subaltern on the Russian Front, but was quickly transferred with his unit to the Western Front. Realizing that the day of the cavalry had passed, he transferred to the German Flying Service and again operated on the Russian Front.

His transfer to fighter aircraft came from selection by the leading fighter ace Oswald Boelcke. The first of his confirmed victories came with the shooting down of an F.E.2b on 17 September 1916. Practically all his 80 victories were achieved along the British sector of the Western Front. He rose to command Jasta 11 and then Jagdgeschwader Nr 1 (JG 1), a grouping of Jasta that became widely known as Richthofen's Flying Circus, partly through its mobile base and also because of the bright finishes of its aircraft, Albatros biplanes and Fokker Dr.I triplanes.

Manfred's younger brother Lothar, who scored 40 victories, was, like Manfred, awarded Germany's highest decoration for gallantry, the Ordre Pour le Mérite. Lothar, surviving three woundings, died in an air accident post-war. Manfred, shot down on 21 April 1918, opened a controversy alive to this day as to who fired the fatal shot. Officially credited to Capt Roy Brown from his combat report, he was, however, seen to fall to earth under fire from the rifles and machine guns of Australian infantrymen who claim that no other aircraft was in the vicinity at that time.

Roe, Sir (Edwin) Alliott Verdon (1877-1958)

A. V. Roe, born on 26 April 1877, aviation pioneer and founder of the famous Avro aircraft firm, was a keen cyclist from the age of six. After engineering training he went surveying in Canada from 1892. At the turn of the century he became interested in aeronautics and on an Atlantic voyage in 1902 he launched model gliders from his ship to observe their flying characteristics.

Turning his interests to powered flight, in 1906 A. V. Roe patented the 'joystick' method of single-hand control to warp control surfaces. From prize money in a *Daily Mail* model aeroplane competition he worked on a full-scale-craft. His Roe I biplane, basically an enlargement of his model, made short hops from 8 June 1908. In partnership with the JAP engine designer J. A. Prestwick, he built the Roe I triplane which first bounded into the air 5 June 1909. In June 1910, with financial help from his brother, H. V. Roe, he founded A. V. Roe and Company. A series of triplanes, biplanes and monoplanes ensued. He built a Curtiss-type aircraft in 1911, and he produced the first practical British floatplane. It was his 504 (the series started at 501) biplane that went into large-scale production during WWI and for some subsequent years that made Avro aircraft famous.

Well established, the firm continued after WWI, but A. V. Roe left the company in 1928 and was knighted the following year. He died in 1958.

Above: A museum photograph of A. V. Roe beneath a model of the Roe 1 biplane. (Brooklands Museum)

Above: Sir Henry Royce. (Bruce Robertson collection)

1906 the firm of Rolls-Royce was formed and two years later its Derby works opened. The Hon C. S. Rolls, seeking new fields, became a pioneer airman, taking up the No 2 British aviator's certificate. He was killed when his aircraft broke up in the air on 12 July 1910.

Rolls-Royce as a car firm expanded rapidly. Early in the 1914-18 War it received contracts for making Renault aero engines. This induced Royce to create a team to design in this field. Thus the famous 'Birds of Prey' series evolved, culminating in WWI with the 375hp Eagle 12-cylinder 'V' aero engine. Royce, in poor health, worked on designs at St Margeret's Bay, near Deal, then West Wittering, for his famous Kestrel and the 'R' Schneider Trophy Contest engines, forerunners of the Merlin. F. H. Royce, who was knighted in 1930 and had taken up farming, died on 22 April 1933.

Short, Horace, Eustace and Oswald (1875-1932/1872-1917/1883-1969)

The oldest established aeronautical firm in the UK is that of Short Brothers, registered in November 1908. While acquiring rights for making Wright biplanes, the firm persisted with designs of its own. In WWI it became the major producer of float-planes for the RNAS and the main manufacturer of flying boats for Britain between the wars. Its Short Empire flying boats of the late 1930s linked the British Empire by air routes and its armed version, the Sunderland, was the RAF's main British maritime reconnaissance flying boat of WWII.

Horace (1872-1917), the eldest, with an inventive turn of mind in several fields, was supportive of the aeronautical interests of Eustace (1875-1932) and Oswald (1883-1969), who were balloonists from the turn of the century. Horace proposed a stratospheric balloon and the following year the brothers had War Office contracts for conventional balloons. Horace led the way into aviation and the brothers followed.

Horace was intimately concerned with torpedo-carrying aircraft and his folding-wing designs facilitated stowage for carrier borne aircraft. Eustace, concentrating on airship and balloon design and construction, died in 1932 in the cockpit of a Short

Royce, Sir Henry (1863-1933)

Royce and Rolls are names associated with élite automobiles and successful aero engines. The two founders of this great company had differing backgrounds Born in 1863, Frederick Henry Royce found employment in jobs such as telegraph boy until an aunt paid for his apprenticeship to the Great Northern Railway. After working for various firms he set up his own engineering workshop in Manchester and built cars. One of these, in 1904, caught the eye of the Hon C. S. Rolls, born in 1877, a balloonist and racing driver who sold continental cars. In

Mussel he had just landed. Oswald, who took over Horace's work in 1917, went on to become Life President of Short Brothers & Harland Ltd and lived to see his firm produce the RAF's famous Sunderland flying boat, the service's first four-engine monoplane bomber, the Stirling, and post-war the Short SC.1 experimental vertical take-off jet aircraft.

Sikorsky, Igor (1889–1972)

There are three distinct phases in the life of Igor Sikorsky, and he achieved fame in all three. Born in Russia at Kiev on 25 May 1889, he began the construction of a helicopter as early as 1909, but after visiting Western Europe he turned to fixed-wing aircraft design and received orders for his biplanes from the Russian Army. Just prior to WWI he built the world's first four-engine aircraft, later produced as a bomber in the war.

Above: Igor Sikorsky at the controls of his VS-300 helicopter during its first flight on 14 September 1939. (Bruce Robertson collection)

Leaving Russia after the Revolution, he emigrated to the United States, where, with associates, he founded the Sikorsky Aero Engineering Corporation which later became part of United Aircraft. By 1937 his flying boat designs were in service on long distance routes, notably by Pan American Airways.

Sikorsky revived his quest for a successful helicopter in the late 1930s and on 14 September 1939 he made his first flight in the VS-300, the first practical machine. The firm went on to produce a wide range of military and commercial helicopters, his basic designs being also built under licence by Westland in Britain, by Sud (later Aérospatiale) in France and by Agusta in Italy. Sikorsky retired as engineering manager in 1957 but he remained a consultant. He died at Easton, Connecticut, on 26 October 1972.

Smith Barry, Robert (1886–1969)

The man who contributed more to the art of airmanship than any other pilot is said to be Robert R. Smith Barry AFC. Born the son of a Grenadier Guards officer, he spent some time at Eton, failed university entrance and soon resigned from his initial post in the Consular Service. Learning to fly at Larkhill in 1911, he went on to instruct at the Bristol School. Commissioned in the Royal Flying Corps on 10 August 1912, he joined the No 1 Course at the Central Flying School. After proceeding to France with No 5 Squadron on 14 August 1914 he was severely injured four days later in a B.E.8. After convalescence and training duties he returned to the Front with No 60 Squadron, which he commanded from July to December 1916.

Late in 1916 he wrote a paper on improving pilot training by having trainers fitted for full dual control, advocating the Avro 504 series, with the pupil occupying the pilot's seat from the outset. Commanding No 1 Reserve Squadron at Gosport, he put his various ideas into effect with the result that his Gosport System of Pilot Training was adopted by the RAF and eventually the world.

After relinquishing his commission as a lieutenant-colonel in 1921, he rejoined the RAF in 1940, serving as an instructor and station commander in

Above: Thomas (later Sir Thomas) Sopwith at his desk in about 1916. (Bruce Robertson collection)

the UK and India until mid-1943, when he resigned his commission in the rank of Squadron Leader. He died in February 1969.

Sopwith, Sir Thomas (1888–1989)

The name Sopwith would have had a far greater impact but for the reticence of this pioneer airman and aircraft manufacturer. T. O. M. Sopwith was first a balloonist, but he flew aeroplanes from 22 October 1910 and in that year broke the British endurance flight record. During 1911 he toured America, giving displays and passenger flights.

He entered the aeronautical design field in 1912, and success came the following year when his Tabloid-type biplane, mounted on floats, won the 1914 Schneider Trophy Contest. Orders for aircraft from the Admiralty and War Office ensued, increasing with the war in 1914. His 1½ Strutter biplane of 1916, in two-seat fighter and single-seat bomber versions, was

Above: Wg Cdr Stanford Tuck is seen in the centre of this group at a ceremony organized by the Croydon Airport Society. Sir Peter Masefield is on Tuck's right. (Author)

built in France in its hundreds and in its hundreds by British contractors. The firm's later Pup, Camel, Dolphin and Snipe fighters brought Britain air supremacy in WWI.

After WWI the firm closed through lack of orders, but in 1920 Sopwith founded H. G. Hawker Engineering, named after his former test pilot who had been killed flying. Had Sopwith chosen to put his own name to the firm, the RAF's mainstay Hawker aircraft between the wars would have been known as Sopwith aircraft. Similarly the famous Hawker fighters Hurricane, Typhoon and Tempest would have borne names alliterative with Sopwith, making his name even more famous. Sir Thomas Sopwith CBE, born on 18 January 1888, died on 27 January 1989.

Stanford-Tuck, R. R. (1916–1987)

After leaving the Merchant Navy at the age of 19 in 1935, Tuck joined the RAF and rose through the ranks to be a flight commander with No 92 Squadron in time for the Battle of Britain, having over a three-day period a little earlier scored six consecutive victories in aerial combat – no doubt due to his keen study of tactics, on which, believing those officially advanced to be outdated, he held his own theories,. In September he had gained sufficient seniority for these ideas to be tried out, and his theories were vindicated.

By the following year Robert Roland Stanford-Tuck was at Biggin Hill in command of a Wing, but only a month after this promotion he was shot down near Boulogne, ground fire having set

his aircraft alight. Taken prisoner-of-war, he was confined for three years, eventually escaping back to England in 1945. He left the RAF with a total of 29 kills to his credit, and holding the rank of Wing Commander, to enter mushroom farming, although he was always ready to assist historians with his accurate appraisal of WWII air fighting. This inevitably led to his assisting at the Royal Air Force Museum, Hendon, where he proved to have a flair for public relations and where those who met him could not fail to be impressed by his still-active, incisive mind. He could occasionally be persuaded to give public talks on his wartime experiences, and on these occasions he proved to be a forward-looking believer in aviation. Post-war he and Adolf Galland (q.v.) formed a strong friendship.

Above: Kurt Tank, Technical Director of the Focke-Wulf organization. (Bruce Robertson collection)

Tank, Kurt (1898–1983)

Kurt Tank was an aircraft designer who raised the Focke Wulf organization from a workshop to a factory. He joined the firm on 1 November 1933 to head its design office and soon became its technical director. The FW 187 twin-engine fighter and the FW 200 four-engine airliner bear testimony to his design versatility. As early as 1942 he was involved in studies of a jet fighter, the Ta 183, but it was his piston-engine FW 190 and its Ta 152 successor that brought him renown.

The son of a sergeant in a grenadier regiment who became a hydraulics engineer after leaving the army, Kurt Tank was born at Bromberg on 24 February 1898. Volunteering to serve in the German Army during WWI, he was severely wounded, decorated for bravery and commissioned. Continuing engineering studies during his service, he went on to the Technical High School at Berlin-Charlottenburg.

He sought work with various manufacturers and was responsible, *inter alia,* for designing the internally expanding brakes on an RAF prototype of the 1920s, the Beardmore Inflexible. After WWII he spent time on design work in Argentina and India, but returned to Germany to work for Panavia. He died at his Munich home in the summer of 1983.

Trenchard, Viscount (1873–1956)

Hugh Montague Trenchard, born on 3 February 1873, joined the Army in 1893 and had the distinction in later life of being called 'The Father of the RAF' by becoming its first Chief of the Air Staff and holding that position for ten of the formative years of the Service. Although severely wounded during his Boer War service in 1899–1902, he continued to serve in African colonial regiments. In 1912, after learning to fly in England, he transferred to the Royal Flying Corps and became Assistant Commandant of the Central Flying School. During WWI he rose to command the RFC in France and the Independent Force in 1918.

As Chief of the Air Staff in the 1920s, Trenchard founded Cranwell and Halton for officer and technical training, opened the RAF Staff College and inaugurated the Auxiliary Air Force, University Air Squadrons and the Special Reserve. On leaving the RAF he became Commissioner of Metropolitan Police in 1931–35 and was a trustee of the Imperial War Museum from 1937 to 1945. After the war he continued his pre-war appointments as Chairman of the United Africa Company and as a director of the Goodyear Tyre & Rubber Company (GB) Ltd. Marshal of the Royal Air Force Viscount Trenchard GCB OM GCVO DSO DCL LLD died on 10 February 1956 and was buried in Westminster Abbey.

giving away plans developed into the Messerschmitt Bf 110. Released with Russia at war, he again headed a design bureau where the developed ANT-58 prototype, as the ANT-61, became the Tu-2; this, its variants and developments served in WWII and into the 1960s.

After the war Tupolev's bureau produced its version of the Boeing B-29 Superfortress and, using the basic Tu-2 configuration, adapted it for turbine power. An original design, the Tu-104, made Russia the second country in the world to produce a gas-turbine airliner; from this the swept-wing Tu-16 bomber evolved. A series of jet airliners ensued, the Tu-124, 134 and 154 matching those of the Western world. When Eng Lt-Gen A. N. Tupolev died on 23 December 1972, his son, Alexei A. Tupolev, took over most of his responsibilities.

Voisin, Charles and Gabriel (1888–1912/1886–1973)

The Voisin brothers, having experimented with kites at the turn of the century, built a float-mounted glider with Louis Blériot. That same year, foreseeing the development of aviation, they established an aircraft factory, Les Frères Voisin, at Billancourt. An early customer was the wealthy Brazilian Alberto Santos-Dumont. Their 1907 biplane enabled Henry Farman to make his record flight of one kilometre on 13 January 1908, and Britain's first certificated pilot, J. T. C. Moore-Brabazon, first learned to fly on a Voisin.

Gabriel carried on the factory after Charles died in a motoring accident in 1912. Even before WWI reconaissance aircraft were being made by Avions Voisin for the French and Russian Armies. During WWI the firm's steel-framed pusher biplanes went into large-scale production, limited numbers being supplied to the RNAS and RFC. A characteristic of the wartime Voisins was their four-wheeled undercarriages. The Types 8 and 10 bombers equipped 28 French escadrilles and, in advance of their time, a few were armed with 37mm cannon. Gabriel faded from the aviation scene to produce cars from 1919 to 1939, taking over first an unused Citroën design. His cars, like his aeroplanes from 1914, bore the firm's motif, 'Avions Voisin'.

Above: Marshal of the Royal Air Force Viscount Trenchard presents a trophy to a Halton apprentice. (Crown Copyright)

Tupolev, A. N. (1888–1972)

Andrei Nikolaevich Tupolev held office heading a Soviet bureau longer than any other designer. His association with aircraft started in WWI at the Duks factory in Moscow. After the Revolution he helped to build up Soviet aircraft production plants. In 1922 his appointment to chair a commission for metal-framed aircraft construction resulted in an aircraft series designated by his initials – ANT. Some of the world's largest aircraft followed, including the ANT-20 *Maxim Gorki* of 1934.

Tupolev was imprisoned from 1936 after visiting Germany and allegedly

Wallis, Sir Barnes (1887–1979)

Sir Barnes Wallis CBE, who had two doctorates and was a member of several learned societies, is associated with his persistent experimentation to provide a dam-bursting bomb in WWII that breached the Mohne and Eder dams; however, that was but one facet of his inventiveness.

Barnes Neville Wallis, born on 26 September 1887, trained as a marine engineer with J. S. White & Co. of Cowes, Isle of Wight, after which he was employed on design work for air-

Above: Dr Barnes Wallis (right) with Air Chief Marshal the Hon Sir Ralph Cochrane CBE KCB AFC in the shadow of an Avro Lancaster bomber. (Crown Copyright)

ship development by Vickers from 1913 to 1915. Joining the Army and then the Royal Navy at the start of WWI, he was released for further airship design work with Vickers. During 1923–30, as Chief Engineer of the Airship Guarantee Company at Howden, he designed Britain's most powerful airship, the R.100.

With the age of the airship passing, he returned to Vickers to become Chief Designer (Structures), and progressed to Chief of Aeronautical Research and Development of Vickers-Armstrong. During this time he introduced his geodetic method of airframe construction, first on the Wellesley and then on the Wellington, built in its thousands during WWII. Apart from his dam-busting bombs he was involved with several specialist weapon projects. After the war he pioneered the variable-geometry (swing-wing) concept as now used on the Tornado and some US aircraft. He died in 1979.

Watson-Watt, Sir Robert (1892–1973)

Watson-Watt will always be associated with radar as its most prominent pioneer. That he developed it at a time when it became vital to the air defence of Great Britain and of general benefit to the air world gives him a status equal to any personality in aviation.

Born on 13 April 1892 in Scotland, Robert Alexander Watson-Watt first started on an academic career. In 1915 he changed to a scientific career when asked to join the Meteorological Office branch at the Royal Aircraft Factory, Farnborough. There he conceived the 'Instantaneous Visual Radio Direction Finder', which had to await advances in the manufacture of cathode ray tubes before development. Watson-Watt himself wrote that in the decade 1922–32 the germs of radar became visible; they became viable in 1935. From that time he headed a team that devised the radar detection chain that was instrumental in winning the Battle of Britain, and then helped its further development. For security reasons radar was then known as RDF (Radio Direction-Finding), and then radio-location. During the years 1943–45 he was Deputy Chairman of the War Cabinet's Radio Board and he remained in government service until 1952.

Sir Robert Watson-Watt CB DSc LLD FRS, who received his knighthood in 1942, set up, with partners, firms in the United States and Canada and in his later years spent much time in these countries. He died in 1973.

White, Sir George (1882–1916)

Sir George White, born in 1882, was the founder and builder of the British and Colonial Aeroplane Company, which was registered at the same time, in February 1910, as the better known Bristol Aeroplane Company. A financier, Sir George headed for many years George White & Co. of Bristol. He was described by C. G. Grey as one of the legendary Bristol merchant venturers, although his fortune was not made in ships but in land transport – trams, buses and taxis. By venturing into aviation he made Bristol one of the largest aircraft constructing centres in Europe.

A memorial to his fame in the aeronautical field still stands in his buildings for aircraft construction near Bristol. These include the spacious sheds from the Filton terminus of Bristol tramways that enabled the firm, with its other plants, to produce 5,252 aircraft in WWI, and these sheds continued in use throughout WWII. But Sir George died suddenly on 22 November 1916. He is remembered today through a Chair of Aeronautics at Bristol University endowed in his name.

His brother, Stanley (later Sir Stanley), also of George White & Co., was elected Chairman of the Bristol Company in January 1917 and after a long association became Deputy Chairman in later years.

Whittle, Sir Frank (1907–1996)

Frank Whittle was 22 years old when he took out a patent, that he later allowed to lapse, for a turbojet engine. This invention, by his persistence and engineering competence, revolutionized military aircraft and gave Britain a lead in civil aviation.

Born on 1 June 1907, Whittle inherited his inventiveness from his father. After joining the 1923 entry of the RAF's apprenticeship scheme, he was awarded a cadetship. Later, as a fighter pilot and flying instructor, his true *métier* was found to be in specialist engineering. Involving British Thompson Houston in his ideas, he formed Power Jets Ltd for developing a jet engine.

Above: Sir Frank Whittle as an RAF Group Captain. (IWM CH. 11367)

Working closely with George Carter of the Gloster Aircraft Company, he evolved the Gloster Whittle jet-powered prototype to Air Ministry Specification E.28/39. The first flight, made from Cranwell, was on 15 May 1941. As a serving officer, reaching the rank of Air Commodore, Whittle was appointed to technical posts associated with the development of the jet engine. His eminent work brought him the OM, a knighthood (KBE 1948) and an award of £100,000 at the age of 41. After retirement from the RAF in 1948 he became a consultant. He died in America in August 1996, aged 89.

Zeppelin, Count (1838–1917)

The German aristocrat Count Ferdinand von Zeppelin, founded Luftschiffbau Zeppelin, which produced 119 of the world's 161 rigid airships, built between 1897 and 1933.

Born on 8 July 1838, he took up a military career, retiring as a German Army general in 1890. Not until then did he devote his time to designing lighter-than-air craft and advocating their use to the Army and Navy for Germany's defence and security. The petrol engine being exploited by Daimler at this time gave the light power unit he sought. In 1898, at the age of sixty, he started building his first rigid airship, 420ft in length and of 399,000 cu ft capacity, in a floating dock on Lake Constance. As the LZ1, his airship, first flying on 2 July 1900, alerted the German government and commercial firms to the possibilities of the airship as a reconnaissance medium and as a passenger transport.

Count Zeppelin persisted in spite of many mishaps. The five Zeppelins LZ4–LZ8 were all wrecked or burnt in the years 1908–11. The very size of succeeding Zeppelins, up to 650ft long, captured the imagination of the German people, particularly during WWI. When the Count died, on 8 March 1917, his nephew took over control of his affairs. Due to the emphasis of post-WWI literature on the Zeppelins' bombing of Britain and the loss of seventeen Zeppelins in the process, their real worth to the German Navy – their continuous reconnaissance patrolling – is often overlooked.

AFTERWORD

The dawn of mankind's *en masse* fighting propensities on land is lost in the mists of time, while that of maritime warfare is open to debate, although there is little doubt that some type of national war fleet was created by Alfred the Great in AD 897. Only the beginnings of air fighting can be traced with certainty, so that in practical terms it may be said to be as old as the twentieth century, man's ability to fly being achieved at the same time as the huge industrialization of Europe, foreshadowed by the Paris Exposition of 1847 and Britain's Great Exhibition four years later. This is perhaps best illustrated by the evolution of the strategic bomber at the end of World War I, compared with the early struggles even to stay aloft suffered by the Wright biplanes that first equipped the United States Army only ten years before. A further illustration of the growth of air warfare may be found in the figures for the British Royal Flying Corps and Royal Naval Air Service, which expanded from a strength of 197 officers with 1,647 other ranks in August 1914 to 30,121 officers and 263,410 men, plus 25,000 members of the WRAF, by the time of the Armistice in 1918. In terms of equipment, the original 272 landplanes and seaplanes, plus seven airships, had grown during the same period to a total of 22,647 machines with 103 dirigibles, while the results of operations in the air over the Western Front from July 1916 and other fronts from 1918 claimed 8,000 enemy aircraft accounted for, 250 balloons destroyed, 8,000 tons of bombs dropped, 500,000 photographs taken and 12,000,000 rounds fired at ground targets, although at a cost of 3,000 aircraft missing, 8,136 personnel killed or posted missing, with 7,245 wounded or otherwise injured.

The twenty years of declared peace which separated the two great World conflicts so briefly — some said that the Treaty of Versailles was no more than the half-time whistle in some macabre killing match — brought with it the advantages of two decades of improved technology, but until the closing years of World War II certain tactics and attitudes bore the stamp of the earlier conflict, and these were not finally dispelled until the appearance of unmanned bombers, the first missiles and the associated functions of electronics, atomic science, chemistry and biological warfare.

The cost of all this had been massive, the United Kingdom alone in June 1944 calculating a total of £19,000m, re-assessed at £30,000m two years later, with the other combatants having to find the following equivalent sums:

Belgium	£812.5m
Canada	£3,920m
China	£49,000m
Czechoslovakia	£200m
France	£3,750m

Above: Equally, refinement of traditional aerodynamics could result in the adoption of airframes similar to that of the EFA Eurofighter mock-up. (Author's collection)

Germany	£67,500m	Soviet Union	£48,000m		
Greece	£55m	USA	£85,372.75m		
Italy	£23,500m	Yugoslavia	£50m		
Japan	£14,000m				
Latin America	£250m				
Netherlands	£231m				
Poland	£387.5m				

These figures are totals, but may be given practical form by the abbreviated list of aircraft lost: Germany 28,000, Great Britain 15,992, Italy 52,272 Japan 31,500 (763 at Okinawa, 1,000 in Manchuria), Soviet Union 56,000 (3,900 in Manchuria) and USA 22,948.

If these figures seem to concentrate on World War II, it must be real-

Above: The shape of military wings to come is still problematic at the end of the century, but the development of 'stealth' techniques may well result in an aircraft resembling this Lockheed F-117A single-seater of the US 37th Tactical Fighter Wing. Fifty-nine of these 52,000lb AUW aircraft were produced. (Lockheed)

286

ized that this is because the period may be taken as the watershed of aerial fighting, following which tactics and weapons would follow fresh courses that would affect all future wars and shape their conduct as the century drew to its close.

An illustration was the Gulf War waged against Iraq in early 1991, in which the changes in aerial warfare that had taken place were indicated not only by the brevity of the encounter but also by the tactical considerations enforced by the new weaponry. To this conflict the US Air Force contributed 48 bombers, which were at first directed by strategic demands, keeping up ceaseless attacks that wore down the enemy not only because of their frequency but also on account of the seeming invincibility of the sophisticated weaponry being used. Indeed, so successful were these raids that it became possible after a comparatively brief period to switch them to the role to which the remainder of the Coalition Force's air arm was dedicated, namely tactical strike sorties, the importance of which is shown by the following figures: France 38, Great Britain 60, Saudi Arabia 38, United States 1,000. Against this, the opposing strength of the Iraqi Air Force has been quoted as 500 machines.

Certainly, the half century between these two historic encounters saw wars in Korea and Vietnam, but by their very location they were encounters calling for specialist equipment and tactics, and both took place before the adoption of two key developments, laser-guided weaponry and stealth aircraft. Many believe that, of the two, the latter will prove the more significant, since guided weapons such as those which dominated the Gulf War seem likely with the passage of time to yield to electronic countermeasures as yet undeveloped, in the same manner those against radar, from which it was once believed there was no escape. Indeed, uncorroborated reports are seen by some as indicating that such a super-stealth warplane is already in being, allegations made twelve months after the end of the Gulf conflict naming a US Aurora (if such an aircraft exists under that title) as having been used there operationally. The Aurora is variously described as being of delta planform and some 90 feet in length, or else resembling the B-70 in appearance and measuring two and a half times the length of the preceding; the former description would appear to be the more likely. If the aircraft is capable of making protracted reconnaissance from an altitude of 132,000ft — some 25 miles — the span of such a machine would be little more than 50ft, with a sweep to the wing leading edges in the region of 75 degrees. Having no need for defensive armament, Aurora, operating in the rarified atmosphere more familiar to space-shuttle designers, would be capable of a velocity calling for heat-dispersal measures round the flight-deck, the most likely method of achieving this being by the circulation of the liquid methane used to fuel the engines capable of giving speeds in the region of Mach 8 (6,000mph). It naturally follows that, although radar-absorbent material such as is already incorporated in stealth aircraft construction would be called for, the main structure would be of titanium alloy such as is used for space vehicles. The range of such a seventy-ton machine would be in the region of 6,000 miles and the unit cost a staggering $15,000 million.

However, the question remains, after half a century of peace since global conflict, how much of this achievement is due to a reformation of man's basic instincts and how much to the fear of extinction — in short 'peace through terror' — which the major nations adopted with the introduction of the atomic bomb and the threat of the hydrogen weapons which have never yet been dropped in anger. In reply to this, it must be stated that *homo sapiens* alone among the living creatures on this planet is given to strife until death, and it is a sobering thought that, distinguished from his fellow creatures by his articulation, man lays himself open to the manipulation of his senses of loyalty — what appears to be 'right', corrupted honour, territorial gain far beyond the inborn hunger for food, and political indoctrination.

These factors seem to point to the fact that the most basic fear of all, that of extinction, has triumphed over the other tendencies, since it is allied to the propaganda of man's species. Given this, it seems that, as far as one can tell, there will always be fighting forces, including the most potent of them all, and mankind will hope for the best but prepare for the worst. Perhaps in some perverse way the baser instincts, borne by human beings alone, have begun to tame man's desire to kill on a global scale, and — who knows? —perhaps in some yet undawned future will also tame his wish to kill by means of even limited conflicts.

Yet if one believes that the future of air warfare rests with aircraft designed along the 'stealth' principle, there is, as the century draws towards its close, much to point in that direction. As early as 1994 reports were being made of a leap forward in such designs in Japan. These described a fighter designated the FI-X with a blended wing and fuselage carrying canard foreplanes, its main parts constructed of a graphite epoxy composite allowing them to flex under the stress of high manoeuvres and fitted with canted twin fins and rudders, the whole covered with radar-absorbing material. Twin, buried, lightweight turbofans offer some 22,400lb of thrust, thus giving a thrust to weight ratio of 8 to 1, and are also capable of two-dimensional thrust vectoring, so that the efflux nozzles become in effect an additional control augmenting the standard controls operated by 'fly-by-light' fibre optics. The comprehensive electronic equipment is reported to include computerized displays incorporating 'virtual reality' techniques, and aft-looking radar as standard.

But of one thing we may be certain: there will always be, for our children, grandchildren and their heirs for many generations, preparation for air warfare, if not warfare itself, so perhaps the last word on the subject should be left to Orville Wright, who uttered the following remarks long after the idyllic days of Kitty Hawk but before the scientist, the politician, the engineer and the chemist had prostituted the art of navigating the heavens for the purposes of destruction: 'What a dream it was. What a nightmare it has become!'